DATE DUE

ILall		
5/5/12		

STRATEGIC SPORT COMMUNICATION

Paul M. Pedersen, PhD

Indiana University

Kimberly S. Miloch, PhD

Indiana University

Pamela C. Laucella, PhD

Indiana University

Human Kinetics

Library of Congress Cataloging-in-Publication Data

Pedersen, Paul Mark.
  Strategic sport communication / Paul M. Pedersen, Kimberly S. Miloch, Pamela C. Laucella.
    p. cm.
  Includes bibliographical references and index.
  ISBN-13: 978-0-7360-6524-5
  ISBN-10: 0-7360-6524-5
  1. Sports--Management. 2. Communication in sports. I. Miloch, Kimberly S., 1972- II. Laucella, Pamela C., 1964- III. Title
  GV713.P43 2007
  796.06'9--dc22

                                        2007003995

ISBN-10: 0-7360-6524-5
ISBN-13: 978-0-7360-6524-5

The Web addresses cited in this text were current as of January 2007, unless otherwise noted.

Acquisitions Editor: Myles Schrag; **Developmental Editor:** Maggie Schwarzentraub; **Assistant Editor:** Jillian Evans; **Copyeditor:** Julie Anderson; **Proofreader:** Kathy Bennett; **Indexer:** Marie Rizzo; **Permission Manager:** Dalene Reeder; **Graphic Designer:** Fred Starbird; **Graphic Artist:** Kathleen Boudreau-Fuoss; **Cover Designer:** Keith Blomberg; **Photographer (cover):** © David Sanders; **Photo Asset Manager:** Laura Fitch; **Art Manager:** Kelly Hendren; **Illustrator:** Al Wilborn; **Printer:** Sheridan Books

Printed in the United States of America   10   9   8   7   6   5   4   3   2   1

Human Kinetics
Web site: www.HumanKinetics.com

United States: Human Kinetics
P.O. Box 5076, Champaign, IL 61825-5076
800-747-4457
e-mail: humank@hkusa.com

Canada: Human Kinetics
475 Devonshire Road Unit 100, Windsor, ON N8Y 2L5
800-465-7301 (in Canada only)
e-mail: orders@hkcanada.com

Europe: Human Kinetics
107 Bradford Road, Stanningley, Leeds LS28 6AT, United Kingdom
+44 (0) 113 255 5665
e-mail: hk@hkeurope.com

Australia: Human Kinetics
57A Price Avenue, Lower Mitcham, South Australia 5062
08 8372 0999
e-mail: liaw@hkaustralia.com

New Zealand: Human Kinetics
Division of Sports Distributors NZ Ltd.
P.O. Box 300 226 Albany, North Shore City, Auckland
0064 9 448 1207
e-mail: info@humankinetics.co.nz

To my best friend, Jennifer, and our four beautiful treasures,
Hallie, Zack, Brock, and Carlie

Paul M. Pedersen

To my husband, Matt, for your love and friendship
and for your endless patience and encouragement

Kimberly S. Miloch

To my parents, Kenneth and Marie Laucella,
for their unconditional love and unwavering support.

Pamela C. Laucella

Contents

Preface

Sport is big business that continues to witness unparalleled growth. In the United States alone, sport has exploded into a $200 billion industry. Internationally, in preparation for the 2008 Olympic Games, advertisers, broadcasters, and sponsors will have contributed more than $4.5 billion toward the Beijing Olympics—in addition to the $40 billion spent by the Chinese government (Payne, 2006). Along with this significant growth and expansion has come increased competition, which has increased the need for individuals well versed in communication practices and management principles. The demand for the sport product—from Chuck Taylor Converse shoes, NASCAR die-cast collectibles, and World Cup tickets to Wimbledon tote bags, World Series podcasts, and *Swimming World Magazine* subscriptions—and the development of new technologies have shaped the way sport industry professionals and organizations communicate with both internal and external publics. In recognition of the growing need for specialists in sport communication, academic units across the United States and abroad have increasingly modified their curricula to include courses and specializations in sport communication.

Although several textbooks have been published in the past decade on the management and marketing aspects of the sport industry, there is a need for an in-depth examination of the complex and expansive sport communication field. This introductory textbook addresses the void in the literature by focusing on the full scope, rather than on one facet, of the discipline. The entire field of sport communication—which ranges from newspaper sports sections and all-sport cable channels to sports satellite radio and sports Web logs—is covered in this text. Readers will find topics ranging from communication skill enhancement and sports writing to Web site management and sport media relations. This macroanalysis of sport communication

is accomplished through an examination of the field from interpersonal, intra- and inter-organizational, and external perspectives. The text is organized to provide readers with a foundation for pursuing a career in the field or simply for acting as prudent consumers of sport communication.

We designed the first three chapters (part I) to familiarize students with the field of sport communication. Chapter 1 defines sport communication and illustrates how it fits into the study and practice of sport management. Chapter 2 provides readers with an extensive discussion of jobs and career preparation in sport communication. The unit concludes with an analysis (chapter 3) of the history and growth of the field.

The next 10 chapters (part II) discuss the Strategic Sport Communication Model (SSCM). Built on communication theories and the unique structure of sport communication (chapter 4), this innovative model bridges theory and practice by detailing the three main components of the field. The first component consists of the personal (chapter 5) and organizational (chapter 6) processes and aspects of sport communication. The second component involves the various sport media. The three chapters in this component include sport publishing and print sport communication (chapter 7), electronic and visual sport communication (chapter 8), and the new sport media (chapter 9). The third component of the model includes three chapters that cover sport communication services and support systems. Included in this component are sport advertising (chapter 10), public relations and crisis communication in sport (chapter 11), and sport communication research (chapter 12).

Readers, after familiarizing themselves with the Strategic Sport Communication Model, are now ready to explore the critical ancillary components of sport communication. Therefore, the final two chapters (part III) of the textbook examine the major issues surrounding this field of study. These issues include the sociological (chapter 13) and legal (chapter 14) aspects of the field of sport communication.

This textbook serves as a primary resource for academicians and students in sport communication and may be used as a reference for industry professionals. Although most of the students who read this book will be majoring or taking courses in sport management and sport communication, this textbook is also appropriate for students in numerous other programs (e.g., journalism, English, communications, photojournalism, radio, telecommunications, advertising, marketing,

and management). As sport communication and sport marketing professors working under a sport management umbrella, we recognize the multifaceted nature of the sport industry but also address the necessity of specialization in sport communication. We believe that this text reflects the full scope of the sport communication discipline within the field of sport management and examines the key research, current trends, industry demands, and organizational value of sport communication. Our goal is for readers to become thoroughly familiar with and excited about the field of sport communication.

Acknowledgments

Thanks to the support from our mentors, colleagues, reviewers, interviewees, friends, and family. A few of these—listed in alphabetical order—are Kelle and Matt Acock, the late Peggy Blanchard, Elizabeth Brockelman, Tom Bowers, Galen Clavio, Annie Clement, Coyte Cooper, Dick Crepeau, Carrie Docherty, Andrea Eagleman, Phil and Susan Estes, Larry Fielding, Jean Folkerts, David Gallahue, Joanne Gerstner, Betty Haven, Rick Huff, David Koceja, John Koluder, Kelly Krauskopf, Dan Migala, David and Judy Miloch, Matt Miloch, Claudia Montgomery, Greg Norman, Barbara Osborne, Sean Parker, Harold and Candy Pedersen, Jennifer Pedersen, Andy Pittman, James and Danielle Reed, Bruce Renfro, Kathryn Rogers, Ron Semiao, John Shea, Shelley Smith, Chuck Stone, Tom and Nancy Sutton, John Sweeney, Jerry Wilkerson, Eric Wright, and Richard Zamoff. We are very grateful for the encouragement and expert guidance provided by Myles Schrag, Maggie Schwarzentraub, and the other professionals at Human Kinetics.

PART I

Introducing Sport Communication

Sport is a dynamic, multibillion dollar industry. Its popularity spans the globe. From neighborhood pick-up games and intercollegiate athletics to Australian Rules Football and the Olympics, sport captivates audiences and transcends borders. As a result, it is experiencing tremendous growth at all levels. Just one example of this was Super Bowl XLI in February 2007. One newspaper (*The Indianapolis Star*) sent 16 people to cover the event. Furthermore, *The Star* printed eight special sections (194 pages), posted 104 photo galleries, and witnessed combined sales of its Super Bowl coverage in the hundreds of thousands above its normal circulation. As sport has grown, the need for individuals well versed in communication has increased, and the discipline of sport communication has emerged as an integral area within sport management. This text defines the evolving field of sport communication and its role within sport management. It outlines the nature, breadth, and scope of the discipline as illustrated by the Strategic Sport Communication Model. We begin with the three chapters in part I.

Chapter 1 introduces you to the sport industry and the field of sport communication. It begins with an examination of the industry, the growth and segments of this broad field, and the place that sport management and sport communication have within the sport industry.

Because education is the foundation for a profession in the sport industry, the chapter emphasizes the study of sport communication. Included in this chapter are the content areas, programs, and options available to students interested in learning about the field. The chapter concludes with steps you can take to increase your marketability as a sport communicator.

The quest to understand and appreciate the complexity of sport communication begins with a knowledge of sport communication career options. Chapter 2 details careers in five distinct segments: management, mass media (e.g., print, electronic, visual), support services (e.g., advertising, public relations), entertainment (e.g., video gaming, movies, music), and ancillary opportunities. The chapter provides you with keys to entry into the field, including self-evaluation, education, networking, experiential learning, and the job search. With a clear understanding of the available opportunities and suggestions regarding their pursuit, you will have a strong foundation on which you can expand your knowledge and your overall educational endeavors.

Chapter 3 covers the historical developments and growth of sport communication from the 19th century to the present. It discusses sports coverage in newspapers, magazines, radio, television, cable, and emerging technologies and how sport media interact with other key entities within the field. Examining the historical development enables you to fully understand sport communication's skyrocketing growth, the full scope of how changes evolved over time, and the opportunities in such an expansive and burgeoning field. From Grantland Rice and Mel Allen to Roone Arledge and Pete Rozelle, sport communication professionals in print, radio, television, cable, and emerging technologies all have contributed to its foundation as a powerful cultural force. By understanding sport communication's history, you can understand the trends in sport communication as well as the vast opportunities you'll have in the field.

Study of Sport Management and Sport Communication

PROFILE OF A SPORT COMMUNICATOR

John K. Koluder

© Paul M. Pedersen

The road to a career in sport communication is often paved with varying intentions. Although some individuals know from an early age that they will work in the field, others decide to enter this segment of the sport industry after finding open doors. Most opportunities, however, only come about as a result of educational pursuits and practical experiences. As Louis Pasteur once said, "Chance favors the prepared mind." John K. Koluder is an illustration of such a situation. When Koluder was leaving high school, he intended to enter music school and prepare for a career as a music teacher. A decade after graduation, however, he has built a strong resume in sport communication rather than music education. His shift of intentions came during his undergraduate education.

After working in the student radio station throughout his first 2 years on campus, Koluder discovered that his interests were in covering and promoting soccer rather than teaching music. "I thought that a shift to sport communication would be a better fit," says Koluder. The switch has worked out well, and he is now the manager of media relations for the Chicago Fire of Major League Soccer. "The most rewarding aspect of my position is simply getting the opportunity to work in the sport industry," explains Koluder. "Although the hours might be long and days off few and far between, it's very rewarding to see the hard work that you and the rest of the staff put in during a week culminate with a great game-day experience."

Although Koluder's job is very gratifying, it is by no means easy. Two major issues make it difficult. The first is time management, which Koluder explains as "the most challenging part of being in media relations. At times you have to deal with the league's deadline for game notes while also helping plan a press conference and trying to put together two press releases by the end of the afternoon. As soon as you can figure out the most effective ways to budget your time and demands, the easier the position will get." The second major difficulty regarding his position involves securing media coverage for a professional soccer team that is "a 'small fish' in the big pond that is the Chicago sports landscape. Although we scrap and claw for any coverage we can get, it is extremely difficult to change the attitudes of editors and producers." Therefore, Koluder works extremely hard to manage his time for maximum efficiency while cultivating relationships with the media and providing everything he can to facilitate increased attention and coverage. He developed his networking, time management, and sport communication skills during his undergraduate education.

By majoring in sport communication, Koluder was able to take a wide variety of writing, reporting, editing, and public relations courses. For example, his broadcast writing course taught him "the nuances of the styles of writing that are involved in all different types of media," whereas his public relations course showed "students how to take control of situations. It gave us the chance to think on our feet and react quickly to different scenarios." Skill courses help prepare sport communication professionals. However, the theoretical foundation—whether it comes through majoring in sport communication or majoring in another area and taking sport communication courses—must be supplemented with practical volunteer and work (e.g., internship) experiences. "Educational institutions provide many opportunities to gain real experiences," notes Koluder, "but it is up to the students to go after those opportunities."

Koluder took advantage of such opportunities by writing sports articles and soccer columns for his campus newspaper *(Indiana Daily Student)* and joining the on-air sports staff of the student-run radio station (AM 1570 WIUS). "The radio station provided a great way to learn about being a part of the media, whereas my activities with the paper introduced me to the realm of print journalism, making for a more balanced experience," states Koluder. "It was covering major events such as the college cup soccer tournament and Big Ten football and basketball that allowed me to cultivate a sense of professionalism and easily adapt to working in a professional sports environment." He parlayed his undergraduate communication activities into an internship as the main Web site beat writer for D.C. United. "My time at the United allowed me the opportunity to be put in contact with some incredible people from other teams, the U.S. Soccer Federation, and Major League Soccer, some of whom were influential in helping me move into the ranks of full-time employment."

In this chapter we first examine the sport industry in general. The financial and sociological impact of the sport industry on the United States cannot be overstated. We analyze the size and segments of the sport industry and the role and importance of sport communication in this industry. After exploring this significance, we next examine the growth of sport management and the study of sport management. We then discuss the study of sport communication, examining the rationale for studying it as a discipline and highlighting the process and skills involved in studying the discipline. We also highlight the programs, courses, and syllabi specific to the discipline, necessary because some schools have more than 150 students majoring in sport communication. Next, we look at sport management and sport communication publications, such as sport communication textbooks, journals, and books. We conclude the chapter by examining sport management and sport communication academic affiliations, professional associations, conferences, and conventions.

RECOGNIZING THE MAGNITUDE OF THE SPORT INDUSTRY

With economic activity in the hundreds of billions of dollars, sport is often ranked as a top 10 industry in the United States. The *SportsBusiness Journal* estimates sport to be a $213 billion industry, which would make it twice as large as the auto industry and seven times larger than the movie industry ("The Sports Industry," 2007). Sport management professors Brenda Pitts and David Stotlar (2002), in their book *Fundamentals of Sport Marketing,* referred to sport as a $324 billion industry. This figure makes sense if you accept their definition of the sport industry, which is "the market in which the businesses and products offered to its buyers are sport related and may be goods, services, people, places, or ideas" (p. 4). Some of the major economic areas of the sport industry are sporting goods ($26 billion), professional services ($15 billion), spectator spending ($26 billion), and team operating expenses ($23 billion). Sport finance professors Dennis Howard and Timothy DeSchriver (2005) pointed out that many estimates examine only organized sports, therefore leaving out major areas of the sport industry (e.g., personal golf, fishing trips). Therefore, the size of the sport industry might be significantly higher than the figures noted here. For example, some have estimated that sport-related travel alone is a $154 billion segment of the industry (Schneider, 2005). The sport of bird watching attracts more than 60 million Americans who spend $30 billion on travel alone to participate in this sport ("The SportsTravel Files," 2001). Gambling is another major segment of the industry. In the United States, people spend approximately $2.1 billion on fantasy football ("$2.1," 2005).

Growth of the Industry

Although the sport industry is already a major industry, the business of sport continues to expand. "Even more impressive than its size is the extraordinary growth it has experienced over the past several years," noted sport management professor Tom Aaron (2004). Dianna Gray and Chad McEvoy (2005) stated that sport "is intertwined with practically every aspect of the economy—from advertising and apparel, to computer technology and video games, to travel and tourism." The sport management professors added, "It is one of the fastest-growing industries in the United States" (p. 230). Twenty years ago, the gross national sport product— the sum total of value added with respect to sport over 1 year—of the sport industry was estimated at $50.2 billion in 1987 (Sandomir, 1988). This placed sport as the 23rd ranked industry among the top 50 industries in the United States. Last decade, Meek (1997) noted that the sport industry was $152 billion in 1995 and supported another $259 billion in activity based on calculations of the gross domestic sport product—the amount of economic activity supported by the sport industry.

Today, sport is a top-10 industry, and some have even placed it in the top 5. Even though the $213 billion figure noted previously is missing several components that would make it much larger, it is still four times the figure noted in 1987. Other statistics support the size and growth of the sport industry. For example, *Forbes* reported that from 2004 to 2005, the team values of National Football League (NFL) franchises increased an average of 12%. The average value of NFL franchises stands at $898 million, with the most valuable franchise being the Washington Redskins at $1.4 billion (Badenhausen, Ozanian, & Roney, 2006). Teams in other leagues are quite valuable as well. For example, in Major League Baseball (MLB), the New York Yankees are valued at $950 million whereas the 30th team in MLB, the Tampa Bay Devil Rays, is valued at $176 million (Ozanian, 2005c). The National Hockey League (NHL) might have low ratings, but it is still big business. The most valuable franchise in that league, the Toronto Maple Leafs, has an operating income of $85 million and is valued at $325 million (Badenhausen & Ozanian, 2005).

Outside the United States, where most view soccer as the most popular sport, the United Kingdom's Manchester United is valued at $1.3 billion, whereas Spain's Real Madrid and Italy's AC Milan are the second and third richest soccer franchises with current values of $920 million and $893 million, respectively (Ozanian, 2005b). In addition to the growth in franchise valuations, athletes continue to earn more money. For instance, NASCAR's Nextel Cup champion Tony Stewart set the record for single-season earnings when he secured $13.5 million in prize money in 2005.

The size of the professional segment of the sport industry is not the only component that is growing. Intercollegiate athletics are increasing in size, influence, and revenues. The 100-year-old National Collegiate Athletic Association (NCAA) has grown to an institution that has an astounding 360,000 students in athletic competition, 88 championships, 23 sports, and three divisions. The growth of the NCAA is a direct result of the outstanding growth exhibited by many of its 1,200 members. At the top of the charts is Ohio State University (OSU). Not only does OSU have the most athletic teams (36) and athletes (900) in major college sports, but the athletic program is the top revenue generator in intercollegiate athletics. The Buckeyes made just under $90 million during the 2004-2005 academic year. These revenues came from such sources as merchandise royalties, ticket sales, advertising, and television and radio rights fees. As athletic director Gene Smith was quoted as saying, "You always want to be the biggest and the best" ("Big Money", 2006, p. 1D). Not far behind Ohio State were the University of Texas ($89 million) and the University of Michigan ($78). The University of Florida made $77 million, but that number will increase with the school's winning the men's basketball title in 2006 and the BCS Championship in January 2007.

The size of the sport industry is determined in large part by sport communication, whether it is the commentary of a sportswriter, a promotion by an advertiser, or a discussion at the water cooler about tonight's heated rivalry. "Over the past 20 years, sport organizations have enjoyed tremendous growth in popularity thanks to expanded media coverage (cable television, magazines, 24-hour sports radio, and the Internet) as well as corporate support," stated McGowan and Bouris (2005, p. 354). These sport communication experts added, "This growth has been a boon to the area of sport communications." An examination of the coverage of sports, which continues to grow each year, illustrates the relationship between the sport industry and sport communication.

In addition to the increase in attention given to sports in traditional and legacy platforms such as newspapers and magazines, there is increased sports coverage on terrestrial and satellite radio, mobile units (audio and video games, updates, and data), the Internet (Web sites, streaming video and radio, Web logs), and television (broadcast networks, cable channels, satellite and digital, high-definition television, video on demand, property specific networks). The best indicators of growth in sports coverage are the television rights fees. As Scott Rosner and Kenneth Shropshire (2004) noted, "Today it is the rare sports business model that does not begin and end with television as the main financial driver. This is the case in all major successful sports enterprises around the globe" (p. 139). Mind-boggling media rights fees are paid out at most levels of sport participation in the United States. At the college level, CBS signed an 11-year, $6 billion deal with the NCAA to broadcast 66 championships through 2013. At the Olympic level, NBC Universal will pay $894 million to broadcast the 2008 Olympic Games and $1.18 billion for the 2012 Games ("Sports Media," 2005). At the professional level, the best example is the NFL. The NFL's national television deals that began in 2006 pay the league an average of $3.7 billion every year. The combined contracts, which are more than the other three "major" leagues combined, is 53% more than the previous national TV deals the league had (Badenhausen, Gage, Ozanian, Roney, & Sundheim, 2005). Even the NHL, trying to recover from overexpansion, labor wars, and team relocations, has what many would consider significant media revenues. The league's 2-year deal with Comcast's OLN channel (now the Versus channel) provided the NHL with $135 million in broadcast rights

revenue. Although this is relatively small compared with the NFL, MLB, or the National Basketball Association (NBA), such national media revenue is still quite large compared with other sports or leagues that often have to pay for air time. Furthermore, when the national (league-wide) media revenue is combined with local media revenues, some teams come out very well. "The value of the local broadcasting agreement varies according to a number of factors, the most important of which is the size of the market in which the team plays" (Rosner & Shropshire, 2004, p. 141). For example, the New York Rangers have $28 million in media revenues. Even the lowest media revenue NHL franchise, the Nashville Predators, brings in $11 million in media revenues (Badenhausen & Ozanian, 2005).

Segmentation of the Industry

Because of its enormous size and scope, the sport industry is best understood when its various components are categorized into segments. There are numerous ways in which the industry has been segmented. You can find segmentation with just a couple clicks on the Internet. For example, you can find that the Massachusetts Institute of Technology (MIT) divides the sport industry into five segments: sport media (e.g., marketing, broadcasting, sportswriting, public relations), sports team administration (e.g., personnel in high schools, college, universities, and professional teams), sport-related engineering (e.g., facilities, sporting goods and equipment, electronic games, computer-assisted training devices), sports medicine (e.g., athletic training, nutrition, psychology, rehabilitation, orthopedics), and other (e.g., sport finance, management, law, statistics, retail, wholesale) ("Careers in the Sports Industry," 2007). The Sport Management Program Standards and Review Protocol (2000) segments the industry according to academic content areas. These 10 areas include sociocultural dimensions, management and leadership in sport, ethics in sport management, sport marketing, communication in sport, budget and finance in sport, legal aspects of sport, sport economics, governance in sport, and field experiences in sport management.

Some of the most widely accepted segmentation models have been developed by sport management professors. One of the first—and still widely used—segmentation models was developed by Brenda Pitts, Larry Fielding, and Lori Miller (1994). Their sport model segments the sport industry into product and buyer type. The three main segments are the sport performance segment (e.g., amateur and professional athletics, sport businesses, membership-supported sport organizations, fitness and sport firms), sport production segment (e.g., outfitting products, performance production products), and sport promotion segment (e.g., promotional merchandising and events, the media, sponsorship, endorsement). The theory behind their model "is that every product and business in the sport business industry falls into one of these three segments" (Pitts & Stotlar, 2002, p. 35). The next segmentation model came from economist Alfie Meek, who segmented the sport industry into three sectors consisting of sport entertainment (e.g., events, teams, participants, associated spending), sport products and services (e.g., design, testing, manufacturing, distribution), and sport support organizations (e.g., leagues, law firms, marketing organizations) (Meek, 1997). In their textbook *Sport Marketing,* Bernie Mullin, Stephen Hardy, and Bill Sutton (2007) segmented the industry according to primary marketing functions (e.g., providing "packaged" events to spectators at the venue or via the mass media; providing facilities, equipment, and programming to players, who then produce the game form; providing general administrative support, control, and publicity to other sport organizations and people). Ming Li, Susan Hofacre, and Dan Mahony (2001), in their textbook *Economics of Sport,* placed at the core of their model the firms and organizations that produce sport. Surrounding and overlapping this core are subsectors, each of which includes

Because of the enormity of the industry, segmentation models are used to divide sport into segments or components. Communication—ranging from employee interactions in a sporting goods firm to broadcasts of a fishing tournament through the mass media—plays a vital role in each of the sport industry segments. Ciara's performance during a sporting event is an in-game promotion, part of the marketing component of the sport industry that relies on effective communication among key stakeholders.

firms and organizations that either provide products and services to support sport production or sell and trade products related to sport activities.

Role of Communication Within the Industry

Regardless of the segmentation used, each model illustrates the vital role that sport communication plays in the sport industry. For example, Meek's model includes the media (e.g., television, radio, Internet, publications) in sport entertainment, his model's first primary sector, whereas Li, Hofacre, and Mahony considered the sport media (e.g., television, radio and cable networks, magazines and other periodicals) as one of their six subsectors. In addition to including the sport media, sport communication involves interpersonal and small-group communication, organizational communication in sport, sport public relations, and other components of the field not categorized in the models. In a poll of more than 1,500 readers of *SportsBusiness Journal* and *SportsBusiness Daily,* 41% believed that the biggest threat to sports was a "disconnect with fan base" ("Welcome," 2005). Sure, inflated salaries (20%), rising ticket prices (19%), use of drugs and a perceived decrease in the integrity of the game (14%), and losing competitive balance (6%) are serious threats facing the sport industry, but the biggest concern relates to a sport communication issue: the ability to connect with fans. The only way to keep the sport industry growing is through taking on this disconnect with an effective communication strategy.

Sport communication plays a vital role in the management of sport. Without sport communication, professionals would be unable to set strategy, advertisers would be unable to promote, and members of the media would be unable to cover sports. If sport professionals could not communicate, the sport industry would not experience continued growth. Richard Irwin, Bill Sutton, and Larry McCarthy (2002) noted, "Communication is the foundation of all buyer behavior. . . . Thus, there is a need for more emphasis on educating future

sport promoters about how to communicate with prospective buyers and users" (p. 22). McGowan and Bouris (2005) noted, "Today's sport communications professional needs to have a well-rounded understanding of the role communications plays in the successful operation of the twenty-first century sport organization" (p. 341).

Clearly, sport communication is vital to the continued growth of the sport industry. For the most part, sport communication is learned through academic study and training.

FOCUSING ON THE STUDY OF SPORT MANAGEMENT

Before we examine the study of sport communication, let's first look at the academic field of sport management. Sport management has been defined in several different ways. For example, DeSensi, Kelley, Blanton, and Beitel (1990) defined it as "any combination of skills related to planning, organizing, directing, controlling, budgeting, leading, and evaluating within the context of an organization or department whose primary product or service is related to sport and/or physical activity" (p. 33). A more recent definition was offered by Pitts and Stotlar (2002), who defined sport management as "the study and practice of all people, activities, businesses, or organizations involved in producing, facilitating, promoting, or organizing any sport-related business or product" (p. 3). Their definition incorporates the aspect of sport management education.

The rapid expansion of the sport industry over the past 2 decades has increased the demand for trained and educated individuals able to manage and promote the increasingly sophisticated operations within this field (Pedersen & Schneider, 2003; Stier, 2001). Today, this training and education are most often found in sport management programs. Before the explosion of sport management programs beginning in the late 1980s, there were few opportunities to major in sport management or sport administration. "Early on, sport managers learned from hands-on experiences gained in the industry. However, as the sport industry became more complex, there was a need to train sport managers in a more formal fashion. From this need emerged the formal study of sport management" (Crosset & Hums, 2005, pp. 15-16). After higher education administrators realized the demand for trained individuals and recognized sport management as a valid career path, they worked to put together academic majors and degrees in sport management in an attempt to keep up with the phenomenal growth of the sport industry (Pedersen & Schneider, 2003).

The first sport management program started in 1966 (Mason & Paul, 1988). Programs began to emerge in the late 1960s and steadily increased for the next 15 years until the number of programs approached 100. Sport management scholars Bonnie Parkhouse and Brenda Pitts (2001) commented, "The significant proliferation in curricular development was not observed until the mid-1980s" (p. 5). Since then, sport management offerings have doubled, with more than 200 undergraduate, 100 master's, and a dozen doctoral programs in the United States alone. There are now sport management programs and courses around the world, especially in countries such as South Korea, Japan, Greece, Australia, Italy, Canada, the United Kingdom, China, France, New Zealand, Switzerland, Portugal, and South Africa. Brock University in Ontario, Canada, is an example of this growth. In the 10 years since it was started, the sport management program has grown to upwards of 500 students, nine faculty members, and more than 40 courses.

Some of the sport management programs are quite small, with only a few students and a professor or two. Other programs are very large, with hundreds of students and many professors. For instance, the Department of Sport Management at the University of Massachusetts houses 13 full-time faculty members and offers three sport management degrees to more than 400 students. There appears to be infinite growth potential in sport management degree offerings (i.e., undergraduate, master's, doctorate).

In addition to the traditional undergraduate and graduate sport management programs, a multitude of non–sport management programs introduce students to the sport industry.

For example, MIT takes an interdisciplinary approach to the study of sport. As its brochure for the study of sport states, "Preparation for many of these areas can be found in a variety of different majors/areas of study" ("Careers in the Sports Industry," 2005, p. 4). MIT's Center for Sports Innovation was launched in 1999 as an opportunity for undergraduate and graduate students to learn about the development of sport technology and products.

Beyond the traditional sport management and interdisciplinary programs offered throughout the United States at undergraduate and graduate institutions, dozens of sport management programs are now offered at 2-year institutions and sport management courses are even offered at the high school level. Furthermore, online programs are available that specialize in sport management.

FOCUSING ON THE STUDY OF SPORT COMMUNICATION

The study of sport management includes many content areas. Sport management programs are structured in unique ways, but for the most part they typically have courses in such areas as sport marketing, sport finance, legal aspects of sport, management and organization of sport, sport governance, sport facility planning and management, event management, and a variety of other courses. All of these courses (the careers involved in each are discussed in chapter 2) involve aspects of sport communication. As we cover in chapter 4, sport communication is defined as a process by which people in sport, in a sport setting, or through a sport endeavor share symbols as they create meaning through interaction. So, regardless of the area of sport management, sport communication plays a part. As Brad Schultz, founder of the *Journal of Sports Media,* stated in *Sports Media: Reporting, Producing and Planning* (2005), "The study of sports media is important, both in a theoretical and practical perspective." Although Schultz's focus is specific to the sport media (e.g., television, radio, newspaper, Internet), his statement is just as applicable to sport communication. Studying this field helps people understand and appreciate the vital role that sport communication plays in all sport organizations. "Sport communication is essential to the industry," notes Adam Neft, a sports reporter and talk-show host for ESPN Radio in Louisville, Kentucky. "Athletes, coaches, teams, and everything else survive because of the publicity. Major athletic programs, for all intents and purposes, get free advertising worth millions yearly on the front pages of newspapers and in magazines, Web sites, and several other places."

If you are a sport management or sport business major, most likely you are required to take at least one sport communication class. If you are not a sport management major, you still can take sport communication classes in programs that specialize in sport media and journalism. Furthermore, many communication, journalism, and media programs have a sport-focused communication class. Regardless of where the course or program is housed (e.g., business, education, telecommunications), there has been an increase in sport communication offerings just as there has been a growth in sport management offerings.

The increase in sport communication educational programs and courses is attributable to both the increase in sport coverage and the demand for skilled sport management professionals. "Sport organizations rely on communication to survive," noted Gillentine, Crow, and Bradish (2005, p. 22). The growth of the sport communication segment of the industry has also prompted increased course offerings in sport communication. Catriona Higgs and Betsy McKinley (2005) pointed out three reasons why people study sport. The first reason is that sport is omnipresent. The third reason is that sport provides role models. But reason number two is that "sport coverage has increased dramatically over the past decade" (p. 12). Thus, the increase in sports coverage is one of the top three reasons we study sport. Although there are no specific figures on the size of the sport communication segment of the sport industry, some significant figures are reported that involve this segment. For instance, the *SportsBusiness*

Journal notes that advertising makes up more than $27 billion of the industry. Advertising is a key component of sport communication and is covered in chapter 10. Sponsorships and endorsements combine to add more than $7 billion themselves. Licensed goods ($10.5 billion), multimedia and the Internet ($2.5 billion), and media broadcast rights ($7 billion) all are critical aspects of sport communication. As Gillentine, Crow, and Bradish (2005) noted, "It is essential that sport managers have a strong appreciation of the power of contemporary communication mediums, both as a means of connecting with key constituents and as an advantage that requires increasingly greater management skill and coordination" (p. 22).

Public relations professionals Noah Gold and Meghan Powers interact during a skateboarding competition at the Dew Action Sports Tour. Powers (right) has been a sport public relations and corporate communications professional working with the NFL and Brener, Zwikel, and Associates, Inc. Gold (left), a soccer player at Indiana University, has sport industry experience that ranges from the IMG and the Super Bowl to the junior world golf championships and the California State Games.

© Paul M. Pedersen

PREPARING FOR A CAREER IN SPORT COMMUNICATION

Closely affiliated (and often intertwined) with the academic aspects of sport management is the study of sport communication. In fact, the sport communication field of study is built on (and requires) interdisciplinary knowledge, with disciplines and courses including advertising, broadcasting, communication, cinema, electronic media, journalism, film, finance, informatics, information services, law, management, marketing, mass communication, new media, public relations, speech, and writing. Take, for instance, someone pursuing an educational path to become a sports broadcaster or sportswriter. "Today's students rarely concentrate solely in sports broadcasting or print, and they must be able to write and perform across a variety of media platforms," noted sport media professor Brad Schultz (2005). "Even someone hired as a 'sports broadcaster' will likely be expected to make contributions to a web site, newspaper, or magazine" (p. xix).

Students have increasing opportunities and options to study sport communication, and the growth in this academic area is outstanding. Penn State University is an excellent example of this growth. The university launched the Center for Sports Journalism in 2003. In two short years, the center had 174 undergraduates enrolled. Furthermore, the center received a $1.5 million grant in 2005 from a foundation to create the Knight Chair in Sports Journalism and Society. The president of the foundation, Alberto Ibarguen, noted at the press conference that his foundation "had a V8 moment when we realized that sports and sports journalism is one of the major reasons that people watch TV, read newspaper and go online" (Knight Foundation, 2005). Also in 2005, the University of Maryland created the Shirley Povich Chair in Sports Journalism, named after the late *Washington Post* sports columnist. Although Penn State's and Maryland's programs and endowments are two of the largest, over the last 15 years many sport communication programs, majors, and courses have been introduced at institutions

of higher learning. As Viseu (2000) wrote at the turn of the century, "Only after 10 years, the new emerging fields Sport Economics & Sport Management as well as the major field 'Sport, Communication & Media' have become a strategic supply [in] universities' academic programmes" (pp. 2-3). In the United States, the options within the numerous programs and offerings allow students to either take selected sport communication classes in a sport management or a related program or major in sport communication. The way one goes about securing this education is not important as long as sport communication courses are taken, education is secured, and training is acquired. As sports broadcaster and educator Ted Hedrick noted, "Absorb all the education possible, and be aggressive in pursuit of on-the-job training along the way" (2000, p. 22).

Options at the Undergraduate Level

Undergraduate students can take four distinct avenues to learn more about sport communication. These avenues include majoring in the field, studying sport communication while majoring in a closely related field, enrolling in specific sport communication courses, and developing skills through experiential classes and practical experiences. Each of these avenues is detailed next.

Major in Sport Communication

An academic program focused on sport communication provides the most courses and opportunities to learn about the field. "I believe sport communication deserves its own program because the positions it entails are becoming more expansive," notes John K. Koluder, media relations manager for the Chicago Fire. "As far as media relations goes, the days of just writing press releases are over. More and more, people in these positions will be required to have knowledge in areas from Web page design and graphics software to event planning and basic accounting and budgeting skills—things that will not be covered in typical telecom or sports marketing courses." Therefore, for those institutions that provide such an opportunity, majoring in sport communication or sport media is an obvious choice for some who pursue academic study in sport communication. Although only a few programs offer the option of actually majoring in sport communication (as opposed to simply offering some courses), for those who have pursued the major the rewards are obvious. Adam Neft, a graduate of a sport communication program who is now a sports reporter and talk-show host for ESPN Radio-Sportszone WSZ in Louisville, Kentucky, notes that sport communication "is worthy of its own program because it will help students learn a specific craft."

One of the best programs in the United States is at Ithaca College, which prepares students to become sport communication professionals in the areas of mass media, sport information, and public relations. The undergraduate program in sport media has the traditional courses such as sport history and sport management, but it also offers sport communication courses such as The Evolution of Sport Media, Sport Media Relations, Sport Publications, and Sport Internet Marketing. Although there are very few sport communication/media programs, most students who graduate from such programs are well qualified to enter the field of sport communication. Brenda Stidham, who has a degree in sport communication and works as a sports reporter and anchor for an NBC affiliate in Flint and Saginaw, Michigan, adds, "I think prospective employers (along with possible internships) are impressed by learning or reading on a resume that an applicant has a degree in sport communication." Stidham adds, however, that "any class that could help train people for tasks such as reporting, anchoring, or writing press releases is worthwhile."

Study Sport Communication Within Another Program

Other options in securing sport communication education are to study sport communication within a sport management, journalism, broadcasting, or telecommunications program. Many institutions offer sport communication as a minor or emphasis within another major.

The programs most frequently offered include such options as sport management and sport administration. For those nationally approved programs, emphasizing communication and offering sport communication courses are requirements. Two academic associations—the National Association for Sport and Physical Education (NASPE) and the North American Society for Sport Management (NASSM)—work together to develop the standards for sport management programs. According to the Sport Management Program Standards and Review Protocol (2000) published by the Sport Management Program Review Council (SMPRC), communication in sport is one of the 10 content areas that the NASPE–NASSM program approval standards require. Although all of the content areas have a sport communication component, the premise of the sport communication content area in particular, according to the guidelines for undergraduate programs, is that the "student will be familiar with the principles of interpersonal communication, mass communication, and interaction with the public, particularly as they relate to the sport agency. Emphasis will be placed on interactions, which are internal and external to the sport agency. Information will be geared toward public relations at entry-level sport management positions" ("Sport Management," 2000, p. 7).

According to the NASPE–NASSM standard, the following content is required—that is, topics must be addressed in the program—for communication in sport: interpersonal communication; small-group communication; media and sport; electronic media; e-mail, Web sites, graphics, and desktop publishing; print media; public speaking; mass communication and sport; and computer application. Furthermore, the following content is recommended—with a minimum of half of these items addressed—for communication in sport: customer service, team building, meeting management, business writing, sport journalism and broadcasting, ratings and shares, organizational communication, and writing press releases. Programs often meet these requirement standards by either offering sport communication courses or covering sport communication topics during the delivery of closely related courses. The sport management program at the University of Michigan is an excellent example of a sport management program with **sport communication courses.** The program (http://www.kines.umich.edu) was started in 1985 and is housed in kinesiology, a division that has 25 faculty and 800 students. Sport communication is an obvious part of the sport management undergraduate program, which "familiarizes students with the diverse aspects of sport management, including: organizational strategy and behavior; promotion and marketing; finance and economics; ethical and legal issues; media; and research methods" ("Sport Management," 2007, ¶4). While offering traditional sport management preparation, the program trains majors for "jobs as sports information and communication specialists" (¶5). In addition to taking the required course, Public and Small Group Communication, students also have the option of taking two sport communication courses, Sports and the Media and Advertising and Promotion Strategy.

Take Individual Sport Communication Courses

Another option for those who attend institutions of higher education that do not offer sport communication or sport management programs is to take individual sport communication courses. Some of these courses are offered as electives, whereas others lead to either a certification or a minor in sport communication. The University of North Carolina at Chapel Hill offers a certificate in sport communication for students who complete three sport communication courses—Sports Communication; Ethical Issues and Sports

---

Examples of Sport Communication Courses

Whether a university offers a program complete with numerous sport communication courses or just one or two classes in the field, a wide variety of sport communication courses are available in higher education today.

COURSES AT THE UNDERGRADUATE LEVEL

A sample of some of the typical sport communication course titles are Sports Writing and Reporting (George Mason University); Sport Communication (Slippery Rock University); Sport Communications (University of Massachusetts at Amherst); Public Relations in Sports (Clemson University); Sport Media Relations (Rice University); Sports, Media, and Society (Penn State University); Ethical Issues and Sports Communication (University of North Carolina at Chapel Hill); Sport Video Production (Ithaca College); Sport Media and Public Relations (Old Dominion University); Sports Reporting (Ashland University); Sports Journalism (University of Texas at Austin); Sports Information Management (Waynesburg College); Introduction to Sport Communication (Indiana University); Sport Public Relations (Wichita State University); Sports, Gambling and the Media (Springfield College); Sports

Broadcasting I and II (University of North Texas); Public and Media Relations (York College); and Sports Communication Internship (Mississippi State University). Sportswriting—offered by Ohio University and many other institutions—is an example of a popular and extremely valuable course for the future sport communication professional.

COURSES AT THE GRADUATE LEVEL

Other sport communication courses at the master's level include such titles as Public Relations in Sport (Baylor University), Seminar in Integrated Marketing Communications (San Diego State University), Reporting and Writing about Sports (University of California, Berkeley), Sport Public Relations and Information Systems (University of Northern Colorado), Sport Marketing and Public Relations (East Carolina University), Sport and the Media (Florida State University), Public/Media Relations (Neumann College), Marketing and Public Relations in Sport and Recreation (Temple University), Sport Publicity and Promotion (University of Louisville), Sport and Media Issues (University of Tennessee), and Public Relations for Sport Organizations (Western Illinois University).

Communication; and Sports Marketing and Advertising. As the university's Web site notes, "The program, which aims to lead the nation in educating young practitioners about important issues of sports in the United States and beyond, provides courses about sports and the media, offers internships and scholarships for students, and brings visiting lecturers to the school" (School of Journalism, 2006). Although the certification is rare, many universities offer sport communication courses.

Sport communication classes will continue to increase to meet both the demands of approval agencies such as NASPE–NASSM and the needs of a well-rounded sport management student. As we cover in the analysis of scholarly publications and ancillary outlets, sport communication is a recognized and growing part of the academic sport management discipline. Whether the courses are offered in full sport communication programs or as individual elective classes, most universities provide some type of sport communication course work because they recognize that preparation is needed for sport communication careers.

Supplement With Additional Courses and Practical Experience

"Working with ESPN during my studies has helped me gain an understanding of the numerous production aspects of sports broadcasting," states Coyte Cooper, who complemented his sport management graduate education with practical experience by working for ESPN for many years, including his experience as a cameraman for the ESPN College Football production team. Although individuals can learn about sport communication through a variety of majors, it is vital for students "to accumulate coursework or volunteer or work experience that helps in understanding the fundamentals of public relations, communications, marketing, advertising, and journalism," explained McGowan and Bouris (2005). "Public speaking skills, writing skills, and knowledge of TV/video production and computer technology are a must for all future sport communications professionals" (p. 355). Important in the study of sport—according to

Doug Anderson, a former sports editor and current dean of the College of Communications at Penn State University—is learning how to write and describe with correct grammar and with accuracy. Anderson (1994) noted in *Contemporary Sports Reporting*, "Students interested in careers in sports reporting must realize that masterful use of the language and knowledge of style are as important on sports pages as on page one" (p. 13). He added that, "A working knowledge of the sport being covered also is a necessity" (p. 14). Adam Neft, a sports reporter and talk-show host, notes that writing is "a big deal" in all of sport communication. "Poor grammar is my number one pet peeve; I can't and won't stand for a lack of understanding of the English language," explains Neft. "It's one thing to do a bit and make fun of a coach or player for poor grammar, but quite another to write a report or voicer with dangling modifiers and other grammatical errors." In addition to writing courses, many industry professionals recommend learning another language. Legendary sports columnist Bud Collins' first jobs in the field included positions as the sports editor of a small-town weekly newspaper in Ohio and with his college newspaper. He offers sound advice for those wanting to break into the business. "Learn Spanish," states Collins, who was pursuing a graduate degree in public relations from Boston University when he joined the staff of the *Boston Herald* for $60 a week. Fluency in Spanish is "helpful in communicating comfortably with the growing number of Hispanic athletes. Study business/finance and some law. Writing sports is much more than covering games" (Glatzer, 2007, ¶9). Sportswriter Joanne C. Gerstner concurs by adding, "Some of the athletes on your team may not speak English, so knowing another language or two is very helpful."

Key components of any sport communication educational program are the opportunities for skill development. "Sport communication classes can give the aspiring professional some wonderful tools," says Galen Clavio, a former sports broadcaster and current sport management doctoral candidate. "Practical experience shows them how those tools should be used."

In the chapters that follow, we cover many of these aspects of sport communication as we look at the development of skills in such areas as interpersonal relationships, organizational communication, and oral and written communication. Although formal education and textbooks provide the framework for the development of skills and expertise, critical aspects of sport communication education are the internship, practicum, and volunteer experiences that are provided. As McGowan and Bouris (2005) explained, "It is no longer acceptable to enter the sports communications field, even as an intern, without some practical, first-hand experience" (p. 355). Neft says his internship and work experiences began during his freshman year when he joined the staff of the campus radio station. "This experience was very valuable as I learned the radio craft," explains Neft. "From there I interned at ESPN Radio in Pittsburgh and also at the network headquarters in Bristol, CT. When back at school, I started working for AM1370 WGCL as a news reporter, producer, and anchor and did some high school sports coverage. I also worked at WRTV-6

in Indianapolis in both the news and sports departments along with the Fox Sports Radio affiliate in Pittsburgh for a couple summers. It is very valuable to get these experiences because professors and classroom work can only teach students so much. A classroom cannot re-create a coach or athlete getting upset with a reporter's line of questioning or teach a potential reporter how to cultivate relationships with athletes, coaches, or media relations staff. The nuts and bolts are put into place in the classroom but the experience that makes someone go from average to good or good to great as a reporter or media member is learned by doing in the field."

Options at the Graduate Level

Although there are not as many programs in sport management or sport communication at the graduate level as there are at the undergraduate level, numerous options are still presented to the graduate student. The first option is to pursue a master's or doctorate in sport communication. The second option at the graduate level is to pursue a concentration or emphasis

An interest in sports is only the first step to a career in sport communication. Here a student takes his own picture with sports broadcaster Dick Vitale.

Spotlight on a Graduate Program for Working Students

An example of a graduate program that offers sport communication courses for **working students** is one of the most popular programs on the west coast of the United States. This is the master of arts program in the College of Arts and Sciences at the University of San Francisco. USF's sport management program is designed for working students in the San Francisco and Los Angeles areas. Its purpose is to provide "professional preparation for management and leadership positions" in a variety of sport industry segments (e.g., professional sports, amateur athletics), including "communication firms that service the larger marketplace" ("Graduate Programs," 2007, ¶2). The curriculum, which is offered at the main campus in San Francisco as well as the area campus in Los Angeles, is interdisciplinary in scope and involves 36 units spread over 23 months. In the USF program, some of the courses—which are offered in the evening to accommodate the working professionals—include Sports on TV: "Real" Reality Programming (taught by Tom Pellack, the marketing director for Fox Sports Net Bay Area) as well as Public Relations in Sport Management, which is taught in both the northern and southern California programs. For instance, in San Francisco,

the course is taught by Shana Daum, the director of public relations and community relations for the San Francisco Giants, and by Ben Drew, the vice president of public affairs for Manning Selvage and Lee. In Los Angeles, the course is taught by Dennis Bickmeier, the director of public relations at the California Motor Speedway. The course, similar to most sport communication and sport management programs, invites many professionals from the field to talk to students. Some of the frequent sport communication speakers for the USF program include announcer Joe Morgan, Ken Arnold (director of media relations for the San Jose Sharks), Joan Ryan (columnist for the *San Francisco Chronicle),* and Julie Miller (marketing development manager of interactive media for the Ladies Professional Golf Association, or LPGA). Its alumni work in all segments of the industry, including firms in sport media (e.g., ESPN, Fox Sports, Fox Sports Net), sports radio (e.g., Clear Channel [SFX]), electronic sport communication (e.g., ESPN Videogames, EA Sports, Sega), and new sport media (e.g., MLB Advanced Media, CollegeSports Online, CBS Sportsline).

in sport communication within the study of another discipline (e.g., sport management, journalism). The third option is to take sport communication courses as electives in the pursuit of a degree in another field or concentration. For example, it would be difficult to find a quality sport management master's or doctorate program that did not offer at least one sport communication course.

Study Sport Communication in Graduate (Master's) Programs

Over the last 2 decades, the study of sport management and sport communication at the graduate level has dramatically increased. Most sport management programs, as noted previously, have at least one sport communication course, and several programs have multiple courses. Therefore, they offer sport communication education through either

sport communication courses or sport communication content covered within the study of another subject. For approved graduate programs, the emphasis on the sport communication component is a requirement. Each of the nine NASPE-NASSM content areas for a master's degree has sport communication areas, in particular the fifth content area: public relations in sport. The premise of this requirement is that "managers communicate with a variety of publics. Internally, for example, they communicate with the staff, coaches, and athletes and members of the board. Externally, they may communicate with the press, alumni, the media, consumers, and fans. Students will acquire and refine effective ways to communicate with all their constituencies" ("Sport Management," 2000, p. 14). The required topics that must be addressed for this content area are employee relations, community relations, media relations, customer relations, and image enhancement.

As noted, there are three distinct ways in which sport communication can be studied at the graduate level. In addition to these options, there are a variety of avenues to pursue within a sport communication or sport management education. Some graduate programs are found in business schools (e.g., Arizona State University, University of Central Florida, Florida Atlantic University, San Diego State University), whereas others are in physical education or human performance schools (e.g., Bowling Green State University, Barry University, Ithaca College). Some are 1-year programs whereas others require a 2-year commitment. Some require a thesis and others do not. Most are traditional programs but a few are online programs. Some require an internship and others do not. Some are for full-time students and others are for working students.

Study Sport Communication in Graduate (Doctoral) Programs

Although there are still relatively few doctoral programs that specialize in sport management, the number of programs is steadily growing. All of these programs have sport communication courses, and some have a sport communication concentration. NASPE/NASSM-approved doctoral sport management programs include sport communication in their content areas. Familiarity with communication in sport is a prerequisite for all doctoral students entering an approved program ("Sport Management," 2000). Pursuing a doctorate in sport management or sport communication prepares an individual for leadership positions in academics and athletics. Regardless of which track one takes (e.g., academician, practitioner), communication is a major requirement of the position. For leadership in academics, professors need to possess the ability to write (research) and speak (present, lecture). For leadership in athletics, communication skills are needed all the more. Leadership is, according to Dr. Carla Green Williams, "the ability to share a vision and get the right people to follow; the ability to serve all in the organization." Williams, who is the associate athletic director at the University of Georgia, adds, "If I am an effective communicator, people will follow my vision." Williams, who had a sport management concentration for her doctoral studies at Florida State University, is now a sport leader with numerous responsibilities. The duties of her position involve supervising academic support services, compliance services, CHAMPS-Life Skills, women's gymnastics and basketball, men's and women's swimming and diving, and equestrian sports. She is also the point person in her department for Title IX and gender equity issues. Her busy schedule requires constant communication. "My day is spent communicating with coaches in every sport and most staff members," notes Williams. Although most of the time she communicates with coaches, academic counselors, and compliance officers, she frequently speaks with staff members of her athletic conference. For those who plan to pursue a doctorate in sport management or communication, the development of strong communication skills should be a foundation of their studies. "Focusing on sport communication in my doctoral work has allowed me to not only learn more about the field of sport communication but has also opened doors for me to learn about other disciplines," notes Andrea N. Eagleman, a former motorsports public relations manager.

Whether pursuing an undergraduate, master's, or doctoral degree, all sport management students are expected to leave their programs with a strong background in sport communication. All of the sport communication content areas presented here are for any position in any level of the sport industry. Any academic preparation in sport communication—whether it is one course or an entire major—will provide you with education, background, skill development, confidence, and networking opportunities. Regardless of the sport communication career (examined in the next chapter) you decide to pursue, education in sport communication will make you more attractive to organizations and employers in the sport industry.

INCREASING YOUR MARKETABILITY THROUGH ANCILLARY ACTIVITIES

Just as courses and practical experiences in sport communication will make you more marketable, taking a proactive approach to your educational and professional pursuits is highly recommended. There are two crucial components that will make you—the sport communication student—more marketable. First, read sport communication literature such as books, academic journals, and trade publications. Second, become affiliated with and involved in professional organizations.

Read Sport Communication Literature

There are numerous publications that sport communication students should read during the course of their studies. Among these are sport communication textbooks, trade publications, and academic, popular, and industry journals and magazines.

Books That Focus on Niche Segments

Students are encouraged to supplement their reading of this textbook by looking at other academic publications that focus on certain areas touched on in each course. This textbook's broad communication perspective gives students a taste of the entire field; it provides insight into the sport communication discipline, whereas other texts focus on certain niche segments of the field. Although we introduce you to the field of sport communication, other textbooks and book chapters can be used as supplemental materials for certain areas where you wish to gain even more understanding. For example, although we introduce you to sport public relations in chapter 11, there are other publications where you can find additional information. For a full analysis of sport public relations, we recommend *Sport Public Relations: Managing Organizational Communication,* by Clay Stoldt, Stephen Dittmore, and Scott Branvold (2006). Others in this area include *The Dream Job: Sports Publicity, Promo-*

tion, and Marketing (Helitzer, 1999), *Coach's Communication Playbook* (Hessert, 1998), *Complete Communications Manual for Coaches and Athletic Directors* (Mamchak & Mamchak, 1989), and *Media Relations in Sport* (Nichols, Moynahan, Hall, & Taylor, 2002).

Numerous books can help you learn more about sports broadcasting. Although this subject is covered in chapter 8, for a more in-depth examination of the sport media, our recommendation is Matthew Nicholson's (2007) *Sport and the Media: Managing the Nexus,* or Brad Schultz's (2005) *Sports Media: Reporting, Producing and Planning.* Schultz explained the focus of his book in the preface: "The emphasis today is on converged media, where television, radio, newspaper, and Internet coverage all blends together in a coherent mix" (p. xvi). For sports radio, you can supplement your reading by picking up books such as *Sports-Talk Radio in America* (Dempsey, 2006) and *Sports Talk: A Journey Inside the World of Sports Talk Radio* by Alan Eisenstock (2001). For sports television broadcasting (also covered in chapter 8), in addition to *Sportscasting* (Hitchcock, 1991), one of the more popular and helpful books on sports broadcasting is *The Art of Sportscasting: How to Build a Successful Career* by Tom Hedrick (2000). Hedrick is a legendary broadcaster with more than 4 decades of experience as the voice of teams such as the Kansas City Chiefs, Cincinnati Reds, Texas Rangers, Dallas Cowboys, University of Kansas Jayhawks, and Nebraska Cornhuskers. In addition to the practical sports broadcasting books, a host of biographies and autobiographies of past and present sports broadcast personalities are available (Dick Enberg, Marv Albert, Gary Bender, Curt Gowdy, and Red Barber).

For students seeking specific instruction in the print media, sports reporting, or sports writing, numerous exceptional books that go beyond the scope of this book (chapter 7) can assist with this pursuit. Some of these books are *Sports Journalism: Context and Issues* (Boyle, 2006), *No Time Outs: What It's Really Like to Be a Sportswriter Today* (Walsh, 2006), *Sports Journalism* (Andrews, 2005), *Inside the Sports Pages* (Lowes, 2000), *Contemporary Sports Reporting* (Anderson, 1994), *Sports Writing* (Craig, 2002), *Sports Reporting*

(Garrison & Sabljak, 1993), *Associated Press Sportswriting Handbook* (Wilstein, 2002), *Sports Writing* (Kervin, 1997), *The Sports Writing Handbook* (Fensch, 1995), *Writing Sports Stories That Sell* (Butler, 1999), *The Mulligan Guide to Sports Journalism Careers* (Mulligan & Mulligan, 1998), *The Coverage of Interscholastic Sports* (Hawthorne, 2001), and analyses by sportswriters such as Christine Brennan (*Best Seat in the House,* 2006), George Castle (*Baseball and the Media,* 2006), and Leonard Koppett (*Sports Illusion, Sports Reality,* 1994).

Beyond the practical and biographical examinations of sport communication, you can also learn more about sport communication by reading cultural, sociological, and critical books in the field. We introduce you to the sociological aspects of sport communication in chapter 13, but if you have an interest in studying this subject in more detail, we suggest *Critical Readings: Sport, Culture and the Media* (Rowe, 2004a), *Representing Sport* (Brookes 2002), *Power Play: Sport, the Media, and Popular Culture* (Boyle & Haynes, 2000), *The Meaning of Nolan Ryan* (Trujillo, 1994), *Handbook of Sports Studies* (Coakley & Dunning, 2000), and *Sport, Culture and the Media: The Unruly Trinity* (Rowe, 2004b). If you are interested in upper-level critical media analyses, several books are very useful: *Handbook of Sports and Media* (Raney & Bryant, 2006), *Sport, Rhetoric, & Gender: Historical Perspectives and Media Representations* (Fuller, 2006), *Exploring Media Culture: A Guide* (Real, 1996), *Sport, Media, Culture: Global and Local Dimensions* (Bernstein & Blain, 2003), *Case Studies in Sport Communication* (Brown & O'Rourke, 2003), *Out of Bounds: Sports, Media, and the Politics of Identity* (Baker & Boyd, 1997), *Women, Media, and Sport: Challenging Gender Values* (Creedon, 1994a), and *Mediasport* (Wenner, 1998a).

Academic and Trade Journals

Further reading in sport communication can be found in academic publications. Journals provide the research and theory that support, enhance, and advance the activities of academicians and practitioners. Many fields of study do not have their own journal. When a discipline gets its own journal, however,

this "can be interpreted as a sign that the demand for and supply of research by [sport communication experts] is now large enough to necessitate a field journal" (Jewell, 2006, p. 16). In sport communication this occurred in 2007 when Human Kinetics announced the launching of the *International Journal of Sport Communication (IJSC).* This refereed and multidisciplinary quarterly promotes the understanding and advancement of the relationship between sport and communication. The mission of the journal is to provide a platform for academics and practitioners to disseminate research and information on the unique aspects and divergent activities associated with any communication in sport, through sport, or in a sport setting. Although a plethora of sport communication articles are published in academic journals, it was not until recently that there was a journal solely dedicated to advancing the body of knowledge in this area. The *IJSC* fills this void. Furthermore, another journal—the *Journal of Sports Media*—began in 2006. This journal received its impetus during a conversation between sport communication professors and researchers at a scholarly convention in 2004. One of those in the meeting, Brad Shultz (2005), explains the vision at the time: "The journal would fill a niche in the academic and research community by focusing on all areas of sports media, including broadcasting, print, and the Internet" (p. xvi). In addition to these stand-alone publications, many journals have special issues dedicated to sport communication topics. Some of these academic publications include the *International Journal of Sport Management and Marketing,* the *Journal of Sport Management,* and the *Journal of Sport and Social Issues.*

In addition to these publications, numerous broad and segmented academic journals publish sport communication articles. Some of these publications average several sport communication articles a year, whereas others only occasionally publish an article on this topic. For example, in 2006 a new journal was launched called the *International Journal of Sport Finance.* The very first issue of this quarterly publication contained an article by Harry

Arne Solberg, "The Auctioning of TV-Sports Rights." Most sport management-related journals publish at least an occasional article on sport communication. In addition to the three "special issue" journals mentioned previously, some of the journals that publish sport communication articles frequently include *Sport Marketing Quarterly; Journal of Sports Economics; Entertainment and Sports Law Journal; The Physical Educator; Women in Sport and Physical Activity Journal; Sociology of Sport Journal; Sport Management and Related Topics Journal; Journal of Quantitative Analysis in Sport; Journal of Legal Aspects of Sport; Journal of Physical Education, Recreation, and Dance; Quest; Research Quarterly for Exercise and Sport; Sport, Education, and Society; Journal of Contemporary Athletics; Sport in Society; European Sport Management Review; International Review for the Sociology of Sport; Sport Management Review; (ICHPER-SD) Journal of Research; International Journal of Sports Marketing and Sponsorship;* and *European Journal for Sport and Society.*

Numerous history, sociological, and communication journals publish scholarly articles on sport communication topics. Published research on any of the topics covered in the remaining chapters of this textbook can often be found in such journals as *Journal of Sport History; Journal of Communication; Sex Roles: A Journal of Research; Public Relations Quarterly; Newspaper Research Journal; New Media and Society; Journal of Advertising; Public Relations Quarterly; International Journal of Sport History; Mass Communication and Society; Journalism: Theory, Practice and Criticism; Journalism Quarterly; Communication Teacher; Sport History Review; Sport in History; Critical Studies in Mass Communication; Journal of Broadcasting and Electronic Media; Journal of International Communication; Quarterly Journal of Speech;* and *Women's Studies in Communication.*

Although it is beneficial to read academic journals and popular press publications (e.g., *Sports Illustrated, ESPN The Magazine, The Sporting News*), a well-rounded sport communication student will also keep updated with information from practitioners in the field of sport communication. This is accomplished through reading trade journals and professional publications in the areas of media, communication, journalism, and sport management. Practitioner-based publications in these areas that frequently cover sport topics are *SportsBusiness Journal, NCAA News, Coach and Athletic Director, Columbia Journalism Review, Amusement Business, Editor and Publisher, SportsTravel, Advertising Age, SportBusiness International, Adbusters, Athletic Business, American Photo, Migala Report, Sports Forum, Design, PRWeek, RTNDA Communicator, Athletic Management, Quill and Scroll, Athletics Administration, Team Marketing Report, The American Editor,* and *Media Ethics.* Reading practitioner publications is a great way to keep updated on your chosen area of specialization. Another way is to subscribe to sport management and sport communication academic listservs. Furthermore, subscribing to information sources such as College Athletics (www.collegeathleticsclips.com), which provides summaries of intercollegiate athletic news and issues, or the Sport Business Education Network (www.thesmn.org), which provides networking opportunities for students and recent graduates, is recommended.

Join Academic and Professional Organizations

To give yourself the best opportunity for entering the field of sport communication, join sport management, marketing, communication, or media academic and professional organizations. This will provide you with more educational and networking opportunities. Examples of practitioner-based associations include the College Sports Information Directors of America (COSIDA), Associated Press Sports Editors (APSE), Association for Women in Sports Media (AWSM), American Sportscasters Association (ASA), United States Basketball Writers Association (USBWA), Football Writers Association of America (FWAA), and National Collegiate Baseball Writers Association (NCBWA).

Some of the best academic associations for future sport communication professionals are the North American Society for Sport

Management (NASSM), North American Society for the Sociology of Sport (NASSS), Association for Education in Journalism and Mass Communication (AEJMC), and the Sport Marketing Association (SMA). Most of the academic and professional associations have conferences, seminars, and workshops at least once a year. Most of the organizations and associations entertain and discuss sport communication topics and issues during their annual gatherings.

CHAPTER WRAP-UP

Summary

In this chapter we have attempted to outline some of the basic issues related to the study and practice of sport communication. We have argued that much of the growth related to the sport industry can be attributed to sport communication. Some of this growth comes from the fact that no other segment of the media is growing as fast as sport (Andrews, 2005). The mass media's coverage and financial backing have tremendously affected the sport industry. However, without the interpersonal and organizational communication in and between sport organizations, the sport industry would not be as enormous and influential as it is today. Therefore, much of the credit for the enormity of the sport industry can be traced to some aspect of sport communication (e.g., interpersonal, organizational, mass mediated, support services). In this chapter, we advanced the notion that there is a need for strong academic preparation for future sport industry leaders, in both sport management and sport communication. We concluded the chapter by offering suggestions to make sport communication students as marketable and knowledgeable as possible through reading outside materials and participating in academic and professional activities.

Review Questions

1. What are the size and scope of the sport industry? What has contributed to its growth?
2. How is the sport industry segmented?
3. What are the size and scope of sport communication?
4. What is the global impact of sport communication?
5. Why is academic training vital to a career in sport communication?
6. What are some typical courses in sport communication? How do these courses help prepare students for a career in the field?
7. What books are useful when studying the field of sport communication?
8. What academic and trade journals focus on the field of sport communication?
9. What academic and professional associations further the advancement of sport communication?
10. Why is professional development important when preparing for a career in sport communication?

Discussion Questions

1. How has sport communication contributed to the growth of the sport industry?
2. Why are communication skills important in any position within the sport industry?
3. What are the various segmentation models of the sport industry? Which models do you believe most appropriately address the size and scope of the sport industry?
4. How do these models classify sport communication?
5. Why is skill development important for a career in sport communication?
6. How can learning additional languages benefit you when preparing for a sport communication career?
7. Why is studying sport communication important?
8. How do academic and trade publications facilitate the growth of sport communication as a discipline?
9. How does the growth of academic programs facilitate the development of professionals in sport communication?
10. How do professional associations contribute to the field of sport communication?

Group Activities

1. With your group members, select one segmentation model presented in the chapter. Prepare an outline of the key aspects of the model. What is the role of sport communication in the model? What should be included in the model or modified to better address the role of sport communication in the growth of sport management? Present your outline to the class.
2. For each member of your group, select two or three academic or trade publications in the field of sport management and sport communication. Identify how these publications affect and reflect the nature and scope of the field of sport communication. Report your findings to the class.
3. For each member of your group, choose a professional position in sport communication. Write a one-page summary outlining the position and how it fits within the realm of the discipline. Present your findings to your group members.

Individual Exercises

1. Identify and research a professional association. How could membership in the association facilitate your skills in sport communication?
2. Choose a sport, sport entity, or segment within the realm of the sport industry. Write a one- or two-page summary statement illustrating how this sport, sport entity, or segment has contributed to the growth of the sport industry. Share your findings with the class.
3. Select a recent academic journal serving the sport management or sport communication discipline. Select an article from that journal that focuses on an aspect of sport communication. Review the article and write no more than a two-page summary illustrating how the article represents the nature and scope of the field or a current trend in the field. Present your summary to the class.

Internet Sites for Additional Learning

Center for Sports Innovation: web.mit.edu/aeroastro/www/labs/csi/

Center for Sports Journalism: www.comm.psu.edu/sports/

Franchise Valuations: www.forbes.com/2006/04/17/06mlb_baseball_valuations_land.html

International Association for Sports Information: www.iasi.org/home.html

Sport Industry: http://ww3.sportsline.com/u/sportscareers/industry.htm

CHAPTER 2

Careers in Sport Communication

LEARNING OBJECTIVES

▶ To recognize the breadth and width of professional opportunities in the communication segment of the sport industry

▶ To learn about the five key areas of sport communication careers

▶ To become acquainted with the many career options in sport communication

▶ To understand the trends in and the current status of the sport communication job market

▶ To comprehend the integral components, resources, techniques, and skill development necessary to prepare for a position in sport communication

PROFILE OF A SPORT COMMUNICATOR

Ron Semiao

With all respect to Linda Cohn, Dan Patrick, Michael Wilbon, and any other popular personality at ESPN, Inc., there are few more influential people in sport communication than Ron Semiao. As the senior vice president of ESPN Original Entertainment, he oversees all entertainment-related ventures for the company. He is a key decision maker for movies (e.g., *The Junction Boys),* scripted series programming (e.g., *The Bronx Is Burning),* events (e.g., ESPY Awards), and unscripted reality (e.g., *The Contender)* and development projects. Although he plays a vital role in defining the vision for the world's most powerful sports network, this sport communication executive always will be best known for creating the ESPN X Games.

When ESPN2 was launched in 1993, a major thrust of the programming was the emergence of extreme sports. Semiao, who moved to the programming department 2 months before the new network went on the air, had little knowledge of extreme sports. He explains, "I went to a Barnes and Noble Bookstore and walked out with a big stack of magazines on such sports as skateboarding, biking, in-line skating, sky diving, and climbing. That is where the idea [X Games] came from." After he perused the publications one weekend it dawned on him to create an "Olympics of extreme sports." His original idea was for ESPN to bring together a collection of the extreme sports under a large umbrella of competition to showcase not only the athletic abilities of the participants but also their accompanying lifestyles and cultural aspects. Most important, however, was his concept of ownership. Television networks and cable companies typically rent the broadcast rights from a league, college conference, or governing body

and bring their cameras in and cover the event. With the X Games, however, Semiao used his creative mind and effective communication skills to sell the unique idea of media event ownership where ESPN would create, market, stage, and broadcast the sports event.

Semiao presented his proposal to colleagues, supervisors, and eventually the company president (Steve Bornstein, now the president and CEO of the NFL Network), who gave his approval. Today, extreme sports—thanks in large part to Semiao and his idea—is a multibillion dollar segment of the sport industry. Although Semiao is thrilled with the success of his X Games, he takes pride in three specific statements that have been relayed to him over the years. "In one of our focus groups, a 39-year-old man told me that he watched the X Games every night with his 13-year-old son and they had a blast together. That was cool. Also, Dave Mirra [the event's most decorated bike stunt rider] once told me, 'If it wasn't for you, I'd be working at Burger King.' Last, I have an autographed picture of Tony Hawk [skateboarder] in my office that says, 'To my hero, Ron, thanks for finally giving us a chance.'"

Semiao was not always a high-ranking sport communication executive. After college he worked in the audit departments for Capitol Records and NBC Entertainment before joining ESPN. Over the past 20 years at the network he has worked his way up through the ranks. He started as a finance analyst and advanced to titles such as production operations coordinator, operations producer, senior operations producer, programming acquisition and planning specialist, director of programming, and vice president of programming before assuming his current leadership position.

Ron Semiao's story illustrates the professional activities of a sport communication executive, one of the five career segments outlined in this chapter (see figure 2.1). In addition to discussing the executive or management segment, this chapter highlights four other career categories in sport communication: the mass media, support services, entertainment, and other opportunities in the field of sport communication.

Sport is a multibillion dollar industry that is full of exciting and challenging career opportunities. A relatively recent estimate had the sport industry accounting for nearly five million jobs (Pedersen, Whisenant, & Schneider, 2005). In addition to the fact that each job in the sport industry has some component of communication (i.e., writing, speaking, interacting), the sport communication segment of the industry is particularly vibrant and attractive. This chapter introduces students to the broad range of careers in this field. It is designed to answer questions such as, "What kind of jobs are available in sport communication?" and "How do I prepare myself for a position in sport communication?"

The various occupations in the field typically involve some aspect of covering, delivering, publicizing, financing, and even shaping sport. Professionals in sport communication craft and send messages in different ways and may alter modes of communication depending on the nature of their position as well as audience needs and desires. Although the nature (e.g., managerial, publicity, writing) and scope (e.g., print, electronic, public relations) of the positions within sport communication vary, at the core of the various career paths is the ability to communicate with key audiences. Key audiences vary based on the type of sport entity and are usually those audiences deemed to be most valuable to the organization. Key audiences may include fans, members of the public, politicians, owners and investors, athletes, and even members of the media. Regardless, sport media professionals as well as sport communication professionals working for sport organizations must communicate appropriately with each key audience.

Furthermore, the growth of sport communication as a discipline (e.g., the increase of sport communication academic publications, programs, and courses) and the convergence of the mass media (the process of overlapping relationships between media entities) have affected the development of sport management and sport communication professionals. Both of these fields require that professionals possess skills that will allow them to work across the landscape of the sport communication industry.

The convergence of media entities provides a wide array of opportunities for professionals with strong skill sets and adaptable mind-sets. For example, editors of newspapers often work with both the print and the online versions of their publications. Similarly, it is common for sportswriters to cross over into sports broadcasting while continuing their writing careers. This is the case with sportswriters Christine Brennan of *USA Today* and Mike Lupica of *The New York Daily News*. Both Brennan and Lupica, along with many other reporters and columnists, are regulars on ESPN programs. Sportswriters Woody Paige (*Denver Post*) and Stephen A. Smith (*Philadelphia Inquirer*) are two of the most visible columnists on television.

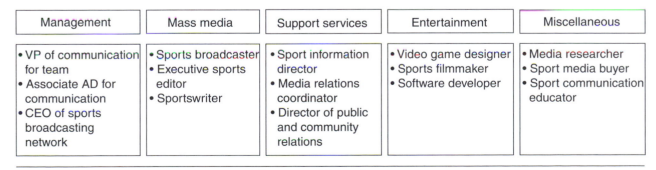

Management	Mass media	Support services	Entertainment	Miscellaneous
• VP of communication for team • Associate AD for communication • CEO of sports broadcasting network	• Sports broadcaster • Executive sports editor • Sportswriter	• Sport information director • Media relations coordinator • Director of public and community relations	• Video game designer • Sports filmmaker • Software developer	• Media researcher • Sport media buyer • Sport communication educator

Figure 2.1 Careers in sport communication fall into one of five major areas.

© Paul M. Pedersen

William C. Rhoden, a sports columnist for more than 2 decades with *The New York Times,* began his sport communication career as the assistant sport information director at Morgan State University. He is a frequent guest on ESPN's *Sports Reporters.* Here, Rhoden interviews United States Senator Mitch McConnell.

When ESPN announced that Smith would have his own show, the columnist explained, "The newspaper business still serves as my foundation." He added that the "principles and the integrity associated with (print journalism) serve as the backbone for all that I'm about and hope to be professionally."

This chapter begins by detailing the various leadership, management, and administrative positions in the field. Next, the chapter covers the plethora of careers in the sport mass media. These careers are in the broad areas of print sport media, sport electronic and visual media, and new and emerging sport media. The chapter continues by describing the professions involved with the support services of advertising and public relations. Sport communication professionals in support services also use a variety of media to disseminate messages. The chapter then illustrates the many career opportunities in sport communication entertainment and some of the nontraditional

positions in the field. The final section of the chapter details the critical components that are necessary to gain entry into a sport communication career.

CAREERS IN MANAGEMENT

Managers and administrators in sport communication are the leaders in the field. Many have been employed in sport communication for decades and have worked their way up in the ranks just as a young professional athlete would work her or his way through the minor or developmental leagues and into the majors. These leaders in sport communication are owners, publishers, producers, presidents, vice presidents, and entrepreneurs. All oversee the day-to-day sport communication operations of the sport-focused organization, and most are required to perform a wide variety of functions. They manage employees, plan strategies, organize campaigns, and deal with budgetary, staffing, policy, legal, and ethical issues. Furthermore, they foster mutually beneficial partnerships with stakeholders (e.g., sport advertisers, sport organizations, sport media outlets, sports clients, fans) and possess a wide range of skills.

Later sections of this chapter detail the traditional positions in sport communication. However, there are numerous managerial and administrative tracks for individuals to pursue in this field.

In sport organizations, these positions range from vice presidents of communication to corporate communication specialists to sport media managers. For example, the sport management leaders of the Miami Heat are the team's owner (Micky Arison), president (Pat Riley), general manager (Randy Pfund), and business operations president (Eric Woolworth). Under these top management professionals is Tim Donovan, who is the team's vice president in charge of sports media relations. He is charged with overseeing all aspects—both sport media and business media—of the team's communication efforts. Under Donovan are sport media relations and business media relations directors and assistant directors as well as managers, staffers, and other professionals in broadcast management, broadcast services, announcing, media production, and press room operations.

An example from intercollegiate athletics is Claude Felton, the associate athletic director for sport communication for the University of Georgia. Felton heads all communication aspects (i.e., radio, television, public relations, sports information, *Bulldog Magazine*) of the athletic department. This includes overseeing the four associate and assistant sport communication directors, publications and systems coordinator, office manager, Web site managers, editors, interns and graduate assistants, and office personnel. Sport communication leaders such as Donovan and Felton have numerous duties that may include broadcast rights negotiations, strategic planning for communication, and a host of other typical managerial and leadership responsibilities.

In sport media enterprises there are similar executive positions and opportunities. For example, *Sports Illustrated* is led by its publisher, Dave Morris. Under this top executive, however, are numerous managerial and administrative professionals who lead hundreds of employees. Some of these leaders have titles such as publishing director, editorial projects director, advertising revenue manager, director of positioning, director of book makeup, director of plant operations, regional directors, advertising directors, sales managers, account managers, production staffers, and a host of other noneditorial employees.

According to the *SportsBusiness Journal,* the most influential person in sports business is George Bodenheimer, the president of ESPN/ABC Sports ("The 50 Most Influential," 2006). The publication notes that the most influential sport media executives are Bodenheimer, Dick Ebersol, David Hill, Sean McManus, Brian Roberts, Steve Bornstein, Mark Shapiro, Chase Carey, Fred Dressler, and James Dolan. These sport communication leaders work for media giants such as ESPN/ABC Sports, Fox, CBS Sports, Comcast, NFL Network, DirecTV, Time Warner Cable, and Cablevision. Bornstein, for example, provides the perfect illustration of career progression and leadership in sport communication.

Before taking his current position as president and CEO of the NFL Network, Bornstein served as president of ABC Entertainment and as a consultant to the NFL. He negotiated the NFL Sunday Ticket renewal with DirecTV, which increased the annual rights fees from $144 million to $400 million per year. In the renegotiation, DirecTV also agreed to carry the NFL Network, which was in its infancy. Today, the NFL Network reaches almost 22 million homes and rights fees have increased to $700 million per year (which amounts to $3.5 billion from 2006 to 2010). Bornstein, known for his strategic thinking ability as well as for his tough negotiation tactics, began his career working at two local television stations while attending the University of Wisconsin. After graduation he worked as a remote crew chief for a television station in Milwaukee and as a freelance cameraman for the Marquette Warriors, the Milwaukee Bucks, and the Milwaukee Brewers. He later served as an executive producer of an Ohio television station before beginning a 2-decade stint at ESPN and ABC Sports, where he was instrumental in establishing ABC as a premier network for college football.

Although sport communication managers and administrators hail from varying backgrounds and positions, they move into the executive and leadership positions by honing their skills and building relationships at lower levels of the organization. They then rely on the experience gained as they work their way through various positions to prepare them for managerial and administrative opportunities at higher levels. Whether the organization is a sport media entity or a sport team, the rapid growth of the sport industry has resulted in an increase of sport communication professionals and a need for people to lead these professionals. As McGowan and Bouris (2005) noted, "Twenty years ago it was generally a one- or two-person public relations staff handling a team, but today there are staffs of six to ten individuals with titles ranging from the vice-president level to directors, assistant directors, and the other staff" (p. 354). Such expansion has increased the demand for leaders who can manage the sport communication aspects of sport organizations and for those who can run the business and administrative areas of sport media enterprises.

CAREERS IN MASS MEDIA

Where do most sports fans find news and updates about their favorite teams and players? For the most part, these enthusiasts get their information through media sources. They either buy the newspaper and read the sports section, turn on the television and flip to a sports broadcast, or rely on the Internet to provide basic and in-depth sports coverage. Although the sports action takes place on the field, rink, or court, the production and transmission of sport information to the public typically come about through the work of sport communication professionals in the mass media.

The mass media make up the segment of the sport communication field that houses the major outlets for the transmission of ideas. This segment—which informs, educates, persuades, and entertains masses of sports viewers, listeners, and readers—employs thousands of professionals. In the past, the primary sport occupation in the mass media was sport journalism, and the sports departments of newspapers housed many of these professionals. Although newspapers still represent a sizable portion of the mass media, people interested in a career in the sport mass media today have myriad additional options from which to choose. Professionals in this segment work for numerous and varied mass media. The divergent positions in the sport media involve the gathering, selecting, processing, and presenting of sports news and coverage to the masses. Careers include writing sports books, taking photographs for sports magazines, programming for sports radio stations, delivering sports news on television, writing scripts for sports movies, and designing sports Web sites. This section examines the unique sport communication careers within the mass media.

Print Media

The print sport media component of the mass media involves several broad areas. Newspa-

pers (e.g., *USA Today, San Francisco Chronicle*), wire services (e.g., Associated Press), magazines (e.g., *Golf Digest, Runner's World*), and books (e.g., *Friday Night Lights, A Season on the Brink*) are some of the most prominent and attractive print sport media options available to those interested in a career in sport communication. Within each print sport medium are numerous and varied careers ranging from business operations to production occupations to editorial professions.

The sports coverage in the print media is a major source of information for fans. Even with the increase in new technology and the dwindling in the number of daily newspapers, there are still exciting and abundant careers in newspapers, wire services, magazines, and books. On the business operations and production sides of the print sport media there are jobs in publishing, accounting, administration, finance, sales, marketing, human resources, promotions, corporate communications, business development, and strategic planning. For instance, there are sales representatives in all areas of the sport mass media. These professionals contact prospective businesses to sell advertising for the print and Web-based media and radio and television time for the broadcast media. The sales representative also works with a copy writer, creating advertisements for sports publications and broadcasts.

On the journalistic side of the print sport media, many full-time and freelance positions are available in writing, reporting, editing, designing, and photography. These journalists in the print media and wire services research and gather information and then communicate their work to the public through their words, creative endeavors, and photographs. Many of these print media activities are performed for radio and television broadcasts and Web-based publications as well. The leader of the newspaper sports department or sports magazine is the sports editor. This professional, who often works closely with an executive sports editor or managing sports editor, is responsible for planning coverage and breaking news, juggling deadlines, handling assignments and special projects, dispatching reporters, supervising coverage and production, and setting and upholding the standard for sports department or magazine practices.

Does everything newsworthy get covered by the local sports section? What about that sporting event that had thousands of spectators but received only limited coverage in a sports publication? Because that event was not covered does not necessarily mean it is any less important than the event that did receive coverage. However, it does illustrate the power of the sports editors—the gatekeepers—in sport communication. These are the key decision makers because they decide what a newspaper (whether it is a national, regional, local, tabloid, broadsheet, daily, weekly, or specialized publication) or magazine will cover and what information does not make the cut. Below the sports editor and managing sports editor are the copyeditors. These professionals inside the sports department or wire service read, edit, update, and put headlines on stories. Other editorial positions include designers, graphic artists, and layout specialists. These are the creative individuals who—through their skilled use of images, graphics, and designs with software programs such as Quark Express and Adobe Photoshop and Illustrator—make the sports pages more appealing.

Sports columnists lead the way with respect to the writing aspect of the print sport media. These professionals provide subjective opinions and analyses. Other careers in sportswriting include beat and feature writers, general assignment reporters, agate clerks, and photographers. Sportswriters and photojournalists cover events, issues, and personalities. The subjects they cover range from interscholastic athletics to college and professional sports, depending on the size of the newspaper, the wire service, and the market. Sportswriters and photojournalists attend games, interview subjects, and provide information and expert analysis for fans and readers. In addition to employing staff reporters and photographers, many print publications rely heavily on correspondents and freelancers to complete sports coverage requirements. Freelancing is for those who want to be sportswriters and photographers but do not want the restrictions of a full-time position with a newspaper, wire service, or magazine. Although most freelancers have years of experience before they decide to become independent professionals, any prospective sportswriter or photographer can embark on a career in freelancing. To work as a freelancer, one needs to develop contacts with Internet sites, newspapers, magazines, and other media.

In addition to the storied publications such as *Sports Illustrated* and *The Sporting News,* there is a magazine for just about every sport. Titles such as *Mountain Biking, Black Belt,* and *American Snowmobiler* show that most sports magazines are niche publications. Although sports magazines—including sponsored magazines, trade journals, and news rack publications—cater to narrow audience segments, they offer countless career opportunities. Many of the occupations found in newspapers and wire services also exist in sports magazines. Depending on your interests, abilities, and experience, professional opportunities in sports magazine publishing can be found in such areas as management, production, editing (e.g., editor-in-chief, editorial director, executive editor, managing editor, senior editor), writing, designing, advertising sales, promotion, marketing, public relations, circulation, art, and photography.

No analysis of the print sport media can be complete without including what is often considered the first and most respected mass medium: books. Hundreds of sport-related novels, biographies, commentaries, histories, trade books, and textbooks are released each year, and a small number are even made into movies (e.g., Norman Maclean's *A River Runs Through It,* Bernard Malamud's *The Natural,* Peter Gent's *North Dallas Forty*). Those who choose this profession have plenty of writers of classic sports books to emulate. A few of these authors are Roger Kahn (*The Boys of Summer*), Jim Bouton (*Ball Four*), Dan Jenkins (*Semi-Tough*), George Plimpton (*Paper Lion*), Terry Pluto (*Loose Balls*), Rick Telander (*Heaven Is a Playground*), David Halberstam (*The Breaks of the Game*), and Roger Angell (*The Summer Game*). The publishing of sports books involves many occupations in addition to that of author, biographer, or chronicler.

There are positions for sport communication professionals in publishing, acquisitions, press agentry, sales, promotion, layout, and design at both the large publishing companies and the thousands of small publishing ventures. As publishers of sports books move to more digital and Web-related publications, there will always be plenty of career opportunities in sports books.

Electronic and Visual Media

Rapid changes are occurring in sports broadcast communication. Such a dynamic field has produced a need for professionals in the management, production, and news sides of these media. The opportunities—whether for 24-hour sports ventures or sports departments and productions—are in local television and radio stations, nonprofit and federally funded noncommercial enterprises, independent production facilities, sole proprietorships, networks, satellite, and cable companies. It is not uncommon for many sports broadcast communication careers to begin in radio, which is considered the first broadcast medium. Sports radio broadcasts—ranging from campus and local endeavors to regional and national networks—reach people in various markets and sometimes throughout the United States with sports-related opinion, news, entertainment, business, and advertising. Each sports station and sports program has managerial, on-air, production, sales, marketing, engineering, research, and programming job possibilities for those interested in such a career. Furthermore, the broadcasting of these sports radio stations and programs on the Internet has increased the opportunities for sport communication professions with technical expertise.

Television—often considered the most influential medium—has similar career on-air and behind-the-scenes offerings. The most appealing—and most competitive—are found in sports cable and other multichannel sport services. For instance, ESPN—the sport network that is a subsidiary of the American Broadcasting Company (ABC)—has created a generation of sports enthusiasts who want to become the next Chris Berman. An opportu-

nity to work for this sport network will come more quickly, however, for those interested in working in other areas (e.g., business affairs, production, engineering, facilities, operations, research, Web design, information services, new media). The growth of digital cable companies and satellite radio and television programming has increased the demand for sport communication professionals. An example of this is the commercial-free Sirius Satellite Radio, which offers sports programming for numerous sports in addition to six all-sports talk channels (ESPN Radio, ESPNEWS, Sport Byline USA, Sirius Sports Action, Sirius NFL Radio, Sports Play-by-Play). In addition to the traditional career opportunities in sports radio and television, sports broadcasting opportunities are available in producing sport training materials, sport videos, commercials for and of sport, and sport education materials.

A career behind the camera can be just as exciting and rewarding as one in front of the camera.

Countless managerial positions are available in production, programming, sales, administration, research, marketing, and promotions in the sports broadcasting, cable, and satellite industry. Some of the careers include the sports director, director of sports broadcasting, tape librarian, film editor, news writer, engineer, corporate officer, advertising sales coordinator, media buyer, market researcher, business manager, account executive, general manager, station manager, operations staff, and operations manager. Other off-camera and off-microphone options have titles such as sports producer, technical director, video technician, media production assistant, and audio consultant. Similar to the sports editor in the newspaper or sports magazine, the sports producer is the leader of the radio or television sports department. This person sets assignments, coordinates programming, keeps stories and programs on schedule and budget, finds new sources for stories, sets and upholds the department's standards of operations, and works to keep the sports show entertaining, profitable, and organized.

For those who wish to go into the performance side of the sports broadcasting, cable, and satellite industry, there are also plenty of career options. Some of these options involve on-air or on-camera opportunities in sports radio, sports television, and sports programming (e.g., anchors, broadcasters, reporters, photographers, talk-show hosts). Although the median annual salary for a sports radio anchor is relatively low at $27,000, these positions are highly competitive (RTNDA, 2005). For television sports anchors and reporters, the pay can be similar to their radio counterparts. The median annual salary for television sports anchors ranges from $24,000 to $90,000 and for television sports reporters from $23,000 to $40,000, depending on the size of the station (RTNDA, 2005).

New and Emerging Sport Technology

The amount of Web-based sport information continues to increase exponentially with the proliferation of the Internet. The Web has become an accepted method for presenting and retrieving sport information. Digitization has played a major role in the transition of some traditional sport media to the Web. The Internet has an abundance of sport-oriented sites ranging from sports news (e.g., CBS SportsLine.com, ESPN.com) to athletes to teams. Public discourse—including sport—has increased with the arrival of the information superhighway. Content created online by individuals other than sport journalists is known as consumer-generated media (CGM). This content is made available to other consumers through the use of Web logs, online forums, message boards, and other digital technology.

This emerging global mass medium has opened career opportunities for many who never would have found a position in traditional sportswriting and sports broadcasting. One such career is that of Web development. Web developers are responsible for planning, creating, and updating sports sites for intercollegiate athletic departments, newspapers, television stations, sports teams, and other sport media outlets and sport organizations. The professional in this field of sport communication has expertise in interacting with the Web (e.g., mastery of the mechanics of scripting languages such as HTML, CSS, and JavaScript) and its users to create appropriate and effective messages suited to the medium. Typical careers include Web site design, multimedia project management, marketing, business development, online and off-line promotions, sales, Web content writing, organizational Web maintenance and management, Web animation, Webmaster, and Internet content coordination. These positions pay $37,000 to more than $80,000 annually depending on the position and one's years of experience (*Salary Guide,* 2005).

Some of the communications system technology and computer networking careers include e-commerce, network design, analysis, and administration. The support services in this field include careers in computer-assisted design, consulting, graphics and animation, operations, database administration, desktop publishing, management, sales, technical support, technical writing, Web page design and maintenance, and word processing (Milbrandt

& Stephenson, 2001). Other career opportunities in this area of sport communication can be found in multimedia endeavors, Web logs, digitization, wireless sport communication, and informatics.

CAREERS IN SUPPORT SERVICES

Few organizations could operate effectively without support services, and sport-related organizations are no exception. Many opportunities are available within the realm of support services, which are vital to the overall mission of the organization. This section highlights the main support services within the broad scope of sport communication. Professionals in each of the main areas must be creative and must possess a keen ability to communicate persuasively, both orally and in writing, with supervisors, coworkers, and key publics.

Sport Advertising

As the number of sport-focused organizations has increased, so has the need for professionals well trained in the principles of advertising. Advertising managers and managers in advertising-related fields held approximately 645,000 jobs in the United States (Bureau of Labor Statistics, 2006). Advertisers carefully craft and communicate messages regarding their products to key audiences, with the specific purpose of convincing members of those key audiences to purchase the organizations' products. In sport, these products range from sports sections in daily newspapers to tickets to sporting events. The manner in which the message is crafted and communicated will vary based on the nature and profile of each key audience. Sport advertising professionals should expect to travel frequently, work under deadline pressure, and work long hours, including evenings and weekends. Approximately two-thirds of professionals in advertising and advertising-related positions report working more than 40 hours per week (Bureau of Labor Statistics, 2006). Students preparing for a career in sport advertising should possess knowledge of advertising trends, strong

visual communication skills, and an ability to generate creative content for print, broadcast, and electronic media. Advertising positions in sport may involve crafting advertising campaigns for the sport organization or selling sponsorships in which the sport organization is used as a vehicle for advertising by various companies and corporations. Positions range from advertising sales, advertising management, and advertising placement to sport media buying and sponsorship sales.

Sport Public Relations

Sport public relations is related to both marketing and advertising in that its goal is to generate awareness for the products of sport organizations. However, the key focus of sport public relations is to manage information flow between the sport-focused organization and its key publics, both internal and external. In managing information flow, sport public relations professionals are most concerned with crafting positive images that present the sport-focused organization and its stakeholders in the most favorable manner possible. This is accomplished through fostering mutually beneficial relationships with the public, with the media, and with the local community of the sport-focused organization. Public relations professionals are responsible for determining the concerns and expectations of the organization's publics and explaining these concerns and expectations to management. Most often in sport, public relations is considered synonymous with media relations. However, the nature and scope of sport public relations are broader and encompass many functions including message development and creation, community relations, collaboration, and communication with the sport-focused organization's key constituents (e.g., stockholders, boosters, season ticket holders, casual fans, and sport media consumers).

Sport entities are growing and are becoming more sophisticated in the manner in which they communicate with their key internal and external publics. As these communication efforts have become more refined, these organizations and sport public relations professionals have adapted by changing the functions of these positions. Traditionally, sport public relations professionals were considered glorified statisticians who provided information to the media. More recently, sport public relations professionals are integral in shaping the messages and images of the organization. They play a key role in managing the complex issues facing sport organizations and in assisting management in understanding and gaining support from key constituents.

Wayne Weaver, majority owner of the NFL's Jacksonville Jaguars, has noted the importance of involving his communication director in efforts to create, shape, and disperse the franchise's messages. Weaver's mentality demonstrates a shift in the NFL, with many owners and top-level executives stressing the need for public relations staff to use their communication skills to aid member franchises in a proactive attempt to manage a positive and influential brand image. Sport receives much free press and is covered in the mass media daily. Dan Edwards—the communication director for the Jaguars—sees the coverage as an advantage, and he understands the importance of using that coverage to send key messages to fans and to citizens of Jacksonville. Top-level executives at franchises across the NFL have followed suit and are using the

skills and talents of these sport public relations professionals to enhance the image of their respective franchises. The Baltimore Ravens produce two weekly television shows and two radio shows from an in-house studio, whereas Pat Hanlon, vice president of communications for the New York Giants, hosts a weekly television show discussing Giants news and notes with local newspaper writers. Miami Dolphins senior vice president of media relations Harvey Greene notes that the cost of operating an NFL franchise warrants a concerted effort by the marketing, public relations, and community relations departments to cultivate a positive brand image in the host city (Schoenfeld, 2005).

Many public relations positions in organizations now include community relations. Community relations managers usually work under the direction of public and media relations directors and are responsible for planning and initiating active participation within the organization's community. The goal of this active participation is to maintain and enhance the local environment to benefit both the community and the organization. Community relations managers work closely with colleagues in public and media relations, marketing, and advertising to initiate and develop community-based programs. Often these sport public

Sport Information Director: Public Relations at the Collegiate Level

Like their counterparts in the major leagues, collegiate sport information directors must now meet the demands of their ever-changing environment. Hardin and McClung examined these professionals in a study published in 2002. The authors noted that the position of a sport information director is considered one of the best jobs in the sport industry. Furthermore, the commercialization of collegiate athletics has forced sport public relations professionals at this level to respond to the demands of their athletic departments, their educational institutions, and their external publics, including fans and boosters. The profession at this level is often characterized by long hours and requires

exceptional writing skills, excellent technological skills including HTML and video streaming, and experience gained as a student or intern. Typical duties of sport information directors include drafting media releases; coordinating media conferences; scheduling interviews with student-athletes, coaches, and athletic directors; developing and producing game notes and media guides; and working with colleagues at other institutions to share information when their teams face each other in competition. Although most public relations professionals earn a median salary of $53,000, only 26.5% of collegiate sport information directors earn more than $55,000 (Hardin & McClung, 2002).

relations professionals work with marketing and promotions executives at various charitable organizations such as the United Way, the Children's Miracle Network, and the American Red Cross. The organization may partner with charitable organizations to combine resources and enhance overall efforts to establish a mutually beneficial environment for the community, the charity, and the organization. These organizations are increasingly community minded and recognize the value of establishing a favorable image as good corporate citizens.

Professionals in sport public relations must use research to determine the attitudes and behaviors of key publics. This enables professionals to plan, implement, influence, and measure changes in stakeholder attitudes and behavior. Sport public relations professionals must also develop skills in relationship building. They often serve as key advisors to management regarding the image and perception of the sport-focused organization. Many times sport public relations professionals are expected to make recommendations to managers regarding the most effective and efficient manner in which to craft messages consistent with the mission and values of the organization. This requires that sport public relations professionals work with various organizational units within the organization as well as with management staff at other corporations and charitable organizations.

CAREERS IN ENTERTAINMENT

Sport consumers are becoming more technologically savvy. Technology allows sport communication professionals to have a direct link to loyal, casual, and potential fans. As sport consumers have increased their technological demands, sport communication professionals have been forced to become more creative in the manner in which they communicate messages to their publics. Often this communication takes the form of entertainment like video games, music, and movies. Sport consumers not only want access to a variety of sport information but also want it to be convenient and readily accessible. Thus, sport and entertain-

ment combine to send powerful messages to sport consumers. This technological trend has created a demand for sport communicators with skills in software development, computer technological support, video editing, sound recording, and Web programming.

Video Gaming

Online video gaming has been noted as one of the fastest growing components of the video game market. It already reaches a majority of sport consumers with companies such as EA Sports as a driving force. EA Sports produces video games for each of the major leagues as well as the NCAA. Sony developed the Playstation Portable (PSP), which has wireless capabilities and can automatically connect to any other Playstation located within 350 feet. The PSP includes a real video highlight feature allowing gamers to obtain video highlights from real major league games. Currently, 6.5 million consumers subscribe to online game services (Bernstein, 2005d).

Positions within this realm of sport communication include graphic artist, designer, and quality assurance game tester. Graphic artists and designers are typically very familiar with software design programs such as Maya and Photoshop. These sport communication professionals often collaborate with members in other areas (e.g., engineering staff) involved with the production of video and online games. Graphic artists and designers must understand trends in the sport industry, texturing and modeling techniques, and the best ways to clearly and openly communicate with all parties involved in the development process. Quality assurance game testers must possess advanced software troubleshooting skills because they are required to identify software defects with video and online games. Sport communication professionals in these positions must also possess strong verbal and written communication skills.

Movies and Music

The increase in sports films and movies has generated a growing need for sport communication professionals with the ability to write screenplays, direct, produce, and serve as technical directors in film and movie production. For example, seven sports movies—led by *The Longest Yard*—ranked among the top 15 gross revenue producers in the United States in the summer of 2005 (Johnson-Reid, 2005b). Sport communication professionals are also needed in various aspects of nontraditional sport events. These careers can be found in the sport management areas of certain music tours, entertainment districts, and ancillary activities. For example, Major League Baseball specifically wants to target its noncore consumers by communicating its key messages through the music and pop culture scene and capitalizing on its MLB Road Show, a 53-foot trailer that unfolds to reveal a "cyber ballpark" with batting cages, video games, and coupons for merchandise (Adams, 2005d). MLB relies on sport communication professionals to assist in designing the Road Show, developing the league's key messages, and disseminating them to its target audience.

CAREERS THROUGH OTHER OPPORTUNITIES

Most professional careers in sport communication are in management, mass media, support services, and entertainment. Beyond those major areas, however, numerous other positions are available in some nontraditional aspects of the field. In fact, some of the best opportunities in sport communication are behind-the-scenes occupations. These include the production and operations sides of the industry and range from equipment technicians and audio engineers to sports videographers and technical writers. Many sport communication positions can be found in sports arenas and stadiums (e.g., electronic technicians, master control operators, public address announcers, video engineers). For example, the Phoenix Suns recently advertised for a public address announcer. The basketball team's job announcement noted that the prospective employee would have to have strong ad-libbing skills, a knowledge of the

league's rules, and an ability to work all 41 home games during the regular season (and postseason games as well).

Another example of an oft-ignored but rewarding career is in sport media buying. This includes sport sales and sport marketing professionals who work to secure media purchases for sports teams and organizations, or they work with a private enterprise to secure media purchases on sport media outlets (e.g., sports broadcasts, sports pages, sports Web sites). The media buyer attempts to make sure every media investment—whether in sports or through sports—works hard for the sport or nonsport organization. This is done through investing in online media purchases (e.g., a company pays the LPGA a certain amount based on the number of ad views for the company that are generated through the www.LPGA.com Web site). The sport media buyers create media plans (e.g., research distribution, goals, market share, media mix, monitor schedules) that ensure effective media buys (e.g., purchasing impressions, dispersing the schedule among media outlets and programs).

Teaching sport communication is a career possibility for those interested in pursuing an advanced degree—usually a doctorate—in the field. Many of the sport communication positions are found in sport management programs that we examined in the first chapter. "A byproduct of the growth of the sport industry and the demand for trained sport management professionals has been the growth of sport management academic programs," noted Pedersen, Whisenant, and Schneider (2005). They added, "The rapid expansion of programs has resulted in a high demand for qualified sport management faculty" (p. 155). Professors can teach in a variety of sport communication areas including sport journalism, communication, sport public relations, telecommunications, sport media, and sports radio and television. In addition to teaching sport communication classes, professors in higher education often conduct sport communication research. They also guide students through internships, practicums, and other practical experiences that provide students with opportunities to build their resumes through working for sport organizations and sport media outlets. Other educational careers in sport communication can be found in some community colleges and secondary schools (e.g., teaching a sport communication course) and technical schools (e.g., the sports broadcasting elective at the Connecticut School of Broadcasting). Closely associated with education are the professional careers in corporate consulting and training (e.g., organizational communication) as well as motivational speaking (e.g., oral communication). Sport speakers bureaus and sport talent agencies such as Playing Field Promotions and Burns Entertainment and Sports Marketing provide speakers for personal, motivational, and endorsement appearances.

In addition to the theoretical research in academia, there is applied research. For the most part, sport media organizations are more interested in the latter. Sport media research involves, as is noted in *Profiles of Sport Industry Professionals,* "a knowledge of advertising and broadcasting business principles such as market share, Nielsen ratings, designated market areas (DMAs), cost per thousand (CPM), cumulative audience over time, and return on investment (ROI)" (Robinson, Hums, Crow, & Phillips, 2001, p. 241). Applied sport media research professionals work with the latest technology and software to provide crucial information for sport organizations, sport media entities, and sport media buyers. Sport market and news research (e.g., surveys, interviews, focus groups, sales figures, press runs) tell the sports team about its consumers and the sport media entity about its audience. Therefore, practical sport communication research involves careers working with both sport media organizations (e.g., conducting research to determine audience information) and nonsport organizations that research sport organizations. Some organizations such as the Sport Information Research Centre (SIRC) provide opportunities for both practical and theoretical research and sport information. SIRC has more than six million pages of sport information and research for coaches, athletes, sports medicine professionals, and sport organizations.

YOUR KEYS TO ENTRY INTO THE FIELD

The preceding sections examined the numerous career opportunities available to students in sport communication. In addition to understanding the nature and scope of occupational options, students need to initiate key steps to prepare for and enter into one of those professional occupations (see figure 2.2). This section details career preparation (i.e., development of skills, knowledge, experience, distinction) for those looking to enter and succeed in this competitive field.

Self-Evaluation

The first step in career preparation is evaluation. If you desire a career in sport communication, assess your potential by examining your skill set and passion for the field. Self-assessment involves exploring and evaluating one's needs, interests, personality, skills, values, work style, and expectations. These explorations and evaluations can be accomplished through a variety of means (e.g., personal reflection, reading, consulting with a friend), but they are most often examined through career counseling that includes surveys such as the Strong Interest Inventory (SII), Knowdell Career Values Card Sort, Campbell Interest and Skills Survey (CISS), and the Myers–Briggs Type Indicator. Those preparing to enter the field should know their interests and determine which aspect of sport communication appeals most to them and for which aspects they possess a great passion. As noted previously, scores of career options in management, mass media, and support services are available. People who have a passion for any of the career options within sport communication may reveal this passion in actions that are often unseen by others and cannot be added to a resume. For instance, to develop his skills as a young broadcaster, the late Chris Schenkel "rigged up a primitive speaker system that carried high schooler Chris's game description out onto the street" (Hammel, 2005, p. A13). College students and young professionals today often attend games

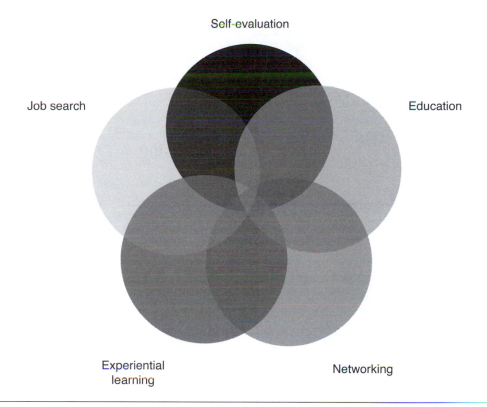

Figure 2.2   Keys to successful entry into a sport communication career.

and perform mock broadcasts as a way to develop their craft. Such actions come from a passion for communication and reveal a deep interest in a career in sport communication.

Because of the wide and divergent career options in sport communication, professionals in this field require varied abilities and skill sets. These skills and abilities range from being open to change and detail oriented to being able to think strategically, set goals, and motivate oneself. Above all, as noted by the authors of *Profiles of Sport Industry Professionals,* "Whereas excellent oral and written communication skills are important in most segments of the [sport] industry, they are the foundation of communications in sport. Advanced skills in computer and electronic technologies, news and feature reporting and writing, the ability to work well with diverse populations, statistical expertise, creativity in a variety of publications, and a thorough knowledge of a wide range of sports are all necessary skills for professionals in the sport communications field" (Robinson et al., 2001, p. 241). After individuals have performed a

self-assessment and evaluated their knowledge, skills, interests, and abilities, it is then time to begin strengthening the areas that need improvement (i.e., refining skills, developing abilities, increasing knowledge).

Education

To pursue a career in sport communication, individuals generally have some college preparation and most often must hold a college degree in sport communication, communication, journalism, broadcasting, public relations, advertising, telecommunications, or other closely related disciplines. Individuals in sport communication usually major in interdisciplinary programs that provide them with the most appropriate background in the field. These interdisciplinary programs are often housed in the areas of sport management, journalism, telecommunication, or mass communication.

Instruction in sport communication is widely available at colleges and universities in the United States and has experienced rapid growth in Canada and other countries

© Paul M. Pedersen

Communication is an integral part of careers in sport management and the mass media. Here, ESPN's Holly Rowe interviews Rod Brodersen, the vice president of marketing for Champs Sports. Part of Brodersen's job responsibilities involves communicating with various stakeholders—including the media. Rowe's job responsibilities include communicating with interviewees, production personnel, colleagues, and the television audience.

worldwide. Some institutions offer degrees in areas of sport communication, and others offer degrees in communication allowing for specialization in mass communication, interpersonal communication, public relations, advertising, broadcast, print, electronic, or visual media.

Those interested in obtaining a sport management degree may search the list of sport management programs on the North American Society for Sport Management (NASSM) Web site at www.nassm.com/InfoAbout/SportMgmtPrograms.

Don't limit your education to the classroom. Regularly read sport communication publications, observe best practices, and volunteer in sport communication activities with sport

organizations and media outlets. Gaining experience, along with networking, is essential to becoming a successful professional in sport communication. These activities all contribute to the knowledge base of the prospective sport communication professional.

Networking

To advance in sport communication, professionals must be willing to build relationships and network with colleagues in the field and in those fields related to the discipline. "Working in the sport industry requires an individual to establish a web of intersecting relationships that reach across business industries and business segments (operations, marketing, sales, finance) within both the public and the private sector," explains University of Miami sport management professor Warren A. Whisenant. "Although an individual's career path will influence his or her level of position power in the sport industry, a continually evolving and growing network of personal relationships will enable the individual to amass a significant level of personal power and loyalty, which can ensure a successful and fulfilling career in sport." The old adage "it's not what you know; it's who you know" is true in sport communication. Oftentimes, top-level positions are not advertised and people in those positions are recruited through existing relationships. The field of sport communication is highly competitive, and building a sound network of relationships will prove advantageous in advancing a career.

To begin networking, be flexible and remain open-minded. Being versatile increases your chances of being presented with opportunities that are uniquely suited to your talents. Be willing to conduct informational interviews, attend conferences and meetings of professional associations, and read articles and publications pertinent to the field. Becoming a student member of a professional association allows you to make contacts and build a solid knowledge base of the field of sport communication. Consider such organizations as the Sport Marketing Association, the National

Association of Broadcasters, the National Sportscasters and Sportswriters Association, and others listed in the Web site reference section at the end of this chapter.

Be persistent in meeting colleagues and those in decision-making roles with various organizations. Remember the names of those you meet while networking and maintain a level of communication to establish a favorable relationship, which may generate word of mouth in your favor.

Experiential Learning

Those desiring a career in sport communication should make every effort to cultivate opportunities to volunteer and work in an applied capacity within the field. The value of real world experience enhances one's chances of landing that all-important first job and provides individuals with the opportunity to further advance and acquire new skill sets. There are many ways to volunteer and work in internships. Sport events rely heavily on volunteers, and this provides an excellent opportunity to gain valuable practical experience to combine with educational training. Sport franchises and events need volunteers to assist in all aspects of operations, including sport communication. Volunteers may provide media relations and public relations assistance to a professional sports team or at a sports event or may work as a writer or editor of the school newspaper. Other opportunities exist within sports radio and television broadcasting and with the Internet for a sports team or sport media organization. Individuals desiring a career in sport communication should actively seek these opportunities. Typically, the amount and quality of practical experience that a person possesses on entering the field determines the quality of his or her first position in the discipline. The quality of the initial job in the field can sometimes set the tone for opportunities throughout the remainder of one's career.

Brenda Stidham—a sports reporter and anchor for an NBC affiliate in Michigan—vigorously pursued experiential learning during her undergraduate studies. While pursuing her degree in sport communication, she interned with a television station and worked for 3 years covering sports for a radio station. She offers her perspective regarding the best way for undergraduates to position themselves to take advantage of job opportunities: "It can't be said enough—hands-on activities and internships," she says. This involvement can range from the campus newspaper, radio station, or television station to the local public relations firm or the sport information department. "Get involved, meet people from other fields and interests, do as much as you can."

Internships are an important avenue in advancing a career in sport communication. "An internship truly is the best way to get a foot in the door because it allows you to trumpet your work ethic and skills in a professional setting," notes John K. Koluder, media relations manager for Major League Soccer's (MLS) Chicago Fire. "Make friends with your academic and internship advisors as soon as you can!" Koluder adds, "Whether students are seeking a job with a professional team or in the media, my advice would be to take an internship as an undergraduate as early as possible. Although networking with professors and guest lecturers at classes can prove valuable, I don't think they can match the contacts that can be made during a successful internship in your chosen field. I also highly advise students looking to break into the media to seek opportunities with as many media outlets on campus as possible, whether it be in television, radio, or print." Internships may be paid or unpaid positions with a sport-focused organization. Individuals may perform a variety of tasks that have been established for a fixed period of time and may be assigned college credit. Because the field of sport communication is quite broad in its nature and scope, securing an internship most often helps students determine which aspect of the field they most want to enter and pursue. Competition for internships, as with jobs, in the field is quite fierce. Students should approach the process as they would approach a full-scale job search, complete with resume and interview preparation.

Job Search

Beginning the job search is similar to finding an internship. Carefully select positions for which you are qualified and craft your resume and cover letter to best highlight your talents, abilities, and key strengths as they relate to the specific position. Typically, resumes should not exceed two pages, and cover letters should be limited to one page. Cover letters allow you to draw attention to your skill set and explain how these skills would be advantageous to the sport-focused organization. Create a resume that is professionally presented, is graphically pleasing, and includes a list of your accomplishments as well as past job responsibilities.

Prepare for the interviewing process. First, research the sport-focused organization to acquire as much information as possible. Next, research the backgrounds of those who will conduct the interview to get a feel for the type of questions that might be asked. Dress slightly conservatively for interviews, arrive on time, and be ready to market your skills to the potential employer. The interview is an ideal time to gauge the culture of the organization and determine if this is indeed a place in which you would like to be employed.

CHAPTER WRAP-UP

Summary

Countless professions are associated with sport communication. The growth of the multifaceted sport industry combined with the sport consumer's increased demand and desire for sport information has produced a need for such professionals. This chapter highlighted many of the key career paths—including traditional, nontraditional, and emerging positions—within the vast and diverse field of sport communication.

This chapter offered suggestions to help you assess your skills, interests, and abilities and evaluate your potential for a satisfying and successful career in the field. The activities, resources (i.e., Web links for education, job searches, professional associations), and references at the end of this chapter are provided to help you further examine your interests, abilities, and career options.

Review Questions

1. What has driven the demand in the sport industry for professionals well versed in sport communication?
2. How have careers in the field of sport communication increased in the past decade?
3. What are some of the emerging positions in sport communication?
4. What are the duties, responsibilities, and functions of sport communication management professionals?
5. In the early years of the media, what was the primary sport media occupation?
6. What are the positions on the journalistic side of the print sport media?
7. What are some of the key off-camera sport communication positions at a major media outlet such as ESPN?

8. How do sport public relations professionals play integral roles in the activities of sport organizations?

9. What are the keys to entry in the field of sport communication?

10. What are some of the traditional positions in sport communication?

Discussion Questions

1. In what ways are careers in sport media organizations and careers in the sport communication areas of sport organizations different? In what ways are they similar?

2. How has technology changed the manner in which professionals in the field perform their job functions and duties?

3. What are the major trends in sport communication careers? Do these trends differ according to medium?

4. How would you rank the five major areas detailed in this chapter according to those with the highest and those with the lowest demand for sport communication professionals?

5. What influences the ways in which sport communication professionals communicate with their key publics, both internal and external?

6. Why are opportunities in the field described as having "breadth and width"?

7. How do the varying roles of sport communication professionals affect the overall effectiveness and efficiency of the sport-focused organization?

8. What is the current status of the sport communication job market?

9. How do trends in the industry and trends in the global economy influence the demand for sport communication professionals?

10. What are the most crucial skills required for entrance into a sport communication career? Do these skills differ depending on the mode or medium? Do they differ depending on the sport communication occupation?

Group Activities

1. Plan a sport communication career day. Divide your class into groups and select one of the major areas of sport communication for each group. Contact sport communication professionals in each area and invite them to speak to the class. Prepare background and biographical information on the selected speakers.

2. Divide into groups. Each group should contact two or three professionals in the field of sport communication to determine the skills that professionals perceive as pertinent for entry and advancement in the field. After compiling the list of skills from the professionals, evaluate your current skill set and identify your strengths and weaknesses. Then devise a plan for enhancing your strengths and improving skills that were identified as weak.

Individual Exercises

1. Arrange to spend a day or an event with a sport communication professional. Reflect on this time and write a three-page paper detailing the encounter. Specifically note the duties and responsibilities of the professional, the professional's

role within the overall organization, the professional's work environment, and the professional's interactions with other staff members.

2. From the list provided at the end of this chapter, conduct a Web search of online job-posting sites for sport communication jobs. After you find a job posting that might be of interest, prepare a cover letter and one-page resume for submission. Although you most likely will not submit the documents, make sure your cover letter is tailored for that position and your resume includes an objective along with your education, work experience, and extracurricular activities. If you do not have much information to put for the work experience section, now is the time to volunteer in some facet of sport communication.

3. Identify three sport-focused organizations for which you would like to work. Within these organizations, ascertain at least two positions in sport communication for which you would apply and denote why these positions are appealing. Write a job description for each position selected.

4. Select a sport communication professional to interview and profile. Develop a set of interview questions, write a synopsis of the interview, and present the profile to the class.

Internet Sites for Additional Learning

American Copy Editors Society: www.copydesk.org/jobbank.htm

American Society of Newspaper Editors: www.asne.org/index.cfm?id=2

American Sportscasters Association: www.americansportscasters.com/

Associated Press Sports Editors: http://apse.dallasnews.com/

Association for Women in Sports Media: www.awsmonline.org/

Book Jobs: www.bookjobs.com/

Broadcast Employment Services: www.tvjobs.com/intern.htm

Career Builder: www.careerbuilder.com/

College Sports Careers: www.collegesportscareers.com/

College Sports Information Directors of America: www.cosida.com/

Collegiate Sports Video Association: www.csva.com/

Creative Hotlist: www.creativehotlist.com/

ECAC Sports Information Directors' Association: www.ecac-sida.org/

Entertainment Careers: www.entertainmentcareers.net/

ESPN's Employment and Internship: www.joinourteam.espn.com/joinourteam/

Football Writers Association of America: www.sportswriters.net/fwaa/

Game Face: www.gamefacesportsjobs.com/

Hot Jobs: hotjobs.yahoo.com/

International Association for Sports Information: www.iasi.org/

Jobs in Sports: www.jobsinsports.com/

Jobs Page: www.freep.com/legacy/jobspage/

Journalism Jobs Bank: journalism.berkeley.edu/jobs/othersit.html

Mass Media Jobs: massmediajobs.com/

Media Job Links: www.geocities.com/Hollywood/Bungalow/5014/joblink.html

National Association of Broadcasters: www.nab.org/bcc/

National Collegiate Baseball Writers Association: www.sportswriters.net/ncbwa/

National Diversity Newspaper Job Bank: www.newsjobs.com/

National Sports Employment News: www.sportsemploymentnews.com/

North American Society for Sport Management: www.nassm.com/

Online Sports: www.onlinesports.com/pages/CareerCenter.html

Rodeo Announcer: www.rodeoannouncer.com/

Sporting Goods Manufacturers Association International: www.sgma.com/jobbankdisplaylistings.cfm

Sport Management Club: www.sportmanagementclub.com

SportsBusiness Journal: www.sportsbusinessjournal.com/

Sports Careers: www.sportscareers.com/

Sportscasting Jobs: www.sportscastingjobs.com/

Sports Resume Writing: www.sportsresumewriting.com/

TeamWork Online: www.teamworkonline.com/

Telecommuting Jobs: www.tjobs.com/index.shtml

United States Basketball Writers Association: www.sportswriters.net/usbwa/

Women in Sports Careers: www.wiscnetwork.com/

Women Sports Jobs: www.womensportsjobs.com/default.htm

Work in Sports: www.workinsports.com/home.asp

CHAPTER 3

History and Growth of Sport Communication

LEARNING OBJECTIVES

▶ To understand the historical development of sport communication

▶ To learn about sports coverage from newspaper sports pages, magazines, radio, television, cable, and the latest technologies

▶ To recognize the influence of the 1920s "golden age of sport" on contemporary sport coverage

▶ To become acquainted with key pioneers in sport communication's ascent and to consider the evolution of sports coverage and its relation to cultural history

▶ To understand the longstanding significance of sports coverage from its roots to its infinite potential

PROFILE OF A SPORT COMMUNICATOR

Grantland Rice

Babe Ruth, Babe Didrikson, Jimmy Braddock, Jack Dempsey, Ty Cobb, Knute Rockne, and Red Grange are still remembered nearly a century later for their heroic feats on the field, in the stadium, or in the arena. Although athletes and coaches during the 1920s "golden age of sport" receive merited attention, the writers who reported their swings, hits, runs, and strategies contributed to sustaining athletes' and coaches' legacies, and the longstanding influence of these writers continues with sports coverage and communication today. John Kieran (1948) of *The New York Times* wrote the following about these pioneers:

Play-by-play announcing on the radio has been an integral part of the sport industry since the "golden age of sport." The World Series was covered live on the radio for the first time in 1922. The play-by-play announcer was Grantland Rice.

© Paul M. Pedersen

What is sometimes overlooked about that glorious era of competition is that there were writers worthy of the great competitors of those dazzling days. What would we have known of Achilles, Hector, Aeneas, Ulysses, Ajax, and other heroes of ancient times if it were not for Homer and Virgil? So the champions of a great era in American sports found their personalities and their performances chronicled by a great group of writers, men who were outstanding in their own part of the field, the press section. (p. ix)

Grantland Rice has been touted as "the first important American sportswriter" with more than 67 million words, 22,000 columns, 7,000 sets of verse, 1,000 magazine articles, and books that set the agenda of American popular culture before television (Fountain, 1993, p. 4; Rice 1954). Charles Fountain (1993), whose biography of Rice provides the framework for this vignette, noted that up to 100 newspapers published his daily

"Sportlight" column with a circulation of more than 10 million. Unlike most sportswriters of the day who used journalism as a springboard to careers in fiction or politics, Rice remained true to his profession and worked as a sportswriter for more than 50 years. His legacy has endured through such verses as, "For when the One Great Scorer comes to mark against your name, He writes—not that you won or lost—but how you played the game" (Rice, 1954, p. 169). Rice's most famous lead, which began his story on the Notre Dame versus Army college football game in 1924, is discussed later in the chapter.

Rice epitomized a Renaissance man. After graduating Phi Beta Kappa from Vanderbilt University with a bachelor of arts in Greek and Latin in 1901 at the age of 20, he worked for such publications as the *Nashville Daily News, Atlanta Journal, New York Sun, New York Tribune, New York Herald Tribune, Nashville Tennessean, New York Mail,* and *Collier's.* Rice wrote more than 500 articles for *Collier's* in 35 years, including the "All-America" football articles appearing annually in December from 1925 to 1947. In addition to maintaining a 53-year sportswriting career, Rice conducted the play-by-play for the first World Series game covered live on radio in 1922. He continued his work in radio by hosting a weekly National Broadcasting Company (NBC) show in the 1920s and 1930s, reporting at big sporting events, and appearing as a guest on other talents' radio shows. He interviewed everyone from baseball legend Ty Cobb to Olympic swimmer Martha Norelius and fellow sportswriter Ring Lardner (Harper, 1999). In addition to his journalistic pursuits, Rice dabbled in more creative ventures. He received two Academy Awards for short subject features for his Sportlight Films and even wrote a play called *The Kick Off.* In 1926, he won the Baseball Writers' Association "most valuable writer" award for his story on 37-year-old Walter Johnson of the Washington Senators and game seven of the World Series. Rice was also credited with popularizing the game of golf and helped create the Masters in 1938 with Bobby Jones.

On July 13, 1954, Rice died of a stroke in his Sportlight office at the age of 73. His life philosophies included the principle "know thyself," and from Emerson's "Self-Reliance" and "Compensation" he learned that "when things are at their worst, brighter days are just beyond. Conversely, when skies are bluest, then is the time to look out for black clouds" (Rice, 1954, p. 353). Although the saccharine rhyme of Rice's optimistic and embellished words might not appeal to readers today, he shaped American sportswriting through his mellifluous and vivid prose. Fountain (1993) even called him the "Matthew, Mark, Luke, and John of American sport" (p. 4). Not only did Rice captivate a public weary from World War I and later the Great Depression, but his unwavering commitment to journalism, the sources he covered and protected, and his principles undoubtedly contributed to the ascent of sport's popularity and journalists' treatment of athletes, coaches, and games. Until Howard Cosell, no one rivaled Rice's impact on sports coverage. Although some consider his verse prosaic and overly sentimental, Pulitzer prize–winning sportswriter Red Smith extolled Rice's literary style, character development, images, and attention to detail with journalist Arthur Daley in a *New York Times Book Review* (November 21, 1954, cited in Fountain, 1993, p. 6). "Grantland Rice was the greatest man I have known," noted Smith. He added that Rice was "the greatest talent, the greatest gentleman."

This chapter traces the early stages of sport communication in the United States from the 19th century to the present, focusing on golden age pioneers like Rice, who made an indelible mark on sport, the profession of sport journalism, and American culture. Although the chapter begins with print journalists, it also discusses other sport communication professionals in radio, television, cable, and emerging technologies. By studying the history of sport communication (see figure 3.1), we can see how it has evolved and how it will continue to emerge as an important industry in America's economic and social fabric.

As we will cover starting with chapter 7, sport and media organizations have shared a symbiotic, mutually beneficial relationship that began with early sport in the United States. In the early 20th century, America changed dramatically with an influx of individuals to cities and the mechanization of life. As a result, individuals turned to sport and communication activities to connect with others and for social cohesion. Sport communication has evolved with cultural changes and the expansion of technology in the industrialization, urbanization, and modernization of America. According to Garrison and Sabljak (1993), sport journalism developed over six periods. These periods—which are covered in this chapter—include the pioneer era (up to 1830), the period of acceptance (1830-1865), the era of consolidation and growth (1865-1920), the golden age (1920-1930), the perspective period (1930-1950), and the transition years (1950-1970). Garrison and Sabljak (1993) provided the framework for this analysis. After covering these periods we look at two

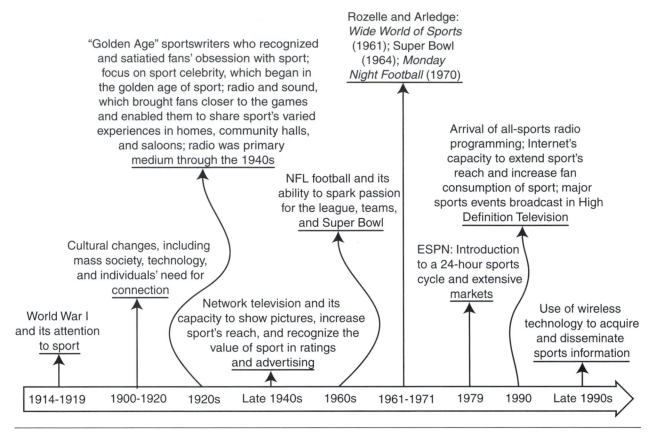

Figure 3.1 Key events in the development of sport communication.

leaders of sport and the media, and we finish the chapter with an examination of today's sport communication arena.

EARLY ERAS OF SPORT JOURNALISM

Although individuals have played sports since the beginning of time, activities were generally more recreational (Garrison & Sabljak, 1993). During the colonial pioneer era in the United States, which is pre-1830, individuals participated in leisure activities—including fishing, hunting, boat races, cricket, horse racing, cockfighting, gardening, swimming, skating, billiards, and wrestling—but newspapers offered limited coverage.

Coverage of Leisure Activities Begins

In the 19th century, daily newspapers and weekly papers on the leisure life began appearing in the United States. William Trotter

Porter's *Spirit of the Times* started in 1831 and allegedly had 40,000 subscribers nationwide by the middle part of the century. Sporting sheets like the *New York Clipper* and *Sporting News* appeared in the latter part of the century, and the *National Police Gazette* was the highest selling weekly newspaper, covering all areas of entertainment and leisure activities. Because of increasing literacy rates and technology, more and more newspapers arose (Rader, 2004). The first sporting journal, the *American Turf Register and Sporting Magazine,* appeared in 1829 and covered horse racing. Many of the journals covered outdoor activities as well. When newspapers reported on sport, they included horse racing, boxing, and wrestling, but it was not until the period of acceptance that sport gained notoriety and attention (Garrison & Sabljak, 1993).

New York–based "penny" newspapers initiated coverage of sport in the 1830s. They were called penny papers because they sold for a penny initially before their prices increased to a few cents. They made news more accessible and available to the mass public and generally exuded a partisan and sensational tone (Blanchard, 1998). William Trotter Porter's *Spirit of the Times* and the *New York Clipper,* founded by Frank Queen, both became popular sports journals in the mid-19th century (Betts, 1953a). Porter's *Spirit of the Times* took over the *Turf Register* in 1839 and covered such sports as cricket, baseball, rowing, and yachting (Harper, 1999). James Gordon Bennett and his *New York Herald* offered front-page coverage of such sporting events as trotting matches, thoroughbred racing, and boxing bouts in the 1840s (Betts, 1953a). With the advent of the electric telegraph in 1844, sports news quickly disseminated and offered instantaneous reports of games, horse races, boxing bouts, and other events (Betts, 1953b). Sport's popularity further developed after the U.S. Civil War, propelled by the popularity of baseball (Fountain, 1993). The game not only entertained the Union and Confederate armies but also bypassed class and geographic lines after the war concluded. Baseball clubs expanded in the 1870s and the National League formed in 1876.

A key pioneer in baseball's popularity and development was writer Henry Chadwick, often called the "father of baseball." Not only did he create the first rule book for the game, but he invented the box score and earned a place in the Baseball Hall of Fame (Hiestand, 2004; "Henry Chadwick," n.d.). His Hall of Fame plaque reads: "Henry Chadwick baseball's preeminent pioneer writer for half a century. Inventor of the box score. Author of the first rule-book. In 1858 Chairman of rules committee in first nation-wide baseball organization." (National Baseball Hall of Fame, 2006).

Newspapers Recognize the Importance of Sport

As baseball gained popularity, sport became a daily feature of the larger newspapers in the 1870s and the press realized the importance of recurrent and innovative sports reporting (Betts, 1953a; Fountain, 1993). Charles A. Dana of the *New York Sun,* Joseph Pulitzer of the *New York World,* and William Randolph Hearst of the *New York Journal* were credited with creating the first regular sports pages (Betts, 1953a; Garrison & Sabljak, 1993). By the 1880s, football, boxing, baseball, horse racing, cricket, croquet, yacht racing, homing pigeon racing, bicycle racing, and lacrosse were covered in the sports pages. According to Fountain (1993), the "style was languid, leisurely, chronological narrative typical of much nineteenth century journalism, with salient information . . . often lost in the morass of secondary detail" (p. 59). The invention of the telephone in 1876, the typewriter's improvements (1869), and the web printing press (1865) all propelled sport journalism and its expansion. By the turn of the 20th century, *new journalism* and *muckraking* described journalists' and writers' attention to a life full of transition with modern advancements and the problems individuals encountered in life (Emery, Emery, & Roberts, 2000, p. 213). "New journalism" sought social reform as evident in articles appearing in mass-produced, sensationalized newspapers. Journalists depicted the life of immigrants, outcasts, and degenerates and described society's systemic problems. Muckraking sustained this focus with investigative reporting emphasizing reforms for an increasingly modern and technological society. The drama of muckraking exposed society's problems with a critical yet optimistic tone (Blanchard, 1998).

Although crusading muckrakers depicted political and economic injustices in American life, newspapers viewed sport as performance. In literature, realism was a primary form of describing life, and often the newspaper and novel covered similar stories, events, and characters. Novelists like Stephen Crane, Ernest Hemingway, and John Steinbeck began their careers as journalists. Stephen Crane is best known as the author of *The Red Badge of Courage,* yet he also wrote feature stories, travel pieces, and even sports articles during his career. In journalism, urban reporting on city life and war correspondence were primary forms of this "fact–fiction" discourse, which bridged the novel and journalistic prose (Robertson, 1997, pp. 3-5).

Only a handful of sport periodicals existed, mainly such trade papers as *Sporting News* and *Sporting Life,* which merely covered the facts (Halberstam & Stout, 1999). These stories were succinct and offered readers the bare minimum on the games and athletes. Whereas trade papers adhered to facts, magazines like *Harper's Weekly, Illustrated American,* and *Leslie's Illustrated Weekly* included photographs of athletes and sportspeople (Betts, 1953b). Because sports coverage described events, more individuals sought to participate. According to sport historian Michael Oriard, "Sport accommodated participants' desire to play, while at the same time enabling the advocates of sport to harness the play impulse to the new industrial order" (Oriard, 1991, p. 11). Efficient transportation and communication in the first 3 decades of the 20th century triggered the expansion of city life, wealth, and leisure time (Noverr & Ziewacz, 1983). Mass production instigated a more rigid and structured work environment, and such technological developments as the railroad, telegraph, electric light, and streetcar led to a workweek of 48 hours from 60 hours in the 1920s (Inabinett, 1994). Living standards increased and the Sunday blue laws disappeared, thereby offering Americans more time for leisure and money for related activities. This meant that Sundays were no longer off-limits for games, competitions, and other activities as work laws dissipated. The universe of "abundance–leisure–consumer pleasure orientation" allowed more time for individual gratification, and sport was one way to attain this (Susman, 1984, p. 112).

People Turn to Sports for Sense of Cohesion

Although technology freed workers from grueling hours, it increased urbanization and dehumanization. Between 1870 and 1920, the population in the United States increased by 44 million people, and individuals turned to sport as an escape from the complexities of a bustling world (Hardy, 1997). Sport offered an outlet for celebrating individual achievements and provided a respite from this faceless existence (Inabinett, 1994), creating a sense of community and social cohesion.

Cities and their inhabitants became a central focus, and the interplay between the cities' infrastructure, groups, organizations, and systems created much of sport's historical narratives (Riess, 1990). The millions of Europeans who migrated to America's cities possessed dissimilar faiths, customs, and rituals. Community building followed in the form of sports clubs, jockey clubs, yachting associations, baseball leagues, and athletic conferences that sought to unite dissimilar groups. This melting-pot ideology comprised a vision where games and sports promoted unification and means for overpowering racial, ethnic, and class divisions (Hardy, 1997). The organizations not only facilitated the transition but also unified cultures and identities, creating heroes and evoking pride among ethnic team members and fans (Riess, 1990).

Sport increased in respectability among the middle class as people connected it with individual growth and rebirth, societal restoration, and the will to live a healthy and fulfilling life (Evensen, 1993). By 1928, Americans spent a fourth of the national income on leisure, and $200 million of that was used for sporting goods and equipment (Noverr & Ziewacz, 1983). According to one historian, "Sports, and media attention to it, had significantly rationalized the leisure time of a growing fraction of the middle class and was celebrated in the popular literature of the youth culture as a proving ground for the thoroughly modern man and woman" (Evensen, 1996, p. xiii).

Military Legitimizes Interest in Sport

As Noverr and Ziewacz (1983) explained, from 1900 to 1920 the United States developed as an industrial nation and formidable world power as American imperialism and military power escalated under President William McKinley and President Theodore Roosevelt. Physical strength and conditioning took the forefront of priorities because America needed to protect and defend its interests. Sport was no longer a trivial activity but was viewed as a means to gain an advantage in life and for physical fitness. Progressive supporters of athleticism touted sport's function in readying individuals and nations for life's tasks, and communication and journalism bolstered the legitimacy of sport (Dyreson, 1989). The American military legitimized sport's utility for the masses in World War I as the armed services made sport central to military life by advancing a "national sport culture" (Pope, 1995, p. 436). More than four million men and women participated in intercamp competitions in football, baseball, basketball, soccer, boxing, and track and field during World War I. In 1918 and 1919, soldiers read the *Stars and Stripes* for information on service sports and they also read articles in the *Sporting News*. The *New York Herald, Chicago Tribune,* and *London Daily Mail* published 190 items on the Inter-Allied Games of 1919 where 1,500 athletes from 18 Allied countries competed (Pope, 1995).

Before World War I, heroes came from business, industry, and science, but soon after the war, athletes soared to celebrity status (Inabinett, 1994). The rise of sport celebrities and mass-mediated hero worship represented a generation's quest for meaning during a turbulent and changing time in America's history and a response to a complicated and bureaucratic society (Evensen, 1996; Inabinett, 1994). Sport represented a postwar optimism, an escape and a means for exalting the human spirit, and some even viewed it as "the religion of health mindedness" (Noverr & Ziewacz, 1983, pp. 69-70). "Sport had become an opiate which allowed the average person to cope with the 'Big Society,'" noted Dyreson (1989). "It offered an arena in which the masses could turn their eyes away, if only briefly, from the grim political and economic realities of the modern world" (p. 269). Journalist Grantland Rice asked, "Just why was this period from 1919 to 1930, in the wake of the Marne, the Meuse, Cantigny, Belleau Woods, Sedan, and the Hindenberg Line, called the Golden Age of Sport?" He responded, "It is because this postwar period gave the game the greatest collection of stars, involving both skill and color, that sport has ever known since the first cave

man tackled the mammoth and the aurochs bull" (Rice, 1948, p. 1).

GOLDEN AGE OF SPORT

Throughout history sport has reflected cultural values, and this is especially true in the early 20th century, when individuals sought to assimilate into modern, mass society while escaping postwar struggles. Sport was one means of doing this through either participation or spectatorship, and its popularity increased exponentially, especially from 1920 to 1930. The "golden age of sport" was an appropriate title for this decade because athletes, coaches, and sportswriters all gained iconic status. Athletes like Babe Ruth, Ty Cobb, Red Grange, Bill Tilden, and Bobby Jones along with writers like Grantland Rice, Paul Gallico, and Damon Runyon became household names. The writers set the agenda for sports coverage by documenting coaches' and athletes' unique stories and athletic achievements. For the first time in history,

Pat Riley interacts with the media following a Miami Heat game. While professional leagues and public relations professionals often dictate the agenda regarding what should be covered, during the 1920s it was the newspaper reporters who set the agenda for sports coverage through their documentation of the activities and achievements of coaches and athletes.

individuals were obsessed with sport and its many participants.

The golden age of sport had implications for sportswriting and the ensuing culture. During this period, sportswriting appeared in general interest and sport magazines as well as newspapers (Halberstam & Stout, 1999).

Athletes Given Celebrity Status

Golden age sportswriters created champions, and their images elevated athletes to celebrity status (Inabinett, 1994). Sport journalists' descriptive and sentimental words set the scene so individuals could feel excitement through mental pictures that they formulated from the writings. Immediacy and words mattered (Laucella, 2004). Few sports fans regularly saw their heroes in action, so athletes became "bigger than life" as icons (Starr, 1999). Sport journalists no longer just reported from the playing fields but also analyzed strategy, provided background, and illuminated character on such athletes as baseball's Ty Cobb, football's "four horsemen" of Notre Dame, golf's Bobby Jones, and tennis' Bill Tilden (Inabinett, 1994). Other famous sports figures who were covered in the golden age included Babe Ruth, Joe DiMaggio, Knute Rockne,

Babe Didrikson, Red Grange, Jack Dempsey, Suzanne Lenglen, Gertrude Ederle, Walter Hagan, and Helen Wills Moody. According to Rice (1954), "Sport—games, hard competition played under the rules, is the greatest thing a country can know. Sport offered the greatest fund of national entertainment. It offered relief from the drabness and dullness of making a living. It was a cure for lonesomeness, the dark spectre so many people face" (p. 349).

Sportswriters Develop Unique Prose

Sport's magnificent athletes required sport journalists to use descriptive, imaginative, and vivid language, which has rarely been experienced since the golden age of sport (Danzig & Brandwein, 1948). The 1920s experienced a restructuring of sport's ideology in American culture, and the newspaper sports section became an indispensable part of the daily newspaper (Dyreson, 1989; McChesney, 1989). The space devoted to sports coverage expanded from 1.7 percent of news space in 1875 to more than 20 percent in 1927, and the popularity of sport depended on the daily sports section for survival (Jordan, 1927). Newspaper circulation rose to 36 million in

Key Characteristics of the Golden Age of Sport

- Significant events graced front-page headlines.
- Writers embellished prose with literary devices like metaphors and analogies.
- Such athletes as Babe Ruth, boxer Jack Dempsey, and Notre Dame football coach Knute Rockne were the subject of hero worship.
- Writers used emotional and gripping language with vivid imagery.
- Meticulous detail was used in describing events and defining agendas.
- Leads were high in drama and description and low in factual content.
- Writers used few quotes.

- Stories were written in a conversational tone.
- Columns reflected frivolity of sport, yet merely hinted at deeper implications like race relations and politics.
- Writers used war and mythology references and "rags to riches" stories.
- Writers used humor, slang, romance, and drama.
- Storytelling was paramount.
- Stories relied on expert description and commentary for pretelevision society.
- Writers extensively used nicknames and Grantland Rice created many of them, including the "Sultan of Swat" for Babe Ruth.

1926, and one of four readers purchased a newspaper solely for the sports section, the single most significant catalyst to circulation (Evensen, 1993; Inabinett, 1994). Just as circulations increased because of the interest in sports coverage, the number of writers covering sports increased during this time period. Examples of this are the sportswriters who covered the Boston Braves during the 1920s. For instance, when the Braves ventured south in 1922 for their first spring training in St. Petersburg, six New England sportswriters traveled with the team on the train to Florida (Pedersen, 1997). This type of coverage for such a mediocre team (it had losing records in 4 of its previous 5 years) reflects the increased attention devoted to sports by newspapers and covered by sportswriters. "They [journalists] invented along the way an often brilliantly different and always special kind of rhetoric and style," explained cultural historian Warren Susman (1984). "Their unique prose delighted readers, sold more copies, appealed to more advertising agencies with products to sell" (p. 143).

Sportswriters used imagination to develop stories using hyperbole, similes, metaphors, and other literary devices that illuminated their culture and era (Lipsyte & Levine, 1995). These writers became nearly as famous as the heroes personified in their texts and attained fame based on how they covered the "dope" (analysis and inside information) rather than on pure writing style (Fountain, 1993). This continued and is now evident in today's style, content, and celebration of celebrity athletes. Sportswriters today still refer to this period and its importance, as in the following quoted by Roger Kahn (1999):

The so-called "Golden Age of Sport," the 1920s, is identified with athletic stars—Dempsey, Babe Ruth, Bill Tilden, Bobby Jones. Reading newspapers from the twenties, I began to see the time as first a Golden Age of Sportswriting. After World War I, a gorgeous flowering burst forth in American newspapers: Heywood Broun, Paul Gallico, Ring Lardner, W.O. McGeehan, Westbrook Pegler, Grantland Rice, Damon Runyon. The general approach was tough-guy romantic, as "when Homer smote his bloomin' lyre," and their best work is belletristic—writing that is not merely informative but also beautiful to read. (p. 443)

There were two classifications of sport journalists during this era. Grantland Rice and Paul Gallico epitomized the "Gee Whiz!" style with florid prose that venerated athletes and reveled in their heroic attributes and feats (Inabinett, 1994, p. 21). Other "Gee-Whizzers" included Heywood Broun, Damon Runyon, Joe Vila, and William B. Hanna (Fountain, 1993, p. 133). "Aw-Nuts!" sportswriters like W.O. McGeehan, on the other hand, were skeptics who wrote with a "how-can-you-let-these-guys-break-your-heart-they're-scarcely-worth-the-bother attitude" (Fountain, 1993, p. 133). They wrote in a coarser and less glorious approach, often using sarcasm and irony to debunk or humanize athletes and events (Fountain, 1993). Most of the writers, however, were Gee Whizzers who characterized a postwar period full of hope and levity.

During the 1920s and continuing into the 1930s, significant sports events were often described in newspapers' front-page headlines with descriptive and florid language. Writers sought to instill excitement in their readers through vivid imagery and stylistic devices. Rice's writings unquestionably possessed unity, lyricism, and eloquence. He informed and commented through his elaborate, yet mellifluous prose and excelled at scene-setting techniques, which instilled a feeling of immersion and participation among the readers (Laucella, 2004). His writings enabled American fans to experience the excitement of events through his tone, language, and intimate commentary. Stories, according to Slote (1996), emulated romance with "color, action, and narrative speed" that described heroes' actions and quest for perfection (p. 63). Rice and Gallico embodied this era's obsession with romance, heroes, war references, and the unwavering human spirit. Rice is most remembered for a column written about the Notre Dame versus Army football game, which referenced Vicente Blasco-Ibañez's novel, *The*

Four Horsemen of the Apocalypse, in detailing the moves of Notre Dame backfielders Harry Stuhldreher, Jim Crowley, Don Miller, and Elmer Layden (Fountain, 1993). Rice and other writers used leads that were high in embellishment and low in factual detail, which dramatically differed from the inverted pyramid journalistic style. Rather than using statistics, quotations, or the who, what, when, where, and why of sportswriting, the writers intricately detailed events and their significance with impact, emotion, and gripping language (Laucella, 2004). Rice wrote this lead in 1924 when Notre Dame beat Army 13-7, yet these eloquent words still resonate with fans today:

> Outlined against a blue gray October sky, the Four Horsemen rode again. In dramatic lore they are known as Famine, Pestilence, Destruction, and Death. They are only aliases. Their real names are Stuhldreher, Miller, Crowley, and Layden. They formed the crest of the South Bend cyclone before which another fighting Army football team was swept over the precipice at the Polo Grounds yesterday afternoon as 55,000 spectators peered down on a bewildering panorama spread on the green plain below. (Rice, 1924, p. 1)

Whereas Rice is the most remembered of journalists during this era, Gallico gained the reputation as the "Hemingway of the sports page" (Tuite, 1995, p. 9). The ex–Columbia University oarsman wrote for the New York *Daily News* before devoting his career to writing fiction (Harper, 1999). After working as sports editor, he wrote freelance articles for *Vanity Fair* and the *Saturday Evening Post,* served as a World War II correspondent, and wrote books while living in England, Mexico, Lichtenstein, Monaco, and Antibes (Gallico, 1946). Gallico's scene setting, detailed descriptions, embellished language, and heroic treatment of athletes captured heroic depictions of valor and competitive spirit (Laucella, 2004). He believed athletes were mirrors for their times, reflecting the innocence and unwavering zeal for sport and its participants. Like many of the era's writers, he considered athletes legends and recounted the fairy tale

nature of their "rags to riches" stories (Gallico, 1965, p. 26). He considered the heroes champions of athletic performance as well as models of character and moral integrity.

Rice, Gallico, and other journalists during this era served as catalysts in propelling the growth of sport's popularity and in changing perceptions toward the profession. They clearly made an indelible mark because their names and verses are still remembered and quoted today by sportswriters and fans alike, and their enthusiastic and praising tone appeared to instill athletes with heroic status and spark excitement in the war-weary public. For the first time, sportswriters enjoyed celebrity status like their subjects. In 1925, Rice signed a contract for $52,000 annually as associate editor of the *New York Herald Tribune,* an amount equal to Babe Ruth's salary (Fountain, 1993). Their narratives sparked interest in sport and athletes and restored and energized Americans before the commercialization of sport and television. These writers also engaged individuals in their writings and offered renewed hope in the American dream and the sports hero. This marked the beginning of mass-mediated hero worship and the celebrity treatment of athletes, and it remains today an important era for sport, journalism, and American culture (Laucella, 2004).

Whereas the golden age of sport included lighthearted and embellished prose, celebrating athletes and heroes in a joyous and romantic tone, the ensuing period reflected changing perceptions of American culture and the journalists who transported readers to playing fields.

PERSPECTIVE PERIOD

During the perspective period between 1930 and 1950, the "giddiness and devil-may-care attitude" in the United States changed dramatically after the Depression and during the period before World War II (Harper, 1999, p. 474). According to Rice biographer William A. Harper (1999), "What was fading out in sport was what a colorful athlete could bring to the fore: drama, the sense of the unexpected, romance, the joy of life" (p. 475).

Four Trends Alter Coverage of Sports

Four primary areas of change occurred, which included different perceptions of sportswriting. Although Americans revered the writers of the golden age of sport, they began to question the ethics and importance of the profession. Additionally, sports sections began editing their own copy and professional sport gained popularity over college sport during this period. Newspapers now had to compete against radio, so they had to adapt to this rising medium and adjust content and style appropriately.

Change in Public Perception

The first trend of the perspective period was that some people began to view sportswriting as a trivial and sometimes crooked occupation in the 1930s. As Harper (1999) noted, readers questioned sportswriters' professionalism, objectivity, and ethics with the laudatory coverage of such athletes as Babe Ruth and the liaisons between journalists, promoters, and owners. The Great Depression drastically affected newspaper revenues and writers' salaries, so team owners started paying for writers' expenses on the road in return for positive publicity. These charges of graft and "tainted sportswriters" warranted discussion at the 1926 American Society of Newspaper Editors' annual meeting, where editors debated key topics (Towers, 1981, p. 16). There was a mutually beneficial relationship between journalists and owners and promoters. Journalists needed owners and promoters for stories, and the owners and promoters rewarded journalists with gifts based on their coverage (Harper, 1999). Emotional graft also existed through journalists' camaraderie with athletes and coaches, developed from sharing trains and social outings with their sources (Towers, 1981). Friendships and ties between sources and journalists potentially eroded writers' objectivity, neutrality, professionalism, and ethics.

Reorganization of Newspaper Structure

Another trend of the perspective period was that newspaper organizations reorganized and sports departments began to edit their own copy and were free from the bounds of newspapers' editorial structures (Towers, 1981). For syndicated columnists like Rice, work routines also changed to minimize newspapers' expenses. When Rice left the Tribune syndicate for the North American Newspaper Alliance in 1930, he began to "batch" his columns, writing seven at once, thus restricting the timeliness of his work (Harper, 1999).

Expansion of Coverage

The third trend of this period was a shift in popularity from college to professional sport during the 1930s. Whereas baseball, boxing, and horse racing had dominated newspapers during the golden age of sport, they now branched out to cover football and basketball (Garrison & Sabljak, 1993).

The one major exception was Seabiscuit. In 1938, according to writer Laura Hillenbrand, "The year's number-one newsmaker was not Franklin Delano Roosevelt, Hitler, or Mussolini. It wasn't Pope Pius XI, nor was it Lou Gehrig, Howard Hughes, or Clark Gable. The subject of the most newspaper column inches in 1938 wasn't even a person," said Hillenbrand (2001). "It was an undersized, crooked-legged racehorse named Seabiscuit" (p. xvii). Seabiscuit was a cultural phenomenon and was the subject of stories in major U.S. newspapers and magazines during the Great Depression. He overcame adversity and defeated the heavily favored War Admiral, a Triple Crown winner, at Pimlico in 1938. Seabiscuit and his hard-luck jockey Red Pollard won the "one hundred grand" race at Santa Anita in 1940; 78,000 people attended his final race and millions listened on the radio.

Development of Radio

The development of radio as a medium was the fourth trend of this period. This trend further led to realism and objectivity in reporting and a flair for verbal commentary in covering sport. The Chicago Cubs broadcast games as early as 1924, and the *Chicago Tribune* experimented with baseball coverage on a "bare news basis," showing the impending trend toward radio coverage of sporting events (Towers, 1981, p. 18). As Covil (2005) explained, Westinghouse, General Electric (GE), American Telephone and Telegraph (AT&T), and Radio Corporation of America (RCA) all covered sporting events on radio. Frank Conrad, a Westinghouse engineer, built KDKA in Pittsburgh. This was the first licensed radio station that was not considered an experiment. Its first sports broadcast was the Johnny Ray–Johnny Dundee fight. Other stations like RCA's WJH followed suit and broadcast the Jack Dempsey–Georges Carpentier title fight in 1921. Westinghouse's Newark, New Jersey, station WJZ broadcast the 1921 World Series with Tommy Cowan narrating, and the following year, that station featured Grantland Rice as lead in the broadcasts. Universities, teams, and conferences feared that radio would affect attendance. This was especially true during the Great Depression when the Eastern Colleges Athletic Conference, the Southern Conference, and the Southwest Conference banned or limited broadcasts. By December 1935, however, all restrictions were lifted.

Nation's Mood Influences Coverage

Although the four trends noted here changed sports coverage, perhaps the greatest influence on sportswriters' work during the 1930s was the gravity of the era. More serious and simple writing followed as priorities and life continued changing, and the Olympics transformed sport into an international spectacle of political proportions (Harper, 1999). Peace, equality, teamwork, and perseverance are just a few of the requisite attributes of athletes and nations seeking Olympic victories. This especially proved true during the Depression and a tumultuous period of world dissension with psychological and financial impact (Towers, 1981).

Impact of the Depression

The U.S. stock market crash in 1929 caused national income to plummet from $81 billion to $41 billion by 1932, with 85,000 businesses declaring bankruptcy and 5,761 banks failing to survive (Tallack, 1991). Even with Franklin

Delano Roosevelt's New Deal and its economic recovery efforts, 10 percent of Americans were still unemployed in 1940 (Hunnicutt, 1996; Tallack, 1991).

At newspapers, advertising revenue fell, leading to substantial reductions in stories along with narrower columns and larger fonts. With this diminished style, tabloid newspapers and pictures took the forefront, and by 1938, some city newspapers devoted as much as 38 percent of space to pictures. Technological developments in radio, photography, and film changed communication and created social cohesion in an evolving environment of reform. Within this era, sport and sport sponsorship gained prominence in mirroring and influencing American culture and sport became more democratized (Harper, 1999; Susman, 1984; Towers, 1981).

Primary newspaper sportswriters included Westbrook Pegler of *The New York World-Telegram,* Arthur Daley of *The New York Times,* Red Smith of the *Philadelphia Record* and *The New York Times,* John Kieran of *The New York Times,* and Shirley Povich of *The Washington Post.* Radio sportscasters during this period included the National Broadcasting Corporation's (NBC) Graham McNamee, Columbia Broadcasting System's (CBS) Ted Husing, baseball announcer Mel Allen, and Jack Buck at St. Louis' KMOX-AM. During this epoch, sport magazines like *Sport, The Sporting News,* and *Sports Digest* gained prominence with their attention to fact, statistics, and literary writing. In the 1940s, specialized magazines like *World Tennis, Golf Digest, Yachting, Football Annual,* and *Daily Racing Form* emerged as the market for niche writing arose (Garrison & Sabljak, 1993). These magazines covered events like the Joe Louis–Max Schmeling fights and Jackie Robinson's integration of baseball as he took the field for the Brooklyn Dodgers. At this time, the alternative press gained momentum in covering such sporting events.

Impact of Alternative Press

By 1900, nearly 200 African-American newspapers were published in the United States (Blanchard, 1998). Throughout history, the media have shown and reflected the friction between traditional and mainstream cultures and diverse subcultures in the United States (Folkerts, Lacy, & Davenport, 1998). African-American newspapers specifically offered opposing viewpoints from mainstream papers and published articles promoting positive depictions of race and the "Negro cause," and they instilled pride in their advocacy and activism (Strother, 1978, pp. 92-99).

In addition to African-American newspapers like the *Chicago Defender, Baltimore Afro-American, Pittsburgh Courier,* and *New York Amsterdam News,* the American Communist press actively promoted alternative voices and social activism. By the late 1930s, the *Daily Worker* and *Sunday Worker* in New York had a circulation of 100,000 (Emery, Emery, & Roberts, 2000). With the increasing apprehension about fascism and the Depression, Communists advocated equity among races, genders, and classes in American society (Rusinack, 1998). Readers could choose from divergent voices that expressed varying ideas and perspectives on issues of the day.

As Chris Lamb wrote in his book *Blackout: The Untold Story of Jackie Robinson's First Spring Training* (2004), "The unabridged story of the integration of baseball in America—like the story of civil rights in America—cannot be found in the mainstream press but in the alternative press" (p. 178). The African-American and Communist presses "captured the spirit of the times and emphasized the longstanding significance of Robinson, using historical context, extensive front-page stories, photos, direct quotations and reactions from numerous sources" and were "primary promoters and catalysts for baseball's integration" (Laucella, 2005, p. 209). In the case of Jackie Robinson, the alternative press played a role in "progress, equality, and justice" whereas the mainstream press failed to elucidate the significance of Robinson and instead bolstered the status quo. Alternative publications actively worked together to help integrate baseball by propelling change in perception and policy through their articles and actions and additionally portrayed all athletes in a fair and equitable manner rather than using racially

marked language and bolstering stereotypes (Laucella, 2005).

TRANSITION YEARS

Whereas newspapers devoted much attention to sport and promoted various agendas, a new medium enabled fans to experience sport instantly and visually. With World War II in the past, nearly 100 television stations across the country, and more discretionary money in the pockets of the working class, there was a spike in the purchase of television sets over the final years of the first half of the 20th century. According to sport historian Benjamin G. Rader (2004), "Nothing was more central to the history of organized sports during the second half of the twentieth century than television" (p. 249). Television was the primary medium during the next phase, the transition years.

Network Television Increases Sports Coverage

During the transition years from 1950 to 1970, print journalists modified style and content to compete with the new medium of television and its coverage of sport. Television brought events live to fans and visually captured the key moments and plays. This required journalists in the print media to search for different angles to maintain a fresh approach. The number of features and human interest stories increased as well as stories on the overarching significance of sport (Garrison & Sabljak, 1993). Television made sport an American and global phenomenon by transporting viewers to the events instantly (Rader, 2004, p. 249). By 1952, television broadcasting matured as a medium and more than 15 million homes had a television (Emery, Emery, & Roberts, 2000). The major networks—National Broadcasting Company (NBC), Columbia Broadcasting System (CBS), and American Broadcasting Company (ABC)—sought to expand their reach through affiliates, with NBC leading the way at 64 (Emery, Emery, & Roberts, 2000). National broadcasting was achievable because of coaxial cable lines, and television was mostly live during this era (Emery, Emery, & Roberts, 2000).

Gillette broadcast boxing bouts through the 1950s, and basketball, bowling, and baseball additionally gained attention (Garrison & Sabljak, 1993). Television broadcast such events as the World Series and the Olympic Games, and the advent of teletype systems enhanced communication from reporters in the field to workers in the newsroom (Garrison & Sabljak, 1993). Network executives realized that sports fans were a commodity to lure advertisers like Coca-Cola and McDonald's to sponsor events and promote their products. Professional football was the first to maximize television's technology with multiple cameras, slow motion, graphics, music, and telegenic announcers. In the beginning of this phase, none of the major networks viewed sports programs as important to their long-term sustenance, but ABC was the first to recognize and implement the power of sport. In the 1950s, ABC was third in ratings; however, by the 1970s it cata-

pulted to the top by using sport as a vehicle for network exposure and high ratings (Rader, 2004). Chapter 8 extensively addresses television along with other electronic media and their impact on sport communication.

By the 1960s, sports journalism gained even more momentum and status as the types and diversity of stories increased. Participation, attendance, and circulation numbers rose. Topics broadened to include the legal, political, economic, and social issues in sport to address fans' obsession with athletes' and coaches' lives on and off the field. In-depth analysis, international stories, and women's sports became more important also (Garrison & Sabljak, 1993).

Women Enter the Field

Female reporters entered the scene with Dorothy Lindsay of the *Boston Herald,* Janet Valborg Owen of the *New York Evening World,* and Olympic skater Maribel Vinson of *The New York Times* (Creedon, 1994b). Mary Garber of

Bernadette Cafarelli is the sport information director at Notre Dame. Over the past 30 years, women have increased their presence in sport communication careers. Pioneers such as Dorothy Linsay, Maribel Vinson, and Mary Garber are legendary female sports journalists who paved the way. Cafarelli oversees the day-to-day operation of the sport information office as well as media relations and publicity material for all of the university's Olympic sports teams.

the *Twin Cities Sentinel* (later the *Winston-Salem Journal*) was one of the first full-time women sportswriters. Previously the newspaper's society editor, she replaced the sports editor in 1944 when he joined the Navy (McGillan, 2005). At the time, she could not conduct post-game interviews in the locker rooms and sat with athletes' wives rather than in the press box with male colleagues. Through the mid-1970s, she was the only female sportswriter in the southeastern United States and she covered athletes at African-American high schools and colleges during the Civil Rights movement. A member of the North Carolina Sports Hall of Fame and the Basketball Writers Hall of Fame, she has won at least 40 writing awards (McGillan, 2005).

Sports Illustrated Is Launched

In 1954, Henry Luce created the weekly magazine *Sports Illustrated*. As Michael MacCambridge (1997) covered in his book, *The Franchise: A History of Sports Illustrated Magazine*, *Sports Illustrated* opened more avenues for sport journalists. Although aides scoffed at Luce's idea, calling it "expensive, misguided, and inherently trivial folly," (p. 4), *Sports Illustrated* satisfied fans' fascination with spectator sports. During this era, sport was more "compartmentalized, regionalized, marginalized" (p. 4) as attendance plummeted after World War II and game shows captured viewers' attention. This same year, RCA manufactured color televisions and networks broadcast more games. Additionally, teams expanded to smaller cities, and *Sports Illustrated* gained popularity among middle-class subscribers of the postwar period. Whereas *Sport* magazine focused more on personalities, *Sports Illustrated* legitimized sport with its sophisticated and colorful journalism, captivating readers and influencing the skyrocketing growth of sport in the 1950s and 1960s. Although historians credited the state of the economy and the invention of television as crucial contributions to sport's growth, *Sports Illustrated* also influenced its expansion, according to MacCambridge (1997):

It served as a counterbalance to the persistent hype of television, offering a way for new and educated fans to put the endless rounds of games and matches into meaningful context. It made an art out of in-depth reporting on those games, and thereby made the games themselves more important to more Americans. By setting the agenda of just what sports were important, *[Sports Illustrated]* pointed the way for much of the television revolution that would follow. (p. 6)

PETE ROZELLE AND ROONE ARLEDGE AND THEIR PIONEERING VISIONS

Sports coverage in newspapers, magazines, and television expanded exponentially with television. Technology enabled more fans to experience games on network television, on radio, and in newspapers and magazines. The technology of a new medium coupled with technological inventions and advancements for television sports coverage especially influenced sport's development within the social fabric of America and the world. Two men crucial to sport and television were Pete Rozelle and Roone Arledge.

National Football League (NFL) commissioner Pete Rozelle and ABC president Roone Arledge were pioneers whose visions shaped television sports coverage. Today's field of sport communication would not exist without their innovative ideas, inventions, and brilliance. They contributed to the development of sport marketing, communication, and broadcasting singularly and collaboratively to promote and use sport as a powerful and lucrative business vehicle in television and American culture.

Posthumously, *The Sporting News* named Rozelle as the 20th century's most powerful person in sports (Carter, 2000). When he took over as commissioner of the fledgling NFL in 1960, each of the 12 football franchises competed against each other and garnered less than $20 million in total revenues (Lewis, 1998). Today, the NFL is known according to

Forbes as the "most valuable and profitable team sport in the world" where the average team is valued at $733 million (Ozanian, 2005a). This can be attributed to Rozelle's business savvy and acumen. Rozelle imagined the role that television could play in sport's popularity and growth and especially in prime-time viewing (Shapiro & Maske, 2005). He saw the importance of pooling broadcast rights together into one bidding package for networks, which grouped teams into a cohesive and single entity rather than stand-alone, fragmented franchises. With "league think," NFL team owners considered the league's welfare over their own teams' individual needs while increasing the value of the NFL brand. Rozelle used this philosophy to develop a business strategy forged around a national television package (DeGaris, 2003). By persuading Congress to legalize single-network contracts for professional leagues, he forced networks to compete for the pooled rights (Carter, 2000). The ensuing 1961 Sports Broadcasting Act enabled professional leagues to bundle their rights for sale in one television package for networks ("Sports Law," 2005).

Under Rozelle, NFL Properties became the league's independent marketer in 1963 (Lefton, 2002). In addition to laying the foundation for today's NFL business model, Rozelle merged the NFL and the American Football League (AFL) in 1970, which led to the AFL–NFL World Championship Game and the Super Bowl. According to communication scholar Michael R. Real, the Super Bowl is "the most lucrative annual spectacle in American mass culture" (Real, 1975, p. 31). Real wrote his seminal article more than 30 years ago, but it is still relevant today. Real wrote that not only does the Super Bowl unite electronic media and sport in a "ritualized mass activity," but it also propagates American cultural values and ideologies in a "mythic spectacle" (Real, 1975, p. 31). Today, corporations vie to reach the more than 86.1 million viewers who watch the "most-watched television event of the year" ("Super Bowl ratings down 4 percent," 2005). Viewership has ranged from 73.9 million in 1990 to 94.1 million in 1996 ("Super Bowl ratings down 4 percent," 2005).

Super Bowl advertising spots in recent years have surpassed $2.5 million for a 30-second spot ($2.6 million in 2007).

In 1970, Arledge and Rozelle together masterminded *Monday Night Football,* which "created a national pastime" (Boss, 2002). After CBS's *60 Minutes, Monday Night Football* is the second longest running prime-time show on television in America (Lewis, 1998). In its first season, *Monday Night Football* featured the legendary Howard Cosell, former Dallas Cowboys quarterback Don Meredith, and Keith Jackson. Frank Gifford replaced Jackson in its second season. Cosell's "tell it like it is" candor attracted huge audiences for the show (Shapiro, 1995). "He was described over the years," according to sportswriter Leonard Shapiro (1995), "as a social phenomenon, a broadcaster and crusading journalist who broke the pretty-face, perfect-hair, former-jock mold of network sports personalities with his unique style and delivery" (p. A1).

CBS paid $9.3 million for 2 years to televise games in 1962. With the new NFL contract extended in 2004-2005, ESPN and NBC also signed $1.1 billion and $600 million annual rights fees to broadcast NFL games (Bernstein, 2005c). This shows how the value of the NFL has skyrocketed in 40-plus years. Networks recognize how important sports programming is to ratings and exposure. NBC hopes to use sports programming to boost its last-place ratings among viewers age 18 to 49 by promoting other shows during the Sunday night broadcast, which the network will carry through 2011 (Isidore, 2005). Fox continued its affiliation with the NFL and will spend $712.5 million a year until 2011 (Isidore, 2005). Fox realized the power of sport in 1993 when it first acquired broadcast rights to the National Football Conference (NFC) package, establishing itself as a fourth major television network (Sweet, 2002a). The 4-year agreement averaged $1.1 billion a year ("Tagliabue's Tenure," 2006). Networks are willing to spend exorbitant amounts of revenue on NFL broadcast rights because NFL broadcasts are some of the most watched programs, and the networks can promote other shows in primetime to young male viewers (Sweet, 2002a). At Fox, 10 of the network's highest-rated shows are with the NFL, reinforcing the network's commitment to sport, and specifically the NFL (Fox Sports, 2006). In 2006, *Monday Night Football* moved to ESPN, and for the first time in 35 years it was on cable, with Mike Tirico, Tony Kornheiser, and Joe Theismann broadcasting the games. Although the ratings of *Monday Night Football* have dwindled, it still adheres to Rozelle's and Arledge's plan to showcase the league, its key players, and coaches; to present sports reporters as experts and celebrities; and to use the most up-to-date technological advancements in sports broadcasting.

Like Rozelle, Arledge was a visionary in sports broadcasting. Arledge gained recognition as one of *Life* magazine's most important Americans of the 20th century (Boss, 2002). In addition to cocreating *Monday Night Football,* Arledge introduced technological innovations to sports broadcasts, including instant replay, slow motion, handheld cameras, split-screen, end-zone cameras, and underwater cameras.

Arledge created the longstanding show *Wide World of Sports* in 1961, offering viewers opportunities to experience every sport imaginable from football to bobsledding and luge. *Wide World of Sports* also featured international events via satellite and enabled viewers to connect with athletes through in-depth human interest stories. After Arledge's death in 2002, ESPN.com's "Page 2" columnist Ralph Wiley (2002) wrote the following about Arledge's contributions to sport while president of ABC sports and news:

> "The thrill of victory and the agony of defeat." His. "Up close and personal." His. "Wide World of Sports." His. Epic Olympic coverage. His. Breaking spot news on terrorism. His, really. "Monday Night Football." His. Howard Cosell. His. Dandy Don Meredith (TV version). His. Frank Gifford. His. "American Sportsman." His. "Nightline." His. "20/20." His. Isolated camera. His. Instant replay. His.

© Paul M. Pedersen

Former heavyweight boxing champion Muhammad Ali (center) and his wife Lonnie (right) listen as one of his twin daughters, Jamillah Ali, speaks at the dedication of the $80 million, six-story Muhammad Ali Center in Louisville. Ali was one of the most media-savvy athletes of all time, and he captured worldwide attention and fame through his pragmatic use of television interviews and press conferences. He embraced the idea of athletic celebrity throughout the 1960s and 1970s.

All totally his. Sports as storytelling. His, in a big way (¶5).

As the "Mark Twain of TV sports" (Wiley, 2002), Arledge recognized that "stars sell" in an age before celebrity athletes and endorsers Michael Jordan, Shaquille O'Neal, Tony Hawk, LeBron James, and Tiger Woods entered the scene (Harris, 2002, p. 11). Arledge focused on the drama, action, and characters in sport to create vivid pictures, memories, and experiences for fans. Arledge captured the entertainment element in sport and transported it to a different level, paving the way for the technology we now experience and expect in sport communication and broadcasting.

TODAY'S SPORT COMMUNICATION

Lawrence A. Wenner (1998b) coined the term "MediaSport" as the "mediation of sport" within culture and the "broader public sphere" (p. xiii). According to Real (1998), "No force has played a more central role in the Media-Sport complex than commercial television and its institutionalized value system—profit seeking, sponsorship, expanded markets, commodification, and competition" (p. 17).

Cable Television Increases Influence of Sport

Although network television primarily influenced the development of sport in the 1950s through 1970s, cable television and especially the Entertainment and Sports Programming Network (ESPN) advanced sport's reach exponentially in the late 1970s and 1980s and contributed to its monumental place in society today. Ironically, when Bill Rasmussen thought of broadcasting sports 24 hours a day on cable television, networks and newspapers downplayed its impact, never envisioning cable's reach and fans' obsession with the 24-hour-sport cycle (Freeman, 2001). From Keith Olbermann to Chris Berman, Bob Ley, Dick Vitale, Dan Patrick, Linda Cohn, and Robin Roberts, ESPN has featured many compelling and

talented anchors and reporters since its first broadcast on September 7, 1979, at 7:00 p.m. (Freeman, 2001). Shows like *The Sports Reporters, Pardon the Interruption* (PTI), *Outside the Lines,* and particularly *SportsCenter* offer provocative commentary, wit, keen writing and reporting, and charismatic personalities on and off the field. Today, ESPN is the largest cable network in the United States with more than 94 million viewers per week on one of ESPN's more than 40 business entities. From domestic cable networks to radio, print, broadband, wireless, and on-demand, ESPN offers programming and entertainment for sports enthusiasts and fanatics alike. With Walt Disney as 80 percent owner, ESPN stays true to its expansive mission of serving "sports fans wherever sports are watched, listened to, discussed, debated, read about, or played" ("Our Mission and Values," 2005, ¶1). ESPN earned Disney most of its $1.92 billion in cable earnings in 2004 (Bernstein, 2005h). ESPN.com also has been the leading sports Web site each month since its launch as ESPNet SportsZone in 1995 (King, 2005b). More than 10 million unique visitors access the site monthly according to Nielsen/NetRatings (Adams, 2005b).

Technology Alters Communication Strategies

As King (2005b) explained, in a fragmented media environment with more than 400 television channels, broadband, satellite radio, and cell phones, media fight to reach and retain audiences. Although 87 percent of U.S. adults consider themselves sports fans, media executives now believe they must reach people at home, in the office, in the car, and everywhere. After all, sports fans consume 9 hours and 13 minutes of media daily. Sports properties of all types actively participate and use technology, and teams, leagues, and sport media are altering their sport communication strategies. One example is the use of blogs, or Web logs. At ESPN.com, there is one blogger for each major sport and for fantasy sports and businesses. Leagues and teams also have blogs. One such example is Dallas Mavericks' owner Mark

Cuban, who started Blog Maverick in 2004 to discuss various topics from media coverage of his team to inside knowledge about players. Another example is SportsBlogs, which consists of 25 teams from Major League Baseball. President Tyler Bleszinski believes that blogs differ from traditional journalism because they offer a big picture of teams, leagues, and sports over daily events and games (Show, 2005). Technology is discussed extensively in chapter 9.

According to *SportsBusiness Journal,* the following technologies are transforming the way fans consume and experience sport. Video on demand (VOD) offers fans a way to see condensed versions of games and events as well as coaches' and athletes' press conferences. Digital asset management enables networks to store and edit digitized video in archives for later use. Optical tracking systems provide a means for tracing an object or player with a camera. 3G, or "Third Generation," is a type of mobile communication technology that will offer live, 24-hour television stations, made-for-mobile channels, and channels with on-demand clips. Portable people meters, high-definition television, personalized sports tickers, Internet Protocol Television, online video gaming, and satellite radio are other technologies in use or soon to be incorporated into sports coverage (Bernstein, 2005d).

Sports Arena Expands

As the use of technology increasingly enables sport organizations and properties to reach fans, it is evident that the sports arena has become increasingly diverse, fragmented, and competitive. In the golden age of sport, journalists focused on games and athletes' heroic feats on the field. Today, journalists focus not only on games but more on legal, political, economic, and cultural implications of sport, athletes, coaches, owners, and managers. Writers like Gary Smith, Frank Deford, Christine Brennan, Michael Wilbon, Kelli Anderson, and Mike Lupica all possess unique styles that spark interest and detail action on the field and off. There are more in-depth analyses, interviews, and opinions and

a movement away from the celebratory tone that emerged during the golden age of sport. The journalist–source relationship has also changed. Whereas reporters and their subjects fraternized during the 1920s and 1930s, there is a more detached relationship between reporters and their sources. The relationship can even become contentious as evident in media incidents with Barry Bonds and coach Bob Knight and in harassment cases like Lisa Olson's with the New England Patriots football team. Journalists feel the need to delve deeper because television and the Internet and emerging technologies bring coverage to fans in real time. In the past, individuals did not know the scores or key game plays until they read the newspaper, but in today's information-rich society and splintered media environment, fans have infinite choices and opportunities. Today, writers care more about being watchdogs than storytellers as in the 1920s and 1930s. "Opinion today is more adversarial, more intrusive, more inclined to pander to the public's 'desire' to know under the guise of its 'right' to know," according to Joe Fitzgerald of the *Boston Herald.* "I see too many columnists measuring celebrities against litmus tests we ourselves could not pass" (McCleneghan, 1994, p. 72). Legendary sportswriter Will McDonough pointed out another aspect of today's sport media coverage. "TV has changed everything. . . . Ethics are nonexistent," noted the *Boston Globe* writer. "It's OK to make something up as long as you don't get caught. It's sad" (McCleneghan, 1994, p. 72). Conversely, others believe there is a trend toward leniency and a noncritical approach. According to *Sports Illustrated*'s Steve Rushin (2000), "The new non-judgmentalism may merely reflect a disingenuous desire among public figures to preempt criticism. When nobody judges, everything is condoned" (p. 24).

As salaries have skyrocketed for athletes, coaches, and owners, content has changed with more of a focus on sport's economic impact as well as the implications of endorsement deals and celebrity status. Additionally, women's sport and international events warrant more coverage. Sport executives also recognize the value of positive fan experiences and forging relationships with the "hard-core" fan as well as the more "casual" fan through technology, marketing, promotions, and amenities ("Executives Focus," 2005). Media companies like Rupert Murdoch's News Corporation, Robert Iger's Walt Disney Company, and Richard Parsons' Time Warner Inc. all are active participants in bidding wars for media rights. Although they have always realized the value of these deals, they now use sport as the "centerpiece" of their programming (Bernstein, 2005h, p. 1). In 2005, Major League Baseball renewed with ESPN for 50 percent more, and the Outdoor Life Network on cable signed a 2-year $135 million deal with the National Hockey League (Bernstein, 2005h).

With the differences between journalists from yesterday and today, the technological advancements of sports coverage, and the variances in content, sport communication has evolved and emerged as a potent force in contemporary American culture. Sport and the media exert a powerful influence and are at the center of our social, economic, and cultural lives today. "Ignoring MediaSport today would be like ignoring the role of the church in the Middle Ages or ignoring the role of art in the Renaissance," noted Real (1998). "Large parts of society are immersed in media sports today and virtually no aspect of life is untouched by it" (p. 15). By analyzing the origins of sport communication and tracing its development from the 19th century to the present, we find that key trends and pioneers contributed to the infinite possibilities in all facets of sport communication from print journalism to electronic media, public relations, marketing, advertising, interpersonal communication, research, and emerging technologies.

CHAPTER WRAP-UP

Summary

This chapter outlined sport communication's development, offering an overview of sports coverage in newspapers and magazines and on radio, television, cable, and emerging technologies. It elucidated the importance of the 1920s golden age of sport, where journalists chronicled athletes' and coaches' outstanding and heroic feats, setting the agenda for readers through their dramatic and vivid prose. Journalists transported readers to stadiums, arenas, and tracks, describing events, athletes, and fans with meticulous precision. The journalists set the foundation for sports coverage in an era before radio and television, and their legacies live on through their quotes and their impact on the importance of sport in popular culture. Although radio entered the scene in the 1920s and television's growth skyrocketed in the 1950s, the golden age of sport set the foundation and had a profound impact on sport and sports coverage.

The electronic media, radio, television, and cable contributed to sport's growth by bringing fans events in real time and adding sound and pictures to stories. Fans could supplement game experiences with continuing coverage on their favorite medium, and those who did not attend the games could listen on the radio, watch on television or cable, and feel like they were actually in the stadium or arena. From early radio announcers like Mel Allen to television pioneers Pete Rozelle and Roone Arledge to ESPN's founder Bill Rasmussen, technology, talent, and vision combined to promote sport's value and utility and to maximize fans' experiences. Today, the field of sport communication integrates sport media with other entities that are crucial for the sport enterprise.

Review Questions

1. What cultural changes influenced the ascent of sport and how did this affect sport journalism?
2. What are some of the names and types of early sport publications?
3. How did the American military contribute to sport communication's growth?
4. What are some characteristics of journalism from the golden age of sport and how did they contribute to the development of sport and sport communication?
5. Who are the key sportswriters from the 1920s, and what were their key contributions?
6. How and why did sport become an "opiate" during the golden age of sport? What role did sport journalism play in this process?
7. Why did the alternative press gain momentum in the 1930s? How was this reflected in sport communication?
8. What changes did radio and television bring about in sport coverage?
9. Why are Pete Rozelle and Roone Arledge pioneers in sport communication?
10. How have cable and emerging technologies changed the playing field of sport?

Discussion Questions

1. How has sports coverage evolved from the penny press in the 19th century? Discuss the types of sports covered as well as the treatment of athletes and events.
2. Why is "MediaSport" an important term today? How does it relate to the media choices and options you have when watching games, obtaining scores, and gaining insider information?
3. What elements of the Super Bowl make it a "mythic spectacle" in the words of Michael Real? Discuss elements of this article that are still relevant as well as those that are no longer relevant.
4. How did television change sport and sports coverage? Address technological changes as well as changes in content.
5. How is today's media environment fragmented, and what are the implications, good and bad, for sport communication?

Activities and Exercises

1. Read Grantland Rice's column from the Notre Dame versus Army football game in 1924. What are your impressions? What works and doesn't work? How does this differ from game stories you would read today?
2. Watch *Monday Night Football* and analyze the broadcast, from the announcers to the on-the-field technology to the fans. What elements are important developments in sport communication?
3. Discuss all the current media rights deals of the major leagues. Why are these so important to major corporations? Consider consolidation, vertical integration, horizontal integration, and how corporations use sport to promote other holdings.

4. Watch, read, play, or experience five different entities of ESPN. How has the network changed sport communication and media coverage?

5. Who are some of your favorite sport journalists and reporters? Why do you like them?

Internet Sites for Additional Learning

Babe Ruth: http://espn.go.com/sportscentury/features/00016451.html

Babe Ruth: www.baberuth.com/flash/about/viewheadline.php?id = 1723

The Four Horsemen by Grantland Rice: http://und.collegesports.com/trads/horse.html

Gertrude Ederle: http://sportsillustrated.cnn.com/2003/writers/frank_deford/12/03/viewpoint/

Jack Dempsey: http://espn.go.com/classic/biography/s/Dempsey_Jack.html

JournalismJobs.com: www.journalismjobs.com

Pete Rozelle: www.time.com/time/time100/builder/profile/rozelle.html

Roone Arledge: www.museum.tv/archives/etv/A/htmlA/arledgeroon/arledgeroon.htm

Sport Journalism Jobs: www.americanpressinstitute.org/content/3962.cfm

PART II

Examining the Strategic Sport Communication Model

Photos © Paul M. Pedersen

Part II contains nine chapters that examine the conceptual and practical aspects of sport communication, which the textbook defines as the process by which people in sport, in a sport setting, or through a sport endeavor share symbols as they create meaning through interaction. This part opens with chapter 4, which explores the concepts of communication and sport communication from a broad perspective and leads to the framework on which the textbook is structured: the Strategic Sport Communication Model (SSCM). Sport communication involves the sport communication process, its components, and how sport industry professionals and organizations communicate with both internal and external stakeholders. Therefore, the SSCM illustrates the sport communication process and categorizes the many varied aspects of communication in the sport industry into three major components. The model details the complex nature and tremendous breadth of sport communication. The process provides a microview of the field, whereas the rest of the model presents a macroview of sport communication. This model was developed to provide the first conception of sport communication as a discipline. After the chapter introduces the process of sport communication and the three components of the model, it then concludes with a discussion of sport communication effects and the sport communication consumption communities (i.e., the sport communication audiences and consumers).

The SSCM divides sport communication into three components: personal and organizational communication in sport (component I), sport mass media (component II), and sport communication services and support (component III). The first component is covered in chapters 5 and 6. Chapter 5 examines personal communication in sport. The three segments of personal communication in sport are intrapersonal (the inward communication, or the speech going on inside one's mind), interpersonal (the two-way flow of information between two or three individuals), and small-group (the communication systems among individuals in small gatherings) sport communication. When communicators in sport interact in an intimate and direct manner, they are participating in one of these three forms of personal communication. Chapter 6 covers the communication in and between sport organizations. Organizational communication in sport is the process in which messages are created, exchanged, interpreted, and stored within a system of human relationships in sport. Therefore, this chapter introduces the theoretical, conceptual, and practical aspects of communication that occur within a sport organization and between a sport organization and another organization. Intraorganizational communication in sport involves the communication with internal publics, whereas interorganizational communication in sport includes the communication a sport organization has with external publics.

The sport mass media—the second component of the SSCM—could be defined as the sport reporting and commentary on sport and the various associated activities that surround sport and the influences that shape sport. In addition to covering the sport industry, the sport mass media often reinforce and reflect the institution of sport and sometimes even help to shape sport. The sport mass media can be grouped into three major segments. Therefore, the sport mass media component of the model involves sport publishing and print sport communication, the electronic media, and the new sport media. Chapter 7 covers the first segment of the sport mass media—sport publishing and print sport communication. Sport publishing is the business or profession of the commercial production and dissemination of information related to sport (e.g., sports books, sports sections of newspapers, sports magazines, sports Internet sites, annuals, team newsletters, fan magazines, media guides, game programs, fact sheets). Print sport communication involves any medium that disseminates printed matter related to sport. Chapter 8—which covers the second segment of the sport mass media—divides the electronic and visual communication in sport into four categories: radio, television, cable television, and films and documentaries. Chapter 9 covers the third segment of the sport mass media—online sport communication and the new sport media. Included in this final chapter of the second component of SSCM are analyses of the Internet, the Model for Online Sport Communication (MOSC), and new sport media and communication channels (e.g., wireless technology, blogs, glogs, video on demand). The online sport communication framework includes the areas of content, design, performance, usability, commerce, and consumer motivations and needs.

Chapters 10 through 12 cover the third component of sport communication, sport communication services and support. The three segments within this third component of the SSCM are sport advertising, public relations and crisis communication in sport, and sport communication research. Sport advertising, as covered in chapter 10, takes many forms and includes advertising of sport products as well as non-sport-related products. Included in this chapter are the history of sport advertising and analyses of sport sponsorships and endorsements. Chapter 11, which examines public relations and crisis communication in sport, covers the two topics from historical and managerial perspectives. The chapter begins by discussing sport public relations, which is the management of sport information flow between a sport entity and its key publics to present the sport organization in the most favorable manner possible and to establish mutually beneficial relationships. The chapter concludes with an examination of crisis communication for sport organizations and outlines strategies for managing crisis situations internally and externally. Chapter 12 provides information on sport communication research, applying the topic to the mass media, sport management, and the scholars and students in academia. The chapter begins with a discussion of how both the media and sport industries use research. It then examines the uses of research in academia and the specifics on writing research and choosing methodologies in sport communication.

CHAPTER 4

Sport Communication and the Strategic Sport Communication Model (SSCM)

PROFILE OF A SPORT COMMUNICATOR

Greg Norman

Just the mention of his name conjures up images of a swashbuckling style, competitive spirit, black wide-brimmed hat, and trademark logo. In addition to having a charismatic persona, Greg Norman is one of the greatest golfers of all time with more than 80 victories—including two British Open Championships—and a place in the World Golf Hall of Fame. In addition to holding an iconic status in golf, he has transcended the sport through his ability to communicate with various publics. His actions outside the competitive arena of golf provide a perfect illustration of the connection between communication theory and praxis.

The Shark has engaged in sport communication throughout his career. Even his nickname was given by a media scribe who was looking for a way to describe the aggressive style of the golf legend. Although Norman's playing days are winding down, he still works with the media by granting interviews, writing books (*The Way of the Shark,* 2006) and magazine golf columns, producing golf videos, endorsing video games, and appearing on golf shows. Of his many media engagements and activities, his most demanding involves Greg Norman Interactive. This company runs his Web site (www.shark.com), which offers sponsorship, advertising, and e-commerce in addition to posted information about golf news, biographical and statistical material, a "Sharkive" of links to his career accomplishments, and a photo gallery. The Web site also features comments, instruction, and fitness tips from Norman. As the official site of Norman and his businesses, the Web site—through the "Ask Greg" link—allows interaction between Norman and his fans through online chatting. One fan recently asked Norman about his approach to work and

The Shark, professional golfer Greg Norman, has built his Great White Shark Enterprises into a corporate empire. As a business leader, Norman communicates with stakeholders through a variety of means. Even his likeness on the billboard for one of his real estate developments is part of his strategic communication activities.

the golfer responded, "I am certainly not afraid to get my fingernails dirty and I'm not afraid to go at a task myself and just get it done. I pride myself on hard work, and I think that is probably why I have achieved the level of success I have. I don't ask anyone in my organization to put in any more effort than I'm willing to put in." Such interaction with fans and Web site visitors is becoming more and more common in the sport industry.

Beyond his involvement with the media, the Australian native communicates the most with business colleagues, company employees, financial strategists, public relations officers, and a host of other sports professionals. "White papers, mission statements, business plans (are) all necessary parts of the equation," Norman once told one of the authors of this textbook. "It's the same for golf, business, whatever."

As the leader of Great White Shark Enterprises (GWSE), Norman has become one of the wealthiest golfers. In addition to his solid golf performances and victories, he built the multinational

GWSE into a corporate empire valued at more than $200 million. His numerous business ventures—the majority of which bear his image—are owned under the umbrella of the GWSE. They include such enterprises as the Greg Norman Collection (apparel line with Reebok), Greg Norman Turf Company (turf growing and licensing of turf grass), Greg Norman Australian Grille (restaurant chain), Greg Norman Production Company (event management), Greg Norman Expedition Yachts (custom boats), and Greg Norman Estates (wine label).

Although he has talented employees within each business entity, Norman takes a proactive approach to communication. "I'm definitely a Type A personality," said Norman, "and I make sure everything is done correctly." His involvement demands that he have the ability to communicate across several levels. These levels—which are called contexts of sport communication—involve all aspects of sport communication. For instance, in his role as leader of the Greg Norman Golf Course Design Company, Norman communicates with developers, architects, designers, salespeo-

ple, and a host of other stakeholders. Because he is so involved in each step of the design, construction, and opening of his golf courses, Norman is constantly engaged in communication.

Although his competitive playing days are coming to a close, there appears to be nothing but smooth sailing ahead for the Great White Shark and his enterprises. Because Norman owns and operates so many businesses, maybe that's why one of his favorite hobbies is fishing. Even when he is all alone with his rod and reel he cannot escape communication. That's because when he talks to himself he is involved with intrapersonal communication. All of Norman's communication—whether it is with fans (interpersonal and small-group sport communication), employees (interorganizational and intraorganizational communication in sport), reporters (sport media), designers (sport communication services and support), or any other message sender or receiver—embodies the sport communication definition, process, elements, and theoretical framework on which this chapter (and the rest of this textbook) is based.

As we have illustrated in our analyses of the educational, career, and historical aspects of sport communication in the book's first unit (chapters 1-3), the field of sport communication is evolving with tremendous growth potential. This expansion is directly connected to the growing prevalence and impact of the sport industry. "Sports are pervasive through our society and culture," noted sport marketing experts Scott W. Kelley and Kelly Tian (2004). "Most of our lives are touched daily in some respect by sports, whether we realize it or not. The entertainment we seek out, the media we are exposed to, and our interactions with others are often influenced by the world of sports," (p. 27). As Kelley and Tian detailed, sport is pervasive and much of this involves communication (e.g., entertainment, media, interactions).

Communication in sport encompasses everything from interpersonal relationships, public relations, and advertising to theory, research, emerging technologies, and, of course, the

print and electronic media. Although a few individuals still possess a narrow view of the field (e.g., some might view sport communication as only dealing with sport journalism), more and more practitioners and scholars are endorsing a broader perspective of this discipline. We too advocate the latter approach because the field of sport communication includes everything from water-cooler conversations between two front-office colleagues in sport organizations to NBC's broadcast of the Olympics watched by millions of television viewers. With such an expansive view of the field, there is a need for segmentation. One of the best ways to do this is through modeling, which creates a theoretical framework on which a concept can be expressed.

This chapter explains the framework—what we call the Strategic Sport Communication Model (SSCM)—that encompasses the sport communication process and three unique components of the field of sport communication.

Although the mass media receive the most visibility, sport communication involves many additional components, facets, activities, and professionals beyond the electronic and print sport media. This exchange between coach and athlete illustrates interpersonal communication.

DEFINING SPORT COMMUNICATION

Studying sport communication is more than simply looking at the sport message. This means that an examination of sport communication must go beyond the end product; such an analysis requires an investigation beyond the sports section of a newspaper or the sports broadcast on the radio. Sure, sport communication involves texts (i.e., the products or materials that are produced through the sport communication) and representations (i.e., the version of subject matter that is in the sport text). However, as noted British communication scholar and author Graeme Burton (2005, 2002, 2000) detailed, there are many additional aspects of communication and media. Many of these facets are quite distinct from the sport message or end product. For example, some of the facets of sport communication include such aspects as institutions (e.g., the organizations that own, run, and finance sport media or sport communication departments), production systems (e.g., the activities involved in putting a sports message together), conditions (e.g., the environment in which the communication in sport or the sport media material takes place), meanings, audiences, content, and context.

Although there is clearly more to sport communication than the sport media or sport communication product itself, arriving at a definition of sport communication is quite difficult. Old Dominion University's Fred Battenfield (2004), in his analysis of sport information departments at intercollegiate institutions, noted, "Because the process of communication is so complex, a precise definition is arguably impossible to put forward" (p. 26). We agree with this sport communication expert. Although it is seemingly impossible to put forth a universally accepted definition of sport communication, we believe that the best definition to date is the one offered by Pedersen, Laucella, Miloch, and Fielding (2007) and depicted in figure 4.1.

At its basic level, sport communication could be defined as the exchange of either information or sport information by or through sport. We prefer, however, a more complex, detailed, and expansive definition of sport communication (Heath & Bryant, 2000). Sport communication is a process by which people in sport, in a sport setting, or through a sport endeavor share symbols as they create meaning through interaction (Pedersen et al., 2007).

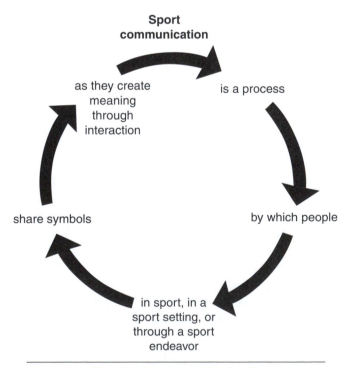

Figure 4.1 The definitional components of "sport communication."

In addition to its cultural approach, this definition integrates the communication aspects that are involved in and through sport.

Try to picture a hypothetical scenario that could occur in the sport industry. For example, say the owner and chief executive officer of the Indianapolis Colts, Jim Irsay, motivates his front office personnel by stopping by the team's headquarters to give a rousing pep talk to the team's president, Bill Polian, and his top managerial team. Could this action be considered sport communication? Sure. Through his expressive talk to the executive administrators, Irsay is sharing verbal and nonverbal messages in a sport setting. Through his interaction with the team, a meaning is created (i.e., the team appreciates his visit and is motivated). Any example that you can think of in which there is communication in and through sport will fit into this definition of sport communication. It is broad enough for interpersonal sport communication, group and organizational sport communication, mediated sport communication, and any other type of communication that occurs in or through the sport industry.

EXAMINING THE THEORETICAL FRAMEWORK OF SPORT COMMUNICATION

Before we analyze what is involved with the Strategic Sport Communication Model (SSCM), let's first examine how it was developed. The study of communication theory provides insight into the study of sport communication. "The word theory refers to the processes of observing and speculating. It is similar to making an educated guess about some phenomenon," stated communication scholars Robert Heath and Jennings Bryant (2000). They went on to say, "A theory is a systematic and plausible set of generalizations that explain some observable phenomena by linking concepts (constructs and variables) in terms of an organizing principle that is internally consistent" (p. 10).

The SSCM is built on numerous theories and models of communication and information. As Battenfield (2004) noted, "Many differ-

ent approaches to the theoretical study of communication have arisen" (p. 26) over the years. Each communication theory, when defined in a broad way, is used to represent a concept or explain a phenomenon (Chaffee, 1996; Littlejohn & Foss, 2005). These conceptualizations of communication range from social scientific theories that have been refined by researchers to normative theory that has been proposed to improve human communication. They also include working theories that are under development and commonsense theories that are just that, common sense. To embrace as many theories and models as possible, the broad approach of the SSCM is based on past research into the genres, contexts, and process of communication and information.

Genres

First, the **genres** of communication involve theories that come in various shapes and sizes. Some of the communication theories are valid and accurate whereas others are invalid or inaccurate. There are, according to Littlejohn and Foss (2005), several main groups of communication theories. These are structural theories (focused on language, social systems), functional theories (focused on how organized systems function), cognitive and behavioral theories (focused on the individual), interactional and conventional theories (focused on the process and effects of interaction), interpretive theories (focused on the discovery of meaning in actions and texts), and critical theories (focused on inequality, oppression, domination).

The study of sport communication involves all of the main groups of communication theories. For instance, critical communication theories are applied in chapter 13 (Sociological Aspects of Sport Communication), cognitive and behavior theories—which often focus on the individual—can be found in chapter 5 (Personal Sport Communication), and structural and functional theories are evident in chapter 6 (Organizational and Leadership Communication in Sport). Therefore, all of the communication theories influence sport communication and the SSCM.

Contexts

Second, regardless of the theoretical approach that is taken, there are **contexts** of communication. It is impossible to analyze sport communication without examining contexts or the levels of communication involved. The dominant communication contexts (i.e., interpersonal, group, organizational, mass-mediated) can be associated with any one theory. Sport communication involves all of these contexts because they are included in component I (interpersonal, small group, and intra- or interorganizational communication in sport), component II (sport mass media), and component III (sport communication services and support) of the SSCM. This is very similar to the segmentation approach found in marketing. In fact, sport marketing experts Brenda Pitts and David Stotlar (2002) created the sport marketing segmentation model, which contains all of the components of sport marketing. Similarly,

all of the components (entities) of sport communication are contained in the four levels or contexts of sport communication. The specific levels or contexts of sport communication are discussed in greater detail later in this chapter and in the next eight chapters.

Process

Third, the definition of sport communication clearly states that sport communication is a dynamic **process**. The sport communication process—whether it results in profits or individual gratification—is vibrant, interactive, multidimensional, and infinite. Taking a process approach to any aspect of communication is nothing new. This process of communication involves the theoretical analysis of information. As Battenfield (2004) noted, "Information theory is concerned with the transmission and reception of messages, rather than the meaning of the message" (p. 29).

Sport communication is interactive and multidimensional with communication flowing multilaterally. Here, April Priest (87)—the tight-end, linebacker, and co-owner of the Indiana Speed—sends and receives many messages even though her direct communication is with the team's head athletic trainer, Marie DeWolf.

Sociologist Harold Lasswell—through asking a famous question about media effects ("who says what in which channel to whom with what effect?")—developed a formula that is considered the first transmission model of communication (sender–message–channel–receiver). The Lasswell formula (1948) was created to explain mass communication. However, it can be applied to all forms of communication including sport communication, as we will see later.

Around the same time as Lasswell's question, media scientists Claude Shannon and Warren Weaver developed the influential general model of communication. The Shannon–Weaver model (1949)—a linear creation similar to the Lasswell formula—proposes six elements in the communication process: a source, an encoder, a message, a channel, a decoder, and a receiver. These early models reduced communication to a one-way process of transmitting information. They failed to allow for the fact that senders and receivers often fail to send messages smoothly. For example, when someone sends a message, the message may be affected by the channel, interference (noise), and context (environment). In sport communication, an example of this would be fan noise produced by capacity crowds in facilities such as Duke University's Cameron Indoor Stadium.

Despite the limitations of the early transmission models (e.g., failure to consider context, channel effects, sender–receiver relationships), they led to the widely accepted model by communication scholar Wilbur Schramm. His simplified communications model (and the ensuing Schramm–Osgood model) allow for both understanding in the communication process and the involvement of feedback and two-way communication (Greenberg & Salwen, 1996). Schramm's model involves the elements of sources (encoders), messages (signals), and receivers (decoders). In addition to taking into account the behavioral aspects of the communicators and the environmental circumstances in communication, this updated model illustrated a circular communication process. In sport communication, this process is evident in NBC's broadcasts of the Dew

Action Sports Tour. The words of the commentators and the images from the camera are broadcast to the network's viewers. Those who tune in to the broadcasts interpret and process the messages. They then exercise power in the process by either staying tuned, switching to another channel, or turning off the television.

The early communication models—although groundbreaking and useful—have been updated and criticized over the decades. Some of these criticisms have focused on the need for the models to include a broader social component and a movement to more critical and cultural communication analyses. One of these analyses is the ritual model of communication, which takes an interactive and interpretive approach to the study of communication. The impetus for viewing communication as a ritual can be traced to philosopher John Dewey, who stated that individuals in society "live in a community in virtue of the things which they have in common; and communication is the way in which they come to possess things in common" (1916, ¶10). Carey (1989) and Pauly (1997) noted that the ritual view of communication includes the perspectives of conversing, sharing, participating, and associating.

The process and ritual models of communication can be used to explain how sport communication works and allow for the development of a critical perspective of sport communication. As Burton (2002) noted, "All acts of communication are a process. This process includes a source, a message and a receiver of the message . . . any one of these factors within any communication process will affect the content and treatment of its messages" (p. 30). Sport communication—whether face-to-face or mediated—can be conceptualized (see figure 4.2) as the process of producing and delivering messages to an audience of one person, a couple of colleagues, or a massive group of sports radio listeners around the world. This is a component system that is made up of many components. Sport communication is intentional or unintentional, complex, circular, irreversible, transactional, unrepeatable, and dynamic. Although effective communication in

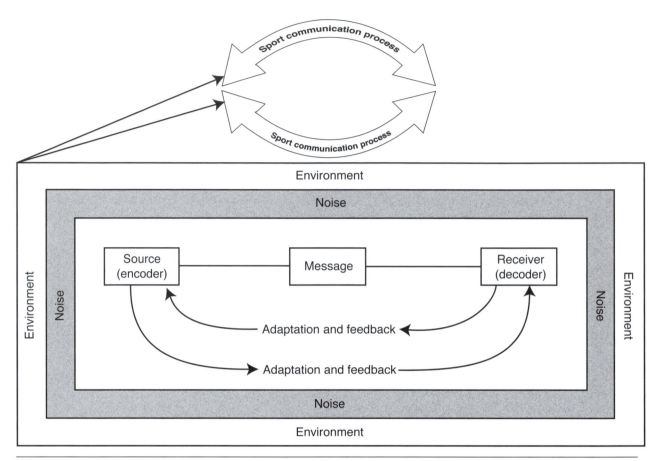

Figure 4.2 The sport communication process.

IDENTIFYING THE ELEMENTS OF SPORT COMMUNICATION

As we stated previously, sport communication is a process by which people in sport, in a sport setting, or through a sport endeavor share symbols as they create meaning through interaction. In addition to providing the various fields (e.g., communicator, message, medium, audience, effect, noise, feedback, context) of communication, every action, aspect, and activity of sport communication can be traced to at least one of the unique components of this process definition. Therefore, this definition of the process of sport communication provides—through the cumulative grouping of the components—the framework for the Strategic Sport Communication Model.

Sport Communication Is a Process

Sport communication is a dynamic process, one that is active and interactive. Receivers of sport communication messages can accept or reject the message, intensity, direction, duration, or type of effects. Sports journalists constantly communicate with their sources, editors, managers, and readers through conversations, gestures, e-mails, letters, and articles. Fans communicate with organizations through e-mails, letters, and ticket sales and with other fans through chat rooms, fantasy leagues, and daily discussions of their teams' progress. A front-office employee for a team communicates with the media, other managers, colleagues, and fans through daily job routines and responsibilities.

sport is often difficult to accomplish because of interference and poor listening skills, at its foundation sport communication is quite simple.

The communication process in and through sport includes interdependent communication. It also allows for feedback, which includes such actions as eye contact, verbal responses, phone calls, e-mail messages, talk shows, or turning off the television set. Furthermore, the communication has an effect. For example, communication within a sport organization may have the effect of motivating, instructing, facilitating, encouraging, and various other results. Communication involving the sport mass media may have effects such as increased ratings, fan support, and purchases of advertised goods and services. There are many variables in the process, such as the communicator's personality, status, expertise, trustworthiness, prestige, physical attributes, relationship to group or individual, and psychological attributes. Furthermore, there are variables before (e.g., knowledge levels, opinions, needs, expectancies, motivation, participation), during (e.g., situation, filters, physical constitution, psychological constitution, evaluation of content, evaluation of communicator, agreement, disagreement), and after (e.g., selectivity and capability of memory) the communication process.

Added to the process of sport communication is the concept of gatekeepers, a concept identified by White (1950). This work defined gatekeepers as editors who—through subjectivity and value-based judgments—selected the news stories for newspapers. The gatekeepers included and excluded certain stories based on what they considered to be important. Their decisions affected the content and the mass communication process. In the sport media, these gatekeepers (e.g., sports editors, sports producers, sport media managers) function as message filters. Certain sports are covered on television whereas others are ignored. Some sporting events receive front-page articles whereas others receive only agate type (i.e., the small font generally used for scores and schedules). Someone—the gatekeeper—is deciding what should be broadcast or printed and what is not going to receive as much (or any) coverage. These are just some of the subjective decisions that are part of the sport communication process. There are—according to Greenberg and Salwen's (1996) model for communication—processes of selection (e.g., determining message, content), creation (e.g., developing message, content), dissemination (e.g., diffusing information), and reception (e.g., decoding and uses of content) in all communication processes.

Senders and Recipients Are Involved

In sport communication, there are senders (communicators) and recipients (receivers or audience). These senders and recipients can range from individuals and small groups to public discussants and the masses. The senders in sport organizations can be any stakeholder (e.g., owner, employee, supervisor, colleague, fan) engaged in communication in or with the sport entity. An example of this would be a team's general manager who sends a message (communicates) to consumers when she greets season ticket holders during a fan appreciation day. The recipients in sport organizations are the same stakeholders noted previously, only this time they are taking on the role of receiver or audience. For example, the general manager is a recipient when she listens to her assistant general manager. The senders in sport media outlets are the personnel engaged as communicators. These individuals can be book authors, sports magazine editors, sideline reporters, or production engineers. The sport media recipients are listeners, viewers, fans, corporate sponsors, and any other audience member or media stakeholder engaged as a receiver of communication.

Communication Takes Place in a Sport Context

As noted in figure 4.3, sport communication is communication in sport (e.g., teammates supporting each other with words of encouragement), in a sport setting (e.g., athletic apparel executives exchanging ideas during a brainstorming session), or through sport (e.g., salespeople using a sport event to entertain prospective clients).

The medium through which communication takes place in or through sport is known as a

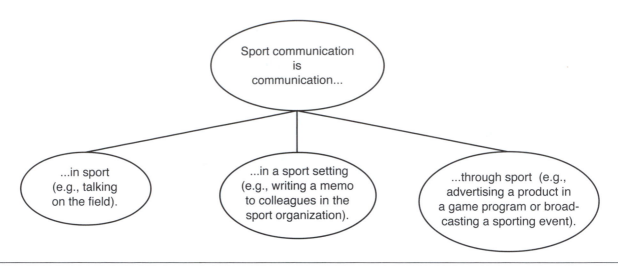

Figure 4.3 Places where sport communication occurs.

communication channel. A sport communication channel can range from e-mail or phone text to a nonverbal or auditory channel. Sport mass media outlets—the management and production of which involve similar communication channels as those listed previously—use channels such as radio and satellite signals and visual and verbal means in the delivery of their mediated communication.

Therefore, some of the means of communication in and through sport organizations and sport media entities involve computers, Web sites, cell phones, interpersonal interactions, oral projection, written material (e.g., memos, articles, press releases, documents, books, briefs, media guides), faxes, intranet, newsgroups, forums, internal repositories, and a host of other channels.

Shared Symbols Are Transmitted

Sharing symbols is the transmission of messages in and through sport. These messages can be words, sports reports, game stories, signs, programs, texts, images, sounds, advertisements, or any other shared symbols that are communicated. The sharing of symbols in the sport industry is the manner in which communicators use language to create symbolism in and through sport. The language that is used may create or reinforce certain beliefs and values that are held by sport participants and entities as well as external stakeholders and publics. The symbolism that is created

conveys meaning that is influenced by context and content.

Sport organizations attempt to create organizational identity and reinforce organizational culture through the use of symbols. A symbol in a sport organization can be a formalized and repeated event (e.g., the seventh inning stretch, singing of the national anthem) that is sustained by the sport entity, specialized or unique language (e.g., company slogans such as Under Armour's "Protect This House"), and tangible manifestations (e.g., trademarks, copyrighted images, branding and marketing elements) that are specific to the organization (Vaughn, 1995). A symbol in a sport organization can be as simple as a story that is passed along throughout the years of the organization. These stories (e.g., narratives, histories, myths) can help sport organizations create, sustain, and reinforce their desired images. For example, the New York Yankees have used stories to enhance perception and brand image. Stories of Babe Ruth and the Bronx Bombers, Pinstripes, and Yankee Stadium are just a few of the ways in which this team uses symbols to convey meaning, history, and culture.

Meaning Is Created Through Interaction

For the sport communication to produce a created meaning, there must be action and interaction between the communicators and recipients. Language—"the system of verbal or gestural symbols a community uses to communicate with one another" (Griffin, 2004, p. 276)—is central in this relationship. Language, despite its ambiguities and varieties across cultures, is the way in which individuals in a society create meaning. In the process of sport c2ommunication, meaning is created through the interactions of the participants (i.e., communicators, subordinates, recipients, colleagues, fans, viewers, listeners).

FOCUSING ON THEORIES OF MASS MEDIA EFFECTS

Let's now look at some of the theories that examine how the sport mass media send (encode) and the audiences interpret (decode) communication. Communication scholars have long studied the mass media audience—which receives messages (e.g., broadcasts of sports events) and provides feedback (e.g., continuing to watch, switching channels, turning off the television). Mass communication research and studies of mass media audiences have primarily focused on mass media effects.

- *Unlimited effects.* The model of unlimited effects—also known as the hypodermic needle model and the magic bullet theory—theorized that mass media audiences had no power to resist the messages delivered by the mass media. Audiences were considered unable to resist the powerful and persuasive messages selected and communicated by the mass media. The model of unlimited effects led to increased research into media effects, a few of which we'll examine later.

- *Uses and gratifications.* Following the research into unlimited effects, empirical research by Klapper (1948) found that the mass media had limited effects. The hypodermic needle model had theorized that the mass media were all-powerful, but the uses and gratifications theory noted that audience members reacted to the mass media and sought to use the mass media for specific uses based on their individual unique characteristics, social categories, and relationships. This theory focused on the audience members' psychologi-

cal attributes as reasons they selected certain content and avoided other content.

- *Agenda setting.* The power of the press also attracted the attention of communication researchers. The seminal work by McCombs and Shaw (1972) resulted in the agenda-setting theory. This pioneering work theorized that although the mass media may not have the power to tell the audience what to think (as noted by the hypodermic needle model), the mass media do have the power to tell the audience what to think about. Burton (2002) examined this when writing about the relationship between participation rates and media exposure in the United Kingdom. "Media sports programmes may not be the only factors causing people to join sports clubs in greater numbers, but sometimes they seem to have been the major factor (as in the case of snooker and the rise of local halls and clubs in the late 1970s)," explained Burton. "American football is a more recent example, where the development of active club interest has coincided with the featuring of the game first on Channel 4, and then on satellite channels" (p. 245). Because gatekeepers such as editors and producers select what they are going to cover and place their stories in order of priority, they influence their audiences' perceptions of reality. This is particularly the case in the sport industry, when certain sports are selected and covered whereas others are trivialized or ignored. For example, when stories about female athletes are nonexistent, are provided in inequitable amounts, or contain sexualized and trivialized portrayals, such coverage can potentially shape the perceptions of the readers relating to female athletes and women in sport (Pedersen, 2002a).

- *Innovation.* Another limited effects theory that has received attention is the adoption of innovation theory. This theory has been described as the process through which consumers or audience members are receptive to and adopt an innovation. This innovation may be a new ideology in the sports world (e.g., strict enforcement of drug testing by Major League Baseball), a new design trend (e.g., the new official uniforms unveiled by the NFL for the 2006 season), or a new technology

The agenda-setting function of the mass media is a theory proposing that although the media may not have the power to tell the audience what to think, they do have the power to tell the audience what to think about. Although the sport media may not be able to tell the viewers and readers what to think, their coverage decisions (i.e., what is covered, how it is covered) can set the agenda for what is discussed the next day at the water cooler.

used by sport (e.g., high-definition television). Although sources of information can be personal contacts such as friends, associates, and family, the mass media are often the sources of information about new inventions. Yoh, Pedersen, and Park (2006) noted that the two major information sources on which consumers rely are "personal references, (i.e., family, peers [colleagues], salespeople) and nonpersonal references (i.e., television, newspapers, product catalogs, the Internet)" (p. 127). Innovation theory can be applied to the sport industry by examining the speed at which sports fans purchase subscription packages such as the Tennis Channel.

• *Diffusion of information.* In our discussion of innovation theory, we noted the personal contacts (e.g., friends, colleagues, family) who often act as sources of information. This process relates to the two-step flow theory and the concept of diffusion of information, which take into account that audiences often acquire mass media messages from personal contacts. Because of the overload of information and media messages, information is often spread (diffused) through opinion leaders or other personal contacts. When sports enthusiasts are unable to watch several sporting events occurring on the same evening, they will often rely on their friends and family to provide information on what they might have missed.

• *Modeling and cultivation.* Modeling theory and cultivation theory are two media effects theories that often come up when the discussion centers on children or young adults. According to modeling theory, the audience members model their behavior on actions viewed on television, listened to on the radio, read in the newspaper and magazine, or any other way they receive messages from the mass media. After seeing the play and advertisements of Shaquille O'Neal on television many times a year, children might be inclined to ask their parents to purchase Shaq Attaq shoes, a Burger King or Nestle product, a Verizon phone, or some other product that the 7-foot-1, 325-pounder endorses. As O'Neal states, he has a "certain niche (that appeals to) children" (Pedersen, 2005c, p. Z64). According to George Gerbner's research in cultivation theory, television audience members view the world as more violent than nonviewers because of the amount of violence on television they watch. Thus, those who watch the broadcasts of brawls in hockey, the "Ultimate Fighting Championship," and other violent sporting activities view the world as more violent than those who do not watch them.

ANALYZING THE STRATEGIC SPORT COMMUNICATION MODEL

All of the preceding pages in this chapter lead to the formulation of a unified and dynamic model of sport communication. In an effort to identify the "big picture" while detailing the interrelationships between the various components, the conceptual analysis presents both micro and macro perspectives of the discipline. This model—the Strategic Sport Communication Model (SSCM)—illustrates the uniqueness of sport communication. The model is built on the elements of theory (i.e., communication genres), context (i.e., levels and segmentation), and the communication process that were outlined in the previous pages. The SSCM (see figure 4.4) explains systematically and rationally the relationships among the key variables in sport communication. The framework for this model works to bridge theory and practice through combining the process of sport communication and the main elements (categories) of the field. Therefore, it is both a process-based and structurally based approach.

The SSCM encompasses—and is highly influenced by—the many areas and perspectives associated with communication and marketing. The major influence from marketing is

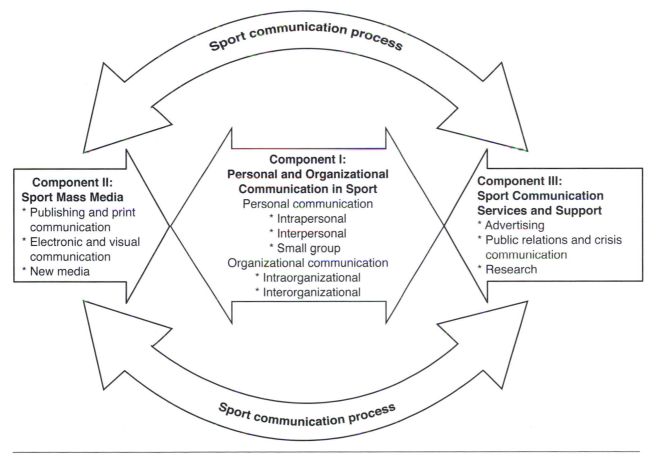

Figure 4.4 The Strategic Sport Communication Model (SSCM).

segmentation. Through segmenting sport communication, the model includes all of the major levels, contexts, and content areas of the field (e.g., advertising, broadcasting, communication studies, communication technology, journalism, public relations). The context or levels of sport communication consist of component I (personal and organizational communication in sport), component II (the various sport media), and component III (sport communication services and support systems). The use of models is nothing new in sport management circles. Within the field of sport management, sport marketing involves numerous theories and models for both research and practice. Some of the more popular models come from the major sport marketing textbooks authored by Mullin, Hardy, and Sutton (2007), and Pitts and Stotlar (2002). The major influence on the model from the field of communication is through its providing the process on which sport communication is based. As communication scholars Kevin Lee and John Baldwin (2004) noted, "Models utilize written symbols in an orderly structure to demonstrate a communication process" (p. 61). The SSCM, which uses modeling to illustrate both the sport communication process and the sport communication components, is also influenced by the areas of applied communication (e.g., communication needs of sport organizations and social interaction in sport, ways to improve communication between sport supervisors and employees); public address, speech education, and communication education (e.g., speech communication, pedagogical contexts); communication theory (e.g., analyses of communication in social interactions); gender communication (e.g., differences and similarities in styles and characteristics); international communication; intercultural communication; legal communication; performance communication; political communication; and a host of other communication perspectives.

Suffice it to say that the SSCM requires both communication and marketing perspectives. Understanding communication theory and the process of communication is necessary to look at the entire field of sport communica-

tion. Within each area, the communication process is evident. Sport communication is a process, but that process has to be played out within some context: The sport communication process does not occur in a vacuum. This is where context, segmentation, and structural analysis comes in. This context or level is where the process takes place in settings as varied as personal (e.g., face-to-face, small group) and organizational (e.g., between two sport organizations) settings, mediated sport communication (e.g., a sports report on the Web), or sport communication support services (e.g., sport research). Beyond the sport communication process illustrated in the model, the other components of the model provide a comprehensive segmentation of the entire field of sport communication. Every activity and career in sport communication as well as every attribute and aspect of sport communication fits into either the process or a component of this model. Therefore, this model combines the process view with the structural analysis of sport entities.

Component I: Personal and Organizational Communication in Sport

In our discussion of the model, we first explain component I, which involves two segments: personal communication in sport (i.e., intrapersonal, interpersonal, small group communication) and organizational communication in sport (i.e., intraorganizational, interorganizational).

Personal Sport Communication

The most common communicative act among sport professionals or sport media professionals is **intrapersonal communication.** This is the communicating that one does within himself or herself (i.e., internal communication). Although this is where the highest percentage of communication in sport takes place, it is also the area that is nearly impossible to examine because it is done individually and is generally kept private. The only exception is mediated intrapersonal communication, which is internal communication that is revealed through some media such as the sharing of one's personal diary or the posting of one's thoughts in a blog on the Internet. Beyond intrapersonal communication, the most common form of daily communicative action in sport organizations occurs between sport professionals. Therefore, most of the communication among sport professionals occurs in either interpersonal or small-group settings. **Interpersonal communication in sport** is the two-way flow of information between individuals (typically two or three persons), whereas **small-group communication in sport** is the flow of information within a small group (typically three or more persons) who are in a sport environment or are involved with a sport-related subject.

The interpersonal communication process is both contextual and developmental with specific application to sport communication and the sport industry. In interpersonal sport communication, few sport communication participants are involved, and those who are involved are in close proximity, use many sensory channels, and provide immediate feedback. Therefore, interpersonal communication can involve all communication between stakeholders in a sport organization or sport media outlet. In addition, interpersonal communication involves communication between all sport professionals, both inside (intra) and outside (inter) the organization.

The communication can be face-to-face, verbal, nonverbal, written, through e-mail, or through any other mediated or nonmediated avenue of communication. Interpersonal communication includes the communication culture of the sport organization and its personnel, their interactions, and their daily routines.

In addition to providing more detail on what interpersonal sport communication is, the next chapter examines the functions, patterns, and conflicts in interpersonal sport communication. Furthermore, the chapter includes a discussion of how face-to-face communication in sport is similar or dissimilar to other forms of sport communication (e.g., sport mass media). Interpersonal sport communication is not anonymous (at least most of the time it is not). It is most often thought of as communication that is one on one. This basic or interpersonal communication in sport involves communication behaviors in dyads (pairs) and their impact on personal relationships and activities in sport. Closely affiliated with interpersonal sport communication, small-group communication in sport involves the communication systems among individuals (typically three or more) who interact around a common purpose and who influence one another. Furthermore, even though there are many audience members and communication is often one way, the components of interpersonal communication are often found in public speaking.

Organizational Sport Communication

Communication in sport can take place outside organizational environments. For instance, a freelance sports reporter may interview a retired professional golfer. The two have no direct organizational affiliation yet they are involved in interpersonal communication. For the most part, however, communication in sport occurs either within a sport organization or sport media outlet or between sport organizations or sport media outlets. The latter—the communication between sport organizations or sport media outlets—involves the idea of **interorganizational sport communication**. This is the communication that takes place between a sport organization and its external publics (e.g., boosters, media, consumers, league).

The former—the communication within a sport organization or sport media outlet—is known as **intraorganizational sport communication**. The prefix *intra* simply means within. Therefore, this type of communication is the communication between a sport organization's internal publics. This includes the communication among employees and colleagues of an organization as well as the communication and organizational culture, staff rituals, tradition, and other organizational issues that affect communication. Our analysis of intraorganizational sport communication—which takes place in chapter 6—looks at the structure, management, production, activities, and role of communication inside the sport organization. This is followed by an application of leadership concepts to the field of sport communication. Such an examination requires a look at sport communication leadership topics ranging from followership in sport communication and sport communication leadership traits to transformational leadership, power, and influence in sport communication. Furthermore, the analysis must include a discussion of sport communication topics related to leadership in sport communication groups, sport communication organizational leadership, leadership and diversity in sport communication, and leadership development in sport communication.

Component II: Sport Media

The sport media component of the Strategic Sport Communication Model involves the most readily apparent segments of sport communication, because this component includes the discrete elements of sport mass media. Bernstein and Blain (2002) noted that "sport and the media have become associated to such an extent that it is often difficult to discuss sport in modern society without acknowledging its relationship with media" (p. 3). The sport mass media segment of sport communication—which constitutes myriad industries and merchandise, from Ken Burns' baseball documentary to sports infomercials after the running of the Daytona 500—is particularly visible and important because adults spend about 40 percent of their day with mass media. All of the activity surrounding the media (e.g., watching television, listening to the radio, surfing the Web) has helped to make media activity the number one activity of adults (E.D. Smith, 2005). The word *media* is plural for medium, and each medium helps to make up the mass media. The sport mass media include three major segments: sport publishing and print sport communication, electronic and visual sport communication, and new and emerging sport media.

The **sport publishing and print sport communication** segment of the sport mass media includes the components such as sports magazines, sports books, and the sports sections of newspapers. Included in this are sport journalists (e.g., sportswriters, sports columnists, sports editors, sports designers) and sport publications (e.g., sports magazines, sports books). Other sport communication topics related to this segment are the technological and historical developments in sport communication, how print sport communication works, business and ownership aspects of print sport communication, and trends in sport communication.

The **electronic and visual sport communication** segment of the sport mass media includes sports broadcasting on the radio, sports film (movies) and photography, and sports broadcasting on television (e.g., broadcast, cable, satellite). This is critical because adult television viewers watch TV for an average of nearly 241 minutes a day and adult radio listeners tune into a radio broadcast at work, home, or in their cars for an average of over 2 hours each day. It is not a far stretch to think that sport consumes a majority of these minutes, especially with the growth of all-sports cable channels and sports satellite radio stations. Rick Cummings, the president and head of programming for Emmis Radio, a subsidiary of the Indianapolis-based media conglomerate Emmis Communications Corporation, told a reporter that because of all the choices people have regarding media options, there is fierce competition for radio listeners (E.D. Smith, 2005). The other topics associated with electronic and visual sport communication include power, technological and historical developments, challenges, means of production, entertainment and news value, role, influence, regulation, programming, delivery, funding, niches, broadcast rights fees, and effects. There are international aspects related to this segment of the sport mass media. For instance, for the 2006 NFL season, China's national television network (CCTV) simulcast NBC's Sunday night games. The CCTV used its own announcers for the games, which were aired on Monday mornings in China.

Trends are also important to examine. For instance, there has been a boom in sports talk radio where bombastic and controversial personalities debate provocative topics with listeners and cover content outside the traditional journalistic arena. Technology is another area that has a major impact on this segment of the sport mass media. Take a look at digital communication, which has affected computers, cable television, and satellites. Digital communication is the process by which images, texts, and sounds are converted (or encoded) into electronic signals. These electronic signals are then put back together (reassembled, decoded) as a reproduction of a sports magazine article, sports television picture, or any other mediated sport communication.

The last segment of the sport mass media, the **new sport media,** includes the most cutting-edge components and activities. Although the Internet is now a healthy teenager, it continues to grow and become more influential. The digital world has a profound impact on the Internet, because the pages, images, texts, and sounds on the medium are all digitally reproduced and transmitted. Web sites are critical in sport communication. For instance, the *SportsBusiness Journal* provides annual rankings of the major team Web sites. The electronic and emerging sport media segment also includes sport media innovations (e.g., e-commerce, niche sport media) and emerging technologies (e.g., use of sports Web logs) in sport media. When examining emerging sport media we need to look at the history of technology in sport communication, followed by the effects, process, ownership, and demassification (a movement from mass media to splintered, diversified, and decentralized media) of new sport media (e.g., Internet newsgroups, chat rooms). Included in the new media is consumer-generated media (CGM). The sport industry and its uses of the Internet also are critical, as are analyses of the development, ownership (e.g., Web site management), and effects of the Internet related to sport.

Component III: Sport Communication Services and Support

The last area of the Strategic Sport Communication Model is the critical component referred to as sport communication services and support. The segments of this component are sport advertising, public relations and crisis communication in sport, and sport communication research. **Sport advertising** includes both the advertising of sport and advertising through sport. The struggle for companies and products to stand out is increasing. One advertising executive noted that because of all the media choices offered to consumers, "Now, you have (to) run more ads. You have to get more creative to get people to stop and look" (E.D. Smith, 2005, p. C2). Any analysis of sport advertising requires an examination of the history of sport advertising, the structure of contemporary sport advertising industry, sport advertising as persuasive communication, the role of research in sport advertising, and criticism and control of advertising in sport. The second segment of this component—**public relations and crisis communication in sport**—is related to message development and image building through effective management of the sport media. The analysis of this segment includes strategies for effectively managing the media through media relations techniques (e.g., media releases, credentialing, game notes, media conferences, media kits, fact sheets, tools of the trade) and community relations efforts. Public speaking and speechwriting in sport are also included in this component. The last segment is **sport communication research**. This segment involves both academic and practical research in sport advertising, sport public relations, the new sport media, sports broadcasting, and print sport communication.

CHAPTER WRAP-UP

Summary

As we noted at the beginning of this chapter, sport communication is broader and more complex than each of the singular aspects of the field. For example, the public relations aspects in professional sports and the sports information activities in intercollegiate athletics are sometimes considered as the field of sport communication. Those sport industry professionals who believe this view sport communication as synonymous with media relations. Although media relations is a significant segment of the field, sport communication involves the sport communication process at work in any of the components and the ways that sport industry professionals and organizations communicate with both internal and external stakeholders.

To help us understand the field of sport communication, we first defined what we mean by this term. Sport communication is a process by which people in sport, in a sport setting, or through a sport endeavor, share symbols as they create meaning through interaction. We then examined the theoretical framework of sport communication, discussing genres, contexts, process, and the elements of sport communication. An understanding of these aspects of the field allows for a complete understanding of the Strategic Sport Communication Model. This model was developed to provide the first conceptual framework for understanding communication in the sport industry. It is an organizational tool for understanding the field that provides a breakdown of the process and major components of the field. The major influence from communication is the process, whereas marketing's major influence is providing the segmentation. The SSCM is a groundbreaking conceptual model because it is used to explain the sport communication process, all of the elements of the process, and all of the components of the field. All sport communication processes, careers, and activities can be situated within the SSCM. This model provides the outline for the rest of this book and for learning about sport communication.

Review Questions

1. How is sport communication defined?
2. What are the genres on which sport communication is based? What are the major contexts of sport communication?
3. In what ways were the early models of communication lacking in their explanation of the communication process?
4. How do the broader models of the communication process help us understand sport communication?
5. In what way is sport communication a process?
6. What types of people are involved in the sport communication process?
7. In relation to the field of sport communication, how do people create meaning through interaction?
8. What is the difference between the linear–transmission model and the ritual model of communication? What is theory and why it is important in the study and understanding of sport communication?

9. What are the major components of the Strategic Sport Communication Model?
10. What are the segments of mediated sport communication?

Discussion Questions

1. Why is it difficult to arrive at a definition for sport communication?
2. Could anything be added to the provided definition of sport communication to make it more complete?
3. How is a one-way flow of sport communication different than a two-way flow?
4. In what way are the communicators (people) in sport organizations the same as the communicators in sport media outlets? Who are the other people involved in sport media outlets?
5. Why is it important to establish a theoretical framework for studying the field of sport communication?
6. What is the difference between communication in sport, in a sport setting, or through sport?
7. Is the Strategic Sport Communication Model influenced more by communication theories or marketing theories?
8. Is one segment of personal or organizational communication in sport more important than the others? If so, why?
9. Which of the components of sport communication are used most often?
10. In your prospective career, which of the components of sport communication do you believe you will use least often?

Group Activities

1. Divide into groups of three. Each group should create at least three original definitions of sport communication. After all of the definitions are read to the rest of the class, discuss how each definition was helpful. Also, point out what was missing in each definition.
2. Divide the class into eight groups. Each group is responsible for a segment of the Strategic Sport Communication Model (e.g., personal communication; organizational communication; publishing and print communication; electronic and visual communication; new media; advertising; public relations and crisis communication; and research). After the class decides on a league or organization (i.e., WNBA, NHL, USOC), each group should come up with at least five specific examples of communication within its component associated with that league/organization.

Individual Exercises

1. List five career opportunities with each component of sport communication.
2. Select a sport media professional and interview him or her. Focus on determining which aspect of communication is used most often and least often in his or her typical work day.

Internet Sites for Additional Learning

Communication Model: www.aber.ac.uk/media/Documents/short/trans.html

Communication Process: http://novaonline.nv.cc.va.us/eli/spd110td/interper/process/process.html

Communication Theory: http://en.wikipedia.org/wiki/Communication_theory

Greg Norman Interactive: www.shark.com/

Ultimate Fighting Championship: www.ufc.tv/

XXIX Olympics: http://en.beijing2008.com/

CHAPTER 5

Personal Sport Communication

LEARNING OBJECTIVES

▶ To learn about the various forms of personal communication in sport

▶ To become aware of the purposes and process of interpersonal sport communication

▶ To understand the functions and forms of nonverbal communication in sport

▶ To recognize the importance of verbal communication in sport by examining its functions and levels

▶ To become acquainted with the key characteristics of effective interpersonal sport communication

PROFILE OF A SPORT COMMUNICATOR

Kathryn E. Rogers

One of the key reasons Kathryn E. Rogers has excelled in her sport management career is her ability to communicate at the interpersonal level. Rogers has most recently relied on her strong interpersonal communication skills to lead initiatives with the Gary Player Foundation and South Florida Super Bowl XLI Host Committee. At the Gary Player Foundation, she was the focal point for the Gary Player Invitational. This event is a benchmark name to which most sports celebrity fund-raisers aspire. Team captains in this annual high-profile golf tournament have included celebrities such as Leslie Nielsen, Julius "Dr. J" Erving, Don Shula, Michael Bolton, Ivan Lendl, Jerry Bailey, Rush Limbaugh, Beverly Johnson, Bryant Gumbel, and George Brett.

At the head of this organization is Gary Player, a legendary golfer who has won 163 championships—including nine major championships on both the regular and senior tours. Until recently, Rogers was the sport management professional who oversaw Player's charitable organization. She notes that her position placed her "in charge of all public relations efforts, fund-raising initiatives, as well as grants and donations that are given by our foundation to other charities that are in need of funding."

As the executive director of the Gary Player Foundation, Rogers communicated with a wide variety of stakeholders ranging from office colleagues and event volunteers to corporate executives and international celebrities. "I interacted daily with high-profile celebrities, businessmen, sponsors, business executives, donors, and companies involved with the events," says Rogers. "I phoned people like Evander Holyfield to personally invite him to attend the events on behalf of Gary Player and Wayne Huizenga [the owner of the Miami Dolphins who is a close friend of Player].

Photo courtesy of Kathryn E. Rogers

I met with key sponsors such as Coca-Cola to present the event and asked that they become an event or global sponsor. I brought interns and volunteers together to work on special projects, such as helping at the local school that the Gary Player Foundation adopted, or assisting with Gary Player events around the world."

Rogers, who states that she has always enjoyed the sports field, has worked in the sport industry for the past decade. Her background includes working for Tampa's Super Bowl XXXV (Baltimore Ravens vs. New York Giants) Task Force—under the direction of executive director Michael Kelly—and consulting with the PGA of America at the PGA Championship and the Senior PGA Championship. Before Rogers moved into the sport industry, she applied many of her interpersonal communication skills while working in public relations, in marketing, and overseas for the American Embassy and the United Nations. Her college education is from London, where she studied international marketing and public relations. As the daughter of U.S. diplomats, Rogers played sports around the world. She continued her global involvement in sports through her work with the Gary Player Invitational and her involvement as director of VIP relations and hospitality services with the Super Bowl Committee. "Regardless of where you go in the world," says Rogers, "sporting events cross over all borders, often uniting people on a common level regardless of stature, culture, or country. Even if people can't speak the same language, they can communicate through a sport, which is quite fascinating."

With her latest work, during the year—and especially the last 3 months—leading up the Super Bowl, Rogers engaged in countless interactions with groups and individuals. "If I have something important to propose or discuss," says Rogers, "I think about the scenario in advance and how best to converse about the topic. It is important to do so, so that my thoughts are clear and concise." In addition to her "inner speech," Rogers is frequently involved in one-on-one mediated and unmediated communication. "A good portion of my day is spent either on the phone, in in-person meetings, or communicating via e-mail. It seems that a good percentage of people communicate via e-mail because it allows you to track what has been said and perhaps address questions at a more convenient time later in the day. I believe in-person communication is very important, particularly if there is something important to discuss. If I have something to speak to my CEO about, I will go to his office and ask if he has a few minutes to meet. If I can explain a situation in person quicker than I can via e-mail, I will always choose this avenue so that I don't waste his time." Beyond the individual encounters, there are also interpersonal interactions in small-group settings. As Rogers notes, she and her colleagues "typically have small group meetings weekly. During very busy times, we will meet daily."

Any effective professional who works in sport has to possess strong interpersonal communication skills to work with clients, athletes, supervisors, and a host of other individuals in the industry. "I believe it is very important to be sincere, genuine, and organized and to follow through on every piece of communication," says Rogers. "The best feeling is to know that people trust you and they know that you will do what you say."

The personal communicative activities engaged in by Kathryn E. Rogers are examples of intrapersonal, interpersonal, and small-group communication in sport. These three forms of sport communication are examined in this chapter. Additional comments by Rogers are seen throughout many of the communication issues covered in the following pages.

The goal of this chapter is to introduce the reader to three closely related forms of intimate communication in sport: intrapersonal, interpersonal, and small-group sport communication. Your success as an intern on the PGA Tour, an employee with a manufacturer of athletic apparel, a colleague in the front office of an MLS franchise, a supervisor with a sports commission, a broadcaster for minor league hockey, or any other position in the sport industry largely depends on the effectiveness of your personal interactions with others. This chapter introduces you to the concepts behind and the skills needed in this aspect of sport communication. First we must define what is meant by intrapersonal sport communication, interpersonal sport communication, and small-group sport communication. After providing these definitions and illustrating their distinctiveness, we use the rest of the chapter to examine their contextual and developmental processes, characteristics, and functions. After reading this chapter, you should be familiar with the activities, components, and workings of personal communication in sport.

In this chapter we apply the key components of interpersonal communication to the personal communicative activities in the sport industry. Although the various concepts are applied to sport settings, the foundation and framework of this chapter come from the academic study of interpersonal communication.

HIGHLIGHTING THREE FORMS OF PERSONAL COMMUNICATION IN SPORT

As illustrated in the Strategic Sport Communication Model (SSCM), there are various forms of sport communication. The forms can be as simple as a shrug or sigh from a disgruntled assistant ticket manager to as complex as an in-depth sports biography such as Laura Hillenbrand's *Seabiscuit* (2001), the historical equestrian treatise that holds the record for sports books with the longest stay on *The New York Times'* bestseller list. Just as the forms of sport communication can be quite varied, the audiences can be very distinct, ranging from a single sports employee reading an e-mail from a colleague to millions of viewers watching an international television broadcast of the Olympics. But whatever the form or audience, sport communicators interact with one another by sharing meaning with each other. Therefore, at its basic level, sport communication is an interpersonal process. "Although it is common to reserve the label interpersonal for intimate communication between two people in face-to-face interaction," noted Trenholm and Jensen (2004), "clearly all communication is, in a sense, interpersonal" (p. 23). Consequently, although this chapter is focused on personal interactions in sport, the concepts and issues examined here touch all forms of communication in sport.

Sport communication takes different forms as a result of the number of communicators and situations. Communication fundamentally can be reduced to three forms. In the context of sport, these three direct communication forms are intrapersonal, interpersonal, and small-group sport communication (see figure 5.1).

Intrapersonal Communication in Sport

The most often used form of communication by all individuals in sport is **intrapersonal communication.** This occurs when the communicators turn their communication inward—the speech going on inside their mind, where they are both the sender and receiver of messages. When the board meeting gets too boring and daydreaming takes over, the individual is involved in intrapersonal communication. When an executive rehearses in her mind the presentation she is about to deliver, she is involved in intrapersonal communication. This form of personal communication occurs when you engage in internal dialogue and brainstorming such as thinking about creative ways to solve a risk management issue with your facility. Because everyone constantly engages in self-talk, all sports professionals are involved in intrapersonal communication. Although this is where the highest percentage of communication in sport takes place, it is mostly

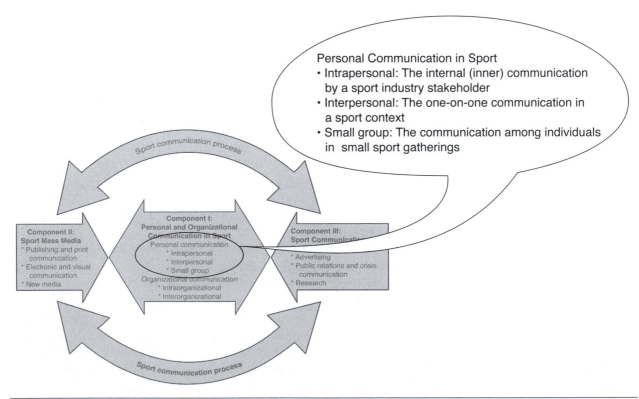

Figure 5.1 The communication forms of intrapersonal, interpersonal, and small-group sport communication make up the first half of the personal and organizational communication in sport component of the Strategic Sport Communication Model (SSCM).

done individually and is private. The only exceptions to this would be mediated intrapersonal communication, which is internal communication that is revealed through some medium such as a diary or a sports blog on the Internet.

Interpersonal Communication in Sport

Beyond intrapersonal communication, the most common form of daily communicative action in sport organizations occurs between sports professionals. Therefore, most of the communication among those involved with sport occurs in either interpersonal or small-group settings. According to Wood (2004), interpersonal communication is a "selective, systemic, unique, and ongoing process of transaction between people who reflect and build personal knowledge of one another and create shared meanings" (p. 22). **Interpersonal communication in sport** is the two-way flow of information between individuals (typically two persons) in a sport setting or regarding a sport issue. Whenever two people communicate in the sport industry they are involved in interpersonal sport communication. This form of communication can be the dialogue individuals have in the hallway or a meeting between executives. The communicators may be interns, athletes, executives, agents, sponsors, colleagues, owners, or any other stakeholders involved in the communicative interaction.

Interpersonal communication is typically a one-on-one or face-to-face (as opposed to an internal) form of communication. Many scholars refer to this as dyadic communication because it involves communication behaviors in dyads (pairs) and their impact on personal relationships and activities in sport. Even when there are more than two individuals in a group (i.e., a triad, small group, even large groups at times), there is often a dyadic primacy in the interactions because many of the interactions are face-to-face between two people.

This form of communication is typically spontaneous, informal, and unstructured and involves close proximity of participants and immediate feedback. Interpersonal sport communication is not anonymous (at least most of the time it is not), although there are exceptions. Because the interactants are senders and receivers, the roles in the interpersonal communication process are flexible.

Small-Group Communication in Sport

Closely affiliated with interpersonal sport communication, **small-group communication in sport** involves the communication systems among individuals in small gatherings

When two people in the sport industry interact with one another, they are engaging in interpersonal communication. Here, sportscaster Bob Costas—a popular public speaker—goes over a script with an event assistant before taking over one of his many master of ceremony assignments.

© Paul M. Pedersen

(typically three or more persons) who interact around a common purpose and who influence one another. This definition separates small groups from just a collection of people (i.e., fans gathering outside the ticket office for postseason tickets). The characteristics of small groups, according to Hartley (1999), involve such aspects as

- interaction (members act and react),
- perception (members view the group as real),
- norms (members have an idea of what others expect),
- roles (members have certain formal and informal positions),
- affective relationships (members are not indifferent), and
- goals (members share purposes and objectives).

Although the characteristics in the preceding list can describe most face-to-face (inter-

personal) communication, there are a few differences between small-group (i.e., intragroup communication, intergroup communication) and interpersonal communication. These differences can stem from issues related to pressure, conformity (i.e., groupthink), and leadership. Regardless, small-group communication is included in the discussion of interpersonal communication because most small groups have dyadic relationships and possess many of the components found in interpersonal communication. The small groups in sports can range from office gatherings (i.e., water-cooler conversation) and conference calls to pack interviews and media days.

Therefore, this form of communication takes place when the flow of information is between a few interactants who are in a sport environment or are involved with a sport-related subject. As Trenholm and Jensen (2004) noted, interpersonal communication becomes small-group communication when a third party enters the interaction. "While the size of

While waiting for the announcement of his name and accomplishments to the spectators, Tiger Woods engages in small-group communication with two members of the event staff at the Ford Championship at Doral.

a small group may vary, it must be small enough that everyone can interact freely," explained these scholars. "In a dyad the participants are connected directly; if the link between them is severed, the relationship no longer exists. In a small group, communication is not destroyed when the link between two of the members is cut" (p. 24). Therefore, even though the link between two small-group members has been broken, members can use other ways to communicate with the members of the small group. Small-group communication in sports occurs in myriad settings such as the war room on draft day, the programming meeting for a broadcast, and the editorial meeting to decide the layout of the sports page.

CHARACTERIZING INTERPERSONAL COMMUNICATION

Although there are distinctions between the basic forms of communication, many of the characteristics, practices, conflicts, and issues involved with all forms of personal communication are very similar. As noted scholar Peter Hartley (1999) commented, interpersonal communication is essentially nonmediated (i.e., generally face-to-face) communication that takes place in a dyadic (i.e., one-on-one) or small-group setting, and its form and content are shaped by the personal qualities of the interactants as well as their social roles and relationships. This thorough definition allows for the inclusion of most forms of personal communication (i.e., two-person or dyadic, three-person or triadic, small-group). Therefore, our use of the phrase "interpersonal sport communication" from here on will be based on Hartley's definition as applied to personal communication in sport. This interpersonal sport communication involves examples such as the following:

- Two colleagues discussing their sport marketing campaign over a meal at the Olive Garden
- An argument between partners of a sport law firm over whether to pursue a certain

high-profile, but controversial, sports client

- A dialogue between a panel discussant at a *SportsBusiness Journal* seminar and three attendees who came forward after the session for a more detailed explanation

Furthermore, because communicators often blend forms and contexts, especially new technologies (e.g., e-mail, chat rooms, instant messages, other computer-mediated interpersonal communication), and because many of the interactions in sport are partially interpersonal, we join Trenholm and Jensen (2004) in preferring to "think of all communication as having an interpersonal element" (p. 25). Using the illustrations and definitions of interpersonal communication provided by Hartley (1999) and Trenholm and Jensen (2004), we propose that interpersonal sport communication occurs whenever individuals in sport, sharing the roles of sender and receiver, create meaning through their personal interactions. This involves all of the face-to-face encounters sports professionals and communicators have with each other, colleagues, advisors, sales managers, media relations professionals, interns, employees, and any other stakeholders. Interactants engage in sport communication for a variety of reasons. Sometimes they engage in interpersonal communication to provide advice (e.g., discussing with an intern the best way to approach his supervisor for a letter of recommendation). On other occasions they participate in this form of communication to learn something new (e.g., learning from a colleague about a new position in the sales department). The purposes for which people engage in interpersonal communication can be reduced to five primary reasons. DeVito (2005) illustrated these five reasons, which all stem from various motivations and often have unique results.

1. Whenever interactants engage in interpersonal communication, they **learn.** Communicators in interpersonal communication learn about the world, people, themselves, etiquette, feelings,

Profile of an Expert at Relating: The Sports Agent

Engaging in interpersonal communication to relate to clients is a critical component of the entire package that is offered by a sports agent. It is involved with every aspect of his or her sport-related activities: negotiating contracts, securing marketing and endorsement deals, providing financial and career advice, engaging in dispute resolution, offering legal counseling, and providing personal care to clients. Such is the case for sports agent Mark Rodgers, whose career progression included sports journalism, teaching, and coaching before moving into the law profession.

Rodgers—whose clients have ranged from former Alabama head coach Mike Shula to professional baseball player Mike Hampton—develops such a close relationship with the individuals he represents that one client felt comfortable enough to ask Rodgers to purchase an engagement ring for his fiancée. Therefore, it might come as no surprise that, according to Rodgers, the most rewarding aspect of his career is the bond that he establishes with each of his clients. "That's easy," notes Rodgers, when referring to friendships as the best part of his career. "Some of my clients have become my best friends. It happens naturally or it doesn't happen at all. I have clients who tell people I'm the big brother they never had. That's flattering" (Pedersen, 2005b, p. Z58).

With upwards of 15,000 sports agents in the United States, the majority of whom are without clients (i.e., it has been estimated that half of all the professional athletes are represented by approximately 20% of the professional sports agents), using strong interpersonal communication skills to develop relationships with clients is not only rewarding—it is pragmatic.

perceptions, and the desires, needs, behaviors, thoughts, feelings, and likes of others.

2. People engage in interpersonal communication to **relate.** They have a need to establish and maintain relationships. Even for the most ruthless negotiator in the sport industry (whomever that might be), there is a desire to love and like and be loved and liked.

3. People engage in interpersonal communication to **persuade,** that is, to influence attitudes and behaviors.

4. People engage in interpersonal communication to **play.** This involves more than simply participating in games but also includes the talks we have with friends about our activities, jokes, stories, and sports.

5. Individuals engage in interpersonal communication to **help** others. This purpose involves offering guidance, consoling, comforting, and advising.

Each of these five reasons for participating in interpersonal communication relates to activity in the sport industry. At various times in each day, sport communication and sport management stakeholders all engage in interpersonal communication to learn, relate, persuade, play, or help.

IDENTIFYING THE ELEMENTS OF THE INTERPERSONAL SPORT COMMUNICATION PROCESS

The interpersonal communication process in sport is similar to the communication process outlined in the previous chapter. To thoroughly understand interpersonal sport communication, one needs to understand the developmental and contextual processes involved. The process of interpersonal communication in sport is not an event or series of events. Rather, it is ongoing (Hartley, 1999) and continuous. Whenever there are two interactants, there is an ongoing process involving interpersonal communication. For instance, let's think about a situation where a recent sport management graduate is invited for an interview with a sports franchise. We might be tempted to view the interpersonal communication process as beginning with an event (i.e., the first question of the interview). However, the process of interpersonal communication was initiated as soon as one interactant communicated the first message to the other. This could be when their eyes met after the administrative assistant ushered the interviewee into the office. Maybe it was when the interviewer noticed the confident posture of the interviewee when he or she entered the interview room. Regardless of when the process began, it was ongoing through verbal and nonverbal messages until the two communicators stopped sending and receiving messages.

Because of the ongoing process of interpersonal communication in sport, the behavior of the interactants influences the outcome. Regardless of the forms of interpersonal sport communication (i.e., verbal, nonverbal), several key elements (or variables) are involved in this ongoing process. The major elements of the interpersonal sport communication process—which are modified from works of Trenholm (1986) and DeVito (2005)—are source–receiver (encoder–decoder), messages, feedback, channel, noise, and context.

Source–Receiver

The first element—**source–receiver**—involves the individuals (generally two) involved in interpersonal sport communication. Interpersonal sport communication has few interactants (or participants), generally either two communicators or a few communicators. Each interactant sends (source) and receives (receiver) messages. The interactants both encode the messages they send (i.e., produce messages such as speaking, writing) as well as decode the messages they receive (i.e., understand them). For interpersonal communication in sport to occur, there must be both a sender and receiver. Without one or the other the process is lost. For instance, when a sports supervisor jumps up and down while yelling to her subordinate who is outside of hearing range, no interpersonal communication is involved because the intended receiver does not receive (and thus cannot decode) the verbal and nonverbal messages.

Messages

The **messages** in interpersonal communication are the expressions of thoughts and feelings of the communicators.

Content and Relational Dimensions of Messages

As Adler and Towne (2003) explained, these messages generally have both content and relational dimensions. The content dimension of the message contains the subject that the communicators are discussing. The content dimension of a message in a ticket sales meeting might be verbal suggestions by the ticket manager regarding ways account representatives can improve their cold-calling techniques.

Along with the content of the message, a relational component is conveyed. The relational dimension of a message "makes statements about how the parties feel toward one another" (Adler & Towne, 2003, p. 24). The relational messages generally deal with social needs such as affection, respect, or control and are usually communicated through nonverbal channels. Most relational messages fit into the categories of

- affinity (e.g., a smile from the ticket manager revealing the degree to which he or she likes one of the salespersons),
- respect (e.g., a motivational talk inspires a salesperson and reveals the degree to which he or she esteems the motivational speaker), and
- control (i.e., the degree one has influence over another person). Control in relational messages includes conversational control (e.g., the person who dominates the conversation) and decision control (e.g., the person who determines what will happen).

Verbal and Nonverbal Messages

The messages of interpersonal communication may be verbal, nonverbal, or a combination of verbal and nonverbal, or they can be relayed through the five senses. "You communicate interpersonally with words as well as with gestures and touch, for example.

Even the clothes you wear communicate, as do the way you walk and the way you shake hands, comb your hair, sit, smile, or frown. Everything about you has the potential to send interpersonal messages" (DeVito, 2005, p. 8). An example of the way in which people communicate interpersonally through the clothes they wear can be found in league- or team-sponsored merchandise and apparel. One estimate has annual merchandise sales of the National Football League at $3.4 billion (Bora, 2006). Through hats, t-shirts, and other apparel, fans are able to communicate and affiliate. Those who purchase and wear this apparel, according to Xavier University's Christian End, "want to communicate to others about their association hoping that the favorable impression of the group rubs off on the group members" (Bora, 2006, p. A5).

Feedback

Feedback is the information we receive from ourselves (by hearing what we say, seeing what we write, feeling the way we move) and others (by hearing affirmation or seeing a frown). The interactants—who have informal communication roles—have the ability to adapt messages to the specific needs of others.

Channels

The medium through which the message is sent is referred to as the **channel.** These channels, according to DeVito (2005), include

- vocal–auditory (carrying speech),
- visual (facilitating nonverbal communication such as through the use of gestures),
- chemical (olfactory, or accommodating smell), and
- tactile (cutaneous, or enabling use of touch).

The interactants use many sensory channels (e.g., speaking, touching, hearing) and have the ability to deliver and receive feedback immediately. In interpersonal communication, the various channels are typically used simultaneously (Hargie & Dickson, 2004). For instance, when the vice president of sales gives a pep talk to her sales team, she speaks to them through the vocal–auditory channel, they see her excitement through the visual channel, they smell the crisp dollar bills laid out as incentive through the chemical channel, and they slap high fives using the tactile (touch) channel. The channels through which interpersonal messages are sent are also referred to as the means (e.g., face-to-face, telephonic, e-mail), which can involve unmediated and mediated interpersonal communication. Pavlik and McIntosh (2004) defined mediated communication as "communication that involves a process by which a message, or communication, is transmitted via some form, or medium" (p. 5). These scholars stated that direct communication (without the use of a medium) is unmediated communication, whereas any communication that involves a medium (e.g., text on paper, words on a Web log) is mediated communication. Mediated interpersonal communication—which is distinct from mass-mediated communication—can involve actions such as talking on the telephone, teleconferencing, instant messaging, and participating in chat rooms. Mediated interpersonal communication often limits some aspect of interpersonal communication (e.g., verbal sounds might not be heard, facial expressions might not be seen—unless a Webcam is used).

Noise

Also involved in the interpersonal communication process are message distortions and interferences. These are referred to as **noise.** The noise in the communication process can come from physical interference such as when sport administrators are unable to hear each other because the crowd noise is too loud at a basketball game or an ambulance siren interrupts a golf tournament. There can also be psychological noise in the interpersonal communication process. This noise might involve the belligerent acceptance of responsibilities by a sports reporter because of some personal bias or prejudice against an editor or producer. Sometimes physiological or biological noise can distort or interfere with the interpersonal communication process; this kind of noise

© Paul M. Pedersen

Noise—which is a factor in all communication—can cause distortion and interfere with communication. Distortions can come from psychological, physiological, semantic, and other noises. In the sport industry, the noise often comes from physical interference, as when the fans become so loud that effective communication is only accomplished through close and direct contact. Penn State football coach Joe Paterno illustrates this as he leans in to communicate with fellow coaching legend Bobby Bowden.

can include illness or exhaustion. Last, the interpersonal communication process can be affected by semantic noise. Examples of this type of noise include when an employee fails to understand the message that his or her boss is sending or when different languages are involved in the process. When the message is very technical or complex terms are used, often semantic noise distorts and interferes with interpersonal communication. All of these types of noise are evident in sport management and communication.

Context

The **context** (contextual element) in the interpersonal communication process involves the place or surroundings where the communication takes place. "Communication styles do change depending on the environment, and

who is involved with each meeting," says sport management professional Kathryn E. Rogers. "If we are in an office setting or in a lunch meeting with solely internal colleagues, the atmosphere is fairly relaxed. If we are on a golf course, even with other guests, we try to communicate in a fun way. If we are selling a sponsorship to top executives of Coca-Cola for example, we tend to formally introduce ourselves and stick to a structured plan." The form and content of interpersonal communication are influenced by the context, which can range from official and formal dinners to unofficial and casual golf outings. The three dimensions of context are

1. physical (e.g., tangible environment),
2. social–psychological (e.g., status relationship among interactants), and

3. temporal (e.g., time dimension, sequence of communication events).

These three dimensions interact with and influence each other.

As we noted, the process in interpersonal sport communication is both contextual and developmental. The process is evident in every interaction between communicators in sport. Anyone in sport who engages in communication with another individual (e.g., dyadic, interpersonal) or a few individuals (e.g., triadic, small group) is a participant in interpersonal communication. Therefore, interpersonal communication can involve all communication between stakeholders in a sport organization or sport media outlet. Interpersonal communication involves communication between all sport professionals, both inside (intra) and outside (inter) the organization. The communication can be face-to-face, verbal, nonverbal, written, spoken, through e-mail, or through any other mediated or nonmediated avenue of communication. Interpersonal communication includes the communication culture of the sport organization and its personnel, their interactions, and their daily work.

COMMUNICATING WITH NONVERBAL MESSAGES

Interactants communicate through verbal and nonverbal forms of communication. Although these two forms are generally used in combination with one another, for the purposes of inquiry we'll separate the two. We'll first examine nonverbal communication, a component of emotional intelligence (EI) that is often overlooked in the workplace. For those individuals in the sport industry who are effective and efficient, acceptable uses of nonverbal communication are generally an expected, if not required, component of their image—their brand. The ability to be expressive is one vital use of nonverbal communication in sport. Obviously, sport media personalities who are working the sidelines are expected to be expressive and excited in their gestures and delivery. But in the office of a sport organization, expressiveness is just as important. For

example, being able to show an excited facial expression after hearing about the closing of a new luxury suite deal can motivate your sales team. Sport management and sport communication professionals are often required to use nonverbal communication to show that they are empathetic, sympathetic, understanding, and sensitive. A ticket manager expresses sensitivity by showing respect for a colleague's personal space in a crowded ticket office. The president of a sports team must be able to end a conversation with a disgruntled fan in a timely and positive manner, which often requires the use of effective nonverbal communication tactics.

Sport communicators often convey their feelings and attitudes through nonverbal communication. Pat Summit, the legendary women's basketball coach at the University of Tennessee, noted, "There is a lot more to communicating than just plain talking. Take it from someone who spends half her life hoarse. Talking is the least of it. If you really want to get something across, body language, facial expression, eye contact, and listening are all necessary parts of communicating. Sometimes so is yelling" (Summit & Jenkins, 1998, p. 65). As Summit explained, communication involves much more than talking. In fact, UCLA psychology professor Albert Mehrabian discovered nearly 4 decades ago that only 7 percent of meaning in an interaction comes from the words themselves, and 38 percent of the meaning comes from vocal inflection. However, 55 percent of an interaction's meaning comes from nonverbal actions such as facial expressions and body language (Wellner, 2005).

Practicing impression management and projecting personal and social identities are often done through nonverbal communication. As Hargie and Dickson (2004) noted, "The potency of the nonverbal aspects of interaction must be recognized by professionals who should be sensitive to the kind of atmosphere they are creating, the scene they are setting, and the parameters they are placing on an interaction, often before they even begin to speak. Knowledge of the various facets of nonverbal communication, and of their effects in social interaction, can enable us to improve our ability to deal successfully with others" (p. 80). Sport industry practitioners would greatly enhance their interactions with all stakeholders by recognizing, learning, and mastering the functions and elements of nonverbal communication.

We define verbal communication in sport as the actual words and language used in sport communication and nonverbal communication in sport as all other aspects of sport communication. This view of nonverbal communication in sport encompasses the way individuals in the sport industry communicate by using their

- body movements (e.g., posture, facial expressions, physical appearance, gestures, movements),
- nonverbal aspects of speech (e.g., tone of voice, talk speed, volume of speech, intonation), and
- environmental factors (e.g., noise, decorations, architecture, texture, furniture, color).

"People talk to you in different ways—through facial expressions, moods, mannerisms, body language, the tone of their voice, the look in their eyes," noted Mike Krzyzewski, head coach of the men's basketball team at Duke University. "This aspect of leadership is fascinating to me. To figure out what the members of my team are thinking, to determine who they are at one particular moment in time, is not only a necessity for a leader, it's a great challenge. Sometimes, I may be wrong in my interpretation, but if I have built strong relationships and spent quite a bit of time observing and listening, I'll usually be pretty close to the truth" (Krzyzewski & Phillips, 2000, p. 107).

Nine Functions of Nonverbal Communication

Sport communicators and industry professionals use nonverbal communication for a variety of reasons. These functions range from the simple (to enhance verbal communica-

tion) to the complex (to express dominance). Hargie and Dickson (2004) illustrated nine primary purposes for the use of nonverbal communication. Their nine functions are noted subsequently and can be applied to all communication in sport.

One of the main functions of nonverbal communication is to **replace** verbal communication. Using nonverbals (e.g., gestures) as a substitute for words occurs when the communicators are unable (the roar of the crowd demands the use of hand signals) or unwilling (a coach needs secrecy in communicating with a colleague about a possible trade or draft pick) to speak. Examples of this are when a racecourse bookmaker uses the ticktack system of signaling or when a baseball manager such as Bobby Cox uses nonverbal cues to call for a pitch from the dugout.

Nonverbal communication is often used to **complement** verbal communication. The verbal message can be enhanced and clarified through the use of nonverbal actions. When the message is hard to get across in words alone, the overlapping of gestures, illustrators, or other nonverbal movements can facilitate speech. For instance, when Rafael Palmeiro was testifying before Congress regarding the use of steroids in baseball, while reading his opening speech to the members of the Senate subcommittee he pointed at them with an enthusiastic gesture while he verbally proclaimed that he never used steroids. In a sport setting, an executive can increase her effectiveness in a motivational speech by not simply reading the prepared speech but also including enthusiastic gestures and facial expressions.

Another key function of nonverbal communication is to **modify** the spoken word. This includes such actions as stressing certain words in a speech, pausing at crucial intervals in a conversation, or smiling while providing a stern warning to a subordinate. Looking again at the Palmeiro testimony before Congress, when he emphasized his never having used steroids, he raised his voice and spoke with a forceful confidence while proclaiming his innocence.

Although nonverbal communication can be used to complement the verbal communication, it can also be used to **contradict** what is said. This can be intentional or unintentional. The contradictory signals between verbal and nonverbal communication often are quite subtle, such as when someone expresses sarcasm or has a dry sense of humor. Sometimes nonverbal cues can be quite revealing when deception (i.e., lying) is involved. These cues can be heightened stress (e.g., sweating), conspicuous attempts to control the performance (e.g., appearing wooden), or displays of emotion (e.g., anxiety, guilt). Machiavellian individuals, even in their acts of deception, often master the ability to present consistent verbal and nonverbal signals.

Nonverbal communication is often used to **regulate** conversation. To prevent talking over one another, individuals involved in interpersonal communication use nonverbal cues to mark speech turns. This gives the interactants information regarding acceptable times to speak. This is done through gestures, tone of voice (e.g., downward vocal inflection), and eye contact.

Another purpose of nonverbal communication is to **express** emotions and interpersonal attitudes. The emotional states can be revealed in facial expressions (e.g., anger, surprise, disgust, happiness), body movements, and gestures, whereas the attitudinal nonverbal behaviors are expressed in smiles, gazes, proximity, touching, and more heightened behaviors that reveal relationships.

Using nonverbal communication to **negotiate** relationships is another function of this form of communication. This involves issues of dominance and control (e.g., louder voice, longer talk, focal position [raised platform, behind desk, head of table, impressive chair], interrupting) as well as affiliation and liking (e.g., immediacy, expected interpersonal distance, gazes, posture, comfort levels).

The final two purposes of nonverbal communication are for conveyance and contextual purposes. Nonverbal communication is often used to **convey** personal and social identity. Individuals send messages about who they are and what group they belong to by their dress, adornments, accent, size of office, office furnishings, and other identifiers. Furthermore, when individuals wish to **contextualize** their interactions, they often do so through the use of nonverbal communication. This can be accomplished through the creation of a particular social setting. People are expected to comply with certain codes of communication conduct depending on the social setting (e.g., informal office water cooler gathering, formal staff meeting, funeral of a colleague, opulent dinner with international contingent).

These nine purposes are the uses to which nonverbal communication is put in interpersonal communication in sport. The exercise of these functions can be independent or simultaneous, depending on the complexity of the communication and situation.

Seven Forms of Nonverbal Communication

There are several codes (forms) of nonverbal communication. What follows are seven nonverbal forms applied to sport from the work of Hargie and Dickson (2004) and Wood (2004).

Haptics

The first type (form) of nonverbal communication is **haptics.** This form involves physical touching or the sense of touch, which can be used to comfort, calm, offer support, or nurture. "It is always a good idea to shake everyone's hand when you first meet them," says Kathryn Rogers, director of hospitality services and VIP relations for the South Florida Super Bowl XLI Host Committee. Some of the beneficial outcomes of a person touching another can be positive evaluations and increased compliance with requests. Touch, however, is a rule-based behavior where there are only certain times, people, and places in which touch can be used. Touching affects the context and the relationships involved as well as the power relations. For instance, in sports, in a social or polite context there are handshakes and embraces. In a friendship or warm context there are pats, soft touches on the hand, expressions of interest, positive feelings, encouragement, expressions of care, shows of concern, demonstrations of understanding, and provision of support. Touch can also be used to reveal negative feelings, manage interaction, and gain control through symbolic, ritualistic, and accidental methods.

Kinesics

Kinesics—communication through body motion—is the second form of nonverbal communication. This type of communication includes gestures and movements of hands and arms (e.g., pointing, scratching, rubbing), head nods (e.g., turning, nodding, dropping), facial expressions, eye gaze (e.g., looking at facial area while communicating, mutual gazing, eye contact, gaze omission, gaze avoidance, staring, and all work to express personal information, regulate conversation, and monitor feedback), and posture (e.g., standing, sitting, relaxing, leaning forward, slumping, showing rigidity, and all work to reveal status, emotions, and interpersonal attitudes). In particular, those communicators who supplement their words with gesture cues "usually arouse and maintain the attention of their listeners, indicate their interest and enthusiasm, and tend to make the interaction sequence a stimulating and enjoyable experience for all participants" (Hargie & Dickson, 2004, p. 61). When gesture cues are used people can more readily identify objects, recall stories, and increase comprehension. With facial expressions, people are able to reveal and recognize emotional states such as sadness, anger, disgust, fear, surprise, happiness, contempt, shame, guilt, pride, embarrassment, and amusement. The face can make more than 1,000 expressions, which is why facial signaling is the most studied and debated nonverbal information source. *Display rules* regulate when it is acceptable to show certain facial expressions. Furthermore, *emotional contagion* is when a certain facial expression is signaled and adopted by another (e.g., infectious smile). The smile is the most common form of facial expression.

Proxemics

The perceptions we have and how we use space in personal and social settings constitute **proxemics.** This is the third type of nonverbal communication in sport. Four cat-egories of proxemics affect the interpersonal communication process.

- First, there is territoriality—the claims of rights to a certain geographical area. Within this are primary territory (exclusivity by occupier), secondary territory (held by habit rather than ownership), public territory (open to anyone), and interaction territory (temporary space where interactants are meeting).

- Second, there are personal space and interpersonal distance. Personal space is the invisible area that surrounds and envelops us. The size of the space is dependent on personality (e.g., introvert), situational variables, and the relationship between the interactants. Personal space violations disturb and affect individuals and how they function in interpersonal relationships. Interpersonal distance is the distance communicators keep during their interactions. Interactants can be as close as a handshake or as far as a noise in the distance. There are numerous reasons for distance (e.g., culture, gender, age, status, topic). It affects the comfort level of the interactants and reflects the relationship and regulation interaction. The four categories of physical closeness are

1. intimate (touch to 18 inches), for close friends and family,
2. casual–personal (18 inches to 4 feet), for informal interactions between friends and acquaintances,
3. visual–consultative (4-12 feet), for professional interactions, and
4. public (12 feet to the limits of sound and vision), for speeches and public addresses.

- Third, orientation is the angling of the body (e.g., direct facing, shoulder to shoulder, side by side) that a person uses in communication. This angling is used to reflect intimacy, inclusion, and exclusion. The position most conducive to communication is when people sit at 90-degree angles to each other.

- Fourth, interpersonal communication is affected by seating arrangements. Interaction is encouraged through sociopetal layouts (e.g., semicircle) and discouraged through sociofugal seating arrangements (e.g., conventional classroom setup). Whether the speaker wants interaction or a central position will affect the seating arrangement and affect the interpersonal communication process.

Physical Characteristics

The fourth form of nonverbal communication is **physical characteristics.** These are used by the communicator to make judgments. They include height, dress, body shape and size, adornments (e.g., jewelry, false nails), and hair color and style. Impressions are formed by how people look. Hargie and Dickson (2004) noted, "Before we even know what people sound like or what they have to say we begin to form impressions based on physical appearance. At the center of most of these will be evaluations of physical attractiveness" (p. 73). Pat Riley, the head coach and president of the NBA's Miami Heat, realizes that he gains certain advantages through his ability to pres-

Physical characteristics, including people's attire, are a form of nonverbal communication. These two fans are communicating their allegiance to the University of Florida, winners of the NCAA D-1 men's basketball title in 2006 and the BCS championship in January 2007.

ent himself positively in an attractive and stylish light. People view individuals who are perceived as being attractive as possessing more charisma, popularity, persuasiveness, and confidence. These perceptions are important in professional relationships because work relationships and evaluations are sometimes influenced by such nonverbal communication. People make assumptions about people, their occupations, and status by looking at physical characteristics such as body size (e.g., weight, shape), baldness, height, and dress. Those professionals in impressive dress (dark suits, corporate attire) command respect, secure compliance, and increase credibility. As Hargie and Dickson (2004) noted, however, although physical characteristics affect likeability, confidence, and perceived competence, they are often viewed as less important than facial expressions, spoken words, and gesture cues.

Environmental Factors

Environmental factors comprise the fifth type of nonverbal communication. Interpersonal interactions can be enhanced, impeded, and shaped by physical settings. Is the locker room open and inviting for the players and media, or is it crowded and restrictive? Is the office layout of the team headquarters dominated by partitions and privacy or is it warm, expansive, and inviting? Perceptions, judgments, and impressions are often heavily influenced by the organization of the fixed (e.g., architecture, size, shape, concrete) and semifixed (e.g., movable or modifiable materials) environmental elements. Office space arrangements communicate status, authority, position, and personality. Separation from others with a desk or administrative assistant (gatekeeper), openness, elevation, barriers, lighting, and styles all influence interpersonal communication. There is typically more than one arrangement in an organization that can be used for an interpersonal interaction. "The more effective professional will select that area of the office more appropriate to the task to be carried out with a particular client or colleague" (Hargie & Dickson, 2004, p. 77).

Vocalics

The sixth form of nonverbal communication in sport is **vocalics.** Although nonverbal communication does not involve the actual words or language, it does include some aspects of speech. "In my opinion, it is very important to show respect in the way that you speak to someone," says Rogers. "You should never speak to a person in an office setting in a harsh or loud tone. You can always get your point across by stressing certain key words, or repeating words if necessary." Paralinguistics involve the components of speaking related to the tone of voice, talk speed, volume of speech, intonation, articulation, pitch, quality of voice, rhythm, rate, moans, sighs, and fillers (e.g., *uh, er*). Changing the meaning of words through vocal variations (prosody) and variations in accents (extralinguistics) is also involved in vocalics. People make judgments about the speaker and message through vocalics. Impressions are often made regarding age, gender, personality, occupation, temperament (e.g., someone who is angry will often talk fast), and emotional state. Similarly, people make decisions concerning the message because of vocalics: an excited delivery, a monotone reading, vocal techniques, and clues as to how content should be received (e.g., joking, sober, respectful). According to Hargie and Dickson (2004), "How information is delivered paralinguistically has important consequences for how much of the message is understood, received and acted on" (p. 79).

Chronemics

Chronemics—how time is perceived and used by individuals—is the seventh form of nonverbal communication. A standard practice in sport (and most other industries in the United States) is for subordinates to be punctual. The expectation is that they will be on time to meetings, assignments, and sporting events. Although showing up on time is a sign of respect, it is often accepted that sports leaders and those in high ranking or status positions can keep people waiting. This conveys the message that the leader's time is more valuable than the subordinates' time. In addition to including punctuality and timeliness, chronemics involves the duration of time that people spend with one another. Interpersonal priorities are revealed by the decisions sport managers make in their daily interactions. For example, this is evident when athletic directors spend more time with important boosters who often make million dollar donations to the athletic department than with those who are just season ticket holders.

Overall, the seven forms of nonverbal communication—haptics, kinesics, proxemics, physical characteristics, environmental factors, vocalics, and chronemics—illustrate the complexity and importance of the nonverbal messages individuals send and receive.

COMMUNICATING WITH VERBAL MESSAGES

We also interact with others through our verbal messages. The verbal system of communication is accomplished through the use of language. "Language is symbolic," according to Adler and Towne (2003). Because of this, "there's only an arbitrary connection between words and the ideas or things to which they refer." Language, through its symbolic nature, enables human beings to communicate "about ideas, reasons, the past, the future, and things not present" (p. 177).

Functions of Language

In sport, language is used for everything from talking with colleagues about a new marketing scheme or detailing the advantages and disadvantages of making a controversial trade to telling the event production staff about the script for that evening's game or writing out the strategic plan for a minor league hockey franchise.

There are eight unique functions for which language is used (Trenholm & Jensen, 2004). All of these apply to the use of language in sport settings:

1. To break the silence and to conquer the unknown
2. To act as an outlet to vent our emotions

3. To express or conceal our true thoughts and motives

4. To either engage in contact with another person or to avoid contact (e.g., talking to avoid communicating)

5. To express our individuality (creating our own image) as well as our identification with a group (using jargon)

6. To facilitate the exchange of information (either providing or seeking)

7. To influence, control, and persuade

8. To engage in metacommunication (i.e., to communicate about and monitor the communication process)

Levels of Meaning

To analyze and understand language and its structure, scholars typically look at three levels of meaning (Trenholm & Jensen, 2004).

First Level: The Word

In our examination of language in sport, the first level (or unit) of meaning is the **word.** This type of study is known as semantics. In semantics, word meanings can be either denotative (i.e., the generally accepted meaning of the word) or connotative (i.e., the way an individual might give his or her own meaning to the word). As Wood (2004) noted, "**content meaning** deals with literal or denotative meaning. . . . **Relationship meaning** refers to what communication expresses about relationships between communicators" (p. 27). Networking has a unique meaning in the sport industry and among those involved in sport. The University of Miami's Warren A. Whisenant provides the denotative (or content or literal) meaning of the word. This sport management professor defines networking as "the development and maintenance of formal and informal relationships with individuals both internal and external to one's own organization." Whisenant adds, "Effective networks—which require strong social and political interpersonal skills—allow individuals to become well informed; sustain levels of loyalty among colleagues; leverage cross-functional alliances to assist the individual and his

or her workgroup in securing the necessary resources to be successful; and provide access to those who may have the power to influence an individual's job, career, and even social relationships." The connotative (or relationship) meaning for networking ranges from a simple greeting to an aggressive pursuit and follow-up activities between job seekers and professional decision makers. For instance, sport management students are incessantly told to network in order to learn, make contacts, and obtain a competitive edge. Their concept of networking and how they go about it reflect a wide range of meanings of the word. To some students, networking means going beyond the traditional networking activities. These individuals enhance their networking activities by engaging in virtual networking. Those who engage in this practice develop relationships, exchange information, and sustain contact with sport management and communication professionals over the Internet. Regardless of whether communicators in the sport industry are networking or simply performing their job duties, they must have semantic competence to communicate effectively, feel a part of their group or organization, and avoid arguments over connotations and semantic differences.

Second Level: The Sentence

The second unit of meaning is the **sentence,** or how words are grouped together. This type of study is referred to as syntactics. Words must be combined in an orderly fashion to make sense of the phrase or sentence. Judgments are passed and impressions are made by syntactic competence, or lack thereof. Grammatical mistakes and violations of accepted rules of sentence construction and form have kept many otherwise qualified candidates from securing a desired position in sport or advancing within the sport industry.

Third Level: The Speech Act

The third level of meaning in the study of language is the **speech act.** How to use words and sentences in interactions is the study of pragmatics. Words and sentences are used intentionally to criticize, promise, warn, question, compliment, threaten, request, or any number of other intentions. We must clearly communicate our intentions as well as accurately perceive the intentions of others. Interpersonal interaction in sport requires pragmatic competence. "Communication is a complex, rule-bound process," explained Trenholm and Jensen (2004). "If we learn to do it well, our relationships will be easy and rewarding. If we have trouble with pragmatic rules, the world can be a hostile place. In fact, it's been argued that many interpersonal problems result from differences in pragmatics" (p. 94). The exceptions to this are those who are effective with the speech act but have to hide their reading or writing deficiencies. Take for instance former National Hockey League (NHL) coach and general manager Jacques Demers, who admitted in 2005 that he was illiterate throughout his years in coaching and management. Demers, who was unable to read and write, relied on his speaking ability and delegation skills to help him in his career. "When I was given the possibility of talking, I could speak well and I think that really saved me," explains Demers. By claiming that his English was not good enough, he was able to hide his illiteracy by having his secretaries and media relations professionals write everything for him. In fact, during his general manager (GM) days at Tampa Bay, Demers brought in two assistants (Cliff Fletcher and Jay Feaster) to handle contracts he could not read. "I never really was a GM," he stated. "I hired [Fletcher and Feaster] because I knew I couldn't do that" ("Ex-Coach Confesses," 2005, p. D2). Demers was definitely the exception to the rule. The ability to read, write, and speak is a basic requirement for those entering the sport industry.

IMPROVING YOUR INTERPERSONAL COMMUNICATION

Learning about interpersonal communication in sport would not be complete without learning what it takes to be effective in interpersonal interactions. Success in interpersonal communication involves many variables, some of which are out of your control. Some of the most successful people in sports have many detractors. For example, Mark Shapiro had one of the most successful runs as a television executive, but there were some who did not like his interpersonal skills. As entertainer and sports aficionado Bill Cosby once stated, "I don't know the key to success, but I do know the key to failure: Try to please everyone." Because you cannot please everyone, some of your effectiveness in interpersonal communication is out of your control. Furthermore, there are times when certain characteristics produce effective interpersonal interactions, yet at other times those same qualities produce ineffective interpersonal interactions. Speaking candidly and openly might be judged with favor when the team owner is specifically asking for it, but doing so on a regular basis will most likely produce problems. Communicators in sport need to be able to judge (and then select) when it is appropriate to use each particular interpersonal skill.

Although there is no definitive approach to effectiveness, effective communicators often exhibit several general characteristics. These are based on the work of DeVito (1990, 2005) and Wood (2004) and applied here to interpersonal communication in sport.

Skills Possessed by Effective Communicators

To be an effective communicator in interpersonal relationships, you need to possess four general skills. The first of these critical skills is the possession of **mindfulness** (i.e., awareness, attentiveness). As a future sport industry professional, you should learn to be cognizant of your communication situation and options. An ability to shape climates through the use of effective communication techniques can only come about when you are mindful of your communication situation and your options within that situation.

Knowing your communication situation and options is a key, but being able to communicate effectively after possessing that knowledge is important. Thus, **flexibility** is the second critical skill for effective interpersonal communication in sport. This is the ability to vary your responses according to the stakeholders and situation involved. **Diversity sensitivity** is the third critical skill: Being aware of differences and then accommodating them are vital to your success as a sport communication or management professional. This involves an awareness and accommodation of not only differences related to individuals and cultures but also the differences in communication choices and relationships. As Wood (2004) noted, "We should strive to respect a range of communicative choices and relationship patterns" (p. 232). The fourth critical skill related to interpersonal communication is **metacommunication,** the metalinguistic ability to convey and understand messages by communicating about the communication. For example, an assistant general manager, when criticized by his general manager in front of the office staff, will use metacommunication skills to talk with his boss about his public communication.

Qualities of Effective Interpersonal Communication

In addition to mastering the four skills noted previously, sport management professionals should be aware of 10 specific qualities that directly affect their effectiveness in interpersonal communication. These 10 qualities are self-disclosure, empathy, supportiveness, positive attitude, equality, confidence, immediacy, interaction management, expressiveness, and other-orientation.

- The first characteristic of effective interpersonal communication in sport is the ability to provide appropriate **self-disclosure.** Sport communication professionals, especially those in leadership positions, need to embrace openness. After trust has been established, they must be willing to disclose information about themselves such as their fears and feelings. Along with this comes the need to listen to others' thoughts and feelings. There must be a willingness to react honestly and spontaneously. Furthermore, such an openness requires accepting responsibility for one's own feelings and thoughts.

- **Empathy** is the second quality of effective interpersonal communication in sport. This is the ability to experience or sense what another person is feeling or experiencing. When an executive can put herself in the place of a subordinate who just lost a relative and feel to a certain level what he is feeling, the executive is empathizing with her employee. Sympathy is feeling for a person, whereas empathy is actually feeling the feelings that the other is experiencing. As Wood (2004) noted, "Expressed empathy confirms the worth of others and our concern for their thoughts and feelings" (p. 226). Empathetic communication allows us to understand at an emotional and intellectual level what another person is experiencing. Effective communicators need to both experience empathy and be able to communicate this understanding. "I believe a sense of empathy is one of the greatest qualities a person can have in life and in business," says Rogers. "The only concern is as a manager, you can't be too empathetic if an occurrence is happening over and over again. For example if someone is out sick several times a year, I am very forgiving; however, if that person is sick on a weekly basis I start to think perhaps the person is actually taking advantage of the situation." Whereas empathetic expressions reveal concern and worth, "Neutral communication implies a lack of regard and caring for others. Consequently, it disconfirms their worth" (Wood, 2004, p. 226). A chief executive of a sport organization exhibits neutral or detached communication if he appears distant or withdrawn from his subordinates. On the other hand, expressing empathy, according to Wood (2004), "fosters a supportive communication culture that helps people discuss their differences openly and productively" (p. 227).

- The third characteristic of effective interpersonal communication in sport is **supportiveness.** Working relationships require acknowledgement, acceptance, and confirmation of others. Being supportive means that rather than evaluate and judge, you describe. This leads to a supportive communication culture. Those we communicate with feel less threatened when they hear a request or a description rather than a judgmental statement or evaluation. People immediately erect barriers when there is nonsupportive communication. For example, using a critical, evaluative, judgmental approach with a young sales associate will not be as effective as using a supportive and descriptive approach that instructs in a nonthreatening way. Skills can be improved through effective and supportive communication. Part of being supportive in communication is to be provisional rather than fixed in our views. This means being open-minded to situations, open to others' points of view, and willing to change positions. Once we truly understand that we don't know everything or always have the answer, then a supportive communication approach can be acquired.

- The fourth quality of effective interpersonal communication in sport is **positive attitude.** This involves being positive, uplifting, and encouraging in our communication and interaction with others. Positive attitudes come from those who are optimistic and confident. The ability to express these attributes is a key to effective interpersonal communication. Uplifting others involves acknowledging your satisfaction with them as well as acknowledging their importance and significance. You are not indifferent to their existence and contributions. This uplifting can be verbal (e.g., word of encouragement) or nonverbal (e.g., smile, hug).

- **Equality** is another key quality of effective interpersonal communication in sport. This is the ability of a communicator to be accepting and approving. It is the opposite of superiority, which takes a condescending attitude. According to Wood (2004), "Equality is confirming and fosters a supportive interpersonal climate" (p. 227). There will usually be some inequality in positions (e.g., someone making more money, higher positions). However, the atmosphere can still be one of equality where everyone is viewed as a key contributor and a valuable and worthwhile member. Establishing this equality takes work, because it must permeate all listening and speaking.

Key to Equality: Effective Listening

Listening is, according to Adler and Towne (2003), "the most frequent form of communication." These communication scholars add that "listening is arguably just as important as speaking in terms of making relationships work" (p. 268).

For success, career advancement, and effective interpersonal communication in sport, one of the best skills to hone is listening. As Adler and Towne (2003) illustrated, the process of listening includes the elements of hearing, attending, understanding, responding, and remembering. Hearing is the element of listening that involves the physiological (i.e., sound waves striking the ear), whereas attending is the element that involves the psychological (i.e., the selectivity of what one wants to attend to). The remaining elements of understanding (i.e., making sense of what is heard), responding (i.e., providing visible and verbal feedback), and remembering (i.e., recall ability) complete the listening process. For equality to be manifested in interpersonal communication, ineffective listening must be reduced.

Some of the types of ineffective listening that you should avoid were detailed by Adler and Towne (2003):

- Pseudo-listening (giving the appearance of listening)
- Stage-hogging (turning conversation to yourself)
- Selective listening (responding only to parts that are of interest)
- Insulated listening (ignoring or avoiding a topic)
- Defensive listening (taking comments personally)
- Ambushing (listening only to collect information for an attack)
- Insensitive listening (taking comments at face value without understanding hidden meanings or nonverbal clues)

In an environment of equality, although there will be inevitable differences, participants attempt to understand and solve disagreements and conflicts through effective communication. "It is very important to be as kind, professional, and courteous to everyone regardless of stature," says sport management professional Kathryn E. Rogers. "This really shows and is often remembered. The worst mistake a person can make is to take care of the very 'important' guests or clients and behave badly or treat those considered less important in an insignificant way. This type of behavior is very transparent. However, certain people such as celebrities do tend to require more personal attention regarding travel arrangements and accommodations."

• The sixth characteristic of effective interpersonal communication in sport is **confidence.** For interpersonal communication in sport to be effective, the communicators must express social confidence. This is done through being relaxed, flexible, controlled, and comfortable with other individuals and situations. Although there will typically be some apprehension and shyness, these variables should not be allowed to interfere with the communicator. Along with this confidence comes the ability to assert oneself through honest, respectful, and direct communication. Assertive communication is simply stating one's feelings, needs, or wants with clarity and without judgment.

• **Immediacy** is the seventh characteristic of effective interpersonal communication in sport. This involves bringing the speaker and receiver together through an expression of interest. The communicator shows a liking or attraction in the topic being discussed. This immediacy joins the interactants. This can be accomplished through keeping close (interpersonal distance), using the name of the person with whom you are interacting, providing relevant feedback, reinforcing, rewarding, complimenting, and being attentive to the other's remarks.

• The eighth characteristic of effective interpersonal communication in sport is **interaction management.** This positive characteristic involves controlling the interaction. This takes work because it involves making sure neither of the communicators feels ignored. The communicators need to feel they are contributors in the communication. This management of the interaction includes maintaining roles, both speaking and listening; keeping the conversation flowing; and making interactants feel they are contributors. Effective interaction management involves self-monitoring skills. "Simple words such as, 'I will get back to you shortly,' or 'let me call you back,' or 'perhaps we can discuss this a bit later' all indicate to the person that you do not have the time just then but you will in the future," says Rogers. "If you are in the middle of something, a distraction such as someone coming into your office can really delay the task at hand."

• The ninth characteristic of effective interpersonal communication in sport is **expressiveness.** This communicates involvement. Similar to openness, it conveys the thought that the communicator is active rather than passive in the process. It involves accepting responsibility for what you are thinking and feeling. Providing honest and direct feedback, encouraging individuals to be expressive and open, stating disagreements directly, and accepting responsibility are all part of being expressive in interpersonal communication. Part of this includes the ability to respond in a nondefensive and constructive way when others offer criticism. The ways to embrace constructive criticism are to seriously contemplate the validity of the criticism and request more information for clarity.

• The ability to be **other-oriented** is the tenth and final characteristic of effective interpersonal communication in sport. This involves not being self-focused. The effective communicator listens and talks, watches and observes, and is not focused on self. Through eye contact, facial expressions, and other verbal and nonverbal cues he or she communicates an interest in what the other person says. For example, Jack Cuchran—the group sales manager of the San Antonio Spurs, San Antonio Silver Stars, and San Antonio Rampage—expresses other-orientation through his mediated interpersonal communication skills. He is, as sport management professor Bill Sutton (2005) noted, "the only salesperson in the NBA to pass the $1 million mark in group ticket sales" (p. 25). Cuchran's boss, Joe Clark—who is the vice president of ticket sales and service with the three teams—told Sutton, "Jack is one of the most amazing ticket salespeople I have encountered" (p. 25). Part of what makes him so successful was pointed out by Sutton when he noted that Cuchran's phone style "at times seems as comfortable as a porch conversation between two friends" (p. 25). Cuchran, in doing some self-analysis, said, "I have found that my approach and style—which people describe as personable—make it more difficult for people to say 'no' to me" (p. 25). His interpersonal skills and ability to be other-oriented have helped him interact effectively with interns, colleagues, executives, customers, and other stakeholders.

CHAPTER WRAP-UP

Summary

The first component of the Strategic Sport Communication Model (SSCM) includes personal and organizational communication in sport. This chapter focused on the first aspect of this component: personal communication in sport. A mastery of personal interaction skills should be the goal of all individuals in the sport industry. This is because most communication in sport involves communicating with oneself, another individual, or a few interactants. This chapter examined these areas of personal communication by looking at the intrapersonal, interpersonal, and small-group forms of communication in sport.

In an effort to synthesize the various forms of personal communication in sport, we defined interpersonal sport communication as occurring whenever individuals in sport, sharing the roles of sender and receiver, create meaning through their personal interactions. This involves all of the mainly face-to-face encounters sport professionals and communicators have with colleagues, advisors, sales managers, media relations professionals, interns, employees, and any other stakeholders.

After analyzing the reasons people engage in interpersonal communication, we examined the process of interpersonal sport communication. This process includes the major elements of source, receiver, message, feedback, channel, noise, and context. We next covered the topic of nonverbal communication in sport, which included analyses of the communicative movements of the body, nonverbal aspects of speech, and environmental factors. We looked at the nine purposes or functions of nonverbal communication in sport as well as the seven codes or forms of nonverbal sport communication. Next we detailed verbal communication in sport by examining the eight functions of language and the three levels of meaning (words, sentences, and speech acts) in the use of language in sport. We concluded the examination of interpersonal sport communication by applying DeVito's (1990, 2005) 10 characteristics and qualities of effective interpersonal communication to the interpersonal communication that occurs in sport settings.

Kathryn E. Rogers commented about various aspects of interpersonal communication throughout this chapter. Rogers also presents a list of characteristics that she looks for in people with whom she does business and prospective employees. "The following characteristics are among the most important (in my opinion) in a professional. When I am looking to hire staff, or do business with others, I look for someone who is genuine, well spoken, polite, diplomatic, attentive, able to follow through, and able to treat everyone from top CEOs to volunteers as equals while understanding the hierarchy structure." To this list of characteristics, Rogers says, "I believe one of the best tools you can learn in school is how to communicate effectively."

Review Questions

1. What is intrapersonal communication and how is it manifested in sport?
2. Beyond intrapersonal communication, what form of communication is used most often in sport? What is the definition of this form of communication?
3. What are the characteristics of small-group communication in sport? Why is it included in the discussion of interpersonal sport communication?
4. Why do people engage in or what are the purposes of interpersonal communication in sport?
5. What are the essential elements in the process of interpersonal sport communication? How do they relate to each other?
6. What are the differences between verbal and nonverbal aspects of communication and what is an example of each?
7. What are the functions of nonverbal communication in sport?
8. What are the seven codes or forms of nonverbal sport communication?
9. What are the functions of verbal communication in sport?
10. What qualities make for effectiveness in interpersonal sport communication?

Discussion Questions

1. How are the three forms of personal communication examined in this chapter similar to each other?
2. As you contemplate your career in sport management or communication, would you consider one of the three forms of personal communication more important to sports professionals than the other two?
3. Why is necessary for interactants in sport to be effective in their interpersonal communication?
4. What are at least 10 professional positions in the sport industry that require intensive interpersonal interactions?
5. What are some positions in sport communication or sport management that require nominal interpersonal interactions?
6. Do communicators in sport use verbal or nonverbal communication more often?
7. What are two or three examples of how verbal and nonverbal communication are used at the same time in the sport industry? What are some instances when they would not be used simultaneously?
8. How can you use the concepts of semantics, syntactics, and pragmatics to improve your interpersonal communication in sport?
9. Rate the four skills related to interpersonal sport communication. What is your rationale for rating them as you did?

10. From the list of 10 characteristics or qualities of effective interpersonal communication in sport, which would you consider the most important? Please explain your answer and provide examples to support your argument.

Group Activities

1. The class is separated into four-person groups. The small groups are given 10 minutes for each member to work on a short (1-minute) improvisational speech about some aspect of the sport industry. Each member takes a turn and delivers his or her speech to the small group. All members make a record of the verbal and nonverbal communication used in each presentation. After the last speech, the group discusses the most effective uses of verbal and nonverbal communication.

2. As a class, decide on a debate topic. Choose something that has at least two distinct and accepted sides (e.g., payment of college athletes, placement of advertising on uniforms, movement of a professional sports franchise). Select five people (volunteers would be the best) to represent each side of the issue. After a few minutes of preparation, have the sides debate each other. At the conclusion of the 5-minute debates, have the class discuss the forms of interpersonal communication used in the debates. Which were the most subtle forms? Which were the most effective?

Individual Exercises

1. You have just accepted an entry-level position in the sales department of a professional sports franchise. Rate from 1 to 10 the key qualities (or characteristics) of interpersonal communication in sport. Which two should you focus on to be an effective salesperson? What behaviors should you use in demonstrating these two qualities?

2. Select a sport-related article about a topic that has been in the news over the past month. The topic, which needs to involve some aspect of interpersonal communication, can come from an article from a local newspaper, a newsstand magazine (e.g., *Sports Illustrated*), a trade publication (e.g., *SportsBusiness Journal*), or the Internet. While reading the story, think about the elements of the interpersonal communication process. After you finish the story, write down the source, receiver, message, feedback, channel, noise, and context involved. Share the story and your findings with the class.

Internet Sites for Additional Learning

American Communication Association: www.americancomm.org/

Articles: www.pertinent.com/articles/communication/index.asp

National Communication Association: www.natcom.org/nca/Template2.asp

Research Topic (Questia): www.questia.com/library/communication/

Tips: http://humanresources.about.com/od/interpersonalcommunication/

CHAPTER 6

Organizational and Leadership Communication in Sport

LEARNING OBJECTIVES

▶ To learn about the components of sport organizations and the features that influence (and are influenced by) communication in and between them

▶ To consider the formal, informal, and cultural communication in sport organizations

▶ To recognize the various forms of organizational sport communication

▶ To understand the importance of communicating in sport leadership

▶ To become aware of the leadership communication styles in sport organizations

PROFILE OF A SPORT COMMUNICATOR

Kelly Krauskopf

Effective communication is vital for the success of any sport organization. A prerequisite of successful organizational communication in sport is leadership. "Leadership," according to Kelly Krauskopf, "is the ability to develop a vision and path for your organization and then the ability to motivate and influence your troops to reach the goal." Krauskopf does more than talk about leadership; for more than 2 decades she has exemplified it. She commenced her distinguished career in sport leadership during her college years at Texas A&M. "My love of sports started there," says Krauskopf, who earned a journalism degree from the university. Through her participation in sports she learned the value of developing leadership skills. But in a move that many athletes have found challenging to accomplish, she has made the successful transition from directing teams on the court to leading people in sport organizations. She has assumed leadership positions in intercollegiate athletics (Texas A&M and the Southwest Conference), broadcasting and marketing corporations (Liberty Sports Media and Host Communications), and professional sports (Indiana Fever and the Women's National Basketball Association [WNBA]).

Krauskopf, who has run the Indiana Fever since 1999, worked as the director of basketball operations for the WNBA when the league began in 1996. Her responsibilities at the league headquarters included everything from organizing schedules and draft camps to determining officiating policies, playing rules, and medical policies. As the chief operating officer and general manager of the Indiana Fever, Krauskopf is the leader of the organization. "I oversee the overall direction of the franchise from the business direction to signing players," states Krauskopf, whom Dodds (2005) noted is the highest-ranking woman at any professional team in Indianapolis and one of the city's most influential

© Paul M. Pedersen

sportswomen. Krauskopf, who is also a key decision maker with USA Basketball, is a leader because she knows how to communicate. "Communication is integral to leadership," she explains. "This is true for both direct interactions—person to person—and indirect interactions—by example."

Communication in sport organizations involves interacting with stakeholders at all levels. "As a leader of a franchise," notes Krauskopf, "I am in constant communication with my staff, colleagues in the WNBA, and league officials." Some of her most important times to share information are when she communicates with her superiors. "My communication upward is to my ultimate boss, Donnie Walsh, and to his second in command, David Morway," says Krauskopf, referring to the president and senior vice president of Pacers Sports and Entertainment. "Donnie and David both have been tremendous mentors to me and use an 'open door' policy. I can usually go into either office and discuss the direction of our basketball team or the many challenges we face in the marketing and sales area."

Although she communicates with many internal and external publics, the group she interacts with the most is her staff. This communication—which takes place daily—involves discussing issues such as "the direction of the business and what is being done to reach our goals." Her participative and "inclusive" style of leadership communication is particularly effective. "I like to engage in a think-tank process in which everyone who is involved or affected by the decision has input and is encouraged to think about the pros and cons. I often use this to encourage ownership and validation of my group as individuals and as a team." She adds, "I really try to push my staff into thinking for themselves and coming up with solutions or new ideas without me having to tell them what to do all the time."

Kelly Krauskopf's views of organizational leadership and communication are highlighted throughout the following pages. Her comments and experiences illustrate the thrust of this chapter, which is to show the importance of communication in sport organizations and the role that leaders have in facilitating a culture of communication.

"Why is communicating important?" asked Pat Summitt. "Because you can't do anything without it. Communication is necessary in order to avoid confusion. It's vital to any successful organization to be clear. When you communicate, you eliminate mistakes. Everybody understands the system and understands his responsibilities within the system, so that he can carry them out" (Summitt & Jenkins, 1998, p. 67). Summitt, the winningest basketball coach in NCAA history, provided a thorough dissection of communication in her answer. That is because all communication includes both situational (e.g., organizational) and personal (e.g., stylistic) aspects (Hattersley & McJannet, 2005). Individuals in the sport industry interact with one another through personal communication and organizational communication. Personal communication in sport involves the intrapersonal, interpersonal, and small-group forms of communication. The elements and functions of these three major forms of personal communication in sport were detailed in chapter 5. Although the formats for and aspects of personal sport communication are intertwined with communication in the organization (remember, communication is both situational and personal), the emphasis in chapter 6 is on organizational communication in sport. Therefore, the two chapters—personal (5) and organizational (6) sport communication—are unique but still so tightly connected that combined they make up the first component of the Strategic Sport Communication Model (SSCM).

Our definition of communication in and with sport organizations is a slightly modified version of the definition of organizational communication offered by Modaff and DeWine (2002). **Organizational communication in sport** is the process in which messages are created, exchanged, interpreted, and stored within a system of human relationships in sport. "Without effective communication," noted sport management scholars Jeremy S. Jordan and Aubrey Kent (2005), "people in the organization would not know what to do and would not know what others were doing" (p. 51). Although other aspects of sport communication such as sport public relations and the sport media often get more attention in casual conversation and scholarly discourse, the importance of the frequently overlooked communication in sport organizations cannot be overstated. "Communication is the glue that holds organizations together," stated communication and leadership consultant John Baldoni (2003). "The aim of organizational communications is to ensure that everyone understands both the external and internal issues facing the organization and what individuals must do to contribute to the organization's success" (p. 2). Organizational communication in sport includes elements of interorganizational as well as intraorganizational sport communication. Therefore, the goal of this chapter is to introduce the theoretical, conceptual, and practical aspects of communication that occurs within (intra) a sport organization and between (inter) sport organizations. We will define these terms, illustrate their uniqueness, and examine their elements and functions. After having read this chapter, the student should be familiar with the activities, components, and workings of communication in sport organizations. "The study of organizational communication helps people understand and appreciate communication as the central process in the organization" (Modaff & DeWine, 2002, p. 18).

UNDERSTANDING ORGANIZATIONAL SPORT COMMUNICATION

The importance of communication to organizational success has been noted for decades. Nearly a half-century ago, Rensis Likert (1961) noted that communication was a prime component of an effective organization. His assertion is just as valid today for all organizations. Research has linked organizational communication to effective leaders and organizations, integrated organizational units, and job and communication satisfaction (Shockley-Zalabak, 2006). The same linkage can be found in the sport industry. A prerequisite of successful sport organizations and productive and satisfied sport employees is effective organizational communication. This section of the chapter examines the definitions and elements of organizational sport communication. By taking an organizational behavior approach (i.e., a perspective that includes examining the collective behavior of groups and individuals within the sport organization) to the topic of sport communication, we analyze the organization, management, and production of the collective communication by the individuals and groups in sport organizations. In this discussion, we explain the impact that organizational structure, culture, and climate have on the formality and complexity of communication. Organizational communication theories provide the framework for this chapter. These perspectives of organizational communication range from the mechanistic approach (i.e., transmission of messages through channels) and psychological approach (i.e., interpretation of messages by receivers) to the interpretive–symbolic approach (i.e., the shared meaning shapes and is shaped by the communication in organizations) and systems–interactive approach (i.e., communication sequence patterns predict organizational outcomes). Although these organizational communication theories underlie any discussion of communication in sport organizations, the focus of this chapter is not an analysis of organizational communication theories.

Definition of a Sport Organization

A **sport organization** is a group of people working in or through sport to achieve one or more objectives. This definition, which is a modified version of Lussier's (2005) definition of an organization, encompasses the local golf club repair shop, the global IMG, and everything in between. When a group of stakeholders (e.g., employees, volunteers, marketers, advertisers, lawyers) work toward some purpose, goal, or objective, they are part of a sport organization. This could be a nonprofit enterprise or a for-profit business. The size or focus (e.g., goods, services) of the company or group does not affect its status as a sport organization.

Sport organizations exist in a variety of forms:

- Knowledge-based or learning organizations (knowledge is shared throughout the organization)
- Cross-functional teams (work is accomplished across departments)
- Virtual or network organizations (major business functions are outsourced to allow for a focus on core competencies)
- Boundaryless organizations (organizations that combine the use of outsourcing, participative decision making, cross-functional teams, networked computers between the organization and its suppliers and customers, and other characteristics)
- E-organizations (organizations that use the Internet, intranets, and extranets for sales [e-commerce], to connect with suppliers [business to business], and to run a business [e-business])

According to Barnard (1938), for organizations to exist they must consist of three major elements. What he noted in the 1930s is applicable to all organizations today. Therefore, we'll apply his three essential elements to sport organizations.

1. The first essential element of the sport organization is that its members must be willing to **contribute and cooperate.** Although there will be some individualism and dissension from time to time, as a whole a sport organization will not exist without a certain level of cooperation and contribution from its members. For instance, the Detroit Pistons as an organization cannot exist without contri-

butions from and cooperation between the various units ranging from the personnel, marketing, and ticket operations to the facility, sales, and media relations departments.

2. The second essential element of a sport organization is that it has a **common purpose or objective** that focuses the efforts of the organization's members. For instance, the main mission of the athletic department at a Division III institution might be to provide students with competitive athletic opportunities in an academic environment. The employees of the athletic department are aware of this purpose and work to provide such an environment.

3. The third essential element of the sport organization is **communication.** This fundamental element is necessary for the survival of a sport organization because without it the purpose of the organization could never be communicated and there could be no interactions between the organization's members. Some scholars emphasize that this element—communication—makes the organization what it is. "Communication is the organization," noted Pepper (1995). "The communication behaviors of organization members are what constitute the actual organization" (p. 3).

Because communication and the sport organization can be viewed as the same activity, one does not follow the other. Even for those who do not consider the two as synonymous, at a minimum communication is one of the three essential and intertwined elements of a sport organization: cooperation, common purpose, and communication.

Communication In and Between Sport Organizations

Organizational communication in sport includes communication in sport organizations and communication between a sport organization and another organization (see figure 6.1). The "communication in" aspect

of organizational communication refers to the **intraorganizational** issues involved in sport communication. This is communication with internal publics—within the sport company. Communicating internally involves exchanging information within the sport organization. This is often a managerial activity because it generally involves such communicative activities as attending staff meetings, engaging in telephone conversations with internal stakeholders, and responding to procedural issues within the sport organization (Luthans, Rosenkrantz, & Hennessey, 1985; Whisenant & Pedersen, 2004b). "Communications belongs to everyone in the organization," said Baldoni (2003). "Communications must become a core competency—the responsibility of everyone within the organization" (p. 2).

The "communication between" aspect of organizational communication refers to the interorganizational issues involved with sport communication. This is communication with external publics—between businesses in the sport environment. When an individual within a sport organization interacts with someone outside the organization (e.g., media member, sales client, prospective sponsor), she is communicating with an external public. Whether a baseball bat salesperson is interacting with a college baseball athletic department or with an agent of a prospective bat client, the communication is **interorganizational** because it involves two organizations (e.g., bat company and athletic department, bat company and sports agent firm). "There is a real sense of togetherness among the WNBA teams," notes Kelly Krauskopf. "We often communicate ways to help each other with our business growth, but when it comes to players, we often keep that to ourselves—like true competitors." Communication between organizations often results in career opportunities and upward mobility for those who chose to interact with others outside their organization. "There is that expression that says, 'It's a small world,'" stated Jay Monahan, the former executive director of the PGA Tour's Deutsche Bank Championship. "You have to spend a lot of your time and energy making certain that you are staying in contact

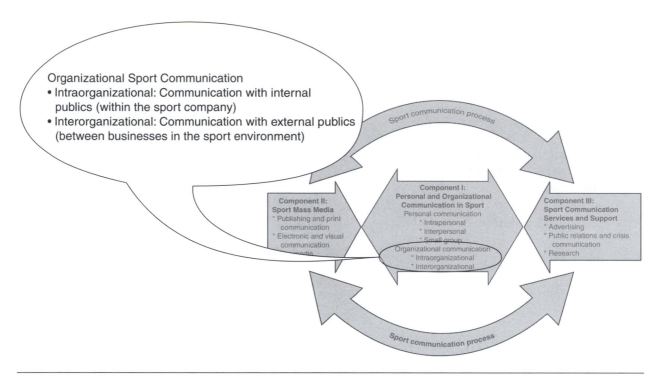

Organizational Sport Communication
• Intraorganizational: Communication with internal publics (within the sport company)
• Interorganizational: Communication with external publics (between businesses in the sport environment)

Sport communication process

**Component II:
Sport Mass Media**
* Publishing and print communication
* Electronic and visual communication media

**Component I:
Personal and Organizational Communication in Sport**
Personal communication
* Intrapersonal
* Interpersonal
* Small group
Organizational communication
* Intraorganizational
* Interorganizational

**Component III:
Sport Communication Services and Support**
* Advertising
* Public relations and crisis communication
* Research

Sport communication process

Figure 6.1   Organizational sport communication is the second segment of the first component of the Strategic Sport Communication Model (SSCM).

with people. This business (sport) feeds itself off of relationships, so it is being diligent . . . just to check in with people every so often. It's the feeder system to being in the front line of this business" (McClung, 2005). Monahan, an alumnus of the sport management program at the University of Massachusetts, focuses on marketing and sales nationwide in his new position as the executive vice president of new business development for Fenway Sports Group.

RECOGNIZING THREE ORGANIZATIONAL FEATURES THAT AFFECT COMMUNICATION

Communication is central to the success of a sport organization. Bob Williams commented on this when he was named the managing director of media and public relations at the NCAA national office in Indianapolis in 2005. "Communicating to a variety of key stakeholders is critical to the NCAA's success," noted Williams, who came to the NCAA after an extensive career in leadership communication positions in the armed forces. "I'm excited

about joining the team communicating the NCAA's goals and priorities with student-athletes and their families, the membership and the public" (Barrett, 2005). The view that the success of an organization is contingent on communication is true whether we view organization in sport as a process (i.e., the process of organizing by a group of individuals in sport) or as an entity (i.e., the result [organization] of organizing efforts). As Pepper (1995) noted, "Communicating and organizing are two sides of the same coin. The process of communicating is the act of organizing, and efforts to organize are communication bound" (p. 7). The sport organization is created, developed, and maintained through the communicative actions of its stakeholders. These forms that make up the organizational structure involve transactions at the individual, dyadic, small-group, intergroup, and technological levels. Therefore, as we have noted before, communication in the sport organization occurs in both the interpersonal and contextual levels. We examined the interpersonal levels in the previous chapter. Of particular interest in this chapter is the fact that communicators use their skills in a certain context or setting—the sport organization. The skills needed for effectiveness by organizational communicators in sport come from an awareness of the relationships in sport organizations as well as knowledge of how to communicate within these relationships.

"Communication is central to the existence of the organization," noted Modaff and DeWine (2002, p. 4). If we apply their analysis to the sport industry, communication is integral in the creation (and re-creation) of the structure of the sport organization. Although communication creates that structure, what is created then has an effect on the communication activities within that structure. Therefore, the sport organization is both shaped by and shapes the communication activities of its stakeholders. In particular, three features of the sport organization—its formal structure, informal networks, and culture—are influenced by and influence the communication flow (see figure 6.2).

Formal Structure in Sport Organizations

The structure of an organization is often viewed as essentially physical (e.g., the organization's building, walls, hallways, desks) or conceptual (e.g., charts, titles, positions, levels, bureaucracies). However, "organizational structure is that which is experienced by organizational members much more than anything built of bricks and mortar," noted Pepper (1995). "Structure includes working relationships, experiences and interpretations, and power relationships" (p. 10). Keep this in mind as we discuss the formal, informal, and cultural influences on organizational communication. The formal structure of a sport organization—as opposed to simply the structure of the organization—refers to the design (i.e., arrangement) of the organization's divisions, departments, and units. A sport manager works to design her organization's

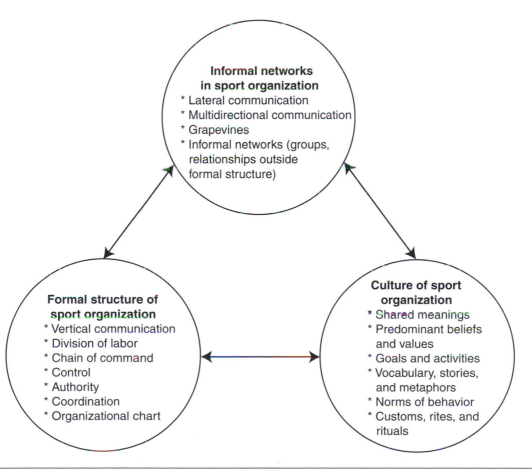

Figure 6.2 Features that influence (and are influenced by) the communication activities in (and between) sport organizations.

structure in such a way as to best achieve the organization's goals and objectives. This is accomplished through an understanding of the five principles of a sport organization.

1. The sport manager must understand the organization's **division of labor** and departmentalization. This involves how the work of the sport organization is subdivided and how the related activities are grouped into units (e.g., marketing, ticketing, sales personnel).

2. The sport manager needs to understand the **chain of command.** The organizational chart illustrates the sport organization's formal structure and line of authority from top to bottom. The chart represents reporting structures (i.e., the people to whom departments and individuals should report).

3. The sport manager must understand the span of management or the span of **control.** This involves the number of individuals and departments that report to each manager.

4. The sport manager needs to be aware of the centralization or decentralization of **authority** in the sport organization. If the leaders make the important decisions, then the sport organization has centralized authority. If the middle and front-line managers make decisions where the action occurs, then the authority is decentralized. "The trend today is toward decentralization so that decisions can be made quickly to take advantage of opportunities to solve problems. Decentralization allows more input into decision making and greater employee commitment to carrying out the decisions" (Lussier, 2005, p. 150).

5. The sport manager needs to be aware of the specific roles and **coordination** of work. This involves getting the sport employees and departments to work together. Although decentralization encourages greater participation among the employees, it adds to the difficulty of coordination. Therefore, job duties,

hierarchy of positions, relationships between members, and other components are involved in the formal structure of organizations.

Decentralization Versus Centralization

The formal structure in sport organizations has evolved over the years. The changes are a result of efforts to create a healthier bottom line (e.g., downsizing) while increasing the satisfaction and production of an organization's members (e.g., encouraging more communication and input through decentralization). More and more sport organizations are moving from a hierarchical (tall) structure to a more decentralized (flat) structure. Tall formal structures have "many layers through which messages and instructions must go before reaching the workers" (Modaff & DeWine, 2002, p. 9). Flat formal structures have fewer reporting levels. This means that the span of management is wider because sport managers have more individuals and departments reporting to them. These flat structures affect the communication in sport organizations because managers must now direct (and communicate with) more people. The increase in communication and complexity consumes a lot more time for sport managers. However, the increased communication and decreased layers allow individuals more input and power in the decision-making process. This participative decision making is reflected in the changing climate of sport organizations from more authoritarian to more empowerment (e.g., coaching). We discuss these changes later in this chapter in our analysis of sport leadership in organizations. Overall, communication in many sport organizations has been changed by decentralization as managers have moved from a more top-down (centralized) approach to a more multidirectional (and often more complicated) approach.

Chain of Command

The formal structure of the sport organization has a tremendous influence on communication within that sport organization. Communication in a sport organization generally follows the reporting structures as illustrated in the organizational chart. For instance, a corporate account manager for the Columbus Crew who has an ethical dilemma regarding her job is not likely to seek clarification from the team's general manager, or even the team's senior vice president of sales and marketing. Rather, she will run the scenario by her immediate supervisor (e.g., the director of ticket sales, the senior director of ticket sales) or one of her ticket sales colleagues. This "chain-of-command" communication (i.e., following the organizational chart) is not always followed but is the generally accepted process of communication in sport organizations. The formal organizational structure in sport organizations generally influences the way employees proceed in their communication within sport organizations.

The direction that communication follows in the organizational chart is categorized as vertical communication. This formal communication (or intraorganizational communication) is the official communication of the organization because it flows upward and downward according to the sport organization's chain of command. Downward communication in sport organizations occurs when subordinates receive communication (e.g., job instructions, results of decisions, procedural information, feedback, job rationale, indoctrination efforts) from those in superior positions. When an assistant ticket manager receives instructions about her job, information concerning her duties, feedback, or an evaluation from her ticket manager or another individual up in the chain of command, the communication is considered to be downward.

Upward communication in sport organizations occurs when subordinates send messages up the organizational chart (e.g., information about the subordinate, information about the subordinate's peers, communication about policy, questions and comments about work). This type of communication occurs in sport organizations when an employee makes a suggestion, airs dissatisfaction, seeks information, attempts to impress a superior, or does any number of actions meant to communicate with someone up the chain of command. Sports leaders should value and encourage this type of communication because it provides information to superiors for decision making

Barriers to Upward Communication

Upward communication can involve several barriers to communication flow. These barriers include hiding thoughts and feelings by subordinates, viewing superiors as not caring or inaccessible, offering misleading information just to please superiors or make the subordinate look better, and using information to subvert the position of the superior (Pepper, 1995).

Several major factors affect the communication between superiors and subordinates. These factors—as examined by Pepper (1995)—include

- trust,
- subordinate mobility (desire to move upward),
- superior upward influence,
- openness,
- overloaded or underloaded channels (more information coming to superiors through more channels, not enough information coming to subordinates),
- gender,
- power (unequal relationships, poor communication sometimes), and
- message clarity (gaps in message intention and the understanding of the message).

Regardless of the barriers, top-level managers in sport can increase the flow of upward communication throughout the organization by being cognizant of the factors that affect the communication and by reducing the barriers noted here. This can be done through implementing an open-door policy, facilitating employee meetings, conducting attitude surveys, and initiating suggestion systems. "I have an open door policy with my subordinates," notes the Indiana Fever's Kelly Krauskopf. "They don't have to make an appointment to see me to discuss something."

as well as information regarding how the followers are doing and to what degree they understand their roles, duties, and activities.

Suggestions for Communicating Formally

Individuals in sport management have a chance to be more effective in their communication within the organization and between organizations if they understand the formal structures of the organizations involved. Communicating in formal structures involves two suggestions.

First, individuals should learn the formal structures of sport organizations. They should ask for and obtain a prepared organization chart to be aware of formal chains of command and lines of communication.

Second, individuals should follow the proper channels (i.e., formal lines) of communication in the sport organization. Bypassing the formal lines often results in alienation and anger, so it is best to stay with formal lines of communication until the informal lines (discussed subsequently) are understood. "I think it is very important for leaders to come together and communicate effectively among each other at a higher level," says Kathryn E. Rogers, former executive director of the Gary Player Foundation. "The same leaders should then go back to their various teams and communicate to those beneath them. This ensures that everyone is on the same page."

Informal Structure in Sport Organizations

In addition to the communication that occurs through the formal channels of sport organizations, some communication in sport organizations is informal or unofficial. This communication involves lateral communication, multidirectional communication, grapevines, and informal networks.

Lateral Communication

Lateral (or horizontal) communication in sport organizations occurs when individuals on the same level (i.e., assistant sports information directors) communicate with each other. This

Informal communication is vital in any organization. Here, Indiana High School Athletic Association (IHSAA) commissioner Blake Ress casually communicates with another sports leader after a contest.

informal communication is not official communication of the sport organization because it does not follow the chain of command. However, this form of communication across the same hierarchical level in sport organizations is essential in coordinating tasks, solving problems, sharing information, resolving conflicts, establishing support systems, and facilitating cooperation among individuals and departments. As Mike Krzyzewski noted, "Too often, people take talking for granted. Around the coffee bar, at the lunch table, or in the locker room, people are always talking to one another. But leaders should not assume that people are going to talk to one another when they are performing their jobs. As a matter of fact," the legendary coach and leadership expert added, "in business, an employee is less likely to talk to a member of the team when he's doing his job than when he's on a break. Leaders have to remind people to talk to one another. They have to teach people to talk" (Krzyzewski and Phillips, 2002, pp. 71-72).

Multidirectional Communication

Multidirectional communication in sport organizations involves communication in a variety of directions. Take for instance a new sport marketing initiative. Downward communication would involve the supervisors' communicating the goals to the sales staff. Horizontal communication would involve the salespeople's communicating with each other to reach the goals. Upward communication would be, at the conclusion of the campaign, the salespeople's communicating the success (or lack thereof) of their effort to the supervisors and upper management. A multidirectional approach is needed for a sport organization to share information, solve problems, and efficiently coordinate its activities. Because information can be secured, problems solved, and coordination achieved through multidirectional communication, individuals should determine when it is appropriate and follow through with their communication with superiors, subordinates, and colleagues.

Grapevine Communication

Grapevine communication in sport organizations is an often overlooked avenue of sport communication. This is the unofficial and informal method of moving messages in all directions throughout a sport organization. Although the accuracy and effects of rumors within an organization are debated by scholars, the important of this form of communication should not be overlooked. "Rather than ignore or try to repress the grapevine, tune into it," noted Lussier (2005). "Identify the key people in the organization's grapevine and feed them information. To help prevent incorrect rumors, keep the information flowing through the grapevines as accurate and rumor-free as possible. Share all nonconfidential information with employees; tell them of changes as far in advance as possible. Encourage employees to ask questions about rumors they hear" (p. 156).

Informal Networks

Groups and relationships are formed outside the formal structure of the sport organization. These informal networks—such as a group of colleagues participating in a weekly golf outing or watching certain games together—are established and maintained through proximity (e.g., working in the same office suite), the development of friendships and political alliances, and other relationships. People make decisions on what information should be shared, with whom it should be shared, and what issues should be raised. The informal communication is often interpersonal sport communication (examined in the previous chapter) but can often involve several individuals. Meetings after work and during lunch often make up the information communication in organizations. The functions of informal communication in sport organizations include

- supporting the formal structure (e.g., interacting and coordinating with others without the chain of command),
- developing emotional and support networks,
- increasing the willingness of individuals to cooperate in the achievement of organizational objectives, and
- increasing job and communication satisfaction.

Suggestions for Communicating Informally

Kelly and colleagues (1989) offered suggestions for communicating informally. These include cultivating informal relationships (e.g., establishing mentors), exercising restraint (e.g., being aware of hidden agendas), and being discreet (e.g., not betraying confidences, not flaunting the benefits of your informal network). The informal communication in sport organizations can sometimes lead to conflicts. "If there's one thing in business that's inevitable, it's squabbles between co-workers," noted Jennifer Gill (2005). "Put a group of people together in a high-pressured office for 40-plus hours a week and hostility about missing food in the fridge and loud telephone conversations is bound to flare up . . . sometimes, they can spiral out of control, poisoning the whole office" (p. 40). Whether the conflict is about job duties or personality issues, squabbles are often handled through clearing the communication channels, reassigning an employee to another department, releasing the employee from the organization, or enlisting an organizational ombudsman who listens to the problems, asks questions, and works with the employees and organization to resolve the problem.

Culture of the Sport Organization

Similar to formal structures and informal networks, the culture of a sport organization is influenced by and influences communication. In fact, some scholars postulate that "culture is communication, or, to be more precise, a cultural approach to organizations is a focus on the everyday ordinary and extraordinary communication of organization members" (Pepper, 1995, p. 3). Sport organizations have their own way of life, or unique culture. Each organization has shared meanings and predominant beliefs, goals, activities, values, rites, vocabulary, stories, metaphors, norms for behavior, customs, rituals, and other indicators of organizational culture. A sport organization creates, shares, and alters its culture through verbal and nonverbal communication. As Carla Green Williams explains, the culture of the University of Georgia Athletic Department is communicated to the various stakeholders through the use of "supervisors, a policy book, media guides, and word of mouth." Furthermore, just as communication influences the culture of the organization, the organization influences the communication. As organizational and leadership communication scholar Patricia D. Witherspoon (1997) noted, "Not only do organizations *have* their own cultures, organizations *are* cultures—systems of values, beliefs, artifacts—that are constituted through the process of communication" (p. 74).

In this section we apply Witherspoon's (1997) writings on organizational culture to the sport organization. After examining the factors, functions, and forms of culture in sport organizations, we then look at how organizational members can effectively communicate in sport organizations.

Factors

The **factors** that help shape the culture of a sport organization include its environment, task, leadership, structure, resources, and climate. The general manager and chief operating officer of the Indiana Fever, Kelly Krauskopf, illustrates many of these factors when she comments on her view of culture within her sport organization. "Since we operate within the structure of Pacers Sports & Entertainment, all of our staff works under the same guidelines in terms of organizational regulations," notes Krauskopf. "The culture is communicated by our HR department and seems to be pretty well understood by all employees."

Functions

The **functions** of organizational culture include providing knowledge about the organization so employees know how to act or behave (e.g., rules, procedures, and rumors provide information about dress code, interactions with superiors, prescribed working hours), providing a shared sense of emotional involvement in and commitment to organizational values, helping members identify and affiliate with the organization, assisting members in processing (collecting, disseminating, using) information, assisting in the solving of problems, defining the organization's boundaries that distinguish members from nonmembers (e.g., physical boundaries, identification badges), providing a system of control (e.g., rules, behaviors), and enhancing organizational performance. Regarding the last function, Witherspoon (1997) noted, "A strong culture is characterized by a continuity in leadership, stable group membership, numerous commonly held values and shared behavior patterns among organizational levels, and organization-wide success" (p. 81).

Forms

There are three predominant **forms** of culture in a sport organization. These are the ways in which a sport organization creates its culture through information processing through the use of

- symbols (i.e., a sign such as a logo, slogan, metaphor),
- schemas (i.e., stored knowledge that helps the organization's members make sense of information), and
- scripts (i.e., the typical behavior or sequence of events used in a situation).

For example, the culture of a Major League Soccer (MLS) franchise is created, developed, and sustained through the interaction of symbols (e.g., wearing shirts with the team's logo), schemas (e.g., a thorough interest in and knowledge of soccer), and scripts (e.g., how employees are expected to treat superiors or season ticket holders). The team's employees and internal stakeholders—through the organization, interpretation, and use of the information secured about the interaction noted previously—develop common interpretations (or shared meanings) of activities and events within the professional soccer franchise. The forms of communication in a sport organization's culture include

- language (i.e., common and understood words, terms, phrases),
- myths (i.e., repeated stories), and
- ceremonies and rites (i.e., elaborate activities, planned functions, dramatic endeavors, regularly scheduled rituals, special ceremonies).

The rites in a sport organization may include rites of passage (e.g., training sessions), rites of enhancement (e.g., rewarding performance), and rites of integration (e.g., picnics, parties). Referring again to the soccer example used previously, all of the team's employees participate in these forms of communication. Therefore, these forms not only create the organizational culture of the sport organization but also reflect and reinforce that organizational culture.

The culture of the sport entity can be viewed as the manifestation of the organization's internal operational influences, practices,

beliefs, norms, and values. This inner self of the sport organization is reflected through the interactions between internal stakeholders and their communication with external stakeholders. Effective communication in organizational cultures can be accomplished if stakeholders listen carefully, observe others (e.g., model effective communicators, realize inappropriate behavior), and fulfill their roles (Kelly et al., 1989). The three features of sport organizations that affect communicators—formal structure, informal networks, organizational culture—need to be understood and appreciated for effective communicative interactions in sport organizations. Information needs to flow between the various levels of the sport organization. Therefore, leaders need to facilitate the movement of information through formal (up, down, across hierarchical levels) and informal communication channels as well as the organizational culture.

For instance, we noted earlier that one type of sport organization is the learning organization. A learning sport organization makes changes based on the information and feedback it receives through systematic inquiry. A sport organization that is labeled as a learning organization accomplishes this because of its culture of communication. As Torres, Preskill, and Piontek (2005) explained, an organization creates a culture of learning through activities. Taking their suggestions and applying them to the sport organization, we can see the various ways in which organizations in the sport industry can create and develop a learning culture. For a sport organization, some of the activities that can accomplish this include implementing the organization's findings from systemic inquiry, establishing feedback loops so the sport entity's members can learn from past activities, developing a new mind-set that reframes problems as opportunities, and encouraging collaboration. Other activities include enhancing individual learning and team knowledge development, appreciating conflict as an aspect of the process of changing and growing, reevaluating the reward structure to include both productivity and new learning measures, and creating a structure that increases and enhances communication within the organization. Furthermore, a sport organization can create a culture of learning by establishing a mechanism for easy storage and retrieval of information, implementing new technology to improve the transfer of information, and examining the perceptions, norms, values, assumptions, activities, and policies surrounding the sport organization and its internal stakeholders.

EXAMINING FORMS OF COMMUNICATION IN SPORT ORGANIZATIONS

Communication in sport organizations includes numerous interaction levels, audience types, and channels. This organizational communication could involve talking at the team headquarters with colleagues, making a presentation at an awards banquet, holding a strategic meeting with upper management, sending a written evaluation to subordinates, soliciting advice from a mentor in a different organization, making a videotape for employees, training salespeople in effective presentation skills, establishing an e-commerce Web site, or preparing a Heisman Trophy campaign. As Hattersley and McJannett (2005) stated, "Since most business communications involve a variety of audiences, you may need to use a number of different channels to accomplish your goal" (p. 83). Carla Green Williams of the University of Georgia notes that she engages in all forms of communication (face-to-face communication, meetings, interviews, presentations, e-mail, letters, memos, reports). She adds, "50 percent of my time spent communicating is face to face; 30 percent is e-mail; and everything else falls in the remaining 20 percent."

The communication channels in sport organizations—or the forms in which messages are transmitted—include both the verbal and nonverbal forms of discourse. This discourse is vital for effective sport organizations because, as quoted in Grant, Keenoy, and Oswick (1998), "Organizations exist only in so far as their members create them through discourse. This is not to claim that organiza-

tions are 'nothing but' discourse, but rather that discourse is the principal means by which organization members create a coherent social reality that frames their sense of who they are" (p. 3). The discourse includes all forms of formal and informal—mediated and unmediated—spoken dialogue and written text. In this section we concentrate on oral and written communication in sport organizations.

The most effective way to illustrate the forms of communication in sport organizations is to arrange the channels into categories. In this section we use the three categories created by Torres and colleagues (2005) to accomplish this. These scholars noted, "Use of these interactive strategies to facilitate dialogue and reflection within a particular organizational context can contribute to a cumulative body of knowledge that informs issues and decisions related to broader organizational goals" (p. 8). Their three categories—least interactive, potentially interactive, and most interactive—include forms of communication arranged according to the degree to which they involve interaction by the audience. "Generally," noted Hattersley and McJannett (2005), "you're well advised to choose the most personal medium, or combination of media, capable of carrying your message" (p. 85).

Least Interactive Formats: The Written Word

The **least interactive** formats involve written forms that can be delivered to an audience without verbal or face-to-face interaction. These formats can be delivered through the mail (e.g., postal, intraorganizational), e-mail, overnight service, news media, the Internet, or an intranet. The most common communication channels for written communication in sport organizations are e-mails, short written communication, faxes, and reports such as annual reports, proposals, and project updates. The short written communication—correspondence such as memos and postcards—can be used for updates, reminders, limited amounts of information, recaps, summaries, and follow-ups. Other forms that are frequently used include text messages, letters, executive summaries, briefs, discussion outlines, chart packs or decks, news media communications, Web site communications, bulletin board notices (general announcements, sign-ups, general information), in-house publications (brochures, newsletters, magazines), and posters or signs. As this list indicates, there are both mediated (e.g., e-mail correspondence, text messaging) and unmediated forms of written communication.

Using E-Mail: Advantages and Challenges

E-mail is the most commonly used—as well as an often abused and inefficient—form of communication in sport organizations. "I really like the phone or in-person (communication) better," notes Kelly Krauskopf, general manager of the Indiana Fever, "but it seems in this era of business, everyone has less time for 'in-person' (communication) and we have adapted well to e-mail communication." It is a preferred form because of its unique uses. For example, when a sport manager receives an e-mail, she can read and respond at her own pace. She can use e-mail as she works on several tasks, thus assisting her in multitasking. Overall, its other advantages are that it is fast, immediate, efficient, cost-effective, and easily distributed to a broad range of stakeholders, and it creates a communication trail. Brandon Steiner is the founder and chair of Steiner Sports Marketing, a $35 million marketing and collectibles company with more than 500 professional athletes. In his book, *The Business Playbook: Leadership Lessons from the World of Sports*, Steiner (2003) noted, "If someone e-mails in the morning or midday, get back to the person by the end of the day. It is called e-mail, after all, not the Pony Express; so don't keep correspondence waiting. If it takes more than a day, what is your response worth? It may be too late to offer the assistance they requested. It's simple consideration" (p. 88).

Although e-mail has many positive uses, there are challenges with using this format of written communication. "New ways of working are now commonplace, but understanding and using the new virtual workplace well is not easy, especially when processes and technology change rapidly" noted Lieberman, Simons, and Berado (2004, p. 67). Some individuals in sport are not interested in any new communication technology. Take for instance Joe Paterno, the legendary football coach at Penn State University. "I don't have e-mail," he told reporters in 2005. "I don't know the first thing about a computer. I don't have a cell phone." He then added, "I go around and do my job as best I can" ("Paterno Turned It Around," 2005). Most professionals in sport organizations, however, work with communication technology throughout the day. Sometimes, according to Lieberman and colleagues (2004), the use of e-mail can be very problematic. These scholars note that delays in answering e-mails sometimes indicate problems or issues that need to be resolved in face-to-face meetings. Also, sometimes informal e-mails that are sent in a friendly gesture come across as short and rude. Information that a person sends in confidence through an e-mail message can sometimes be passed on to others, thus betraying a confidence knowingly or unknowingly. Furthermore, professionals should exercise caution when sending personal e-mails or e-mails not related to their employment.

Sports leaders and organizations should set norms for when and how they will use e-mail, who gets copied on e-mails, how long e-mails should be, how responses should be formulated, and the formality (or lack thereof) of the e-mail correspondence.

The best way to send an important message, resolve a conflict, or convey a confidential matter, however, is the use of a face-to-face meeting or some other more personal approach to communication in sport organizations.

Importance of Writing Skills

The development of writing skills is important for success in sport organizations. Whether you want to be a sports reporter or a ticket manager, you will frequently rely on your written communication skills to be effective and efficient with your communication and interactions. "The higher up in the organization you plan to go, the more important writing skills are to get there. Probably nothing else can reveal your weaknesses more clearly than poor writing. People judge you on your ability to write your thoughts effectively and correctly" (Lussier, 2005, p. 160). Even those in prominent positions in the sport industry must be able to communicate with words. A legendary television sports executive penned the following note—which was found in the archives of the Jack Nicklaus Museum in Columbus, Ohio—to Jack Nicklaus after the golfing great won the Masters in 1986: "Dear Jack, Not since the United States hockey team in 1980 has anything in sports given me such a wonderful sense of satisfaction and sheer enjoyment as watching you win your sixth Masters on Sunday. You've always been a credit to the game of golf and a hell of a guy, and it's wonderfully rewarding to see something like this happen. I am delighted you're going to be associated with us, and I look forward to seeing you in the future. Kindest regards, Roone Arledge." Arledge—despite his status as the pioneer of *Monday Night Football*, groundbreaking Olympics coverage, innovative technological enhancements in sport broadcasting, and the *Wide World of Sports*—still took the time to write a note. As Rick Pitino, the basketball coach and former president of the Boston Celtics, noted, "The message you want to give is that the person you're dealing with is important and the best way to do this is to deliver the message yourself. Pick up the phone yourself. Write the note yourself. Write the memo yourself. Deal with it yourself, especially if you want this message to be accurate" (Pitino & Reynolds, 2000, p. 22).

The demand for sport employees with strong writing skills has increased with the increased use of e-mail in sport organizations. "The inability to create a clear and coherent document has hindered countless business careers. Even something as apparently innocuous as an internal e-mail can hurt you and your organization," noted Deborah J. Barrett, business communication scholar and author of *Leadership Communication* (2006). "Once you are in a leadership position, your documents become powerful and can change the entire direction of your company. By knowing the importance of every document you create, you begin to appreciate the importance of making

Writing is one of the most used forms of communication in the sport industry. University of Louisville men's basketball coach Rick Pitino (left) might use verbal communication more often than written, and SID Kenny Klein (seated far right) may use written communication more often than spoken. Both use multiple forms of communication to be effective. As Pitino says, "Pick up the phone yourself. Write the note yourself. Write the memo yourself. Deal with it yourself, especially if you want this message to be accurate."

sure you approach the writing of all documents with utmost care, from the simplest e-mails to the most complicated reports" (p. 46).

Potentially Interactive Formats: Verbal, Video, and Poster Presentations

The **potentially interactive** formats—which can be delivered to an audience with or without interaction—include verbal presentations, video presentations, and poster presentations. For those in management and leadership positions in particular, oral communication is the overwhelming communication choice. As Barrett (2006) noted, "Much of the 70 to 90 percent of their time that managers spend communicating is spent in conversations or in presenting, either talking to others one-on-one or speaking in groups or to groups" (p. 116). "All employees should be skillful in oral communication in its various forms, because oral skills are important on a daily basis," noted Kelly and colleagues (1989). "As people move up in an organization, their oral skills become more and more important" (p. 39). Oral communication, according to Lussier (2005), "is the appropriate medium for delegating tasks, coaching, disciplining, instructing, sharing information, answering questions, checking progress toward objectives, developing and maintaining human relations, and interviewing" (p. 159).

Oral communication in sport organizations includes a variety of formats. The most frequently used oral communication is the one-on-one delivery (and receipt) of messages. As with all the forms of oral communication, this form can be one-way or two-way (interactive). Personal oral communication is generally face to face, over the telephone, or Web based. These interactions, which may be impromptu or planned, are "one of the most powerful forms of communication [and] can facilitate insight, understanding, and new knowledge" (Torres et al., 2005, p. 30). Although the telephone is useful for getting information quickly or checking on progress, it should not be used for disciplining employees or other such personal matters. These are best done

in face-to-face settings. For more information on interpersonal communication, refer to the previous chapter.

Other forms of oral communication in sport organizations are meetings (e.g., committee, departmental, executive), interviews (e.g., hiring, performance appraisals, counseling), internal (e.g., to employees) and external (e.g., to audiences at trade shows, conventions, media) presentations and speeches, and training sessions. Just as Barrett (2006) noted for traditional businesses, the common types of presentations in sport organizations are roundtable presentations, stand-up presentations, and impromptu presentations. The roundtable presentation involves sitting at a table and interacting with the audience members as opposed to standing in front of the audience. Therefore, it has the potential to be very interactive. The stand-up presentation is an extemporaneous delivery that allows an individual to present information to and establish rapport with an audience. The impromptu presentation is the one in which someone is called on to talk without warning. These presentations can range from a request for an update from a superior to a request for comment from a media personality.

Presentations in large-group meetings and small-group meetings can be very interactive or one sided, depending on the setting and purpose of the meeting. Meetings can range from informal get-togethers to more formal meetings that involve coordinating activities, delegating tasks, and resolving conflicts. A leader needs to be able to communicate in a variety of settings to effectively run a sport organization. "We have mandatory weekly staff meetings," notes Kelly Krauskopf, a former executive with Host Communications sport marketing agency in Dallas. "I think this is important for the once-a-week in-person discussion. The rest of the time spent is a lot of e-mail communication."

In addition to the unmediated forms of oral communication in sport organizations, there are mediated forms of oral communication (e.g., telephone calls, telephone conference calls, video messaging and conferencing). Videos allow the audience to see the verbal

Meetings, Meetings, Meetings: Survival Tips

Some individuals, such as industrialist Simon Ramo, have attended more than 40,000 meetings in their careers.

In his book, *Meetings, Meetings and More Meetings: Getting Things Done When People Are Involved* (2005), Ramo noted that those who call meetings should

- be prepared,
- know the subject and goals of the meeting,
- determine which individuals to invite based on their ability to contribute,
- keep objectives in mind throughout the meeting, and
- be ready to move discussions along by tactfully and gently interrupting those who might dominate the meeting.

For those who doze off at meetings, Ramo suggested that they should pinch their cheek or thigh to stay awake and if they fall asleep, the best way to recover when you are called on is to say "Why?" as opposed to "What?"

Obviously, it is best not only to stay awake but also to listen. "It is a good idea to listen and pay attention to what the speaker is saying," states Kathryn Rogers. "I tend to bring a note pad with me to all meetings, so that I can take notes to keep my mind engaged in what the speaker is talking about."

To ensure that people will stay awake and listen when you are chairing a meeting or making a presentation, the most effective way to make the event a success is to include audience interaction as well as visuals such as slides, transparencies, handouts, or flip charts. The visuals are particularly important when the sport communicator is conveying information on a topic that is complex or specialized.

---

and nonverbal communication of the presenter. Similar to video presentations, live broadcasts convey immediacy and can be done through an in-house network, satellite hookup, or mass media (Hattersley & McJannett, 2005).

"So much of good leadership rests on your ability to get your message across," noted Pitino and Reynolds (2000). "The ability to communicate effectively is one of your best weapons. From establishing your vision at the very first meeting to constantly reinforcing that vision at every opportunity, good communication is key" (p. 26). To effectively engage in oral communication in sport, communicators need to work on overcoming their fear of public speaking. "Regardless if you are the CEO of a major company, there are always some nerves when speaking in front of large groups or important clients," notes Kathryn Rogers, former executive director of the Gary Player Foundation. "The best advice is to be well prepared and know your topic, so that regardless of the audience you can get back on track quickly if fear starts to overwhelm your thought process. I like to think of the crowd as my friends or family; that calms my nerves and forms an immediate relationship in my mind." In the end, however, there are few leaders who are exceptional orators (Baldoni, 2003). Rather, leaders are individuals who "lead in thoughts, words, and deeds, and in that, all are exceptional leadership communicators" (p. 2). Therefore, although it is important to always work to improve your oration skills, failure to become a great orator is not a fatal blow to your career in the sport industry.

Most Interactive Formats: Working Sessions, Synchronous Electronic Communication, and Personal Discussions

The **most interactive** formats include working sessions, synchronous electronic communication (e.g., chat rooms, teleconferences, videoconferences, Web conferences), and personal discussions (e.g., over the telephone, via the Internet, in person). "I make myself accessible to my staff 24/7 by either Nextel, e-mail, phone, or my favorite—in person," noted high school athletic director Michael Stutzke (Pedersen, 2004b, p. Z50). The approachability and visibility with such an interactive approach, when combined with trustworthy and supportive actions, help to maintain open communication lines and a culture of fairness and equity. As noted previously, there are other highly interactive formats besides personal discussions.

Individuals in organizations are often put into working sessions that encourage collaboration, discussion, and often decision making by the participants. Individuals in sport organizations often find that it is impossible or impractical to have a face-to-face meeting with certain stakeholders. This is the result of separation by geography. For instance, when the general manager of the Los Angeles Dodgers is attending a business meeting in Hawaii, he still might need to disseminate information, seek input, or participate in communication for any number of reasons with his subordinates based in California. Such communication often involves the fully interactive format of synchronous electronic communication. The general manager and the other participants communicate in real time without being in the same physical location. An example of real-time office communication through Web conferencing is "Live Meeting" from Microsoft. This media-rich toolkit is a meeting solution that allows participants to communicate with each other without having to leave their desks. The interactive tools offered by this system are integrated into the office's computer system and productivity applications. These tools allow for sport industry personnel to work on projects, brainstorm ideas, edit files, collaborate on whiteboards, and negotiate with clients with just a personal computer and an Internet connection. As such technological advances make their way into the sport industry, the highly interactive formats will improve productivity and increase efficiency in all communication. In addition to working sessions and synchronous electronic communication, personal discussions between two individuals fit into the most interactive format category because they are interactive by nature.

APPRECIATING LEADERSHIP COMMUNICATION IN SPORT

An integral component of effective communication in sport organizations is leadership. More than a half century ago, scholars noted that leaders were responsible for developing and maintaining a communication system (e.g., Chester Barnard's 1938 book, *The Functions of the Executive*). The same holds true today. "A key element of organizational communications is the messages from the leader," noted Baldoni (2003, p. 2). Included in this section are examinations of sport leadership, leadership communication in sport, and sport leadership communication styles. There are several fundamental elements of and competency requirements for effective communication of leaders in sport organizations. These are important for organizational performance and career success. They include leadership attitudes, behaviors, styles, and strategies that help sport management professionals communicate effectively. The goal of this section is to help readers—and future sport management leaders—competently share, persuade, and present their ideas to others. The "definite dozen" is what Pat Summitt called "a blueprint for winning" and "a formula for success" (Summitt & Jenkins, 1998, p. 7). The dozen statements make up the principles that Summitt and her teams have followed for 3 decades. On the list at number 4—following respect, responsibility, and loyalty—is, "Learn to be a great communicator" (Summit & Jenkins, 1998, p. 8). That is our hope for each of you. Certain key organizational and interpersonal communication skills can support and enhance effective leadership in sport organizations. The ability to use these skills to create commitment to organizational vision, goals, and workplace culture is a specific focus. Although Collins (2001) appropriately advised that we place leadership in its proper perspective and not attribute everything (i.e., organizational success or failure) to leadership, the importance of leadership communication in sport cannot be overstated. As Bobby Bowden noted, "Everything that occurs within an organization reflects back upon its leader"

(Bowden & Bowden, 2001, p. 11). Therefore, this section covers the theory and application of leadership communication in sport organizations.

Definition of Sport Leadership

Thousands of articles and books are published on the subject of leadership. The sport industry has its share of leadership publications. As Jeremy S. Jordan and Aubrey Kent (2005) noted, "Researchers in the field of sport management have likewise been enamored with the concept of leadership, whether it concerns how coaches deal with their athletes, how Athletic Directors motivate their employees, or how people create successful sport companies" (p. 47). The thousands of publications on leadership have revealed hundreds of definitions of the word. In fact, most individuals have their own thoughts of what leadership means to them. For instance, if you go to a sport organization and ask 10 of its employees to define leadership, you will probably get 10 unique definitions. Some would say that leadership is an act that brings about a response or is the art of influencing or persuading. Others might think that leadership is simply the way one motivates subordinates, how one coordinates people and activities, or the approach one takes to guiding and directing the behavior of people or groups. What the many definitions reveal is that there are many types, attributes, and perceptions of effective leadership. The hundreds of leadership definitions are a result of the fact that there is not one standard leader.

Regardless of the definition of leadership, an integral part of leadership is communication. In their analysis of sport organizations, Jordan and Kent (2005) noted, "The vast majority of a leader's time is spent communicating with others" (p. 51). For effective leadership, however, there must be effective speaking, listening, writing, and reading on the part of the leader. "Effective leadership requires effective communication," noted Daniel

Popular Definitions of Leadership

Here's your textbook's definition of sport leadership:

Sport leadership is the communication in and through sport that influences the attitudes and behaviors of others to meet shared group goals and needs.

Sports leaders on and off the field of play have their own unique definitions:

- Kelly Krauskopf, the general manager of the Indiana Fever, noted at the beginning of this chapter, "Leadership is the ability to develop a vision and path for your organization and then the ability to motivate and influence your troops to reach the goal."
- Pat Williams, the general manager of the Philadelphia 76ers when they won the NBA championship in 1983, reduced leadership to one word when he said, "Ultimately, that's what leadership is all about: Winning" (Williams & Denny, 2002, p. 215).

- Bobby Bowden, the winningest football coach in major college football, stated in his book, *The Bowden Way: 50 Years of Leadership Wisdom*, "A leader is someone people look up to. A leader is someone people choose to follow because they believe in him" (Bowden & Bowden, 2001, p. 26).
- Yet another leadership angle is provided by Ulice Payne. "Leadership is helping people do what they think they can't," noted Payne, who in 2002 became the first African-American team president in MLB history when the Milwaukee Brewers named him the president and CEO. "It's about unleashing their energy" (Stanford-Blair & Dickmann, 2005, p. 97).
- Mitt Romney, the past president and CEO of the Salt Lake Olympic Committee, noted, "Leaders establish vision and values that motivate and create unity of purpose" (Romney, 2004, p. 20).

Covell, Sharianne Walker, Julie Siciliano, and Peter W. Hess in their book *Managing Sports Organizations: Responsibility for Performance* (2003). "Every leadership task—from providing direction, support, and encouragement to providing inspiration and meaning—can be accomplished only through effective communication" (p. 292). Effective communication by a leader—communication improves organizational and individual performances—can be best understood by viewing it as a continuous cycle made up of three major components that a leader participates in daily (Baldoni, 2003).

1. A leader needs to **develop** her leadership message (e.g., vision statement, mission statement, calls for change or action). In this step, the leader determines what she wants to say or do and selects the proper communication channel.

2. The leader needs to **deliver** the leadership message. In this step, the leader takes the message and proclaims it to an audience. Without knowing the audience and its perceptions, the leader will fail in her delivery of the message.

3. The leader needs to **sustain** her leadership message. In this step, the leader keeps the message alive and meaningful through feedback, reiteration, and coaching.

Because of their symbiotic nature, the words *leadership* and *communication* have been combined into one phrase by some scholars. "Leadership communication," according to Barrett (2006), "is the controlled, purposeful transfer of meaning by which leaders influence a single person, a group, an organization, or a community. Leadership communication uses the full range of communication skills and resources to overcome interferences and to create and deliver messages that guide, direct, motivate, or inspire others to action" (p. 5). The definition of sport leadership that we propose reflects this connectedness. It is a slightly modified version of the communication-driven definition of leadership offered

by Hackman and Johnson (2004). We believe that **sport leadership** is the communication in and through sport that influences the attitudes and behaviors of others to meet shared group goals and needs. This definition makes it clear that at the core of sport leadership is communication. "People who can't communicate can't lead," noted Ulice Payne, the chair of the board of directors for the Bradley Center Sports and Entertainment Corporation (Stanford-Blair & Dickmann, 2005, p. 102). As Barrett (2006) noted, *"Effective leadership depends on effective communication*. It is through effective communication that leaders guide, direct, motivate, and inspire. Good communication skills enable, foster, and create the understanding and trust necessary to encourage others to follow a leader" (p. 3). Baldoni (2003) concurred with this by stating, "Every successful leader is at heart an effective leadership communicator." He supported his argument by adding that leaders "have a personal leadership style that is rooted in communications as a means of accomplishing their vision, mission, and goals as a leader for the good of their organization and for themselves as contributors to the organization" (p. 2). These communication styles are examined next.

Styles of Sport Leadership Communication

You can take advantage of opportunities to advance in sport leadership positions by knowing and applying what effective leaders do when they communicate with followers. Thus, it is crucial to understand the behavior approaches or communication styles that leaders exhibit toward those they lead. The way a leader behaves toward and interacts and communicates with followers is her **sport leadership communication style**. As Witherspoon (1997) noted, "The way leadership and communication styles are integrated in the process of leader-follower interaction is an important subject of study" (p. 50). It is important because the degree to which this integration takes places has a direct relationship on the effectiveness of the process. "A leader's communication style may reflect a philosophical belief about human nature or may simply be a strategy designed to maximize outcomes in a given situation," stated Hackman and Johnson (2004). "The communication style a leader selects contributes to the success or failure of any attempt to exert influence" (p. 36).

The organizational context, specific situation, and follower capability and perceptions dictate the most effective communication style for a sports leader. As Jordan and Kent (2005) pointed out, "The best advice for leaders is to understand your own predominant communication style, but then also endeavor to match your communication style with the situation and with those with whom you are trying to communicate" (p. 52). Professional basketball player Grant Hill illustrated this when he commented on different approaches that his college coach, Mike Krzyzewski, had with his teams. "Every team I was on over my four years at Duke, he coached differently," noted Hill (Krzyzewski & Phillips, 2000, p. 3). The degree to which sports leaders provide supportive and directive behaviors varies depending on contextual, situational, and subordinate influences.

Task-Oriented and Relationship-Oriented Communication

Sport leadership communication styles consist of two dimensions: task-oriented communication and relationship-oriented communication.

When a sports leader closely supervises a performance and tells a subordinate what to do, she is exhibiting **task-oriented communication**. Some of the other labels for task-oriented communication include task behavior, production-oriented communication, initiating structure, Theory X management, and concern for production. Task-oriented communication involves such activities as having a greater interest in completing the task than in the people completing it, disseminating information, often ignoring feelings, exhibiting rigid communication, interrupting others, demanding, and focusing on information relevant to task and productivity.

When the sports leader is not closely supervising the performance of subordinates and works to listen and provide a supportive, trusting, and respectful working environment, she is exhibiting **relationship-oriented communication.** Some of the other labels for relationship-oriented communication include relationship behavior, concern for people, employee-oriented communication, Theory Y management, and consideration. Relationship-oriented communication involves such activities as being concerned with interpersonal relationships, soliciting opinions, recognizing feelings, engaging in open communication, listening to others, and making requests.

Four Situational Supervisory Styles

Depending on the amount of emphasis placed on the dimensions during the communicative process, the task-oriented communication and the relationship-oriented communication are described as either high or low. Therefore, there are four situational supervisory styles (see figure 6.3) in the communication process (Hackman & Johnson, 2004; Lussier, 2005).

Autocratic Communication Style

When sports leaders exhibit a high task-oriented communication (i.e., high directive behavior) and low relationship-oriented communication (i.e., low supportive behavior) combination, they are demonstrating an **autocratic communication style.** "My leadership style is more of a service style than control style," noted Mike Lindgren, a high school athletic director. "Most of the time, if I try to just stay out of their way, support them when needed and let them coach, that is all the motivation they need to be successful" (Pedersen, 2004b, p. Z20). Lindgren's approach is contradictory to the autocratic communication style. The autocratic or authoritarian communication style is evident when a leader regulates policy, procedures, and behavior to maintain strict control over followers. Some of the communication patterns of this style of leadership are setting goals individually, engaging in one-way or downward communication, controlling discussions, setting policy and procedures unilaterally, dominating interactions, directing

High task-oriented communication

Autocratic style

" A dictator-style leader has all the answers and no questions. This kind of boss demands performance according to unbending and unchanging personal ideas. And, it can work. However, a leader who incorporates the creativity of others makes it work better."
(Wooden, 2005, p. 28)
—*John Wooden, former basketball coach*

Consultative style

"I am a servant leader. As a former student-athlete and former coach, I don't ask anything of my coaches or expect anything of our student-athletes that I didn't ask of myself or expect of myself. For example, I understand what it means to return from a trip and have to get up and go to class...I expect that of our student-athletes."
—*Carla Green Williams, college athletic administrator*

Low relationship-oriented communication

High relationship-oriented communication

Laissez-faire style

"The team lacked discipline under Pete (Rose). He was too nice. He didn't have many rules and those he had were not enforced. The younger players may have been in awe of him until they saw what was going on—and that changed quickly. People took advantage of him."
(Nightingale,1990, p. 8)
—*Rod Oester, former second baseman for the Cincinnati Reds*

Participatory style

"Communicating is not just about giving great speeches. It's about allowing others to express themselves...The more I have listened to our players, the better I have known them and understood them." (Summitt, 1998, p. 87)
—*Pat Summitt, basketball coach*

Low task-oriented communication

Figure 6.3 Situational supervisory styles in sport communication.

tasks personally, providing infrequent positive feedback, rewarding obedience and punishing mistakes, exhibiting poor listening skills, and using conflict for personal gain (Hackman & Johnson, 2004). Input and responses from subordinates are not solicited or valued.

Therefore, communication that is autocratic in nature generally has an expectation of compliance. Those who are on the receiving end are expected to comply with the communication. Furthermore, the autocratic communication style is generally one sided. This means that the communication often involves detailed instructions to, close supervision of, and limited input from those to whom the message is directed. Pat Summitt (1998) explained the autocratic communication style by stating, "Often a strong, dominant leader is the worst listener. He or she is too busy telling everyone else what to do and what to think." She then offered this advice, "While you are listening to someone, don't just take in the words. Study the speaker. Be aware of the speaker's voice and mannerisms. Notice what his effect is on you. Become aware of your own voice and body language, too. Are you dismissive of someone without realizing it? Do you project vulnerability or a loser's limp?" (Summitt & Jenkins, 1998, p. 87). A recent study assessed the communication skills of 250 entrepreneurial leaders. The study, commissioned by *Inc. Magazine*, placed individuals into three categories based on whether they persuade through expressing ideas, criticizing, or supporting. The leaders—often stereotyped as hard-charging bullies who have an autocratic communication style—scored higher than 82% of the population on their ability to express encouragement and support. McFarland (2005) noted that the findings show that in assessing communication skills, "CEOs succeed by helping other people—their employees, partners, investors, suppliers—become successful themselves" (p. 159).

Consultative Communication Style

When sports leaders exhibit a high task-oriented communication (i.e., high directive) and high relationship-oriented communication (i.e., high supportive) combination, they are demonstrating a **consultative communication style.** Although the sports leader who uses this style of communication is interested in determining if the subordinate is interested in the message (e.g., explaining why the task should be completed, answering questions, showing empathy) and accepts her influence, there is little openness with regard to the subordinate's acceptance of the task itself (i.e., sports leader has final say). Therefore, throughout the project the instructions are specific, tasks are explained, and performance is overseen.

Participative Communication Style

When sports leaders exhibit a low task-oriented communication (i.e., low directive) and high relationship-oriented communication (i.e., high supportive behavior) combination, they are demonstrating a **participative communication style.** This participative or democratic style is evident when interaction between followers and the leader is encouraged and occurs through supportive communication. Some of the communication patterns of this style of leadership are involving followers in setting goals, engaging in two-way communication, facilitating discussions, soliciting input, focusing on interactions, providing suggestions and positive feedback, rewarding good work while punishing only as a last resort, and exhibiting effective listening skills (Hackman & Johnson, 2004). According to John Wooden, "Cooperation—the sharing of ideas, information, creativity, responsibilities, and tasks—is a priority of good leadership" (Wooden & Jamison, 2005, p. 29). The sports leader uses this style of communication with subordinates who are highly capable and who can provide information. Subordinates are consulted to determine how to solve a

Legendary basketball coach John Wooden—who had a record of 885-203 in 40 years of coaching—is still an outstanding communicator. The most successful coach in college basketball history explains his participative communication style by stating, "Cooperation—the sharing of ideas, information, creativity, responsibilities, and tasks—is a priority of good leadership." Wooden's UCLA Bruins set all-time records with four perfect 30-0 seasons, 88 consecutive victories, 38 straight NCAA tournament victories, 20 PAC-10 championships, and 10 national championships, including seven in a row.

problem or reach an objective. They are also encouraged and supported throughout the process. Communication is open (two-way), directions are general, and the relationship between the communicators is helpful and supportive.

Laissez-Faire Communication Style

When sports leaders exhibit a low task-oriented communication (low directive) and low relationship-oriented communication (low supportive) behavior, they are demonstrating a **laissez-faire communication style.** This style, also referred to as nonleadership or avoiding leadership, is used when a sports leader accepts the messages and decisions of subordinates and conveys to them that they are in charge. After informing subordinates of the task and answering any questions, the leader provides little direction because the followers are highly motivated and highly capable. Some of the communication patterns of this style of leadership are allowing followers free rein to set their goals and set policy and procedures, engaging in superficial communication, avoiding discussions, avoiding interactions, providing suggestions only when asked, providing infrequent feedback, and avoiding offering rewards or punishments (Hackman & Johnson, 2004).

Leadership Grid

Blake and McCanse (1991) created the "leadership grid," which plots five communication styles based on the degree to which leaders exhibit task-oriented (concern for production) and relationship-oriented (concern for people) behaviors:

- The impoverished leader (low concern for task, low concern for relationship)
- The authority–compliance leader (high concern for task, little concern for relationship)
- The middle-of-the-road leader (adequate concern for both task and relationship)
- The country club leader (low concern for task, high concern for relationship)
- The team leadership approach (high concern for both task and relationship)

The team leadership approach is considered the most effective because work is accomplished through relationships that are built on trust and respect, which are the result of interdependence and a push for a common objective in the sport organization. This style results in increased productivity, increased profitability, effective communication, and positive relationships. Kelly Krauskopf, the chief operating officer and general manager of the Indiana Fever, illustrates the team leadership approach. "Since we operate as a small unit, I need to have strong people and I urge them to take a proactive approach in their respective areas," notes Krauskopf. "It is less of an 'org' chart approach although we have reporting structures for clarity. I try to give staff members leadership roles in their areas so that they feel ownership of the goals we are trying to achieve." Ulice Payne concurred. "You have to give up power and share it," noted Payne, a former collegiate basketball player and baseball executive. "If people take ownership in something, they will lead. It's the toughest thing (ownership), but when it is not there, it's only a job. It's like the difference between owning a house and renting. You will do the extra upkeep if it's yours" (Stanford-Blair & Dickmann, 2005, p. 95).

Those in sport leadership positions generally embrace and exhibit one leadership communication style. This is their dominant style that they use in most of their interactions with people. In addition to having one dominant leadership communication style, leaders generally have a backup style, or second orientation. Regardless of the style that a leader exhibits, leadership is a requirement for success in sport organizations. This is confirmed by Pat Williams, the senior vice president of the Orlando Magic. "Every team, company, club, organization," noted Williams, "needs leadership. Whenever even two or three people gather together around a task or a purpose, there must be direction. If not, the task won't get done and the people will fail" (2002, p. 2).

Four Variables That Affect Leadership Style

After understanding the various styles of leadership communication, people in sport organizations next need to consider the variables that affect leadership communication selection. Although sports leaders "may change their communication styles to accommodate organizational context, specific situational demands, or to adapt to individual listeners," (Witherspoon, 1997, p. 68), they should consider four specific variables when determining which communication style to use: time, information, acceptance, and capability.

• Regarding **time**, the sports leader needs to determine if there is time for two-way communication. If there is such time, the sports leader can use the consultative, participative, or laissez-faire communication style. If there is no available time, the autocratic communication style is used.

• With **information**, the sports leader needs to determine if she has enough information for communicating, making a decision, or taking action. The sports leader can use the autocratic approach if there is no need for information, the consultative approach if only some of the information is known, and the participative or laissez-faire communication style if she has little information.

• Regarding **acceptance**, the sports leader needs to determine if the follower will simply accept the message (use the autocratic approach), will accept with some reluctance (use the consultative), or will reject it (use participative or laissez-faire to gain acceptance). As Pat Summitt noted, "Each situation requires a different tone. We all know people who yell at every opportunity. They yell in the office, at home, in a restaurant. After a while, we tune them out. Too much of one thing tends to dull your listener's sensibilities. If all you ever do is yell, then you will be heard less and less. That's why, sometimes, saying nothing at all can be just as powerful" (Summitt & Jenkins, 1998, p. 66).

• Regarding **capability**, the sports leader needs to determine both ability and willingness (i.e., motivation). The sports leader can use the autocratic style if there is low capability (unable, unwilling), the consultative style if there is moderate capability (moderate ability and motivation), the participative style if there is high capability (high ability but low confidence and motivation), and the laissez-faire style if there is outstanding capability (very capable and highly motivated).

As Lussier (2005) noted, "Successful managers understand different styles of communication and select communication styles based on the situation" (p. 191).

CHAPTER WRAP-UP

Summary

A sport organization is a group of people working in or through sport to achieve one or more objectives. We began the chapter by looking at the three essential elements of a sport organization, of which one is communication. Organizational communication in sport is the process in which messages are created, exchanged, interpreted, and stored within a system of human relationships in sport. In particular, three features of the sport organization—its formal structure, informal networks, and culture—are influenced by and influence the communication flow. Formal communication in sport organizations is the intraorganizational or official communication of the organization because it flows upward and downward according to the sport organization's chain of command. The informal communication in sport organizations is the unofficial, lateral, multidirectional, and grapevine communication. Similar to formal structures and informal networks, the culture of a sport organization—the sport organization's own way of life, predominant beliefs, goals, behaviors, customs—is influenced by and influences communication. A sport organization creates, shares, and alters its culture through verbal and nonverbal communication.

We next examined the forms of communication in sport organizations. To help with the understanding of this topic, we categorized the forms into least interactive formats (i.e., involving written forms—e-mails, short communications, text messages, faxes, Web site communication, posters, notices, reports—that can be delivered to an audience without verbal or face-to-face interaction), potentially interactive formats (e.g., presentations and meetings delivered to an audience with or without interaction), and most interactive formats (e.g., working sessions, synchronous electronic communication, personal discussions). Because leadership is crucial to effective communication in sport organizations, we finished the chapter by examining this topic. We first defined sport leadership (the communication in and through sport that influences the attitudes and behaviors of others to meet shared group goals and needs) and then examined sport leadership communication styles (i.e., autocratic, consultative, participative, and laissez-faire). After looking at the dominant and backup styles of leadership communication, we concluded the chapter with an examination of the four variables—time, information, acceptance, and capability—that affect leadership communication selection.

Review Questions

1. What are the definitions for a sport organization and organizational communication in sport?

2. What are the three major elements and the three features of a sport organization?

3. How does the structure of a sport organization affect its formal communication?

4. What are the five principles of a sport organization?

5. What are the directions in which communication flows in a sport organization?

6. What types of communication are involved in informal sport communication?

7. How does the culture of a sport organization affect the communication in the organization? How is the culture affected by the communication?

8. What are the three categories of communication forms in sport organizations?

9. Effective communication by leaders is a continuous cycle. What are the components of this cycle?

10. What is a sport leadership communication style and what are the two dimensions that influence this style?

Discussion Questions

1. Compared with the other two elements, how important is communication as an element of the sport organization?

2. Which of the three categories of communication forms is used the most in sport organizations?

3. How are interorganizational communication in sport and intraorganizational communication in sport similar?

4. How are interorganizational communication and intraorganizational communication in sport different?

5. How has the structure of some sport organizations evolved over the years, and how has this evolution affected the communication within these organizations?

6. Why is sport leadership included in a chapter on organizational communication in sport?

7. What is your definition of sport leadership?

8. When have you demonstrated a task-oriented communication style? A relationship-oriented communication style? Which was most effective?

9. Of the four situational supervisory styles of leadership communication, which would you consider your dominant style? Your backup style?

10. How often do you consider the four variables when determining an effective communication style?

Group Activities

1. Divide the class into two or more groups. Each group is assigned a sport organization. Determine the predominant intraorganizational communication activities and the predominant interorganizational communication activities of that organization. For each organization, determine the formal communication, informal communication, culture, categories of communication, and leadership communication styles.

2. As a class, come up with a list of five leaders of sport organizations. These can be international, national, regional, or local leaders. Divide the class into groups; discuss as a group the various leaders' communication styles. Determine a sport leadership communication style for each of the leaders and then share your findings with the class.

Individual Exercises

1. Select a sport organization and determine its organizational chart. What is the chain of command in the organization? Identify a couple departments within the sport organization. What is the span of management for each departmental manager? Is authority in the sport organization centralized or decentralized?

2. Reflect on your career ambitions: Where do you hope to be in 10 years? Make a list of five people who have jobs similar to what you are hoping to have. Contact these five people and ask them to define the term *sport leadership*. What are the similarities and differences in their definitions? How is communication intertwined with their definitions?

3. Describe your sport leadership communication style. How do you lead? Which style do you like to be under when you're a follower? What about when you're a leader?

Internet Sites for Additional Learning

Baldoni Consulting: www.johnbaldoni.com/directions/thoughts5.html

Indiana Fever (WNBA): www.wnba.com/fever/

John Wooden: http://uclabruins.collegesports.com/sports/m-baskbl/spec-rel/ucla-wooden-page.html

Leadership: www.nwlink.com/~donclark/leader/leader.html

Pat Summitt (Tennessee): www.coachsummitt.com/

Sports Leader: www.bst.org.uk/Home/Default.aspx

Sports Leadership Institute: www.adelphi.edu/communityservices/sli/

CHAPTER 7

Sport Publishing and Print Sport Communication

LEARNING OBJECTIVES

▶ To consider the various types of sport publishing and print sport communication entities within the Strategic Sport Communication Model (SSCM)

▶ To understand sport publishing and print sport communication

▶ To become acquainted with the growth and functions of newspaper sports sections

▶ To become aware of the professionals in sport publishing and print sport communication

▶ To recognize the activities associated with sports books, wire services, sports magazines, and the affiliation between print, publishing, and the Internet

▶ To learn about the activities, qualifications, principles, and pressures of sport journalism

PROFILE OF A SPORT COMMUNICATOR

Joanne C. Gerstner

She is one of those rare individuals who determined as a child what she wanted to do for the rest of her life. The seed was planted when she began to notice that women could make a career in the print sport media. "I saw that women were writing for the sports section in my local paper, the *Detroit News,*" says Joanne C. Gerstner, a sportswriter for the *Detroit News.* "Sports journalism is the only thing I've wanted to do since I was in third grade."

Gerstner sums up her passion for sport journalism in five words, "love sports, love to write." This combination has led her to encounter many of the aspects of the print sport media that are examined in this chapter. From niche sports magazines and national newspapers to independent publications and corporate chains, Gerstner has built a career as an editor and writer for a variety of print media outlets. Her career progression commenced in the early 1990s when she earned a bachelor's degree in journalism from Oakland University. After working at the *Flint Journal* and Quarton Publishing (where she was an assistant editor for NBA *Inside Stuff* magazine and *PGA Magazine)* she moved to Chicago and enrolled in the prestigious Medill School of Journalism at Northwestern University. Since her graduation with a master's in journalism in 1995 and for the majority of her career, Gerstner has worked for the Gannett Company. Her involvement with this international news and information conglomerate has taken her from the *Cincinnati Enquirer, Lansing State Journal,* and *USA Today* to where she is today at the *Detroit News.* In August 2005, Gannett sold the *Detroit News* to another large mass media corporation, MediaNews Group.

Gerstner has been an athlete from as far back as she can remember. Her involvement in highly competitive sports culminated with her par-

Photo courtesy of *The Detroit News*

ticipation as a varsity intercollegiate tennis player. As a sportswriter, her interest in and knowledge of sports go far beyond tennis. "My job varies depending on the time of year," says Gerstner. Although her primary duties involve covering professional basketball (Detroit Pistons), her byline regularly appears on feature articles and stories about hockey (Detroit Red Wings), intercollegiate football and basketball (University of Michigan and Michigan State University), golf, tennis, and Olympic sports. "I literally do anything and everything at the *(Detroit) News.*"

Although her primary responsibility is to cover teams and write stories for the newspaper, Gerstner is also required to communicate with a wide variety of internal and external publics. In doing so, Gerstner communicates with various stakeholders (e.g., athletes, managers, colleagues, fans) through various means (e.g., online chats, television appearances, radio interviews). She uses her strong verbal, writing, and interpersonal skills to be an effective reporter. "A typical day has me answering and sending dozens of e-mails, talking live to sources, and making phone calls to sources," says Gerstner. "I talk to coworkers at the office via cell and e-mail and in person."

Joanne C. Gerstner has risen to the top of her profession—including a presidency of the Association for Women in Sports Media (AWSM)—through education, experience, talent, and the development of numerous communication skills. "I have been blessed to go to Australia for the Olympics, cover Stanley Cup and NBA Finals, go behind the scenes and meet a lot of very interesting people," said Gerstner. "And most of all, my job lets me be a storyteller, something I love the most. I think the best characters and stories are in sports, allowing a writer to be creative in ways that other sections would never allow."

The next three chapters cover the second component of the Strategic Sport Communication Model (SSCM)—the sport mass media. The word *media,* at its basic level, refers to a variety of means through which communication takes place. The words *mass media* denote the segment of media that is focused on reaching the masses or large numbers of people. Mass media come in various types (e.g., newspaper, radio, television, the Internet, and other new media platforms), and different modes of delivery are used (e.g., print, radio signals, the World Wide Web). The roles and functions of these mass media are quite varied and oftentimes include

- informing (e.g., presenting newsworthy stories),
- creating (e.g., producing a story or event),
- influencing (e.g., reporting that results in a change of mind-set or action),
- entertaining (e.g., providing a diversion for people to hear, see, read, or experience),
- telling (e.g., publishing commentary and opinions),
- delivering (e.g., bringing the message to the audience), and
- reinforcing (e.g., supporting cultural values).

Although the mass media cover a multitude of areas and beats such as national and local news, politics and religion, science and entertainment, and business and finance, one of the major roles of the mass media is to cover sport.

The phrase *sport mass media* involves sports reporting and commentary on sport and the various associated activities that surround and the influences that shape sport. In addition to covering the sport industry, the sport mass media often reinforce and reflect the institution of sport and sometimes they even help to shape sport. Sure, there are plenty of sports that fail to receive media coverage. Although sports are not dependent on the media for their survival, most sports that do not receive much attention from the media often struggle to attract fans or see financial success. The inability to make it as a mediated sport—or at least a television mediated sport—directly affects the awareness levels of a specific sport. A lack of media coverage results in a lack of awareness, and this can make it difficult for a sport entity to achieve sustained success. The National Hockey League (NHL) and its low television rights revenue provide an appropriate example. This affects the fan base, the salaries, the promotion of the sport, and, most important, the financial viability of the league. It could be said that the sport media are dependent on sport and sport is dependent on the media: It is truly a symbiotic relationship. This intertwining of sport and the mass media occurs across the United States and around the world. "Here is the potent formula behind the booming sports economy: A global business partnership between the sports industry and the sports press," explained Soren Schultz orgensen (2005). "Together they have created an industry that excites and involves young and old all over the world and in Europe has an estimated turnover of 165 billion Euro (6 percent of Europe's total GNP) and a turnover of 213 billion dollars in the US—annually" (p. 1).

Although at certain times and at different levels one needs the other more, both sport and the media need each other to some degree. The sport media rely on sports to help fill programming schedules and newspaper columns, to sell advertising, to increase profits through higher ratings, to improve circulation figures, and to increase Web hits, and the sport industry depends on the media to provide visibility (e.g., coverage of a track meet), promotion and marketing (e.g., preview of a local hockey game), credibility (e.g., what is covered is often viewed as legitimate or popular), information (e.g., analysis of trade rumors), advertising and publicity (e.g., coverage without having to pay for space or time), and revenues (e.g., the broadcast rights fees such as NBC's payment of $3.5 billion to broadcast the Olympics). One of the predominant reasons for the growth of the sport industry is the influence of the sport media. This industry segment—which ranges from newspaper sports sections and all-sports cable channels to satellite radio and Web logs—has had a profound impact on sport through its myriad of activities associated with covering, delivering, publicizing, financing, and at times even shaping sports. As Pulitzer Prize–winning sport journalist Dave Anderson (2005) explained, "Today you have so much more media. Newspapers are only a portion of it." He added, "Today you go to a ball game, let's say a midseason, Tuesday night ball game between the Yankees and Kansas City. Years ago, you would have had roughly 10 writers at a game like that; today, you have 50 to 60 to 70 writers, radio or television voices, and cameramen" (p. 42). According to the sport information department at Penn State, the Nittany Lions attract an average of 450 media members (reporters, broadcasters, technicians, announcers, photojournalists, videographers, support staff) for every home football game ("Beaver Stadium," 2006). Along with their growth in numbers, the sport mass media have grown in influence. They are pervasive in everyday life, play a key role in society, and are viewed by some as the most influential form of sport communication. The mass communicators in sport

reach audiences through the sport mass media, which consist of numerous channels and programming arrangements. These include mediating sport through movies, photography, videography, emerging technologies, live transmissions (e.g., broadcast of a sports event on radio, Internet, local or network television, cable or satellite television), delayed and rebroadcast transmissions, the magazine format (e.g., sports news, interviews, reportage, documentary journalism), activity programming (e.g., active participation by the audience), made-for-television events (e.g., organizing and broadcasting of events such as X Games, Dew Tour, Outdoor Games), paid programming (i.e., program for which event organizer pays for broadcast time, or time-buys), the Internet (e.g., Web sites, news, updates, broadcasts, games, chat rooms, Web logs), and print (e.g., newspapers, team newsletters, magazines).

This chapter focuses on the first segment of the sport mass media: sport publishing and print sport communication (see figure 7.1). This includes an analysis of the rise of the print media as it relates to sports. In the chapter we examine the development of newspaper sports sections, sport journalists,

Figure 7.1   According to the Strategic Sport Communication Model (SSCM), there are three major segments of the sport media. The first of these is publishing and print communication.

sports books, sport information through wire services, sport information on the Internet, and sports magazines. Other sport communication topics covered in this chapter include how print sport communication works, business and ownership aspects of print sport communication, trends in sport communication, and practical advice and information relating to careers in sport publishing and print sport communication.

What is sport publishing? What is print sport communication? Although this chapter covers these questions in much detail, we'll provide short answers to these two questions now. These answers will provide the foundation on which the rest of this chapter is based.

> Sport publishing is the business or profession of the commercial production and dissemination of information related to sport.

This definition, which is a sport-related spin-off of the dictionary definition of *publishing* (2006), is broad enough to include all forms (i.e., sports books, sports sections of newspapers, sports magazines, sports Internet sites, annuals, team newsletters, fan magazines, media guides, game programs, fact sheets) of sport-related publishing.

Although the definition of print sport communication is similar to the definition of sport publishing, there is a slight difference.

> Print sport communication involves any medium that disseminates printed matter related to sport.

Therefore, all print sport communication could be considered sport publishing, but not all sport publishing is print sport communication. For instance, electronic sport publishing—the distribution of sport information by means of a computer network—is sport publishing but not print sport communication. Because electronic sport publishing involves both sport publishing and the new media, this aspect of sport communication is covered in both this chapter and the chapter on new media (chapter 9).

With the increase of convergence (i.e., partnerships across various mass media) and the advances of electronic and digital communication, many sport media entities are involved with more than one genre of sport communication. For instance, sport media giant ESPN, Inc., is most known for its television programming (e.g., *SportsCenter, Outside the Lines, Baseball Tonight*), domestic television networks (e.g., ESPN, ESPN2, ESPN Classic, ESPNEWS, ESPN Deportes, ESPN Now, ESPN Today), and other electronic and digital media (e.g., ESPN HD, ESPN Radio, ESPN.com, ESPN Broadband, ESPN Wireless, ESPN Video-On-Demand, ESPN Interactive, ESPN PPV). This multinational and multimedia corporation, however, is also heavily involved with sport publishing and print sport communication. The company, in addition to operating the top sports Web site and releasing sports books, publishes *ESPN The Magazine*. For an analysis of the connection between ESPN entities, please see the study by Clavio and Pedersen (2007).

NEWSPAPER SPORTS COVERAGE

Both at the macro level (i.e., structural, organizational) and micro level (i.e., relationships, interactions), the institution of sport has a symbiotic relationship with the mass media. Although all of the mass media influence and are influenced by sport, one could argue that the most powerful of the media is the broadcast media through its influence on the growth of sport over the past 3 decades. But those sports and sport organizations that receive consistent coverage by local dailies know that their bottom line is bolstered and sustained through the coverage, information, and hype provided by newspapers. In fact, newspapers are the major source of news for many Americans, with more than half of all adults reading a daily newspaper every day ("Facts About Newspapers," 2004). Many of these readers purchase and read their daily newspapers for the variety and in-depth coverage of sports that newspapers provide.

For example, Dennis Ryerson (2006), editor of the *Indianapolis Star*, explained how his newspaper is trying to "focus our local coverage on topics we think are key to the lives of our readers." Regarding the sportswriters and sports photographers in his publication's sports section, Ryerson explained, "We cover games and what teams do to prepare for those games. But sports help define Indianapolis and dominate the lives of many families. We must do more to report about the impact of sports off the court or playing field" (p. 1E).

Background of Sports Coverage in Newspapers

Sports have not always received coverage in the newspapers, which have a history in the United States that goes back 4 centuries. Although paper was invented nearly 2,000 years ago, the first newspaper was published in China in the 8th century. The first newspaper in the United States did not arrive until 1690. Another century almost slipped by before the country witnessed its first daily newspaper, in the 1780s. Today, according to the Newspaper Association of America, 1,457 dailies are published in the United States ("Newspaper Circulation," 2005). This number does not include the weekly newspapers, community newspapers, online services, and wire services. Daily newspapers are categorized by circulation size. Florida newspapers may be used to illustrate this. Large circulation newspapers could be considered any newspaper in Florida that has a circulation greater than 200,000. The Florida dailies that fit into this category would range from the *Miami Herald* (365,000) to the *Tampa Tribune* (251,000). Nationwide there are 36 newspapers with circulations greater than 200,000. The top circulation dailies are *The Wall Street Journal, USA Today, The New York Times, Los Angeles Times,* and *The Washington Post.* Medium circulation newspapers could be considered any newspaper that has a circulation of between 100,000 and 200,000. There are 67 newspapers across the nation that fit into this category, with the newspapers in Florida ranging from the *Sarasota Herald-Tribune* (109,000) to

Palm Beach Post (180,000). Small circulation newspapers would be those with circulation sizes of fewer than 100,000. In Florida, these would range from the *Daytona News Journal* (98,078) to the *Daily Okeechobee News* (4,000). The country's nearly 1,500 daily newspapers mainly consist of local and regional newspapers that have circulation sizes of fewer than 50,000, with 85% of all of the papers fitting into this category. There are only 217 daily newspapers in the United States with circulation sizes greater than 50,000 ("Facts About Newspapers," 2004).

Most dailies were owned and operated by individuals, families, and private groups for most of the history of newspapers. However, the 20th century brought about a concentration of ownership. For better or worse, most newspapers today are owned by newspaper chains or newspaper groups. Some of the leading newspaper chains are The Gannett Company, Knight-Ridder, The New York Times Company, Cox Enterprises, The Tribune Company, The E.W. Scripps Company, and The Hearst Corporation. As detailed by Pavlik and McIntosh (2004), although there are benefits to the newspaper chains (e.g., shared resources, not having to rely on—and possibly be influenced by—one major advertiser or industry), there are many problems with chains (e.g., reduced connection with local communities, reduced local reporting in favor of material from wire services or the chain's other papers, increased pressures to be profitable through reducing staff and quality control). Folkerts and Lacy (2004) added that with the increasingly competitive, corporate, and concentrated landscape, there has been an increase in the attention paid to "circulation numbers of newspapers. . . . Entertainment has assumed more importance. Although journalism has always been a business, during the last thirty-five years it has evolved into big business. . . . The corporations that increasingly own large news outlets require ever-higher profit margins. . . . The tension between profit and quality journalism will continue as long as journalism is a commercial enterprise" (p. 44). Sport journalists are often caught in the middle of this tension. Remember the story about Joanne C. Gerstner at the beginning of this chapter? This sportswriter has spent most of her career working for mass media conglomerates, including nearly a decade with The Gannett Company. This is an international news and information conglomerate that includes 99 daily newspapers, 21 television stations, and more than 130 Web sites in the United States alone. With a combined daily paid circulation of 7.6 million, Gannett is the largest newspaper group in the country. Gerstner's involvement with Gannett took her from the *Cincinnati Enquirer, Lansing State Journal,* and *USA Today* to where she is today at the *Detroit News.* In August 2005, Gannett sold the *Detroit News* to MediaNews Group. This mass media company, which also owns television and radio stations, operates 40 daily newspapers with a combined daily circulation of 1.7 million. The new media division of the company, Media-News Group Interactive, is the host of all of the company's 40 newspaper Web sites.

Although newspapers have been affected by competition (e.g., when advertising expenditures are spent on retailing or broadcast media rather than on buying space in newspapers) and changes in readership and consumption patterns (e.g., readers gravitating toward the immediacy of communication offered by the Internet), newspapers are not going out of existence. The combined daily newspaper circulation in the United States is 54.6 million for the weekday morning and evening editions and 57.7 million for the Sunday editions. This means that more than 54 million newspapers are sold daily and more than 57 million are sold every Sunday. In addition to dailies, there are 6,704 weekly newspapers (published fewer than four times a week) that have a combined total circulation of just over 50 million ("Facts About Newspapers," 2004). The publication of local, regional, and national sports stories by the daily and weekly newspapers is a major reason for today's circulation figures. The type of coverage, quality of analysis, credible reporting, and consistency in packaging all combine to keep many Americans as newspaper subscribers even in the midst of intense competition. It has only been in the last 120 years, however, that publishers have realized the value that sports bring to newspapers and circulation figures.

In 1733, the *Boston Gazette* published an article on a boxing match. This article has been referred to as the first sports story printed in an American newspaper. Ever since, dailies have provided more and more sports coverage for their readers. Throughout the 1700s and most of the 1800s, newspapers covered sports, but only in a sporadic and isolated manner. That began to change in the last 2 decades of the 19th century. The initiator of this change was Joseph Pulitzer, who, in 1883, created the first newspaper sports department for his *New York World* (Brian, 2001). Pulitzer's sports pages covered boxing, baseball, football, and many types of races (e.g., horse, bicycle, roller skate). Twelve years after Pulitzer's creation, sports began to be covered to an even greater degree when William Randolph Hearst established the first sports section—the "modern sports section" (Belts, 1953, p. 56)—in a newspaper. Hearst, who realized that the attention he gave to sports helped to increase his circulation figures, created this innovative section in his *New York Journal.* Over the next few decades sports received increased coverage in newspapers. Sport sections became more pervasive and specialized in the 1920s with expanded pages, extended coverage, improved sportswriting, and the arrival of the "golden age of sports." This was a time when people had increased leisure time, increased literacy rates, economic prosperity, and a desire to put World War I behind them, so they turned to their newspapers to read about their favorite sports and heroes. They had many to choose from, with such legends as Babe Ruth, Jack Dempsey, Suzanne Lenglen, Bobby Jones, and Red Grange playing a prominent role in sports during this time.

The coverage of sports has remained a major component of newspapers throughout the ensuing decades. Today, it is difficult to find a newspaper that does not cover sports to some extent. Sports sections can range from single pages inside small publications to 20- or 30-page stand-alone productions with additional pullout sections (e.g., the high school football section in a Saturday paper in Odessa, the college football section in a Sunday paper in Miami, the professional football section in a Monday paper in Pittsburgh). The size differences result from many variables such as the newspaper's circulation size, availability of sports news in the area, and interest of the publisher and managing editor in sports coverage. It took some time for a few newspapers to finally join their competitors in offering a sports section. For instance, *The New York Times* was one of the latest to add a section devoted to sports coverage every day. As the former managing editor of the paper, Arthur Gelb (2003), stated, "The paper had long been criticized for the haphazard way it covered sports. From its inception, *The Times* had looked upon sports as an uncouth country cousin, acknowledging its existence but treating it as though it didn't quite belong at the same table as 'real news'" (p. 625). As the newspaper grew and new printing presses ushered in production flexibility, the prestigious publication eventually went to a daily sports section. The *Times*' veteran sports columnist, Dave Anderson, confirmed Gelb's comments when he talked about the biggest change in sport journalism over the past half-century. "One thing is that the editor—the executive editors and the managing editors—of the newspapers are giving more attention and more space and more importance to sports," noted Anderson (2005), who began working in the newspaper industry as a copy boy in 1945. "For years the *Times* had a sports section almost hidden in a cave somewhere in the paper. I always joked that you had to call AAA every morning to find out where the sports section was. Now we have our own section; now we have color. The progress of printing and everything else and also the importance of the public's devotion to sports has made editors realize that sports can sell their papers" (p. 42).

Just as there is a disparity in the size or output of sports sections, the personnel of sports departments can range from a lone part-time journalist (i.e., someone assigned as the writer, photographer, layout artist, and editor of the sports page while also being assigned to another section of the newspaper) to a staff of more than 50 employees. In an

extension of the quip about sports being the toy department of life, some individuals have referred to newspaper sports departments as the toy departments of journalism. This labeling comes about because sportswriting is often very different from other journalistic endeavors. "You have a little more leeway, more fun writing sports than most other news," explained legendary sportswriter and tennis commentator, Bud Collins. "After all, it is the paper's toy department, and people usually read sports for enjoyment as well as the results. Although, at times, subject matter can be very serious, it isn't genuine life-and-death" (Glatzer, 2006, ¶3). Although Collins provides a solid explanation for the phrase, most of the time when it is used it is unfair labeling and unjustified stereotyping. Sure, there are some professionals in the print sport media who fail to live up to the high standards of journalism. Because some sport journalists have been unable to balance the reporting and presenting of information and entertainment, they have reduced standards for the sake of "infotainment." The blurring of these lines has caused some to lose credibility and has hindered the profession. However, most professionals in sports departments are dedicated and professional journalists just as much as their counterparts in other sections of the newspaper.

Organization of the Newspaper Sports Department

Newspaper sports departments are operated in a similar manner as the news, business, feature, or any other section of the newspaper. Although some small circulation newspapers combine departments, most newspapers have a sports department that is a separate entity. This separate entity can range physically from one desk with a shared phone and fax machine to multiple distinct units that include multiple desks, phones, fax machines, rooms, computer terminals, televisions, and any other device needed to help produce a quality sports section. The professionals who gather, select, process, and present sports for newspaper sports sections are similar to those who work for sports magazines and sports wire services. These trained and experienced individuals can be grouped as writers and photographers and editors and production staffers.

Writers and Photographers

The writers and photographers consist of general assignment reporters, correspondents, stringers, wire reporters, feature writers, beat writers, staff photographers, freelance photographers, and columnists. The sports columnists are the top writers—in prestige, salary, and often experience—on a sports staff. They are expected to provide expert commentary, and their position comes with a lot of expectation and power. Take, for instance, one of the most established and respected sports columnists in the business, Bill Plaschke of the *Los Angeles Times*. Matt Welch (2005), associate editor and media columnist for *Reason* magazine, explained a scenario that unfolded in Los Angeles. Former Dodgers general manager Paul DePodesta, according to Welch, was someone Plaschke had "been

trying to run out of town for 20 months." When DePodesta was fired by the owner of the Dodgers, Frank McCourt, ESPN's Peter Gammons commented, "McCourt, ever sensitive to the Los Angeles media, changed direction" (¶1). It is not uncommon for sports columnists and media personalities to affect the sport industry with the columns that they write or the words that they speak. The subjectivity of the columnist's viewpoints can often create hostility from athletes, coaches, management, and fans. For instance, Bob Kravitz, a sports columnist for the *Indianapolis Star*, informs, surprises, entertains, and enrages readers. One subscriber once wrote a sarcastic note to the sports editor: "For me, his [Kravitz] penchant for playing general manager/team president is growing tiresome and stale. A columnist should have strong opinions and is not expected to agree with everything team management does. But he annoyingly overplays that hand. I have often wondered why some NFL or NBA team hasn't tapped his brilliant mind to lead its team" (Heeter,

© Paul M. Pedersen

The columnist—such as Bob Kravitz of the *Indianapolis Star*—is the top writer for the sports section of a newspaper. This individual is responsible for interpreting the activities in the sport industry, writing opinion pieces about athletes and activities, and delivering key commentary and insight to the readers. There are hundreds of popular sports columnists, such as J.A. Adande, Mitch Albom, Barbara Barker, Christine Brennan, Peter Schmuck, Stephen A. Smith, Michael Wilbon, and Mike Wise.

2005, p. C2). Although not everyone is happy with a columnist's opinions and insights, the job of a sports columnist is not to please all stakeholders (e.g., readers, team managers, athletes).

Photographers add much of the visual element to the sports page. Without their pictures, most sports sections would lose their appeal to subscribers. Sports photojournalists gather images for newspaper sports sections, sport-related Internet sites, sports magazines and books, and any number of other outlets. The photo department at *Sports Illustrated* receives more than 4,000 images every day from freelancers, staff photographers, wire services, and picture agencies. For a recent Super Bowl, the *Sports Illustrated* editors (Steve Fine, director of photography, and George Washington, deputy photo editor) worked on site to process more than 16,000 digital pictures to identify the best cover shot and inside photographs for the magazine. The *Sports Illustrated* photographic workflow for an event, which is covered in detail in an outstanding article by Eamon Hickey (2004), includes a 6-hour time frame that culminates when Fine and Washington make their final decisions.

There are numerous opportunities to work in sports photojournalism. Many of these are freelance assignments, but there are full-time positions with newspapers, teams, and organizations. Veteran sports photojournalists such as *Sports Illustrated* veteran Peter Read Miller make a career out of providing photographic images to editorial and commercial clients. The editorial clients are generally the sports sections of the newspapers and sports magazines, whereas the commercial clients can be any company that needs a photograph for advertising or business-related purposes. Some legendary sports photographers have additional activities such as photographic exhibits and books. Take for instance Walter Iooss. For more than 4 decades Iooss has captured some of the best sports photographs that *Sports Illustrated* has published. At a time when many photographers positioned themselves in the press box, Iooss worked alongside the action on the field of play to capture his images. During his time at *Sports Illustrated* he has had numerous cover shots and assignments,

Tips for Sports Photojournalists: Advice From an Expert

Professional sports photographer Mark M. Hancock (2004) offered suggestions to photographers who cover games in poorly lit sport stadiums and facilities.

Hancock encouraged photographers to get as many shots as possible in the first game of the season because many of these photographs will be used throughout the year when stories are written about the sports team. Hancock explained that photographers should make sure the photograph includes the ball (for sports such as basketball, football, and soccer). There are exceptions (e.g., sideline shots and celebrations), but for the most part photographers should get the action and ball-focused shots. Photographers should also take their photographs in a kneeling—rather than standing—position. This allows photographers to get the players' expressions and helps to make the players appear "larger than life." Hancock advised photojournalists to learn to jump (in case the play comes your way), to know the strategies and rules of the sport that is covered, and to be ready to photograph and report unique or special interest stories that happen during the game.

In addition to knowing when to use a flash, eliminate red-eye, and use the lowest film speed and fastest lenses possible, sports photographers should take follow-up shots of the players involved with the action (because even if the photograph is great, if the players cannot be identified the photograph will not be published) and take a couple of "dead" shots (hand covering the lens) after you know that you just took a great photograph. This last exercise helps to save time during editing, especially if the photojournalist is on a tight deadline.

The sport industry has many opportunities for photojournalists. Photographers often work as freelancers or staff employees for newspapers, magazines, and organizations. Here, Sam Upshaw, Jr., of the *Louisville Courier-Journal,* asks Rahman Ali, the brother of Muhammad Ali, for verification of a photo that Upshaw took of Ali's twin daughters. Even if a photograph is a great shot at a sporting event, the photograph will most likely not be published if the individuals and athletes involved in the photograph cannot be identified.

including shooting the *Sports Illustrated Swimsuit Edition* several times. His work has been in exhibits, the most recent of which were his three traveling exhibits. These distinct exhibits were titled Classic Baseball (80 photographs), Classic Golf (65 photographs), and Classic Basketball (80 photographs). A 210-page book on each feature accompanied each exhibit, which cost between $15,500 and $16,500 for a nearly 2-month booking. In addition to his photographic exhibits, his photographic books (e.g., *Sports People, Lifetime Shooting Sports & Beauty, Shooting for the Gold, Classic Golf*) and essays with athletes (e.g., *Rare Air* with Michael Jordan, *Cal on Cal* with Cal Ripkin, *Junior* with Ken Griffey, Jr.) have been received with much acclaim. Iooss admitted that sports were his first interest when he started at *Sports Illustrated.* Although he is passionate about photography, his love of sports continues be driving force in his work. "I've been to every

Super Bowl," Iooss once explained to Charlotte Lowrie (2005), "and I continue to go because I love pro football" (¶14).

For those who plan to enter this field, Nancy Ford (1998) explained that "you should make sure that journalism is in your blood and that you love it, because frankly, you are not going to get rich doing it" (¶1). Ford went on to say that, "If you don't feel that passion, that drive to learn everything about photography, journalism, and photojournalism that you can, then please find what is in your heart. It is important to feel passion for whatever you choose to do" (¶3).

Editors and Production Staffers

Editors are the decision makers and rewrite professionals with titles such as executive sports editor, managing sports editor, deputy sports editor, copyeditor, and night editor. Sports editors are known as the gatekeepers, because they decide if an event or personality is worth receiving coverage in the sports section. The ability of these editors to decide what should be included and what should be deleted from the sports section is essential, because everything cannot be included. The gatekeeping function is an important and extremely difficult duty to fulfill. At the sports desk there is often intense debate on what should or should not be covered, and sports editors struggle with the issue of giving their readers what they want and giving their readers what they need. Although the marketplace has a tremendous influence on the struggle, in the end the sports editors set the agenda and act as news filters. The content of sports sections often influences society's opinion of what is important. If the sports editors publish only certain major commercial sports, then those sports often will be the sports that society views as important. Therefore, through their gatekeeping function, the sports editors are the agenda setters. Although there are natural limitations associated with their gatekeeping role, most sports editors work hard to perform their duties in an equitable and professional manner through providing coverage that is newsworthy, interesting, timely, and reflective of the interest of readers.

The editorial side of sports sections consists of agate clerks (i.e., those responsible for working with agate material, which is the small type used for scoreboard pages, statistics, and box scores), copy desk editors, night editors, deputy sports editors, executive sports editors, designers, layout specialists, and graphic artists. Although many newspapers have multiple clerks, editors, designers, and layout and graphic artists, not all newspaper sports sections have all of these positions. For instance, many small circulation newspapers will have only one sports editor who acts as the editor, copyeditor, layout artist, and any other role required to produce the sports page.

For each day, the newspaper sports department is given a certain number of pages that the editorial staff will need to fill with stories, photographs, graphs, statistics, and agate material. The typical day begins with the editorial meeting to discuss what stories, photographs, graphics, and illustrations might be included in the sports section for that day. The staff make a mock layout of the paper (dummy sheet) and then determine which stories will come from wire reports and which stories will need to be assigned to staff reporters, correspondents, and freelancers.

Production Process of a Newspaper Sports Story

The assignment of stories involves four major aspects. First, the reporters are told what type of story is needed. Sports articles are typically gamers (i.e., a game story written during and completed shortly after an athletic contest), previews (i.e., an article about an upcoming event), features (i.e., a human interest story about an athlete, coach, team), and follow-ups (i.e., an article that takes a second look at a game or event after the activity or original article has been published). Second, the reporters are informed if any additional stories (e.g., sidebars, which are articles that accompany a game story) will be needed. Third, the length of each story is assigned to fill a certain news hole in the sports section. Therefore, reporters are told if the game story needs to be 20 inches (approximately 600 words, depending on the width of the column) or the sidebar needs to be 7 inches (approximately 210 words). Fourth, the reporters are informed of the deadline for each assigned story. Some stories such as investigative analyses or feature articles have deadlines of a few days or even weeks. However, most stories in sports have a deadline at some point that very evening. This is the time in which the story has to be delivered to the editors at the copy desk so they can edit the story and get it to the presses in time. Although deadlines are challenging for editors, they are most exhilarating and stressful for the writers. "There are a lot of wonderful journalists who will never be sportswriters for one simple reason: seriously tough deadlines," says Joanne C. Gerstner. The veteran sportswriter adds, "Sometimes you only have a mere two minutes to write an entire story. Factors such as overtime, television broadcasts of the game, acts of God such as weather or power outages, and even your own laptop dying can make even the most seasoned journalist freak out. You learn how to control your own stress, calm your nerves to the point where you can write effectively." Once the game has been covered or written, sportswriters submit their stories through some electronic method to the copy desk. A copyeditor then reads the submitted article, makes editorial changes to the story, and puts a headline on the piece. The story is then passed to the night editor who, after giving approval, passes the story on to the layout artist. In the past, film negatives were used in the plate-making and printing process. Now, the editors and layout professionals of sports pages compose their pages on computers using sophisticated publishing software. They send the pages directly from the computer to the printing plate, which is then processed and made ready for the presses.

SPORTS BOOKS

Sports books are forgotten in most discussions about print sport media delivery systems. The writing and publishing of sports books, however, are major aspects of sport communication. Each year thousands of sports books are published, covering a wide variety of areas such as sports commentaries, novels, self-help books, biographies, histories, and a host of other categories.

According to communication scholars Pavlik and McIntosh (2004), some of the major functions of books in society include transmitting culture, entertaining, and diffusing information, ideas, and knowledge. Although sports books play a key role in entertaining readers through escapism and diversion, they also can inform (e.g., sports books that cover history or business) and transmit culture (e.g., sports books that teach right and wrong, socially acceptable behaviors, rules, norms, morals, values).

According to the Association of American Publishers (AAP), the book publishing industry in the United States had net sales of just under $24 billion in 2004 ("Industry Statistics," 2005). The major categories in book publish-

ing are trade ($5 billion in sales); professional and scholarly ($4 billion); elementary, high school, and young adult ($4 billion); higher education ($3.5 billion); religious and self-help ($1.3 billion); book club and mail order ($1.2 billion); and mass market paperback ($1.1 billion). There are sports books that fit into each of these categories. An example of a trade publication is the book by David Williams and School Graham (2006), *The Baffled Parent's Guide to Coaching Six-and-Under Soccer*. Barry Smart's (2005) *The Sport Star: Modern Sport and the Cultural Economy of Sporting Celebrity* would be placed in the category of professional and scholarly sports books. An example of a sport-focused publication in the elementary, high school, and young adult category would be Michael Benson's (2006) *Althea Gibson*. A sports book in the higher education category is *Human Resource Management in Sport and Recreation*, by Packianathan Chelladurai (2006). *Business Leadership and the Lessons From Sport* by Hans Westerbeek and Aaron Smith (2005) is a sport-focused publication that fits into the self-help category. Many sports autobiographies, historical examinations, leadership manuals, and other trade books can be purchased through such outlets as an audio book club or a traditional book club such as the Doubleday Book Club. The latest craze in mass market paperbacks is exemplified by the licensing agreement between the publisher of contemporary romance fictions, Harlequin Enterprises Limited, and NASCAR. The first publication for the NASCAR Library Collection was Pamela Britton's (2006) *In the Groove*.

Sports authors have a wide variety of options in terms of possible topics and publication outlets. They can publish their books through major conglomerates, niche publishers, contract basis (i.e., book for hire), vanity presses, and self-publishing. Although there are some self-published sports books, most sports books are published in the major companies that dominate the book industry (e.g., Random House), electronic outlets, and niche publishing houses such as Griffin Publishing Group, McFarland Sports Publishing, and Taylor Publishing Company that specialize in sport-related topics. For those interested in the authorship side of sport publishing, Doug Looney—former senior writer for *Sports Illustrated* and author of the bestselling sports book *Under the Tarnished Dome*—told Mulligan and Mulligan (1998), "If your book involves major sports celebrities and really takes off, it's possible to realize income on the order of $300,000 to $500,000. But that's very unusual, and it's more likely that writing a sports book will put you in the neighborhood of $50,000—and that's if it is really good" (p. 308). Mulligan and Mulligan (1998) also noted that more than 150 book publishers are listed in the *Writer's Market*—a sourcebook for prospective authors—who are interested in sport-related books. The publishing of sports books includes career opportunities on the writing, editorial, business, production, and marketing sides of the business.

WIRE SERVICES AND TECHNOLOGICAL ADVANCEMENTS

Numerous wire services supply sports news to print and nonprint media organizations and customers. The content that these wire services provide includes text (i.e., articles), graphics, audio, video, and photographs. Sport journalists provide the sport-related content for the wire services, which then distribute the articles, photographs, and other content to print publications, Web sites, and multimedia companies.

The most popular wire services are Reuters, United Press International (UPI), and the Associated Press (AP). Because of its associated information services (e.g., financial information) in addition to supplying news, Reuters is the largest international multimedia news agency. In terms of organizations that primarily focus on news, the AP is the largest (with 3,700 editorial, communications, and administrative employees, 242 bureaus) and oldest (started in 1846) news organization in the world. UPI turned 100 years old in 2007, but this news agency—which began as the United Press Associations and provided

an alternative to the monopoly that the AP enjoyed—has struggled in the past 2 decades with market share issues, credibility assaults, and numerous owners. Although it has offered breakthroughs in recent years including being the first news agency in which consumers could directly purchase their content, UPI remains a distant third to AP and Reuters.

Wire Service Employees

Similar jobs as those listed previously for newspaper sports sections can be found with a wire service company. Most of the wire service positions related to sports involve writing, editing, and photography. Wire services employ writers and editors who are bureau journalists to serve as reporters, editors, generalists, beat writers, and correspondents. Other professionals in the wire services include photographers, graphic artists (i.e., those who produce maps, drawings, illustrations, logos), online employees, technicians, programmers, engineers, and developers. On the business side, the wire services employ salespeople, marketers, administrators, managers (i.e., bureau chiefs, communications managers, business development and strategic planning leaders, office managers), accountants, administrative assistants, and executive positions in finance, corporate communications, marketing, and human resources.

Web Sport Journalists

Print sport media professionals are increasing their activities with and presence on the Web, as they use the Internet to find background information on stories, search for sources, and interview sources through e-mail (although e-mail interviewing provides convenient and sometimes more detailed and thorough written communication, it does not allow for the immediate follow-up questions, informal conversations, and observational reporting that often accompany face-to-face interviewing). The presence of sport journalists has increased on the Web through Internet publishing (i.e., posting of stories on the Web, creating Web logs or blogs) and interacting with readers in chat rooms. What Mulligan and Mulligan predicted nearly a decade ago has come true. In 1998, these authors stated, "It's obvious that millions of Americans are and will be gaining much of their sports news electronically and on-line in a variety of ways. Students and experienced sports communicators must come to grips with this reality and become skilled in its ways, or they may find themselves on an off-ramp of the Information Superhighway rather than part of the traffic flow" (p. 275). The demand for print sport media professionals to work with the Internet is a result of the advancement of online activities and increased content provided on the Internet by newspapers and sports magazines (in addition to other media). According to the Newspaper Association of America, more than 1,500 daily newspapers in North America have Web sites.

The convergence of the media, as noted in the preceding paragraph, along with entrepreneurial sports endeavors on the Internet has produced Web sport journalists. Although many of these individuals are professional and credible journalists who value strict editing, accuracy, and reporting, some of the people who call themselves sport journalists (e.g., some sports bloggers, sports Web site owners and operators, sports newsletter creators) are more interested in speed and sensationalism that in upholding high journalistic standards. The new sport media (i.e., blogs and other Internet activities) have opened up the field of sport journalism to everyone.

Without the controls imposed in traditional sport journalism, much sensationalism and gossip are available on the Web. Many stories, insights, and commentaries are published on the Web that never would have been published by more traditional avenues. Furthermore, many sports stories are first released to the public through blogs or Web sites rather than traditional media outlets. Take for instance the organization eSports Media Group. This self-described "sportswriting community" is one of many Web sites that uses the Internet to syndicate sport-focused articles for use by other media organizations and outlets. More than 100 "freelance journalists" are employed who write sports analyses and commentaries that can be syndicated within 24 hours. The

categories of articles available range from "amateur" and "baseball" to "women's sports" and "youth sports" with more than 20 other categories in between. Ten years ago the traditional media were breaking stories. Now nontraditional outlets often scoop the print and broadcast media. As is noted on its Web site, "eSports Media Group primarily utilizes the efficiencies of the Internet to organize, collect, and distribute content products allowing it to be first to market with the newest information in the sports arena" ("About Us," 2006, ¶3). Although eSports Media Group explains that it "provides a unique approach to sport journalism while maintaining the highest level of journalistic standards" (¶7), not all Internet sources can make such a claim.

Many Web-enabled publishing systems and Internet publishing outlets fail to uphold the ideals that are typically adhered to by print sport journalists. Therefore, although the publishing of breaking sports stories on the Internet by independent agencies and outlets has dramatically increased, because of credibility issues with some of the independent Web sites many Internet users remain most confident in the articles and commentaries associated with established media outlets such as newspapers, magazines, television networks, and radio stations.

SPORTS MAGAZINES

Media consumption patterns and increased competition have eroded some of the influence of sports magazines over the past few years. However, those publications that are able to make adjustments in this age of demassification (specialization) will have a bright future. They already have a storied history. Similar to newspaper sports sections, sports magazines started in the latter part of the 19th century. *The Sporting News* (a publication that started in the 1880s) and *Sports Illustrated* (the preeminent sports magazine, which dates back to the 1950s) are two of the legendary sports publications that have stood the test of time. According to Megargee (2004), *Sports Illustrated* received its impetus when Bob Cowin, an employee at Time Inc., sent a three-page memo in 1950 to the founder (Henry Luce) of the company. "My wife likes to say I was the founder of *Sports Illustrated*," Cowin once told a reporter. "That makes me squirm. I had the idea, yes. But somebody else would have come up with the idea sooner or later. Ideas are often a dime a dozen" (Megargee, 2004, p. 3C). Cowin had done some door-to-door research in Ohio earlier that year and discovered that there was an interest in more sports publications. After determining that the nation needed a general interest sports magazine, Cowin presented his proposal to Luce. In August 1954, the first issue of *Sports Illustrated* was published and even with the changes in reading habits and subscriptions, the magazine remains the top-selling sports publication.

The top sports magazines in the United States are those with circulations greater than 300,000, with *Sports Illustrated* leading the way with a circulation of more than three million. In the most recent release by *SportsBusiness Journal* of advertising totals for sports magazines, *Sports Illustrated* again led the way followed by *ESPN The Magazine, Golf Magazine, Golf Digest, Runner's World, Cycle World, The Sporting News, Golf World, Transworld Skateboarding,* and *Tennis* (Johnson-Reid, 2005a).

Types of Sports Magazines

The hundreds of sports magazines that are published each year are part of the nearly 19,000 magazine titles in circulation in the United States, according to the Magazine Publishers of America. The popular magazines, those known to the general public, are called *consumer titles*. More than 7,000 consumer titles are in circulation. Consumers either subscribe to the magazine or purchase single copies in retail outlets. For example, 25 consumer titles are devoted to fantasy football alone, with sales of the successful titles (i.e., *Fantasy Football Index, Pro Football Weekly*) as high as nearly 400,000 (King, 2005d). The majority of magazines are trade or business-to-business publications. There are nearly 12,000 such publications, most of which will not be found at the local newsstand. These have limited circulation to specific readers

within the profession ("Making the Switch," 2005). Examples of sports trade publications are *Tennis Industry Magazine* and *American Quarter Horse Racing Journal.*

There has been a tremendous increase in the number and variety of sports magazines over the past decade. Mulligan and Mulligan (1998) noted that an average of more than 40 new sports magazines are launched annually. There are sports magazines for every sport. These niche newsstand publications aim for narrow audience segments and range from bowling and running to snowboarding. Some magazines have targeted professional athletes. At the turn of this century, a new magazine was launched that targeted professionals in the field of play. This magazine, *Pro,* lasted only four issues. In 2004, another upstart magazine, *OT (Overtime Magazine: The Business and Lifestyle Guide for Professional Athletes),* arrived on the scene. The quarterly is targeted toward active and retired professional athletes, sports agents, coaches, sport management executives, and other sport industry professionals with average annual incomes of $1.5 million. In *OT*'s media kit, Ryan McNeil (2006) stated that his publication's "mission is to produce the premier magazine for all professional athletes and sports industry insiders. By leveraging our extensive networks of colleagues and industry experts within and outside professional sports, we will offer rare insight into the industry as it relates to former, current and future professional athletes." He added, "OT will become both the business lifestyle manual for all professional athletes and required reading for the professional athletic industry as a whole" (p. 3). By 2006, this quarterly—created and published by former professional football player Ryan McNeil (with between $250,000 and $500,000 out of his pocket)—was a profitable magazine with a circulation just under 40,000 (Mickey, 2006).

OT represents a trend in the sports magazine publishing business. As Schultz (2005) noted, many sports magazines "have carved out a successful niche by catering to specialized groups, which is almost essential given the growth in media options and the fragmentation of today's audiences. The general interest sports magazine has given way to a highly specialized and specifically targeted publication, usually based on the type of sports or interest involved" (p. 59). Even the traditional publications have attempted to make changes because of the competition in the magazine industry. Stuart Marvin, the senior vice president of marketing and promotions for *The Sporting News,* said, "We're not a broad-reach publication, so we kind of position ourselves to more serious enthusiasts" (Adams, 2005a, p. 8).

Functions of Sports Magazines

Sports magazines are journalistic and visual innovators that continue to serve numerous functions.

First, sports magazines expose consumers to sport. Through their work in this area, consumers are encouraged to participate, become spectators, or in some way involve themselves in the sport. This often occurs with teenagers. According to Teen Research Unlimited ("Media Tracker," 2005), sports magazines are popular among teenagers, especially males. Teenage males selected *Sports Illustrated* as the their favorite magazine, whereas *Sports Illustrated* and *Transworld* magazines (snowboarding, skateboarding, and surfing magazines) were the only two sports publications to make the favorite list (13th and 15th, respectively) for female teenagers. Aside from videogame publications, some of the other popular magazines among teenage males included *ESPN The Magazine* (2nd), *Sports Illustrated for Kids* (6th), and *Transworld* magazines (11th).

The second function of magazines is to serve as sources of information, advertising, and a host of other offerings. In their role as a provider of information, sports magazines include detailed, longer, more developed, and more in-depth articles than a sports fan typically finds in a newspaper sports section (Schultz, 2005).

Third, sports magazines provide profits for publishers. Within this function, they also enhance corporate synergy by helping to promote other related businesses. For example, *Sports Illustrated* can promote its

Web site (www.cnnsi.com, a joint operation with media giant CNN) and assorted products through the magazine. *ESPN The Magazine* can promote ESPN's programming options, upcoming ESPN movies, ABC programming, and a host of other associated products and offerings of the sport media conglomerate (Clavio & Pedersen, 2007). As John Skipper explained at the launch of *ESPN The Magazine* in 1998, the magazine helped ESPN become "the principal source of sports entertainment. Print completes our ubiquity. The magazine can take advantage of the network's status and newsgathering resources" (Ryan, 1998, p. 66). In addition to providing profits to publishers and media conglomerates, magazines also promote athletes and sports teams. For instance, professional athletes are often placed on the cover of magazines—both sport and nonsport publications—as a way to increase circulation sizes. Athletes such as Michael Jordan and Danica Patrick have graced the covers of numerous and varied magazines. Even professionals such as Ron Artest are attractive to magazine publishers and editors. Artest, the oft-troubled professional basketball player, has been on the cover of magazines such as *GQ, Sports Illustrated, ESPN The Magazine,* and *Penthouse.* As one journalist explains, "Artest is a natural media darling. Aside from all of his controversies, he's photogenic and complex. The image of the player who has been suspended so often doesn't jibe with the soft-spoken family man" (Montieth, 2005, p. P11).

Organization of the Magazine Industry

According to the Magazine Publishers of America, there are two distinct entities involved in publishing a magazine, which are very similar to those found in the newspaper business. The editorial side provides content for a magazine, and the publishing side involves the business aspects of publishing a magazine.

Editorial Side

The editorial staff at sports magazines are responsible for creating all of the magazine's content including stories, photography, and design. Anything regarding the content and look of the magazine is covered by the editorial staff, designers, and photographers. "For writing and editing, you need to have strong writing skills, an eye for detail, the ability to generate unique story ideas and time management. For graphic design, you need to be artistic, precise and trained in photography, illustration, or graphics" ("Making the Switch," 2006, p. 3).

Publishing Side

On the publishing side, there are numerous key areas as detailed in the industry publication *Building a Career in Magazines* (2006). Advertising sales in sports magazines involve meeting sales prospects, researching leads, developing sales packages, selling as many ad pages for each issue as possible, and generating revenue for the sports magazine. Marketing and promotion involve creating materials that will be used during sales calls and presentations, planning events, designing sales materials, producing videos, promoting the magazine, and keeping projects on time and budget. Consumer marketing—also called circulation—is the department responsible for selling the magazine to readers. Business, management, and finance professionals work in sports magazine publishing. These individuals hold positions such as publisher (head of the business department) and upper management (the individual at smaller magazines or the several people—such as associate publisher, chief

---

Planning to Work at a Sports Magazine? Learn the Lingo

Professionals who work for sports magazines, and any magazine for that matter, have their own language. Prospective magazine employees need to be cognizant of jargon and terminology. Some of the lingo, as explained by the Magazine Publishers of America and the American Society of Magazine Editors, is examined here.

For instance, the *ad-to-edit ratio* is the proportion (percentage) of magazine pages used for advertising and for editorial (the averages are 47% and 53%, respectively). Ryan McNeil, publisher of the *OT* magazine, has a specific ratio in mind for his sports publication. "To me a good ratio is 60/40, but we started out at 70/30," explained McNeil (Mickey, 2006, ¶7). The magazine has grown from 100 pages to 154 pages, the last issue more in line with McNeil's desired ratio.

Another term—*book*—refers to each issue of the magazine. When a copyeditor prepares the manuscript for final publication, his or her action is referred to as a *line edit*. The *masthead* is the box inside the magazine that lists the editorial and business personnel. Although the words *circulation* and *readership* are often confused, circulation is a magazine's total net paid subscriptions, single copies, and requests and qualified recipients, whereas readership or audience is the number of people who read the magazine.

The *close date* is the final date an order can be placed by an advertiser to reserve space in the next issue, whereas the *material due date* is when the advertisement is due. The first look at a manuscript by a senior editor to determine if an assignment is satisfactory is called a *top edit*.

The *rate card* is the official price list for advertising space in the magazine. For example, in the original media kit for *OT*, the rate card was a six-by-four grid. These six rows (spread, full page color, cover 2, cover 3, cover 4, and half page) by four columns (1x, 2x, 3x, and 4x) included all the prices for advertisements, ranging from $4,795 (this is the cost for each half-page advertisement with a four-issue commitment) to $19,985 (this is for one advertising spread) (McNeil, 2006, p. 7). *Selling off the rate card* is when a salesperson offers discounts to a client, reducing the cost of an advertisement from the official price printed on the rate card. For instance, *The Sporting News* had its largest issue ever in terms of ad sales with its 2005 publication of the NASCAR Chase for the Nextel Cup preview issue. The special issue included approximately 40 ad pages; "at full rate card prices, that would generate about $2 million" (Bernstein, 2005f, p. 9).

financial officer, general manager—at larger publications responsible for the magazine's profitability, promotion, and overall operation). There is also the production side with positions that involve coordinating several key aspects, creating the sports magazine's layout, determining which pages will feature editorial and which will carry advertising, receiving all the advertising and editorial materials in proper format, making sure the magazine goes to the printer on time, and overseeing buying the paper and distributing the magazine. The research positions involve examining through surveys and focus groups the nature of the sports magazine's readership to help shape the focus and content of the magazine's editorial and advertising efforts.

Careers Within the Sports Magazine Segment

Numerous career opportunities are available in sports magazine publishing. These careers can be in areas such as circulation, research, ad marketing, editorial and graphic design, and selling ad pages. For those interested in editorial careers in magazines, an in-depth knowledge of sports and the ability to write well are two essentials for entry-level positions. Taking classes in writing and magazine publishing can help, as can contacting local or regional publishers and inquiring about writing an article. Even if you do not receive compensation for the work, writing stories and building a portfolio of published works are important for entry and advancement in sports magazines ("Making the Switch," 2006).

As Schultz (2005) noted, "The role of the sports magazine continues to evolve in today's changing media environment, but while it can certainly carve out a profitable niche, it's likely that the sports magazine will never again have the level of prominence it did during the heyday of *Sports Illustrated*" (p. 60). They might not be as prominent as they were years ago, but sports magazines have a strong presence among the media, with 80% of Americans still reading sports and nonsports magazines, according to the Magazine Publishers of America. A key measure

of a magazine's standing in the advertising community is its ranking in *Adweek's* Hot List. In 2005, *ESPN The Magazine*—which was launched in 1998 by veteran media professionals John Papanek, John Walsh, and John Skipper—was ranked eighth among magazines, generating more than $50 million in ad revenue and *The Sporting News* was ranked sixth among magazines posting less than $50 million in ad revenue (Adams, 2005a). Although the environment surrounding sports magazines is in a state of flux and some of the publications will come and go, sports magazines as a whole are a sport communication component that is here to stay.

LIFE AS A SPORT JOURNALIST

No 2 days are alike for a sport journalist. This can be an appealing aspect of the job (e.g., new experiences), but it also can make for some difficult days. One day the game story just falls into place. The next game you miss the deadline because sentences are nearly impossible to put together. One day your interviewee appreciates your obligations and fills your tape recorder with exceptional quotes. Another day you can't get a good quote from anyone. Most sportswriters know the quotable and approachable subjects. For instance, *Sports Illustrated*'s Rick Reilly (2003a) praised one athlete in particular for his helping the media. "Of all the thousands of athletes I've interviewed, Jack William Nicklaus is the most helpful, the most giving, and the most thoughtful. The man just never dodges a question. He answers every one, whether you're from *60 Minutes* or the *Toledo Blade*" (pp. 232-233). However, just as there are excellent interviewees, there are times when a subject is unapproachable because of his personality or simply because he is having a bad day. On these occasions, the one you need a quote from either avoids you or won't talk. For instance, Joe Paterno, the legendary football coach at Penn State University, told reporters before his turnaround season in 2005, "I don't like you guys anymore." His reasoning for this change was, "I can't trust you guys anymore." He added, "I'm just being honest with you. It

The career of a sport journalist can be challenging at times, especially when a legendary figure in the sport industry—such as Penn State football coach Joe Paterno—is on your beat. Covering a team and interviewing the key participants can be very difficult, especially when the sport entity is struggling or the athletic figure has just had a bad outing.

is no fun." A few weeks later he was conciliatory with the reporters. "I know what kind of job you guys got. It's a tough job. I got a tough job, you got a tough job. And once in a while, you write things that I think you're jerks, and once in a while I say things and you think I'm a jerk. OK? But that's the way it works out" ("Making Amends," 2005).

Definition of Sport Journalism

Sport journalists write game stories and report on anything related to sports. Oftentimes, this includes much more than reporting on athletes and events. "Being a good sportswriter is a blend of many things," notes sportswriter Joanne C. Gerstner. "Sports today is business, sociology, medical issues, agents and contract disputes, crime, and lots of games and practices." To understand activities and duties faced by sport journalists, it is best to start with an understanding of journalism. Although there are many definitions, at its core journalism could be defined as an act, a

ritual, or simply the dissemination of information (Folkerts & Lacy, 2004). The same definitions for journalism could be applied to sport journalism.

1. Sport journalism could be defined as an act because there is a method to the collection, presentation, and distribution of sport information through a medium.

2. Sport journalism could be defined as a ritual because the reporting on sports helps to sustain, enrich, and challenge societal norms.

3. Sport journalism—because it informs the public about sport-related activities, personalities, and events—could be defined as the dissemination of sport information.

Regardless of the definition of sport journalism, its delivery systems can include such outlets as sports sections of newspapers, sports magazines, sports radio and television stations, and sports Web sites.

Journalists have been involved in informing the public throughout the history of the United States. Although the work of reporters was prevalent in the 1600s and 1700s, the role of journalism as an occupation did not evolve until the 1830s. Similarly, sports reporters were around long before the arrival of newspaper sports sections. Although sports articles were published in the first half of the 19th century, Henry Chadwick, who is known as the first sports reporter, covered baseball for the *New York Herald* in the late 1850s and 1860s (Garrison & Sabljak, 1993). In 1870, Middie Morgan became the first female sports reporter when she covered track races for *The New York Times*. Over the years, sport journalists and the print sport media have been quite influential. For instance, journalists were instrumental in giving Purdue University its nickname. In the story covering the Purdue football team's 44-0 defeat of Wabash College in 1894, a newspaper referred to the "burly boilermakers from Purdue." Since that nickname was coined more than a century ago, the distinctive mascot of Purdue has held strong (Manring, 2005).

Qualifications of Sport Journalists

Today's sport journalists are expected to have several qualifications.

Knowledge of Sports

Sportswriters and editors need to possess some knowledge of sports. Journalists involved with writing and editing sports books, sports magazines, and newspaper sports sections need to have a background in sports. This does not mean that journalists need to have played competitive sports. It does mean, however, that there must be some familiarity with competition and sports in general. Interest in sports is not a prerequisite, but at a minimum a sport journalist needs to be familiar with the sports with which she or he works. Because this is a prerequisite, the field of sport journalism is wide open to anyone—female or male—who has knowledge of sports. "People raise an eyebrow when they hear I'm a sportswriter, as there aren't too many women doing that job,"

says Gerstner. This is not surprising when you look at the sports sections of newspapers. As Pedersen, Whisenant, and Schneider (2003) noted, "While some females break through the barriers and into positions as sports editors, reporters, and photographers, males continue to dominate the sports newspaper media" (p. 378). They found in their study of Florida daily newspapers that all of the positions were dominated by males. The positions examined were executive sports editors (100%), prep sports editors (95%), sportswriters (91%), and sports photographers (79%). Gerstner goes on to explain that her gender is not the only thing that people are surprised by when they discover that she is a sportswriter. "Some people imagine me sitting at games, eating popcorn and drinking a beer, cheering away. Others wonder what I'm doing in a men's locker room, imagining some pretty crazy things. My answer is always the same for the curious: My job is nothing like what you think. Yes, I'm at games, from the NBA Finals to the Olympics, but I'm never cheering. Yes, I'm in men's—and women's—locker rooms, interviewing athletes. But no matter where I am, I am always at work, trying to be impartial, handling tough deadlines, and doing the very best job I can."

Strong Writing Skills

Most sportswriters and editors have developed strong writing skills through experience and reading. "I think [the state of sportswriting today] is better than ever overall, by far. There are better writers, especially better young writers," explained sports columnist Dave Anderson (2005). "To me, writing goes back to reading. If you don't like to read, what would make you want to become a writer? And if you want to be a writer, there's no better training than reading" (p. 42). In addition to reading a lot and mastering grammar and language, effective sport journalists avoid the use of exaggerations, colloquialisms, and clichés. Through their writing style they have the ability to pull readers into their stories and sustain the readers' interest. This commences at the beginning of the story with the lead (or "lede," which is the opening line of the article). The most famous sports lead was written by Grantland Rice (1880-1954), the legendary sportswriter whom we examined in detail in chapter 3. Sports editors of today would have changed his 1924 "four horsemen" lead if it were submitted by a sportswriter today. Although Rice's lengthy introduction was missing some of the key elements of the five *W*s and *H* (who, what, when, where, why, and how), it was written for a different audience at a different time. What it does illustrate is great sportswriting. Rice is one of the best writers to cover sports, and prospective sportswriters could learn a tremendous amount by reading how he communicated his thoughts through exceptional prose. Because of tight deadlines imposed on today's sportswriters, many of their leads are written during the game without the luxury of in-depth contemplation and poetry. "You often have to write a lead while the game continues, and keep subbing to make the editions, with one eye on the game, the other on your typing," explained Bud Collins. "You're under the gun, as the saying goes. If you're not fast in pounding out stories that make sense, another form of journalism with more lenient deadlines may be the way to go" (Glatzer, 2006, ¶6).

Ability to Create Structure and Write Effective Leads

Mastery of the inverted pyramid is also a necessity for sportswriters. The inverted pyramid is the way in which sport journalists guide their writing. Furthermore, it is the natural way to tell a story, it provides readers the essential information quickly, it aids headline writers, and it makes it easy for editors to trim the story. At the top of the inverted pyramid is the first section, which includes a strong lead. According to Anderson (1994), "The most difficult task when writing a sports story is to structure the most appropriate, effective lead. Story flow often will fall into place naturally if the article begins with a suitable lead" (p. 32). Anderson explained that there are several categories of sports leads:

- Summary sports leads present the most important information in the first paragraph.

- Narrative sports leads paint the scene for a feature story.
- Descriptive sports leads immediately thrust the reader into the action.
- Contrast or comparison sports leads establish relationships between news angles, issues, or timeframes.
- Background sports leads provide background material before the article or story is developed.
- Staccato sports leads give information in short and rapid bursts.
- Direct address sports leads pull the reader in by putting the reader in the lead.
- Question sports leads pose a question to move into a story.
- Quotation sports leads start the article with a quote that encompasses the thrust of the story.
- Literary sports leads allude to literature.

Anderson (1994) cautioned, "Always remember, however, to make the lead accurate, readable, grammatical, and understandable. You also want to entice the reader to stay with the story to its conclusion" (pp. 32-33).

The second section of the inverted pyramid contains the main facts, and the third section develops the story with facts less significant near the bottom. The fourth section includes facts that are interesting but dispensable.

Versatility

The ability to write a variety of stories is also a requirement of sport journalists. In traditional journalism there are varying kinds of news. These kinds include soft (i.e., human interest), hard (i.e., serious), and deep (i.e., investigative) news stories. In sport journalism, the articles range from long investigative features to short recaps. Media expert Helitzer (1999) noted that sports pages contain "1) news stories that report the results and description of recent action, 2) statistics, standings, and schedules, 3) features that interpret people's actions, 4) features that encourage fan expectations" (pp. 109-100). Helitzer (1999) added that there are

Typical Game-Day Activities for a Sportswriter

At some point, most sport journalists are involved with writing a game story. For a professional baseball beat writer, this happens 162 times a year (not counting spring training and off-season coverage requirements).

- *8 a.m.-4 p.m.* The typical game procedure for sportswriters—often the beat writers—starts at the office (for a home game) or in the hotel room (for an away game) with some initial research and formulating of stories and story ideas.
- *5 p.m.* Contact sports editor to determine what is needed (e.g., game story, sidebars).
- *5 p.m.* Go to press box and find assigned seat. Press boxes are considered home for sport journalists who cover athletic contests. Generally, the media relations and sport information staffs work to make the press box as accommodating as possible to the working members of the media.
- *5-6 p.m.* Go to field, locker room, or team office and conduct pregame interviews with players, coaches, and team executives.
- *6 p.m.* Call sports editor or copy desk to confirm submission agenda and deadlines.
- *6-7 p.m.* Grab a bite to eat with colleagues in the press lounge.
- *7-11 p.m.* Receive pregame notes, media guides, fact sheets, and other materials before, during, and after the game.

- *7-11 p.m.* While in press box during game . . . do not cheer. Pay attention to press box public address announcements, sheets of information with play-by-play, scoring summaries, team and quarter statistics, player participation summaries, drive charts, quote sheets, player updates, and injury reports.
- *8-10 p.m.* Begin formulating plot line for story and write sidebars about interesting aspects of the event as the game progresses.
- *10:30 p.m.* Head to field with 6 minutes left in the game. Interview key participants either on the field or in the locker room after a 10-minute cool-down period.
- *11 p.m.* Insert quotes into story, finish the article, and send it to the copy desk.
- *11:01 p.m.* Call to make sure the article was received.
- *11:15 p.m.* Call the copy desk to determine if there are any questions regarding the story.
- *11-11:45 p.m.* Continue to update the article and insert quotes for the later editions of the newspaper.
- *12 a.m.* Leave the press box for the parking lot when everyone is asleep.
- *8 a.m.-4 p.m.* Wake up the next morning and begin working on postgame analyses, feature stories, and advances for the next game.

eight feature formats including championship stories; profiles; roundups; the next game; sidebars, quotes, anecdotes, and humor; statistics; the wrap-up; and photo layouts and line illustrations. A recent advertisement for a "sports reporter" position at a small newspaper explained the responsibilities and activities that such a position requires: "Responsibilities include covering three county high schools, along with other school and community sporting events. You'll work in a fun, fast-paced environment. Writing/photography/design experience preferred, but will train the right person. We're looking for a highly-motivated self-starter who loves writing and sports" ("Member Bulletin Board," 2005, p. 2).

Principles Associated With Sport Journalism

In their book *The Elements of Journalism*, Kovach and Rosenstiel (2001) noted that the principles of journalism include telling the truth, maintaining loyalty to citizens, practicing the discipline of verification, maintaining independence from those covered, undertaking independent monitoring of power, providing a forum for public criticism and comment, making the significant interesting and relevant, keeping the news in proportion and making it comprehensive, and having an obligation to personal conscience. Sport journalists are held to these same principles.

Truthfulness, Accuracy, and Credibility

Sport journalists must produce stories and sports sections that are truthful and accurate. If they are not accurate, readers will not return to that source for information. Texas Tech basketball coach Bobby Knight is not a fan of the print media. He once stated, "Absolute silence—that's one thing a sportswriter can quote accurately." If all readers were convinced of this, sports reporters would soon lose all of their readers and be out of business. This is why there was such a controversy when Mitch Albom, a legendary sports columnist from Detroit, wrote a story about an event before the event took place. When the story was published with inaccuracies, Albom had to apologize to his readers and the profession. For the sake of truthfulness, accuracy, and his readers, Albom will not take that chance again. Closely associated with truthfulness and accuracy is the issue of credibility, which can be lost through errors (e.g., factual, grammatical), biases, and sensationalism.

Objectivity and Independence

Sport journalists must uphold the principle of independence or objectivity. Although missing a deadline, getting a name wrong, or arriving late to a game are offenses that cannot be tolerated, Bud Collins listed "failing to get all sides of a story" first in his list of worst mistakes sportswriters can make (Glatzer, 2006, ¶13). According to Mindich (1998), the five components of objectivity are

- detachment,
- nonpartisanship,
- reliance on facts,
- balance, and
- the inverted pyramid style of writing.

Some have wondered whether sport journalists, just by the nature of their field, can comply with the objectivity components appropriately when compared with traditional journalists on the news or business sides. For example, sports beat assignments rely on sources. If you report on something that is not acceptable to the source, the source may not continue to provide the much-needed information. Therefore, although sport journalists often claim independence, in all reality they often blur the line between upholding journalistic standards and sustaining a relationship with their sources (e.g., athletes, coaches, administrators). Folkerts and Lacy (2004) noted that objectivity is "looking at a story as though through a perfect lens uncolored by a reporter's thoughts about a subject; trying to view a story from a neutral perspective. Some critics believe pure objectivity is impossible and that fairness and balance are more important" (p. 43). To provide fair and balanced reporting, sportswriters and sports editors cannot be homers (i.e., fans unable to provide both sides of the story) of the teams they cover. They are writing and publishing stories to inform the public, not to promote the sports team or athlete. Their role is to provide readers with objective critical analysis, unbiased reporting, and full disclosure. Although sport journalists have to balance reporting and entertainment, the refrain, "no cheering in the press box," must be upheld on the sports pages of newspapers and magazines. In fact, the Football Writers Association of America (FWAA) has a policy that there is no cheering in the press box. Involved in this issue of objectivity is determining what should and should not be published. Sport journalists must look at the public's right to know versus the person's privacy. We discuss legal ramifications of such decisions in chapter 14.

Pressures Experienced by Sport Journalists

Print sport media professionals face numerous pressures in their line of work (see figure 7.2). Some of these pressures are faced only by sportswriters (e.g., interviews), whereas some pressures are faced by all print sport media professionals (e.g., deadlines). Although some professionals consider these pressures undesirable, others view them as the positives associated with the profession. For instance, there is intense pressure to cover a beat. But sportswriters often enjoy this pressure because it provides them a sense of accom-

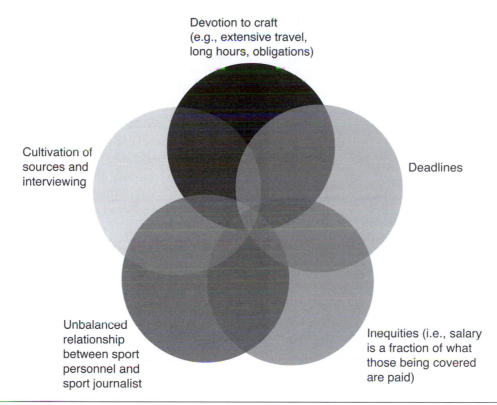

Figure 7.2   General pressures faced by print sport media professionals.

plishment and satisfaction while fulfilling their competitive needs. So, pressure in sport journalism does not necessarily have a negative connotation. Some pressure is good in sport journalism, but too much pressure can cause burnout, frustration, improper decision making, and ethical missteps.

Devotion to Craft

First, there is the pressure of devotion. This is a pressure because a sport journalist must be devoted to his or her craft. This devotion involves extensive travel, odd and long hours, in-season excesses, and off-season obligations. Covering a beat can be very stressful. A beat writer must know everyone and everything about his or her beat (i.e., the team or sport that the journalist is assigned to follow). For example, beat writers and investigative journalists broke the stories in 2005 about steroid abuses in professional baseball. When the scandal reached the front page of every newspaper, Barry Bonds went on the defensive, pointing a finger at the media and blaming sport journalists for not letting the story go

away. Karen Crouse, who at the time was with the *Palm Beach Post* but has since moved on to *The New York Times*, turned the spotlight back on Bonds. "To blame us ink-stained wretches for the stain on baseball caused by the unfolding steroids scandal is to badly miss the mark," she explained. "Like a lot of baseball people, Bonds addressed the issue of performance-enhancing drugs by attacking snitches like Jose Canseco and any scribe intrepid enough to sidestep the myth in search of the truth. If, as Bonds inferred, Canseco is motivated by jealousy and journalists are either 'jealous, upset or disappointed,' what does Bonds' own morality have to do with it?" Crouse, who was a journalism major and member of the swim team at the University of Southern California, added, "If not for reporters uncovering the dirt in baseball's recent past, there would be no hope for cleaning up its future. . . . One person's snooping is another's supervision" (Crouse, 2005, p. 4C).

Deadlines

The second pressure is deadlines, which can be overwhelming. All stories must be sent by a certain time. Although we covered deadlines previously, we reiterate that these impositions by sports editors can be exhausting, frustrating, and exhilarating all at the same time.

Inequities in Salary

The third pressure is unconscious jealousy regarding salary differentials between sport journalists and the often wealthy athletes they cover. "At one time there was probably more camaraderie among reporters and athletes," noted sports columnist Bud Collins. "Neither side was making much money—reporters sometimes more. But now, so many professional athletes are millionaires. Having decided feelings of entitlement after being fawned over in high school and college, they take themselves extremely seriously, and can be very difficult to deal with" (Glatzer, 2006, ¶5). Sport journalists are not in the profession to get rich. Although there are some relatively wealthy journalists writing columns for the major papers or authoring sports books, for the most part print sport journalists earn a fraction of what those who are covered earn.

Unbalanced Relationship Between Sports Personnel and Sport Journalists

Fourth, there are different pressures depending on the level of sports (e.g., interscholastic, intercollegiate, amateur, minor professional, major professional) being covered. It is much more intense to cover the Philadelphia Eagles than it is to cover the youth flag football championship in a Philadelphia suburb. Involved with the different levels are differences in accessibility. Often, the most accessible sports and organizations are the least covered. Some individuals, teams, sports, and leagues are more accessible than others. The symbiotic relationship that exists between sport and the media is tilted in favor of sports personnel in major commercial sports. Although the sports personnel need the coverage for their own public image and promotional exposure, they have the upper hand in the relationship. They can ignore sport journalists or work with them. Sport journalists know when they can inter-

view the sports personnel and what questions and subjects are acceptable. Not knowing or failing to follow accepted protocol can mean the loss of access, information, sources, and eventually the beat assignment.

When Nick Saban joined the Miami Dolphins in 2005, the much heralded coach and football executive was available at a press conference and then went to work putting his management and coaching team together. Throughout his work in this area, the media were not allowed access to the media work room and there was an information lockdown with the team. "Bill Belichick, Saban's mentor, wastes neither words nor effort in New England. He is not warm and fuzzy. He is nothing at all, except a winner," explained veteran sports columnist Dave George. "If the same thing happens in Miami, Saban can coach the team from an undisclosed location, for all I care, and he can seat reporters in the nosebleed section. If it goes the other way, giving us the stiff-arm won't be the priority it is today. He'll be hiding from you instead" (George, 2005, p. 10C). Saban left the Dolphins for the University of Alabama in 2007. Although the major commercial sports teams often have the upper hand in dealing with reporters, if a working relationship is not established with the media there will be nothing but trouble when the team is losing or if negativity surrounds the franchise (e.g., New Orleans Saints during the 2005 season).

Probably the best (or worst) example of the unbalanced relationship between an organization and the press is found in Oakland, California. The Raiders, under their renegade owner, Al Davis, have a unique approach to working with the sport media. For the most part the NFL franchise simply abides by the minimum requirements handed down by the league. The organization sometimes even fails to do that much, as when the NFL fined the franchise $50,000 in 2003 for not abiding by the league's media accessibility requirements. Traci Curry (2003) explained, "Among the cadre of sportswriters who regularly cover the team—indeed, throughout the NFL—the Raider franchise is known as the toughest, most secretive, and most paranoid to report and write about" (¶2).

Although the Raiders are an extreme exception to the rule, they do represent the uncooperative side of media relations. Lawrence Wenner noted that "conventional cooperation is typical in the professional sports leagues." He added, "The reason cooperation is generally given is that it contributes to positive good will, with access being the primary commodity in the sport press" (Curry, 2003, ¶85-86). Despite the obvious benefits (e.g., free publicity, access to fans) from having a strong relationship with the press, some teams, administrators, coaches, and athletes believe that they do not need to work with or accommodate the media to advance their agenda. "The relationship between the Raiders and the press is reminiscent of the chicken and the egg," says Curry (2003). "Is the team's widespread and dedicated following a result of a carefully crafted public image channel through the media? Or do the press flock to the team because of its organic popularity?" (¶98).

The individual working relationships between sportswriters and the sport industry participants they cover is often a challenging and uneasy association. Although intense confrontations (e.g., Ryan Leaf and Jason Williams) are rare, there is often an adversarial relationship between the two parties. "Generally athletes feel that writers don't really understand their sport and endanger the athlete's livelihood with unfavorable reports," explained *Boston Globe* sports columnist Bud Collins. Even the most approachable athletes can be offended by a story or sportswriter. Rick Reilly (2003a) detailed such a situation in his book *Who's Your Caddy? Looping for the Great, Near Great, and Reprobates of Golf.* Professional golfer Tom Lehman is known as one of the nicest players on the PGA Tour. His relationship with Alan Shipnuck, whom Reilly describes as "a particularly aggressive golf writer for *Sports Illustrated*," had been strained when Shipnuck approached Lehman for an interview. According to Reilly, "The last time they spoke, it went something like this. Shipnuck: Can I talk to you? Lehman: No. Shipnuck: Why not? Lehman: I don't like you. Shipnuck: Oh. Lehman: What do you want to talk about? Shipnuck: (Tour pro) Joe

Durant. Lehman: Oh, OK. Here's my quote: Joe Durant is a great guy and if you rip him, I'll stick my fist down your throat and remove your heart. Shipnuck: Oh" (p. 141). Other well-known personalities (e.g., Ted Williams, Bobby Knight, Barry Bonds) have had frequent clashes and overt hostility toward many members of the sports press. Knight once explained his feelings for sport journalists. "I do not hate the press," stated Knight. "Some of you are really good at what you do. A lot of you are good friends and I really respect you. I think there are a lot of sorry bastards in the press, but there are a lot of good people, too" (Ryan, 1992, p. 33). Just as sports participants are frequently frustrated with sportswriters, the same could be said for the other side. "Naturally reporters feel that athletes don't understand their business, the responsibilities of both to the public," explained Collins, "and that the reporter has a job to do, too, which is not being a cheerleader" (Glatzer, 2006, ¶4).

Some athletes do understand the relationship. Nicklaus once explained to Reilly (2003a) about his approach to the media. "I just always thought if you fellas thought enough of me to wait around after my round and ask me a question, I ought to stop and answer it. I figured it was part of my job and part of yours" (p. 233). Fellow professional golfer Tom Watson explained in John Feinstein's *Caddy for Life: The Bruce Edwards Story* (2004), "It's my duty as a player to talk to the media." Former NBA All-Star and current television commentator Charles Barkley once explained on the show *The Big Idea With Donny Deutsch*, "I learned early on to be nice to the media because the media are nice to those who are nice." One of the most media-friendly sports figures is Bobby Bowden, head football coach at Florida State University. Bowden (2001) explained his philosophy of dealing with the media: "The news media is the most powerful force in athletics today. As most seasoned coaches know, you'd better get them on your side, and for heaven's sake don't lie or try to deceive them, because they will eat you alive" (p. 205). The legendary coach added, "I've enjoyed a favorable reputation with the media since being at Florida State, and I've worked hard for that reputation. Part of my success owes to my appreciation of the difficult job they have. Sportswriters are obligated to write a new story every day. They've got to dig up something interesting to say, without fail, day after day after day. Goodness, I couldn't write an interesting new story once a month, much less once a day! Consequently, I try to make myself accessible and give them something interesting to write about, perhaps some insight or observation they might be interested to know" (p. 206).

Cultivation of Sources and Interviewing

The fifth pressure involves the cultivation of sources and the process of interviewing.

Beat reporters have to walk a delicate tightrope because they are obligated to break stories and cannot be scooped by other journalists, but at the same time they have to nurture their relationship with sources. The sports reporter must establish a network of sources and stay on top of every story. "Covering a beat takes endurance, as you will be faced with travel, finding unknown places, covering games and practices, dealing with coaches, managers, players, trainers and front office staff, as well as trying to be a creative writer producing interesting and factual copy," explains veteran beat writer Joanne C. Gerstner. Involved with the beat assignment are the demands of getting the inside stories and breaking the important stories, or getting the "scoop." "The competition is fierce," says Gerstner. "Today's wired world means the competition could be anybody from a sports Web site in Serbia to ESPN to the TV or radio stations in your own town. A lot of rumors fly around, making the cultivation of good sources a critical factor. Some sources just want to be first with news, no matter if it is accurate or not. I want to be first and accurate, which can be tough."

Sport journalists need to get the participants' perspectives. To get their quotes, journalists need to ask the right questions and avoid clichés. They often have to enter the locker room to secure these quotes. The locker room can sometimes be a challenge because of confrontational and even hostile comments and actions by some sports personnel against reporters. Furthermore, some athletes, coaches, and team officials do not make themselves available. For instance, in the NFL, if an assistant coach doesn't want to talk, he doesn't have to. A number of head coaches (e.g., Bill Belichick) in the league put their assistants off limits. The only time a player or coach has to talk is media day at the Super Bowl. They submit to interviews or are fined. Although interviewing can be stressful, it can also be enjoyable, especially with talkative, intelligent, and humorous sport industry participants and leaders. Dave Anderson, a sports columnist with *The New York Times* since 1971, was recently asked about his more memorable interviewee. "Muhammad Ali," stated Anderson (2005). "We've never had anybody like Muhammad Ali, and we'll never have anybody like him ever again." The Pulitzer Prize–winning sportswriter added, "Somebody would ask him a mundane question and he would go into a monologue for the next 20 minutes. You very rarely had a sit-down question-and-answer session with him" (p. 42).

CHAPTER WRAP-UP

Summary

This chapter covered the first segment of the second component of the Strategic Sport Communication Model (SSCM), sport publishing and print sport communication. Sport publishing is the business or profession of the commercial production and dissemination of information related to sport. Print communication involves any medium that disseminates printed matter related to sport. The first print delivery system examined was newspaper sports sections. In the United States, 1,457 daily newspapers are published, most of which have sports sections that range from one page to dozens of pages. Sports sections, first established in 1895 by William Randolph Hearst, now employ thousands of professional journalists who gather, select, process, and present sports for newspapers.

In addition to newspaper sports sections, sport publishing involves sports books, sports news delivered through wire services, sports on the Web, and sports magazines. Sport journalism can be defined as an act, a ritual, or simply the dissemination of sports information. Some of the qualifications of sport journalists are knowledge of sports, strong writing skills, the ability to develop stories, a mastery of the inverted pyramid style of writing, and the ability to write various types of sports stories. Some of the principles of sport journalism include accuracy, truthfulness, credibility, objectivity, and independence. The pressures that confront sport journalists are numerous and include devotion, deadlines, inequitable salaries, unbalanced relationships, cultivating sources, and interviewing.

Review Questions

1. What are the definitions for sport publishing and print sport communication?
2. How is the phrase "symbiotic relationship" evident in sport and the mass media?
3. When did a newspaper create the first sports department and sports section?
4. Is there a difference in the size (output) of and personnel behind sports sections? Who are the journalists involved with providing and editing the written material for newspaper sports sections?
5. Why are sports editors known as gatekeepers?
6. What are the avenues an individual can pursue to publish a sports book?
7. In what ways do some sports bloggers affect the credibility of journalism?
8. Why are some sports magazines considered niche publications? What are their functions?
9. What are the qualifications to become an effective sport journalist? What pressures are associated with the job?
10. What is the role of wire services and technological advancements in print sport journalism?

Discussion Questions

1. In what ways does the "symbiotic relationship" between sport and the media affect print sport communication? Provide examples.
2. How does print sport media coverage affect the profitability of sport entities? How has it affected specific sport entities?
3. How has print sport communication evolved?
4. How are sports editors and publishers gatekeepers? How do their decisions affect the symbiotic relationship between sport and the media?
5. How has newspaper sports coverage evolved to what it is today? How has competition from other media affected the manner in which sport journalists operate?
6. How does sports coverage in newspapers differ from that in other media?

7. Of the qualifications necessary to be an effective sport journalist, which do you perceive as most important and why?

8. How has some print sport coverage become "infotainment" rather than a means to inform the public?

9. Why is it important for print sport journalists to cultivate and maintain relationships with sources? How can this relationship sometimes become strained? How does the relationship affect the credibility of the print sport journalist?

10. How have the growth and demand for niche sports magazines affected print sport communication?

Group Activities

1. Select three daily newspapers: one with a small circulation, one with a medium circulation, and one with a large circulation. How do the sports sections at these daily newspapers differ? How are they similar? What does your examination of these daily sports sections tell you about the symbiotic relationship between sport and the media?

2. Have each member of your group identify two niche sports magazines. Why are the sports magazines that you selected considered niche sports magazines? What segment of sport consumers do these niche sports magazines serve? How are the niche sports magazines similar and how do they differ? How do the niche sports magazines compare with sports magazines with mass appeal?

3. Have your group interview a print sport journalist and write a feature story on him or her. Present your feature story to the class.

Individual Exercises

1. Examine newspaper Web sites to determine their coverage of sports. This content analysis can include a determination of what sports are covered, what links are provided, and what type of advertising is on the site. You can access many of the nearly 1,500 newspapers that have Web sites by going to www. newsvoyager.com and clicking on one of the newspaper links.

2. Write a game story on a sport event of your choice. You must attend the event in person and submit your story via e-mail to your instructor by 10 p.m. the evening of the event. After submitting your story, write no more than a two-page mini-analysis summarizing your experience. Did you meet your deadline? What hindered or facilitated the meeting of your deadline? What pressures were associated with meeting your deadline? What type of information did you need to write an appropriate game story?

3. Select a print sport journalist of your choice. Interview the journalist regarding his or her daily activities and responsibilities. Write a one-page summary of the interview.

Internet Sites for Additional Learning

Associated Press: www.ap.org/

Bill Frakes: www.nppa.org/competitions/best_of_still_photojournalism/2004/winners/still/index.cfm?category=SPY&place=1st

Campus Photo Shoot: http://gostanford.collegesports.com/sports/m-baskbl/spec-rel/022304aaa.html?page=1

Editor and Publisher: www.editorandpublisher.com/eandp/index.jsp

John Biever: www.getthatgig.com/dayof_SIphoto.html

Local Newspaper Directory: www.newsvoyager.com/voyager.cfm

Magazine Publishers of America: www.magazine.org/home/

National Sportscasters and Sportswriters Hall of Fame: www.salisburync.gov/nssa/

NFL Stadium Specs for Photojournalists: www.photojournalism.org/football.html

Photo Gallery: http://sportsillustrated.cnn.com/multimedia/photo_gallery/

Photojournalism: www.poynter.org/content/content_view.asp?id = 15422

Peter Read Miller: www.peterreadmiller.com/

Reuters: http://about.reuters.com/home/

Sports Columnists: http://sports.espn.go.com/nba/news/story?id = 1929084

Sports Illustrated: http://sportsillustrated.cnn.com/

Sports Shooter: www.sportsshooter.com/index.html

Sportswriting Community: www.e-sports.com/pages/About-Us

United Press International: http://about.upi.com/

Walter Iooss: www.walteriooss.com

CHAPTER 8

Electronic and Visual Sport Communication

LEARNING OBJECTIVES

▶ To learn about diverse types of electronic media and their coverage of sport

▶ To become aware of key pioneers and media practitioners in sport and to consider the growth of technology through radio, television, cable, and emerging technologies and their impact

▶ To understand the progression and changes in sport journalistic content

▶ To recognize advertising's role in the development of sport media

▶ To consider media challenges and opportunities for reinvention and growth within sport communication

PROFILE OF A SPORT COMMUNICATOR

Shelley Smith

In the post-Watergate era when many students wanted to become the next Bob Woodward, Shelley Smith thought, "Wouldn't it be great to write about sports?" Smith says that when she was a journalism and political science major at the University of Nebraska, "If you didn't like sports, there was nothing else to do." A self-described "rabid football fan," she found that sport was a natural progression for her. After she took a newswriting class, she was hooked.

Smith admitted that team sports weren't "a cool thing to do" when she was growing up, so she skied competitively and played club tennis. "We still had P.E. classes where they would teach square dancing," says Smith. Although she jokes about her sports background, she clearly has demonstrated her expertise as a sport journalist in many arenas. After she graduated from college, her first job was with the Associated Press. One of her formative experiences occurred at a grain elevator explosion in Iowa. She remembers running a mile to a farmhouse to use a phone for updates because there were no cellular phones or laptops. "There were men trapped in the grain elevator," says Smith. "I learned to think on my feet and to write in my head quickly. Whoever thought that would pay off in television?"

And pay off it has. She has written for the *San Francisco Examiner* (1984-1987), and she lived in Japan and wrote for the United States military's *Stars & Stripes* (1987). During her time as a newspaper sports reporter she won a Randolph Hearst Award for her coverage of Title IX in 1986. From 1989 to 1997, she wrote at *Sports Illustrated*. She has effectively used the interviewing, reporting, and writing skills gained from her experiences as a print journalist in her current job at ESPN.

Smith believes that ESPN is unique because the network hires reporters from newspapers and

© Rich Arden, ESPN

magazines and "wants the same standards as print." She began working part-time at ESPN in 1993 and became full-time in 1997. In explaining the various aspects of what she covers for the network, Smith notes, "It's gangs in sport, cardiomyopathy, salary cap issues, and social issues of every area." Everything somehow has a sports angle. On the day of Hurricane Katrina when everyone was evacuating New Orleans, Smith arrived. And when the O.J. Simpson story broke, she was on a vacation on a houseboat and returned to cover the story. "There is no typical work week. It's like being an ER doctor," says Smith. "You're on call constantly."

Smith has covered everything from the NBA finals to the BCS championship game, NHL Stanley Cup championships, USC football, golf, tennis, and boxing. Smith says that stories at ESPN are assigned according to "who can get there the fastest and whose schedule will allow them to do a story." Smith lives in Los Angeles but covers more than just the West Coast. Among her greatest accomplishments, she broke the story on athletes with gang ties for ESPN's *Outside the Lines—Turf Wars, Gangs & Sports*. She also won a Sports Emmy for her coverage on Magic Johnson and AIDS, which appeared on ESPN's segment on AIDS and athletes.

Like many journalists, she has also written books, including *Just Give Me the Damn Ball* with NFL playmaker and friend Keyshawn Johnson and *Games Girls Play: Lessons to Guiding and Understanding Young Female Athletes* with sport psychologist Carolina Silby. This helps her relate to her daughter Dylann, who is a journalism major and soccer player at the University of Oregon. Despite her busy schedule, Smith still finds time to see the Ducks play one game a weekend in Eugene, Oregon.

"Learn to do everything. Intern, intern, intern," Smith recommends to aspiring sport journalists. "Don't be afraid to ask for help and advice. Don't be afraid to take a chance." She encourages students to meet people and attend sporting events. "People rely too much on e-mails and phones—go get the story." For those students interested in broadcast journalism, she recommends hiring a voice coach to work on inflection and suggests watching tapes. And for women, Smith says, "Realize the standards are different. Make sure you ask good questions. Everything you do is scrutinized—the way you act and the way you comport yourself in interview and social causes, so be aware of that."

Smith highly recommends the career to students with a keen interest in all facets of sport. "Sports is not limited to games. It's personality, controversy, crime, corruption, and scandal." The veteran reporter adds, "That's what makes it the most diverse field to cover. You have the fun of games and drama and immediacy, yet you have social issues that touch athletes just like other people."

This chapter divides electronic media into four categories: radio, television, cable television, and sport documentaries. It offers an overview of each medium and then discusses sport and sport communication. In earlier chapters, you learned sport communication's definition and the components of the Strategic Sport Communication Model (SSCM). You also learned about sport communication careers, theories, and the history of sport communication as well as sport publishing and print sport communication, organizational communication, and interpersonal sport communication. This chapter on electronic media offers an overview of each electronic medium from its invention and early stages to maturation. The chapter starts by providing a macroscopic view of each medium and then delves into how each medium covers sport and fits into the sport communication model.

Alina Bernstein and Neil Blain (2002), in their seminal work on sport and media, wrote, "It is often difficult to discuss sport in modern society without acknowledging its relationship with the media" (p. 3). The media's attention to sport not only is vital in sport's popularity and development but has been influential in sport's social impact. Each electronic medium has transformed sporting events into intimate experiences, bringing fans close to the action through audio, pictures, and dialogue. Fans experience events in real time and gain insider access to athletes, coaches, and sports. The media additionally focus on issues transcending sport. This started with television, which forced other media to change the content and style of stories and gave fans more outlets to satiate their desire for sport information. Although the media still offer game stories and feature stories, they also provide detailed information on social, cultural, political, and historical issues. They additionally discuss the longstanding historical significance of an event and implications for future impact. From the skating scandal at the Salt Lake City Olympic Games to the dearth of African-American coaches in men's division I-A football to NBA star Kobe Bryant's trial, all is fair game. With HDTV, fans can view games with keen clarity. With ESPN mobile, fans can get updated sports scores and trivia on their mobile phones. "ESPN Full Court" enables fans to follow their favorite college basketball teams for the entire season. With "Mike and Mike in the Morning," fans can tune in to ESPN Radio for their daily morning dose of sports news. These are just a few of the options available on electronic media that enable fans to experience sport at their convenience 24 hours a day. The electronic media, more than anything, have introduced sport to more fans and sustained the passion through vivid pictures, provocative commentary, and real-life stories. The electronic media begin with radio and end with cable television and emerging technologies. Figure 8.1 illustrates this segment of the second component. Each medium has contributed to sport's growth and each medium possesses unique attributes that enable fans to fully experience the excitement and drama of sport.

Shelley Smith (this chapter's opening vignette), Gayle Gardner, Lesley Visser, Andrea Kremer, and other veteran female sportscasters paved the way for sideline reporters such as Erin Andrews. Here, Andrews—after working the sideline in the Orange Bowl—interviews Penn State quarterback Michael Robinson. Andrews, a former studio host for the Atlanta Braves and Thrashers with Turner Sports, secured a position with ESPN/ABC after she gave the network some of her tapes. She has stated that she prefers the sideline over reading a Teleprompter in a studio. The number of female sportscasters has increased dramatically over the past 2 decades. In the early 1990s there were fewer than 50 female sports reporters working in the 630 network affiliates.

This chapter serves as a precursor to chapters on new sport media, advertising, public relations and crisis communication, sport communication research, sociological and legal issues, and future trends. Singularly or together, electronic media have a profound impact on sport communication, from sparking and satiating fans' desire for sports knowledge and trivia to showcasing live sport and uniting fans through a common communicative experience. This is especially true with radio, which united people in the early 20th century as they listened to boxing bouts and sporting events in their homes or in the public arena.

EXPERIENCING SPORT THROUGH RADIO

As the first electronic medium, radio had an effect that was powerful and immedi-

ate. According to communication and journalism professor Susan L. Brinson (2005), "Since 1920, broadcasting has been one of the defining features of modern American sociocultural, political, and economic life" (p. 1). We cannot ignore or escape its pervasive and puissant influence on American culture because it directly affects every element of our lives. Although we have many forms of electronic media today, radio was first among the national mass media and gave people the chance to connect via programs, music, drama, sport, or political messages.

On November 2, 1920, the first broadcast informed Americans of Senator Warren G. Harding's victory over Governor James M. Cox from a 100-watt transmitter in a dilapidated shack. Pittsburgh's KDKA became known as "The Pioneer Broadcasting Station of the World" with this presidential election night coverage (Harbord, 1929, p. 61). For the first time individuals heard election results and

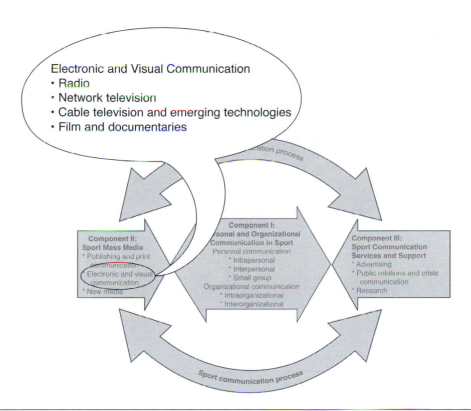

Figure 8.1 Electronic and visual communication is the second segment of the second component of the Strategic Sport Communication Model.

returns live, and the Jack Dempsey–Georges Carpentier boxing bout of 1921 drew thousands of listeners to shops, halls, and many other places where they shared a communal experience. By the beginning of 1922, 30 stations broadcast their music and messages to 60,000 receivers in America (Ackerman, 1945). Westinghouse was the first company in radio with station KDKA and then WBZ in Springfield, Massachusetts, and later Boston.

Adam Neft expresses the feelings of many of the professionals in sports radio. "The most rewarding aspect is to have a job I enjoy, get paid pretty well to do it and to get access to games, practices, and press conferences, that very few people get," explains Neft, a sports reporter and talk-show host for ESPN Radio-Sportszone WSZ in Louisville, Kentucky. In addition to hosting pre- and postgame shows and a call-in show, Neft prepares and plans daily morning sports shows. "Typical daily duties include making calls to local sport information offices and other media contacts,

setting up pertinent interviews, doing an air shift, cutting a daily promo, and doing other radio production (commercials, liners)." The sports radio profession is attractive to many individuals and has an exciting and storied history.

History of Radio and Sport

Sport was important for radio networks in the 1920s and 1930s. Networks like NBC with its Red and Blue networks and CBS as well as Mutual Broadcasting System helped establish radio as a primary medium. Listeners wanted to hear about boxing bouts, their favorite horses, football teams, and baseball teams. "Fandom" was one element of radio's ability to connect the nation and overcome differences in race, gender, age, and locations. Grantland Rice made his radio debut for WJZ in Newark, New Jersey, for the Western Union Telegraph Company's broadcast of the 1922 World Series between the Yankees and Giants. Rice used a radiophone to broadcast the game to more than one million people within 300 miles. This was his only play-by-play, but he regularly appeared on radio shows as a guest, interviewer, or commentator. For NBC radio, he interviewed sports and media celebrities such as Ty Cobb, Bobby Jones, Babe Ruth, Walter Hagan, Ring Lardner, and Knute Rockne (Blanchard, 1998; Harper, 1999; Vaillant, 2002).

The "golden age of radio" began in the 1930s and continued through the 1940s, when the medium reached maturity as more listeners tuned in for entertainment and information on news, sports, and politics. As mentioned in chapter 3, individuals had more leisure time and people relied on radio and the movies for entertainment and enjoyment. During the 1930s, the number of homes with radios increased from 12 to 30 million and advertising revenue expanded from $40 to $155 million. Although the Great Depression affected all aspects of American life, radio recovered quickly and sustained its place in American life. According to media historian Margaret A. Blanchard (1998), "Radio became the one widely available distraction from the awful daily struggle" (p. 239).

Radio has appealed to individuals for different reasons. It added sound to listeners' experiences while using words as primary means for communicating messages. Although newspaper journalists in the early 20th century used imagery and stylistic devices to transport readers to the events, radio incorporated the sounds fans would hear if they were at a game, bout, or match. This included crowds' cheers and boos, referees' whistles, the sound of a baseball bat or basketball dribble, car engines, tennis balls being hit, or any number of things. The term *actuality sound* (Andrews, 2005, p. 122) refers to sounds you would hear if you were live at the event, enabling listeners to imagine the event, the players, the fans, and the stadiums or arenas. Radio incorporates the journalist's voice with sound, music, interviews, and commentaries. Key radio play-by-play sportscasters included Mel Allen, who started broadcasting Yankees games in 1939. He was baseball's first nationally recognized voice and was known for his

"How about that!" Other prominent baseball announcers appeared in television like Dizzy Dean, who hosted *Game of the Week* beginning in 1953. Dean and other baseball players like Pee Wee Reese, Phil Rizzuto, Tony Kubek, Joe Garagiola, Bob Uecker, and Tim McCarver have offered play-by-play and color analysis (Andrews, 2005; Jicha, 2004).

Emergence of All-Sports Radio Format

Today, fans still catch games on radio as they did in the 20th century, but now sports radio has its own place on radio. In 1988, there were no stations with the sports format; however, in less than 10 years, WFAN in New York reaped $50.3 million. From Lee "Hacksaw" Hamilton and "Mike and the Mad Dog" to Eddie Andelman and Papa Joe Chevalier, sports radio caters to the much-coveted male demographic with its sharp and often off-color dialogue and commentary. From Sports Byline USA, airing in 1988, to ESPN Radio, which debuted in 1992, and One-on-One Sports Network, which started in 1993, all reach fans through affiliates nationwide. Fans tune in daily to hear their programs, ranging from irreverent, edgy shows to the more straight-laced programs. Listeners can debate topics of the day, express their views, and engage in lively discussions.

Some radio station owners have chosen to not go with the all-sports radio format. "What we have management to find is that unless you're in a town with a major league franchise, it just doesn't work," reasoned Greg Wyatt, a former ESPN anchor who now owns and operates three radio stations in Florida with his wife (Pedersen, 2005a, p. Z24). Many radio station owners, however, refuse to buy into that line of reasoning. That is why by 2005, there were 470 all-sports radio stations across the United States (Pedersen, 2005a). The power ratios appear to back up the all-sports radio stations. It is not unusual for sports or talk radio to be the top billing format in terms of power ratios. These ratios, according to Stark and Schiffman (2000), "measure the sales strength of individual formats by showing how many cents on a hypothetical dollar each format returns in ad revenue" (p. 116). This means that if sports talk had a power ratio of 1.82, in a market where each audience share is valued at $1 million in ad revenue, a sports talk station would bill $1.82 million per share. Hosts like Fox Sports Radio's *The Morning Extravaganza's* Tony Bruno have gained popularity and hosted the in-game show in EA Sports' video game Madden 2005. Sports radio's core demographic is the 25- to 54-year-old male, and its ratings remain steady and consistently show gains in each ratings period. For example, Katz Media Group revealed that sports radio stations had a 2.5 share of the 25-54 male audience during the ratings period from June 30 to September 21, 2005. This is 4 percent higher than that same time period in 2004 and 9 percent higher than the summer of 2003. During that time, however, sports radio's rating decreased 5 percent among males aged 18 to 34. Arbitron found that New York City's WFAN had a 2.7 rating; Chicago's WMVP had a 2.1 rating and WSCR had a 2.0 rating; Philadelphia's WIP had a 3.2 rating; and Boston's WEEI had a 6.6 rating (Berardini, 2004; Brown, 1998; Grossman, 2005b).

Although males are the coveted demographic in sports radio, the targeted audience consists of different levels of interest in sport. The first segment of the targeted audience could be called the main target of this format. It consists of sports nuts who thrive on scores, trades, suspensions, and playoffs. This audience makes up the bulk of listenership to any all-sports formats. Although it is the largest audience, it is not the only targeted audience. The audience that is made up of fans who are interested in just one particular sport is another target. These fans will not tune in 24 hours a day, but they will tune in when their favorite sport is being played or discussed. The last targeted audience consists of those who like sports but are not devoted faithfully or fanatically to any particular team or sporting event. This group just tunes in to catch up on sporting news and to become aware of the sports scene. These are three targeted audiences of the all-sports radio stations. They all have one thing in common: They all have at least some interest (whether passive or active) in sports.

In 1994, Nanci Donnellan, the "fabulous sports babe," became the first woman host of a national sports talk radio show, and she was also the first to run her own program. Although women such as Lesley Visser, Gayle Gardner, Andrea Kremer, and Robin Roberts worked as sports reporters and anchors on network or cable, most of the sports radio stations across the United States are dominated by male employees. In fact, 89.8 percent were men in 2002. From 1994 to 2001, Donnellan was heard nationally on ESPN Radio and SportsFan Radio Network until she took time off because of breast cancer. Her autobiographical book *Babe in Boyland* details her experiences. Today, some popular sports radio hosts are Ralph Barbieri and Tom Tolbert at KNBR in San Francisco, Mike North at WSCR in Chicago, and Glenn Ordway at WEEI in Boston (Schultz, 2005; Sweet, 2002b).

Radio's Popularity and Its Ability to Adapt

RCA founder David Sarnoff set up a boxing bout to promote radio on July 2, 1921. For 30 years, radio was stable, steady, and solid. Television took advertising revenue away from radio in the 1950s, but radio adapted by seeking the local sports fan interested in high school and college sports. Two of the benefits of radio are its low costs and simple technology. Live radio coverage generally is reliant on telephone transmission, especially at small stations that can only send one reporter to cover an event. Larger stations use microwave signals or Cellcast, which uses cellular phone technology to transmit signals. All stations use mixers allowing talent to mix their voices with other audio. Additionally, reporters and producers use microphones for interviews with athletes and coaches and for extraneous noises like crowd cheers and boos (Schultz, 2005).

Although radio cannot offer the same visuals and technology as other electronic media, it has adapted with new technology and targets of its own. High-definition (HD) and satellite radio, local audiences, and an emphasis on sports talk radio all have enabled the medium to thrive and cater to diehard sports enthusiasts and fanatics. Often, radio is used to supplement other media. A fan might watch a game on television and then go online to discuss its outcome with other fans in chat rooms or might call a sports talk radio show to debate issues or share ideas.

Viacom Infinity Broadcasting chairman and CEO Joel Hollander thinks that radio's power lies in its intimacy and prevalence in American culture. Upwards of 250 million people listen to radio daily in the U.S. alone, and four million are satellite radio subscribers. Sirius and XM have gained the most attention in satellite radio, especially for their affiliation with sport. Sirius signed a $107 million contract for 5 years with NASCAR starting in 2007. XM has a multiyear deal to broadcast the Indy Racing League as well as the 2005 Indianapolis 500. Sirius also broadcasts the NFL, the NCAA men's basketball tournament, the NHL, English Premier League Soccer, and the NBA to its 1.14 million subscribers, whereas XM's 3.2 million subscribers can hear MLB, college sports, and *The Washington Post*'s *The Tony Kornheiser Show*. 20.5 million satellite radio subscribers are expected by 2009, further reinforcing radio's adaptability and commitment to progress and change (Bernstein, 2005d, p. 15; Bruscas, 2005; "Infinity Boss," 2005).

Although radio is a pervasive medium, radio executives are aware of increasing competition from cable television and emerging technologies and recognize the importance of local business in markets. From savvy cable television marketers to teams opting for in-house radio production and sales, radio faces challenges yet adapts to changes. One example is the courting of Howard Stern fans. According to Bridge Ratings & Research, 1.4 million of the 6 million listeners who weekly tuned into Stern's show will follow him to satellite radio, which means that 4.5 million will be fair game. Because sports radio shares the same audience as Stern, it is natural for them to seek his listeners. Another example is sports radio's brand extension through themed restaurants and publications. WQXI in Atlanta seeks to

be like a sport marketing company as evident in its weekly magazine, *Score Atlanta;* sports guidebooks authored by on-air talent; and plans for a high-tech restaurant with plasma televisions, high-speed Internet access, radios, televisions, and other media and technology choices for clientele. Kansas City's 810 Zone is WHB-AM's restaurant, which boasts partners and Kansas City Royals players George Brett and Jeff Montgomery. Minneapolis' KFAN The Restaurant is another example of brand extension as the radio station in the name bolsters awareness and exposure. From HD radio (digital) to satellite radio, the medium has adapted to changes in technology and addressed its competition. Although its strength is sound and audio, its reach and power are infinite. It enables sports fans to interact on issues with other sports fans. It enables sports fans to hear their favorite games in their cars, homes, or offices. And it enables sports fans to gain insider information on teams, players, and coaches (Grossman, 2005a, 2005c).

Career Opportunities in Sport Radio

Because of the extensive programming and technological developments, different career opportunities are available for those interested in pursuing jobs in radio. All stations, regardless of format, contain certain management and administrative departments. There are owners, general managers, office managers, sales managers, accounting managers, and engineers. There are also operations directors, promotions directors, and program directors. The size of departments varies from station to station, but the roles remain the same. Sports radio builds its audience on the strength of its personalities. The objective of the all-sports radio formats is to have foreground personalities, or very opinionated personalities that will bring forward the content in a lively and vivacious manner. The on-air staff need to be personable, knowledgeable, and easy to listen to in order to sustain audience interest. To succeed in sports radio, shows should have a local flavor. This means they will sound like the city and will discuss the specific city. Because

Bob Lovell (right) is a veteran sports announcer who hosts the popular radio program, *Indiana Sports Talk*. The program, which airs for nearly 3 hours on Network Indiana on Friday and Saturday nights, is broadcast throughout the state on more than 50 stations. The Indiana Broadcasters and Sportswriters Association named Lovell the Broadcaster of the Year in 1999.

most all-sports formats are in cities where the myriad of sports cannot satisfy the thirst of all fans, programming for the masses is easy. The programming for sports radio includes play-by-play, sports news and information, interviews and telephone talk, sportswriters' commentary, health and fitness shows, and shows with very broad appeal. There are also memorabilia programs, fantasy football nights, and sports handicapping shows ("All-Night," 1989; "Listening," 1991; "Sporting Times," 1987; Viles, 1992).

Because of the vast functions at the numerous radio stations in U.S. towns, cities, and metropolitan areas, there are many opportunities in radio. A majority of play-by-play

announcers start in radio because every local radio station covers sports, and radio is open to entry-level applicants. Radio gives vital experience in play-by-play because announcers tell stories with imagery and detail. From how a pitcher throws the ball to how a batter swings, fans rely on play-by-play announcers for images, storytelling, and sports updates. Hall of Fame Brooklyn Dodgers announcer Red Barber was especially talented at this medium.

Daily sports production deals with prepping stories for presentation and producing live events. Producers in broadcast create regular sportscasts, stories, shows, and special programs. Producers decide which stories to air and how they will be presented, including such issues as time constraints and story orders. In live production, the producer supervises every element of production, from preproduction through postproduction. From positioning commercials to communicating with on-air talent, producers need to make decisions instantly and decisively.

EXPERIENCING SPORT THROUGH TELEVISION

Although print journalism and radio clearly influenced sport and sport communication's development, the most powerful and significant of all media is television. According to Douglas Kellner, American television is "one of the most far-reaching communication apparatuses and information and entertainment transmitters that has ever existed" (1981, p. 31).

Bruce Garrison reinforced this in writing: "Television's love affair with sports, especially major professional sports and college football and basketball, was the most important factor in creating a sports-oriented American society" (Garrison & Sabljak, 1993, p. 235). Although many believe that the media transformed sport, sport definitely has transformed the media as well.

History of Television and Sport

In the late 1940s, broadcasters used sport as a vehicle to increase demand for television, which in turn would boost advertising revenues. As noted earlier, the networks sought first and foremost to sell television sets, and by 1950 that figure reached 10.5 million in the United States alone. Early on, boxing, wrestling, baseball, and football were easy to broadcast because the first two were in small, lighted gyms and the second two were played outside. With heavy camera equipment that needed bright lights for maximum efficacy, broadcasters restricted broadcasts to certain events, sports, and locations. On the positive side, sport was inexpensive because no writers, actors, props, or sets were needed. In 1939, a single camera on the third-base line transmitted the first televised sporting event to fans—a college baseball contest between Columbia and Princeton. NBC's *Gillette Cavalcade of Sports,* however, became the first network sports broadcast in 1944, and it stayed on air for 20 years, offering variety sporting events for fans. NBC broadcast the first college football game on September 20, 1945, and Columbia defeated Lafayette by the score of 40-14. That same year on December 1, NBC's new image orthicon camera brought viewers the annual Army versus Navy football rivalry. The late George Halas, founder of the Chicago Bears, only received $900 a game for broadcasts of his team in 1947. Although television programming began as a prime-time event, it moved to weekends during the 1950s. One example included college football, which was now only broadcast on NBC Saturday afternoons with one "game of the week" (Baran, 2006; Bernstein & Blain, 2002; Castleman & Podrazik, 2003; Garrison & Sabjlak, 1993).

In the 1960s, the sports audience increased as advertisers valued sport despite its rising expense. Television, and specifically the camera, could tell each sport's unique story in a visually aesthetic way. ABC broadened its sports coverage in 1960 by contracting to broadcast the first Olympic Games on television in Squaw Valley, California. It paid $167,000 for the first televised Winter Games and tried to acquire broadcast rights for the Rome Summer Games. When CBS outbid ABC for Rome, however, ABC canceled its contract for Squaw Valley. CBS broadcast the games without sponsors and enjoyed high ratings for both games. Jim McKay broadcast from Rome and the network's use of videotape enabled viewers to see events from the same day for the first time (Baran, 2006; Castleman & Podrazik, 2003).

In 1963, the Army versus Navy football game featured instant replay, improving fans' at-home viewing experiences of the game. As discussed in chapter 3, Arledge revolutionized sports broadcasting and the way we experience sport. Not only did he recognize fans' desire to learn more about the human interest side of athletes through "up close and personal segments," but he revolutionized broadcasting's technical elements to capture sport's most dramatic moments on the field and off. His *Wide World of Sports* debuted in 1961 with Jim McKay as host. It showcased many different sports from numerous venues and locations using live and taped segments. It also highlighted popular mainstream sports as well as lesser known sports like bowling and racing. In the Summer Olympics of 1972, Arledge, McKay, and Howard Cosell used satellite transmissions and averaged a 52 percent share for prime time during their coverage. During the 1976 Olympic Games, Arledge's crew of Frank Gifford, Howard Cosell, and Chris Schenkel presented "up close and personal" segments on athletes, adding emotional human interest stories that gained top ratings during most time slots. According to Castleman and Podrazik (2003), "Over the years it established the network's reputation as an effective and innovative source for sports" (p. 137) (Castleman & Podrazik, 2003; Hilliard & Keith, 2005).

On September 21, 1970, Arledge and Rozelle brought *Monday Night Football* to prime time. As sport historian Richard Crepeau (2005) noted, "It certainly has been an institution of historical significance for broadcasting and for American popular culture as well as sport" (¶1). Arledge's ABC paid $8.5 million for the rights to 14 games. In 1970 the Cleveland Browns defeated the New York Jets 31-21, with Cosell and Keith Jackson offering play-by-play and Don Meredith provid-

Tips for Becoming a Successful Radio or Television Sports Reporter

- Take all the classes you can in college in sport, writing, and reporting.
- Obtain an internship so you can gain experience and put together a resume tape.
- Gain practical experience, the most important thing in broadcasting.
- Be persistent—ask to shadow reporters for the day, ask for informational interviews.
- Don't be afraid to ask for help—that's how you learn and perfect your skills.
- Be curious—listen all the time for great tips!
- Be willing to go to great lengths to get a great story—follow-up is key!
- Ask good questions—open-ended questions requiring explanation rather than close-ended questions with yes or no answers.
- Develop a network of sources.

- Take voice lessons to improve diction and articulation.
- Always seek self-improvement—critique your tapes.
- Because sport affects every branch of life and everything has a sports angle, delve into social issues, politics, and other provocative topics.
- Be willing to work all the time even when you're on vacation because if a story breaks, you need to be there.
- Find out things no one else knows.
- Remember that some of the most important quotes come as someone is walking away.
- Go with your gut instinct on stories—use your intuition.
- Build drama through your words and visuals.
- Learn to do everything to maximize your marketability.

ing color. When asked about Arledge, CBS Sports president Sean McManus (he is also the son of Jim McKay) said, "He understood the importance of on-air talent and building stars, whether it was Peter Jennings, David Brinkley, Ted Koppel, Jim McKay or Howard Cosell. He understood how much of your identity really is placed in the people who are in front of the camera. No. 2, he understood that all good television basically comes down to storytelling" ("CBS's McManus," 2006). *Monday Night Football* captured both of these through charismatic and witty announcers and state-of-the-art technology that captured emotion and intimate stories. There were nine cameras on the field and two production units for the beginning shows. As the number of cameras increased, the "sports as soap opera" method of showing athletes' emotions with tight camera shots and angles enabled fans to see firsthand the struggle and conviction of their favorite athletes and teams. The NFL's broadcast rights package was $50 million compared with the

NBA's $2 million and Major League Baseball's $18 million. This was the first time networks realized that "major league sports meant major league broadcasting" (Baran, 2006). As Crepeau (2005) pointed out about *Monday Night Football*, "The amazing thing is how much the habits of the nation were transformed. The football weekend was extended, reducing some of the gloom that is Monday. The ratings exceeded everyone's wildest expectations. MNF became the king of the Monday night television. The other networks could not compete and sometimes gave up trying. People gathered in bars and homes in groups to watch these games and see what outrageous thing would happen next" (¶7). After 36 years, ABC's *Monday Night Football* ended after the 2005 season. ESPN's *Sunday Night Football* moved into the Monday slot in 2006 (Baran, 2006; Castleman & Podrazik, 2003; Schoenherr, 1999b).

ABC also pioneered the celebrity sports announcer, with Howard Cosell on *Monday Night Football*. This lawyer-turned-announcer is considered one of the greatest legends in sports broadcasting. *The Washington Post's* longtime sports writer Shirley Povich wrote the following after Cosell's death in 1995: "Cosell was identified as the foremost sports television journalist of his time. He would have accepted it all with his trademark comment, 'That's telling it like it is'" (Povich, 1995, p. E2). Cosell entertained and recognized the importance of communication skills. He considered himself a "communicator with a human perspective" and someone who would "bridge the gap between entertainment and journalism" (Schultz, 2005, p. 128). Robert Lipsyte called him the "most valuable property in American sports," and he stood up for his beliefs regardless of consequences. Cosell was controversial, and at times, caustic. He supported legendary boxer Muhammad Ali's refusal to join the U.S. Army during the Vietnam War, which cost him his heavyweight title, and he idolized Jackie Robinson for integrating professional baseball in the 20th century. Cosell was also outspoken about baseball's reserve clause and the commercialism in collegiate athletics and the Olympic Games.

Fans loved Cosell's unique style, and according to Povich, "All of this, with his flow of language, was unmatched in the television trade. He didn't merely address the microphones, he articulated into them. And always at length, in that nasal tone that told everybody it was none other than H.C. who was putting on another show. And damn the polysyllables, he used as many as he liked," said Povich. After his controversial departure from *Monday Night Football* in the mid-1980s, he had two radio shows on ABC radio, *Speaking of Sports* and *Speaking of Everything* (Shapiro, 1995, p. A1). *The Washington Post's* Leonard Shapiro wrote the following: "Cosell was arguably the best-known and most controversial sports broadcaster in the history of the medium, attacking the hottest subjects and helping attract a huge audience to ABC's 'Monday Night Football'" (1995, p. A1).

In other sporting events, ABC's broadcast of the 1973 "Tennis—Battle of the Sexes" between Bobby Riggs and Billie Jean King in the Houston Astrodome with Gifford and Cosell gained high ratings during primetime. In the September 20th match, King defeated the 1939 Wimbledon champ 6-4, 6-3, 6-3. King was top-ranked in the world for 5 years and won 12 Grand Slams, 6 of which were Wimbledon titles. She made it acceptable and fashionable for women to be athletes, and she started the Women's Tennis Association, *WomenSports* magazine, and the Women's Sports Foundation (Castleman & Podrazik, 2003; Schwartz, 2000).

ABC broadcast the Montreal Olympic Games in 1976 after paying $25 million for the rights and charging sponsors like Sears, Schlitz, and Chevrolet $72,000 per minute for spots. In the 74 prime-time hours with Jim McKay as host, the network used 25 color cameras, including four electronic sports gatherer (ESG) minicameras. In the late 1970s with the continued expansion of sport coverage, WTBS, WGN, HBO, and ESPN all offered cable sports shows. Additionally, college football and basketball were syndicated nationwide or broadcast through conferences or school-related networks. Broadcast networks recognized that amateur sport especially evokes loyalty, allowing fans to identify with their favorite team, players, and fan bases (Schoenherr, 1999b).

Emergence of ESPN

As noted in chapter 3, ESPN changed sport, and *SportsCenter* arose as a cultural phenomenon through its charismatic, witty anchors, flashy technical tricks, and nonstop sports coverage. Whether broadcasting FIFA World Cup soccer, *Monday Night Football*, PPV boxing bouts, or sports documentaries, ESPN is the best-known TV sports franchise in the world by mixing sport and entertainment. From founder Bill Rasmussen's conception and ESPN's first president Chet Simmon's vision, ESPN now no longer just offers the major leagues and NCAA sport but also includes original series, films, reality shows, and even game shows to appeal to everyone. From its foundation, ESPN has stood apart with creativity and the innovative use of technology. A few examples include ESPN's electronic cut-ins during the 1980 NCAA Tournament where clips of games in progress were interspersed within another game's broadcast. In 1983, ESPN broadcast the first time in stereo, and in 1985, *ESPN Sports Update* offered scores concurrently while televising another event on the television screen. Now, of course, ESPN owns SportsTicker, where scores and information appear simultaneously at the bottom of the picture. Among other advancements, ESPN presented in-game box scores during MLB in the mid-1990s and "K Zone," where viewers could see the strike zone through the box shown in their television screens. It is not surprising that ESPN has won more than 87 Sports Emmy Awards (Hill, 2004a).

In addition to taking advantage of technical innovations, ESPN's shows continue to expand and evolve as the network grows and offers cross-platform buying for advertisers with varied networks and programming options. ESPN is a special brand that has always targeted young males, but when college football became a foundation for the network in the 1980s, it was clear that ESPN sought to widen its audience. This continues to hold true with such shows as ESPN2's *Cold Pizza*, which debuted in 2003 and offers 2 hours of early morning talk, news, and information. What began as a sports-based program now also includes political coverage, news, and pop culture pieces with hosts Skip Bayless, Woody Paige, Dana Jacobson, and Jay Crawford ("Cold Pizza TV," 2005; Hill, 2004a; Reynolds, 2004b; Whitney, 2004).

Although ESPN has changed during the more than 25 years it has been on air, certain things remain constant. Perhaps the most celebrated and famous anchor is Chris Berman, otherwise known as "Boomer," who started at ESPN when he was 24 years old. The National Sportscasters and Sportswriters Association has selected Berman as Sportscaster of the Year six times, and he hosted one of cable's most popular shows, *NFL Prime Time*. This Brown University alumnus shouts "Boomerisms" and has become the "voice and face of ESPN" (Hill, 2004b).

Mutually Beneficial Relationship Between Sport and Television

Networks recognized the importance of sports in ratings in the 1980s, and the three major networks broadcast 1,500 hours of sports in 1985. In 1989, CBS paid $1 billion for rights to broadcast the NCAA basketball tournament for 7 years. That same year, Major League Baseball received $500 million from television and radio for one season. In 1990, NBC paid $150 million per year for 4 years of NBA broadcasts. Additionally, CBS carried the rights for Major League Baseball for four seasons at a price tag of $1 billion. ESPN paid $400 million for rights to 175 games and Sunday night games during that same time period. Networks paid these huge amounts of money to keep sporting events away from their competition and to solidify and differentiate their networks from others. For the first time, sport was part of an overall promotional effort for the entire network.

TV and Football

Live sports continued to draw larger audience numbers, and by 1991, a Super Bowl 30-second advertising spot was drawing $800,000. In 1993, Fox gained NFL rights, paying $1.58 billion for 4 years, and used professional football as a means to gain exposure for the upstart network. With anchors John Madden and Pat Summerall, the network used innovative graphics and introduced cutting-edge technology. In the late 1990s, the networks paid $17.6 billion to cover NFL games, and with the most recent contract, *Monday Night Football* appears on cable. ESPN gained rights to the longstanding show in 2005, and Mike Tirico, Joe Theismann, and Tony Kornheiser do play-by-play and color for the broadcasts (Al Michaels is on NBC with John Madden). ESPN will offer advertisers new media options through the Internet and cellular phones. Additionally, ESPN will broadcast the game on ESPN HD, ESPN Deportes, ESPN Phone, and ESPN.com. During the 2005-2006 season, advertisers like Fidelity Investments, Domino's Pizza, Comcast, Geico, Anheuser-Busch, Lexus, Toyota, and FedEx paid $350,000 for a 30-second spot.

Ex-ABC and ESPN veteran Steve Bornstein now heads the NFL Network, a cable channel launched in 2003 and seen in 35 million households. Although the NFL can threaten to broadcast games exclusively on its own network, it has not used this bargaining power. It has used satellite operator DirecTV and its distribution rights. DirecTV has a $700 million-a-year contract with the network for the *Sunday Ticket* broadcasts of games through the 2010 season. The network also offers off-season programming like HBO's *Hard Knocks* with the Baltimore Ravens, player profiles with *In Their Own Words, How They Were Built* about the NFL divisions and teams, and NFL Europe games. For 2006, the NFL televised a 30-minute show with Super Bowl ads for its video-on-demand platform.

TV and the Olympic Games

The NFL is anticipated to earn $23.9 million in television revenue between 2005 and 2013 with a profit of $3.7 billion yearly and is the most lucrative of sports properties. The Olympic Games, however, rival the NFL in prestige and power. In 1984, ABC paid $91.5 million for the Sarajevo Winter Games and $225 million for the Los Angeles Summer Games. As the Olympics gained profitability, the rights fees reflected this. In 1992, the Barcelona Olympic broadcast rights reached $610 million. Recently, NBC paid $2 billion to win the rights to the 2010 and 2012 Games, which is a 32.6 percent increase over the $1.5 billion the network spent for the 2006 Torino Winter Games and the Beijing Summer Games. In the 2004 Athens Games, NBC sought the youth demographic, focusing on the 18-34 and 12-34 groups. It used text-messaging with AT&T Wireless and presented messages on nbcolympics.com with tie-ins to sponsors like McDonald's, Visa, and Choice Hotels. Best Buy, Circuit City, and Sears broadcast ads in their stores. Sponsors' expenditures averaged $730,000 per prime-time spot. NBC began targeting the younger demographic in Salt Lake City where it enjoyed a 27 percent increase. This could have something to do with the fact that U.S. skiers won 10 medals in 2002, making the

Winter Games more interesting to Generation Y. Skiing has gained media attention because of its increasing popularity, and $13 million is expected from revenue, sponsorship, and television rights in 2005-2006 from the 20 sponsors and NBC (Garrison & Sabjlak, 1993; Higgins & McClellan, 2004; Reynolds, 2005; Stanley, 2004; Woodward, 2005).

There was more televised coverage of the 2004 Athens Games than the "combined total from the previous five Summer Olympics" ("NBCU's Olympics," 2004, p. 8). NBC televised 1,210 hours on NBC, USA, Bravo, MSNBC, CNBC, and Telemundo, including high-definition programming. NBC Cable televised 100 gold medal finals and twice the number of hours than the network broadcast, providing coverage 24 hours a day (225 hours). NBC strengthened its cable broadcasts with veteran anchors Keith Olbermann, Mary Carillo, Pat O'Brien, and Fred Roggin. The use of narrowcasting on niche cable channels enabled fans to see more events and competitions between athletes. Randy Falco, president of NBC Universal Television Network Group, seeks to use more platforms to spark publicity and buzz around prime-time shows, news shows, and cable networks, and the Olympic Games maximize this exposure. Olympic viewers saw all commercials, promotions, and other marketing efforts from the NBC stations and partners. According to Nielsen Media Research, this means that 203 million viewers tuned in, making it "the most viewed non-U.S. Summer Games in history" (Reynolds, 2004a, p. 3). The four cable networks captured 69 million unduplicated viewers. Fifty-four percent of viewers who watched daytime coverage of the Games watched NBC for continued coverage during prime time. NBC earned $70 million on the Athens Games, proving that the Olympics is "the most profitable sports property for any network" (Bernstein, 2004b, p. 19). In 2002 at Salt Lake City, NBC netted $75 million for the Winter Games. For the Torino Olympic Games in 2006, NBC provided ESPN with next-day video clips, which was the first time the network had licensed clips to another network. ESPN had links to NBC's Olympic site, and this promotional arrangement was

Stars of the Gridiron: The Super Bowl Ads

The Super Bowl is consistently one of the highest rated television programs, and some viewers watch the event exclusively for the ads. As a result, the value of Super Bowl ads has increased more than 6,000 percent from 1967 when NBC charged $37,500 for a 30-second spot.

Experts believe that the value of the Super Bowl ad is far greater than media research indicates and the ads might even "generate twice the marketing value from the buzz" (Mandese, 2005, p. 14). Viewers watch the ads for entertainment and as a subject for discussion rather than tuning them out or changing the station as in other shows (p. 14). The event is typically the highest rated program in the United States with 89 million viewers for the 2005 game between the New England Patriots and Philadelphia Eagles. For this reason, advertisers seek to maximize exposure by paying $2.5 million per spot.

The event lures advertisers because of increased viewer engagement. Viewers are much more likely to watch commercials during the Super Bowl than during regular programming. In fact, Starcom's research indicated that 45 percent of Super Bowl viewers pay attention to advertisements compared to only 17 percent for regular programming. A Super Bowl ad's reach is about three times more than that of a regular commercial, and around 10 million Americans watch the Super Bowl exclusively for the ads. Products that appear in ads also sell better and faster. Films advertised during the Super Bowl earned twice as much first-week revenue than those not appearing during the Super Bowl. Perhaps the main draw is the longevity of the ads. Consulting firm Penn Shoen & Berland discovered that 58 percent of polled respondents admitted that they discussed the ads more than the game the following day. The hype and interest in the game continue past game-day also (Atkinson, 2005; Baran, 2006; Bernstein, 2004a; Castleman & Podrazik, 2003; "DirecTV," 2004; Fisher, 2005b; Grover, 2005; Hilliard & Keith, 2005; Lafayette, 2005b; Mandese, 2005; Neff, 2005).

After the game, advertisements dominate conversations and media outlets. Advertisers offer copies of ads on Web sites, and the NFL Network and satellite channel rebroadcast them for fans. Market researcher InsightExpress found that 25 percent of viewers would access the Web to see some of the ads. TiVo also enables fans to record and replay ads if they want to see them again. Talk shows, newspapers, and magazines discuss and judge the winners and losers, interacting with fans and differentiating between creative strategies. This continued attention and exposure affect recall, as evident in studies. According to Don Bruzzone of Bruzzone Research Company, the top 20 percent of ads as far as recall possess eight times the impact a week later than the lowest rated 20 percent of ads. As a "showcase mainly for first-run ads," Cadillac uses the Super Bowl as a means for exposure. Cadillac has advertised since 1999, and since 2002, Cadillac has been the "official vehicle" of the Super Bowl and has "sponsored the MVP award" (Neff, 2005). It is the subsequent buzz that convinces corporations to buy as well as the "viral" marketing and other intangible benefits (Mandese, 2005; Neff, 2005).

---

also a first (Bernstein, 2004b, 2006; Lafayette, 2004a, 2004b, 2004c; "NBCU's Olympics," 2004; "Profile: NBC Sports," 2004; Reynolds, 2004a).

As this section indicated, sport and television share a mutually beneficial relationship. Networks seek high ratings and advertising revenue, and sport fans' loyalty and zeal make it a perfect fit. From monumental global events like the Super Bowl and Olympic Games to regional and local team coverage, television captures the dramatic victories and defeats, tells athletes' and coaches' human interest stories, and offers vital scores, statistics, and overall sport information and knowledge. From television's inception to today, it has changed the way Americans experience sport.

Television's Effect on Sport Journalism

In addition to changing prime-time programming and sporting events, television has also changed sport journalism and improved and expanded the content. With the increasing number of media outlets and options, journalists have focused more on the "why" of events and have interpreted their significance for fans. Television provides pictures, so writers include more opinion pieces and in-depth reporting to differentiate their stories from broadcast packages. Competition stiffened with Internet sites, 24-hour sports talk radio, and cable stations like ESPN, which force newspaper sportswriters to focus more on "enterprise, feature, and investigative pieces" over typical game stories (Strupp, 2001, p. 10). Although the "golden age of sport" created hero worship, sport journalists and reporters today delve into scandals like the O.J. Simpson case, Kobe Bryant's trial, and Barry Bonds' alleged use of steroids.

Journalists continually create new angles to compete with nonstop sports coverage and reinvent by integrating trends, novel subjects, and local stories. According to Red Zone LLC CEO and ex-ESPN wunderkind Mark Shapiro, reporters need to ask difficult questions. "They have to be willing to put themselves out there. And too many of them are worried about how it might affect their friendship with athletes, the coach, the teams and the league," said Shapiro. "What they don't realize is if they have a pattern of asking tough but fair questions, they'll be respected for it and more people will be willing to open up to them" ("Exit Interview," 2005, p. 1). A few examples include *The Washington Post*'s coverage of additional high school sports and New Orleans' *The Times-Picayune*'s focus on youth sports (Garrison & Sabjlak, 1993; Strupp, 2001).

Pulitzer Prize–winning author David Halberstam sums up the state of sport journalism. "It's in such flux because the technology has changed so much. Sport journalism was once a place where print was completely in charge and the columnist was a god, people like Grantland Rice and Red Smith and Jimmy Cannon. The only thing they competed with was the daily story in the paper and radio broadcast. Then you moved into an age of television, when, in fact, print was no longer the prime carrier. Now you've moved into the age of ESPN, which is an astonishing universe of its own and where the sports fan probably goes to get his or her

fix" ("One-on-One With David Halberstam," 2005, p. 34).

The role of the journalist has also changed. Before television, journalists were confined to playing fields and sports arenas, but now with television, cable, and emerging technologies, journalists have more competition and more time pressure to produce stories in real time. As Halberstam says, the reporter must "go where the camera can't go and find the stuff that's not being said on the air" ("One-on-One With David Halberstam," 2005, p. 34). This means journalists must use unique angles to captivate viewers by setting the scene and illustrating action within vivid prose. Although the role of the sport journalist is still to "fill space," journalists need to be versatile and well-rounded while still specializing in certain areas (Andrews, 2005, p. 9). As writers, public servants, watchdogs, entertainers, and personalities, sport journalists must inform, interpret, investigate, and focus by relaying key and supplemental sports news to sports-hungry enthusiasts. Game stories initially touch on the basics of the victory and defeat, but subsequent stories cover the significance and implications of the result for both sides. Beat reporters covering a certain team year-round must intersperse "details, analysis, and reaction" within their articles because they immerse themselves in the life of the beat and grant insider analysis (Schultz, 2005). Feature writers must enliven copy and use anecdotes and creativity to bring athletes, coaches, and action to fans. All journalists must go beyond the playing fields and discuss the significance, implications, and context of key players and events.

In addition to changes in coverage and content, photographs also supplement and enhance articles. Whereas television brings us live pictures and images, magazines like *ESPN The Magazine* and *Sports Illustrated* capture still shots of athletes, coaches, and fans, portraying unique moments in time. *Sports Illustrated* even has a Web site, www.SIpictures.com, that showcases more than three million images from the magazine. Although *ESPN The Magazine* appeals to a younger demographic with its "visually and editorially appealing product,"

(Adams, 2004c, p. 35), *Sports Illustrated* won Time Inc.'s Luce Award honor for "Magazine of the Year" in 2004. *Sports Illustrated* contains high-quality writing and vibrant pictures (Adams, 2004a, 2004b, 2004c).

Career Opportunities in Television

For individuals interested in careers in television, internships are vital because the competition is keen for positions. The hours are very long and pay is low compared to other jobs. In the world of "sports speak," there are options in opinion journalism, where the sports reporter gives opinions to stir up discussion (Rowe, 2004b). Homers are reporters who are sympathetic to local teams, athletes, and fans, whereas a critical sport journalist is quite harsh in stirring up emotion. With first-person reporting, the journalist enters the story, which is considered participatory sport journalism. Social commentary reporting discusses provocative issues like race, gender, and sexual preference. It is best to learn all techniques to increase your marketability. Connect with working reporters and be persistent. Go on any story to gain experience and exposure. For students interested in radio or television reporting, a voice coach is a good investment. Because jobs are very limited, the more and diverse experience you have, the better (Schultz, 2005).

Anchoring and play-by-play are other options for on-air talent. An anchor sits behind a desk and reads copy for evening sportscasts or for sports shows. Good anchors have a great deal of control as far as appearance, voice, knowledge, personality, and creativity. Think about your favorite anchors. Most are charismatic, confident, eloquent, witty, and professional. Play-by-play announcing requires more spontaneity than anchoring and much research. Announcers learn everything they can about players, coaches, teams, and conferences before game day. Play-by-play announcers join a sideline reporter and analyst, and all need to study in-depth statistics and information to inform fans and describe key plays and penalties. John Madden, Keith Jackson, and Brent Musburger are legends in this area.

In television production as in radio, the crew takes care of every part of the broadcast. For television this usually includes a satellite truck and uplink and equipment, and crews are much larger than in radio broadcasts. There can be more than 50 crewmembers depending on the event (Schultz, 2005). All are committed to bringing the most up-to-date and visually aesthetic production to the fans.

Although today's sports fans still turn to television and newspaper as their top choices for sport content, by 2010 three out of four Americans will rely primarily on the Internet or a wireless device for sports knowledge ("How We See It," 2005). This focus on technology has come about partly as a result of cable television and its use of technology.

RECOGNIZING THE INFLUENCE OF CABLE TELEVISION

It is all about choices in today's information-rich media society. Sport has no boundaries in today's technologically advanced society and is a 24-7 passion. According to *SportsBusiness Journal,* 200 million Americans are sports fans, 170 million have cellular phones, and 15 million play fantasy sport games; in addition, Americans bought $24.5 billion worth of video games in 2004, and 2.7 billion hours were logged at sports Web sites in January 2005. Although the average American consumes more than 8 hours of media daily, sports fans log more than 9 hours. The Internet actually feeds the fire because fans usually use it to supplement television, radio, newspaper, and other media. Although most people recognize that newspapers, radio, and television have covered sport awhile, cable also has existed for more than 30 years ("How We See It," 2005; King, 2005a).

History of Cable and Sport

Cable television originally was believed to sharpen reception for regular television viewers. It began in the late 1940s and was known as community antenna television, spreading throughout small areas in the United States. It provided customers with network affiliates, educational television, and sometimes independent stations. Two developments in the 1970s helped propel its growth and acceptance as a modern medium. They include the FCC's Cable Television Report and Order of 1972, which laid a foundation for rules and regulations in the industry, and the use of satellites in the mid-1970s to allocate services to cable systems and networks. Subsequently, the Cable Communications Policy Act of 1984 eradicated the regulation of cable rates, and 1992's Cable Television Consumer Protection and Competition Act reinstated regulation for basic cable and allowed cable companies to fix prices on their premium stations (Blanchard, 1998).

In 1972, HBO was the first premium channel, and by 1980, CNN and ESPN had formed. Although CNN is currently a staple of 24-hour news coverage, it lost $2 million a month in its early stages. Founder Ted Turner used profits from superstation WTBS to keep CNN on the air. Although ESPN also struggled in the beginning, it now has a "church-and-state relationship" with its major properties, and control of the market ("Exit Interview," 2005, p. 1). In 1984, the U.S. Congress passed the Cable Communications Policy Act of 1984, which enabled cable to compete with broadcast. By 1987, more than 50 percent of American households had cable. Cable expanded in the 1990s with original content and additional networks. Multimedia communications now were the new medium. Cable in the mid-1990s offered more specialized content with the advent of the History Channel and Home and Garden, and in 1997, cable's prime-time share was 32.4 percent. As with radio and television, mergers, monopolies, and consolidation were rampant. By the late 1990s, the 10 largest multiple system operators comprised 74 percent of cable subscriptions. By 2000, cable reached 66 million of the 99.6 million U.S. homes that television reached. Strangely enough, the highest rated shows on cable were professional wrestling shows because of their entertainment factor (Blanchard, 1998; "Exit Interview," 2005; Folkerts & Lacy, 2004; Hilliard & Keith, 2005).

Growth of Cable Television and Diversity of Programming

With the new millennium, Comcast purchased AT&T Broadband and served 21 million cable subscribers in the United States. Ted Turner's WTBS became the first superstation on cable, mostly attributable to Atlanta Braves baseball team coverage. Now the top cable networks include Rupert Murdoch's News Corporation, with 2004 revenue at $20.45 billion and key assets Fox Broadcasting Company, Fox Cable Networks, DirecTV, and BSkyB (Bernstein, 2005h). Brian Roberts' Comcast Corporation had $20.31 billion in 2004 with 21.5 million cable subscribers and the assets Outdoor Life Network, Comcast SportsNet, the Philadelphia 76ers and Flyers, and the Wachovia Center. Comcast's first national television advertising campaign described Comcast as the "high-definition sponsor of ABC's *Monday Night Football*" in 2005 (Bernstein, 2005e, p. 13). Other corporations include Rogert Iger's Walt Disney Company with $30.75 billion and ownership of ESPN Networks, ABC, theme parks, and studio; Richard Parsons' Time Warner Inc., with $42.09 billion revenue and Turner Broadcasting, AOL, Time Warner Cable, and Time Inc.; and Bob Wright's NBC Universal (General Electric), with $12.89 billion worldwide in 2004 and assets NBC, USA Network, Bravo, CNBC, MSNBC, and Telemundo (Bernstein, 2005h; Hilliard & Keith, 2005; Jicha, 2004).

The proliferation of sport on more networks and outlets gives viewers many choices. With the increasing interest in niche markets, regional sports networks like Fox Sports Network continue to expand exponentially. In fact, 30 regional sports networks broadcast approximately 80 percent of MLB, NBA, and NHL games. There's Comcast SportsNet Chicago with 3.4 million households, Comcast SportsNet West with 2.2 million, Comcast SportsNet Mid-Atlantic with 4.5 million, and Comcast Philadelphia with 3 million. Other examples include the New York Mets' venture with Time Warner and Comcast in 2006, Fox College Sports, and ESPNU. In other cable networks, Turner Network Television carries the NBA, NASCAR, and the Professional Golfers' Association (PGA); TBS broadcasts the Atlanta Braves and NCAA football; WGN superstation carries MLB's Chicago White Sox and the NBA's Chicago Bulls; USA Network broadcasts United States Open tennis, the PGA, and World Wrestling; FX carries NASCAR and MLB playoffs; and Spike TV also carries wrestling and other male-oriented sports. More and more professional sports teams are developing their own regional networks. The Cleveland Indians organization is one of around 30, which include the New York Mets' and Jets' SportsNet New York, the New York Yankees' YES Network, and the Boston Red Sox' New England Sports Network (Dobrow, 2005; "Growing Number of Professional Sports Teams," 2006; Reynolds, 2005).

ESPN still covers more sports programming than any other network. In 2002, ESPN was the first network to televise four major professional leagues in 1 year. This trend continues with ESPN's broadcasts of Major League Baseball under an 8-year, $2.4 billion contract through 2013. This $296 million per year is a 51 percent increase on ESPN's previous agreement and will include the broadcast of more than 80 games a year including Sunday games. This also includes "broadband, wireless, and fantasy-sports rights" where the network can stream broadcasts via wireless phones through ESPN360 (Umstead, 2005, p. 4). XM Satellite Radio also has a $650 million deal with MLB from 2005 to 2015 (Bernstein, 2005g; Reynolds, 2005).

Although ESPN is a pioneer in sports programming and offered more than 51,000 hours of programming in 2005, smaller cable networks seek to offer sports programming also. One such network is the Outdoor Life Network, which originated in 1995. In addition to acquiring the rights for the National Hockey League (NHL) for $135 million, the Outdoor Life Network also broadcasts the Tour de France. The network started televising cycling in the network's early stages and in 2005 offered 320 hours of the Tour de France to its more than 64 million households. Additionally, it broadcasts Professional Bull Riders

(PBR) events. For 10 years, the Outdoor Life Network has focused on outdoor sports, but now it seeks to add more mainstream sports. Although the Outdoor Life Network seeks to expand its content and programming, other channels like the Outdoor Channel in 25.6 million households, and the Sportsman Channel in around 13 million homes, seek to stay small and focus exclusively on field sports. Other niche sports like paintball, arm wrestling, and table tennis have been broadcast, and ESPN even considered airing a "rock, paper, scissors" tournament (Brown, 2005; Fitzgerald, 2004; Hill, 2005; "How We See It," 2005; Nethery, 2005; Prospero, 2006; Thomaselli, 2005).

Expansion of Content Through Cable Technology

As sports programming diversifies, more organizations, leagues, and teams are updating and expanding content through traditional and new ways. One such example is the National Basketball Association (NBA), which believes content is not just about games and postgame press conferences. In addition to ESPN's 6-year $2.4 billion contract with the NBA, the NBA markets its product in other ways. Technology enables fans to supplement television and cable viewing with in-depth and real-time scores and analysis. According to Brad Schultz (2005), the Internet influences how sports content is "created, distributed, and consumed."(p. 89). Technology and the Internet not only offer content in real time but enable fans to interact with other fans, players, coaches, and media professionals. They also enable fans to purchase merchandise and participate in fantasy leagues and other sports events. The NBA is one league that shows just how to maximize marketing power through technology. The league creates one package for NBA TV's shows, a second for Comcast's Video on Demand platform, a third for Verizon Wireless' Vcast service, and a fourth for Nokia's wireless service and Web site. NBA TV was the first of the professional sports leagues' cable channels and also has an EA Sports "bottom line" graphic offering scores, statistics, and other information for viewers. During the

An NBC television camera operator and several still photographers record the Skateboard Vert action while professional skater Neal Hendrix (left) watches a competitor. In addition to his career as a professional skateboarder, Hendrix made an appearance as a skateboarding stunt double in the movie *The Grind*.

2004 season, NBA Entertainment, which runs NBA TV, built a computer program with intrusion detection systems (IDS) called Digital Television Interface (DTVi), which enables graphics to be linked into the NBA's database and is used with any character generator with a serial interface. It also experimented with Courtside Confidential to link sport and Hollywood. Using their remote, fans could press the SAP button and hear Spike Lee, Star Jones, or actor Tom Cavanaugh's perspectives about the games. TNT, ESPN, and ABC currently have broadcast rights to the NBA, but NBA TV is furthering the league's reach with 66 million homes. It distributes such programs as *NBA Talk*, *NBA TV Insiders*, *NBA TV Live*, and NBA TV's *Fantasy Hoops*. Additionally, the NBA signed a video download agreement with Google Inc. Video.google.com will offer full-length videos for download of every game in the 2006 season (Fisher, 2006; Kerschbaumer, 2004b; Lafayette, 2004d, 2005a; Reynolds, 2005; Stump, 2005).

With technology, "the games, the stats, the players, the other fans—they're everywhere," said *SportsBusiness Journal* writer Bill King. "Thanks to the proliferation of niche TV channels and sports talk radio, the popularity of the Internet and the evolution of wireless devices—170 million Americans carry cell phones—content is available any time, any where in almost any way you want it" (King, 2005a, p. 23). Fans expect and crave content, and technology works together to satiate this need. The sports fan truly is a "24-7 fan" (King, 2005a, p. 23). Technology is especially necessary in reaching the 18- to 34-year-old demographic. "To advertisers, 18-34-year-olds are precious gems, rare and uncut," said King. "Their preferences in programming pull them far from TV mainstream. The Internet, cell phones, video games and digital video recorders promise to make them even more elusive in the coming years" (King, 2006, p. 1). In today's fragmented media environment with niche markets, sport communication organizations must use technology to reach fans and fully exploit marketing potential and profit.

NASCAR also has tapped into new technology as its stock continues to rise with networks. Most races require more than 25 HD cameras. Fox and FX aired the first half of the 2005 season, and NBC and Turner Broadcasting ended the season as part of a $2.4 billion contract expiring after the 2006 season. The new NASCAR contract, which runs from 2007 to 2014, is a $4.48 billion deal with Fox, ABC/ESPN, and Turner Broadcasting. This is a 40 percent increase on average per year from $400 million in the old contract to $560 million in the new. Fox will air the Daytona 500 exclusively (Bernstein, 2005j; Grossman, 2005; Kerschbaumer, 2005).

Although television and cable continue to seek the highest technological advancements, certain challenges come with maximizing innovations. High-definition television—or HDTV—presents challenges in the technical and financial arenas for networks. All the networks airing the NFL will use HDTV, and college football games and postseason baseball playoff coverage will also be available in high definition. Although this allows individuals to enjoy clear, crisp pictures of games, only 9 of the 110 million total television households in the United States had high-definition televisions in 2004. Additionally, the high-definition broadcasts cost nearly 20 percent more than traditional television telecasts. Certain cameras and trucks are necessary, and technical glitches include the need for 5.1 surround sound. There is currently a shortage of trucks for the technology. Additionally, HD takes up a lot of bandwidth, limiting the other content on telecasts. Nevertheless, 15 million American households are expected to use HDTV by 2009. The most popular models include rear-projection LCD televisions and flat-paneled plasma televisions, which can cost up to $10,000. Media conglomerates have prioritized HDTV, as evident in Comcast SportsNet's more than 125 games in 2005, ESPN's 425 games, and MSG's airing of home games in HDTV (Bernstein, 2005d; Kerschbaumer, 2004a).

In addition to new technology, networks' focus on local and regional appeal includes efforts to tap into other underdeveloped markets. This is especially true of the Latino market. Fox Sports en Espanol was the first American network to create a Spanish-language station in 1996, and Fox also has Fox Latin America and Fox Sports World. New York's Madison Square Garden Network was the first regional network to offer Spanish audio through a secondary audio programming (SAP) channel. Comcast has also tapped into this market with their Spanish broadcasts of Atlanta Falcons NFL games on Comcast Sports Southeast. Other Spanish-language stations like Gol TV, ESPN Deportes, AYM Sports, and TyC Sports all specialize in different programming and target demographics. ESPN Deportes has distribution agreements with many cable operators like Adelphia Communications Corporation and Cox Communications. Although the stations offer a lot of soccer and boxing, they also offer other sports like baseball (Morales, 2004).

Cable television and emerging technologies have taken sport and made it a 24-7 passion. The number of media outlets has increased more than 250 percent over the last 40 years, which leads to more shows and programs, more diversity, and more choices for sports fans. From newspapers and magazines to radio, network television, cable, satellite, and Web-based choices, technology has created infinite opportunities for sport communication and its practitioners (Powell, 2003).

SHOWCASING SPORT THROUGH FILMS AND DOCUMENTARIES

In addition to radio, television, and cable, films showcase sport's emotion, its powerful pictures, and athletes and coaches' commitment to competition and their sports. Motion pictures developed from photography and moving picture devices and evolved from peep shows and vaudeville acts. In the 1920s, the film industry was located in California, and by 1930 Warner Brothers, Lowe's, Inc., Metro-Goldwyn-Mayer, Paramount, RKO, and Twentieth Century Fox controlled the industry. When television gained popularity in the 1950s, the film industry responded to the competition by adding color, larger theater screens, and the technical advancements of Cinerama, 3-D, and Panavision. Cinerama produced wide-screen pictures, 3-D gave the audience depth when viewing images, and Panavision used lenses to create depth in a natural manner. Hollywood also released older movies for network broadcasting in the 1950s (Folkerts & Lacy, 2004).

Documentaries began in the late 1890s with actualities, which were short pieces of nonfiction. Inventor Thomas Edison produced sporting actualities like boxing bouts before the turn of the 20th century. Although fiction gained prominence in the 20th century, social documentaries and propaganda appeared during the World Wars, and later in the 1950s to 1970s, television documentaries, direct cinema, or cinema verité were produced. As portable sound film recording equipment developed, documentarians could produce longer, continuous productions. Although sports films have been around for many years, networks like HBO focus on the genre. Ross Greenburg, president of HBO Sports, has been an innovator in sports documentaries and storytelling as evident in *When It Was a Game* (1991), *Fists of Freedom* (1999), and *Nine Innings from Ground Zero* (2004). HBO seeks to delve into the social and cultural significance of events and athletes. Greenburg has effectively presented sport in a dramatic and entertaining way and executive-produced *Real Sports With Bryant Gumbel* and the movie *61** about Roger Maris. In his nearly 30 years at HBO, Greenburg has won 30 sports Emmys, 21 CableACE awards, six Peabodys, and other awards. HBO has also presented *Mantle, Ali-Frazier—One Nation Divisible,* and *Dare to Compete—The Struggles of Women in Sports,* just to name a few (Paige, 2005, p. 16). Other documentarians include Bud Greenspan, an Olympic filmmaker who has documented the 1984 Los Angeles Games, 1988 Calgary, 1992 Barcelona, and 1996 Olympic Centennial Games in Atlanta. Some of his other works include *16 Days of Glory, Los Angeles, Triumph and Tragedy: The 1972 Olympics, The Measure of Greatness, An Olympic Dream,* and *Time Capsule: The 1936 Berlin Olympic Games.* In an interview with ESPN Page 2's Jim Caple, Greenspan said his goal in films is longevity and immortality. The depth and breadth of his work clearly reinforce his desire to produce meaningful, provocative, and socially progressive films that document important moments in sport and cultural history (Bernstein, 2001; Blanchard, 1998; "Bud Greenspan," 2005; Caple, 2005; Clarke, 2005).

In network and cable films, Fox Sports Net broadcast a series, *Beyond the Glory,* which included boxer Mike Tyson, the NBA's Manute Bol, and former Major League Baseball's Cy Young award winner Denny McClain, who became a felon. In other shows, ESPN's *SportsCentury,* which began in 1999, and *Outside the Lines,* from 1990 to present, both take a different approach to sport. The Tennis Channel aired the documentary series *No Strings* about Pete Sampras and *Net Films* about past tennis greats. These and other programs resemble ABC's syndicated series *Greatest Sports Legends,* which was televised from 1973 to 1993. Many of the shows and documentaries deal with strong and compelling content, affirming that sport transcends the playing field and both humanizes and celebrates athletes, coaches, and their athletic and personal feats. In 2005, the top-grossing sports movies according to *SportsBusiness Journal* were *The Longest Yard, Coach Carter, Herbie: Fully Loaded, Cinderella Man, Kicking and Screaming, Racing Stripes, Fever Pitch, Bad News Bears, Dreamer: Inspired by a True Story,* and *Ice Princess* (Paige, 2005; "Top Sports Movies of 2005," 2005).

CHAPTER WRAP-UP

Summary

As technology matured from newspaper and magazine to radio, television, cable, new technologies, and film, sport coverage and the way fans perceive sport evolved, making one thing clear: Sport remains a constant pastime, passion, and vital marketing tool with expansive reach and infinite potential in the economic, social, cultural, legal, and political arenas. This chapter builds on the previous chapters, which set historical context and a foundation for sport communication's development. Like the other chapters, it reinforces the symbiotic nature of sport and the media, which is especially evident with electronic media. From athletes, teams, and leagues using the media to promote their sports, products, and brands to the electronic media using sport's popularity to gain advertising revenue and high ratings, it is evident that both sides work together in a mutually beneficial manner.

The "golden age of radio" started where the "golden age of sport" left off in 1930. Radio enabled listeners to connect with each other in homes as well as the public arena. Radio still used the words of print journalism but added sound to the mix. This meant that fans could hear live commentary from sports announcers, interviews with their favorite players, and crowd noise that enlivened their experience of the event. Today, radio still includes those features but has adapted to technology and variances in content preferences. Two examples are sports radio and satellite radio.

Although print journalism and radio have singular strengths, television more than any other medium has catapulted sport into mainstream America. As noted in chapter 3, Pete Rozelle's and Roone Arledge's role in sport as entertainment and television as a vehicle for showcasing sport cannot be understated. Their contributions to sport television are enormous. It is difficult to fathom a culture without *Monday Night Football* or the Super Bowl and the technology, spectacle, and celebrity that come with these events. The "big three" networks of NBC, ABC, and CBS dominated the airwaves until the advent of cable with ESPN and HBO in the late 1970s to early 1980s. Today, hundreds of stations are available with cable television and satellite, showing how electronic media evolved and matured as times changed and fans' preferences fluctuated. ESPN single-handedly made sport a 24-hour addiction, and *SportsCenter* has a cult following among men and women alike. Although *SportsCenter* often defines ESPN, the network also offers films, reality shows, game shows, and a wide array of programming.

In 2006, for the first time in *Monday Night Football's* history, it appeared on cable television on ESPN. ESPN, like many sport communication outlets, recognizes the importance of emerging technologies, as discussed further in chapter 9. Radio, television, cable, and technology are used by all segments of sport communication organizations to inform, protect, persuade, and justify. More than any other entity of sport communication, the electronic media have the power to reach the greatest number of people and influence perceptions.

Because individuals can only experience a finite number of events, they rely on the media, and especially radio, television, and cable, to inform them about important people and events. This is also true in sport because we can only attend to a finite number of games and events. From the O.J. Simpson trial to the Torino Olympic Games, the media transmit moving pictures and set the agenda for what we see and hear. To be informed citizens, we need to obtain information from as many types of sources as possible to gain extensive insight and to potentially overcome or balance biases at divergent sources. Today's information-rich society enables us to be as informed or uninformed as we choose. It is obvious that fans, sport communication practitioners, and others follow sport passionately and obsessively, which will only escalate with the continued expansion of sport at the local, regional, national, and international levels.

Review Questions

1. Describe key individuals, companies, and networks in the development of radio and sport coverage.
2. How did radio adapt sports coverage to compete with television?
3. Why has sports talk radio skyrocketed in growth and popularity?
4. How has sport on television evolved from the mid-20th century to the present?
5. What are vital skills for sports reporters to possess?
6. Which firms control media content? What are their sport entities?
7. Why are so many advertisers drawn to the Super Bowl?
8. What challenges does high-definition television pose for networks, and what opportunities exist in sport communication?
9. What is the NBA doing to maximize technology and sport marketing through the media? How about the NFL?
10. Who holds the broadcast rights to the Olympic Games, and what are some of their marketing strategies?

Discussion Questions

1. Who are key pioneers in electronic media and sport?
2. How do electronic media outlets and their coverage of sport differ from print journalism?
3. How did radio, television, cable, and emerging technologies expand and improve on previous electronic media outlets' coverage of sport?
4. Who are some of your favorite sports reporters and announcers? What makes their style and techniques effective?
5. How is *Monday Night Football* different now that it's on cable television? Do you prefer ESPN's coverage over ABC's past coverage? Why or why not?
6. What are some of your favorite shows on ESPN? Why do you think it is such a successful network?
7. Discuss several sports films or documentaries. What do you like about them? What don't you like?
8. Given your knowledge from chapter 2 on careers and the brief discussion of jobs in this chapter, what do you think are the most demanding jobs in sport communication? Why?
9. Where do you get most of your sports news? Why do you prefer a certain media outlet over another one?
10. How has sport journalism changed over the years? Address content, style, and coverage.

Group Activities

1. Read your local sports page, watch a local affiliate sportscast, and watch ESPN's *SportsCenter* on the same day. What sports did the reporters focus on? What were their styles of coverage? What differences did you observe?

2. Listen to a sports talk radio program. What was the tone of the host? What did listeners discuss? Write a log of what was covered and your overall observations.

3. Watch a sport documentary. How do sound and images work in tandem in creating the film? How is this genre different from other media? What are the strengths and weaknesses of this medium?

Individual Exercises

1. Write a media diary for a week. Discuss the strengths and weaknesses of the format, media outlet, host, and writers.

2. Conduct an informational interview with someone in the media (either at your university or locally). Ask what drew him or her to the job, the biggest challenges faced, and the typical career progression for someone in that field. Tape the responses or write them down.

3. Watch *SportsCenter* and observe the content of the show and the anchors' verbal and nonverbal gestures. What makes the show so popular?

Internet Sites for Additional Learning

Association for Women in Sports Media: www.awsmonline.org/

Bud Greenspan: http://espn.go.com/page2/s/questions/budgreenspan.html

ESPN: http://espn.go.com/

HBO Sports: www.hbo.com/sports/index.shtml

Kenn Tomasch: http://kenn.com/work/tv/index.html

NBC's Olympic Web site: www.nbcolympics.com/index.html

Sportscasting Jobs: www.sportscastingjobs.com/index.asp

The Olympic Movement: www.olympic.org/uk/index_uk.asp

Women's Sports Foundation: www.womenssportsfoundation.org

CHAPTER 9

Online Sport Communication and the New Sport Media

LEARNING OBJECTIVES

▶ To become acquainted with the Model for Online Sport Communication (MOSC)

▶ To understand the Internet's impact on new and emerging media and sport communication channels

▶ To be cognizant of the factors influencing online sport communication

▶ To understand the components of effective online sport communication

▶ To become aware of new and emerging media in sport communication

PROFILE OF A SPORT COMMUNICATOR

Sean Parker

From the penalty box to center ice, the Web site of the Washington Capitals provides fans with a hat trick of information, interactivity, and identification. The person in charge of completing this hat trick for site visitors is Sean Parker, the director of new media for this franchise of the National Hockey League (NHL). Parker's efforts bring the thrill of hockey straight to fans' fingertips. Responsible for the franchise's online vision, Parker and his team of online sport communication professionals have consistently created one of the top-ranked Web sites in professional sport. "Our content and design are key elements in making our site what it is," notes Parker, whose site includes such features as pregame stories on game days and postgame notebooks. "We maintain a level of consistency with our content." Parker attributes the content of the Web site to the franchise's senior writer. "He's a fantastic sportswriter."

Content and design are two primary factors enhancing a sport entity's online presence, and the Capitals provide site visitors with the best of both. "We get high traffic through our site with many fans going to the message boards and providing opinions on the state of the team," states Parker. "Allowing for fan interaction is a feature that makes our site a top site. Our message board is really a core piece of the site." A recent addition to the message board is the ticker that the Capitals added to encourage posters to return to the home page, read a story, and return to the message board to discuss it. To further foster interactivity with stakeholders, the Capitals provide video and audio files in easily downloadable formats. The goal is to provide fans with formats that are widely available and easily used. Although file formats are available that may provide better quality, Parker illustrates the importance of using

Photo courtesy of Washington Capitals

more mainstream formats. "In the future, we will look to new formats, but we will wait until these technologies are adopted in the mainstream by the majority of users," says Parker. "We have to find the middle ground. We want to provide high-quality interaction, but we have to make sure that the majority of people visiting our site have the capability to use it." The affordability of high-speed Internet has allowed the Capitals to provide more video and audio feeds for their fans. In addition to providing video clips after each game, the franchise provides fans with video clips of interviews from both the Capitals' and the visiting team's locker rooms after every home game.

The online demands of sport consumers force the Capitals to remain current and use new media and communication channels to better provide fans with information on the franchise. "Expectations are much higher for sport Web sites," explains Parker. "Sport consumers are different from other online consumers because of their expectations. They demand current statistics and injury reports as well as the latest news and information on the franchise. Therefore, we are always interested in using new media and technologies to provide them with this information." This is evident given that the Capitals are on the forefront in this area: They were among the first professional sports teams to provide information in new ways such as live video streams for each game, live chats, and podcasts.

New communication channels can be advantageous in communicating and reaching fans as well as providing the sport entity with measurable return on investment (ROI) data. "The immediate nature of the technology allows us to actually measure our ROI," notes Parker. "We can determine how many people are clicking on each page, how many people downloaded an audio clip or podcast, and if someone opened an e-mail. The measurability helps us better communicate." New technologies also allow sport entities to make instantaneous changes to the medium. This is unique compared with traditional media. "With print or broadcast media, Tuesday's story is always Tuesday's story," explains Parker. "With the Internet and new mediums, we can communicate with our fans as stories evolve. We can add a link, or we can add a video."

The Capitals understand the value of their Web site in marketing the franchise. They brand the Web site just as they would the franchise by

placing the Web site address on all promotional pieces. "Everything is branded with www.washingtoncaps.com, whether it is in print or broadcast," states Parker. "We are constantly sending traffic to the site. We will self-reference and link stories back to the site. We meet with marketing and we meet with search engine organizers to generate more traffic and more ticket sales." Sean Parker's approach to new technologies, branding, and Web site management has broadened the appeal and promotion of the Capitals. The various components of the team's Web site—touched on in the preceding paragraphs—embody many of the aspects outlined in the following pages.

The two previous chapters highlighted the first two key segments (publishing and print sport communication and electronic and visual sport communication) of the sport mass media component of the Strategic Sport Communication Model (SSCM). This chapter covers the third segment—new media—and completes the discussion of the second component (see figure 9.1).

The goal of this chapter is to introduce you to the new media that have drastically altered and are incessantly changing the manner in which sport-focused organizations and sport media outlets communicate with their key publics. A little more than 10 years ago, sports fans followed the progress of their favorite sport entities by reading the sports section of the newspaper, listening to sports talk radio, or watching a segment on the evening news. Today, sports fans are much more sophisticated in charting the progress of their favorite sport entities by logging on to various Web sites, downloading video clips and podcasts, and partaking in online chats with other individuals sharing their same sport interests. Podcasting has become increasingly popular because it enables sport consumers to download media and audio files from their favorite sport Internet sites. Sport consumers can then play or view the files on their MP3 players. Technology has dramatically influenced the growth of new sport media. Some believe the

new technology often does more harm than good. Bill Self fits into this category. "One thing I think has hurt college athletics more than anything is the technology age," noted the head coach of the Kansas Jayhawks. Because chat rooms and message boards allow anonymous users to criticize athletic participants, Self commented, "I think the Internet stinks" (Tucker, 2006, pp. 2-3). Although there have been many abuses of the new technology in sport, for the most part the advances in the Internet and new media have been positive. Advancements in technology continue to spur a more sophisticated level of communication and affect the manner in which organizations associated with sport disseminate information. From e-mail, live video streaming, and real-time sport scores to podcasting, web logs (blogs), and game logs (glogs), technology provides the foundation for the growth of the new sport media. These technologies and new media will continue to have a significant impact on sport communication through their ability to provide an instantaneous link between the sport-focused organization and its publics.

This chapter examines the use of the Internet and new media in sport communication. This examination is followed by a discussion of the Model for Online Sport Communication (MOSC). The MOSC highlights the key components of effective online sport communication,

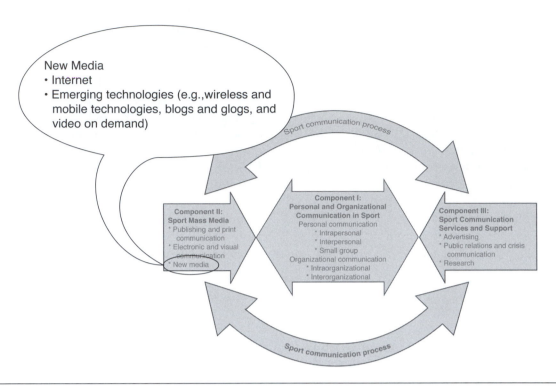

Figure 9.1   The third segment of the second component of the Strategic Sport Communication Model is the new sport media, including the Internet and emerging technologies such as wireless and mobile technologies, blogs and glogs, and video on demand.

focusing on seven important aspects central to sports Web sites. A discussion of technological advances that are affecting sport communication, such as wireless technology and blogs, is included in the final section of the chapter.

SURVEYING THE NEW SPORT MEDIA: INTERACTIVITY AND THE INTERNET

The phrase "new sport media" incorporates the aspects of sport communication and new media. Sport communication, as we discussed in chapter 4, is the process by which people in sport, in a sport setting, or through a sport endeavor share symbols as they create meaning through interaction. But when people talk about the new media, what are they referring to? This must be examined before we discuss the new sport media and online communication in sport. This section examines the application of the new media in sport communication.

The new media were described by McQuail (2002) as "linking information communication technologies with their associated social contexts, bringing together three elements: technological artifacts and devices; activities, practices and uses; and social arrangements and organizations that form around the devices and practices" (p. 38). Aspects of the new media include

- interconnectivity,
- interactivity,
- accessibility, and
- multiple usages.

"New media is a catchall term for various forms of digital communication and technology. Some examples include 3-D animation; streaming video for the Web; virtual reality environments, such as that for video games; content, such as video or audio, for cell phones; and interactive television" (E. Smith, 2005, p. 1A). Many members of society, including millions of sports fans and consumers, have transitioned from reliance on traditional mass media to use of more interactive communication and commercial interfaces, which the Internet provides (Stafford, Stafford, & Schkade, 2004). Although the Internet has been around for more than a decade, we still consider it a new medium because it is different than the traditional media, has dramatically affected communication at all levels, and continues to influence the manner in which organizations and individuals communicate. Compared with traditional sport media, the Internet is immediate and instantaneous. It is a complex medium, but it provides an additional communication channel, serving as an alternative mechanism to establish communication (Peterson & Merino, 2003). Moreover, "the Internet possesses a powerful capacity for efficiently and effectively searching, organizing, sharing, and disseminating stored information, as well as information generated dynamically through various protocols" (Peterson & Merino, 2003, p. 103). The immediacy, instantaneousness, and connectivity of the Internet are often best illustrated in the sport industry. For example, at the official Super Bowl Web site (www.superbowl.com), sport consumers may obtain information such as game recaps and game stats for all past Super Bowls. Additionally, the site includes details and lists outlining award winners, all-time standings, national anthem singers, performers, halftime shows, number of Hall of Fame players in the Super Bowl, a comprehensive list of Super Bowl records, and the regular season statistics for each team to ever make it to the Super Bowl. The site also includes similar information for playoff games. This information is easily accessed, usually within one or two clicks of a mouse, from anywhere in the world with Internet access.

Verizon is a leader in new media technology and sport sponsorship. The company affects the sport industry through its product and service offerings that range from allowing sports reporters to e-mail voice mail through iobi Home to providing Internet access and mobile applications to entire sport organizations. Verizon has national sponsorship deals with sport organizations such as USA Luge and the New York Yankees. The company's sign shown in this photo is directly above the press box at Dolphins Stadium.

The Internet allows consumers to be interactive, which provides a unique communication channel. As Ko, Chang-Hoan, and Roberts (2005) noted, the interactivity on the Internet is a key factor in making it a unique medium when compared with traditional media. By going beyond the interactivity of traditional media, the Internet provides unique interaction tools that help organizations strengthen their relationships with consumers (Bei, Chen, & Widdows, 2004). This interactivity makes the Internet a distinctive medium, and it provides opportunities to access a product without having to experience it in person (Porter, 2001). On sports Web sites, this means that individuals may be particularly active in the communication process by selecting which sections of the site to visit, determining what game clips to download, and even choosing to vote for specific players in competitions such as All-Star games.

EXAMINING INTERNET USAGE IN SPORT

The Internet is a "new normal" for Americans: It has become part of everyday life. The majority of Americans log on to the Internet daily, with those not logging on "constituting an ever-shrinking minority" (Rainie & Horrigan, 2005, p. 59). The affordability and availability of high-speed Internet access have enhanced the quality of the Internet and the experiences of Internet users. This is considered a primary reason for the increased use of the Internet among all populations (Madden, 2003). Sport entities should capitalize on this increased use among populations when communicating their key messages. One advantage to online communication via the Web is that sport entities can essentially eliminate the "gatekeeper." When sport entities disseminate messages through traditional media, they are often edited. However, sport entities are able to craft and shape their key messages and disseminate them directly to the sporting public using the Internet. In other words, sport entities can shape their own agenda rather than having the media shape it for them. McCombs

and Shaw (1972) developed the agenda-setting theory, which centers on the media's ability to stimulate dialogue about certain topics among the public. Essentially, the media, through its ability as a gatekeeper, shapes public opinion by choosing to cover and report on specific issues. This creates the perception in the public's mind that certain topics deserve more dialogue than others. When sport entities use their Web site to communicate with the masses, they are essentially becoming the gatekeepers. Therefore, they can influence the perceptions of their key publics based on the manner in which they craft and disseminate their online messages.

Who Uses the Internet?

The Web has been transformed from a niche medium primarily used by young Caucasian males to a mainstream medium used by the masses (Rainie & Horrigan, 2005). The vast majority of Americans reported that the Internet is a good place to gain everyday information, to communicate and interact with others, to conduct daily transactions, and to entertain themselves (Fallows, 2004, p. i). Research reveals that almost two-thirds of Americans access the Internet, and the majority of Internet users log on to gather information related to specific inquiries as well as to gain information on hobbies and entertainment (Madden, 2003). Fifty-two million Americans reported accessing the Internet to check sports scores and information, with 14 million reporting daily access (Madden, 2003). Similarly, 55% of those using the Internet indicated that when they desire information on sports—such as scores and statistics—they will first go online to obtain the information (Fallows, 2004). Males are more likely than females to access sport information online, and Americans age 18 to 29 are more likely to search for sport information than those older than 30 (Rainie & Horrigan, 2005).

The Internet has also spurred an increase in participation in online sport fantasy leagues. Approximately 11 million people in the United States participate in a sport fantasy league, with 8 percent of American Internet users indicating participation in online fantasy leagues (Rainie, 2005). Online sport fantasy participants tend to be males younger than 40 with more than 6 years of Internet experience. Half of these participants indicate daily use of the Internet, and more than 60% have broadband access to the Internet at home. Online sport fantasy participants are also likely to earn household incomes of more than $75,000 per year (Rainie, 2005).

The Internet has laid the framework for new and emerging media in sport communication, and more than any other medium, the Internet has allowed sport consumers to feed their craving for information regarding their favorite sport products. Technology has enabled sport-focused organizations and media entities that cover sports to provide this information almost instantaneously through the Internet. Although this instantaneous distribution of information can be advantageous, the means by which it is distributed are often complex. Therefore, the manner in which sport information is relayed becomes paramount.

What Makes a Good Sports Web Site?

Sport entities began using the Internet to communicate with sporting publics in 1995. Initially, sports sites were intended to inform franchise and league personnel of the potential for online media usage (M.T. Brown, 1998). Currently, sport organizations rely on Web sites to provide immediate communication with both internal and external publics and key stakeholders. For example, the Indianapolis Colts had just completed a 14-2 season and were hosting a playoff game at the RCA Dome in January 2006. Before this contest against the Pittsburgh Steelers, the Indiana football franchise was fearful that too many of its ticket holders would sell their tickets to others who just might show up to support the rival club. So the Colts e-mailed the following signed note from head coach Tony Dungy and team president Bill Polian: "In an effort to keep the RCA Dome a 'sea of blue' we are asking those of you who have tickets but cannot attend the game to do everything possible to make sure

that your tickets end up in the hands of Colts fans. Our fans are critical to our success on the field, so if you cannot be there please make sure that someone who bleeds blue is in your seat" ("Keep Dome Blue," 2006, p. 1). Teams that are able to effectively use the Internet and other new media have a competitive advantage over those that rely on traditional print communication. Sport entities rely on the Web, according to sport management professor Matt Brown (2003), to "provide information on the organization to site visitors, to generate awareness of their organization, to project a favorable organizational image, and to establish an interactive channel of communication with visitors" (p. 52). Thus, the sport organization's Web site becomes an integral aspect of its communication and marketing strategies.

It is of the utmost importance that sports Web sites reflect the mission and values of the sport organization as well as provide a high-quality online atmosphere and experience for publics. Sport-related Web sites should meet the overall business objectives of the organization. These objectives may range from selling season or group tickets, educating consumers on specific aspects of the sport-related product, fulfilling key components of a sponsorship package, providing an appropriate resource tool for the sport media, or promoting, reinforcing, and maintaining a favorable image of the organization.

Sport organizations rely, to a large extent, on service when promoting and selling their products. An effective Web site can serve as a supplementary service for sport consumers (see figure 9.2). For example, an appealing Web site allows a professional sport franchise to reinforce its image among fans while at the same time creating a sense of identification between consumers and the team. It also creates a social network for fans through message boards, blogs, and live chats. Additionally, it provides essential information for both casual fans (who may log on to check game times, parking restrictions, or other game night policies) and fans who consume the product more heavily (who may desire information on specific players, statistics, or general news on the franchise). As we illustrate in chapter 10 (Sport

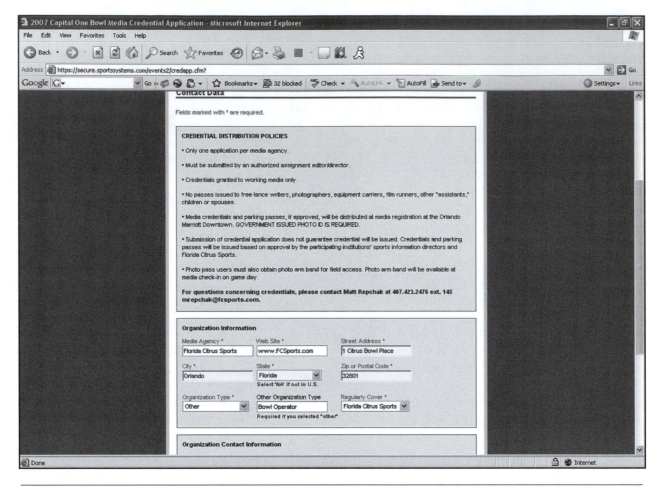

Figure 9.2 The Internet has enhanced many aspects of the sport industry. For example, the sport information and media relations departments for sport organizations often use the Internet for handling media and credential requests. This is the Online Credential Media Manager used by Florida Citrus Sports (FCSports).

Florida Citrus Sports

Advertising) and chapter 11 (Public Relations and Crisis Communication in Sport), these aspects are of key importance when fostering a certain brand image and when selling the sport-related product to the masses.

Although in existence for more than a decade, the Internet continues to be considered a new medium that provides a level of interactivity beyond that of traditional media. This level of interactivity combined with ever-improving technology can benefit the sport entity when communicating with key publics both internally and externally. To use the unique capabilities of the Internet to the maximum potential, sport entities must understand the key aspects of online sport communication. The key aspects of online sport communication are examined in the next section, which presents a model for online sport communication that outlines the primary focal points for establishing effective communication online.

INTRODUCING THE MODEL FOR ONLINE SPORT COMMUNICATION

To understand the nature and scope of online sport communication, one must understand the key aspects influencing online sport communication as well as the factors that are instrumental in cultivating effective sport communication via the Internet. The factors influencing online sport communication are numerous, and several are highlighted in this chapter. In the sections that follow we explain this through the use of an illustration called the Model for Online Sport Communication (MOSC). The factors that influence online sport communication and the components of the model are detailed in the following pages.

A myriad of factors influence effective online sport communication. The MOSC highlights seven factors considered most pertinent to online sport communication. These factors include

1. individuals' level of involvement with the respective sport entity,

2. motives for Internet use,

3. the content of a sport entity's Web site,

4. the design of a sport entity's Web site,

5. the performance of a sport entity's Web site,

6. the usability of a sport entity's Web site, and

7. the commerce of a sport entity's Web site.

The first and second components of the MOSC illustrate the role of people's involvement with the sport entity and their motives in determining Internet use. These components are presented first because together they form the basis for individuals' desires, needs, and expectations when using the Internet and when visiting a specific sport entity's Web site. Depending on the person's needs, one component may influence the effectiveness of the communication more than another component. For example, if someone desires to download a podcast, the performance and usability components of the model may be most pertinent to that person. If the podcast takes too long to download, the individual will not be satisfied and the opportunity for effective and enhanced communication will be lost. In contrast, if someone visits a specific entity's Web site to retrieve game statistics for a specific player, the content, design, and usability components are likely to be most important in the online communication process. The person will want the content quickly,

and the Web site should direct that individual to the desired content through its design and through its usability.

The influence of one's motives in the online sport communication process should not be overlooked when establishing effective online sport communication. These motives influence people's needs, and online sport communication should address these needs. The following components of the model address the online needs of sport consumers. The third component of the MOSC focuses on Web site content. A sport entity's Web site should develop content that not only will meet user's needs but also will reflect positively on the mission and values of the organization. Users will desire a range of content, and the sport entity should provide it quickly. The fourth component of the model illustrates the importance of design in online sport communication. The design of a sport entity's Web site will influence user interaction, which is the element that differentiates online sport communication from other media. This interaction can greatly enhance communication with sport consumers. The fifth component of the MOSC focuses on the performance of a sports Web site and the importance of the user being able to access and download certain features within a reasonable amount of time. The sixth component of the model involves usability, people's ability to use the features of a sport entity's Web site to gather the sport information desired. If a sport entity's Web site is not usable, online sport communication becomes much more challenging, and the sport entity will have difficulty disseminating its messages to publics. The seventh and final component of the model focuses on commerce. Although the Internet is a most effective communication tool, one must not overlook its potential to promote and market the products of the respective sport entity. The role of online sport communication in marketing the sport entity is examined as part of the commerce component of the MOSC. The aspects of the MOSC are instrumental in cultivating quality communication and in assisting the sport entity in gaining an online presence. The factors are very much interrelated and each

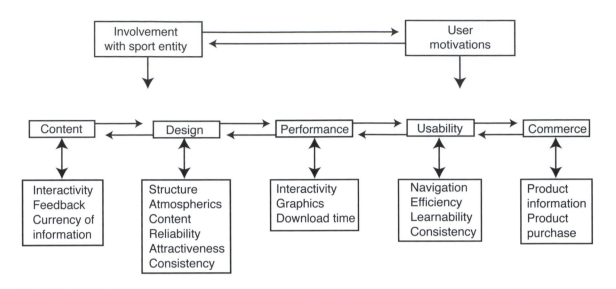

Figure 9.3   The Model for Online Sport Communication.

affects the other. The Model for Online Sport Communication (see figure 9.3) is presented to illustrate these factors.

Involvement With the Sport Entity and User Motivations

As mentioned earlier, the Internet is now a mainstream medium. Because it is used widely by the masses, we need to examine motivations for its use. Just as sports fans' motivations vary for attending a specific sport event or for purchasing a certain sport product, people's motives also vary for acquiring sport-related online information. However, it is often people's level of involvement that affects motivations, needs, and desires when using the Internet. Level of involvement with the respective sport entity must be considered when identifying and discussing sport consumers' motives. People consume the sport product for a variety of reasons, and this consumption can be linked to their level of involvement with the sport entity. Similarly, people's level of involvement with the sport entity determines their motives, needs, and desires when visiting the Web site and will determine why an individual visits and uses a certain Web site. This is linked to Blumler and Katz's (1974) uses and gratifications theory, a well-known communication theory stating that media users are active in selecting which

media to use. The theory suggests that individuals are goal-oriented when using media and will seek the source that best addresses their needs. Uses and gratifications address the "'how and why' of media use motivations, since gratifications are typically defined as some aspect of satisfaction reported by users" relative to a specific medium (Stafford et al., 2004, p. 261). This theory asserts that individuals use the media to satisfy certain needs and wants. Therefore, when people visit a specific sports Web site, they are usually doing so with a specific goal in mind. This goal will likely vary based on the involvement with the sport entity.

For example, someone who has an interest in the Chicago Blackhawks may log on to the franchise's Web site to examine the team's game schedule and purchase a ticket. However, a season ticket holder may log on to the franchise's Web site to download a podcast, read a game recap, or to engage in a live chat with other season ticket holders. Although these two users both have an interest in the franchise, the season ticket holder is much more involved in consumption. Similarly, a sports enthusiast may log on to the French Open's Web site during the Grand Slam to see if a well-known player such as Maria Sharapova or Andy Roddick advanced to the next round. However, a person who is an avid tennis fan may log on to the site to watch video highlights of the day's matches, review match statistics, find the broadcast schedule of matches, or read a player blog. People exhibiting different levels of involvement with the sport entities will visit Web sites for different reasons. They will each have different goals and motives for visiting those sites based on that involvement and, thus, their online needs and desires will vary.

Although the Internet is ever-changing as a mainstream medium, the factors motivating individuals to log on have remained consistent since its inception. The majority of individuals log on to

- check or send e-mail,
- gain information,
- be entertained, or
- engage in e-commerce (Rainie & Horrigan, 2005).

Rainie and Horrigan (2005) noted that although there has been exponential growth, "the hierarchy of metaphors that describe it has remained constant: the Internet is most of all a mail pigeon, then a library, then an amusement park, then a shopping center" (p. 63).

To effectively communicate their message online, sport entities must understand the motives of their key publics when designing, developing, and maintaining online sport communication. Motives influence people's online needs, and they also tend to influence people's strategies in acquiring the desired information. For example, a tennis player in need of a new tennis racket may log on to the Web sites of three different racket manufacturers to compare and contrast different rackets. The player's motive is to gain information regarding the tennis racket to determine which racket is the best option

NBC and Clear Channel—two media entities leading the way in both traditional and new media offerings—joined forces in sports programming in 2005. NBC needed to get back into action sports, so the network partnered with Clear Channel Motor Sports, secured a title sponsor in Mountain Dew, attracted more than 100 action sports athletes, and put together a five-stop phenomenon known as the Dew Action Sports Tour. In 2006, the tour included five cities, three sports (skateboarding, BMX, motocross), a competition series, and a season-ending championship.

for purchase. To gather this information, the player desires to find certain content about each racket, access this content with navigational ease, possibly view the rackets from varying angles, possibly engage in an online chat with other tennis players about a racket's performance, and gain information about the cost of a racket, where it may be purchased, and if it may be purchased online. When any of these components are missing, the sport entity has failed to communicate effectively. Therefore, sport entities must understand not only the motivations of their publics but also the method in which their publics obtain the information.

Methods and Approaches Used in Searching

When people choose to use the Internet, they have two key methods for obtaining the information. These methods, described by Sandvig and Bajwa (2004), are searching and browsing. In using either method, people type queries into a search engine and the documents pertaining to that query appear on the screen. **Browsing** is characterized by more simplistic queries in which several documents are returned and people "browse" through the documents to find the ones that are most pertinent to the information needed. Browsing is also characterized as "navigating through linked chains of hyperlinked documents" (Sandvig & Bajwa, 2004, p. 14). **Searching** refers to a more detailed and strategic search often facilitated by professionals serving as a liaison between the user and the database being searched. Users choose their information-seeking method based on several factors. Most searchers, however, are influenced by their previous searching experiences on the Web site and other Web sites, the information being sought, the formulation of search terms, and search feature accessibility. Browsing with hypertext can be advantageous because searchers do not need to formulate search terms. For example, someone desiring information on Wimbledon might simply type *Wimbledon* into a search box. This will pull up a series of links to pages relating to the Grand Slam event. The searcher may then browse

the links to find the one deemed most appropriate. Some people may simply select the links that they believe are most appropriate in obtaining the knowledge they seek. However, this can be problematic because people sometimes misinterpret category headings. For example, someone desiring information on the U.S. Open tennis tournament may type into a search box *U.S. Open*. Doing so may provide information on not only the Grand Slam tennis event but also the major Professional Golf Association event held each year by the United States Golf Association. In contrast to browsing with hypertext, searching via a search engine can be beneficial because it allows searchers to gain access to specific pages of a Web site without having to navigate through hyperlinks. However, people must be able to develop appropriate search terms for this method to prove effective. Internet users prefer to seek information by browsing because it is perceived as being less difficult than searching. Typically, Internet users navigating sports Web sites are more successful at obtaining the desired information by the browsing method than by the searching method.

The approaches that people use to acquire information when they go online for their searches can be divided into two other groups. These approaches—described by Ylikoski (2005)—are characterized by the reason for the search and are typically considered to be heuristic or analytical. **Heuristic searches** are searches with low deliberation, meaning that an individual will use hyperlinks to navigate through the Web. In contrast, an **analytical search** involves an element of planning, relying heavily on the use of search engines. Heuristic searches are based on trial and error, whereas analytical searches are more focused or more strategic, often requiring more cognitive effort than a heuristic search.

Expectations and Needs of Online Users

As noted earlier, online users' expectations and needs vary widely as a result of sport consumers' involvement level and varying motives for logging on and surfing the Web. Like an individual's level of involvement, these varying motives can also be tied to individuals' uses and gratifications. For example, a sports reporter may log on to the team Web site to gain the most current statistics on players, injury reports, or even the latest press releases. In contrast, a consumer with some interest in the team may read the sports section of the daily newspaper for information on the same franchise. Both people are making choices based on information needs and based on which medium they perceive will best address those needs. Satisfaction is linked to how well the Web site provides information that addresses these users' needs.

Scholars note that motivations for use of a specific medium usually stem from one of two broad reasons:

1. to access content available on a certain medium (e.g., specific information, entertainment) or

2. to gain the experience of using the specific medium including exploring the dimensions of the technology provided by the medium (Stafford et al., 2004).

These two reasons have been defined as content gratifications and process gratifications (Cutler & Danowski, 1980; Stafford & Stafford, 1996; Stafford et al., 2004).

Content gratifications are messages carried by a specific medium, whereas process gratifications are the uses of the specific medium. In other words, content gratifications focus on the message whereas process gratifications focus on the features and technology of the medium itself. For example, a sports fan may log on to a Web site to gain information about an upcoming game or a community relations event hosted by a specific sport entity. However, a different person may log on to a specific franchise's Web site to download a podcast. This user is specifically interested in using the technology provided on the Web site.

Several general expectations and needs are apparent among most consumers. Papacharissi and Rubin (2000) were two of the first scholars to classify individuals' motives for using the Internet. They noted that the motivations include using the Internet for its interpersonal utility, as a pastime, for information seeking, for convenience, and for entertainment. Additionally, online users expect sports Web sites to have both visual and emotional appeal. Most consumers expect to receive an enjoyable and quality experience when they visit a sports Web site just as they would if they attended a live sporting event. This means that most consumers anticipate a certain level of quality in regard to content, graphics, and performance. Consumers' expectations of online quality are raised as they become more sophisticated in their use of technology. Therefore, sport communicators must become more sophisticated in meeting the needs and demands of online consumers while also positively conveying the key messages of the organization. To do so, sport communicators must first understand the general needs and motivations of the online consumer of sport.

Content

Content is a primary component of any sport entity's Web site. It is considered a major factor in an individual's decision to return to a Web site (Rosen & Purinton, 2004). Sports Web site content should be selected based on the mission of the sport entity as well as the needs of its key publics. Sports Web site content, therefore, should reflect the sport entity's objectives as well as the needs and demands of the sport consumer. In other words, what type of information do visitors to the site seek when logging on? The content provided on Web sites must appeal to and be valued by consumers (Yang, Ahmed, Ghingold, & Boon, 2003).

Just as sports fans desire a level of involvement when attending a sports event, they also desire a level of involvement when visiting a sport entity's Web site. The involvement level of online consumers affects their decisions to visit certain sites and their expectations when obtaining information from those sites. Highly involved sport consumers desire much more information related to the sport product than do sport consumers with low levels of involvement. Sport consumers exhibiting low levels of involvement are most attracted and satisfied by entertaining elements of the sport-related Web site. This means that sports Web sites should provide enough content to satisfy highly involved sport consumers while also providing enough interactivity to satisfy the less involved sport consumer. Bei, Chen, and Widdows (2004) suggested that the Internet is an effective complementary communication channel in providing highly involved consumers with significant and varying information regarding a product. Similarly, the Internet provides a means to facilitate decision making among consumers with lower levels of involvement because "online information compensates traditional information sources" (p. 465).

The interactivity of the medium allows consumers to form social networks. This can be especially important in sport, where the social aspect is suggested to influence sport consumption. One of the means to facilitate this social aspect among sport consumers is to provide chat rooms, message boards, and blogs. As Stafford and colleagues (2004) noted, "Building chat capabilities and fostering a sense of community within the context of an Internet access resource could greatly enhance the usage experience for consumers, who appear to have strong social requirements for Internet use" (p. 287). This provides online users with "a new dimension of social discourse previously untapped in communication media innovations of the past" (Stafford et al., 2004, p. 287). Many sport franchises use message boards, online discussions, and live chats with team personnel and players to facilitate an online social network among sports fans. Similarly, sport news Web sites provide blogs and live chats to discuss a myriad of sport-related issues.

Any sport-related Web site should also have a practical benefit for visitors to its site. In other words, the Web site should provide the content necessary to meet the needs of its visitors. The perceived practical value of a Web site is integral in people's decision to use the medium, and it will affect their frequency of Web use (Bei et al., 2004). Sport marketing expert Dan Migala (2004) explained these issues as follows. He began by noting that sports Web sites should all include some basic components such as a "What's New"

section, a search engine and site map, a feedback mechanism, phone numbers, and a privacy policy. Because most sport entities are interested in encouraging repeat visits to their sites, information must be updated each day. Providing search engines and site maps assists consumers in quickly obtaining information. Sport entities should provide direct links to specific people for feedback purposes. This establishes a more effective means of communication between the sport consumer and the sport organization. Many sports Web sites fail to provide phone numbers, and this can be problematic if consumers desire more personal interaction. Additionally, as more sport entities use their Web sites to obtain data on their consumers, consumers should be made aware of the privacy policy and how the data provided to the sport entity may be used (Migala, 2004).

Graphic design on the sports Web site can greatly assist in providing content (Rosen & Purinton, 2004). "Elements of space, use of images, size of images, use of animation and/or audio, number of words per line, color and size of characters are among just a few of these factors" (Rosen & Purinton, 2004, p. 788). Additionally, designing content requires sport entities to determine the placement of these elements (Rosen & Purinton, 2004). Doing so allows sport entities to best communicate with site visitors and enables the sport entity to more effectively communicate its messages.

Design

Equally important as content to a sports Web site is the design of the site, which is influenced by numerous factors. As with every aspect of the MOSC, sport entities must consider the motivations and needs of consumers when designing and modifying their Web sites. As Chan-Olmsted and Park (2000) illustrated, the main page of a Web site is similar to the front page of a newspaper. This main page uses headlines to draw attention to items it deems are significant. The ability of the site to retain visitors is linked to "its ability to demonstrate to its target users, on the 'front page,' that it has the utilities he/she is searching for" (p. 323). Failure to clearly indicate this will cause visitors to navigate away from the Web site. Therefore, if the sport entity's Web site is not designed in a manner to easily communicate content, the sport entity will have difficulty communicating its online message. The design of a sports Web site should include determining placement of links as well as colors, graphics, and interactive features.

Recognizing the Importance of Structure

One of the most important elements of Web site design is the concept of structure. Developing a sound structure enables sport entities to incorporate necessary elements as well as enhance the other components of the MOSC.

Proper design is an integral aspect of any Web site because, as Van Schaik and Ling (2005) noted, it affects user interaction, the primary feature that establishes online communication as unique. It is also the feature that enables sport entities to more effectively communicate and enhance the online experience for sport consumers. Site design is also instrumental in encouraging individuals to visit the sport entity's Web site and in fostering repeat visits to the site. The Web site presents

a unique opportunity for the sport entity to grasp the user's attention and to communicate its message (see figure 9.4). Just as a poorly designed storefront influences a person's decision to enter the store (Auger, 2005), a poorly designed Web site will influence a sport consumer's decision to log on and to return to a specific Web site. Sandvig and Bajwa (2004) noted, "Web designers should be cognizant of the types of information users desire, the high importance they place on finding information, and how ease of use influences their perceptions of web site effectiveness" (p. 21).

Given individuals' preferences to browse rather than search, the Web site should include distinct and concise paths to the information most users seek (Sandvig & Bajwa, 2004). Therefore, sport entities should understand what information is most desired by visitors to their Web sites and relay this information to the consumer with ease. In other words, a season ticket holder should not have to spend much time surfing a franchise's Web site to obtain information regarding parking or game time. Similarly, an individual desiring to purchase single game tickets should be prominently directed to the franchise's schedule

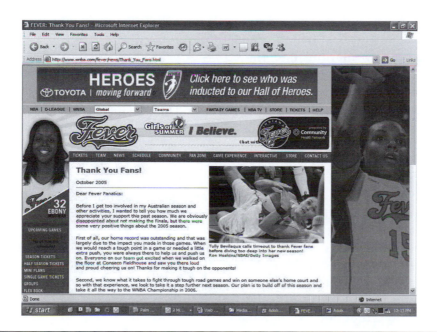

Figure 9.4 Sport organizations use Web sites for numerous reasons, including the opportunity to directly communicate with their fans. Here, a WNBA franchise (Indiana Fever) communicates with stakeholders at the conclusion of the postseason.

Reprinted, by permission, from Indiana Fever, 2006.

and ticket prices without having to search the entire site. Rosen and Purinton (2004) noted that a Web site should strive to provide consumers with access rather than an overload of information. "Web design should not result in information overload," the scholars state. "The goal, rather, should be to give access to the information web surfers desire in the most expedient way possible" (p. 793).

The design of an effective Web site involves structure. A Web site without structure is equivalent to a book with unnumbered and unbound pages (Hackos & Stevens, 1997). To assist in developing structure, Web site designers should include text that is scannable and use highlighted keywords such as hypertext links. The National Hockey League's Washington Capitals provide structure to site visitors by using several highlighted words linking fans to more details on the franchise's prominent news stories, linking fans to podcasts, and linking to posts on its message board. Nielsen (1997) suggested also using meaningful subheadings and bulleted lists when designing a Web site. This is based on the research showing that consumers rarely read Web pages (Nielsen, 1997; Rosen & Purinton, 2004). Most consumers will take fewer than 10 seconds to determine whether to visit a specific site (Rosen & Purinton, 2004). Internet users desire specific information, and they desire to have this information quickly: They will hastily scan Web pages to find the desired information (Sandvig & Bajwa, 2004). More than 79% of consumers scanned a new page online rather than reading the page (Nielsen, 1997).

The aforementioned factors (scannable text and highlighted keywords) as well as the mission of the organization and the needs of its key publics should be at the heart of Web site design. The online needs and desires of the key publics should be considered in conjunction with the organization's business objectives when determining Web site design. The organization should first determine what type of information it will provide to consumers, how the consumers will use this information, how the information will be marketed, the demographics of the consumers, and the needs of the consumers (Hackos & Stevens, 1997). As Theriault (2005) noted, information on a Web site should be displayed and communicated with the specific needs of the key publics in mind. Ideally, the needs of the sport entity should be balanced with the needs of the consumer. For example, if the sport entity wants consumers to return to its site on a regular basis, it will implement a different design strategy than if it simply wants to release specific information on the organization. To encourage repeat visits on behalf of its consumers, the site will need to be designed to meet their needs.

Evaluating Well-Designed Web Sites

To assess the quality of its Web site design, a sport entity should continuously evaluate its design as it relates to each component of the MOSC. Evaluation is key in maintaining effective online sport communication. Kim, Shaw, and Schneider (2003) noted that to determine the effectiveness of a Web site's design, a set of evaluation criteria must be established. These evaluation criteria should be linked to the organization's goals when designing the site. In reviewing current research on evaluation of Web sites, the scholars identified six key criteria:

1. business function,
2. corporation credibility,
3. content reliability,
4. Web site attractiveness,
5. systematic structure, and
6. navigation.

Similarly, Cox and Dale (2002) suggested that key design elements include

- the use of links,
- consistency,
- communication and feedback,
- a search mechanism, and
- fill-in forms.

Cox and Dale (2002) suggested that the color of links should be modified when accessed to remind the consumer that they have been accessed. Nielsen (2004) agreed, listing failure to change the color of a link once it has been accessed by a user as one of the top 10 mistakes in Web design. Additionally, it is suggested that links be clear and concise and that graphics change to text when encountered by the consumer's cursor. Cox and Dale (2002) argued that navigational menus should be simple and should appear in the same place on each page of the site. This increases consumers' satisfaction with the site because it allows them to find their way quickly and without incident. Additionally, a Web site should not deviate too much from the design of other Web sites. The majority of consumers form their perceptions of Web sites based on their experiences on other sites (Nielsen, 2004). Therefore, any deviation from the design norms of most sites will potentially create frustration and confusion among consumers. For example, the uniformity of the Web sites for Major League Baseball (www.mlb.com) and its teams provides online consumers consistency and increased design usability. There are no surprises, and frustration and confusion are limited by this approach.

Web pages should be short and should include a button allowing consumers to return to the top of the page. The transaction process for consumers should also be simple and quick (Cox & Dale, 2002). A feedback mechanism should also be used to inform the consumer if a mistake has been made or if a difficulty exists with the Web site. A search mechanism should also be used to allow consumers to search for specific information on the site. Many consumers prefer to use the search feature before using navigational tools on a Web site. Cox and Dale (2002) noted that any forms that require online completion to order or purchase products should be self-explanatory and should provide the consumer with examples of how information is to be entered.

Layout

In their identification of components of successful Web sites, Scheffelmaier and Vinsonhaler (2003) highlighted the importance of site design. The two explained that successful Web sites include an attractive home page, a common design applied to all pages in the Web site, product descriptions with attractive pictures, and easy-to-read pages. Layout should be a central focus when designing the site. Forman (2003) suggested that to develop an appropriate layout for a site, one must identify the elements (e.g., headings, text blocks, navigation bars) associated with the site. Forman (2003) next detailed the layout process. The first step begins with a clear understanding of the elements and includes listing all the elements on paper or in a document. These elements should be categorized based on their function, content, or visibility. Additionally, it is best to group elements to simplify the layout process and to make the site more user-friendly. Elements should be grouped based on their relevance and relationship and may be visually grouped by location on the page, color, or style. Borders on pages may prove useful when grouping items, and color may be used in conjunction with placement to establish association between elements.

As sport fans become more sophisticated in their use of online media, sport entities must become more responsive to their needs, which includes understanding of several factors relative to layout. Forman (2003) noted three key factors regarding layout relative to audience needs:

- User resolution
- Browser window
- Content familiarity

Resolution refers to users' monitor resolution. According to theCounter.com (2005), 56% of users set their resolutions to 1024 × 768. Browser windows refer to the screen size an individual uses when online. For example, users may use the full screen or only use half screen. Content should be included based on audience needs and the objectives of the site. Layout of the site should be based on what will reach the most people and what will be most appropriate for the target audience.

Atmospherics and Environmental Cues

Similar to layout and central to sports Web site design are atmospherics. Kotler (1973) characterized atmospherics as the purposeful placement and structuring of certain environmental cues. These cues will affect the perceptions and decisions of consumers. Atmospherics are of such importance that they often have a greater impact on consumers' decisions to purchase than the product (Kotler, 1973). Dailey (2004) applied the concept of atmospherics to Web sites and defined Web atmospherics as "conscious designing of web environments to create positive effects (e.g., positive affect, positive cognitions, etc.) in users in order to increase favorable consumer responses (e.g., site revisiting, browsing, etc.)" (p. 796). Similarly, Milliman and Fugate (1993) characterized Web atmospherics as the components of a Web site that stimulate an individual's senses. The Web interface is, according to Dailey (2004), "the portion of the website that is visible to the web user" (p. 795).

As Fink and Laupase (2000) noted, an entity's Web site allows consumers to "experience an organization's atmospherics or ambience without actually being there" (p. 44). This enables the sport entity to provide consumers with a sense of their products in a most convenient manner. Richard (2003) suggested that Internet atmospherics have a dramatic impact on site effectiveness because these cues influence individuals' decisions regarding which pages to view, how long to spend on each site or page, and how much information should be gathered from each site or page. Eroglu, Machleit, and Davis (2001) characterized Web atmospherics by classifying them as either high task relevant or low task relevant. High task relevant cues help individuals reach their online goals, whereas low task relevant cues have no impact on the individuals' attainment of their online goals. Individuals may also rely on different cues based on their association with a specific organization or product.

Appropriate Web atmospherics assist in designing the sports Web site as well as cultivating a level of satisfaction with the online sport consumer. Dailey (1999) suggested that Web sites with appropriate atmospherics will generate greater pleasure and a more positive attitude among site visitors, which will likely result in repeat visits to the site and positive perceptions of the online experience. Van Niekerk, Berthon, and Davies (1999) noted

that "a key element in successful commercial website design is that there be enjoyment during the interaction with the site. The surfer must feel in control of his/her fate, and the design should attempt to encourage or provide the facility for an experience that involves a sense of exhilaration, a sense of enjoyment that is cherished and becomes a landmark of how surfing or interaction should be" (p. 111). An individual's involvement with a site is often linked to the quality of entertainment on the site. Entertainment facilitates a greater emotional pleasure, and this emotional pleasure increases an individual's involvement (Richard, 2003). Additionally, entertaining Web sites foster individuals' exploratory behaviors through a more strategic information search and have favorable impacts on attitudes (Richard, 2003). People with low involvement are likely to spend less time and effort seeking the information required to satisfy their need. Therefore, these people are most influenced by cues rather than detailed content. In contrast, those with high involvement will seek detailed information to assist in decision making and in reaching their goals. These individuals are also more likely to desire interactivity and communication access with the respective organization (McGaughey & Mason, 1998).

Without a keen understanding of Web site design and its relationship with the content, usability, and commerce components of the MOSC, sport entities will not recognize the full potential of the Internet as a communications tool. This section has illustrated the pertinent aspects of Web site design as they relate to sport entities. These aspects include elements such as structure and atmospherics. The design of the sports Web site is integral in providing the sport consumer with information in an quick and efficient manner. The design of the sports Web site is linked closely with peformance and usability, as discussed in the next sections.

Performance

The fifth component of the MOSC focuses on the performance of the sports Web site. Although performance is related to content and design, it is also closely related to usability. For example, if a user cannot download a podcast within a reasonable amount of time or cannot navigate the site in an appropriate time span, the Web site is considered to perform poorly. Also pertinent to performance of a sports Web site is its level of interactivity. Sport consumers have come to expect that sports Web sites be interactive and perform well relative to speed of downloads and navigation. This section highlights these aspects of Web site performance.

The manner in which the performance of a Web site is evaluated has changed from determining its number of "hits" to evaluating its interactivity and the amount of time it takes to complete certain tasks, such as downloading a file. The use of multimedia most often has a positive impact on the consumer if the site performs well. Consumers may become frustrated and agitated if download times take several seconds and tasks are unable to be completed in an appropriate time. Auger

(2005) noted that consumers are most often negatively affected by oversophisticated or graphic-intensive Web sites. This is attributable in large part to the time it takes to access these features. The use of graphics has a dramatic impact on the performance of the Web site (Auger, 2005). Sports Web sites are usually expected to have numerous graphics, and it is essential that these graphics perform well.

Sports Web sites are expected to be interactive as well. Interactivity is also considered to affect Web site performance by enhancing a Web site's value to consumers as well as to the organization (Auger, 2005). Interactivity improves communication channels and provides consumers with an additional avenue of communicating directly with the organization. This additional communication channel allows the organization to better understand its consumers and enables it to better meet their needs. It is suggested that interactivity proves particularly useful when communicating with consumers in dynamic settings. This

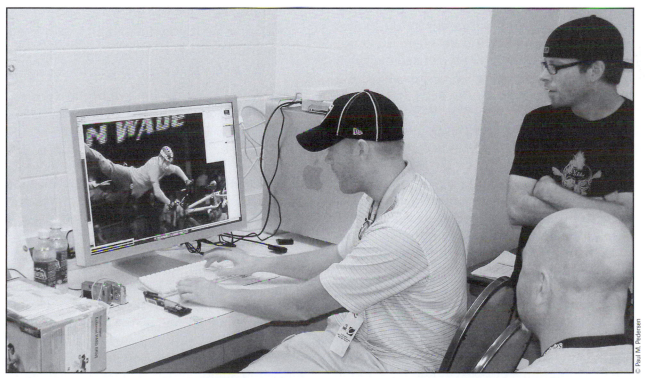

Web site performance is one of the major components of the Model for Online Sport Communication (MOSC). Usability is a key aspect of this component. An example of this is when Web sites provide galleries of photographs that can be accessed and often downloaded by fans and visitors. Greg Hydle (center) is a professional image processor. With the Web site managers of the Dew Action Sports Tour looking on, Hydle downloads images provided by a sports photographer. Selected photographs are then processed and placed on the event's Web site for immediate viewing while the event is still active.

has significant meaning for the sport entity because the nature of consumers as well as the nature of the sport product can vary dramatically (Auger, 2005).

Although content is a key component of any sports Web site, the interactive qualities of a Web site are most useful in attracting site visitors. Interactivity assists a Web site in attracting visitors and retaining visitors who may not be attracted to a site by content. This is likely the case with consumers who are less loyal to the sport product. Including entertaining visuals helps lure less loyal consumers to the site. As Richard (2003) illustrated, "Surfers who do not give much attention to contents are attracted by visuals, giving them the opportunity to pursue the visit because of the entertainment value of the site" (p. 1639). Although interactivity and entertainment features of a Web site have the most impact on the casual sport consumer, these features also positively influence the most loyal sport consumers as well.

Regular consumers of the sport product tend to be information seekers, and research indicates that entertainment adds to the experience for information seekers (Richard, 2003). Sport entities have recognized the value of interactivity on their Web sites and use a myriad of tools to engage in active communication with consumers. The Web site of the Seattle Mariners is a prime example of this. This Web site, which was recently ranked for interactivity as one of the best in major professional sports, provides numerous multimedia avenues for visitors (Liberman, 2005). A review of this site (www.seattlemariners.com) reveals the organization's focus on interactivity. The franchise provides visitors to the site with a multimedia guide in which consumers may learn about the varying features on the site. Additionally, site visitors may search a video database and download and watch various videos. Visitors may access photo galleries as well as franchise commercials. Furthermore, fans of the team are able to log on and secure game-day audio clips, online voting opportunities for numerous contests and polls, and downloadable ring tones for their cellular phones.

The key aspects of sports Web site performance include Web page speed and interactivity. These elements are related to each component of the MOSC but are most closely related to usability.

Usability

When sport consumers visit a specific Web site, they not only expect to find the desired information easily, but they also expect to find it quickly, within two or three mouse clicks. Usability is a key element of any Web site and is a broad term with varying definitions (Hassan & Li, 2005). Jakob Nielsen (2003) characterized usability as (a) a quality attribute that determines the ease of use of user interfaces and (b) the manner in which user interfaces are improved when a Web site is designed. Hassan and Li (2005) indicated that utility refers to the functionality of a system, whereas usability refers to how well a consumer can use the functionality. In other words, for a Web site to be usable,

- it must serve a distinct purpose;
- it must be functional; and
- the consumer must be able to use the Web site's features with ease.

Therefore, usability refers to the relationship between a specific tool and its users. For the tool to perform its intended function, the user must be able to operate it effectively. This means that a person logging on to a certain Web site must be able to use it to satisfy her needs and wants. The Web site should enable consumers to complete their desired goal accurately and completely without creating frustration. Nielsen, one of the world's leading experts on usability and the Internet, noted that usability of a Web site is more than important—it is essential for the Web site to survive. Usable Web sites have few navigational problems and are easy to use. This encourages individuals to remain on the site to acquire information and will usually enhance perceptions regarding the site (Richard, 2003). In contrast, Web sites that are confusing or difficult to use, that fail to state what an entity offers, and that are hard to read will impede information searches and cause consumers to leave the Web site (Nielsen, 2003; Richard, 2003), which means communication cannot occur.

Principles of Web Site Usability

The principles of Web site usability are grounded in engineering principles pertaining to human interaction with machines (Palmer, 2002). The five quality elements of Web site usability, according to Nielsen (2003), include

1. learnability,
2. efficiency,
3. memorability,
4. errors, and
5. satisfaction.

Learnability refers to consumers' ability to accomplish basic tasks during their initial visit to the site, whereas efficiency refers to consumers' ability to quickly perform tasks once they have learned the design of the site. Memorability characterizes consumers' ability to effectively and accurately perform tasks when returning to the site after a period of inactivity. Errors refer to the amount and severity of errors made by consumers and their ability to recover from these errors when using a particular Web site. Satisfaction refers to the appeal of the Web site's design. The manner in which these five elements are addressed on a specific Web site affects online consumers' ability to seek and discover information and knowledge regarding the sport organization and its products; thus, these elements influence the quality of online communication with publics. Because communication is a two-way process, Web sites must be usable for the sport media or the sport organization to convey its messages to the publics. If sport consumers leave the site, the flow of communication is interrupted, and the sport-focused organization loses a key advantage associated with online communication.

Importance of Navigation

One of the most important aspects of usability is Web site navigation. Proper navigation ensures that site visitors can peruse the Web site with ease. Navigation on a sports Web site is just as important as a sports franchise's game plan. Proper site navigation provides a road map for frequent and infrequent site visitors to acquire the information they desire. For example, a Chicago Cubs fan in Boise, Idaho, plans a business trip to Chicago. The fan may log on to the franchise's Web site to determine if the team will be playing a home game during the time of the trip. The fan will visit the site and look for "directions" to the desired information, which will likely include the team's home game schedule, ticket availability and price, and purchase information. Without proper navigation, the fan may not get the information he needs. As Nielsen (1999) noted, users should be able to ascertain at any given moment where they are on the site, where they have been on the site, and where they are able to go on the site. Johnson (2003) suggested that this allows consumers to know if they are close to meeting their needs and goals by finding the information they desire to retrieve.

Hackos and Stevens (1997) illustrated that the most important aspect of navigation is the structure of the Web site. As discussed earlier, Web site structure is also an integral aspect of the design component of a sports Web site. Once a meaningful structure has been developed, a Web site should possess a set of navigation aids and hypertext links allowing users to access additional information with ease and without getting lost on the site. The navigation aids and hypertext links serve as a map for online consumers, enabling them to travel from point A to point B without incident. Forman (2003) emphasized that navigational elements should be grouped in a manner that allows consumers to determine the location of second- or third-level elements. In other words, consumers should be able to easily understand that by clicking on certain buttons, they will obtain certain information. As noted by Rosen and Purinton (2004), "making websites 'user-friendly' requires making them easy to use and easy to understand" (p. 790).

When establishing a Web site with effective navigation, sport entities should always provide a feature that allows site visitors to find their way back to a certain point on the site. Hackos and Stevens (1997) noted that Web sites should provide a home base, which is consumers' point of entry on the Web site. A consumer should be able to access that point of entry or home base by clicking on a "home" button or menu option at any time while visiting to a site. The home base allows consumers an escape option if they become lost trying to access information on the site.

Johnson (2003) noted that minimizing the number of navigation schemes present on a Web site aids navigability and suggested that a left navigation bar may list the content areas of a Web site whereas a navigation bar across the top of the site might list standard organizational aspects like a privacy policy or contact information. Similarly, Nielsen and Tahir (2001) suggested that multiple navigation areas should be avoided. The two further noted that critical components of navigation include grouping similar items next to each other in the navigation area and creating a navigation system that is easily located and noticed by the consumer. Pratt, Mills, and Kim (2004) noted that a review of research on navigation and usability revealed several common best practices: "(a) focusing on consistency, clarity, and conciseness; (b) organizing the site contents to mirror users' desired actions, and (e) making the site intuitive and easy to use" (p. 94).

Commerce

The final component of the model focuses on commerce. The use of the Internet as an effective communications tool is widely accepted. For sport organizations, its use as an effective marketing and commerce tool should not be overlooked (King, 2004a). In 2003, Major League Baseball generated $7.4 million in online ticket sales, whereas 70% of the NBA's non–box office tickets were purchased online (Migala, 2004). As M.T. Brown (2003) noted, "The web has the potential to be more than just a public relations tool" (p. 54). This sport

The University of Louisville offers its stakeholders a Web site with outstanding content, design, and navigation. The sport information department's Webmaster is Garett Wall, who is also the primary media contact for the school's cross country, rowing, and track and field teams.

management scholar suggested that the interactivity of the Internet enhances its ability to market the organization and that sports Web sites should be constructed using specific elements designed to promote user interaction with the sport entity. The advantages of online communication and the mass appeal of sport make it an ideal match for succeeding in online commerce (M.T. Brown, 1998). Some professional athletes use their Web sites to promote their image, increase brand equity, and move products. For instance, Greg Norman is known around the world as one of the best golfers to have played the game. Often overlooked are his brilliant business mind and leveraging skills. As noted in chapter 2, his businesses are far reaching and very profitable. An integral component of his $200 million corporation, Great White Shark Enterprises (GWSE), is his Web site (www.shark.com/index.php), Greg Norman Interactive (Pedersen, 2004a). Through this Web site, fans and visitors read about this popular athlete, encounter numerous advertisements, and have the opportunity to purchase Norman-endorsed products through shopatshark.com.

Internet's Role in Positioning the Sport Product

A sport entity's Web site can be used to create a "virtual fan experience" and can provide a high-quality service experience for key audiences. Many entities use Web sites to enhance customer service efforts and to foster more positive and mutually beneficial relations with consumers (Yang, Ahmed, Ghingold, & Boon, 2003). The Internet's ability to assist organizations in providing information and in enhancing customer relations is significant: The Internet provides organizations with the ability to dramatically improve business and organizational performance (Yang et al., 2003). M.T. Brown (2003) suggested that sport entities "must focus on the online seller/consumer relationship. Without this focus, business may be lost to organizations effectively implementing forms of e-commerce" (p. 54). He noted that other forms of entertainment effectively use the Internet as a viable means for engaging consumers and enhancing commerce. If

sport entities fail to recognize this value they will lose money. For example, "Sport entities should focus on selling merchandise and tickets online and on generating sales leads through web activities" (M.T. Brown, 2003, p. 53). Porter (2001) suggested that the increase in Internet use is linked to its ability to provide easy access to information relative to the price and to the product and provide an easy way to make a purchase at a relatively low cost. "Compared to the era without the Internet, consumers can more precisely make purchase decisions because of the abundant information sources on the Internet" (Bei et al., 2004, p. 450). The Internet facilitates better decision making among consumers because it provides a large amount of quality information that is "individually customized" with "minimal effort and cost" (Peterson & Merino, 2003, p. 99).

Migala (2004) noted, "Technology can do wonders to improve revenue-generation," and its power to enhance customer service should not be overlooked (p. 2). To enhance the commerce aspect of a Web site, the expectations, needs, and desires of consumers must be considered when selecting and designing content. Accurate knowledge of consumers' desires and motives for using the Internet provides businesses with a more efficient means of serving their customers (Stafford et al., 2004). Van Niekerk, Berthon, and Davies (1999) suggested that to retain a user's interest in a site, organizations should design the site with specific customer groups in mind. The interactivity of the Internet provides an ideal opportunity to build relations with key customer groups. Web sites that do not provide a satisfactory online experience are less likely to succeed and encourage repeat visitors. To be successful, businesses must be responsive to the online needs and preferences of consumers (Yang et al., 2003). This means that sport entity Web sites should meet the needs of key target markets while also touting the benefits of the specific sport products.

Filo and Funk (2005) noted that sport entities should do more than relay information about the sport product to the sport consumer. Rather, sport organizations should determine what appeals to consumers and use the Web site to reinforce those product attributes. The two sport management scholars suggest that "sport organizations should determine the specific features that drive consumer interest in their sport product and then ensure its presence in Internet marketing communication" (p. 114). Additionally, sports Web sites are advantageous in strengthening the emotional attachment consumers have with sport entities and are useful in generating awareness among less loyal consumers (Filo & Funk, 2005). The design and content of the site can be used to facilitate a greater satisfaction and loyalty among both infrequent sport consumers and those who consume the sport product more heavily. Sports Web sites should be designed to enhance consumer perceptions of the sport product, facilitate a greater sense of product identification, add a greater dimension of service related to the sport product, and enhance consumers' experience with the sport product. The design and content of a sports Web site should focus on the sensory shopping experience. As Rosen and Purinton (2004) explained, a sensory shopping experience facilitates sales and assists in building relationships with customers. "For the e-retailer, the sensory shopping experience must be played out on the template of the web page" (p. 788). Music, color, and lighting have been known to influence customer purchases and, therefore, should not be overlooked in e-commerce.

Internet's Role in Acquiring Consumer Data

Additional factors that should be considered in developing the commerce aspect of the sports Web site include privacy issues and issues related to building the organization's database. Ensuring the privacy of site visitors will establish a sense of trust between the sport entity and its key publics and enhance relations with customers (M.T. Brown, 2003; Yang et al., 2003). Using database mining technologies allows sport entities to track consumers' needs and desires, which will enhance the value and benefits associated with their products (Yang et al., 2003). Additionally, the Web site provides an efficient means of gauging feedback regarding various aspects of the sport product. This feedback can be invaluable when positioning the sport product and when addressing the needs and concerns of key publics.

The sport entity's Web site can be used to obtain customer data (M.T. Brown, 1998; McGowan, 2004). These data can be used to build a database enabling the entity to directly market to consumers who have already expressed an interest in a sport product. The "Devil's Domain" program at Arizona State University entices consumers to provide information to the athletic department via the Web (www.thesundevils.collegesports.com). In exchange for the information, consumers earn a chance to win numerous items and experiences such as mingling with players or traveling with the team. The information allows the athletic department to directly market ticket promotions to consumers via e-mail, which has resulted in 9% redemption rate (Migala, 2004).

EXPLORING NEW SPORT MEDIA AND COMMUNICATION CHANNELS

Advances in technology will continue to enhance communication channels and alter the manner in which sport entities communicate with both internal and external publics. This section highlights technological advances that currently affect sport communication and provides an overview of technologies predicted to affect sport communication in the future. These technologies include wireless technology, blogs and glogs, video on demand, and other new technologies.

Wireless Technology

Wireless technology has enabled people to remain in constant contact with friends, family, and business colleagues at all times from almost anywhere in the world. The same technology is now allowing sport entities to communicate with sport consumers 24-7. Sport consumers may access information about their favorite sport entities at any time using mobile and wireless technologies. Sports fans typically desire information about game or event highlights, interviews, updates on events or games in progress, and feature stories (Bernstein, Fisher, & Kramer, 2006).

Although these aspects are most desired by sport consumers, many other options are available. Sport consumers can download television shows and games. After the Rose Bowl, Apple's iTunes reported three Bowl games in their top five downloads: the Rose Bowl, the Orange Bowl, and the Fiesta Bowl (Bernstein et al., 2006). The popularity of "sports on demand" will continue to increase, which provides a unique avenue for sport entities when communicating with their key constituents. New technologies allow sport entities to further enhance their communication efforts and assist them in promoting and effectively marketing their mission, values, and products.

Blogs and Glogs

Similar to message boards, Web logs (blogs) allow users to post messages on a wide range of topics and engage in a social dialogue. Blogs have been characterized as personal online journals and are defined as "frequently updated webpages with a series of archived posts, typically in reverse-chronological order" (Nardi, Schiano, & Gumbrecht, 2004, p. 222). Web logs can include text, photos, and links to other sport or related Web sites and blogs. Because blogging is a relatively new aspect of the Internet, studies examining its impact on individuals and sport entities are quite limited. However, some research suggests that the growing popularity of blogging is spurred by people's needs to express thoughts and feeling via the written word. In an age of technological advances focusing on interaction, blogs allow people to use the Internet for thinking and reflection (Nardi et al., 2004). Sport journalists often use blogs to supplement their print articles and beats. Sometimes, however, the writers are hesitant to get involved with this new medium. "For almost a month now, my bosses have been threatening to force me to write an

online blog," noted *Indianapolis Star* sports columnist Bob Kravitz in December 2005. "Originally, I was resistant, since until four months ago, I didn't know what a blog was, but was pretty sure it was treatable with a course of antibiotics. More and more, though, it sounds likes a marvelous idea. What's not to love about a forum that allows me to make random comments that don't require transitions or a unifying theme?" (p. C1).

For the sport entity, blogs are a new channel with which to reach and communicate with consumers (Show, 2005). One of the most popular sports Web sites—www.ESPN.com—has a blogger for each major sport plus fantasy sports and sport business, whereas sport media outlets such as www.si.com, www.sportingnews.com, and other popular Web sites have created blogs for sport consumers. Peter King, a legendary football writer, posted his 2005 training camp diaries on a blog, and Major League Baseball created MLBblogs with blogs by various players, sport consumers, owners, media members, and former players. The NBA publishes its Blog Squad in five different languages, whereas the NHL used its blogs to gauge perceptions of the league during the 2004-2005 lockout (Show, 2005). Dallas Mavericks owner Mark Cuban is one of the most accessible owners in professional sport. In fact, he even took time to answer a query we had during the writing of this book. Cuban hosts his own blog where he regularly posts his thoughts and shares links with visitors to the site. His blog—www.blogmaverick.com—features his e-mail and various aspects related to technology and to his charitable work.

"Glogs" are blogs with game logs. Glogs are becoming more common and are typically used by sport media outlets such as www.cbssportsline.com to provide a form of real-time game commentary similar to real-time scoring (see figure 9.5). According to Fisher (2005a), glogs have become the third most popular feature of the game center at the CBS Sportsline Web site. If the popularity of glogs continues, sport media outlets may integrate them as a central aspect of sport journalism.

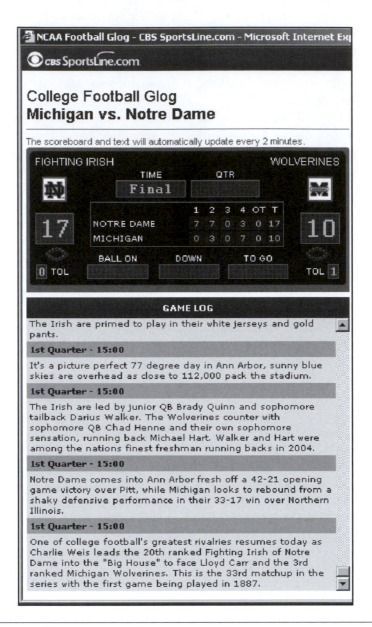

Figure 9.5   Information once reserved for sports journalists in the press box is now readily available for all fans online. Game logs—glogs—are a popular feature of numerous sport media Web sites.

Reprinted, by permission, from CBS Sportsline, 2006.

Video on Demand

Video on demand (VOD) provides sport consumers with the ability to select and watch video by simply pushing a button. This new technology may be accessed as part of an interactive television system or via the Internet. Cable television provider Comcast provides VOD service to approximately eight million consumers with more than one billion programs viewed via VOD (Bernstein, 2005d). VOD featuring sport includes shortened versions of games or feature aspects such as media conferences or game highlights. The NBA recently modified videos on its Web site to more closely align with NBA TV. Sport consumers may now download video featuring game highlights, features, and fantasy segments. Most notably, the videos will include segments developed during games (Fisher, 2005b). Similar to the NBA's initiative, the NFL used VOD technology to provide fans with highlights during the 2005 draft and for 2 weeks after the 2005 draft (Bernstein,

2005d). CBS Sports and College Sports Television teamed in 2005 to offer sport consumers online access to each game of the 2005 NCAA men's basketball tournament. For a minimal fee, sport consumers receive "March Madness on Demand" (Marchand, 2005).

Other Sport Communication Channels

The constant advances in technology provide a wide array of new avenues of communication that are being explored and used by sport entities. Bernstein (2005d) highlighted several of these new technologies, which include 3G, optical tracking systems, digital asset management, and online video gaming. "Third generation"—or 3G—is new mobile communication technology. The implementation of this technology on mobile phones would allow sport consumers to access more video highlights and game packages on cellular phones. **Optical tracking systems** allow moving objects to be tracked using cameras. Examples of this new technology include Pass Trak, which illustrates the height and speed of a football as it is thrown down the field of play, and the first-and-ten line in football, which enables viewers to clearly see the yardage needed and gained for a first down. **Digital asset management** allows sport entities to store video in a network. Once video is placed in the network, it can be accessed instantaneously. Online video gaming is one of the fastest growing aspects of video games. These games are dramatically enhanced by high-definition technologies and allow players to compete online against multiple competitors.

CHAPTER WRAP-UP

Summary

The goal of this chapter was to introduce you to the new media that are drastically altering the manner in which sport-focused organizations and sport media outlets communicate with their key publics. More than ever before, sports fans are using the Internet to research and follow their favorite sport entities. Sports fans' use of the Internet has dramatically increased since its inception, and sports enthusiasts are relying less on traditional media. Today, sports fans are much more sophisticated in charting the progress of their favorite sport entities by logging on to various Web sites, downloading video clips and podcasts, and engaging in online chats with others who share their interests. Technology has dramatically influenced the growth of new sport media. Advancements in technology continue to spur a more sophisticated level of communication and affect the manner in which organizations associated with sport disseminate information. From e-mail, live video streaming, and real-time sport scores to podcasting, Web logs (blogs), and game logs (glogs), technology provides the foundation for the growth of the new sport media. These technologies and new media will continue to have a significant impact on sport communication through their ability to provide an instantaneous link between the sport-focused organization and its publics.

This chapter examined the use of the Internet in sport communication, followed by a discussion of the Model for Online Sport Communication. The MOSC highlighted the key components of effective online sport communication focusing on seven important aspects central to sports Web sites. A discussion of technological advances that are affecting sport communication, such as wireless technology and blogs, was included in the final section of the chapter.

Review Questions

1. Why is it important to understand sport consumers' online needs when maintaining a Web site?
2. What are your expectations when logging on? How do your expectations vary based on the Web site and your needs?
3. What are the general needs of consumers when logging on to a sports Web site?
4. What factors affect online sport communication?
5. What factors influence effective online sport communication?
6. How is the Internet different from traditional media?
7. What new and different media and communication channels are currently affecting sport communication?
8. How does an individual's prior experience with the Internet affect her online sport communication behavior?
9. How does one's level of involvement affect his online needs and desires when visiting a sport entity's Web site?
10. What is the difference between searching and browsing online?

Discussion Questions

1. How are the various factors that influence effective online sport communication interrelated? How do these factors affect consumers' decisions to return to a site?
2. How does level of involvement with the sport product affect online needs and desires?
3. How has the Internet evolved and affected the manner in which sport entities communicate with internal and external publics?
4. How are new media and communication channels affecting sport communication?
5. How do you use the Internet? How does this compare with how your friends and family use the Internet?
6. Of the factors influencing online sport communication, which do you perceive as most important? Which do you perceive as least important? Why?
7. Of the factors influencing effective online communication, which do you perceive has the greatest impact on cultivating a sense of identification with a sport entity?
8. How is the immediacy of the Internet an advantage to the sport entity? How is it disadvantageous to the sport entity?
9. How do blogs affect communication channels and interactivity with sport consumers?
10. How can a sport entity's Web site serve as a "virtual sport service" for sport consumers?

Group Activities

1. Randomly select three professional team Web sites and evaluate the sites using the Model for Online Sport Communication. Write a brief report of your evaluation and share your findings with the class.

2. Using the Model for Online Sport Communication, develop a set of guidelines for evaluation of minor league, collegiate, or nonprofit sports Web sites.

3. Visit a blog that focuses on sport-related issues. Visit the blog daily for 1 week and identify any trends in posting, commentary, and design. Share your observations with your group members. What similarities did your group discover? What differences did you discover? Report your findings to the class.

Individual Exercises

1. Attend a sporting event. While in attendance, note the many ways in which new technologies are affecting communication mechanisms and your overall experience.

2. Develop your own blog related to sport. What components will you include?

3. Visit several of your favorite sports Web sites. What appeals to you about these sites? How does your level of involvement with the sport entity influence your needs when visiting the site?

Internet Sites for Additional Learning

Best Sports Web Sites: www.webaward.org/winners_detail.asp?yr = all&award_level = best&category = Sport

CBS Sportsline.com: http://cbs.sportsline.com/

LPGA Web site: www.lpga.com/default_rr.aspx

Major League Baseball (MLB) Blog: www.MLBlogs.com

National Basketball Association (NBA) Blog: www.nba.com/blog

National Hockey League (NHL) Blog: www.nhl.com/blogcentral

Nike Basketball Web site: www.nike.com/nikebasketball/

Mark Cuban's Weblog: www.blogmaverick.com

Prince Tennis Web site: www.princetennis.com/countrySelector.asp

Web Site Analysis: www.theCounter.com

CHAPTER 10

Sport Advertising

LEARNING OBJECTIVES

▶ To understand the use of sport as a means to advertise to mass and diverse audiences

▶ To recognize how companies use sport when advertising their products to mainstream audiences

▶ To appreciate the unique challenges of marketing the sport product

▶ To become acquainted with the historical context of advertising and advertising in sport

▶ To comprehend the role of sport sponsorship in sport advertising

▶ To understand the role of the celebrity-athlete endorser in advertising

PROFILE OF A SPORT COMMUNICATOR

Dan Migala

Just as "Bo Knows," Dan Migala knows sport marketing. Migala, a marketing leader in sport, publishes a monthly online newsletter, *The Migala Report. The Migala Report* keeps sport industry executives abreast of the best practices and current trends in sport marketing. Executives from a wide variety of sport entities use Migala's expertise including the Los Angeles Lakers, the New York Yankees, the Toledo Mud Hens, and the Ohio State University. Migala also publishes his report in Japanese to better serve the global sport community.

In addition to his work with *The Migala Report,* Migala has worked as an e-sports columnist for *SportsBusiness Journal* and has written several sport marketing books including *Interactive Sports Strategies*. The book provides a guideline for sport entities to develop online marketing efforts. Migala's degree in broadcast journalism, from the University of Missouri–Columbia, has assisted him in his endeavors and served him well when advising sport entities. Migala has advised many sport entities on a wide range of issues such as stadium financing, naming rights, and sponsorship strategies. These sport entities include Major League Baseball, the National Hockey League, Arena Football League, the Ladies Professional Golf Association, Churchill Downs, many minor league baseball and hockey leagues, and numerous collegiate athletic departments.

Through his work, Migala has noted that technology affords sport entities a new mode of communication with which to persuade and influence sport consumers. "It has given teams the ability to communicate with mass audiences on a one-to-one basis. Teams and sports entities have the power to bring fans closer to the action and

Dan Migala is a sport marketing expert who emphasizes the importance of building relationships with consumers whenever companies engage in marketing endeavors. Sport, because of its appeal to mainstream and niche audiences, is an effective vehicle for companies to advertise their products to the masses. One example of this is the numerous company and product names on the signage at this Major League Soccer contest.

to create the perception of them being closer to the organization in a more intimate way while still protecting the sanctity of privacy," Migala says.

In addition, Migala believes that customer relationship management has increased and facilitated better relations with sport consumers. "The concept of customer relationship management has fueled both a sales component through segmentation and a customer service channel that serves both the fan and the team alike. For the fan, it has also created a simpler way of buying and managing tickets. From online renewals to ticket forwarding to buying playoff tickets without having to wait outside, it has never been easier to be a ticket buyer thanks to technology," Migala says. The concept of customer relationship management centers on building relationships with sport consumers. Many sport entities have recognized the importance of quality customer service and the influence of the service encounter in impacting sport consumers' attitudes. Because of the unique nature of sport, this interaction can be integral in cultivating loyalty and repeat purchasing among sport consumers.

Migala also believes that the iPod will tremendously affect the manner in which sport entities communicate and cultivate identification among sport consumers. He says podcasting will become common. Many teams such as the Chicago Blackhawks and Washington Capitals have used podcasting to communicate with fans. "You will see this become a common feature on a team Web site and communication channel as a game-day magazine. It will evolve into video, and fans will soon come to expect it from their teams," Migala says. Sport entities such as NASCAR provide video and clips for fans to download to their iPods. Additionally, clips of the Bowl Championship Series games were also available for download onto the iPod in the 2006 season. Communicating via podcasting provides a sport

entity with a unique means to reinforce its brand image among sport consumers and enhance the quality of customer service.

Dan Migala believes that sport entities should "always keep fans' interest at the forefront of every decision they make. That should be the primary objective in every decision, and revenue will be the result of that objective." Catering to sport consumers' wants and desires is key in marketing the sport entity. Doing so enables sport entities to better communicate with and shape the perceptions of sport consumers, which allows sport entities to illustrate the values and benefits associated with their products. Relating to and communicating with sport consumers are at the heart of sport advertising. This chapter incorporates many of Migala's points and illustrates the importance of relating to sport consumers when marketing and advertising the sport product.

Advertising has long been associated with communication and is closely related to public relations and marketing in its intent to persuade. Figure 10.1 illustrates how this segment fits into the Strategic Sport Communication Model. Because of its appeal to mainstream and niche audiences, sport is an effective vehicle from which to communicate and to persuade the masses. Advertising in sport takes many forms and includes not only advertising of sport products but also using sport as the vehicle for nonsport entities to advertise their products to the masses. For example, a minor league sport franchise may develop various ticket pricing strategies to sell more tickets. Similarly, this same minor league franchise may sell advertising in its game program to varying companies. This company is using sport as a means to reach fans attending the games. Other examples of companies using sport to reach the masses include Peyton Manning's commercials for MasterCard and sport sponsorship. Sport sponsorship and the celebrity athlete endorser are discussed in greater detail in subsequent sections of this chapter.

Sport is a vehicle for reaching a mainstream audience, but sport managers are also faced with marketing the sport product to the masses. Sport is a nontraditional product and has many unique characteristics that can make it challenging to market. However, these unique characteristics are also what make sport so appealing.

Messner, Dunbar, and Hunt (2000) suggested that sport "includes the huge network of multibillion-dollar automobile, snack food, entertainment, and other corporate entities that sponsor sports events and broadcasts" (p. 391). To truly understand the challenges and benefits associated with advertising through sport and advertising for sport, one must understand the historical context of advertising as well as the application of advertising principles in sport. Additionally, one should understand the unique characteristics of the sport product and how these characteristics are used to effectively advertise and market the sport product.

UNDERSTANDING HISTORICAL PERSPECTIVES

Sport was used by advertisers in late 1800s to reach the masses. Early advertisements

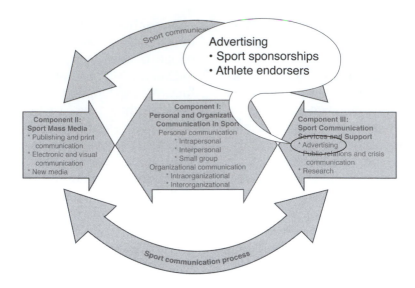

Figure 10.1 Advertising is the first segment of the sport communication services and support component of the Strategic Sport Communication Model.

featuring sport include tobacco ads displaying boxers, hunting, and horse racing. However, advertisers began to seriously use sport commercially in the early 1930s. Early advertisements included Ford Motor Company's advertisements during the World Series, Chevrolet's purchase of advertising during a series of college football games, and Brown & Williamson Tobacco Company's advertisements during the Kentucky Derby.

Sport appealed to advertisers because of its ability to allow companies to differentiate their products from those of others. In the 1920s, marketers used broadcasts of boxing to drive the sale of radios. Sports such as boxing and football were centerpieces in encouraging consumers to purchase new radios or vacuum tubes to maintain quality and clarity. With the invention of television in the 1940s, advertisers realized that sports broadcasts were an effective means of directly reaching a more mainstream audience, specifically a male audience.

General Mills began to capitalize on the mass appeal of sport by contracting real-life sport figures as spokespeople to endorse Wheaties cereal. The company has become synonymous with featuring the faces of famous athletes on its cereal boxes. Through an ad agency, General Mills first contracted with Babe Ruth in the 1930s and the slogan "Break-

fast of Champions" was coined. Wheaties has since featured athletes such as Michael Jordan, Walter Payton, John Elway, Mary Lou Retton, Tiger Woods, and the 1980 U.S. Men's Olympic Hockey Team.

Many companies in the hygiene, transportation, and electronics industries used sport as a means to spark interest in their products. Barbasol Shaving Cream regularly depicted sports such as football, fencing, fishing, cricket, and archery in its ads featuring females admiring clean-shaven men. Hertz Rental Cars portrayed individuals renting vehicles to travel for participation in winter sports. Greyhound Bus Lines and American Airlines featured sports such as football and hockey in their advertisements, whereas New York Central Railroads also used football to promote the ability of consumers to sleep on its Dreamliner. Picture quality and comfortable viewing of sport events were used by General Electric, Motorola, and Magnavox to entice consumers to purchase their televisions.

Advertisements using sport have made a mark on the masses and on advertising agencies. In fact, three sport advertising campaigns were named in *Advertising Age's* Top 100 advertising campaigns, with Nike's "Just Do It" campaign rated as 4 followed by Wheaties' "Breakfast of Champions" at 52 and ESPN's *Sportscenter's* "This Is Sportscenter" at 77. Both

Nike's "Just Do It" and Wheaties' "Breakfast of Champions" ranked in *Advertising Age*'s top 10 slogans of the century.

The broadcast of the Super Bowl each year provides a premier venue for unveiling creative advertising and reaching a mass audience. This annual professional football championship is a perfect example of a sports event that consistently places (and receives) a high price tag for advertising time. "This annual extravaganza provides companies the opportunity to launch new products to or build market share with an international audience," noted Pedersen (2005d). "Despite the fact that some view the money spent as wasted and the price tag for Super Bowl advertising has doubled over the past decades, the [broadcasting networks have] little trouble securing advertisers. Although the return-on-investment may be questionable" (Pedersen, 2005d), there are plenty of Super Bowl advertisers who jump on the 60-plus in-game advertising slots. In addition to the Super Bowl, however, other sports broadcasts offer equally appealing avenues for reaching specific target audiences. The Olympic Games, World Cup, World Series, and NBA finals attract large, diverse audiences. Other sports broadcasts, such as the Kentucky Derby, U.S. Open Tennis Tournament, PGA broadcasts, and X Games, allow advertisers to directly reach specific target audiences. Companies such as Visa, Prudential Insurance, Mercedes, and American Express advertise to target audiences via broadcasts of these sports.

NASCAR has been one of the most successful sport entities with regard to advertising. NASCAR fans tend to be quite loyal to sponsors of drivers, and NASCAR has been most effective in creating a sense of identification between its drivers and its fans. NASCAR is consistently on the cutting edge of sport advertising and produces some of the most effective opportunities for companies desiring access to its key audiences. NASCAR engages in corporate partnerships with companies such as Allstate, DirecTV, Sears, and many

Using Sport to Reach the Masses: McDonald's Sponsorships

Throughout its history, McDonald's has been particularly effective in using sport to reach the masses. In fact, McDonald's has been responsible for many innovations in sport advertising. Lefton (2005) examined and highlighted McDonald's use of sport in its advertising efforts. In the late 1950s McDonald's began sponsoring local Little League championships, and in 1968 the company airlifted hamburgers to American athletes at the Winter Olympics. However, it was McDonald's airing of a commercial in the first Super Bowl broadcast in 1967 that truly marked its commitment to advertising through sport. The company sponsored its first McDonald's high school all-American basketball game in 1978 (Lefton, 2005).

With its opening of international restaurants, McDonald's first engaged in sponsorships with the Olympics. Its first involvement with the Olympics began in 1968 when figure skater Janet Lynn mentioned in an interview that she missed the taste of McDonald's. The company immediately sent its hamburgers to France and provided the broadcast announcers with the hamburgers as well "to make sure there was a lot of talk." Its official involvement with Olympic sponsorships began with the 1976 Summer Games, and in 1984, McDonald's was involved in the most commercial Olympics to date and made a significant investment in grassroots swimming that included title rights to the Olympic swimming facility in Los Angeles. By 1996, the company boasted restaurants inside the Olympic Village in Atlanta. In addition to sponsoring the Olympics, McDonald's is the NBA's third largest sponsor. The company also sponsors 11 Major League Baseball teams, three Major League Soccer teams, fifteen NBA teams, seven NFL teams, five NHL teams, one NASCAR team, and 19 collegiate programs (Lefton, 2005). The unique nature of sport can be advantageous as a vehicle to reach and attract the masses, as illustrated by McDonald's sponsorships.

others. NASCAR works diligently to create sponsorship opportunities that differentiate sponsors' products and cultivate identification among fans.

IDENTIFYING THE CHARACTERISTICS AND CHALLENGES OF SPORT

Marketing the sport product presents unique challenges for sport managers, largely because of the unique nature of sport. When sport managers advertise and market the sport product, they are essentially marketing three key elements: the competition between two teams or the on-field product, the entertainment or fan experience associated with sport product consumption, and the benefits gained through sport product consumption. Although the on-field product lies largely outside the control of marketers, the entertainment or fan experience and the enhancement of benefits associated with sport product consumption lie solely within the marketers' control.

Characteristics of the Sport Product

As many sport marketing scholars illustrate (Mullin, Hardy, & Sutton, 2000; Pitts & Stotlar, 2002), marketing the sport product is challenging for several key reasons. The sport product is

- intangible,
- heterogeneous,
- perishable, and
- simultaneous.

The intangibility of the sport product essentially means the sport consumer cannot judge the quality of the product until the product is purchased. This is directly linked to the simultaneous nature of sport, meaning that the sport product is consumed at the same time it is distributed. One must purchase tickets and attend the event to judge the quality of the product. In more traditional industries, products are not consumed at the time of distribution.

The intangible and simultaneous nature of sport emphasizes the quality of the entertainment experience, because the entertainment experience is within the marketer's control. Additionally, the simultaneous nature of the sport product places a heightened emphasis on the interaction between the service provider and the consumer. Heterogeneity refers to the ever-changing nature of the sport product, which means that the sport consumer's perception of the product can change over time. Numerous factors make the sport product heterogeneous, including but not limited to player injuries, weather, facility amenities, and team performance. As the sport product changes, so too do consumers' perceptions of the product. These changes in the product as well as the changes in consumer perception affect how marketers communicate, persuade, and formulate advertising strategies.

Another unique aspect of the sport product is its perishability. The sport product cannot be stored and has no shelf life. Again, it is consumed at the same time it is produced, and therefore it is perishable. Perishability also forces sport marketers to place a great deal of emphasis on the quality of the experience for the consumer because it may be a one-time interaction. The quality of this interaction will affect the consumer's experience, and the consumer's perception will largely be shaped by this experience. If people have poor interaction with game or event staff, it may reduce the quality of their experience and will affect their decision to return. Similarly, having to wait in long concession lines may give a person an unfavorable perception of the experience. Therefore, sport entities must focus on developing and maintaining a high-quality experience for sport consumers.

Key Distinctions

The sport product has several key distinctions in comparison to more traditional industries. These distinctions are highlighted in the work of sport management scholar William Sutton (1998). Sutton (1998) suggested that demand for the sport product can fluctuate dramatically based on a myriad of factors. Rarely does inventory exist with sport products. Sponsorship inventory is an exception to this, as discussed later in the chapter. In most industries, products and supplies can be replenished. In service industries like sport, consumers must use the product or it is lost forever. For example, if a family of four purchases tickets to a collegiate football game and cannot attend the game, the experience is lost because it cannot be captured and reproduced.

The sport product is most often consumed publicly, meaning that consumers' satisfaction is affected by social stimulation and often depends on others' enjoyment. In traditional industries, other consumers' perceptions and enjoyment of the product are far less likely to affect one's experience. The sport product is inconsistent and unpredictable, which would likely not be tolerated in other industries. However, it is likely the inconsistency and unpredictability of the sport product that appeal most to the masses. The sport marketer has little control over the on-field product relative to performance, rules, and penalties. However, the sport marketer has a central role in crafting the entertainment experience associated with the sports event.

As mentioned earlier, the service provider and client interface is of the utmost importance in sport. The ability of the sport marketer to control the fan experience allows for a focus on quality customer service (Miloch, 2005). Typically, service quality is categorized in two main areas, technical and functional, with technical quality referring to the core service and functional referring to the quality of the service delivery (Gronroos, 1991; Kelley & Turley, 2001). As illustrated by Kelley and Turley (2001), sport marketers have little ability to control the technical quality of team performance. However, they can dramatically affect the functional quality of the event experience. The functional quality of sport influences fans' perceptions of multiple aspects of the experience, including parking, pre- and postgame activities, arena and on-field promotions, concessions and merchandise, public address announcements and musical selections during the game, interaction with game operations staff, amenities of the venue, and other aspects of the event experience (Kelley & Turley, 2001; Westerbeek & Shilbury, 2003). These aspects are elements of Wakefield, Blodgett, and Sloan's (1996) "sportscape" and are considered to enhance the fan's entertainment experience (Chelladurai & Chang, 2000). Because sport fans consume the sport product at the same time it is produced, providing a high-quality experience is a most effective form of advertising for the sport organization.

When sport-focused organizations advertise their products, they must identify consumers' purchase motivations. Individuals consume products for various reasons, and these reasons may vary dramatically. The intangibles associated with sport present unique challenges to sport marketers when identifying consumer expectations (Miloch, 2005). Therefore, marketing strategies should focus on consumer satisfaction and identification with the sport entity (Arnett & Laverie, 2000; Chelladurai & Chang, 2000; Gladden & Funk, 2001; Gladden, Milne, & Sutton 1998; Kelley & Turley, 2001; Pritchard, Havitz, & Howard, 1999; Wann & Branscombe, 1993; Van Leeuwen, Quick, & Daniel, 2002; Zhang, Lam & Connaughton, 2003).

Individuals purchase products to satisfy personal desires and needs. In other words, products must serve some purpose for the consumer, and the consumer must gain a perceived benefit from purchasing a product. Consumers' purchase decisions are also affected by various environmental and individual factors (Mullin, Hardy, and Sutton, 2007). Environmental factors include a consumer's demographics and psychographics. Demographics include aspects such as personal relationships, socioeconomic class, ethnicity, gender, age, and income. Psychographics include elements such as one's cultural norms, beliefs, values, and lifestyle.

Additionally, one's stage in the life or family cycle affects choices regarding product purchases. According to Mullin and colleagues (2007), the life and family cycle includes

- the preparation period,
- the establishment period, and
- the reintegration period.

Sport organizations should establish clear objectives when they formulate advertising campaigns. Here, the Indiana Pacers advertise their schedule and promote their sponsors on a building in downtown Indianapolis.

In the preparation period, youth and individuals are most influenced by peers. In the establishment period, individuals are typically classified as single, married, or with a life partner, and they typically engage in an active lifestyle. Married couples may begin to have children, and thus life priorities change, which alters personal needs and desires. This change in lifestyle affects consumers' purchase motivations, which in turn influence consumers' decisions to purchase certain products. After children enter college or leave home, people have more time and, once again, purchase motivations and decisions change. Finally, people enter the reintegration period, which is characteristic of retirement where individuals have much more free time but typically less income. Individuals in this stage of life may also become single again because of the death of a spouse or life partner (Mullin, Hardy, & Sutton, 2007). When sport organizations advertise their products, they must consider a person's stage in the life and family cycle to most effectively formulate marketing strategies.

Requirements for Effective Sport Advertising

Steve Bloom, an executive with a Minnesota-based research company, teamed with the American Marketing Association to establish guidelines for effective print advertising. Many of these guidelines are illustrated in this section and can be applied in the context of sport advertising. When formulating an advertising campaign, sport managers should establish clear objectives so they can develop effective strategies for implementation. Advertisements should also be developed to either create or reinforce a specific brand image. However, the sport organization must be clear as to what brand image it desires. Once clear objectives have been defined, all elements of the advertising campaign must support the overall objectives. Additionally, campaigns should illustrate the merits and the benefits associated with the sport product, the key in which is to support the consumer's decision to purchase the product. For example, the typical consumer has numerous entertainment options but limited discretionary income. Sport entities are competing for this income with many other options such as other sport teams within a geographic region, restaurants, theaters, and other recreational activities. When formulating advertising campaigns, sport entities must focus on how the benefits associated with the consumption of their product outweigh the benefits associated with the purchase of another related product. In other words, why should consumers spend their money on your sport product over another? Advertising campaigns should also feature the sport product in use if possible, because this allows potential consumers to relate to the sport product and creates a visual sales point.

Advertisements should be straightforward, clear, and consistent in their design and in their messages to build and maintain a brand image for the sport product. Repetition reinforces the messages the sport entity desires to send to its key audiences.

Target Markets and Segmentation

A target market is a segment of consumers with like characteristics who have the ability to purchase the product and are willing to purchase the product. Advertising and marketing strategies should center on reaching the target market. To determine target markets, sport organizations must begin with segmentation, which lays the foundation for identifying key target markets. Through segmentation, sport entities can identify groups of consumers who should be targeted to purchase the sport product. Consumers may be segmented in numerous ways, and some common considerations for segmentation include demographics, psychographics, lifestyle, geographic region, and frequency of product usage. Wyner (2002) noted, "Effective segmentations enable companies to allocate investment resources to target customers that will be most attracted to offers. Success is judged on how well the firm acquires and retains profitable customers" (p. 6).

Understanding the characteristics of segments and target markets is key in advertising. Without this understanding, a sport organiza-

tion cannot effectively communicate its core messages to consumers. Sport entities will likely communicate the features of their products differently based on the characteristics of each target market.

Oftentimes, sport organizations may use consumers' lifestyles to best reach them. Reaching consumers through their lifestyle requires understanding consumers' cultural trends and attitudes and how these influence purchase intentions. To reach consumers via their lifestyle, sport organizations must become involved with the beliefs and culture of its target audience. As Miloch and Lambrecht (2006) illustrated, the sport organization should become involved with the activities that "mean the most to its target consumers" (p. 147). Because it is increasingly unprofitable to advertise and market to a mass audience, lifestyle marketing has become more prominent.

To effectively advertise and market based on consumers' lifestyles, sport organizations must understand the patterns of attitudes and activities of its target consumers. With this understanding, sport organizations can then tailor their products and promotional strategies to fit these patterns. These patterns or recurring patterns denote one's lifestyle (Hanan, 1980; Michman, Mazze & Greco, 2003; Schreiber & Lenson, 1994). Within these patterns, sport organizations should examine the target market's psychographics, product and media usage, and demographics.

RECOGNIZING THE VALUE OF SPORT SPONSORSHIP

Companies have recognized the value of sport as a vehicle for communicating to the masses and consistently use sport as a means to advertise their products. Sport entities have also recognized the value of partnering with companies to assist them in reaching the masses. The most common means for accomplishing this is through sport sponsorship. Sport sponsorship is an effective way for companies to build and support their own brand identity. It also is an excellent way for sport entities to

Businesses recognize the value of sport as a vehicle to communicate their message to the masses. A title sponsorship comes with a high price tag and high visibility. Here, Ford Motor Company promotes its products during the Ford Championship at Doral.

increase revenue, enhance their consumers' experiences, and sometimes enhance their own brand image.

Challenges of Sponsorship

At its most basic level, sponsorship involves a marketing exchange between the sport entity and the sponsoring company. As mentioned previously, sport entities benefit from sponsorship as a revenue generator, as a means to offset expenses, and as a means of promotion. When companies began engaging in sport sponsorship, it provided a sound means for product differentiation. Now, countless companies use sport as a means to reach the masses. Because so many companies use sport as a vehicle to the masses, they must make their products stand out compared with other advertisers seeking to capitalize on the mass appeal of sport. The number of companies using sport sponsorship to enhance their brands has dramatically increased. Because of this increase, sport entities face numerous challenges when soliciting spon-

sors. To meet the challenges, sport entities must focus on

- differentiation,
- research, and
- the needs and desires of sponsoring companies.

Sport entities must be creative in differentiating sport sponsorships, especially when companies are within the same sponsorship category. Sponsorship categories refer to classifications. Usually sponsors are classified according to their products and the service in which they provide. For example, Coca-Cola and Pepsi would be classified in the beverage category, whereas Chase Manhattan and Bank of America would be classified in the banking or service category. Understandably, these companies desire to distinguish their products and services from those of their competitors. The sport entity must ensure that differentiation occurs by designing sponsorship packages that meet the specific motives of each corporate partner.

In addition to differentiating sponsorships, sport entities must conduct research on their consumers. Oftentimes, sponsoring companies will want to tap into the sport entity's demographics, psychographics, and consumption habits. Therefore, it is in the sport entity's best interest to gather this information, so it can better identify potential corporate partners and develop sponsorship packages to meet the needs and objectives of sponsoring companies.

Sport entities must also be cognizant of companies' rationale for engaging in sport sponsorship. Companies engage in sponsorship for a variety of reasons (see figure 10.2). IEG, a company dedicated to researching sponsorship, has noted several reasons why companies partner with sport entities. These reasons include a desire to

- heighten visibility,
- shape consumer attitudes,
- reinforce existing attitudes,

- communicate commitment to a particular lifestyle,
- engage in business-to-business marketing,
- differentiate their products from competitors,
- entertain clients,
- gain merchandise opportunities,
- showcase product attributes,
- combat larger ad budgets of competitors, and
- drive sales.

The exposure of sport events provides a wide range of publicity opportunities for sponsoring companies and allows them to increase the visibility of their products. Companies with highly recalled and highly recognized brands will use sport sponsorship to shape consumer attitudes toward their products and associate their product with a particular lifestyle. Additionally, engaging in certain sport sponsorships allows

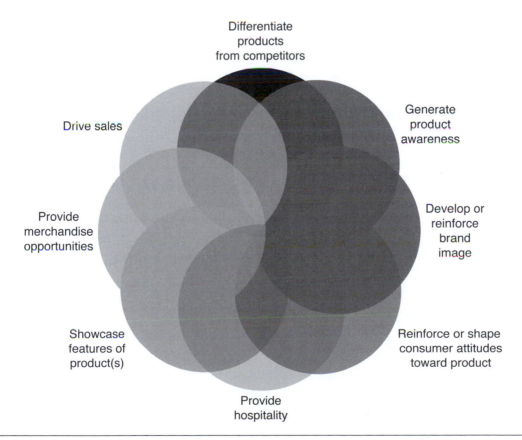

Figure 10.2 Common motives for engaging in sport sponsorship.

a company to communicate its lifestyle to a particular niche market (IEG, 2001a).

As mentioned, sport sponsorship is also used to differentiate products from competitors. This is especially pertinent for companies in the service industry such as banking and insurance. Sport sponsorships provide opportunities for category exclusivity and, in doing so, provide service-oriented companies with chances to create currency with consumers. Category exclusivity means that a sport entity will not engage in another sponsorship with a company within the same category. For example, if Coca-Cola is an exclusive sponsor of a minor league franchise, the franchise would not be able to enter into a sponsorship with competing companies such as Pepsi or Dr. Pepper. Additionally, sport sponsorships provide merchandising opportunities for companies. This is appealing to companies because 80% of product choices are made in-store. Sponsorship allows companies to develop unique and exciting "pop-up" displays at the point of purchase. Sport sponsorship is also cost-effective compared with traditional media advertising (IEG, 2001b).

When developing sponsorships, sport organizations should focus on the sponsoring company's objectives. If a sponsoring company wants opportunities for on-site sales or an opportunity to expose consumers to the features of a specific product, the sponsorship should be designed to account for this. For example, if a car dealership wants to increase awareness of its vehicles and expose consumers to a specific vehicle's features, a sport franchise might allow for the vehicles to be displayed during events and allow for the dealer's salespeople to be on hand to answer any questions consumers may have. Furthermore, the sport entity could develop a contest in which consumers may enter to win a vehicle or incorporate the vehicle into various on-field or in-arena promotions. This would allow the dealer to expose the features of the vehicle while also building a database of potential target consumers.

Objectives for sponsors vary, and the effectiveness of each sponsorship will be measured by the specific objectives. For example, Migala

(2005b) noted that Pepsi-Cola has established six key objectives for sport sponsorship. The objectives include creating assets owned exclusively by Pepsi, developing a cobranded logo with the sport or event, owning the pouring rights within the facility, creating branding opportunities through "bold signature signage," cultivating hospitality assets, and establishing grassroots marketing opportunities. To foster the accomplishment of these objectives, Pepsi pursues relationships that allow the company to deliver retail promotions at the local level. These promotions include activities like Pepsi-branded fantasy camps that are handled by local bottlers. When Pepsi develops a cobranded logo, it uses the logo to separate itself from other team or event sponsors and to further heighten its status as owning the particular promotion or platform. Owning pouring rights means Pepsi is the exclusive soft drink provider in the sponsored venue. Pepsi creates branding opportunities through "bold signature signage" by seeking signage that is prominently displayed and typically larger than other companies' signage. This allows Pepsi to create a more unique branding opportunity. Pepsi cultivates hospitality assets and uses these assets to entertain key customers both during games and on nongame days within sponsored facilities. When establishing grassroots marketing opportunities, Pepsi coordinates efforts with franchises to create opportunities to support the relationship. These activities include on-can ticket redemption programs and other promotions that can be supported at the local and retail level (Migala, 2005b).

Activation Strategies

Increased financial pressures combined with growing numbers of sponsors have forced sport marketers and corporations to become more innovative and creative when designing and activating sport sponsorships (Miloch & Lambrecht, 2006). In turn, these pressures have also increased the need to more effectively assess the return on investment of such sponsorships and have forced sport marketers to pay closer attention to the needs and objectives of corporate partners. Activation refers to the sponsoring entity's promotion of its sponsorship. In other words, the sponsoring company will promote its association with the sport entity and the fact that it is a sponsor. The 2006 Super Bowl XL sponsors provide an excellent example of activation. The NFL provided sponsors with a greater amount of lead time so the companies could better design their marketing campaigns that centered on the game. Many of the sponsoring companies activated their sponsorship of the event. Campbell's Chunky Soup designed print advertising that featured 40 different soups with 40 different Super Bowl logos. The advertisements were distributed nationally in the United States. Sprint, title sponsor of the halftime show, used a text-messaging contest that allowed fans to select a song by the Rolling Stones, and the selected song was then played during the halftime show. Coors focused on the legacy of the Super Bowl and developed a sweepstakes for the event. Additionally, Coors placed NFL logos on its cans and bottles. Pepsi implemented a Super Bowl collectible can series to showcase great moments in NFL history (Lefton, 2006). These activation strategies assisted each sponsoring entity in enhancing and reinforcing its brand image while also celebrating the storied history of the NFL, which in turn enhanced the image of the NFL. This example illustrates best practices in activation and the ability of both parties to maximize their partnerships.

As illustrated in the Super Bowl example, the manner in which sponsors activate their sponsorships may influence the effectiveness of the sponsorship. Therefore, sport entities should strive to include activation strategies as part of the overall sponsorship. This in addition to providing suggestions to sponsoring companies helps both parties reap the maximal benefit from sponsorship. Since 2001, sponsoring companies have increased their

Examples of Successful Activation Strategies

As sponsorship has evolved, the activation of the sponsorship packages has become more sophisticated. Sponsorships now assist in building the brand for the sponsoring company and exposing the sponsoring company's products to potential consumers. For example, when MBNA renewed its sponsorship with the NFL in 2003, it wanted a sponsorship that would encourage consumers to use their credit cards. MBNA offered an affinity card with the NFL, and research revealed that consumers were signing up for the card but were not using the card. Credit card companies earn the bulk of revenue from card usage and, therefore, MBNA needed a program that would entice consumers not only to sign up for the card but to use it regularly. Together the two entities developed a reward system based on card usage. For example, the more consumers used the credit card, the more points they earned. The points could then be redeemed for various NFL merchandise and tickets, even opportunities to acquire tickets to the Super Bowl (Lefton, 2005).

The American Automobile Association (AAA) teamed with Mark Martin and NASCAR to enhance the value of memberships and to also attract new members to the organization. Using Martin as its endorser, the association sponsored 12 International Speedway Corporation tracks and spent as much on activation of their sponsorship as on the sponsorship itself. Some of the ways AAA activated its sponsorship and provided an added value for its members included bestowing its members with roadside assistance at various racetracks, offering 10 percent discounts on Mark Martin merchandise, and presenting question-and-answer sessions with Martin at select races including Daytona and Talladega (Smith, 2006).

During the 2006-2007 NBA season, Lexus and the Minnesota Timberwolves designed a sponsorship to target the franchise's premier season ticket holders. Courtside season ticket holders were treated to what team officials refer to as the "Lexus experience." These fans were granted access to all Lexus-sponsored spaces in the venue and were treated to complimentary dinner and cocktails during each game. These patrons were also entitled to valet parking (Muret, 2006).

spending on activation. Although this spending declined in 2003, it once again increased in 2004. Currently, more than 80% of sponsors report some amount of spending on activation (IEG, 2004, 2005).

Given this research, sport managers should develop sponsorship packages that will enhance opportunities for sponsors to activate or leverage the sponsorship (IEG, 2005; Migala Report, 2005). This may allow sport consumers to identify with the sponsor's products and to associate the sponsoring company with the sport entity. Sponsoring companies have indicated that enhanced public relations efforts, internal communications, traditional advertising, hospitality, internet tie-ins, and enhancement of business-to-business partnerships are ideal forms of activation (IEG, 2005). Sport entities should include these elements as potential pieces of inventory when developing packages to meet sponsor objectives.

Sponsorships and Branding

Sponsorship of niche sport events has dramatically increased as companies seek to appeal to consumers through their lifestyles. Although niche sports do not appeal to mainstream audiences, sponsorship of these sports and of these types of events allows sponsors direct access to target markets. Recent niche sport sponsorships include Panasonic's sponsorship of Major League Soccer's grassroots tournament, Toyota's sponsorship of bass fishing, Re/Max's sponsorship of the World Long Drive Championship, Nextel's sponsorship of the Breeder's Cup, and Mountain Dew's sponsorship of the Dew Action Tour.

Developing and cultivating a specific brand image for the sport organization and its products are referred to as branding. Consumers are more likely to purchase products that possess a well-respected or well-known brand name (Gladden, Milne, & Sutton, 1998; Mullin, Hardy, & Sutton, 2007). Specific organizations and products elicit certain associations or perceptions in consumers' minds. Brand associations include anything in a consumer's memory that is linked to a specific brand (Keller, 1998), and

these associations ultimately create the overall brand image of the product.

Keller (1998) identified three types of brand associations: attributes, benefits, and attitudes. "Attributes are those descriptive features that characterize a product or service, such as what a consumer thinks the product or service is or has and what is involved with its purchase or consumption" (p. 93). In sport, attributes may include features such as a new facility. "Benefits are the personal value and meaning that consumers attach to the product or service attributes—what consumers think the product or service can do for them and what it represents more broadly" (Keller, 1998, p. 99). These benefits are what satisfy the consumer's motivations for consumption. In sport, season ticket holders enjoy many benefits, although the benefits that matter most to each season ticket holder may differ. For example, one season ticket holder may enjoy having the same seat for each game, whereas another may most enjoy a special parking area. Other season ticket holders may simply enjoy the camaraderie they share with other season ticket holders. Consumer attitudes are abstract and difficult to measure but ultimately shape the consumer's overall evaluation of the brand. Brand attitudes significantly affect consumers' actions and behaviors (Keller, 1998). For example, a person's attitude toward a specific sport may have a great impact on his decision to watch the sport on television or attend a live event specific to that sport. Similarly, people's opinions of a specific franchise may also affect their decisions to purchase a single game ticket, a miniseason ticket package, or a full-season ticket package. Sport consumers' perceptions regarding certain equipment will affect their purchase decisions in a similar manner.

According to sport management scholars Gladden and Funk (2002), "attributes of the sport product include team success, star player, head coach, and management" (p. 57). Benefits include "identification of fans, acceptance by peers, escape, nostalgia, and pride" (p. 59). These authors suggest that subjective beliefs, aspects, and cognitive structure are influential in cultivating attitudes. In their research, the scholars developed the Team Association Model. The model illustrates the numerous factors that affect branding in sport. Branding is important because through strong and consistent branding efforts, sport organizations can establish brand equity. Brand equity is considered the added value a specific brand name contributes to a specific product (Aaker, 1991). In other words, brand equity is the premium a consumer will pay for a branded good or service compared with the amount paid for an identical unbranded version of the same item (Keller, 1998). This premium is considered the difference in price between a brand name product and the generic version of the same product.

Building brand equity provides several advantages to the sport organization. Brand equity assists sport entities in enhancing their image and also in generating revenue (Gladden, Milne, & Sutton, 1998). It also cultivates loyalty and repeat purchasing among sport consumers.

FOCUSING ON THE USE OF ATHLETES AS ENDORSERS

The use of celebrities as endorsers has been a significant part of the advertising industry since its inception. Approximately 20% of all commercials use some type of celebrity endorsement (Bradley, 1996). Although companies have long used sport to reach the masses, companies have also recognized the value of having athletes, and celebrity athletes, endorse their products. Endorsements can be quite lucrative for athletes and can have a strong return on investment for companies. Athlete endorsements can range from wearing specific products to speaking on behalf of certain products. Brooks and Harris (1998) identified four key classifications of endorsements. These include the explicit mode ("I endorse this product"), the implicit mode ("I use this product"), the imperative mode ("You should use this product"), and the copresent mode (the endorser appears in some setting with the product).

Many companies view the athlete endorser as a means to set their product apart from the

competition. Petty, Cacioppo, and Schumann (1983) noted that using golf and tennis athletes in advertising resulted in a higher brand evaluation among consumers compared with using the average citizen as an endorser.

Trends in Use of Athlete Endorsers

Research indicates that the most popular athletes are the most likely to endorse products and that these athletes usually come from highly visible sports such as basketball, football, tennis, golf, auto racing, and the Olympic Games (Jones & Schumann, 2000). Jones and Schumann (2000) noted that the use of athlete endorsers has increased since the 1920s. In the 1980s, one of every five ads featured a sport celebrity. Stotlar (2005) noted that few athletes were used as endorsers in the 1960s, but this dramatically changed in the 1980s when shoe companies began using athletes to endorse their products. In sport-related media, the use of the athlete as an endorser is more widespread than in non–sport-related media (Jones & Schumann, 2000). The use of the female athlete as an endorser is also on the rise in the general media. However, in sport-related media, the use of the Caucasian male athlete as an endorser appears to be most prominent (Jones & Schumann, 2000).

The use of Tiger Woods to endorse not only golf-related products but also products marketed to mainstream audiences has proven effective for companies like Buick and American Express, who relied on Woods' talent on the course as well as his well-rounded, clean-cut image to market vehicles and credit card services to the masses. Woods' persona has made him one of the most popular athlete endorsers. However, Nike has capitalized most on its use of Woods. In fact, even in commercials and print ads for other companies, Woods wears Nike branded clothing, a constant reminder to the masses of his association with the company.

Traditionally, female athletes have not endorsed as many products as their male counterparts, but endorsements by female athletes are significantly on the rise. Tennis star Maria Sharapova is one of the highest

Memorable Campaigns With Athlete Endorsers

One of the most infamous and effective campaigns using an athlete endorser was Coca-Cola's use of "Mean Joe Greene" (see table 10.1 for a list of other ad campaigns featuring athlete endorsers). The ad featured the lineman in the player's tunnel. A young boy approached and asked Greene if he wanted a bottle of Coke. Greene declined the Coke, but the boy asked him again and stated, "I just want you to know that you're the greatest." This time Greene accepted the Coke and chugged the soda while the boy began to walk away. Greene then said to the boy, "Hey Kid . . ." and threw him his jersey. With a big smile, the boy said, "Thanks, Mean Joe." This ad capitalized on Greene's persona as a rough and tumble lineman for the Pittsburgh Steelers and left a favorable impression of both him and of Coke's product in the mind of consumers.

Coke's rival, Pepsi, has also capitalized on the use of athletes in its campaigns. Soccer legend Pele and rising star Freddy Adu have endorsed Sierra Mist while professional snowboarders Shaun White and Hannah Teter endorse Mountain Dew. Baseball legends Ken Griffey Jr. and Sammy Sosa have also appeared in ads for Pepsi.

Nike has also long relied on top athletes to reach the masses. Nike has used prominent athletes like Michael Jordan, Bo Jackson, Maria Sharapova, Charles Barkley, John McEnroe, Andre Agassi, Tiger Woods, Roger Federer, and LeBron James to tout its products using the slogans "Just Do It" or "Must Be the Shoes." Recently, James has been featured in a series of ads entitled "the LeBrons." The ads highlight four different personas of James and include scenes on a basketball court and one scene where James dives into a swimming pool.

McDonald's promoted its quarter pounders by featuring on-court rivals Michael Jordan and Larry Bird challenging each other to make unthinkable shots ("off the billboard, through the tunnel, off the floor, nothing but net"). This ad campaign allowed fans to identify with and relate to the two heroes. The ad left lasting memories in the minds of consumers. As noted earlier in the chapter, McDonald's has consistently used sport to reach the masses. It is also heavily involved with the Olympics and claims to "feed the world's top athletes."

Table 10.1 Memorable athlete endorsers

Athlete endorser	Sport	Products endorsed
Andre Agassi	Tennis	Genworth Financial, Canon
David Beckham	Soccer	Gillette, Adidas
Dale Earnhardt, Jr.	NASCAR	Budweiser, Wrangler Jeans
John Elway	Football	Prevacid, Bassett Furniture
Jeff Gordon	NASCAR	Pepsi, Dupont
"Mean" Joe Greene	Football	Coca-Cola
Mia Hamm	Soccer	Gatorade, Nike
Tony Hawk	Professional skateboarding	Kellogg's, Sirius
Bo Jackson	Football, baseball	Nike
LeBron James	Basketball	Sprite, Nike
Michael Jordan	Basketball	Gatorade, Hanes, McDonald's, Nike
Lisa Leslie	Basketball	Gatorade, Nike
Peyton Manning	Football	DirecTV, Sprint, MasterCard
Arnold Palmer	Golf	Pennzoil, Heinz
Danica Patrick	Indy Racing League	Argent, Peak Antifreeze, Motorola
Maria Sharapova	Tennis	Motorola, Tag Heuer, Honda, Nike
Tony Stewart	NASCAR	Home Depot, Old Spice
Serena Williams	Tennis	Wrigley, Nike
Tiger Woods	Golf	Nike, GM (Buick), American Express

paid female athletes in history with average earnings of approximately $19 to 22 million per year (Reimer, 2006; Thomaselli, 2005). Although this is miniscule compared with the earnings of male endorsers such as Tiger Woods, female athletes are increasingly recognized as effective product endorsers. Sharapova endorses Nike, Tag Heuer, Prince Racquets, and Canon cameras. As more girls and women play sports, more female athletes are endorsing products that appeal to the female audience. Indy Racing League driver Danica Patrick has inked deals with fashion company Bebe and endorses racing specific products like Bell, a helmet company. Patrick's success on the track earned her Indy Racing League's Rookie of the Year honors for 2005. Experts note that for Patrick to endorse more mainstream products, she must continue to perform well and be competitive.

Selection Factors

The selection of an athlete as an endorser is not a decision to be taken lightly. Similarly, athletes must carefully choose which prod-ucts or companies to endorse. Similar to sponsorship, the endorsement is a market-ing exchange. It is imperative that both par-ties select the other based on their respective brand images.

Companies' Point of View

Companies must be sure that the athlete appeals to its target market to ensure an appropriate return on investment. Schaaf (1995) identified three key endorsement trends noting determining factors in the selection of an athlete as an endorser: the athlete's accom-plishments, the athlete's personality or "elite" status, and the athlete's participation in an international sport. Athletes who have made significant accomplishments are more likely to have a following among mainstream audiences and to have been established in the minds of consumers as an elite athlete. Athletes par-ticipating in international sports may have more appeal as endorsers as a result of the sport's ability to transcend borders. Former athletes and athletes in niche sports are also becoming more widely used as endorsers. George Foreman, Michael Jordan, and Arnold

© Paul M. Pedersen

The advertising industry frequently uses celebrities as endorsers. Peyton Manning's endorsement deals with AirTran, Marsh Supermarkets, Reebok, Gatorade, DirecTV, MasterCard, Sony, Kraft, and other companies were worth more than $11.5 million in 2006 (in addition to his $19 million salary). His endorsements are found in media including billboards, television commercials, in-store advertising, radio, newspapers, and magazines. In February 2007, Manning was named MVP of Super Bowl XLI.

Palmer have all seen lucrative endorsement deals in their retirement, and extreme athlete Tony Hawk earns more than $10 million per year in endorsements. Oftentimes, companies include conduct clauses in their endorsement agreements with athletes. This protects the company's brand image and allows the company to distance itself from the athlete endorser if the athlete engages in behavior viewed as inappropriate. In this situation, the company seeks to preserve a positive brand image and will likely not want the inappropriate behavior of the athlete to affect public perception of the company.

Additional factors considered in selection of athlete endorsers include the athlete's trustworthiness, the recognizability of the athlete by the company's target market, the affordability of the endorser, the small risk of garnering negative publicity for the company, and the appropriateness of the match between athlete and product (Stone, Joseph, & Jones, 2003).

The use of the sport celebrity as an endorser may be disadvantageous. In its longstanding relationship with the U.S. Open, American

Express developed a series of commercials for the 2005 tournament featuring tennis ace Andy Roddick. The commercials focused on a specific theme: "Have you seen Andy's Mojo?" The theme was meant to entice consumers to log on to the Web and view additional portions of commercials, and it portrayed Roddick as a hard-working athlete who had lost an integral aspect of his game. While Roddick was left searching for the missing pieces of his tennis game, his alter ego, Mojo, was living it up on the streets of New York City. The American Express ads were to change and the story was to develop in the commercials throughout the 2-week tournament. Ironically, Roddick lost in the first round of the tournament, and American Express was forced to modify its commercials.

The use of athletes as endorsers is likely to continue even though many companies have indicated that their return on investment when using expensive athlete endorsers is diminishing. Additionally, top athletes tend to attract more endorsement deals and, in doing so, can be overexposed. Using an overexposed athlete

Equal Opportunities for Hero and Antihero

Indianapolis Colts quarterback Peyton Manning embodies the image of the wholesome, credible, and community-minded celebrity athlete. He was recently identified as the NFL's leading endorser over other top players including Tom Brady and Reggie Bush (Show, 2006). Manning recently signed three endorsement contracts making him one of the most used endorsers in the NFL. Manning entered the NFL 8 years ago, and he and his representatives have taken great care to build his own brand. Upon graduating from the University of Tennessee, Manning appeared in advertisements for a health care agency and a financial institution in Knoxville (Eder, 2007). He built his local endorsements in Indianapolis by first endorsing a local health care agency and a supermarket chain (Schoettle, 2005). Manning's national endorsements include Reebok, Gatorade, MasterCard, Sony, Sprint, and Kraft. Although Manning has yet to earn a Super Bowl Championship, his wholesome image appeals to a mainstream audience. He is perceived as an athlete with credibility

and character who is also community minded. Manning and his younger brother, Eli, organized a relief effort for victims of Hurricane Katrina. Manning was able to use his endorsements to assist him in this effort, and doing so further enhanced his image as a community-minded athlete. This perception has also made him the center of the NFL's national marketing plan. Many sport marketers note that Manning is an attractive endorser because he has a brother who currently plays in the league and a father who formerly played in the league. Marketers are able to use this aspect of Manning's life to reach the masses.

In contrast to the wholesome, well-rounded image of Peyton Manning, many advertisers prefer the athletes that embody the unpredictability of sport. These athletes may represent the antihero or villain, whom sport is notorious for producing. The most notable include the personas of Dennis Rodman, Charles Barkley, and the Oakland Raiders.

as an endorser means that consumers are less likely to listen to the athlete as a pitchperson, and this may also lead to a diminished return on investment for advertisers (Till, 2001). Furthermore, if an athlete's image becomes tarnished, it can have a negative impact on a product or brand (Till & Shimp, 1998).

Athletes' Point of View

Athletes have become extremely marketable and, in doing so, have become their own brands. Just as a company will research the appeal of specific athletes as endorsers, athletes should also take great care in selecting which products or companies to endorse. Recent research has illustrated that athletes'

images can be tarnished if they endorse inappropriate products or products that do not match their personas (Till, 2001). Athletes have well-developed images of their own which should be carefully crafted and maintained. Athletes should endorse products that will not only maintain their current brand image but also enhance it. To ensure that a particular brand image is maintained, some athletes and celebrities have even shifted to voiceover work in advertising to avoid being too closely associated with a specific product and to avoid overexposure (Brandes, 1995). Shuart (2002) also noted that credibility of an athlete can be paramount when endorsing products.

CHAPTER WRAP-UP

Summary

Long associated with communication, advertising is closely related to public relations and marketing in its intent to persuade. Because of its appeal to mainstream and to niche audiences, sport is an effective vehicle from which to communicate and to persuade the masses. Advertising in sport takes many forms and includes not only advertising of sport products but also sport as the vehicle for nonsport entities in advertising their products to the masses.

The sport product is a nontraditional product and has many unique characteristics that can make it challenging to market. The intangibility, heterogeneity, simultaneity, and perishability of sport are what consumers find most appealing. The role of sport advertising in advancing the "media sports cultural complex" is paramount. The historical perspectives of advertising illustrate this. This chapter has highlighted the challenges and benefits associated with advertising through sport and advertising for sport, and it provided the historical context of advertising.

Review Questions

1. What were some of the earliest forms of advertising? How was sport used in early advertisements?

2. Why is sport effective in enabling advertisers to reach both mainstream and niche audiences?

3. What are some of the more prominent advertising campaigns using sport?

4. What makes marketing the sport product unique and challenging?

5. What key strategies should sport entities implement when designing advertising for sport products?

6. What is segmentation and why is it important in advertising? How is segmentation performed?

7. What is a target market?

8. What is branding and why is it important?

9. What is the role of sponsorship in sport advertising?

10. Why are celebrity athletes effective in advertising? What affects the selection of the celebrity-athlete endorser?

11. Who are some of the most prominent athlete endorsers? What characteristics do these athletes possess that make them effective as endorsers?

Discussion Questions

1. What affects consumers' purchase behavior and intentions? Of the factors that affect consumers' purchase decisions, which do you perceive as being most influential and why?

2. What elements should be considered when formulating an advertising campaign?

3. How has sport been an effective tool for advertisers?

4. How has sport influenced advertising?

5. What makes sponsorship valuable compared with other modes of advertising?

6. Why is it challenging to market the sport product? How do these challenges affect marketing decisions?

7. How is an athlete's image also a brand?

8. How is branding important in advertising? Why is branding important when marketing the sport product?

9. Why do companies engage in sport sponsorship? Provide some examples of effective sport sponsorships.

10. How has McDonald's used sport to sell its products to the masses? How have other companies used sport to pitch their products? Provide examples.

Group Activities

1. Develop an advertising campaign for a specific sport franchise, league, or product. Present your campaign to the class.

2. Select two to three advertising campaigns focusing on sport. Examine the campaigns for similarities and differences. Which, in your opinion, is the most effective and why? Present your findings to the class.

3. Contact a sport franchise or sport entity and interview those with the responsibility of marketing and advertising the product. What techniques do these individuals use in selling their products to the masses? What challenges do they face in doing so?

4. Select three to five high-profile athletes. What endorsements do these athletes currently have? How do the athletes' images affect these endorsements? How are they effective as endorsers?

5. Select two athletes who epitomize the antihero or villain. Which products might be appropriate for them to endorse and why?

6. Select a specific sport entity or sport product. What are the primary target markets for the entity? What methods does the entity use to reach and convey its key messages to these target markets?

Individual Exercises

1. Record and examine the commercials during a 30- to 60-minute non–sport-related segment on one of the four major broadcast networks. How do the advertisers use sport to convey messages to key audiences?

2. Record and examine the commercials during a 30- to 60-minute segment of a sports broadcast or on a cable sport network. Examine what types of companies are advertising in the sport context. Who are the target markets for these products? How do these advertisements compare with those of the nonsport programming on the broadcast networks?

3. Attend a sporting event and examine the manner in which sponsorship is used at the venue. How are the sponsorships effective or ineffective?

4. What factors affect your purchase decisions? How would a potential company influence you to purchase its products?

Internet Sites for Additional Learning

Advertising Age: www.adage.com/

Advertising.com: www.advertising.com

American Marketing Association: www.marketingpower.com

IEG: www.sponsorship.com

Institute of Sport Sponsorship: www.sports-sponsorship.co.uk/index.htm

The Migala Report: www.themigalareport.com

Sponsorship Online: www.sponsorshiponline.com/

Sport Marketing Association: www.sportmarketingassociation.com

Sport Marketing Quarterly: www.smqonline.com/

Sport Marketing and Entertainment: www.smenet.com/

CHAPTER 11

Public Relations and Crisis Communication in Sport

LEARNING OBJECTIVES

▶ To understand the value of public relations to the sport-focused organization

▶ To recognize the techniques used to effectively manage media relationships

▶ To become acquainted with and to understand the key components of crisis management

▶ To comprehend the breadth and scope of sport public relations

▶ To appreciate the role of community relations in sport public relations

PROFILE OF A SPORT COMMUNICATOR

Indianapolis Colts

Securing public funding and gaining public support for the development of new sport facilities have become increasingly difficult for sport entities. Franchises such as the Arizona Cardinals, the Chicago Bears, the Arizona Diamondbacks, the Miami Heat, and the Indianapolis Colts have faced these challenges. Sport entities often rely on sport public relations to assist in garnering support for these endeavors. Most often, it is the intangible benefits of such a facility that benefit the local community. Intangible benefits include psychic income, an enhanced community image, and greater community visibility on a national or international scale.

Recently, the Indianapolis Colts were successful in gaining public

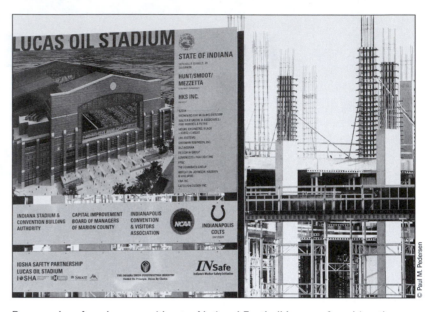

Because Los Angeles was without a National Football League franchise, there had been rumors that the Indianapolis Colts might be ready to head west if the team wasn't given a new home to replace the RCA Dome. The public relations campaign executed by the Colts resulted in Lucas Oil Stadium, a $625 million facility with a retractable roof.

support for their new stadium venture. This NFL franchise focused on the star power of the head coach (Tony Dungy), team president (Bill Polian), league commissioner (Paul Tagliabue), and quarterback (Peyton Manning) in several trips to meet politicians at the statehouse. This allowed lawmakers to meet and interact individually with team personnel. The team also used an economic impact report to identify the value of the Colts to community residents. The Colts' public relations campaign was successful in gaining the support of key constituents. The Colts were also successful in obtaining naming rights for the facility in an agreement with Lucas Oil. Lucas Oil Stadium is set to open in the fall of 2008.

Franchises and sport management professionals can learn from the strategy used by the Colts. David Pierce and Kim Miloch (2006) studied the activities of the Indianapolis franchise as it prepared and delivered its public relations campaign. These two sport management scholars identified key issues that other teams and leaders may

wish to emulate in public relations campaigns. For example, the two suggest that in the years leading up to a stadium funding campaign, team owners should monitor the external environment and identify the areas of greatest concern to community residents. Community relations efforts can then be geared toward satisfying those concerns. Thus, if it appears that the needs of the public school system will be a key argument against using public funds for a stadium, then the sport organization should focus community relations efforts on giving to the local schools. Although the team may already be actively involved with the school system, a more concerted effort can convince the community that the school system benefits from the team's presence. Therefore, residents and lawmakers see a tangible benefit for the school system. The key for sport franchises is to make tangible the otherwise intangible benefits associated with their presence in the community.

For the Colts, the public relations campaign was a crucial component in securing funding and providing a vehicle to make tangible the social benefits that it offers. Therefore, team owners should use the media to convince community residents and politicians that the team provides the area with intangible benefits that improve the quality of life. Exploiting the mutually ben-

eficial relationship between sport and the media provides sport organizations leverage to craft a positive message about the benefits a team can bestow on a city and enhances the franchise's chances of gaining public support for a stadium financing venture.

Using the media to the sport entity's advantage and implementing strategies to enhance public relations strategies are the primary focus of this chapter. This vignette about the Indianapolis Colts highlights many of the key aspects of public relations that are discussed in this chapter. From persuading the public and managing the media to interacting with the community and training for interviews, public relations professionals play a significant role in communicating the messages of the sport entity to its key constituents.

The value of public relations to the sport entity should not be overlooked, especially when trying to influence public opinion. As the vignette illustrates, public opinion was instrumental in facilitating the Indianapolis Colts stadium venture. The Colts organization recognized the importance of clearly communicating its needs, desires, and values to members of its community and developed a public relations strategy to assist in gaining public support. The Colts' sport public relations campaign is an example of the application of sport public relations strategy and highlights the key concepts discussed in this chapter. This chapter examines the public relations aspect of sport communication, including crisis communication (see figure 11.1).

The chapter begins by discussing sport public relations with a special focus on message development and image building through effective management of the sport media. Included are strategies for effectively managing the media through media relations techniques (e.g., media releases, credentialing, game notes, media conferences, media kits, fact sheets, tools of the trade) and building community relations efforts. In addition to containing information on public speaking and

speechwriting in sport, the chapter highlights successful sport public relations campaigns. The chapter concludes with an examination of crisis communication for sport organizations and outlines strategies for managing crisis situations internally and externally. Typical crisis situations in sport are presented along with standard protocol and operating procedures for each situation.

Sport public relations is significant to sport entities. Effective public relations strategies ensure that sport entities communicate in a most favorable manner with key constituents, both internally and externally. Public relations centers on the management of information flow between an organization and its key publics (Grunig & Hunt, 1984). Therefore, sport public relations may best be defined as the management of information flow between a sport entity and its key publics, both internal and external, to present the sport organization in the most favorable manner possible and to establish mutually beneficial relationships. At the heart of sport public relations is the image of the sport entity. To create favorable public opinion, the sport entity must understand the perceptions of its sporting publics. According to the Public Relations Society of America, public relations helps an organization and its publics mutually adapt to each other, implying that communication is a continuing process. This is also illustrated in the works of several public relations scholars.

Bronzan (1977) emphasized that public relations is a function of management that focuses on examining the public's attitudes, identifying organizational policies in light of public opinion, and implementing plans designed to earn positive public support. Similarly, Cutlip, Center, and Broom (2000)

Public Relations and Crisis Communication
• Public relations
• Media relations
• Community relations
• Communication during crisis

Component II:
Sport Mass Media
* Publishing and print communication
* Electronic and visual communication
* New media

Component I:
Personal and Organizational Communication
Personal communication
* Intrapersonal
* Interpersonal
* Small group
Organizational communication
* Intraorganizational
* Interorganizational

Component III:
Sport Communication Services and Support
* Advertising
* Public relations and crisis communication
* Research

Sport communication process

Figure 11.1 The second segment of the Strategic Sport Communication Model's third component is public relations and crisis communication.

wrote that public relations is a management function that establishes and maintains mutually beneficial relationships on behalf of the organization and the publics that are integral to the organization's sustained success. Davis (2004) stressed that the growth and sophistication of the field warrant a more modern definition, indicating that "public relations is a communication with people who matter to the communicator, in order to gain their attention and collaboration in ways that are advantageous to the furtherance of his or her interests or those of whoever or whatever is represented" (p. 4). In the sport industry, this collaboration with publics has traditionally occurred through the media, but as the industry has grown tremendously so too has the need for a more sophisticated means to communicate and shape public perception in a manner favorable to the franchise. Sport-focused organizations collaborate with a variety of publics in numerous ways, and this collaboration may take the form of media relations, community relations, and, in some instances, crisis communication.

An emerging discipline within the realm of sport management, sport public relations has

most often been associated media relations (Mullin, Hardy, & Sutton, 2000). In the past, public relations professionals maintained statistical records, wrote press releases, scheduled press conferences, developed media guides, and scheduled interviews. More recently, the role of public relations within the sport organization has been expanded to better address the complex issues facing franchises (Schoenfeld, 2005). Sport public relations professionals are responsible for determining the concerns and expectations of the organization's publics and explaining these concerns and expectations to management. According to the Public Relations Society of America, the best public relations will tell the organization's "story" to its publics and also help shape the organization and the way in which it performs. Sport entities depend on the expertise of their public relations professionals to not only tell the organization's story but also assist in responding to crises that may occur. More than ever before, sport public relations professionals are being used to support the sport entity's overall objectives by crafting and reinforcing the organization's brand image (Schoenfeld, 2005).

Community relations—such as the interaction of Florida Marlins players and coaches with their young fans during spring training—is one of the main ways in which sport organizations collaborate with their stakeholders.

IDENTIFYING HISTORICAL PERSPECTIVES AND TRENDS IN PUBLIC RELATIONS

The growth of sport public relations has been influenced by several key trends. Seital (2001) identified several trends affecting the discipline of public relations. These include growth in business and the continuous availability of information via enhancements in technology and the Internet. Several of these trends are the driving forces behind the changing nature of sport public relations. As the sport industry has evolved into a multidimensional industry, so too has the need for improved communication with key publics. Regardless of the sport entity's size or scope, assessing and managing public perception are paramount to its sustained success. Public perception is paramount because the public's image of the sport entity may influence product purchases, ticket sales, media coverage, and even organizational poli-

cies. However, influencing the perceptions of sport consumers is particularly challenging because unlike traditional industry, sport elicits strong emotions in the public. Whether supporting or criticizing a particular sport product or franchise, sport consumers often attach more meaning to sport, and this should not be overlooked when developing strategies to persuade and influence the perceptions of the sporting public.

Sport has often been considered a microcosm of society. For this reason, many social issues have played out in the realm of sport and have mirrored the social issues in general society. Many of these social issues are discussed in detail in chapter 13. These social issues have led sport entities to place a greater emphasis on managing public perception. For example, sport has long been considered the domain of males, with few females entering and advancing in the field. Additionally, sport is often criticized for its lack of minorities in management positions. Various incidents of discrimination and harassment have occurred in sport, sparking widespread controversy and dialogue regarding numerous social issues.

The globalization and expansion of sport have placed a greater emphasis on sport public relations. As sport becomes an industry without borders, sport entities must carefully manage worldwide perceptions of the organization. This means that sport entities must pay close attention to the various cultures and demographics that have become a part of the sporting public. The globalization and expansion of sport have been spurred and enhanced by technology and the Internet. This was covered earlier in this book in chapter 9, which provided an in-depth examination of the Internet's impact on sport communication. The Internet, as well as new media such as podcasting, instant messaging, and mobile technology, has created an instantaneous link with sport consumers. Sport consumers may access information relative to the sport product from almost anywhere in the world. This greater access emphasizes the need to effectively manage public perception, because new technologies are instrumental in shaping public opinion as an instantaneous communication channel.

Recent exposés on sport entities and athletes combined with controversial incidents such as the on-court brawl between the Detroit Pistons and Indiana Pacers in 2004, the death of a young girl hit by a flying puck at an NHL game in 2002, and certain issues surrounding player conduct (e.g., Bode Miller, Terrell Owens, and Lance Armstrong) have highlighted the need for sport entities to focus on effective public relations. In the scenarios regarding player conduct, the athletes faced intense scrutiny for comments made during interviews or comments and actions stemming from their performances or contracts. During an interview with CBS' *60 Minutes,* Miller stated, "It's not easy to ski when you're wasted." His statement made headline news and angered donors and sponsors of the United States Ski and Snowboard Association. Miller later apologized for his statements ("Miller Apologizes," 2006). Also scrutinized for his demeanor, actions, and

attitude is NFL standout Terrell Owens. Owens, in conjunction with his agent Drew Rosenhaus, made numerous comments about former teammates including Jeff Garcia and Donovan McNabb. Through his actions and the media's coverage of his actions, Owens is often perceived as a self-centered, egotistical athlete (Spector, 2005). Although the public perception of Lance Armstrong is more positive than that of Terrell Owens, Armstrong's character is often called into question by allegations of doping in sport. Despite Armstrong's constant denial of allegations that he used performance-enhancing drugs, his image as a wholesome, American hero has been jeopardized. His response to these allegations often influences public perception. These types of incidents can tarnish the image of individual athletes and can affect perceptions of the sport entity as well. Therefore, managing public perception regarding such issues is paramount.

Two of the primary influences on sport public relations are the nature and scope of the player–press relationship. As trends in journalism changed, so too did the manner in which athletes were portrayed in the media. Journalists no longer limited their critiques and analysis of players solely to their performance and began to incorporate elements of their personal lives into stories. Additionally, technology and the Internet have created more competition among journalists to attract viewers, listeners, and readers. This shifting focus on reporting in the media has caused sport entities to emphasize and increase public relations efforts. One of the key elements of enhancing public relations efforts is media relations, which is discussed at length in the sections to follow.

Many factors have influenced the growth of sport public relations. The growth of public relations as a discipline combined with the significant growth and expansion of the sport industry has caused sport entities to recognize the value of cultivating and maintaining favorable public opinion. Additionally, sport, as a microcosm of society, brings to the surface many sociocultural issues present in the mainstream society. As a result, sport entities are more cognizant of managing public perceptions. As sport becomes more global, sport entities understand the need not only to reach diverse audiences but to also relate to these audiences. Because sport garners widespread media coverage in both the sporting press and the mainstream media, it is essential for sport entities to manage public perception. This is most often managed through media interaction with athletes and other high-profile members of the sport entity. In managing public perception, public relations professionals often rely on four key models for guidance. These models, and their application to sport public relations, are discussed in the next section.

PRACTICING EFFECTIVE PUBLIC RELATIONS

Cultivating positive relations and perceptions among members of the public is a challenging endeavor. Sport entities serve a number of key constituents, each with varying needs, concerns, and desires. To serve their constituents most effectively, sport entities should focus on the transfer of information, the persuasion of perceptions, and the facilitation and maintenance of favorable relationships. Doing so means practicing effective public relations. Bernays (1952) suggested that the three main elements of public relations consist of informing the people, persuading the people, and integrating the people with the people. The manner in which these elements are applied varies for each sport entity and varies based on which constituents the sport entity desires to reach. For example, in persuading young adults to participate in tennis, the United States Tennis Association (USTA) might use spokespeople such as Andy Roddick, Venus or Serena Williams, or Maria Sharapova. Using these premier athletes as spokespeople may influence the younger generation to learn the sport, because younger adults can better relate to and identify with these players. To encourage older adults to participate in the sport, the USTA might rely on a spokesperson such as Regis Philbin.

Four Models of Public Relations

To establish effective and favorable relations with publics, public relations scholars have suggested four key models of public relations (Grunig & Grunig, 1992; Guth & Marsh, 2003; Hunt & Grunig, 1994). These models are the press agentry–publicity model, the public information model, the two-way asymmetrical model, and the two-way symmetrical model. These models are the most widely accepted and practiced models of public relations. Each model has evolved based on the needs of sport entities and their constituents.

The **press agentry–publicity model** focuses primarily on obtaining positive and favorable coverage from the media. This is the model most frequently used in sport. Sport receives more coverage in the media than any other industry, so sport entities have become quite proficient at providing the media with information such as statistics and injury reports. Many communication elements in sport occur through use of the press agentry–publicity model.

The **public information model** is often used in sport as well. A key element of this model is the distribution of unbiased and accurate information regarding the sport entity. Practitioners using this model are often considered journalists in residence. This is illustrated in sport by the use of sport information directors (SIDs) and media relations directors (MRDs) at professional franchises. These individuals are primarily responsible for disseminating various facts relative to the sport organization to members of the media. The focus is to disseminate accurate information to the sport media as quickly and as efficiently as possible. Although SIDs and MRDs are concerned with enhancing the sport entity's image, the primary concern is providing the media with the desired information.

The two-way asymmetrical and the two-way symmetrical public relations models focus more on shaping and influencing perceptions rather than simply disseminating information. These models require two-way communication between a sport entity and its publics rather than a one-way communication from the sport entity to the public. These models emphasize that feedback from constituents is integral in establishing effective and favorable relations.

The **two-way asymmetrical model** is intended to persuade an organization's key publics through message development. Essentially, the organization shapes its messages with the intent of persuading its publics to behave in a manner in which the organization desires. This model is effective when conflict from the public is minimal. This is pertinent to sport in that a sport entity may research its consumer base to determine consumers' satisfaction level with various aspects of the sport product. However, rather than use this knowledge to facilitate further communication, it may simply modify the manner in which it sends its messages or alter the message to achieve the desired result.

The **two-way symmetrical model** of public relations is often considered the most appropriate model in establishing positive relations with constituents. This model is grounded in research and advocates conflict resolution through facilitation of a mutual understanding between an organization and its key publics. Application of this model is seen in sport in a myriad of ways including when professional leagues enter into negotiations with players unions and when a professional franchise or collegiate athletic department desires public funding for the construction of a new facility. Sport public relations is transcending from a significant reliance on the press agentry–publicity model of public relations to an emphasis on the two-way symmetrical model of public relations. For example, sport entities are becoming more cognizant of the role of public relations in enhancing brand image. To effectively enhance their image, sport entities must understand the needs and desires of their key publics, and they must seek and obtain feedback from constituents to better address their needs. Feedback cannot be obtained in models focusing on one-way communication, so two-way communication is becoming the focus.

When practicing both one-way and two-way forms of communication, sport entities are concerned with persuading the public. An examination of persuasion techniques follows in the next section.

Elements of Persuasion

To truly influence public perception, sport entities must understand the fundamental elements involved in persuasion and use these elements in conjunction with the aforementioned models in shaping the perceptions of sport consumers. Persuasion is defined as "getting another person to do something through advice, reasoning, or just plain arm twisting" (Seital, 2001, p. 56). Seital (2001), who provides the framework for this section, suggested that most individuals do not have strong opinions on any particular issue. This means that a sport entity may, through strategic public relations, influence the perceptions of many sport consumers. However, there are a small number of people who possess strong beliefs and opinions, and changing their opinions and beliefs is most challenging for any organization. This has a particular impact in sport, where consumers may already hold strong beliefs on particular issues such as stadium financing, franchise expansion and relocation, or free agency.

To effectively persuade individuals, organizations must provide evidence that coincides with individuals' existing beliefs, emotions, and expectations. The most effective uses of evidence include

- the use of facts and figures,
- an appeal to the emotions of individuals,
- the personalization of information, and
- a focus on individuals' needs.

Although numbers can be misleading, individuals tend to be persuaded by their use. This is seen in sport through various ranking systems such as the NFL's power rankings, the Bowl Championship Series rankings of the top collegiate football programs, and the ATP's men's tennis rankings. Given these rankings, sport consumers formulate their perceptions of the best and most talented athletes and teams at the professional and collegiate levels.

As mentioned earlier, emotions run high in sport and emotional appeals can be quite persuasive. Sport is often used to persuade the masses, and sport entities often use additional emotional appeals when trying to shape public perception. Examples include framing the Dallas Cowboys as "America's team" and baseball as the "national pastime." These emotional appeals use patriotism to enhance perceptions among sport consumers. Personalization is often used in sport as well. Lance Armstrong advocates cancer research and is viewed as particularly persuasive given his personal struggle with the disease. A final form of evidence in persuasion is focusing on what appeals to consumers by focusing on what's in it for them. Sport entities that persuade using this mechanism are often effective because the focus is placed on the benefits to the sport consumer rather than the benefits to the sport entity. Many sport equipment and apparel companies are quite proficient at touting the benefits of wearing certain apparel and in using specific products to achieve maximal sport performance.

Factors That Influence Perception

A variety of factors influence the perceptions of sporting publics and, therefore, influence the ability to persuade them (see figure 11.2). These factors include motives for sport product affiliation, sport product performance, level of involvement with the sport product, frequency of sport media exposure, and sociocultural influences. These factors are discussed in the following sections.

Individual motives for sport product affiliation influence individuals' frequency of consumption and loyalty to a sport product. Loyalty may lead to repeat purchasing or followership. An individual may be a loyal fan but may not purchase tickets regularly. Therefore, he or she may be a loyal follower of the franchise by watching it on television, purchasing franchise merchandise, and engaging in online chats and discussions on the franchise's Web site. Motives for sport affiliation vary from individual to individual. Common motives include a desire for stress reduction, social stimulation and interaction, or competition (McDonald, Milne, & Hong, 2002). Motives are integral in shaping people's perceptions and should be considered by sport public relations professionals when shaping the opinions of sporting publics. Motives are also linked to perception of sport product performance, which refers to the utility of the

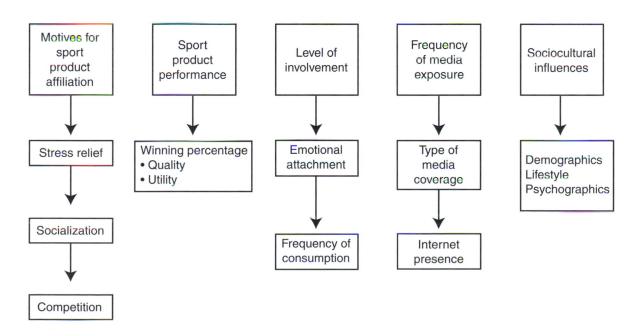

Figure 11.2   Key influences shaping public perception of the sport product.

sport product. Utility refers to the attributes of the sport product that make it capable of meeting individuals' needs and desires (Mullin, Hardy, & Sutton, 2007; Pitts & Stotlar, 2002). Therefore, the sport product must satisfy the desires of sport consumers. Its ability to do so will affect the perception of the sport product, which in turn affects persuasion.

Consumers' level of involvement with the sport product will also affect the ability to influence their opinions. As mentioned earlier, sport elicits high levels of emotions. The more a consumer is involved with the sport product, the less likely it is that her opinions of the product can be changed. However, those who are highly involved typically have more favorable opinions of the sport product.

The frequency and type of sport media exposure affect perceptions. Favorable coverage in the sport media can enhance public opinion by reinforcing existing positive beliefs or by encouraging more favorable public opinion. Similarly, negative coverage in the sport media can reinforce negative opinions and create negative perceptions in the minds of the sporting public. Demographics and sociocultural factors should also be considered when managing the perceptions of the sport entity. For example, demographics include characteristics such as gender, household income, education level, and number of children living at home. Sociocultural factors include aspects pertinent to one's culture and lifestyle. These factors play a role in shaping the perceptions of individuals and should be considered when formulating strategies to manage perceptions. In managing the perceptions of the sporting public, sport public relations professionals often focus on media relations.

MANAGING MEDIA RELATIONS

Sport receives tremendous coverage in the media. Entire sections of newspapers, segments on the evening news, and multiple cable television channels are devoted to covering sport. The media is an ideal way to promote a business and to gain more exposure (Lontos,

2004). Although most companies strategize regarding how to obtain more media coverage, public relations professionals in the sport-focused organization concentrate on how to use this coverage to the full advantage of the organization. Although SIDs and MRDs perform a variety of tasks and serve multiple functions, the primary goal of the position is to "enhance the athletics program's image among key constituents such as the mass media, the fans, the alumni, and other university personnel" (Stoldt, Miller, & Comfort, 2001, p. 45). In doing so, the sport-focused organization must pay close attention to the manner in which it cultivates and manages media relationships. This section highlights the key elements in media relations and provides strategies for enhancing media relationships while presenting the sport-focused organization in the most favorable manner possible.

Strategies for Developing Positive Relationships With the Media

The media should be treated as a direct link to the sport organization's consumers. Sport consumers have instantaneous access to media sources and because of this, sport public relations professionals should cultivate positive relations with the media. The mass media shape public opinion, and oftentimes the media's perception of the sport-focused organization will be the public's perception as well. As Kline (1996) wrote, "A good relationship with the media is important for the success of any business. A good relationship will not insure that the media will present only good news about the business, however, it will insure good communication between the two; which is the foundation for effective public relations" (p. 55).

Both sport information departments and the sport mass media, according to sport media scholar Lawrence Wenner (1998b), shape public opinion. In college athletic departments and in sport franchises, the professionals who work in the sport information and media relations departments are primarily tasked with creating and maintaining a positive image within the communities. To do this,

Sport information offices in intercollegiate athletics and media relations departments in professional sports work to shape public opinion. Those employed in these areas—such as the men's basketball contact at Ohio State, Dan Wallenberg (seated with computer at scoring bench)—create and maintain positive images with the public. Wallenberg is the associate director of the athletic communications office at OSU. He is second in command under associate athletic director of athletic communications Steve Snapp.

professionals must provide the media with much-needed "scoops" on their respective entities. The media's portrayal of the sport entity will have a tremendous impact in shaping public perception. The mass media possess the power to "shape the content of the message generated by a news release, a postgame interview, or another form of indirect public relations" (Nichols et al., 2002, p. 63). Furthermore, Mullin, Hardy, and Sutton (2007) suggested, "Public opinion is one of the most powerful forces in our society, and media relations is designed to formulate and shape favorable opinion via the mass media" (p. 387).

The responsibilities of SIDs and MRDs were stressed by Connors (2000): "It is important to create and maintain an honest and open relationship with the media and to encourage a level of trust between the two parties" (p. 319). Members of the media depend on trustworthy contacts (McCleneghan, 1995). Therefore, SIDs and MRDs must place a prime emphasis

on fostering favorable working relationships with the local, regional, national, and international media.

As Miloch and Pedersen (2006) noted, SIDs and MRDs view cultivating positive and mutually beneficial relationships with the media as integral in shaping the image of their sport entity. The relationship between the sport public relations professional and the media may appear basic in nature, but fostering and nurturing that relationship can be challenging. Additionally, an adversarial relationship can develop quite rapidly if the relationship is not properly maintained. Miloch and Pedersen (2006) noted that fostering a positive and mutually beneficial relationship with the media is a necessity in media relations. The nature of this relationship is thought to enhance coverage.

MRDs and SIDs share many similar views about cultivating relationships with the media. When responding to inquiries about their relationship with colleagues in the media, 87% of MRDs characterized the relationship as mutually beneficial and more than 90% indicated that they have a positive relationship with both the local and the national media. Approximately 66% of MRDs believed that the manner in which they handle the media directly affects the type (positive or negative) of coverage received by the sport entity. Sixty percent of MRDs believed that fostering positive relationships with members of the media increased the quantity of exposure for the sport entity, and approximately 74% indicated that cultivating positive media relationships would increase the quality of coverage for the sport entity.

Understand the Journalistic Environment

To foster positive relations with media entities, sport public relations professionals should understand the environment in which journalists operate, know what is considered newsworthy, and strive to provide this information in a timely and appropriate fashion. Newsworthy items include "anything significant that relates to the main news priorities at the time . . . conflict . . . controversy, anything that affects the community, human-interest stories . . . the unusual or the different . . . interesting data, statistics or research results, interesting 'firsts', anything that links up with famous or infamous people, success in major or prestigious awards, or any other significant recognition" (Frangi & Fletcher, 2002, pp. 19-20). The media will initiate contact with the sport organization for information such as facts, figures, statistics, and attendance figures. The media will also need confirmation or disconfirmation regarding rumors and will also seek the sport entity's reactions to rumors. For example, reporters will contact the sport franchise to obtain quotes or official statements if it is rumored a player may be traded or released or if a head coach may be hired or terminated. Members of the media will also initiate contact seeking reactions to reports, implementation of policies, or reactions to certain events. For example, major league players associations may be contacted for a response to a league's stance on a particular issue pertaining to the renegotiation of a collective bargaining agreement.

Anticipate Contact

Sport-focused organizations should always anticipate being contacted by the media after a major announcement such as the suspension of a player, the hiring or termination of a head coach or general manager, or the sale or relocation of a franchise. Sport-focused organizations may also be contacted when the media need more explanation on certain policies or programs. Oftentimes, the media will want further clarification on legal issues associated with operating the sport franchise such as stadium financing issues and player contract negotiations. Knowing when to contact the media and when to anticipate that the media will initiate contact with the organization allows public relations professionals to carefully craft responses that will reinforce the overall mission and image of the sport-focused organization. It also allows the organization to prepare to provide the media with information it needs in a timely and efficient manner. Members of the media have different deadlines, and to foster mutually beneficial relationships, sport public relations professionals must be timely in relaying and in providing the media with requested information.

Tools for Maintaining Contact With the Media

Sport public relations professionals use several methods when communicating with the media. These tools include the sport media release, the sport media conference, the media kit and media guide, the fact sheet, and the coordination of interviews with key sport entity personnel. This section provides an overview of each of these tools.

Sport Media Release

To initiate contact with the media, most sport public relations professionals will write and distribute to the media a press or media release. According to PR Newswire (2005), media releases should have a significant news angle, meaning that the sport entity's news release should inform the public by providing key information. The media release allows the sport organization to notify the media of specific news in a timely fashion. It also allows the organization to notify all media at once so as not to give the impression that certain members of the media take precedence over others. It is of the utmost importance that sport public relations professionals do not play favorites with the media. Doing so will undermine the organization's credibility and can lead to unfavorable coverage.

Newsworthy Media Releases

Sport entities should not release information to the media unless it is newsworthy and has general interest to the public. This may take the form of a new development within the sport entity such as a change in franchise ownership, the retirement of a legendary athlete, or the groundbreaking of a new stadium.

Media releases may also provide information regarding a dramatic element or present an issue of human interest. Human interest issues take a myriad of forms and may include aspects such as a popular player returning after a serious injury or illness, players working with various charitable organizations, or members of the same family competing against each other in a high-profile competition. Additionally, media releases with local flavor are also considered newsworthy. This may include hometown athletes earning high-profile awards or competing on a national or an international level. As mentioned earlier, sport public relations professionals must be cognizant of what constitutes newsworthy information and must take great care to notify the media when appropriate.

Characteristics of Well-Written Media Releases

Media releases should follow specific guidelines and should be written in Associated Press (AP) style, which is used by members of the media when formulating stories. Communicating with the media in this format helps build the organization's credibility and assists members of the media in performing their duties as journalists. Sport public relations professionals must understand journalists' deadlines and send the release at an appropriate time. This allows journalists to formulate their stories and may enhance the coverage of the sport entity.

The media release should be written using the inverted pyramid. Essentially, as we covered in chapter 7, the inverted pyramid requires that the most important information appear first in the media release. The most important information will be found in the lead sentence, which is the first sentence of the media release. The lead sentence should provide a clear and concise idea of what the organization is conveying by clearly outlining the five Ws: the who, what, when, where, and why elements of the story. The lead sentence should summarize the contents of the release and should encourage journalists to continue reading. In the body of the media release, the sport public relations professional may provide more in-depth information and include quotes from key figures within the organization. The end of the release may include more "fluff" information that is not necessarily pertinent to the information being relayed but rather touts the organization in some way. Examples include the inclusion of ticket information or upcoming promotions for a sport franchise. Additionally, the end of the media release may also include information that describes the sport entity or its products.

One should not distribute a media release to members of the media without being prepared for the information to be made immediately available to the public. Therefore, the release should always include a date and it should always indicate that the information being distributed is for immediate release. These three words—*FOR IMMEDIATE RELEASE*—should appear in all capital letters in the upper section of the release before the headline and contact information. It is not considered best practice for the sport-focused organization to send a media release in advance of when it would like the information to become public. The media should not be expected to withhold information from the public once they receive a media release.

Media releases should always include a headline. The headline should clearly convey the subject matter of the release and should be written in all capital letters. It should be concise, should stimulate reader interest, and, if possible, should not exceed one line.

The media release should always include contact information for the sport public relations professional. This includes office and cellular phone numbers, fax numbers, e-mail addresses, and a Web address. Typically, media releases should be short and concise and not exceed two pages. When media releases exceed one page, page numbers should be included on the release. It is also appropriate AP style for sport public relations professionals to indicate in the media release when no more information will follow. This is usually indicated by using the ### symbol. Recently, sport entities have become more creative and often end the release with the organization's name or slogan.

The better the media release is written, the more likely the sport public relations professional will be able to use the media to convey the organization's message to the masses. Oftentimes, a well-written media release may appear exactly as written in print. This is ideal because the sport organization has now directly linked its message to the public. Sport public relations professionals often craft lead sentences to boost the credibility of their organization. For example, an organization that has recently won a league championship might craft the lead sentence as, "Team A, League Champions, announced today that the . . ." This allows the organization to remind its publics that the organization is of championship caliber. Additionally, it is quite common for sport-focused organizations to e-mail media releases or to post media releases online. Doing so allows the journalist to easily access a wealth of information in addition to the media release. Sport entities should distribute the media release in a format preferred by the media.

PR Newswire (2005) offers several guidelines crafting an effective media release. These include writing in a concise manner, making points briefly, and emphasizing those points by including quotes and evidence.

Sport Media Conference

Many times the sport organization will have information of such high importance that the organization will schedule a media conference. Similar to the media release, the media conference allows the sport organization to disseminate information to all members of the media at once. However, the key difference with conducting a media conference is that it allows members of the media to interact with key personnel to ask questions and obtain quotes to better develop their stories and broadcasts. Information such as the hiring or

Best Practices for Media Releases

When developing a media release, sport public relations professionals should avoid several common mistakes.

- The media release should be clear and concise and it should provide only the necessary background for the journalist.

- Quantity does not equate with quality when writing a media release, and sport public relations professionals should always be cognizant of journalists' time constraints and deadlines.

- Sport public relations professionals should also ensure the newsworthiness of the information contained in the media release. If it is not newsworthy information, it should not be distributed to the media.

- Media releases should not be used as attempts to generate publicity for the sport-focused organizations. The media should only be contacted when the information to be distributed warrants communication.

- Similarly, quotations from key personnel should center on the purpose of the information being conveyed. The quotes included in media releases are often used by the media, and, therefore, these quotes should have pertinence to the information contained in the release.

firing of a coach or the relocation of a franchise will warrant scheduling a media conference, and the sport public relations professional should anticipate that most members of the media will want access to key individuals. The media conference allows the sport-focused organization to grant this access to all media entities in a timely, convenient, and efficient manner.

Like the distribution of a media release, media conferences usually should not be scheduled on a regular basis. However, some exceptions are warranted. Many sport entities host weekly media conferences or media luncheons, especially when in season. This allows the sport entity to cultivate media relationships and provide the media with desired information. Hosting these events regularly during a sport entity's season serves as an effective tool for disseminating key information in a timely manner. Aside from these exceptions, media conferences should only be conducted when information warrants. Sport public relations professionals should schedule the conference considering the various deadlines for the different media and also considering other items that may be newsworthy and require the media's attention; in other words, schedule the media conference at a time when it is less likely to compete with other entities for coverage. The sport-focused organization should provide the media with some advance notice that it will hold a media conference. The amount of advance notice will vary depending on the nature of the announcement.

Sport public relations professionals should script and coordinate the media conference. Typically, media conferences should not exceed 30 minutes. If possible, senior staff members should always speak. Speakers should test microphones and usually should wear dark or neutral clothing because it photographs well. Speakers should be well prepared to make the announcement, and they should always be prepared to respond to the media's questions. Any members associated with the organization should be prepared to field questions from the media even if they are not speaking during the media conference. Many

of the key points discussed in the section on interview preparation should be applied when preparing individuals to speak and anticipate questions at a media conference.

Media Kit and Media Guide

Media kits and media guides are often used to showcase the sport entity. These publications may be online or may appear in print. They will vary in their content based on the needs and focus of the sport entity.

Typical inclusions in media kits are media releases, significant statistics such as franchise "firsts," fact sheets, a frequently asked questions page, a feature story, biographical sketches of key figures within the sport organization, and photos. For major events, such as a bowl game, a media schedule might also be included (see figure 11.3) Media guides (figure 11.4) are much more extensive than media kits and provide a wealth of information on the sport entity including statistics, player rosters, and historical perspectives.

Fact Sheet

The fact sheet is similar to a media release in that it provides the media with concise information regarding a specific issue. Fact sheets typically do not exceed one page and often serve as key points of reference for members of the media. General fact sheets provide background information on the sport-focused organization, and often this background information has historical significance.

General fact sheets may serve as "fluff" pieces for the organization and may tout the organization's accomplishments, legendary athletes and coaches, or the organization's role within the community. Sport-focused organizations may provide fact sheets to the media for specific instances or to supplement announcements. Fact sheets are written in bulleted format and highlight key points associated with an announcement or issue (Irwin, Sutton, & McCarthy, 2002).

Interviews

Integral in managing media relationships and presenting the sport entity in a favorable manner is interviewing. Members of sport

2005 CHAMPS SPORTS BOWL MEDIA SCHEDULE
TENTATIVE & SUBJECT TO CHANGE
ALL TIMES EST

YEARS

CSB: Champs Sports Bowl
Notes:
* Game Day Credential required for admittance to all Bowl events.
* Both Clemson and Colorado will open the first 20 minutes of each practice
  for photo and video purposes. Player interviews will be conducted after practice.

Tuesday, Dec. 20
8:00 p.m.	*New Orleans Bowl - Southern Miss vs. Arkansas State*	*Lafayette, La. / ESPN*

Wednesday, Dec. 21
4:30 p.m.	Colorado Arrives	Peabody Orlando
8:00 p.m.	*GMAC Bowl - UTEP vs. Toledo*	*Mobile, Ala. / ESPN*

Thursday, Dec. 22
10:00 a.m.-5:00 p.m.	Media Registration	Orlando Downtown Marriott (Garland Room)
10:15 a.m.	Colorado Practice	McCracken Field
2:00 p.m.	Clemson Arrives	Marriott World Center Resort
5:00 p.m.-11:00 p.m.	Media Hospitality	Orlando Downtown Marriott (Room 1503)
5:30 P.M.	**CSB TEAM WELCOME DINNER**	**GATORLAND**
8:00 p.m.	*Pioneer PureVision Las Vegas Bowl - BYU vs. California*	*Las Vegas, Nev. / ESPN*
10:30 p.m.	*San Diego County Credit Union*	*San Diego, Calif. / ESPN2*
	Poinsettia Bowl - Colorado State vs. Navy	

Friday, Dec. 23
10:00 a.m.-5:00 p.m.	Media Registration	Orlando Downtown Marriott (Garland Room)
10:00 a.m.	Colorado Practice	McCracken Field
10:30 a.m.	Clemson Practice	Thunder Field
1:00 p.m.	Colorado Universal Studios Visit	Universal Studios
3:30 p.m.	Clemson Disney World Visit	Walt Disney World
5:00 p.m.-11:00 p.m.	Media Hospitality	Orlando Downtown Marriott (Room 1503)
8:00 p.m.	*Fort Worth Bowl - Kansas vs. Houston*	*Ft. Worth, Texas / ESPN*

Saturday, Dec. 24
9:00 A.M.	**GIVE KIDS THE WORLD VILLAGE VISIT**	**GIVE KIDS THE WORLD VILLAGE**
10:00 a.m.-2:00 p.m.	Media Registration	Orlando Downtown Marriott (Garland Room)
10:30 A.M.	**GIVE KIDS THE WORLD VILLAGE PRESS CONFERENCE**	**GIVE KIDS THE WORLD VILLAGE**
12:00 p.m.	Colorado Practice	McCracken Field
2:15 p.m.	Clemson Practice	Thunder Field
8:30 p.m.	*Sheraton Hawaii Bowl - UCF vs. Nevada*	*Honolulu, Hawaii / ESPN*

Sunday, Dec. 25 - Christmas Day
2:30 p.m.	Colorado Practice	McCracken Field
3:15 p.m.	Clemson Practice	Thunder Field

Monday, Dec. 26
All Day	CSB Bash At Universal Orlando Resorts	Universal Studios
9:00 a.m.	Orlando Citrus Parade Float Building	Orange County Convention Center, North Concourse
10:00 a.m.-5:00 p.m.	Media Registration	Orlando Downtown Marriott (Garland Room)
10:30 A.M.	**CSB KICKOFF BRUNCH PRESS CONFERENCE**	**HOUSE OF BLUES ORLANDO**
11:00 A.M.	**CSB KICKOFF BRUNCH**	**HOUSE OF BLUES ORLANDO**
11:30 p.m.	Colorado Practice	Florida Citrus Bowl Stadium
3:15 p.m.	Clemson Band Performance at CSB Bash	New York Library Steps, Universal Studios
4:00 p.m.	Colorado Band Performance at CSB Bash	New York Library Steps, Universal Studios
4:00 p.m.	*Motor City Bowl - Memphis vs. Akron*	*Detroit, Mich. / ESPN*
5:00 p.m.-11:00 p.m.	Media Hospitality	Orlando Downtown Marriott (Room 1503)
9:00 p.m.	Exclusive Champs Sports Bowl Fear Factor Live Show	Universal Studios

Tuesday, Dec. 27 - Champs Sports Bowl Game Day
9:00 a.m.	Orlando Citrus Parade Float Building	Orange County Convention Center, North Concourse
1:30 P.M.	**MEDIA SHUTTLE #1 DEPARTS**	**ORLANDO MARRIOTT DOWNTOWN**
2:00 p.m.	One Cool Tailgate	McCracken Field
3:00 P.M.	**MEDIA SHUTTLE #2 DEPARTS**	**ORLANDO MARRIOTT DOWNTOWN**
3:00 p.m.	Chick-fil-A Youth Rally with former NFL QB Randall Cunningham	Jones High School
5:00 p.m.	**CHAMPS SPORTS BOWL KICKOFF**	**FLORIDA CITRUS BOWL STADIUM**

Figure 11.3 The media relations staff for college football bowl games are busy with press conferences and media outings the entire week of the bowl game. This is the typical media schedule for a college bowl game.
Florida Citrus Sports

entities are interviewed on a regular basis, which can work to the advantage of the sport entity if interviewees are well trained in interviewing. Positive interviews can cultivate positive media relations and shape public perception of the sport entity. In contrast, poor interviews can result in negative perceptions and create negative relationships. Professional athletes have come to understand the importance of interviewing skills and have recognized that developing strong communication skills is as important to their career as on-field performance. Building excellent communication skills can lead to more endorsements for athletes, even after retiring (Williams, 2005). Most important, knowing how to communicate effectively and appropriately can prevent athletes from inciting controversy and tarnishing their image as well as that of their team or organization.

When preparing individuals to interact with the media or to be interviewed, sport public relations professionals should address several key elements. These elements have been emphasized by sport media scholars and communication professionals (Casazza, 2006; Nichols et al., 2002; Wadsworth, 2005; Wielgas, 1990). Their work, in conjunction with the American Psychological Association's "Tips for Interviewing," form the framework

Figure 11.4 Game programs and media guides are two of the many publications included in a media kit. Additional communication activities surrounding events range from creating publications such as a media guide and arranging press conferences to managing the press box and postgame interviews.

Reprinted, by permission, from Indiana Fever, 2006.

Interviewing Tips

Before the interview:

- Brainstorm for questions
- Know and understand context and purpose of interview
- Anticipate questions

During the interview:

- Establish credibility
- Personalize when possible
- Maintain eye contact
- Use action words
- Be truthful and straightforward
- Be aware of posture

of the following paragraphs. The first step is to brainstorm with the interviewee regarding all potential questions that might be asked in an interview. Knowing the context and the purpose of the interview is of the utmost importance because it helps the interviewee anticipate questions and formulate appropriate responses. Interviewees want to establish credibility with not only the audience but with the journalist as well. To establish credibility, interviewees may prepare for the interview by determining three or four key points that reinforce the overall message to be disseminated to the public. Once these key points have been determined, interviewees can determine the best way to convey them regardless of the questions asked by the journalist. Interviewees should look at interviews as an opportunity to relay the sport entity's message to the public, and they should not expect for interviewers to provide them with the opportunity to do so; rather interviewees should take steps to integrate their messages into their responses.

Interviewees should personalize the interview if possible. This helps the interviewee feel more in control, implies confidence, and lends a conversational tone to the interview. If interviewees do not understand a question or have difficulty hearing a question, they should ask the journalist to repeat it.

Interviewees should maintain eye contact with the interviewer to convey confidence to the audience. Interviewees should not chew gum or candy when being interviewed, and they should use simple sentences. Long, technical sentences may confuse the journalists and, more important, may confuse the audience. In preparing for the interview, individuals should practice summarizing technical or complicated answers and strive to paint a mental picture for the audience.

Individuals should always be honest and straightforward with interviewers and should avoid speculating when responding to questions. Interviewees should also be aware of their posture and use a strong voice when speaking. Interviewees should make the interaction pleasant for the journalists and for the audience and, at the end of the interview, should thank journalists for their time.

Preparing members of the sport organization for interviews enhances the quality of the interview and fosters favorable public sentiment. The sport organization's image is enhanced by engaging in positive interviews, practicing positive media relations, and communicating effectively with the media.

MANAGING COMMUNITY RELATIONS

One of the most overlooked elements of sport public relations is community relations. Activities designed to enhance community relations efforts assist the sport-focused organization in cultivating mutually beneficial relationships with key constituents and audiences within the community. Community relations is an invaluable public relations tool, yet most sport organizations do not use community relations activities to the fullest benefit. These activities should be included in any public relations strategy, because they benefit the sport entity as well as the local and regional community.

Irwin, Sutton, and McCarthy (2002) noted that "community relations is the process of interaction and 'connection' between the sport organization and its assets on the one hand and the community or service market and the target population within that community on the other hand" (p. 266). Sport organizations engage in a variety of community relations activities including food drives, reading programs, and involvement with charitable organizations. For example, the NHL's Dallas Stars established the Dallas Stars Foundation to better serve the youth of the Dallas–Fort Worth metroplex. The franchise also donates game tickets to charity and participated in relief efforts after Hurricane Katrina. As part of the relief efforts, the franchise collected donations during preseason games and raised funds through a raffle, generating approximately $25,000 for hurricane victims.

Other sport entities have implemented numerous and varying community relations efforts. These efforts reinforce and communicate the sport entity's image and values to its constituents. The Professional Bull Riders (PBR) partnered with Resistol Western Hats in support of the Resistol Relief Fund, which was developed to support participants of all ages and levels in the sport of bull riding. The fund assists those injured in bull riding by providing them with monetary support for costs incurred due to injuries. The partnership with Resistol enables PBR to give back to its community while also furthering its mission to promote and support the sport.

To support its mission "to promote and develop the growth of tennis," the United States Tennis Association has developed numerous grassroots programs designed to encourage youth to participate in the sport. The USTA

Community relations is an often overlooked aspect of public relations and marketing in sport. This form of public relations—which has an impact on public perception of the sport organization—can range from structured community-oriented programs to spontaneous interactions with fans. Here, former Kansas State University wide receiver Antoine Polite signs a young fan's helmet.

Schools program is "dedicated to introducing youth to the sport in the schools" (USTA.com, 2006). The program provides free and discounted equipment to schools that enroll and training for physical education instructors. The program is specifically designed to facilitate the instruction of tennis to large groups of students who do not have access to traditional tennis courts. The ultimate goal of the program is to teach students the fundamentals of the sport and encourage them to participate in other USTA programs. One such program is the USTA's National Junior Tennis League program established by Arthur Ashe. The mission of the program is to "develop the character of young people through tennis and emphasize the ideals and life of Arthur Ashe by: reaching out to those who may not otherwise have the opportunity to play the sport; by instilling in youngsters the values of leadership and academic excellence; and by giving youngsters the opportunity to fully develop their tennis skills so they can derive a

lifetime enjoyment from the sport" (USTA.com, 2006). These programs are representative of the many community-oriented programs instituted by the USTA and highlight the importance of communicating the sport entity's message and values through community relations.

Similar to the USTA programs is the World Golf Foundation's First Tee program. The World Golf Foundation partnered with the LPGA, the PGA Tour, the United States Golf Association, and the Augusta National Golf Club to develop a program that would allow youth from all backgrounds and socioeconomic classes to participate in the sport. Its mission "to impact the lives of young people by providing learning facilities and educational programs that promote character development and life-enhancing values through the game of golf" (www.thefirsttee.org, 2006) embodies the spirit of golf and reinforces the image and values of the sport in the minds of the public.

Another sport entity that reinforces its values through its community relations is

NASCAR. NASCAR recently implemented the NASCAR Foundation, which supports numerous and varied charitable organizations. As part of the NASCAR Foundation, members of the general public may become involved with many of the community-oriented projects that NASCAR supports. The NASCAR Foundation reinforces the mission and values of the organization while communicating a favorable image within the community.

Numerous community-oriented programs assist sport entities in reinforcing and enhancing their image while communicating the values and mission of the organization to the public. These programs allow sport entities to engage with their communities while emphasizing the key aspects of their organization. Therefore, community relations programs should be included as part of a sport entity's overall public relations and marketing strategy and should not be overlooked as a way to manage public perception. The nature of the sport product is unpredictable, and this unpredictably can influence public perception. Community relations provides an avenue that sport entities can use to maintain a consistent and favorable public perception.

MANAGING COMMUNICATION DURING CRISIS

Sport entities are sometimes faced with crises that could potentially tarnish their image by creating unfavorable perceptions in the minds of the media and key constituents. Any threat to a sport entity's image, reputation, and perception constitutes a crisis, because an entity's reputation is one of its major assets (Mann, 2003). Responding to a crisis often means more than simply responding to media inquiries: It sometimes requires an organizational response.

Examples of Crises in Sport

Crises may arise as a result of comments made during an interview. For example, at the 2006 Orange Bowl, legendary football coach Joe Paterno was asked about his feelings regarding Florida State University linebacker A.J. Nicholson. Nicholson had been removed from the FSU team and sent home before the game as a result of allegations of sexual assault. When asked about Nicholson's dismissal, Paterno responded, "There are so many people gravitating to these kids. Nicholson may not even have known what he was getting into. Somebody may have knocked on the door. A cute little girl knocks on the door. What do you do?" Paterno has long held the image of being a straight shooter who does not mince words. However, his comments sparked a controversy relative to the issue of sexual assault, and the president for the National Organization of Women in Pennsylvania requested Paterno resign. Penn State officials suggested that Paterno's comments were taken out of context by members of the media and by the public (Harlan, 2006; "NOW Upset," 2006). However, the scenario presented a crisis situation for the Nittany Lions as well as the university.

Just as Paterno's comments sparked controversy relative to sexual assault, the Air Force Academy's head football coach Fisher DeBerry's statements relative to African-American athletes spurred a dialogue on racism and race relations. After a 48-10 loss to Texas Christian University in Mountain West Conference competition, DeBerry referenced the lack of minority athletes in his football program and stated, "We were looking at things, like you don't see many minority athletes in our program. It just seems to be that way, that Afro-American kids can run very, very well. That doesn't mean that Caucasian kids and other descents can't run, but it's very obvious to me they run extremely well." In a media luncheon after making the comments, DeBerry was asked about his statements and said, "I just want to recruit speed; we need to find speed as much as anything. The black athlete, statistically, from program to program, seems to have an edge as far as speed is concerned" (Benton, 2005; Limon, 2005). His comments in both instances resulted in an investigation by the Air Force Academy and spurred debates regarding the issue of sport and race.

Sometimes crises arise from volatile situations or from incidents during a sport event.

In November 2004, the Indiana Pacers and Detroit Pistons engaged in an on-court brawl. During the brawl, members of the Pacers entered the stands in a response to fans, and the brawl continued in the stands as well as on the court. Eventually, a fan threw a chair. The actions by players and fans of both teams tarnished the image of the National Basketball Association. In direct response to the brawl and in an effort to immediately begin to reestablish the NBA's image, NBA Commissioner David Stern suspended nine players. Several players were sued for misdemeanor assault charges and ordered to do community service. The NBA was also forced to examine its procedures and policies specific to event security. The scenario provides an example of a crisis situation in which the concerns of key constituents had to be addressed immediately. A tarnished reputation harms not only the league but also the fans and players.

Because millions of people attend sport events each year, leagues and franchises are expected to maintain a safe environment. When incidents occur in the sporting environment, a league's event management policies are called into question and public perception of the entity may be affected. In 2002, a young girl was hit by a puck during the National Hockey League's Columbus Blue Jackets game at Nationwide Arena. The girl died a few days later as a result of her injury. Her injury occurred when Espen Knutsen's shot was deflected off of Derek Morris' stick. The incident raised serious questions regarding risk management and event security at sporting events and specifically at NHL events. To ensure the public's safety and retain a favorable reputation among the public, many NHL franchises now use nets in their venues to prevent injuries to fans.

The NHL was again faced with a crisis when its owners locked out the players in the 2004-2005 season. The image of the owners, the players, and the entire league was at risk. Employees of the league's franchises were laid off, and the players' association launched a public relations campaign to gain favorable public opinion on behalf of the players. Unlike other major league sports, the NHL derived a majority of its revenues from fan attendance. Therefore, franchises were concerned about retaining season ticket holders during the lockout as well as maintaining a favorable image (Blount, 2005). Although the league and the players' association agreed to terms and played the 2005-2006 season, the league lost television coverage on a premier network. The NHL continues to work to repair its image and to acquire positive exposure for its franchises and players.

No stranger to labor strife, Major League Baseball faced a major crisis regarding the use of performance-enhancing drugs by its players. Some of MLB's most well-known players, including Rafael Palmeiro and Barry Bonds, have admitted to having steroids in their systems. Rumors had surfaced regarding steroid use by players such as Mark McGwire. McGwire, Palmeiro, Jose Canseco, Curt Schilling, Commissioner Bud Selig, and players association executive director Donald Fehr were called to testify before Congress regarding the use of performance-enhancing drugs in the league. Members of Congress questioned the integrity of baseball and alleged that MLB's policies and punishments for steroid use were not as strict as they should be. Major League Baseball implemented a stricter policy on the use of performance enhancers as a result of the congressional hearings and public opinion. Many public relations professionals have suggested that MLB should have been more proactive in handling the issue and in managing public perception. However, the league did make a significant statement when it suspended Alex Sanchez and 38 minor league players the first and second days of the 2005-2006 season for steroid use (Adams, 2005c). The crisis affected not only MLB but other professional leagues as well. The crisis caused many in the media and in the public to question the use of performance enhancers in professional sports, and each league had to prepare to field questions regarding the issue.

Guidelines for Responding to Crises

The scenarios described here exemplify the many crises that can face sport entities. Crises in sport may take many shapes and forms and include issues such as player eligibility, player arrest, player death, incidents on the field of play, or the terminations of coaches. The public usually forms its perception of a crisis situation within the first 24 hours of the crisis (Nichols et al., 2002). The manner in which the organization responds to the crisis situation will have a dramatic impact on the public's perception of the crisis.

Preparing for a crisis situation is an integral aspect of public relations (Rovell, 2006; Stoldt et al., 2000; Ucelli, 2002). To prepare for crisis situations, sport public relations professionals should, with other staff members, brainstorm and identify possible situations that may occur throughout the course of a season or a year which could threaten the image of the sport organization. Threats might include a player arrest, the firing of a head coach, or a serious injury to a fan or group of fans. Other crises may relate to various organizational policies that could affect relations with key constituents, such as ticket sales policies, game operational issues, and even locker room policies. Specific plans must be in place to address crises as they arise.

Without proper preparation for a crisis, public perception will usually be negative. Preparation procedures should be kept as simple and straightforward as possible to establish early and regular communication during a crisis. The objectives of any crisis plan should be to quickly and accurately communicate information that can minimize damage to the sport organization's reputation.

To begin preparing for a crisis, scholars and industry professionals (Stoldt et al., 2000; Ucelli, 2002) suggest that sport public relations professionals should follow several key steps (see figure 11.5).

To begin, sport public relations professionals should conduct research within the organization. The organization's philosophy for managing the crisis and the makeup of a "crisis team" should be determined through consultations at all levels of management. The crisis team will be instrumental in managing any crisis situation. Assessment should involve the analysis and prediction of various crisis situations that may arise. As mentioned earlier, crises will vary based on the nature of the sport entity. A clear chain of command should be established to guide personnel during the crisis. The chain of command should specify roles for superiors and others within the organization. Procedures should be outlined for notifying the crisis team when a crisis does occur. Staff should make any necessary modifications in order to control for any issues or risks that might arise.

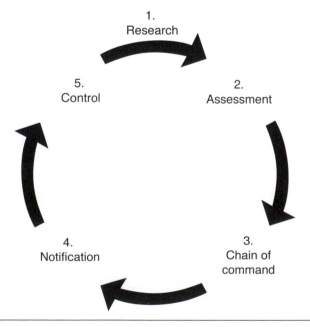

Figure 11.5 Steps in crisis management.

Crisis Kit and Summary

Sport public relations professionals should prepare a crisis kit (Stoldt et al., 2000; Ucelli, 2002). Key components of the kit include a media relations checklist (including guidelines for dealing with the media), a synopsis of policies and procedures, the crisis strategy, and contact information for key personnel. All information in the kit should be checked regularly for accuracy.

Sport public relations personnel should prepare key members of the crisis team to interact with the media, such as having key personnel rehearse the crisis plan. Sport public relations professionals should work diligently to create a cooperative environment with the media during a crisis. Existing media relationships may be key in managing the crisis, and personnel should be responsive and accessible to the media. Failing to return phone calls or using statements like "no comment" may intensify the situation. Sport public relations professionals should strive to meet the demands of the organization while also providing the media with needed information.

Sport entities are sometimes faced with crises that could potentially tarnish their image by creating unfavorable perceptions in the minds of the media and in the minds of key constituents. Crises refer to any threat to a sport entity's image. Crises may arise at any time resulting from many different factors. They can take many forms and include issues such as player eligibility, player arrest, player death, incidents on the field of play, incidents involving other franchises or leagues, or the terminations of coaches. Sport public relations professionals must be prepared to manage a crisis situation when it occurs to maintain a favorable image among key constituents.

CHAPTER WRAP-UP

Summary

The value of public relations to the sport entity should not be overlooked, especially when trying to sway public opinion in a manner that is favorable. As this chapter has illustrated, public opinion is instrumental in cultivating favorable relationships among key constituents. It has been instrumental for numerous sport entities in securing financing for new stadium ventures. Public opinion has also played a key role in causing entities to implement organizational policies that enable them to maintain favorable relationships, such as with the NHL and MLB. This chapter—which is the second of three chapters in the unit that cover sport communication services and support—examined the public relations aspect of sport communication and detailed the central role that sport public relations plays in the field. It provided an analysis of crisis communication in sport. Public relations centers on the management of information flow between an organization and its key publics, and this chapter has highlighted this focus.

In this chapter we have detailed the theory and practice of sport public relations. We provided a special focus on persuasion, message development, and image building through effective management of the sport media. Included in the chapter were strategies for effectively managing the media by using media relations techniques (e.g., media releases, credentialing, game notes, media conferences, media kits, fact sheets, tools of the trade) and building community relations efforts. The chapter, in addition to containing information on public speaking and speechwriting in sport, highlighted successful sport public relations campaigns. We concluded the chapter with an examination of crisis communication for sport organizations and outlined strategies for managing crisis situations internally and externally. Effective public relations is central to the success of the sport entity. Maintaining positive relations with key constituents should be a primary public relations strategy for sport entities.

Review Questions

1. What is public relations? How is public relations practiced in the sport industry?
2. How should sport public relations professionals cultivate relationships with the media?
3. What are the key elements of a media release?
4. What are the objectives of a crisis management plan? Why is a crisis management plan integral in protecting the overall image of the sport-focused organization?
5. What are the key steps in developing a crisis communication plan? What are some typical crises that may arise in the sport-focused organization?
6. How should one prepare for an interview? Why is such preparation instrumental in effective public relations? What is considered best practice during an interview?
7. What should be included in a media kit? What is a fact sheet?
8. What are the models of public relations and how are they illustrated in the sport industry?
9. What individuals were instrumental in shaping the development of public relations as a discipline? How has sport public relations evolved? What trends have shaped the nature of sport public relations?
10. What factors influence perceptions of the sport product?

Discussion Questions

1. How are public relations campaigns used in sport?
2. How can the sport-focused organization use the media to its advantage when communicating with its key publics?
3. What are some typical crisis situations in sport, and how can sport public relations professionals prepare to manage the media in these cases?
4. How are the four models of public relations applied in the sport industry?
5. Which models of public relations can be most effective in the sport industry?
6. Of the trends influencing the growth of sport public relations, which do you perceive as most important?
7. How do motives and level of involvement affect individuals' perceptions? How do these factors influence sport public relations strategies?
8. How can a crisis situation tarnish and also enhance the image of a sport entity?
9. What constitutes a crisis situation? What are some recent crises occurring for sport entities? How were they handled by the sport entity? Was the sport entity's management of the crisis effective? Why or why not?
10. How can interviewing skills tarnish or enhance media relations? Provide some examples.

Group Activities

1. Record two or three radio or television interviews with members of a sport organization. Using the interview guidelines presented in the chapter, write a critique of the interview and rate the interviewee's performance.

2. Select a sport organization and identify three issues that could potentially be a crisis. Develop a crisis communication strategy for each and present it to the class.

3. Select a sport entity. Research the sport entity and develop a community relations program specific to its needs and brand image. Present this program to the class.

4. Select a sport entity. Develop a media kit specifically for the sport entity. What have you included and why? How does your media kit reflect the image and values of the sport entity?

Individual Exercises

1. Each member of the group should visit the Web sites of four sport entities. Provide a report relative to the sport entity's community relations efforts. Compare and contrast the efforts with your group. What similarities are noticed?

2. Conduct a mock interview with a classmate. Evaluate your classmate's interview style and, using the guidelines provided in the chapter, write a critique of your classmate's performance.

3. Identify various stadium financing campaigns. What methods were used to gain public support for these campaigns? How did the methods differ? How would you run a similar campaign in your region? Discuss with your classmates.

4. Select a specific sport entity. Write a media release announcing an important issue related to the entity.

Internet Sites for Additional Learning

American Marketing Association: www.marketingpower.com

Brener, Zwikel, & Associates: www.bzapr.com/

College Sports Information Directors of America: www.cosida.com

Council of Public Relations Firms: www.prfirms.com

Edelman Public Relations: www.edelman.com

Institute for Public Relations: www.instituteforpr.com

Online Public Relations: www.online-pr.com

PR.com: www.pr.com

PRWeek: www.prweek.com

Public Relations Newswire: www.PRnewswire.com

Public Relations Society of America: www.prsa.org

Public Relations Student Society of America: www.prssa.org

CHAPTER 12

Sport Communication Research

PROFILE OF A SPORT COMMUNICATOR

Eric Wright

Research firms such as Joyce Julius and Associates recognize the requisite components of solid research—refined objectives, precise measurement, appropriate implementation, and veritable results. "The biggest challenge we face is that each of our clients has a different objective with sponsorship," notes Eric Wright, the vice president for research and development at Joyce Julius. "So, as a research organization we gain an understanding of what their objective is so we can measure the right components and deliver the data they need." Wright joined Joyce Julius in 1991 after graduating from Michigan State University and serving a brief stint as a small-town journalist in Michigan. He is one of approximately 30 employees at the Ann Arbor, Michigan, firm, 20 of whom conduct research. Conducting entertainment marketing research services like promotions, product placements, and theater surveys; case study research on brand exposure using entertainment programs; and market research and sponsorship studies for brands, venues, and agencies, Joyce Julius services Fortune 500 corporations, league sanctioning bodies, networks, agencies, and individual athletes.

Joyce Julius not only analyzes print, radio, television, and the Internet but also studies specific events, news programs, and entertainment at the local, regional, and national levels. Wright states that he and his associates determine the "full scope of the event" from "how many impressions were generated to who saw the logo, and they follow up with surveys on-site or focus groups" to complete the report. Although Joyce Julius' range is extensive, television makes up 70 percent of its business. "It's a very powerful medium," Wright explains, "and it really overshad-

Companies such as Joyce Julius & Associates perform market research and sponsorship studies to determine return on investment for brands, venues, and agencies. For instance, a racing team sponsor can contract with a research organization to analyze the exposure the sponsor receives in the media, including radio, television, billboards, print, the Internet, and television.

ows all the other media in terms of the number of people who see it, are affected by it, and what you can do with it."

Although some projects and clients are proprietary, some of the company's recent findings have been published. For instance, Joyce Julius found that the 90 million viewers of Super Bowl XLI saw Peyton Manning's name and face clear and in focus for 6 minutes and 5 seconds of the game. Manning was mentioned 86 times and he had 1 minute and 51 seconds of face time and 10 more mentions in CBS' postgame show (Wilson, 2007). In the 2005 United States Open tennis coverage, the top 10 sponsors' logos were clear and in focus for 147 hours and 57 minutes during the 2-week tournament broadcast by CBS and the USA Network ("US Open," 2005). Joyce Julius used image identification technology for the first time at the 2005 event. "The new software system based on pixel patterns," explains Wright, "will go through the digital telecast and automatically track when a pixel pattern appears." This means that the staff could analyze 160 hours of the U.S. Open and have raw data numbers by Wednesday after the men's final on Sunday where before, it would take Joyce Julius 5 or 6 weeks to obtain that information. Although sponsors are happy with the quick results, Wright says that the importance lies elsewhere. "Speed is great, but the real value is the additional information and data we can pull out and provide to clients."

The "Sponsors Report" (2005) is another element of the television research performed by Joyce Julius. This component measures "in-broadcast brand exposure" during sporting events for sponsors. This report breaks down the telecast frame by frame to measure all clear and in-focus

exposure. Joyce Julius next takes that exposure and compares it with the cost of commercials during the specific broadcast. Then, the report details the amount of time on screen as well as the comparable exposure value and where each second of the exposure originated. From this information, the company can determine exactly where to put logos.

As evident in Joyce Julius' numerous research projects, sport communication research is highly technical and valued. "Every dollar spent is scrutinized now more than ever before," states Wright. "Research is a lot more scientific now with more consideration and importance attached to it."

This chapter addresses research from two perspectives—that of the industry practitioner and that of the academic researcher. Both are important for the sport industry. Knowledge is power, and research enables sport communication practitioners to do their jobs better to meet or surpass goals. Research enables investigators in a more theoretical arena to provoke inquiry in important areas and to bolster sport communication's legitimacy in academia. Together, the industry practitioner and the academic researcher can work to promote sport communication and establish it as one of the most important fields in sport, communication, and culture today. See figure 12.1 for an illustration of how research fits in the Strategic Sport Communication Model.

As previous chapters have indicated, sport influences and intersects all aspects of American life. From politics and business to legal and social issues, sport reflects, reinforces, and shapes cultural values. Sociologists James H. Frey and D. Stanley Eitzen (1991) wrote, "Sport is an arena of patterned behaviors, social structures, and interinstitutional relationships that holds unique opportunities to study and understand the complexities of social life" (p. 503). Because sport is a microcosm of society, it is important to study in both the practical and theoretical arenas. "No other institution, except perhaps religion, commands the mystique, the nostalgia, the romantic ideational

cultural fixation that sport does," said Frey and Eitzen (p. 504).

As Frey and Eitzen recognized, it is vital to explore both the practical arena of industry and the theoretical arena of research, which studies various components of sport communication from a sociocultural, historical, and political perspective. In addition to studying sport from a broad, macroscopic point of view, we should focus on the media because of its puissant impact on sport and society. "From a theoretical standpoint, we must try to come to a better understanding of the tremendous impact of sports and sports media on our society," said Schultz (2005, p. xvi). Today's fragmented media landscape and increased choices lead to greater pressure on the media to capture a targeted audience for advertisers and for general sustenance. Today individuals can read sports sections and magazines, listen to sports radio, watch nightly sportscasts or shows, or check the Internet for scores, supplemental sports information, and game plays. According to Neil Postman in *Amusing Ourselves to Death: Public Discourse in the Age of Show Business* (1985), "Each medium, like language itself, makes possible a unique mode of discourse by providing a new orientation for thought, for expression, for sensibility" (p. 10). Even sport journalists recognize the diverse opportunities available in a converging media environment where boundaries

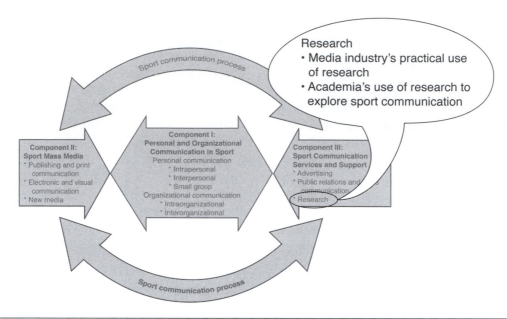

Figure 12.1 Research is the third segment in component III (sport communication services and support) of the Strategic Sport Communication Model.

no longer exist. ESPN's *The Sports Reporters* features newspaper sportswriters who discuss and debate key sports stories weekly while maintaining their role as print journalists at newspapers. From Jason Whitlock at the *Kansas City Star* to Mike Lupica at the *New York Daily News* and Mitch Albom of the *Detroit Free Press*, the show is just one example of how media converge and content coincide from print to broadcast to new technology (Schultz, 2005).

In such a transitory media landscape, research can elucidate factors and implications within the media, media workers, and the audience. As Aristotle wrote in *Metaphysics* (350 bc), "All men by nature desire to know" (Book I, ¶1). Because of the extensive scope of research, it is most effective to use a broad definition. Gratton and Jones (2004) defined research as "a systematic process of discovery and advancement of human knowledge" (p. 4). Our definition will take this one step further by applying it to sport communication. **Sport communication research** is the process by which sport communication practitioners and scholars initiate, discover, and expand knowledge of sport communication texts, audiences, and institutions (see figure 12.2).

This definition is apropos for both industry and academia because it applies to the media industry, sport organizations, academics, and students. This chapter begins with a discussion of how both the media and sport industries use research and then discusses

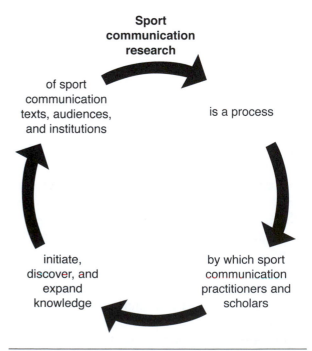

Figure 12.2 Sport communication research definition and components to study.

research in academia and the specifics of writing research and choosing methodologies in sport communication.

MEDIA INDUSTRY'S PRACTICAL USE OF RESEARCH

Industry practitioners use research in a wide array of ways, and Folkerts and Lacy (2004) detailed its many uses. As they and other scholars indicate, the uses and opportunities for media research are infinite, especially for media institutions, advertising agencies, and corporations that use the media as a vehicle to reach targeted audiences. Media management uses research in various ways, such as determining audiences' programming preferences, determining advertising costs, and deciding what news and information choices to offer to audiences.

Research shows what advertisers will spend in a specific medium. With newspapers, the Audit Bureau of Circulations (ABC) measures circulation for daily newspapers and a select group of weekly publications. News organizations survey viewers during election years to determine the frontrunner and to reveal those issues important to viewers. University of North Carolina at Chapel Hill journalism professor Philip Meyer (2002) emphasized the need for precision journalism, or the importance of social scientific research methods in creating news stories. Most newspapers, however, use computer-assisted reporting (CAR), which uses statistics on existing databases to determine specific patterns. A.C. Nielsen Company and Arbitron provide statistics for television and radio, respectively. Advertisers and networks seek audience demographic information and statistics because advertising prices are contingent on the number of households watching or listening and specifics on viewers or listeners for particular shows, measuring demand. Television news stations also distribute tapes of anchors to determine audience preferences. Even movie companies use research when companies test different

© Paul M. Pedersen

Research is used in a wide array of ways by industry practitioners. For an event such as an NBA game, there is research of interest to sport marketers (e.g., sponsorship [ProLiance]) as well as media managers and advertisers (e.g., audience analyses).

endings to determine audience preferences (Folkerts & Lacy, 2004; Meyer, 2002).

Companies seek research for many reasons, but mostly for monetary reasons. As Ben Bagdikian discussed in *The Media Monopoly* (1997), media conglomerates and corporations care about profit first and foremost, which is why they seek such precise information about audiences. Although the media originally viewed themselves as public servants, they now emphasize profit. In radio and television, local stations and national networks focus on ratings to lure advertisers to reach coveted target demographics. The Project for Excellence in Journalism, affiliated with Columbia University and funded by Pew Charitable Trusts, found that local news has decreased enterprise reporting and has increased the number of feeds. News stations emphasize "infotainment" over hard news and focus on profit margins rather than enlightening the citizenry (Rosenstiel, Gottlieb, Brady, & Rosenheim, 2000). In newspaper, there is little difference because it's all about circulation and readers' disposable income. Newspapers seek to sell newspapers to boost circulation numbers, and readers' income is important because of newspapers' reliance on advertisers, who seek to sell products to individuals at certain income levels. In new media, it's about the number of unique visitors on Web sites and revenue spent online. Sites seek new visitors to expose them to their messages and potentially sell merchandise (Schultz, 2005). Sport readers, listeners, and audiences are especially coveted by advertisers and companies because they tend to be very loyal to certain sports, teams, and athletes, and they also enable advertisers to reach the male 18-34 demographic. To gain information on readers, viewers, and Web surfers, organizations and companies have perfected research techniques, which have evolved over the years. The next section discusses how interest in ratings, circulation data, and Web use developed and the methods used for studying these issues.

A.C. Nielsen Company

Nielsen Media Research provides Nielsen television ratings and remains the "official national measurement service of the television industry" ("What TV," 2006). Advertisers, agencies, networks, stations, cable operators, and programs purchase the research to learn more about all audiences. Nielsen Media Research does not provide a qualitative measurement but simply measures how many people watched a specific program or station. Nielsen's Web site likens its role to the board of elections and its function as answering such questions as, "Who is watching TV?" and "What are they watching?" ("What TV," 2006).

Sampling Techniques

The company's researchers conduct a representative sample of about 5,000 houses with more than 13,000 people participating in national ratings studies. Everyone in the population possesses an equal chance of being selected for the study. This is known as random sampling and is often viewed as the most representative sample. In other words, the sample represents the overall population, and everyone in the general population could be selected to participate. Random samples ensure that a study is free from bias. Whether you flip a coin, draw a card, or use a table of random numbers, respondents are chosen by chance.

Other common sampling techniques in research include

- stratified random sampling within subgroups;
- cluster sampling, which randomly chooses groups (not individuals); and
- systematic sampling, where every kth case is studied (Rothenbuhler, 2005).

Stratified samples enable the researcher to see if a certain attribute occurs throughout the sample. This is sometimes called a "quota sample," and if the researcher wants perceptions of certain elements of the population, he or she needs to ensure that the distribution is consistent. Convenience samples are biased in the sense that the sample is affected by proximity. For instance, if a researcher wants to study sport viewing habits among 18- to

24-year-olds and uses names from the Indianapolis phonebook rather than using a more regional or national sample size, this will limit findings. Cluster samples examine certain elements of the population like female collegiate athletes' perspectives toward gender equity. The researcher could decide that each sport at a university represents one cluster and then could select a small number from each team to interview. This is a basic cluster sample requiring one step. Systematic samples occur once a population is determined. For instance, you might want to examine preferences of the Carolina Panthers season ticket holders. You would select a random number as a starting point, and from there, you would select ticket holders at certain intervals for your survey or poll. One in 50 might be chosen or one in 100, depending on the sample size needed. Some researchers use the telephone book in systematic samples, but some individuals' numbers are not listed and therefore using the telephone book may or may not work depending on what is studied. These are a few examples of sampling techniques used in research, and the most effective method will depend on the researcher and the object of study (Bostrom, 1998).

Nielsen's Research Approach

The approach that Nielsen takes to television research is explained on its Web site. Nielsen studies the "amount of TV usage on every set in a sample household" and can provide information on homes, televisions, programs, and commercials to television and advertising companies ("What TV," 2006). Its television meters monitor when televisions are on and the stations they are on, passing along that information to a computer and modem in the form of a central "black box." These data are transferred daily to Nielsen's central computers, which store the information and use it in their research findings. Each television picture contains a coded identification number that identifies the program and episode number. This is called automated measurement of line-ups or AMOL, and locations nationwide amass and store these codes for daily download-

ing to Nielsen's central computer system. In addition to AMOL, Nielsen monitors programs through program listings provided by stations, networks, and systems as well as those that are published. Included in Nielsen's studies are 1,700 television stations and 11,000 cable systems. Nielsen identifies commercials by a signal identification technology where they are "converted into a digital 'fingerprint'" that is compared with others and identified. Nielsen uses the Nielsen "people meter" to study people watching programs. It is a box for the top of the television, containing buttons and lights for each household member and a remote control for easy use. Viewers push a button when they begin watching a program and the light changes from red to green and then back to red when they complete their viewing session. This records the shows being watched and who is watching specific programs ("What TV," 2006).

Although Nielsen evaluates national audiences and programs, it also studies 200 local television markets by television diaries. These are books where viewers write down what shows they watched during a specific week. These studies usually take place during the "sweep" ratings months of February, May, July, and November. Diaries only measure what viewers write down in their logs and their individual perceptions. Nielsen also uses set-tuning meters inserted in the back of televisions in 49 of the largest television markets to record what viewers watch. Nielsen researchers cross-check information from national and local studies and conduct audits and quality checks to ensure the accuracy of their procedures. For instance, they compare the national "people meter" audience information with the diaries from all local markets. Nielsen also conducts "telephone coincidentals," where it calls randomly selected numbers to ask individuals if they are watching television and, if so, who is watching. Nielsen's measurement system for television is similar to Arbitron's for radio except the unit is the household as well as different individuals. Nielsen reports its results in ratings as well as shares, which indicate how viewership is divided among channels and markets (Folkerts & Lacy, 2004).

Uses for Data

Nielsen specifically offers programmers, advertisers, and agencies crucial information on the television audience. Regardless of whether ratings companies use the diary, interview, or meter, they integrate their data to obtain circulation, or the number of people watching or listening to a show at a certain time. Media buyers then use this information to work with advertising agencies in formulating an appropriate media strategy. The amount advertisers charge generally is a "negotiated rate per thousand viewers multiplied by the Nielsen Research audience estimate (in thousands)" ("What TV," 2006). Cost per thousand or CPM equates to the amount an advertiser must spend to reach 1,000 audience members. Generally, additional quantitative research from MediaMark (MRI) or Simmons Market Research Bureau (SMRB) provides the pass-along-rate or the "average number of people who read an issue of their periodical" (Turow, 1997, p. 133). Noncommercial stations also use Nielsen research to effectively make programming choices and decisions (Turow, 1997). *SportsBusiness Journal* regularly passes along information on sports programming to its subscribers, telling readers which sport shows and networks scored highest during each quarter.

Research Challenges

With increasing audience fragmentation, it is evident why research is so vital for local stations, networks, and cable systems and operators. Despite the need for research, it is difficult to measure across media. Each of the previously mentioned methods has limitations. In newer options, Arbitron is developing a "portable people meter" (PPM) with the help of Nielsen. It is a small gadget the size of a pager that "registers an inaudible code placed in radio transmission and in the audio of television and cable programs" (Folkerts & Lacy, 2004, p. 415). Viewers therefore do not have to record their programs, and the PPM's motion detector enables Arbitron to watch

and evaluate usage. The viewer or listener then inserts the PPM in a station at the end of the day, which transfers the information back to Arbitron for evaluation. Because the PPM measures radio, television, cable, and direct broadcast satellite usage, it can compare media usage and preferences. Although the PPM has not yet been adopted as a research method for electronic media usage measurement, it is one example of how ratings companies seek to perfect their studies and measurements. This is just one method for studying audiences (Folkerts & Lacy, 2004).

Relevant Knowledge, JupiterResearch, Media Metrix, and Nielsen/Net Ratings all study Web use, but there is a disparity of opinion on which method is most effective, and individuals' varying uses of the Internet also complicate the picture. Radio and television are used mostly for entertainment, but individuals use the Web for research, e-mail, and other uses. Nielsen/Net Ratings recognizes the need to measure more than the number of visitors and issues a report called *Digital Media Universe* with statistics about people using instant messaging, Web phones, media players, online games, and other features (Folkerts & Lacy, 2004). Among the strengths of Internet research, surveys are cheaper and quicker than traditional surveys sent through the postal mail and the Internet also is more anonymous for participants. Individuals tend to provide more candid and inclusive responses to delicate questions, and data can be collected 24 hours a day from usually unreachable individuals. One problem, however, is the creation of "alternate personas" and several submissions that skew results. As with all research, accuracy is paramount and the best procedures incorporate reliability, validity, and economy because numbers can be "distorted or even misleading" (Ledbetter, 2000, pp. 66-67). Whether there is one poor-selling issue of a magazine that skews results, poor sampling procedures in a broadcast, or a massive disparity between page views and online readers, checking, cross-checking, and integrating methods are key. Turow (1997, p. 140) explained three key aspects of media research:

1. Reliability is the "ability of two researchers using the same methods to arrive at results that are the same from a statistical standpoint."

2. Validity "means that the results can be considered truly representative of what goes on in the population as a whole, outside the survey situation."

3. Economy "points to the need to pay attention to the costs of audience research." It is necessary to understand that "every media audience is a construction of reality" (Turow, 1997, p. 141).

Companies like Arbitron and A.C. Nielsen pose questions with their own agenda and focus on various aspects of research. The power of the public is secondary to the power of the media industry because the latter can "control the basic terms on which audiences are defined" (Turow, 1997, p. 142). According to Bagdikian (2005), the large corporations controlling every mass medium have hurt democracy through restricted ideas that he considers radical right-wing political beliefs. Included in this list are Time Warner, News Corporation, Viacom, Bertelsmann, Disney, and General Electric, whose holdings were discussed in prior chapters. And in radio, Clear Channel owns 2,400 stations. These huge media conglomerates own sport networks, stations, properties, and teams. The success and efficacy of these conglomerates are measured by the ratings provided by Nielsen and Arbitron and by their positions on the stock market. Bagdikian also blamed the FCC, believing that most members consider the maximum profits as the standard in serving the public (Bagdikian, 2005; Cheyne & Ritter, 2001).

Effect of Television Ratings on Sport Communication

According to sport marketing professor Matthew D. Shank, television delivers results like no other media outlet. "Used in the right way," said Shank, "it can be a marketer's dream, harnessing the thrill of top-level competition for a targeted mass audience of interested and involved consumers" (2002, p. 338). The reason companies continue to spend millions of dollars yearly on sport programming is its expansive reach and powerful influence. Sport enables a company to center its message on the audience it wants to persuade. According to Nielsen Monitor-Plus, Anheuser-Busch topped all spenders in 2004 with $293 million and Chevrolet came in second with $220 million. Cingular Wireless, Ford Motor Company, and Coca-Cola USA rounded out the top five.

Importance of Ratings

With audiences, size counts. Networks and advertisers compute cost per thousand, or CPM, which measures the cost and value of advertisements. They also calculate cost per point, or CPP, which computes how much it costs to reach 1 percent of the entire audience. In addition to audience size, the total aggregate of houses and viewers tuning into a program over time is also important. Reach, or cume, denotes the total aggregate of different viewers tuning in over time and calculates the "true audience for sports broadcasts" (Mullin, Hardy, & Sutton, 2000, p. 304). Sponsors look for this before agreeing to long-term advertising contracts. Advertisers also care about an audience's composition or demographic. Younger males are traditionally hard to reach, and sporting events of all types from sports talk radio to television programs draw them in and sustain them (Mullin, Hardy, and Sutton, 2007).

Super Bowl Ratings and NFL Research

According to Shank, "the fragmenting of the network audience in general makes sports —especially the big-ticket events—one of the only television events that can pull large ratings with consistency" (2002, p. 340). Among events, the Super Bowl remains the top sporting event in the United States as far as consistent ratings and advertising revenue. In 2007, Super Bowl XLI between the Indianapolis Colts and the Chicago Bears had a 42 rating and a 64 share, compared to Super Bowl XL between the Pittsburgh Steelers and the Seattle Seahawks with a 41.5 rating and 62 share. Although some believe that "conservative cultural forces predominated" 2005's Super Bowl XXXIX after the Janet Jackson saga of

2004 ("NFL Takes Safe Route," 2005, p. 28), its game-day programs were still the highest rated sportscasts of the week from January 31, 2005, to February 6, 2005. Super Bowl XXXIX between the New England Patriots and Philadelphia Eagles captured a 41.1 rating and 62 share. Ratings show the percentage of every television on a certain show in a specific market. A share discloses the percentage of televisions on at a certain time and a certain show in a certain market. Generally, audiences peak during prime-time hours of the evening. For the 2005 Super Bowl, Jacksonville, Philadelphia, and Boston were at the top of the local market ratings. And the average cost of a 30-second spot was $2.4 million, up from $2.25 million in Super Bowl XXXVIII in 2004. Although Fox's telecast may have been the "most-watched event on television for 2005," it had the fewest viewers for a Super Bowl since 2001 ("NFL Takes Safe Route," 2005, p. 28), when Baltimore routed the New York Giants 34-7. It tied for 28th among all televised Super Bowls. According to *SportsBusiness Journal*'s Andy Bernstein (2005b), "Viewing by men 18 and older was off by 5 percent, the key male 18-34 group saw a 6 percent decline, and the male 18-to-49 group showed the sharpest decline, 9 percent" (p. 31). It must be noted, however, that ratings among younger males also decreased in the Super Bowl in 2004 ("A-B Paces Ad Spending," 2005; Bernstein, 2005b; "Down Time for Prime Time," 2005; Mullin, Hardy, and Sutton, 2007; "Nielsen Weekly Sports Ranking," 2005; "Super Bowl TV Ratings," 2005; "Who's Watching," 2005).

In addition to following ratings, the NFL also seeks and values other practical research. FanLinks, a venture uniting Nielsen's parent VNU and Nielsen Sports, will offer the NFL an opportunity to obtain not only sports data but also consumers' "packaged-goods buying habits" (Kaplan, 2005b, p. 7). This is just one example of how leagues are obtaining more precise and sophisticated information about consumers to determine if fans' lifestyles are affected by companies' affiliations with certain leagues and sports. The NFL also hired Turnkey Sports and Nielsen Media Research to conduct research on its 32 teams. The league wants to give the teams new marketing services and to guarantee that they conduct fan and sponsor research at the local level. Nielsen analyzes sponsors' exposure through its "sponsorship scorecard," and Turnkey provides surveys for season ticket holders (Kaplan, 2005a). The NFL recognizes the importance of research for the league, their teams, and their key sponsors and fans.

Top-Rated Sport Programs

Although the NFL continually tops the ratings charts for singular games and the Super Bowl, other sports programs gain high shares. In top-rated programs, according to the article "Second Best" (2005), the 2005 NCAA Men's Basketball Championship game between Illinois and North Carolina gained a 15.0 rating/23 share for CBS. The NBA Finals game 7 between the Detroit Pistons and the San Antonio Spurs earned an 11.9 rating/22 share for ABC, and NBC's Kentucky Derby coverage in 2005 had a 9.0 rating/22 share. Compared with other sport leagues that have seen increases in advertising revenue in 2005, the NBA did not see the same growth, possibly because of the Los Angeles Lakers' substandard season in 2004. For the 2005-2006 season, T-Mobile was the official wireless communication provider; Toyota, Nokia, Hyundai, Southwest Airlines, and Sony PlayStation were all committed to the NBA in 2005 (Bernstein, 2005i; "Second Best," 2005).

In other sporting events and programs, NBC was happy with the 2004 Athens Games because the 17-day Olympic coverage averaged 14.77 million households, which increased 9 percent from the 2000 Olympic Games in Sydney, Australia. The Indy Racing League's viewership increased significantly in 2005 because of Danica Patrick's success. ABC, ESPN, and ESPN2 will broadcast the league's races through 2009, and in 2005 the ratings increased 50 percent over 2004 with a 0.6 rating on ESPN. ESPN2's one race saw a 100 percent jump in ratings to 0.4. ABC had ratings of 2.0 in 2005 compared with 1.4 in 2004. Whereas the average ratings of U.S. Open men's and women's finals decreased by 44 percent from 1995 to 2004, CBS saw ratings increase in 2005 with a 6.12 rating/12 share and a 2.7 rating/5 share, respectively. This was a 100 percent change over the previous year in the men's and a 22.7 percent increase in the women's ("Equal Opportunities," 2005). American Express was the top advertiser in each with 3 minutes of ad time in the men's and 2:30 in the women's. The Open switched its court color to blue from green in 2005 to enhance ball visibility for fans. Tennis has actively accepted and promoted change as evident in the increasing numbers of ethnic minorities in the sport, more participation at the recreational level, and the emphasis on staying fit. The number of "avid" tennis players increased 10 percent from 2004 to 2005, and racket sales increased 29 percent from 2003 to 2005. The United States Tennis Association (USTA) also has been more proactive with sponsors, devoting $5 million to the U.S. Open Series. Sony Ericsson's $88 million commitment over 6 years to the women's tour makes it the largest in women's sport history ("Equal Opportunities," 2005; Kaplan, 2005c; "Nielsen Weekly Sports Ranking," 2004; Warfield, 2005). As these examples show, sport is highly coveted by stations, networks, and corporations for many reasons, but most of all for profit.

Networks and Research

ESPN and ABC both agree that "sports is big, big numbers, big impact, big passion and most important, big return on objective (ROO)" (Whitney, 2005, p. 17). In addition to ratings, ROO is an important term in the advertising business. It is based on the client's objectives and differs from return on investment, which measures the cost and efficiency of an ad purchase. The client and network come up with goals and subsequently use "sports polls, Internet measurement, focus groups, customized research and data from measurement companies such as Joyce Julius and Nielsen Sports to assess the impact of sponsorship in sports" (Whitney, 2005, p. 17).

ESPN and ABC participate in customized research efforts using focus groups and other methods. One such example is ESPN's affiliation with Nielsen Sports' Web-based "sponsorship scorecard," which helps measure the "return on on-air sports sponsorships" (Whitney, 2005, p. 17). Another example is ESPN and ABC's project with Joyce Julius, which measures product placement and the number of times a brand is cited (brand mention). Joyce Julius has offered sport research since 1985, providing clients with the "Sponsors Report," national television impression value analysis (NTIV), and survey analyses using quantitative and qualitative methods to evaluate sponsorship value. "Econometric modeling, case studies and tracking behavior through TiVo" are other ways to measure ROO (Whitney, 2005, p. 17). ESPN's research has paid off because its total audience increased 3 percent in 2004 to an average of 673,000 viewers any time of the day or night (Bernstein, 2005a, p. 9). In prime time, its audience escalated 5 percent to 1.4 million people. ESPN2's total audience increased 6 percent, and in prime time it increased 8 percent. Despite these increases, ratings were flat for both networks overall (0.8 and 0.3). More important, however, is the increase of 11 percent overall among males in the 18-34 category for ESPN and 9 percent for ESPN2 (Bernstein, 2005a; "Products and Services," 2006; Whitney, 2005). As noted before, young males are difficult to reach, and companies view sport as a surefire way to communicate with them.

CBS Chairman Les Moonves also recognizes the importance of research. CBS' Television City in Las Vegas at the MGM Grand is a monumental research center for audience research and feedback with state-of-the art facilities and technology. Although research is a vital component of broadcasting corporations, according to David Poltrack, chief research officer of CBS Corporation and president of CBS Vision, "a lot of people get lost in the esoteric aspect of research" ("One-on-One," 2006, p. 34). He noted, however, that effective research enables viewers to offer insight on programs from positive feedback to suggestions for improvement.

Challenges Associated With Ratings

Although research on ratings is important to companies and adverting agencies, there are certain challenges and shortcomings, according to analysts. Sponsors and advertisers must ensure they do not annoy their consumers. In Global Marketing Insite's survey about this issue, telephone marketing topped the list of annoyances; telephone marketing, Internet pop-up windows, and junk e-mail were the top three annoyances among consumers in the 30-44 demographic. In this same study, 79 percent of those polled did not believe celebrities added value to products and cited product trial and word-of-mouth testimonials as more valuable.

Some professionals who study consumer behavior in sport believe that sport organizations and marketers place too much emphasis on demographics. Because demographic information constitutes only 3 to 5 percent of attendance, they believe psychographic research is more valuable despite its cost. Some motives for individuals to watch sport, according to sport management professor Dan Wann, include entertainment, escape, economics, eustress, aesthetic, family, self-esteem, and group affiliation. Our attention to sports can be explained by social identity theory, where we are "likely to behave in manners that improve the way they're perceived by others" (King, 2004b, p. 25). This involves social cohesion and looking for similar passions, pastimes, and perspectives. Sport, "stadiums, arenas, sports bars, chat rooms and water coolers" are examples where we bond with others and maintain a group and personal identity (King, 2004b, p. 25). "Deep fans" abound with the 24-hour sports news available on ESPN, online, and with sports talk radio (King, 2004b, p. 25). Although Nielsen has provided detailed information about ratings for many years, up until now, ratings calculations took place for television viewing inside the home. Sports TV therefore has been underreported. Because many fans watch television at sports bars, restaurants, gyms, and other locations, Nielsen and Arbitron are testing the portable people meter (PPM), which can determine "where and when the media is being consumed" (Besser, 2005, p. 22). Because 10 to 20 percent of television viewing occurs outside the home, this is an important development. If the PPM system is implemented, ratings will most likely increase, which increases sport properties' values and potentially advertising costs and revenue. This could have a "permanent and lasting effect on the world of sports and traditional TV real estate" and could be the most important "technological advance in modern sports history" (Besser, 2005, p. 22; Poole, 2005).

This section has elucidated the role of ratings and research in various sport communication entities' daily functions. Companies, leagues, teams, and networks see that research helps them to plan better, spend better, run better, and function in the sport communication market. Just as practitioners have used research over the years, academics have begun exploring the intersecting worlds of sport and communication from many perspectives (e.g., sociological, journalistic, political). All areas from industry to academia are vital for sport communication's acceptance and progression as a burgeoning and provocative field of practical and academic inquiry.

ACADEMIA'S USE OF RESEARCH TO EXPLORE SPORT COMMUNICATION

Compared to other areas examined in educational research, sport has surfaced relatively recently as a topic of academic inquiry. For example, the first journal dedicated to sport media (the *Journal of Sports Media*) started in 2006, and the first sport communication journal (the *International Journal of Sport Communication*) launched its inaugural call for papers in 2007. Research in this area is crucial to fully understand how sport intersects the social, cultural, economic, and political arenas. In an earlier chapter you learned about sport communication theory, but theory and research are inextricably linked and should be considered more as a continuum rather than as separate entities of inquiry. According to Salwen and Stacks (1996), "One cannot conduct good research without theory and good theory development requires good verification" (p. 4). Bostrom (1998) confirmed this statement by adding, "Research is the process of first

Table 12.1   Research Methods (and Their Strengths and Weaknesses) for Sport Communication

Research method	Types	Key characteristics
Quantitative	• Survey • Content analysis • Polling	• Uses numbers and statistics • Can be replicated • Is systematic and structured • Is more statistical • Is objective
Qualitative	• Media analysis • Narrative analysis • Rhetorical analysis • Framing • Observation • Participant observation • In-depth interview • Oral history	• Provides depth of research and meaning • Analyzes words, pictures, and meanings • Is flexible and adaptable • Is more interpretive • Is descriptive

discovering and then examining theories formally and objectively" (p. 19). Table 12.1 shows several different types of research.

Types and Approaches to Research

There are several different types of research: exploratory, descriptive, explanatory, and predictive (Gratton & Jones, 2004; Salwen & Stacks, 1996):

• **Exploratory research** sets a foundation for knowledge in an unexplored area of inquiry. An exploratory study in sport communication could analyze athletes' and coaches' perceptions of television sports reporters versus newspaper sportswriters. It is a pioneering study and sets the foundation for academic inquiry.

• **Descriptive research** describes a phenomenon and what occurs rather than why it occurs. A descriptive study could analyze how sports reporters integrate stand-ups within their daily sports reports. Stand-ups are when reporters are at the actual scene of a story reporting the current event live.

• **Explanatory research** expounds on why something occurs and measures causal relationships. An example of explanatory research could try to explain why sport companies need to be proactive in their marketing strategies.

• **Predictive research** predicts or anticipates phenomena based on explanatory research and its findings. A predictive research study could anticipate how the Internet will change sports coverage and content and the media's attention to it.

Before undertaking research and expanding knowledge about sport communication, researchers need to understand certain philosophical approaches to research, the nature of knowledge, and data collection. Positivism considers scientific knowledge and the methods of natural sciences to be the only veritable type of knowledge. By observing behavior, the researcher can measure facts to create "laws" or theories, which will anticipate future behavior. Although early researchers like the Chicago School of Sociologists often viewed quantitative and qualitative methods as complementary, using both case study and statistics in their studies, the positivist philosophy focuses on statistics. Positivists use the experiment from the physical sciences as a model for research. They believe in universal laws about relationships between variables and the generalizability of findings. Positivists value anything that they can observe directly and model experiments on the physical sciences. Positivists base validity and reliability on the testing of theories and their replication. They have often dismissed qualitative research for not having enough scientific rigor because of subjective data and findings (Hammersley & Atkinson, 2002).

An interpretive approach includes those who view sport as a more "social phenomenon." According to Gratton and Jones (2004), the interpretive researcher studies words or "nonnumerical measures" to delve into meanings and values (p. 19). Naturalists study the social world in its "natural" state rather than in the artificial setting of a lab. Respect for the subject is paramount, and they do not believe individuals' actions are open to the "causal analysis and manipulation of variables" that are part of quantitative research inspired by positivism (Hammersley & Atkinson, 2002, p. 8). Researchers must have access to meanings that direct individuals' actions. By studying individuals' social worlds, we can understand and interpret the world similarly and learn social processes. In naturalism, the description of cultures is most important (Gratton & Jones, 2004; Hammersley & Atkinson, 2002).

Whereas positivists believe in a more quantitative approach to research, interpretivists and naturalists believe in qualitative research because of the depth and breadth of its results. In addition to using different types of measurement, qualitative research and quantitative research vary in their uses of data. According to Gratton and Jones (2004), the quantitative approach uses "numerical measurement and analysis" and involves "measurable 'quantities'" (p. 21). With this approach researchers study data that can be statistically evaluated to see if there is a relationship between variables. Conversely, qualitative research seeks to "capture qualities that are not quantifiable" or those not "reducible to numbers, such as feelings, thoughts, experiences . . . those concepts associated with interpretive approaches to knowledge" (Gratton & Jones, 2004, p. 22). Qualitative research and quantitative research generally apply to methodologies, or the "structured sets of procedures and instruments by which empirical phenomena of mass communication are registered, documented, and interpreted" (Jensen & Jankowski, 1991, p. 8). To be a solid researcher, you should tackle both because they are both useful in social research.

By using triangulation, or combining qualitative and quantitative methods, the researcher gains the depth of meaning from qualitative research and the quantification of results from quantitative research (Gratton & Jones, 2004; Jensen & Jankowski, 1991).

Before the 1920s, much was written about the media, but there was little systematic, scientific study (Lowery & DeFleur, 1995). As statistics became a part of the behavioral and social sciences during the 1920s, quantitative research gained momentum in academia as experiments dominated research with surveys in social sciences (Jankowski & Wester, 1991). McCracken (1988) examined the differences between quantitative and qualitative research. Quantitative research defines and labels categories rigidly before the study begins in order to evaluate the relationships between them. Quantitative research and qualitative research also differ in categories. In qualitative research, the categories evolve and change during the process of research. In quantitative research, the precise categories are the "means of research," whereas in qualitative research "they are the object of research" (McCracken, 1988, p. 16). Qualitative research also seeks interrelationships between many categories, whereas quantitative generally looks for a "sharply delineated relationship between a limited set of them" (p. 16). According to McCracken, "The quantitative researcher uses a lens that brings a narrow strip of the field of vision into very precise focus. The qualitative researcher uses a lens that permits a much less precise vision of a much broader strip" (p. 16). There is also a difference in reporting abilities. In quantitative research, the participant responds quickly to closed questions, whereas in qualitative research there are broader, imprecise questions warranting response. Finally, another difference deals with the sample. In quantitative work, the researcher creates a sample and generalizes it to the general population, whereas in qualitative work, access to culture is an issue. In this sense, "it is the categories and assumptions, not those who hold them, that matter" in qualitative research and it is "more intensive than extensive in its objectives" (McCracken, p. 17).

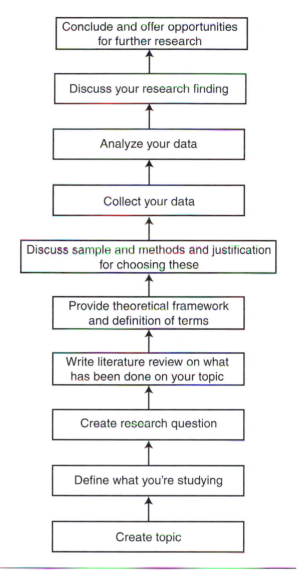

Figure 12.3 Steps in the sport communication research process.

Example of the Research Process

After we understand the approaches to research, the research process can begin (see figure 12.3). The following is an application of sport to the work of Gratton and Jones (2004). The first step in the research process is to decide a topic of study. When evaluating topics, the researcher should consider past literature, current events, social issues, and personal interests. A potential topic is *Sports Illustrated*'s coverage of female tennis players. Next, the researcher discusses and synthesizes past literature on related topics, showing a gap and therefore providing a justification for

further study. With this, the researcher would need to start broad with gender and sport literature. Next, the researcher would need to discuss media portrayals of female athletes. Now the researcher can focus on tennis. There have been studies on the Williams sisters, Billie Jean King, and Martina Navratilova to name a few. The researcher then creates a theoretical framework that defines terms and concepts and presents the theoretical foundations of the study. Here the researcher should define gender for this specific study and could define such terms as sexualization and marginalization (of female athletes) and gender-marked language. Additionally, theories from mass communication, communication, and sport research can be used here to bolster the study's legitimacy. Agenda setting, gate keeping, and critical theory are all examples of relevant theories.

Next comes a clear, coherent research question. With all research, a good question is necessary. Then research will develop the theory behind this question or hypothesis, which in turn expands research in this area. Research questions result from either the **inductive process,** where questions are derived from general assumptions, or the **deductive process,** where questions are derived from rational observation. Deductive reasoning—which is often associated with quantitative research—moves from the general to the specific, whereas inductive reasoning—which is often associated with qualitative research—moves from the specific to the general. When a researcher is contemplating a question, the "so what" factor must come into play. In other words, the social significance of the question is crucial (Bostrom, 1998). Why do we care? Research is conducted to solve problems whether they are theoretical or practical in nature. Before a research question is finalized, the researcher should make sure that he or she can answer questions such as, "What are you going to research? Why is this a topic of interest? How are you going to conduct your research?" (Stokes, 2003, p. 29). In addition to ensuring that the research question is focused, refined, and realistic, the researcher should consider time constraints and accessibility issues. The data must be available and the researcher must be able to conduct the research and deal with all issues related to it. An example of a question for the study mentioned previously could be, How did *Sports Illustrated* frame Martina Hingis' comeback in 2005-2006? The research question must be specific, refined, focused, and doable; it must be narrow yet compelling enough to study. After the research question is determined, the following must still be accomplished: the research design or sample and methodological procedures, the data collection stage, the analysis and discussion of research findings, and finally the conclusion and opportunities for further research. The final section should include any weaknesses in the study and opportunities to expand the study.

For sport communication research, there are a few overall considerations for all communication researchers. According to communication scholar Denis McQuail (1996), these elements are associated with questions such as, "Who communicates to whom? (sources and receivers) Why communicate? (functions and purposes) How does communication take place? (channels, languages, codes) What about? (content, references, types of information) What are the consequences of communication (intended or unintended)?" (p. 9). Researchers must consider all phases and elements of the communication process to create a compelling and significant study.

There are also a few different approaches for studying the communication process. Different approaches to communication research include

- the structural, which studies media systems and how they relate to society (cable television and ESPN);
- behavioral, which studies human behavior in the communication process (job functions specific to sport marketers); and
- cultural, which focuses on mean-ing, language, and cultural context (textual analysis of sports journalists' writings).

Research Procedures

The dominant paradigm of communication research perceived the mass media as powerful and often used social science and methods such as surveys, statistical analyses, and experiments to study communication in an empirical way. The alternative paradigm, on the other hand, rejected the transmission or linear model of communication and contained a critical view of society, using a more cultural approach and qualitative methods (McQuail, 1996). The former often uses more quantitative methods of research, or methods that be quantified by numbers. Surveys are one example because you can count and categorize responses to make a general observation about the population. The latter uses deeper and more meaningful methods like in-depth interviewing or textual analysis. Although the sample size of this type of study is usually small compared to surveys that can be sent or distributed to hundreds or even thousands of people, the alternative paradigm takes a more ritualistic and deeper approach to issues. When conducting a study, maximize your strengths. If interpersonal skills are your strength, you enjoy talking and observing people, and you're a good listener, the alternative paradigm would work well for you. If you enjoy numbers and seek to generalize your results more easily to the general population, the dominant paradigm would be most effective for you.

After determining the research question, the researcher next defines and operationalizes terms and concepts (Bostrom, 1998). Primary sources are those that comprise the researcher's "object of analysis," whereas secondary sources are work done by others, which is used as background information or in the literature review (Stokes, 2003, p. 31). For the study listed previously on Hingis, the researcher would define any relevant terms and justify the research. The researcher then engages in a literature review, which involves the study of all literature pertaining to the research question. Although this body of research propels future studies, it also helps determine what is missing and therefore gives the researcher a justification for doing his or her study. The literature review has several purposes, according to Gratton and Jones (2004). It should show the researcher's comprehensive knowledge on the topic and should sketch an outline for theories, concepts, and past work. It also needs to further focus the question. In addition, it should show the scope of past research while creating a hypothesis, which is the "predicted outcome of the research based upon logical reason or existing evidence" (p. 52). This section should show methodologies used in the past and should identify and define all concepts and variables as well as showing how the researcher's work expands on past research. The literature review must contain a critical synthesis rather than a description of past work. It should include academic journal articles, library books, trade publications, conference papers, doctoral dissertations, government documents, and other secondary sources.

The researcher cannot simply summarize past work but rather needs to organize and synthesize scholars' contributions in a systematic manner to prove that his or her study adds to the body of knowledge in this area of inquiry. The researcher knows his or her literature review is complete if sources repeat themselves in bibliographies and reference lists. Viable methods for the study described could include textual analysis or framing analysis, just to name a couple. The researcher would need to investigate how to conduct the method chosen and the pioneers who created the method and key scholars who implemented it previously.

Generally, researchers write proposals or an outline to guide their research. A proposal includes the research question, a definition of the object of analysis, a description of primary sources, an overview of secondary sources, a literature review, a time frame for the work, a sample instrument like a survey, an explanation of what the researcher anticipates finding, and a bibliography (Stokes, 2003). The next section offers an overview of the history of sport communication research.

History of Academic Research on Sport

Sport communication is a relatively new academic discipline, which began in the age of television. As the media gained prominence and power in the United States with the maturation of television as a medium, more academics focused on the media and sport. Scholars have recognized the importance of understanding the history and sociology of the institutional relationship between the mass media and sport (Rowe, 2004b). Garry Whannel has studied television and contributed to the growing field of sport studies within this arena. Whannel (2002) wrote, "The growth of television as a significant cultural form during the 1960s put the relationship between sport and the media on the public agenda" (p. 291).

Many studies critically analyze television sport coverage in "sociological and semiological traditions" (Whannel, 2002, p. 291). They look at the production of media messages either through the media workers' perspectives and practices or through the organizational and cultural media institutions, legal limitations, and economic pressures. They also look at media content in an age of spectacle and at sport media audiences and the influence of media messages on attendance and participation. Some topics considered in the ongoing research include the commercialization of sport, portrayals of women in sport media, the issue of masculinity in media sport, race and media sport, globalization, and sport and the body (Whannel, 2002).

According to Trujillo (2003), communication scholars published articles about sport in *Journalism Quarterly* beginning in 1934 with Riding's article on slang in newspaper sportswriting. The *Journal of Communication* published Michael Real's seminal work on the Super Bowl in 1975 and even devoted an entire issue to the study of sport in 1977. The *Journal of Broadcasting* published sport articles in the 1980s, and *Critical Studies in Mass Communication* and the *Quarterly Journal of Speech* also published works on sport at that time. Sport media scholar Lawrence A. Wenner

(1998a) noted, "The meanings associated with mediated sport texts often extend well beyond the archetypal heroic myths of the playing field to offer lessons about cultural priorities and the current state of power relations" (p. 5). Wenner's *MediaSport* set the agenda for research in this field. This expanded on his 1989 text, *Media, Sports, and Society.* Wenner explored "sport as communication" and defined *MediaSport* as "the cultural fusing of sport with communication" (p. xiii).

Until the early to mid-1980s, sport was not considered in communication and media studies, but today it is one of the main areas of research. This area integrates sociology, communication, and media studies, offering opportunities to further understand the power of the media in American culture and the impact of sport on American society. From sport institutions to texts and audiences, each enables scholars to further understand the meaning and significance of sport in cultural values and relationships of power and prestige.

Overview of Research Methodologies

Today, all journalism and communication journals include articles on sport. Work in this area can be conducted from diverse theoretical and methodological perspectives. Books such as *Case Studies in Sport Communication* share examples of work in the field and reveal the importance of continuing scholarly inquiry and contributions. When considering types of studies, the researcher can choose between work on texts, the media industry, or audience analysis (Trujillo, 2003; Wenner, 1998a). The researcher can study newspapers, magazines, television audiences, or workers at ESPN. The options are infinite in a world mesmerized by sport and the media. There is a need for more research in all facets of sport communication from marketing, advertising, public relations, and law to print, electronic media, and emerging technologies.

Kinkema and Harris (1998) analyzed the differences and needs of the various types of sport communication research. They noted that more research is needed on production as

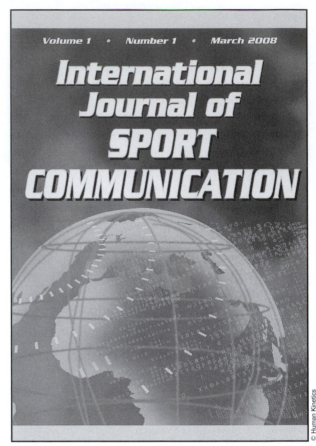

Many scholarly outlets publish qualitative and quantitative research articles related to communication activities and personnel in the sport industry. Only recently, however, has there been a release of journals that are entirely focused on sport media and communication. The *Journal of Sports Media* commenced in 2006 and the *International Journal of Sport Communication* (IJSC) made its initial call for papers in 2007.

well as the audience and specifically the "political and economic dimensions at local, national, and global levels" (p. 53). In textual analysis, more work should be done in sport advertising, the commercialization of sport, drugs and athletes, and teamwork as shown in media texts. Additionally, there is a need for work in emerging technologies as well as sports talk radio and for research reports aimed at making policy recommendations in media sport.

The following section offers an overview of a few methodologies in sport communication. Although this is just a sampling of the endless options, it shows the strengths and weaknesses of each. As noted earlier, triangulation, or integrating different methods, maximizes the efficacy of a study. Although the researcher needs to choose a method based on his or her interests, passions, and objectives, integrating both quantitative and qualitative methods affords the optimal generalizability of results. The next three sections discuss research on texts, the media industry, and audiences. Each has its strengths, and each furthers the understanding of the sport industry, and specifically sport communication.

Research on Media Texts

This section focuses on methods used in studying texts. Content analysis, narrative analysis, and other methods enable the researcher to delve into language, meaning, and media content.

Content Analysis

There are a few benefits to studying texts. One is accessibility, because there are many search engines, research databases, and interlibrary loans that make research simpler. Additionally, texts are social phenomena, part of our ordinary life at work, at school, or in our personal lives. Although texts are often readily available, researchers must be aware of the time-consuming nature and meticulous detail required for this type of research. Gratton and Jones (2004) defined content analysis as the "analysis of the content of communications" (p. 167). Content analysis is a quantitative, yet symbolic method that includes "counting and summing phenomena" (Stokes, 2003, p. 56). Whether the researcher counts mentions of a certain word or subject or the number of stories, he or she systematically uses categories to guide the study. Content analysis is effective when the researcher is trying to see how much of a "given phenomenon there is in a chosen set of texts" and is used in many media studies (Stokes, 2003, pp. 57-58). For instance, you might hypothesize that *Sports Illustrated* has more coverage of male sports than female sports today. You could compare the numbers of articles on each during the 1990s and today by selecting a representative sample. This factual evidence will either support or refute your hypothesis. The strength of content analysis is in its generation of "reliable, replicable facts" (Stokes, 2003, p. 58). It's easy to do even for

beginning researchers and is very clear and straightforward. The researcher can study the written, audio, or visual texts.

As far as challenges and drawbacks, content analysis relies on good categories to provide meaningful results. Often it can be insensitive and very time-consuming, and the researcher must collect a representative sample of the selected texts. The following is an overview of steps in content analysis. After naming the text, specifically identify the data. Then establish a hypothesis or research question. The researcher must have a clear vision of what he or she wants to learn and find from reading the texts. Next, read widely to refine and justify the work. Then define the object of analysis, whether it is a book, magazine, newspaper, or television show. The sample should be representative, yet realistic. Categories should be specific. From here, the researcher will develop a coding sheet, which will be a grid with the objects of analysis and the categories. The researcher will record the findings here, so the more specific the better. Next, test the categories on a small sample to determine if they need refining or revising. If they need revisions or changes, include reasons in the methods section later in the proposal. After the categories are set, collect the data and write down the texts on another sheet of paper. If something does not fall into a category, that must be noted appropriately. The researcher can list findings on a second log sheet and convert raw data to percentages and afterward can see if any patterns either support or refute the hypothesis. If the hypothesis is not supported, it is still useful research. The researcher can then present the results in tables, charts, and written paragraphs, which details how he or she conducted the research and what was found. As mentioned earlier, content analysis is effective in studying quantities and in making "explicit facts about content" (Gratton & Jones, 2004; Stokes, 2003, p. 66).

Narrative Analysis

Narrative analysis, a qualitative methodology, centers on the structure of the story whether it's a newspaper article, novel, film, television show, or magazine article. Through narratives, the researcher can study and further understand cultural values and ideologies. Narratives contain events that are active or communicate a state or condition (change). There is a temporal arrangement with a series of events, and there must be some causal relationships as well as a coherent topic. According to Jane Stokes (2003), the researcher selects a limited number of texts. Because this is in-depth research, be careful not to choose too many. One feature film or one news topic in 5 days would suffice.

Next, the researcher must get acquainted with the text and then define the hypothesis accordingly. Rhetorician Sonja K. Foss believes there are many elements to analyzing the artifact or text. The researcher must analyze the settings, characters, narrator, events, temporal relations and the function of time, causal relations and cause-and-effect relationships, the audience, and the themes. By exploring the text, the researcher can determine the most significant and valuable parts of the narrative. According to Foss (2004), "A narrative, as a frame upon experience, functions as an argument to view and understand the world in a particular way" (p. 339). A narrative can be judged according to the following (Foss, 2004, pp. 338-340):

- "Does the narrative embody and advocate values that you see as desirable and worthwhile?
- What ethical standards does the narrative suggest?
- How readily can the narrative be refuted?
- Is the narrative coherent?
- Does the narrative demonstrate fidelity?
- Does the narrative fulfill the purpose of its creators?
- Does the narrative provide useful ideas for living your life?"

By using these guidelines and focus, the researcher can formulate a research question dealing with what the narrative shows about cultural values or an individual or how it controls the understanding of an event. Among methodologies, narrative analysis is open-ended and creative in its approach, offering much leeway for the researcher.

After analyzing the text, the researcher should include the basic elements in the final paper. The introduction should introduce the question or problem, its contribution to communication research, and its overarching significance. The researcher should next elaborate on the narrative or artifact and fully describe it. Third, a description of the methodology should follow. Fourth, the findings elucidate what the study discovered, and fifth, a conclusion is written in which the researcher discusses the contributions to communication research and theory (Foss, 2004; Stokes, 2003). An example in sport communication would be a narrative analysis of *The Seattle Times'* coverage of the Seattle Seahawks and the *Pittsburgh Post-Gazette*'s coverage of the Pittsburgh Steelers during the 2005-2006 NFL season through Super Bowl XL.

Other Methodologies Used to Study Texts

The preceding are just two examples of methodologies used to study media texts. Others to consider would include rhetorical criticism, semiotics, or textual analysis.

- **Rhetorical criticism** is based on rhetoric, which is individuals' "use of symbols to communicate" (Foss, 2004, p. 4). Rhetorical criticism is a method created for the "systematic investigation and explanation of symbolic acts and artifacts for the purpose of understanding rhetorical processes" (Foss, 2004, p. 6). In sport communication, an example would be to study rhetorical strategies used by sport journalists to describe disabled athletes.

- **Semiotics,** or the study of signs, is also useful in studying texts and developed from Ferdinand de Saussure's *Course in General Linguistics* (1983). Semiotics studies the meaning of artifacts and is especially valuable in analyzing visual texts.

- **Textual analysis** includes the systematic study of films, television shows, sportscasts, newspaper articles, or any other media document.

- **Qualitative document analysis** enables researchers to develop categories and protocols after analyzing documents and emphasizes "process, context, and significance and how the document helps define the situation and clarify meaning for the audience member" (Altheide, 1996, p. 12).

Archival research involves studying history through old documents, and participant observation enables the researcher to study behaviors of workers firsthand by becoming part of their study. Interviews require the researcher to ask subjects open-ended questions to gain insight into their worlds (Altheide, 1996; Foss, 2004; Stokes, 2003).

These are just a few of the examples for researchers interested in media texts. Whether you choose qualitative or quantitative research, texts enable you to study culture and its artifacts.

Research on the Media Industry

This section focuses on the media industry, which enables you to find out information on media workers, stations, networks, and the industry. Archival research, interview, and participant observation are a few examples of methods used to study the media industry (Stokes, 2003, p. 25).

Archival Research

Research on the media industry affords knowledge in how newspapers, magazines, television stations, cable networks, Internet sport sites, and others work to produce sport communication content. This section describes some viable methods for studying people in the industry and the media entities themselves. The most valuable research in this area is qualitative in nature because the most compelling research questions deal with processes. Whether the research wants to find out about sports reporters or how sports fans experience the media, qualitative research elicits more depth than content analysis. University of Chicago sociologist Robert Park began an in-depth study of the news media in the early 20th century when he studied city life, immigrants, and the role of news in social cohesion. Some key works in this area are Gaye Tuchman's *Making News: A Study in the Construction of Reality* (1978), Herbert Gans'

Deciding What's News (1979), and Todd Gitlin's *Inside Prime Time* (1983). When one is studying the media, access is a key concern. Whether the researcher studies the history of a certain network or evolution of a certain technology, documentary evidence or written sources and people serve as the primary means of conducting research. Examples of methods using documents are archival research and those with people are generally interview, participant observation, and oral history. With archival research, the researcher obtains original documents and uses those as the primary basis for research. Whether the researcher is studying the history of women's athletics at Indiana University or the history of public relations in the National Hockey League, he or she must have access to documents. As in other forms of research, the researcher first defines the object of analysis, creates a research question based on past literature, identifies the primary sources, and refines the question if needed, ensuring he or she has access to the documents. The researcher then gathers the data from the documents and synthesizes it, referring back to the hypothesis and expounding on the findings. Archival research is compelling if the researcher has an interest in history and inquiring about a certain time period or topic. The researcher uncovers nuances from primary sources and enlivens history (Gans, 1979; Gitlin, 2000; Stokes, 2003; Tuchman, 1991).

Interview, Participant Observation, and Oral History

Another good methodology for historical research (and for contemporary work) is the interview. Interviews enable researchers to gain intimate information about experiences in the media industry. This way, scholars can learn about the perspectives and attitudes of the audience or the media workers themselves. Whether the researcher seeks a structured interview, semistructured interview, unstructured interview, or focus group, interviews provide insightful, surprising, and meaningful information. According to Grant McCracken (1988), "The long interview gives us the opportunity to step into the mind of another person, to see and experience the

If one were to conduct participant research of the crowd interactions at college basketball games, he or she would have to choose between nonparticipant observation (i.e., the researcher observes, but does not interact with, the crowd) or participant observation (i.e., the researcher observes and interacts with the crowd).

world as they do themselves" (p. 9). Language is vital both as a "tool and the object of analysis" (Jensen, 1991, p. 32). To maximize the work's value, the researcher must choose interviews selectively and must interview more than one person. The researcher can conduct interviews in person, on the phone, via e-mail, or through a survey. The researcher should write the questions beforehand, using mostly open-ended questions, or those that elicit a full response and more than a yes–no answer.

Next, the researcher records the interview, takes notes, and transcribes it later word for word. Afterwards, a determination is made whether the interviewee supports or refutes the research question. As in other studies, the researcher must offer a detailed account of the process in the methods section and then will write findings in the results and discussion sections. McCracken (1988) noted that "time scarcity and concern for privacy" are

limitations of qualitative research, yet the long interview overcomes these, giving the researcher data without "participant observation, unobtrusive observation, or prolonged contact" (p. 11). Additionally, according to Gratton and Jones (2004), researchers could potentially add bias, data analysis is complicated, and the quality of the study relies on the interviewee. Nevertheless, surveys and interviews are the dominant methodologies used in sport research today.

Participant observation requires interviews also but goes further in the process because the researcher immerses himself or herself in the behavior and actions of a specific group of individuals. This type of research is considered the "most neglected research in sport" (Gratton & Jones, 2004, p. 159). Whereas nonparticipant observation requires the researcher to observe phenomenon with no interaction between the researcher, activity, and subjects, participant observation enables the researcher to participate in the research. According to Jankowski and Wester (1991), "The primary purpose of participant-observation research . . . is to describe in fundamental terms various events, situations, and actions that occur in a particular social setting" (p. 61). For instance, in Herbert Gans' seminal work, *Deciding What's News* (1979), he spent several months at *CBS Evening News, NBC Nightly News, Newsweek,* and *Time* between 1965 and 1969. He studied journalists' work routines and values, how they selected stories, and the many pressures of the job. In sport, Jeff MacGregor and Olya Evanitsky (2005) experienced NASCAR firsthand for an entire season and documented their results in a book, *Sunday Money: Speed! Lust! Madness! Death! A Hot Lap Around America With NASCAR.*

In participant observation, researchers use their expertise and experience to gain access to a group of people and read fully about the industry, company, league, or team that they will observe. They write a plan and schedule, making sure the work can fully answer the research question. When conducting fieldwork, researchers fit in and talk to people discreetly, taking notes and being as unobtrusive as possible. They continue to monitor field notes, filling gaps as needed. Once they have completed notes, they reflect and write up their thoughts during the observation phase. Next, they write their findings, which should detail what they found and did not find. Included in this section are any shortcomings with the work. They should reflect not only on whether their findings supported the research question but also on their actions and method. Although most of what they write will be included in the analysis section, the appendix can include field notes.

As in all research, researchers refer back to theories, past literature, and the research question. There are many positives with this type of research. Strengths include the direct and candid reporting of events and phenomena. Whereas researchers generally rely on others, with this method they actively engage in the process. The research occurs in a natural environment rather than an artificial one as with sur-

veys and experiments. Researchers can observe behavior directly and naturally. In surveys, respondents may not admit certain things or may not be as forthcoming. Weaknesses of this approach include researchers' inability to fully understand phenomena, missing observations, or influencing subjects (Gans, 1979; Gratton & Jones, 2004; Jankowski & Wester, 1991; MacGregor & Evanitsky, 2005).

Oral history is one of the oldest methodologies, affording pioneering studies and archival research. Oral history involves interviewing individuals about their past experiences. According to Donald A. Ritchie (2003), "Oral history collects memories and personal commentaries of historical significance through recorded interviews" (p. 19). The researcher then transcribes, summarizes, and uses the interviews for research. The researcher must have access to individuals for interviews and must be well prepared before the interview. It is best to begin an interview with simple, clear questions about the interviewee's background and then progress to more difficult and provocative questions.

Respect for the subject is paramount. Ask good questions and let the subject do most of the talking. It is vital to adequately document the interview (Ritchie, 2003; Stokes, 2003). Tape record and later transcribe the interview; take notes on nonverbal gestures and other information.

An example of oral history research in sport communication could be in-depth interviews of Negro-league baseball players. You could document their experiences in segregated baseball before Jackie Robinson's integration of professional baseball in 1947. This would not only enable contemporary society to understand their plight and what they endured but also grant insight into cultural history.

This section discussed some methods for studying the sport media industry. Equally as important is research on the audience. Some methods already discussed, like participant observation, interviews, and oral histories, can be used in studying audiences, and there are a few others also. In sport, the audience is especially important for ratings, sponsors, and corporations.

Research on Audiences

When one is studying audiences, the most effective methodologies are surveys, interviews, focus groups, and oral histories. Communication research on audiences includes effects as evident in the "all-powerful effects" era with the hypodermic needle theory of effects in the 1930s. Creedon's work (1994b) stated that the "limited effects era" began in the 1940s with Paul Lazarsfeld and later Joseph Klapper's work (pp. 9-10). The "powerful but contingent" era from the 1970s was based on Carl Hovland's World War II research about a "hierarchy of media effects" and Maxwell McCombs and Donald Shaw's legendary agenda-setting research (Creedon, pp. 10-11). This states that the media do not tell us what to think but rather what to think about. Additionally, the knowledge gap and uses and gratifications research fall within this era. See chapter 4 to learn more about theories. In the late 1980s, the "powerful, content and contextual effects" era began, acknowledging that "the media are powerful, *and* that the power is contingent *and* contextual; that is, it accounts for the fact that different individuals view the world differently based on the way they have experienced it" (Creedon, 1994b, p. 12). Work to date in media effects and sport communication centers on "motivations for viewing, locus of exposure and effects of exposure" (Creedon, 1994b). Media effects research can use different methods, including experiments.

Survey Research

Experimental research is replicable—it can be repeated by others with identical findings. Like the early Payne Fund studies and Hovland's research on World War II soldiers, research of this type resembles a laboratory experiment. The survey process begins with a statement of objectives and a clear and coherent proposition on how it will be tested. Next, the researcher creates the propositions to be tested or hypotheses. In social scientific research, causal hypotheses are most important, or those that study the "causes of phenomena" (Weisberg, Krosnick, & Bowen, 1996, pp. 29-30). Next, the researcher must state how the

concepts will be operationalized or "defined in such a way that they can be measured" (p. 30). After determining the objectives of a survey, the researcher determines the target population and then collects survey data via interview, telephone, mailed questionnaires, or e-mail. Next, the researcher determines whether a panel study is necessary with follow-up surveys or whether it is a typical cross-sectional survey with respondents participating once.

Babbie (1998) examined the strengths and weaknesses of survey research. Surveys work well when describing a large population and are flexible in the sense that the researcher can ask many different questions on the same topic. Weaknesses include the inability to adequately study and cover complicated issues and the "context of social life" (p. 273). Additionally, survey research is inflexible in the sense that the study design remains rigid, whereas in qualitative research the study design can be modified throughout the process. Like scientific experiments, survey research can be artificial in the sense that it does not "measure social action" (p. 274) but only past or hypothetical actions of respondents. An example in sport communication would be a mail survey about sports fans' consumption patterns with various questions about media use and buying habits (Babbie, 1998; Weisberg et al., 1996).

Ethnographic Research

Ethnography, which is anthropological in nature, is a qualitative method that captures the depth of experience. It is based on cultural forms and includes the "everyday" (Jankowski & Wester, 1991, p. 54). The ethnographer participates in individuals' lives over time, observing, asking questions, and collecting data that elucidate what he or she is studying. Ethnography studies a specific group or subculture and most often uses observation, participant observation, and in-depth interviews. The researcher uses the emic perspective rather than the etic perspective (Gratton & Jones, 2004). In the former, the researcher takes the perspective of the individuals under study compared with the latter, which takes the perspective of the researcher. If you are

© Paul M. Pedersen

The director of research and development in the Louisville Slugger Division of Hillerich and Bradsby Company oversees all aspects of research (i.e., product development, design, validation, implementation, technology assessment, prototyping, quantitative field testing, feasibility, qualification). The research is then communicated to various stakeholders of the company, which employ approximately 470 people in nine branches across the United States. It's hard to miss the Louisville Slugger Museum and Factory in downtown Louisville as the 120-foot "Big Bat" stands in front of the complex.

interested in the Women's National Basketball Association (WNBA) and the New York Liberty, you could follow the team for part of a season, documenting media coverage of athletes during this time at press conferences and singular interviews.

Focus groups, according to Babbie (1998), enable the researcher to study complicated issues and individuals' opinions and perceptions of them. For subjects, students can use friends or fellow students in their studies, but unlike participant observation or ethnography, subjects are in laboratory settings. Groups consist of 12 to 15 people who are convened for discussion on a predetermined topic relevant to the researcher's work. Generally the researcher selects more than one group to increase the generalizability of the study. Focus groups are considered social research with real-life data. Other strengths

of focus groups include flexibility, high validity, quick results, and low costs. Some disadvantages are that focus groups provide less control than individual interviews, and it is difficult to analyze data singularly and among groups. It is also difficult to convene groups, and the environment must be right for effective discussion (Babbie, 1998). An example could be a focus group on fans, studying their perceptions of a team's treatment of season ticket holders.

These methodologies are only a few of the choices there are available to sport communication researchers. Sport communication researchers should select the best method for their specific study and gear it toward their strengths. For the creative individuals with a background in reporting, in-depth interviewing would highlight their strengths. For those who are interested in storytelling, narrative analysis would work. For those interested in a more scientific approach with numbers, surveys or content analysis would work best. The main consideration should be ensuring accuracy, adhering to ethics, and furthering the discipline of sport communication through significant and thought-provoking topics of inquiry.

CHAPTER WRAP-UP

Summary

This chapter expanded on previous chapters by showing how important research is to athletes, teams, leagues, companies, broadcasting stations and networks, newspapers, and other industry practitioners as well as sport communication academics. It offered facts on how companies have used research and ratings and offered suggestions on how to conduct an actual research study. In today's transitory media environment, it is especially important to be proactive in being informed. Information and power enable the sport entity to function more effectively and to reach future goals. According to Mullin, Hardy, and Sutton, "No organization can exist without considering the future" (2000, p. 83). In industry, this includes being aware of competition, knowing an entity's place in the sport communication arena, and being aware of opportunities for growth and possible challenges.

Techniques that can be used in both industry and academic research include surveys (mail, telephone, computer-based), interviews in an informal or focus-group setting, and textual analysis of newspapers, magazines, and other publications. Academic researchers can also conduct ethnographic research like observation and participant observation, where they become part of the subculture and immerse themselves in the sport communication world. Each method and technique has its strengths and weaknesses, but all are valuable to sport communication's growth. For sport communication to reach its potential as an academic and industry discipline, thought-provoking research must expand awareness and spark dialogue and debate. An ever-changing sport communication environment challenges the professional and academic to be resilient, flexible, and committed to its vision. This chapter serves as a segue to the final chapters in the book, which present sociological and legal issues of sport communication. Research is the commonality among all the chapters because it stresses the requisite components of vision, expanded knowledge, and commitment.

Review Questions

1. What is research and why is it important in the practical and theoretical arenas of sport communication?

2. Why is audience research valuable for media corporations, sport organizations, and advertising agencies?

3. What is the people meter? What are diaries? How do they work?

4. What are the four types of research? Define.

5. What are the primary differences between quantitative and qualitative research in sport communication?

6. Why is a literature review important in sport communication research?

7. What is the difference between primary and secondary sources and how are each used in a sport communication research proposal?

8. What is content analysis? Define and list strengths and weaknesses for use in sport communication research.

9. What is survey research? Define and list strengths and weaknesses for use in sport communication research.

10. What are in-depth interviews? Define and list strengths and weaknesses for use in sport communication research.

Discussion Questions

1. What are some topics for research studying the legal and economic areas of sport communication?

2. How would you trace the development of audience research?

3. How do ratings companies such as Nielsen and Arbitron work?

4. Think about sport shows (e.g., *SportsCenter*) and events (e.g., Wimbledon). Why are ratings vital and how do they fit into the Strategic Sport Communication Model?

5. What is the research process? Start from creating a topic to the final product.

6. Where would you find sources for your research proposal?

7. What types of resources would you use for a research project? Why did you select these resources?

8. What are some topics for research on the social and historical areas of sport communication?

9. What are some methodologies for studying sport communication audiences?

10. What are the strengths and weaknesses of some of the methodologies that are used to study sport communication audiences?

Activities and Exercises

1. Attend a university or community meeting and fully observe participants, the discussions, and the overall environment. Make field notes with verbal and nonverbal communication. Bring the notes into class and be prepared to discuss your observations.

2. Schedule an interview with a classmate. Ask her questions about her experiences playing or working in sport. Tape the interview, transcribe it, and be prepared to tell the class all about your interviewee's experiences.

3. List several potential sport communication studies. What methodology would work best in each one? Why or why not?

4. Attend a sporting event and observe the media, the team, the fans, and other sport communication components. Brainstorm and record research topics and potential research questions for these.

Internet Sites for Additional Learning

University of Wisconsin-Madison's Writing Center, "How to write a research paper": www.wisc.edu/writing/Handbook/PlanResearchPaper.html

Sport Research Center: www.sirc.ca/

Sports Research Center, University of Notre Dame: www.sports.nd.edu

Sport England's Latest Sport Research: www.sportengland.org/index/get_resources/research/latest_research.htm

Sport Research Resources at the University of Illinois Archives: web.library.uiuc.edu/ahx/sports.htm

York University Sport Research Guide: www.library.yorku.ca/ccm/rg/nk/Sports.jsp

Ohio University Sport Research Guide: www.library.ohiou.edu/subjects/sports.htm

University of Central Florida's Institute for Diversity and Ethics in Sport: www.bus.ucf.edu/sport/cgi-bin/site/sitew.cgi?page=/ides/index.htx

PART III

Addressing Issues and Regulation in Sport Communication

Now that you are familiar with the background and components of sport communication, the final two chapters of the book examine two unique ancillary components of sport communication. The first major issue—examined in chapter 13—involves the sociocultural aspects of sport communication. The second major issue is detailed in this textbook's final chapter—chapter 14—and looks at the legal activities surrounding the field.

Chapter 13 explores how and where sport communication and sociological and cultural issues intersect. Discussions within this analysis relate to the emergence, role, function, diffusion, impact, and meaning of sport communication across time and societies. Many aspects of society are reflected and sustained through sport communication. We examine many of these aspects, including looking at how culture, structure, myths (e.g., heroes, villains), socialization, values, social policies, norms (e.g., commentary), and power relationships (e.g., racism, sexism, ageism) are often facilitated through sport communication. Some of the key cultural and sociological issues analyzed are those related to enjoyment, marketability of violence, gender, race and ethnicity, nationalism, and current sociological issues affecting the sport media. Because of the sport media's impact on sociocultural issues, this chapter also examines gatekeepers' ability to reflect, create, shape, reinforce, and sustain myths, values, perceptions, power structures, and societal beliefs.

Chapter 14 examines the legal issues surrounding sport communication. Because of the uniqueness, impact, and history of the relationship between athletes and the press, the chapter begins with an analysis of this relationship. Included in this analysis are the legal rights of those in sport journalism to acquire, report, and publish information relative to athletes and sport entities. The chapter analyzes constitutional issues, such as the First Amendment (freedom of the press) and its connection to sport journalists and the sport media. Included in the examination of the limits of the press are topical analyses of defamation law, right to privacy, copyright and trademark, and right of publicity. The chapter concludes by assessing technology's impact on legal issues in sport communication (e.g., real-time scores, online fantasy sport leagues) and by examining the rights of reporters to access locker rooms.

CHAPTER 13

Sociological Aspects of Sport Communication

LEARNING OBJECTIVES

▶ To understand the impact of the sport media on society

▶ To consider how the sport media create and reinforce social myths and to examine sport media portrayals of sociocultural issues prevalent in society

▶ To appreciate the sociocultural, historical, and political elements of sport communication

▶ To recognize the role of sport communication in maintaining or dispelling the status quo relative to race, gender, nationalism, and violence

▶ To become familiar with the roles of the mainstream versus alternative media in promoting diversity through hiring processes and through portrayals of ethnic minorities

PROFILE OF A SPORT COMMUNICATOR

Bryant Gumbel

For coverage of the mass media, sport, and sociology, there is no better television sports magazine to watch than *REAL Sports With Bryant Gumbel.* The monthly show, which celebrated its 10th anniversary in 2005, has aired more than 100 episodes on HBO Sports. Bryant Gumbel and his colleagues (producers and correspondents) have won Sports Emmy Awards in the category of outstanding sport journalism because they go beyond what is typically covered in the sport media. "Since we are free of the entanglements associated with commitments to leagues and sponsors, we are able to deal with sports in the kind of honest and straightforward fashion that others can't and don't," explained Gumbel ("About the 10th Anniversary Show," 2006, ¶7).

The correspondents are the top sports reporters and commentators in the field, led by Frank Deford. This legendary sport journalist and James Brown are the only two correspondents who started with the program in 1995. Since the first show, the staff has grown in stature and appeal with the inclusion of Mary Carillo (1997), Armen Keteyian (1998), and Bernard Goldberg (1999). Their investigative reports, human interest stories, and exclusive interviews are unrivaled in the business. It is no surprise that the *Los Angeles Times* called the show "flat out TV's best sports program."

The opinionated and controversial Gumbel was not always well received before taking on the position as host of *REAL Sports.* As Alynda Wheat noted (before she provided a positive review of his show), "When we first noticed him, he was pretty and pompous as the smarter-than-thou host of NBC's *Today* show, pounding his interview subjects into submission with his brainpower and unrelenting questions. He didn't mix at all with the fashion and cooking segments" (2003, ¶1). His work and approach on *REAL Sports* mixes well because of the changes in the sport industry. Gumbel has stated that the show was "spawned by the fact that sports have changed dramatically, that it's no longer just fun and games, and that what happens

Disabilities in sport is one of the many sociological issues covered by Bryant Gumbel and his investigative team of sport journalists in their program, *REAL Sports With Bryant Gumbel.*

off the field, beyond the scores, is worthy of some serious reporting" ("REAL Sports," 2006, ¶1).

Before the movie *Glory Road, REAL Sports* examined the Texas Western basketball team that won the national championship in 1966. The Miners had the first all-black starting lineup in NCAA basketball championship history. Five years before the steroids issues became big news in 2005, *REAL Sports* covered the use of steroids in Major League Baseball. The show—which includes four episodes each airing—has produced other captivating reports dealing with issues such as sports violence, leadership in the Olympics, disabilities in sport, participation in sports by children and youth, counterfeit golf clubs, imprisoned athletes, women in all-male golf clubs, health issues in sport, and a host of other sociological and cultural topics. This chapter provides the theoretical overview for many of the topics that are examined in Gumbel's hard-hitting and highly rated program.

Scholars have long suggested that the media have a pervasive impact on society and culture. The media possess the power to make social myths into social realities, shaping our perceptions. The sport media affect the sport culture in the same manner. As Billings (2003) suggested, notable differences in coverage and characterizations mold the manner in which the sporting public and society in general perceive the myths of sport. In this process, these myths become reality and media bias will become society's bias.

The media reflect society, but they are also instrumental in creating society's perception. Lippmann (1922) suggested that what the media report as news is different than truth. In selecting which stories to report as the news, the media create and fortify stereotypes because of the public's limited experience with these issues. As we examined in chapter 4, the members of the media, through their ability as gatekeepers, essentially tell the public what it should think about, and in some instances how it should think. In studies of presidential campaigns, McCombs and Shaw (1972) determined that issues characterized by the public as significant political issues were those issues that were most often discussed in the mass media. Therefore, the mass media play a key role in shaping public opinion. From their research, the two scholars developed the agenda-setting theory, which illustrates that the media, as gatekeepers of information, shape the public's thoughts. In doing so, the media essentially create the perception that certain topics and issues are more important than others (McCombs & Shaw, 1972).

Although the mass media have power to influence and reinforce culture, they also have the power to create culture. Through this power, the media shape our beliefs and values and correspondingly shape our society, shape the dynamics of sport entities, shape the sport culture, and shape the public's perceptions of sport.

In this chapter we explore the intersection of and relationship between sport communication and sociocultural issues such as gender, ethnicity, violence, nationalism, and popular culture. Discussions within this analysis will relate to the emergence, role, function, diffusion, impact, and meaning of sport communication across time and societies. Many aspects of society are facilitated through sport communication, and we will examine many of these aspects, including looking at how culture, structure, myths, socialization, values, social policies, norms, and power relationships are facilitated through sport communication. The first key cultural theme discussed pertains to race and ethnicity.

RACE AND ETHNICITY

The sport media are often scrutinized and criticized for their coverage and portrayals of minorities. Similarly, sport media entities and sport organizations are criticized for not hiring and promoting minorities.

Media's Coverage of African-Americans

Until the mid-1970s, African-Americans received very limited coverage in the sport media. Although coverage has increased, it often focuses on a few sports such as football, basketball, and baseball. The lack of coverage and the manner in which African-American athletes are portrayed in the sport media often places them in secondary or entertainment roles. Many suggest that this reassures members of the majority that their dominance is not being threatened. This type of coverage, or lack thereof, marginalizes the many accomplishments and contributions

Basketball legends John Thompson (left) and Bill Russell talk while observing a game. Both have been sports television analysts at some point in their careers. Russell, one of the greatest players in the history of the NBA, was a leading figure in promoting African-American rights. Tony Kornheiser, a *Washington Post* sports columnist and cohost of *Pardon The Interruption* on ESPN, once wrote that "Russell represented a new type of black athlete: the educated, outspoken, defiant star seeking—no, expecting—respect just for who he was. In 1961, Russell boycotted an exhibition game in Lexington, Kentucky, when two of his teammates were refused service in a hotel coffee shop."

of minority athletes to sport (Bernstein & Blain, 2002).

The marginalization of minority athletes occurs in various ways. Communication scholars note that Caucasians receive more praise and less criticism in commentary examined during NFL games (Murrell & Curtis, 1994). European-American colleges tend to receive more positive story headlines compared with predominantly African-American colleges. In addition to providing praise and criticism, sport media coverage implies a relationship between race and ability (Bass, 2001; Billings & Eastman, 2002, 2003; Denham, Billings, & Halone, 2002; Mathisen & Mathisen, 1991; Sabo, Jansen, Tate, & Duncan, 1996). Often, performances of African-American and minority athletes are characterized by uncontrollable external forces, whereas the performances of European-Americans are differentiated by controllable internal forces. The sport media describe African-Americans

as having natural athletic abilities, noting that these athletes possess a superior physiology and are naturally quick. Furthermore, the sport media focus on the central roles of European-American athletes and highlight their contributions on the field as integral to the outcome of the competition. By focusing on the cerebral or the "thinking" abilities of Caucasians, the sport media create the impression in the minds of the public that minority athletes make poor team leaders, coaches, or administrators because they lack the knowledge and thinking skills necessary to function and succeed in these roles. Because of this type of coverage, society essentially will often view African-American athletes as dunces while considering European-Americans as mentally astute.

Sailes (2000) noted that the dunce stereotype of athletes began in 500 BC when Greek athletes were disparaged for spending significant amounts of time preparing to perform rather than spending time to enhance their mental development. The philosophers and scholars of the time often portrayed these athletes as inadequate and uninformed citizens with inept minds (Coakley, 2004). Sailes (1993) suggested that sport media coverage has helped create a similar perception of athletes in modern society and that this is a predominant theme in American sports culture. For example, college students have expressed various and distinct perceptions relative to student-athletes. College students perceive that athletes cannot function well in the classroom and do not possess the ability to earn high grades. College students noted feelings that professors "gave" athletes grades rather than athletes having to earn grades, and that athletes simply enrolled in "easy" courses to maintain eligibility. College students also believed that African-American athletes were less qualified and less prepared to enter and to attend college and were admitted solely based on their athletic abilities (Sailes, 1993). As Sailes (1993) suggested, college students perceive student-athletes as "dumb jocks," but they perceive African-American student athletes as the most inadequate. Although this perception is widely accepted, no evidence exists to support the belief that athletes, including African-American athletes, are

dunces (Nixon, 1982). This stereotype may be perpetuated by the graduation rates of student athletes and, in particular, the graduation rates of African-American student athletes. Of the football teams participating in the 2005 Bowl Championship Series, approximately 49% had a graduation rate of less than 50%. Additionally, approximately 41% of football teams earned scores less than the NCAA's standard academic progress rate of 925. Of those same teams in 2005, 67% graduated fewer than half of African-American student athletes (Lapchick, 2005).

In addition, the media often portray African-American athletes as deviant and violent. They are characterized or stereotyped as "thugs" who are uncontrollable, excessive in their habits, and addicted to drugs and gambling. Examples of this can be seen in media portrayals of Mike Tyson, Ray Lewis, and Marcus Vick. This fosters the idea that African-American athletes are overly aggressive or "animal-like." It is theorized that these stereotypes resulted as a creation of Caucasians who desired to maintain a superior position in society as African-Americans began to make significant strides and contributions (Coakley, 2004; Leonard, 1998; Lombardo, 1978; Sailes, 2000). A recent example includes media reports focusing on Terrell

Mutual Impact of Sociocultural Issues and Sport

Race issues were covered by the media during the 1968 Olympics because of an event that was broadcast on a large scale, with ABC providing 44 hours of programming that attracted an estimated audience of 400 million viewers worldwide. The event—the "black power" salute by American sprinters Tommie Smith and John Carlos on the medal stand—provides yet another example of sport as a vehicle for highlighting political and nationalistic issues. The salute, commonly referred to as "fists of freedom," was a response to the social and political unrest occurring in the United States at the time. The two wore black gloves and black stockings with no shoes. Smith also had a black scarf on his neck. During the U.S. national anthem, they raised their clenched

fists in the air and bowed their heads in the award ceremony for the 200-meter race. The protest was in response to requests made by noted sociologist Dr. Harry Edwards that African-American athletes boycott the Games to rally against the treatment of African-Americans in the United States and illustrate to the world that the Civil Rights movement was not yet complete. In lieu of the boycott, the two planned the nonviolent protest, and the incident is one of the most memorable medal ceremonies in Olympic history. It illustrates the impact of sport on sociocultural issues and also highlights the influence of sociocultural issues on sport (Bass, 2002; Gettings, 2005).

Owens' contract negotiations and interaction with teammates while playing for the Philadelphia Eagles and the Dallas Cowboys. The sport media's portrayal of Owens has largely affected the public's perception of him.

The influence of media portrayal is also evident in the struggles and triumphs of boxer Jack Johnson. Johnson was the first African-American heavyweight champion of the world. Johnson defeated Caucasian Tommy Burns in Australia to become the heavyweight champion in 1908. According to Randy Roberts, the media's response was one of despair. "The press reacted as if Armageddon was here. That this may be the moment when it all starts to fall apart for white society" (Burns, 2005). Many in the press suggested that John-

son didn't truly win or earn the title because he had not beaten the longtime heavyweight champion Jim Jeffries. Members of the boxing community coerced Jeffries out of retirement to face Johnson, a bout in which the press warned African-Americans "not to be too proud." Johnson won the bout, knocking out Jeffries. As a response to his victory, Congress passed legislation forbidding the transport of films depicting the victory. Johnson was also portrayed by many in the press as a "bad nigger" for dating Caucasian females. He was eventually arrested and jailed for a bogus violation of the Mann Act, which prohibited the transport of females in interstate commerce for the purpose of prostitution or for immoral purposes (Burns, 2005).

Glory Road was a blockbuster sports movie in 2006. The movie—and the book of the same name—is about Texas Western University coach Don Haskins and the first-ever all-African-American starting lineup in NCAA basketball championship history. The victory by the Miners in that 1966 championship broke barriers of segregation and influenced society during a critical time in the history of the United States. Nevil "The Shadow" Shed, posing with a young fan during the 2006 Men's Final Four, hit the free throw that put the Miners up for good in the game *Sports Illustrated* called "a contest for racial honors."

The media also cover race issues in block-buster movies such as *Remember the Titans* and *Glory Road*. The latter, which was released in 2006, highlights sociocultural issues in sport and how sport is a microcosm of society. The film details the plight of legendary NCAA basketball coach Don Haskins. Haskins actively recruited African-American athletes and was the first coach to start five African-American players in an NCAA game. His Texas Western team defeated Coach Adolf Rupp's top-ranked University of Kentucky for the 1966 NCAA Championship. Haskins and his players were often chastised, harassed, and threatened, which reflected the prevailing attitudes in American society during this era.

In general, the sport media have limited their coverage of African-American female athletes (Hardin et al., 2004). However, when the media do cover African-American female athletes, the media marginalize their performances by characterizing them in certain ways. In sport media commentary, African-American female athletes are often compared to animals. For example, a commentator might say, "She's as fast as a cheetah." This has been examined by Collins (1994), Smith (2000), and Williams (1994). These scholars note that African-American female athletes endure great stigmas in the sport media and in society because of their status as females and as African-Americans. They are forced to function in two worlds, one in which they are oppressed and one in which they are exploited. It is theorized that the lack of mainstream media coverage of African-American female athletes is a result of both their gender and their race. According to the scholars noted previously, the African-American female's experience in sport is much different from that of her Caucasian counterparts. A lack of coverage and a lack of research focusing on African-American female athletes have led to a distorted perception of their experiences in sport.

This lack of coverage dramatically limits society's awareness and acceptance of the African-American female athlete. This suggests that "White America, for the most part, is unaware and perhaps even uninterested in the realities of the sport experience for the African American sportswoman" (Corbett & Johnson, 2000, p. 207). Thus, the media not only create but enhance these stereotypes and, in doing so, preserve the status quo in lieu of advocating social acceptance and change (Rintala & Birrell, 1984). The difference in coverage of African-American female athletes between the mainstream Caucasian press and the African-American press parallels the coverage recounting Jackie Robinson's integration of baseball. Lamb (2004) noted that "reporting in the mainstream press was limited by a mindset that prevented white reporters, their newspapers, and their readers from appreciating the historical significance of Jackie Robinson's 1946 spring training. To black sportswriters and their readers, however, the story clearly symbolized the hopes and the dreams of integration, not merely on a ball field but in society" (Lamb, 2004, p. 7).

Media's Coverage of Other Minorities

Similar to the characterizations of African-American athletes are the depictions of Native American, Latin-American, and Asian-American athletes. Much discussion has centered on the use of Native American mascots by sport entities, and the NCAA recently instituted a ban on the use of such mascots. This has affected institutions like the University of Illinois and the University of North Dakota. Similarly, professional franchises like the Washington Redskins, the Cleveland Indians, and the Atlanta Braves make these mascots focal points of their organizations. Many argue that the use of such mascots makes a mockery of Native Americans, their culture, and their contributions to society. As sport management scholar Ellen Staurowsky (2004) noted, "The manufactured images of American Indians that serve to mark and market athletic teams in the United States contribute to the relegation of American Indians to the past, casting them in limited social roles" (p. 12). Strong (2004) supported this, saying that "the use of Indian sports mascots, logos, and rituals are just such normalized everyday activities; they exclude contemporary Native

Americans from full citizenship by treating them as signs rather than as speakers, as caricatures rather than as players and consumers, as commodities rather than as citizens" (p. 83). Many argue that the use of these mascots is intended to honor Native Americans. Others suggest that this is simply another attempt to limit the legitimate role of Native Americans in American society. "Because members of the dominant culture 'identify' with the invented tradition of Indianness embodied in mascots, they believe that their intention to honor the Indian warrior tradition carries more weight than the dishonor and disrespect experienced by many Native Americans" (Strong, 2004, p. 82). This is largely attributable to what was characterized by C.R. King (2004) as an attempt on behalf of Caucasian-centered society to "lay claim to Indianness as well as the authority to delimit how it enters into public culture" (p. 5).

Latin-American athletes are often portrayed in the sport media as "hot tempered," whereas Asian-American athletes are viewed as the "model minority." The model minority stigma suggests that Asian-American athletes are obsessive conformers, rigorously self-disciplined people, and excessively hard workers (Mayeda, 1999; Wong, Lai, Nagasawa, & Lin, 1998). Depictions of Asian athletes born in the United States, such as Michael Chang and Kristi Yamaguchi, differ from portrayals of Asian nationals who play professionally in the United States. The influx of Asian nationals into Major League Baseball has often been characterized by journalists as an "Asian invasion." Journalists characterized the pitching style of Chan Ho Park as "so foreign." It is suggested that this stereotype portrays Asians as hostile foreigners (Mayeda, 1999; Wong et al., 1998).

Employment Opportunities for Minorities

The portrayals of minorities in the sport media may be attributed to the lack of minorities working in the sport media and the lack of minorities working in sport organizations. Caucasian males continue to dominate the media, particularly in sport. Few African-American males are represented, and even fewer African-American women serve in these roles (American Press Institute, 2002). This pattern holds true in sport organizations as well. The NBA has been rated as one of the best in the major leagues for providing minorities with professional opportunities. However, minorities constitute only 29% of employees at the NBA's league offices. Minorities have been presented with fewer opportunities in the other major leagues. The NCAA also is one of the best sport organizations encouraging diversity. African-Americans constitute 23% of NCAA administrators, and this number has increased in the last several years. Although more minorities are now being hired, few minorities are in high-level management positions (Lapchick, 2004). Additionally, Cunningham and Sagas (2005) illustrated that Caucasian head coaches in intercollegiate basketball are more likely to have Caucasian assistant coaches. African-Americans are consistently underrepresented on the coaching staffs in intercollegiate basketball, especially the coaching staffs of Caucasian head coaches. In contrast, African-American head coaches are far more likely than Caucasian head coaches to hire African-American assistants (Cunningham & Sagas, 2005).

These stereotypes of minorities in the sport media and the lack of minorities in positions within the sport media and within sport organizations deny minorities the prestige they have earned by portraying them as less deserving than their Caucasian counterparts. These characterizations limit opportunities for minorities to obtain quality endorsements, play particular positions, and become sport leaders or administrators.

FEMALES AND THE SPORT MEDIA

Just as the sport media have been criticized for their coverage of minorities, they are equally scrutinized for their coverage of female athletes. It is often perceived that the media, through their commentary and amount and type of coverage, devalue and downplay the accomplishments and contributions of females in sport. The sport media characterize females differently than males, focusing on their familial relationships and their physical attractiveness rather than their performances on the fields of play. Similarly, the working environment for women in the sport media is often characterized as challenging. Female sport reporters sometimes face the same type of marginalization as women on the field.

Coverage of Female Athletes

Considered the last bastion of male dominance, the sport media have consistently neglected to provide equitable coverage to female athletics. Females are dramatically underrepresented in sport media coverage. The amount of coverage received by female athletes is usually far less than the coverage for their male counterparts at all levels (Eastman & Billings, 2000; Kane, 1989, 2002; Kane & Greendorfer, 1994; Pedersen, 2002b). This lack of coverage creates the perception that female athletics are less worthy, lack competitiveness, and lack quality for the sport viewer. Bernstein and Blain (2002) suggested that "this severe under-representation creates the impression that women athletes are of little importance in the sporting world" (p. 7). As Kane (2002) noted, the sport media's marginalization of women's sport "denies them the status, power, and prestige that are routinely given to male athletes" (p. 115).

Characterizations of Females in Sport

Not only do female athletes receive less coverage, but the coverage they receive is often biased in characterizations as well as performances. Scholars have long noted differences in coverage based on attractiveness and appropriate gender participation. In fact, sport participation and sport coverage have been classified by some exclusively on the basis of gender bias. Men's sports would include high-contact sports such as basketball, football, or hockey, whereas women's sports would include those requiring more finesse like figure skating or

gymnastics (Harrison, Lee, & Belcher, 1999; Mateo, 1986). Females receive coverage in the sport media when participating in a socially acceptable or gender-appropriate sport such as tennis, figure skating, or gymnastics (Kane, 1989; Matteo, 1986; Reid & Soley, 1979; Tuggle & Owen, 1999). Past research has revealed that NBC focused its coverage of females during the 1996 Atlanta Olympics almost solely on the visually appealing or visually attractive sports rather than sports such as field hockey, softball, soccer, shot put, and discus (Tuggle & Owen, 1999). This feeds into Wolf's (2002) beauty myth, which essentially theorizes that mass media have affected females' concept of beauty and, in doing so, have placed false ideologies of women in society. Wolf (2002) noted that the concept of beauty, sparked during the Industrial Revolution, has evolved over time. However, the media's portrayal of beauty has painted an unrealistic picture in the minds of not only women but society as well. The beauty myth creates a perception in society that if a female is successful, she must not be beautiful. In other words, physical beauty is a tradeoff for intelligence and talent. This is seen in sport in a myriad of ways. Anna Kournikova has consistently been portrayed in the media as a no-talent vixen focusing more on her endorsements and modeling than on the sport of tennis. Although Kournikova never earned a Grand Slam singles title, she was quite successful in doubles with partner Martina Hingis, winning several Grand Slam doubles titles.

Females in sport have consistently been examined based on their physical attractiveness, with many facing the stereotype of looking like a "butch" (Cahn, 1993). "Women athletes invoked condemnation as often as praise. Critics ranged from physicians and physical educators to sportswriters, male athletic officials, and casual observers. In their view, strenuous athletic pursuits endangered women and threatened the stability of society. They maintained that women athletes would become manlike, adopting masculine dress, talk, and mannerisms. They contended that too much exercise would damage female reproductive capacity . . . that the excitement of sport would cause women to lose control, conjuring up images of frenzied, distraught co-eds on the verge of moral, physical, and emotional breakdown. These fears collapsed into an all-encompassing concept of 'mannishness', a term signifying female masculinity" (Cahn, 1993, p. 345.) Golden age of sport journalist Paul Gallico profiled champion all-around athlete Babe Didrikson as a muscle moll who lacked femininity (Harper, 1999, p. 463).

Eastman and Billings (1999) examined portrayals of athletes during the 1994, 1996, and 1998 Olympics and specifically characterized commentators' statements relative to physical attractiveness of both male and female athletes. Their examination revealed that commentators made significantly more statements regarding the physical attractiveness of females than when discussing performances of male athletes in each telecast. Similarly, commentators made almost twice as many statements about the physical prowess and strength of male athletes compared with their comments focusing on the physical prowess of female athletes (Eastman & Billings, 1999).

The differentiation of media coverage for males and females is further defined by the manner in which they are portrayed in the sports pages. Males are most often characterized by their physical and athletic abilities. In contrast, females are depicted in terms related to their physical attractiveness and their femininity (Kane & Parks, 1992). This "sexualization" of female athletes "trivializes them and robs them of athletic legitimacy" (Bernstein & Blain, 2002, p. 8). When photographs of female athletes appear in the sport pages, they most often depict the athletes in nonactive roles. This is in stark contrast to photographs of male athletes (Salwen, 1994). *Sports Illustrated*'s Rick Reilly asserts that "if you are a woman, there are only three ways to get the sports world to notice you: strip down to your panties and bra and wrestle over beer; play crappy tennis but look hot pulling the second ball out of your briefs; or tweak Hootie's nose" (Reilly, 2003b, p. 94). Reilly is referring to the sport media's almost constant coverage of retired professional tennis player Anna Kournikova and the media's character-

ization of Martha Burke's ongoing battle with Augusta National's chairman Hootie Johnson. Kournikova received countless hours of media coverage despite consistently performing poorly in singles events, whereas Burke's disdain with Johnson's refusal to allow females to join the legendary golf club regularly made the sports pages.

Gender Marking

Additional examinations support a sport media bias, determining that coverage and acceptance of females as athletes depend on their ability to manage traditional feminine roles while pursuing a career in athletics. If this balance is not achieved, female athletes do not gain acceptance (Hilliard, 1983). This often takes place through gender marking. Gender marking usually occurs when male athletes are described as affecting the sport through their performance or through some outstanding aspect of their performance. For example, a commentator may emphasize that an athlete's rebounding skills are the best in the sport. In contrast, female athletes are gender marked when commentators purposefully note that their performance is outstanding but only relative to other women's performances. A female athlete may have outstanding rebounding skills but instead of referring to these skills as the "best" in the game, commentators note that these skills are the "best" in women's basketball. This would indicate that female athletes' skills and talents are not significant enough to stand out in the sport, but are only good enough to stand out compared with female counterparts. Halbert and Latimer (1994) noted that gender marking enhances and supports the bias against female athletes by qualifying their abilities. "By using traditional definitions of 'female' and 'femininity' as the antithesis of 'athlete' and 'athletic', the de facto norm or standard against which performance is measured becomes maleness or 'masculinity'" (Creedon, 1998, p. 90).

Naming Practices

Naming practices also are problematic in the coverage of female sports. Female athletes are often referred to by their first names, whereas male athletes are referred to by their last names (Billings, 2003; Halbert & Latimer, 1994; Messner, Duncan, & Jensen, 1993). It is theorized that using athletes' last names distances them from viewers, and this distance assists in creating the perception that these athletes are first-class and heroic (Billings, 2003). Furthermore, the media attribute male athletes' successes to exceptional courage, experience, skill, and composure (Billings, 2003; Eastman & Billings, 1999; Halbert & Latimer, 1994). Females' achievements, on the other hand, are often linked to interpersonal relationships, signifying their dependency on significant others.

Theory of Hegemony

Creedon (1998) asserted that the sports coverage hierarchical model is a manifestation of the hegemony of a gendered media. Hegemony refers to a dominant group's ability to establish and maintain power over other groups (Pedersen, 2002a). Sport is considered a male domain, and according to the theory of hegemony, females threaten the hegemonic structure in sport (Whisenant & Pedersen, 2004a). By increasing the amount of coverage of female sport and by modifying the manner in which female athletes are characterized, the media would essentially reinforce females' threat to male hegemony. Recent research reveals that sport editors make little effort to determine what readers prefer, and many sports editors consider female athletics as inferior to male athletics. Furthermore, some sports editors indicated a lack of obligation to cover women's sport (Hardin, 2005).

Working Environment for Females in Sport

Not only do female athletes and coaches receive less media coverage than their male colleagues, but female sport journalists consistently struggle with opportunities and advancement in sport journalism careers. Sport has traditionally been slow in allowing women to participate in sport as athletes, as coaches, and as administrators and to speak as experts about sport-related topics (Hertz, 2000;

Staurowsky & DiManno, 2002). In fact, some sports editors noted a lack of obligation to hire women to cover women's sport (Hardin, 2005). As noted previously, hegemonic masculinity maintains male dominance in sport, and, thus, males exert power over females (Pedersen, Whisenant, & Schneider, 2003).

Female sport journalists strive to legitimize their role within sport journalism and face numerous barriers in doing so (Humms, O'Bryant, & Tremble, 1996; Neupauer, 1998; Schell & Rodriguez, 2000). Women's entrance into that male domain threatens the hegemonic masculinity associated with sport. Most often, this is manifested and reinforced in the locker room, where the presence of female journalists threatens the traditional power structure. This is especially true when the female is in a position to critique and to make public an evaluation of the male's performance (Kane & Disch, 1993).

This is exemplified through the struggles of *Boston Herald* reporter Lisa Olson. Olson was sexually harassed in 1990 in the New England Patriots locker room by members of the football team who thrust their genitals at her insisting that her purpose in the locker room was specifically to see them naked. After she reported the incident to her editor, it became front-page news, resulting in the then owner of the Patriots, Victor Kiam, to refer to Olson as a "classic bitch." In response, the NFL launched an independent investigation, which in turn prompted much debate on the presence of female sports reporters in the locker rooms. Many justified the treatment of Olson by arguing that she was simply asking for trouble by being in the locker room. Others rejected this claim, noting that females should have equal access to athletes and coaches to perform their duties as sports reporters (Disch & Kane, 1996). Professional sport leagues now have a policy allowing women in the locker room.

Hegemonic masculinity is upheld through discriminatory hiring practices as well as unfair opportunities for advancement, payment, and recognition. Just as women are underrepresented in administrative roles within athletic departments and professional sport organizations, they are underrepresented

© Paul M. Pedersen

Female athletes are often marginalized, trivialized, or ignored by the sport media. This often occurs because of the hegemonic nature of the print and broadcast media (Pedersen, Whisenant, & Schneider, 2003). Although attitudes are changing and there are many opportunities for women in the sport media, there are still many challenges in working in an environment considered by some as a male domain.

in sports departments across the United States (Arnold & Skinew, 1997; Humms et al., 1996; Miloch, Pedersen, Smucker, & Whisenant, 2005). Schell and Rodriguez (2000) noted that "playing, coaching, supervising, and reporting are four occupational aspects of sport dominated by males" (p. 21). Males tend to dominate supervisory roles and sports reporting (Miloch et al., 2005). This trend holds true for the general broadcast media as well, with women holding only 26.5% of management positions in television and 14.4% in radio (American Press Institute, 2002).

Additionally, fewer women are assigned to cover sport than any other beat (Hardin, 2005). This is characteristic of male hegemony. Females did not gain access to male locker rooms until 1990 after the incident involving Lisa Olson. Female sport journalists have faced much harassment from athletes, fellow sport journalists, and other industry workers (Cann & Mohr, 2001; Eberhard & Myers, 1988; Kane & Disch, 1993; Miller & Miller, 1995; Padgett, 1998; Walsh-Childers, Chance, & Herzong, 1996). Female sport journalists must fight for equal pay, face discrimination from male colleagues, and endure unrealistic assumptions, criticism, condescension, sexual harassment, and social isolation (Acosta & Carpenter, 2000; Enda, 2002; Hertz, 2000; Staurowsky & DiManno, 2002). Although more women are covering sports, women have made limited headway in attaining influential roles within their field (Dodds, 2000; Salwen

& Garrison, 1998). The hegemonic structure of sport and the sport media has impeded women sports reporters. "By limiting women's opportunities and rewarding them less for similar performances, the hegemonic ideology persuasively . . . portrays women as less deserving of access to jobs and money" (Schell & Rodriguez, 2000, p. 23).

According to Miloch and colleagues (2005), female sport journalists have endured discrimination, yet improvements have been made. Most female journalists have had limited access to key sources and have faced this discrimination from athletes and coaches. Female sport journalists note bias on behalf of athletes and peers, and many have encountered discrimination before entering the profession. Undergraduates preparing to enter the field have noted facing sexual objectification and sexism in a work environment (Staurowsky & DiManno, 2002). Although there is still much work to be done to improve the coverage of female athletes and the working environment for women in the sport media, females who are interested in sport communication should not hesitate to pursue this career ambition. As Andrew McGowan and Gregory Bouris (2005) noted, "Despite the fact that men seem to dominate most sport organizations, women have an equal opportunity to gain internships and full-time opportunities in the area of sport communications" (p. 354).

NATIONALISM AND THE SPORT MEDIA

Nationalism can best be defined as identification with the life and aspirations of the fellow members of a nation, even when we do not know these citizens or we have not seen the boundaries of the nation in its entirety (Wenner, 1998b). Nationalism is a type of national mythmaking that comes about by using stereotypes that signify the ethical and cultural norms that shape, generate, or reinforce habits among the nation's citizens (Wenner, 1998b). Nationalism is often reinforced through the media and, specifically, the sport media. Sport is the most appropri-

ate means of creating an imagery of national unity. Bernstein and Blain (2002) noted that the media serve as powerful agents providing significant symbolic material to facilitate nationalistic emotions.

Nationalistic images can be seen in the sport media throughout history, and often these images reflect the tenor of society at the time. Many of these nationalistic images can be seen during the Olympics and media coverage of the Olympics. Guttman (2002) noted that nationalism has a prominent theme in the Olympics. In researching the early Olympic Games, Guttman (2002) quoted Charles Maurras as saying, "I see that your internationalism . . . does not kill national spirit—it strengthens it" (p. 19). This sense of nationalism was certainly evident in the 1936 Olympic Games. Referred to as the Nazi Games, the 1936 Olympics were used by Adolf Hitler as a forum to establish his agenda. Hitler exploited the attention surrounding the games to create the perception that Germany was a tolerant and peaceful nation. The anti-Semitic propaganda was removed, and approximately 20 transmitting vans and 300 microphones were provided to the foreign media to encourage more radio broadcasts, which were given in 28 different languages. Hitler perceived hosting the Games as a way to prove to the world that Nazi Germany was the most efficient and most superior race in the world. In promoting the Games, Germany used posters and magazine ads that linked Nazi Germany to ancient Greece. The ads depicted what Hitler believed to be the ideal race: blue eyes, blonde hair, distinct features, and heroic. After the Games, Germany dramatically advanced its Nazi political agenda resulting in an invasion of Poland, World War II, and the Holocaust.

American track athlete Jesse Owens won four gold medals at the 1936 Olympics and disproved the alleged Aryan myth of racial superiority. Pamela C. Laucella (2004) found that sport journalists at mainstream newspapers respected Owens' talent yet were descriptive, stylistic, and evasive in dealing with racial and political issues. They referred to Owens and other African-American athletes as African or Ethiopian and discussed alleged

The mass media often ignore female athletes and women's sports. Furthermore, the print and broadcast media often fail to examine the underrepresentation of females in coaching (e.g., Notre Dame's Muffet McGraw) and administrative positions. A recent survey of 25 intercollegiate sports found that women are the head coaches of the majority of women's teams in only seven of the surveyed sports.

genetic variances between the races, focusing on African-Americans' speed and agility and downplaying their intelligence. Whereas mainstream writers failed to challenge or change the status quo, the journalists of the African-American press "remained passive yet resolute in emphasizing Owens' place in history while denouncing Adolph Hitler and Nazism" (Laucella, 2004, pp. iii-iv). They touted American athletes' accomplishments and established equitable treatment of all athletes while deriding Hitler. The journalists at the American Communist press were forthright and forceful in promoting equal rights and opportunities for all Americans.

"They deprecated Hitler and the Nazis and everything for which they stood, including their propaganda, racial supremacy logic, and ideologies," noted Laucella (2004, pp. iii-iv).

Other examples can be seen in the portrayal of different nationalities in the sport media. Japanese have often been portrayed as possessing a passion for sport. However, it is often noted in the media that the Japanese rarely succeed in sport and that this is a result of their physical limitations relative to height (Mayeda, 1999). Another example includes the media's characterization of the 1980 United States Olympic hockey team's victory over the Soviets at Lake Placid as a "miracle on ice." The victory came at a time when Americans appeared to be losing faith in their leaders and in the country. Confidence was at an all-time low, and many Americans at the time believed that the future was dismal. This was often referred to as a "crisis of confidence." Americans had been taken hostage in Iran, the end of the Vietnam War was still fresh on the minds of many Americans, the Soviet Union had invaded Afghanistan, the United States had endured Watergate, and it was facing an energy crisis and increasing unemployment numbers. Politically, Americans believed the country faced its toughest challenges in years.

The defeat of the Soviets resonated with society and many Americans still believe that defeat was the victory in which the team earned the gold medal when in actuality the team beat Finland in the final round to secure the gold medal. The upset of the Soviets was such a boost to the American psyche that even sport reporters often erroneously forget about the victory over Finland.

Many argue that this victory gave Americans a reason to believe in their country again. Throughout the time leading up the Olympics and during the event itself, the media fed into the stereotypes of Soviet society. The HBO documentary and the movie *Miracle* recount the historic achievement, and these memories and facts are most often recounted with serious nationalistic undertones. Many of these stories characterize the competition for the gold medal as an impossible dream for the American team, referring to it as a "Herculean" task.

Most portrayals of the Soviet players and coaches focus on their work ethic, framing them as robots who showed little emotion and never smiled—even after scoring goals. In many interviews, Soviet team members discussed how playing hockey was their job, and it required separation from their families. These characterizations essentially symbolized the Soviet team as the antithesis to American values and beliefs, setting the tone for a "good versus evil" theme. In fact, members of the American team received many telegraphs before the game indicating American disdain for the Soviet Union and illustrating that the hockey game represented much more to the American public than just a competition between two teams. This is evident in many documentaries in which head coach Herb Brooks discusses the significance of the game to society.

Brooks himself was framed from a distinct nationalistic perspective. He was framed as a magical character with an extreme charisma who brought his team together to defeat the Soviets and move on to capture the gold medal. He was framed as a family man who balanced his familial obligations with his quest for the gold medal, a characterization in stark contrast to the Soviets.

The sense of nationalism, or nation building through sport, is often seen in the sport media. American athletes are often portrayed differently than foreign counterparts, and these portrayals typically reflect American culture. This tends to reinforce stereotypes of certain nations and bonds Americans together in these beliefs. For example, Brazil is synonymous with soccer, rugby is synonymous with New Zealand, and hockey is synonymous with Canada. Sport often builds and reinforces the values, beliefs, and character of nations or regions and, in doing so, unifies its citizens.

CURRENT SOCIOLOGICAL ISSUES AFFECTING SPORT MEDIA

As noted in the preceding pages, the mass media are intertwined with numerous sociological and cultural aspects of sport. Sometimes the mass media reinforce the values and belief in culture, whereas at other times the print and electronic media influence and even help to create sport culture and the public's perceptions of sport. In addition to the sociological issues covered previously (i.e., race, nationalism, sexism), three specific current issues are of particular interest to the topic at hand. The first deals with drugs in sport, whereas the second involves disability in sport. The third issue focuses on sexual orientation and homophobia in sport.

Doping and Steroids

Sport centers on competition, and those who compete desire to win. The desire to win combined with the pressures of high-profile sport often leads athletes, coaches, and administrators to seek means that will assist in winning, and sporting society often turns a blind eye to the use of performance-enhancing drugs. In the 1988 Seoul Olympic trials, American Carl Lewis tested positive for using three stimulants banned by the International Olympic Committee and the U.S. Olympic Committee. Rather than go public with the results, the U.S. Track and Field Federation hid the results from officials and the public (Todd, 2005). Many sport reporters and even Congress allege that Major League Baseball consistently ignored the fact that many of its players were reported to have used performance-enhancing drugs.

Steroids and doping are among the most serious issues plaguing sport. These issues have gripped the global sport community on many occasions and caused the public and members of the industry and media to question the integrity of sport. The Seoul Olympics marked what has been characterized as a benchmark in doping history (Todd, 2005). During the 1988 Seoul Olympics, Canadian Ben Johnson engaged in a legendary 100-meter sprint against American Carl Lewis. Johnson won the race with a time of 9.79. The race has been characterized as one of the best races in Olympic history but also as one of the most tainted races in Olympic history. Two days after the race, Johnson tested positive for stanozolol. Stanozolol is a steroid similar to testosterone, and testing indicated long-term use by Johnson. Johnson, considered the fastest man alive, was stripped of his gold medal. Lewis was awarded the gold medal, and Britain's Linford Christie was awarded the silver medal. Many years after the race, Christie also tested positive. American Dennis Mitchell, who finished fourth in the race, would also test positive later in his career. Johnson's positive tests and revocation of the gold medal created much debate. Canadians began referring to him as "the Jamaican-born Ben Johnson" instead of

the "great Canadian runner," hoping to distance the country from the controversy. Media stories and reports described him as "disgraced runner Ben Johnson" (Todd, 2005). Johnson's time in the 100-meter sprint would not be surpassed until 2002, when American Tim Montgomery would post a time of 9.78. However, Montgomery has since been banned from the sport for steroid use and for his link to the infamous BALCO (Bay Area Lab Co-operative) scandal. His partner, Marion Jones, has also been linked to the BALCO scandal, and her former husband, C.J. Hunter, has alleged that Jones has used banned performance-enhancing drugs. Hunter, a retired shot putter, tested positive for steroids four times before the 2000 Sydney Olympic Games (Gains, 2004).

The BALCO scandal has not only affected the world of track and field but has also dramatically affected Major League Baseball (MLB). In March 2005, high-profile members of MLB were called to testify before Congress regarding an alleged widespread steroid problem within the league. Mark McGwire, Rafael Palmeiro, Jose Canseco, and Curt Schilling, commissioner Bud Selig, and players association executive director Donald Fehr fielded questions from Congress regarding steroids in baseball. All except Canseco denied that steroids were a problem within the league. Canseco had just released his book *Juice* detailing his use of steroids and naming other MLB players who had used steroids as well. One of those players was Palmeiro ("Palmeiro Tested," 2005a). Although Palmeiro denied using steroids, stating that he "never, ever" doped, he later tested positive for stanozolol (Jeansonne & Dobie, 2005). Stanozolol is the same performance-enhancing drug for which Ben Johnson was stripped of his gold medal in the Seoul Olympic Games. After testing positive, Palmeiro claimed he had no idea how the drugs got into his system and said he never intentionally used a steroid ("Palmeiro Tested," 2005b). The congressional hearings served as a catalyst for MLB to initiate a tougher stance and stricter discipline for those players found using performance-enhancing drugs. Palmeiro was the first to be disciplined under MLB's new steroid policy and was suspended for 10 days ("Palmeiro Tested," 2005a). Many still argue that MLB's policy on steroid use is not as strict as it should be and that it lags far behind the standards used by the World Anti-Doping Agency (Jeansonne & Dobie, 2005). Other baseball players admitting to using steroids include Jason Giambi, Jeremy Giambi, Gary Sheffield, Barry Bonds, and his teammates Armando Rios, Benito Santiago, and Bobby Estalella (Jeansonne & Dobie, 2005).

The congressional hearings highlighted the impact of the BALCO scandal not only on MLB but on other sports as well. Although the BALCO scandal seemed to affect MLB and U.S. track and field more than any other sports, its impact was also felt in the National Football League. Bill Romanowski played 16 years in the NFL as a linebacker for the San Francisco 49ers, the Philadelphia Eagles, the Denver Broncos, and the Oakland Raiders. Romanowski retired after testing positive for tetrahydrogestrinone (THG), an anabolic steroid. Other NFL players testing positive for performance-enhancing drugs include Chris Cooper, Barret Robbins, Dana Stubblefield, Johnnie Morton, Daryl Gardener, and Josh Taves. The Carolina Panthers have also dealt with the steroid issue. An alternative medicine doctor allegedly prescribed performance-enhancing drugs to linemen Todd Steussie and Jeff Mitchell and punter Todd Sauerbrum within 2 weeks of the 2004 Super Bowl (Cooper, 2005). The NFL launched an investigation to examine the allegations, and it is anticipated that Congress will use the results to evaluate the NFL's policy on steroids. Congress is also anticipated to discuss implementing legislation to uniformly govern the use of performance-enhancing drugs in all sports (Funk, 2005).

Seven-time Tour de France champion Lance Armstrong has long been accused by competitors and former employees of using performance-enhancing drugs. However, Armstrong firmly denies that he has ever used performance enhancers. It seems that many of the allegations directed at Armstrong stem from the French media and are linked to his 9-year association with Italian physician Michele Ferrari. An Italian court convicted Ferrari of "sporting fraud" in 2004, and Armstrong immediately ended the association. Armstrong has engaged in several legal battles stemming from confrontations with another cyclist during the 2004 event and from various allegations, reports, and the book *LA Confidential: The Secrets of Lance Armstrong*. The book contains allegations by a former masseuse who says she disposed of syringes and collected performance enhancers for Armstrong. Recently, the French newspaper *L'Equipe* reported that Armstrong had tested positive for erythropoietin (EPO), a performance enhancer designed to boost performance by increasing the production of red blood cells. Armstrong denies the claims and has accused the French media as well as Tour de France officials as engaging in a "witch hunt" (Kroichick, 2005). Most recently, Armstrong's former teammate Floyd Landis won the 2006 Tour de France. A short time later, Landis tested positive for elevated testosterone levels. Landis pleaded with the media to provide him with an opportunity to prove his innocence. However, Landis' second test was also positive for performance enhancers. Another of Armstrong's teammates, Frankie Andreu, has disclosed publicly that he used performance enhancers during the 1999 Tour de France in which Armstrong won. However, Andreu has not claimed that Armstrong used performance enhancers (Buckner, 2006; "One Cyclist's Brave Candor," 2006; Robertson, 2006). Regardless, the media often report on and speculate about the many rumors surrounding doping in cycling.

Luschen (2000) illustrated that doping in sport is not a new phenomenon and was considered problematic as early as the 1970s. Recent public concern and governance of doping have resulted from several factors including a wide awareness and acknowledgement of use by numerous athletes, the fact that a small enhancement of performance can lead to a victory, the commercialization of sport and increased salaries of athletes, the wide availability of the performance-enhancing products, and a greater sophistication in methods of control and enforcement (Luschen,

2000). Luschen (2000) also suggested that the media have played a role in cultivating public concern over the issue of steroids through their opinions and stances on the issue. Many in the media have encouraged stricter standards, and, as a result, the public and sporting officials have placed the issue at the forefront of sport (Luschen, 2000).

Disability

As discussed earlier in the chapter, sport reflects society and, in some instances, can spur social change. This is certainly true of sport in its portrayal and integration of disabled people. Disabled athletes face the same challenges as other minority groups in the realm of sport. They struggle to garner much media coverage, and when media coverage is provided, it is often characterized in differing ways. As Nixon (2000) noted, the media have provided more coverage to disabled athletes competing with and against nondisabled athletes in the last 20 years. This coverage has highlighted the participation and prowess of one-armed major leaguers Jim Abbott and Pete Gray. Abbott, a pitcher, and Gray, an outfielder, garnered much attention in the press. Other disabled athletes have received coverage for their participation in sports such as boxing, triathlons, basketball, gymnastics, cycling, sailing, wrestling, swimming, karate, and many others (Nixon, 2000). One of the most prominent disabled athletes gaining much media coverage was PGA golfer Casey Martin. Martin, born with a circulatory defect in his right leg, had a legal battle with PGA officials that resulted in a landmark court decision applying the 1990 Americans with Disabilities Act to sport. Because of his condition, Martin requested to use a golf cart rather than walking the full length of the course during PGA competitions. The PGA argued that this would be an unfair advantage for Martin, whereas Martin argued that the PGA was denying him the opportunity to participate by not allowing him to use a cart during competitions. Ruling in Martin's favor, the court acknowledged that sport at all levels of competition must be accessible to those with disabilities (Agostini, 2005; Bonk, 2005).

Nixon (2000) pointed out that the word *disability* can have a different meaning in the context of sport, an example being when athletes are placed on the "disabled list." Placement on the "disabled list" simply indicates that an athlete is temporarily unable to participate in competition. In contrast, society views "disability" as meaning that a person has a permanent disability, mental or physical, that prevents participation in specific activities but does not necessarily prevent playing and competing in sport. "Thus, a person can be disabled in society, but not be disabled in certain kinds of sports or sports roles" (Nixon, 2000, p. 422). As happened with Casey Martin, sport can assist in shaping the public's perception of those with disabilities in society.

Sexual Orientation

Athletes' sexual orientation is often characterized in the media in a manner to reinforce certain hegemonic ideologies (Butterworth, 2006; Nylund, 2004). "At this historical moment when hegemonic masculinity has been partially destabilized by global economic changes and by gay liberation and feminist movements, the sports media industry seemingly provides a stable and specific view of masculinity grounded in heterosexuality, aggression, individuality, and the objectification of women" (Nyland, 2004, p. 160). Cahn (1993) noted the depictions of Martina Navratilova in the sport media and in the mainstream media, recalling Arsenio Hall's comedic routine in which he asks why we can't put a man on Martina if we can put a man on the moon. Spencer (2003) illustrated that media depictions of Chris Evert and Navratilova are and were quite different now and during the heyday of their rivalry. Navratilova faced a coding of lesbianism, whereas Evert was portrayed as "America's sweetheart." Media framing of Evert reinforced traditional views of heterosexuality and motherhood. Spencer (2003) also noted that Evert's tennis legacy is often linked to current players, including Jennifer Capriati and Martina Hingis. This is in contrast to the tennis legacy of Navratilova, who is often linked to players such as Amélie Mauresmo. Mauresmo was always upfront with the media about her sexual orientation as a lesbian. Because of this, she endured negative comments from fellow players (Spencer, 2003).

Characterizations based on sexual orientation are not limited to females. Many times, portrayals of male athletes also reinforce hegemonic ideologies. Butterworth (2006) suggested that recent media dialogue relative to the sexual orientation of Major League Baseball's Mike Piazza illustrates the perceptions associated with baseball culture. "Piazza's behavior and the discourse surrounding gay identity in baseball call attention to the ways gender is used to mark bodies in sport, to perpetuate normative standards of masculinity, and to discipline those who do not adhere to these norms. . . . Because being gay is equated to being feminine, which in turn is equated to weakness, it is not surprising that very few gay male athletes have publicly disclosed sexuality" (Butterworth, 2006, pp. 138-139).

CHAPTER WRAP-UP

Summary

Scholars have often suggested that the media have a pervasive impact on society and culture. Through their ability to affect society and culture, the media possess the power to make social myths and to reinforce existing beliefs in society. The sport media, through its coverage, affect the sport culture in the same manner. Differences in coverage in the sport media shape the manner in which the public and society perceive sport. The media tell the public what to think about and often tell the public how to think. Through their power as gatekeepers, the media mold our beliefs and values and, in turn, shape our society.

The media reflect society, but they are also instrumental in creating society's perception. Although the mass media might not be able to tell us what to think, they can certainly tell us what to think about. The power of the media to not only influence and reinforce culture but to also create culture must not be ignored. Through this power, the media shape our beliefs and values and correspondingly shape our society, the dynamics of sport entities, the sport culture, and the public's perceptions of sport.

Much of the media's portrayal of sport may be influenced by the lack of diversity in media entities as well as in sport organizations. These entities have become more diverse but minorities consistently remain underrepresented in positions and in managerial roles. This chapter has explored the intersection of and relationship between sport communication and sociocultural issues such as gender, ethnicity, violence, nationalism, and popular culture. The analysis included discussions related to the emergence, role, function, diffusion, impact, and meaning of sport communication across time and societies. This chapter included how culture, structure, myths (e.g., heroes and villains), socialization, values, social policies, norms (e.g., commentary), and power relationships (e.g., race, minorities) are facilitated through sport communication.

Review Questions

1. How do the media shape or reinforce public perception?
2. How do the media often characterize minorities?

3. What are the most common portrayals of females in the sport media?

4. How does male hegemony affect the media's coverage of female sport?

5. What are the ramifications of biased media coverage?

6. What is nationalism and how is it evident in the sport media?

7. How are the sport media a reflection of society?

8. How do the media stereotypes of minorities and females affect sport participation and sport coverage?

9. What are the most common stereotypes of minorities in the sport media?

10. How has doping in sport been characterized in the media?

Discussion Questions

1. In what ways do the sport media characterize minorities?

2. In what ways do the sport media characterize females?

3. How do the sport media assist in building national mythologies?

4. What can be done to encourage more objective media coverage?

5. Why is biased coverage problematic?

6. Is sport media coverage simply a reflection of society or does it influence society's beliefs as the gatekeeper?

7. How do members of the sport media justify biased coverage?

8. What are some examples of biased coverage? Do these biases differ based on medium?

9. What are some examples of nationalistic coverage in the sport media?

10. How have the sport media shaped your perceptions of sport?

Group Activities

1. Form groups of three to five members and select two to three key sociocultural issues prevalent in society. As a group, examine how these issues are portrayed and characterized in the sport media. How do the sport media shape society's beliefs and values on these issues? What are the similarities and differences in characterizations? How would you rate the coverage on these issues?

2. Form groups of three to five members. Each member should select a specific sport medium and examine its sport coverage for 1 week. Examine the amount and type of coverage for female sport compared with male sport. As a group, discuss the amount of coverage given to each gender. How are female athletes characterized? How are male athletes portrayed? How are these characterizations and portrayals similar and how do they contrast?

Individual Exercises

1. Select a sport movie or sport book. After viewing the movie or reading the book, determine what themes are most prevalent. For example, what racial stereotypes are present; how are females portrayed; how are European-Americans positioned within the film or text? Are nationalistic overtones present?

2. Collect the sports section of your local or campus newspaper for 1 week. Examine the photographs included in the section for each day. What ethnic group and what

gender receive the most photographs? How are different ethnic groups and the two genders portrayed in these photographs? How do the photographs reinforce society's existing beliefs about minority and female participation in sport?

3. Collect the sports section of your local newspaper for 1 week. Examine the bylines for the articles and for the photographs. What is the percentage of articles written by females compared with males? What types of stories are crafted by female reporters compared with males? Do the writing styles of females differ from those of males?

4. Tape the sports segment on the evening news for 1 week. Examine the amount and type of coverage relative to minority participation, gender participation, and nationalistic themes. How does the coverage reflect the values and beliefs of society in your region?

Internet Sites for Additional Learning

Association for Women in the Sport Media: www.awsmonline.org/

Institute for Diversity and Ethics in Sport: www.bus.ucf.edu/sport/cgi-bin/site/ sitew.cgi?page = /ides/index.htx

International Sociology of Sport Association: http://u2.u-strasbg.fr/issa/

North American Society for the Sociology of Sport: www.nasss.org/

REAL Sports with Bryant Gumbel: www.hbo.com/realsports/index.html

Representation of Women in Hockey: http://board.uscho.com/showthread. php?t = 39335

CHAPTER 14

Legal Issues in Sport Communication

LEARNING OBJECTIVES

▶ To examine the evolution of player–media relationships and the legal issues related to sport communication

▶ To understand the role of the sport media in informing the sporting public

▶ To become cognizant of the legal cases establishing athletes and coaches as public figures and the evolution of the right of publicity as it pertains to athletes, coaches, and sport entities

▶ To comprehend the legal issues surrounding the legal rights of sport entities to real-time sport information and player statistics

▶ To recognize the legal issues surrounding gender equity and locker-room privileges

PROFILE OF A SPORT COMMUNICATOR

Mark Roesler

Best known for protecting the intellectual property rights of deceased celebrities and sports figures, attorney Mark Roesler is no stranger to key legal issues in sport communication. In fact, Roesler could be considered a sports agent for many deceased celebrities and sports figures. He has represented some of the most high-profile and legendary celebrities and sports figures in many landmark legal battles involving right of publicity, copyright and trademark, and domain name battles. Chairman and CEO of CMG Worldwide, Roesler established the company to provide a range of services instrumental in protecting and marketing the images of deceased celebrities

Baseball great Lou Brock is one of hundreds of entertainment and sports celebrity clients represented by Mark Roesler's CMG Worldwide.

including licensing and merchandising, advertising and endorsements, marketing and public relations, legal representation, consulting and speaking engagements. Central to the company is its specialization in copyright and trademark law and right of publicity. The company represents legendary celebrities and sports figures and their families. Some of the company's most notable clients include Marilyn Monroe, James Dean, Jesse Owens, Jim Thorpe, Robby Gordon, "Sugar" Ray Robinson, Bob Cousy, Babe Ruth, Ty Cobb, Lou Gehrig, Jackie Robinson, Joe DiMaggio, "Shoeless" Joe Jackson, Knute Rockne, Jason Taylor, Arthur Ashe, Andre the Giant, and Howard Cosell.

To put himself through college at DePauw University, Roesler began a roofing company and then became a licensed real estate broker during his years as a law and business student at Indiana University. His first position with Curtis Publishing was instrumental in guiding his career path. He was assigned to legally protect the artwork of Norman Rockwell because the company was the supplier and licenser of *The Saturday Evening Post.*

His work with this art inspired him to explore and protect the legal rights of deceased celebrities and legendary sports figures. He recognized that images of such individuals needed legal protection like those of living celebrities and athletes.

Roesler led the fight for the legal rights of retired Major League Baseball players so they could wear their team uniforms when endorsing products. The case was spawned by Hallmark's use of Babe Ruth in uniform on a jigsaw puzzle packaged with Hallmark cards. Per Major League Baseball's collective bargaining agreement in 1968, players were not allowed to appear for commercial purposes in their uniforms without permission from the league. Since the collective bargaining agreement began addressing this in 1968, Roesler and CMG had a legal license allowing players before 1968 to endorse products while in their uniforms. Roesler and his firm were also instrumental in retaining domain names for clients like Marilyn Monroe and Babe Ruth. As the Internet has expanded in popularity and use, celebrities and sports figures need protection in cyberspace. Roesler was one of the first to recognize this need and is a pioneer in gaining and protecting the legal rights of deceased celebrities and sports figures. Many of the legal issues Roesler addresses are discussed in this chapter and include the right of publicity, copyright, and trademark.

Based on information from www.markroesler.com/about/bio.htm and www.markroesler.com/cmgworldwide/index.htm.

Major League Baseball pitcher Kenny Rogers may be best known as the player who threw a tantrum and shoved a television cameramen. The interview between Pete Rose and Jim Gray at the 1999 Major League Baseball World Series almost upstaged the entire event and spurred ongoing debates at water coolers across the United States. Andre Agassi's breakup with Brooke Shields and marriage to Steffi Graf have been the subject of interviews and color commentary during televised ATP events and Grand Slams such as the Ericcson Open in Miami and the U.S. Open. The media slam-dunked Charles Barkley, printing and broadcasting story after story that he "was not a role model." Magic Johnson, Arthur Ashe, and Greg Louganis were each forced to face the media spotlight and discuss the most intimate details of their lives. Johnson was forced to announce he had HIV, as was Arthur Ashe, and Louganis was forced to admit he was gay and had HIV. Dave Letterman told the world that Jennifer Capriati was banned from Wimbledon because of fears she would "smoke the grass." Billie Jean King and Martina Navratilova were "outted" by the media because of their sexual preference.

Such issues between athletes and the press are now common. Athletes distrust reporters, believing they all have an agenda. Some reporters believe athletes disrespect the journalism profession and are overpaid and uneducated. Laucella and Osborne (2002) suggested that professional respect on behalf of athletes and coaches and the journalist would result in positive and favorable benefits. However, it is often the sport entity's desire to maintain and enhance its image and the journalist's desire to provide the public with much-desired information that lead to an "inherent clash" between sports figures and the media.

Player–media relationships have experienced conflict through history, and the conflict between the two continues to build. It has become the "main event" in the big business of sports. This chapter examines the legal issues surrounding the legal rights of journalists in acquiring, reporting, and publishing information relative to athletes and sport entities. It examines the legal issues surrounding sport communication stemming from the U.S. Constitution. An analysis of freedom of the press as it relates to the sport media is also examined. Furthermore, the chapter highlights defamation law and examines the legal parameters that establish athletes and coaches as public figures, discussing the limitations to their privacy rights as public figures. Other areas included in this examination of the legal aspects of sport communication involve legal cases pertaining to libel, slander, and right of publicity and recent legal issues surrounding sport entities' rights to real-time sport information and player statistics.

EXAMINING PLAYER–MEDIA RELATIONS

Since the genesis of sport, journalists and members of the public have analyzed and criticized the performances of athletes and franchises (Craig, 1994; Deem, 2006). Initially, sport media coverage was limited to on-field performances (Craig, 1994; Robinson, 1998). As the public's desire for more sport information increased, so too did stories outlining the personal lives of athletes and the business aspect of managing a sport enterprise. Recent media exposés on athletes, violence, eligibility issues, scandals, and crime erroneously had led many to believe that controversy is a contemporary phenomenon, despite its existence since the inception of sport (Robinson, 1998). In 1928, baseball writers covering the New York Yankees on a rail trip were sitting in the train's club car, playing nickel-ante poker. Suddenly the door to the club car burst open, and

Although the University of Louisville's Rick Pitino (left) and Robbie Valentine (right) do not have an antagonistic relationship, there is often a distrust between sports figures and the sport media.

Babe Ruth sprinted down the aisle followed by an attractive young woman with a knife. "I'll kill you, you son of a bitch!" she screamed, following Ruth into the next car. The writers observed all the action, then turned and looked at each other. "That'd make a helluva story," one of them said. The others chuckled and nodded, and the poker game resumed (Telander, 1984).

According to Telander (1984), no one reported the incident until Fred Lieb put it in a hot stove league column for *The St. Petersburg Times* in 1976. Lieb says no one reported it because "we were in the business of creating heroes, not tearing them down" (Telander, 1984). In those days reporters refrained from writing stories on athletes' personal issues, perceiving that the public was simply not interested. Reporters often saw athletes as

heroes, and their writing reflected this. Ruth's prowess on the field was all that counted. The media refrained from reporting that baseball great Ty Cobb was mugged and left for dead and that he was allegedly a mean-spirited person (Telander, 1984).

Many issues have cultivated the current state of player–sport media relations. The invention of television provided competition for the newspapers. According to Telander (1984), Ray Sons, a columnist for the *Chicago Sun Times*, stated that telling readers who won and how the runs were scored no longer sufficed because television had already shown the fans the game 24 hours before. Because of this, reporters searched for new angles in their reporting and became more sophisticated in their critiques.

In the late 1960s, Tom Wolfe brought the pizzazz of "new journalism" to writing. Wolfe applied fictional writing techniques in his stories to engage readers. Many sportswriters took note of this and started to develop their own unique angles (Telander, 1984).

Sports reporters may not have disclosed athletes' personal issues because many were friends, many shared similar interests, and many earned similar wages (Robinson, 1998). For example, legendary sportswriter Grantland Rice earned as much as Babe Ruth in the mid-1920s. The deterioration of the relationship may also be attributed to investigative reporting, which has grown since the Watergate scandal in the United States (Robinson, 1998). In addition, sport consumers now have multiple choices to gather sport information. The instantaneous nature of the Internet and mobile technology allows individuals to access information at any time. Most often, sport consumers can obtain information before it is reported on the evening news or in the daily newspapers. This ability to access real-time information requires that newspaper writers dig for more unique and provocative angles when covering their beats and formulating their stories.

Now in the age of constant and interactive media, improvement has been made in athlete–media affairs, with little time for adjustment. With emerging and instantaneous technology, print journalists feel pressured to compete while the contention between print and broadcast reporters grows. Print reporters believe that these "instant" sources of information are a disadvantage when competing for stories (Craig, 1994; Deem, 2006; Nordhaus, 1999; Robinson, 1998). This is largely attributable to the fact that newspaper readership continues to decline. Readership of daily newspapers fell 3.1% in 2005 ("Newspaper Readership," 2005). Furthermore, newspapers must contend with more than television and the Internet. As sport continues to expand as an industry, reporters are forced to lobby for stories. Sports sections now cover double or triple the number of teams as before and, therefore, are unable to provide extensive coverage with limited space. The competition and limited space force reporters to dig for stories to "get the scoop." In some cases, this means "getting the dirt" on athletes, coaches, managers, or owners.

Additionally, newspaper proprietors, editors, broadcasters, and media companies such as CBS, ABC, NBC, and Fox compete for readers and viewers. Without readers and viewers, the business dies. Media entities exist to inform the public, but they must also generate revenue. This forces the media to provide content that will attract mass audiences. The media will often use information on celebrities and even sensationalize stories to ensure captive audiences.

Competition should encourage a better product, but it hasn't necessarily produced quality reporting. The sport media—often citing the public's right to know—shock the public with exposés and exclusive stories or encourage fans to "tune in for 'exclusive' footage" often at the athlete's expense. This often boosts ratings, which ensure advertising profits. Controversies involving athletes capture the attention of audiences. For example, allegations of Lance Armstrong and doping make headlines. Additional examples include steroids in baseball and athletes accused of sexual assault. Other headlines include athletes with "bad boy" images such as Randy Moss and Terrell Owens. The latter's antics and comments have garnered much media coverage. Rumors

of a possible romantic relationship between Andy Roddick and Maria Sharapova have also made headlines. Laucella and Osborne (2002) noted that "journalistic inaccuracies as misquotes and quotes out of context, the use of off-the-record material, and a discussion of an individual's private life" spur sports figures to be leery when interacting with the media (p. 185). The athletes argue invasion of privacy and defamation, whereas the media counter with the First Amendment and freedom of the press. The courts must balance the rights and freedoms guaranteed by the First and Fourth Amendments when hearing cases involving athletes and coaches (Barnett, 1999; Craig, 1994; Deem, 2006; Nordhaus, 1999; Robinson, 1998). Central to these cases is the athletic participant's status as a public figure and the elements of defamation.

ESTABLISHING FREEDOM OF THE PRESS IN THE UNITED STATES: THE FIRST AMENDMENT

The First Amendment guarantees the freedoms of religion, speech, and press. It clearly indicates that the U.S. Congress cannot make laws (a) concerning establishment of religion or prohibiting its free exercise, (b) abridging the freedom of speech or of the press, or (c) denying the right of the people to assemble peaceably and to petition the government for a redress of grievances (U.S. Constitution, AM I). This means the press has almost absolute freedom of thoughts and beliefs (Craig, 1994). U.S. society prides itself on allowing people the freedom to express opinions, to engage in debate, and to be informed. To advance such values, the First Amendment guarantee of free press is crucial.

Freedom of the press encourages the decision-making process in the "marketplace of ideas." As Middleton and colleagues (2000) noted, the concept of the marketplace of ideas was initiated by English poet John Milton and philosopher John Stuart Mill, but Supreme Court Justice Oliver Wendell Holmes coined the phrase "marketplace of ideas." Desiring the freedom to end his marriage, Milton had written and published an essay entitled *Areopagitica*. He had received much criticism for publishing and distributing the essay without the consent of his government. Milton suggested that he should not need a license to distribute his materials and voice his views. He believed that knowledge improved the lives of citizens and that requiring a license would limit knowledge. This censorship, he believed, would limit the distribution of influential ideas. Similarly, Mill believed that freedom of expression was essential to gain the truth and that suppressing statements would be disadvantageous to society. Justice Holmes also believed that freedom of expression led to the truth and noted that whether an idea was accepted in the marketplace of ideas was an ideal test for truth. In other words, the public should be cautiously aware of the ideas that circulate. Being informed and educated about all the ideas would allow individuals to select the idea they deem to be the truth (Middleton, Trager, & Chamberlin, 2000). Milton, Mill, and Holmes believed that the exchange of ideas should always lead to the truth. They believed it was important for people to freely say, read, and hear, so that they could express themselves and contribute to society. A free press fulfills this function by informing the public of ideas. The First Amendment affords the press the protection it needs to fulfill its duty as a "watchdog" over the government by informing the people. This is grounded in the idea that only a truly informed public can make educated decisions, and the role of the press is to expose a potentially hostile government or issues that are a matter of public interest. For a summary of cases involving freedom of the press, see table 14.1.

DEFINING THE LIMITS OF THE PRESS

The First Amendment was intended to be an added assurance that the press was able to serve as a watchdog of the government. However, libel was not to be included in free speech as supported by the Sedition Act, passed 7 years after the ratification of the First Amendment (Rodman, 2001). The Sedition Act essentially prohibited statements, written or oral, that were made against the government, its officials, and its actions. Many argue that the Sedition Act spurred the courts to define the limits of free speech (Rodman, 2001). In defining the limits of free speech, one must consider the parameters specific to defamation, as discussed in the next section.

Defamation

The intent of the First Amendment was to prohibit prior restraint "but allow for punishment after publication" (Craig, 1994, p. 529). Prior

Table 14.1   Cases Establishing Freedom of the Press

Case	Summary of ruling	Relevance to sport communication
New York Times v. Sullivan (1964)	Established two types of public figures: those of high prominence and those serving as figureheads for various organizations	Ruling was pertinent to general managers, CEOs of sport enterprises, head coaches, and those spearheading community and charitable associations relative to sport.
Curtis Publishing Company v. Butts (1967)	Established that public figures would be treated as public officials in the eyes of the law	Ruling meant that athletes and coaches could be considered public figures.
Gertz v. Robert Welch, Inc. (1974)	Established that persons considered private figures did not have to meet actual malice standard and that false opinions are protected by the First Amendment	Private individuals involved in sport have more legal protection than public figures; the opinions expressed by members of the sport media are not subject to defamation claims.

restraint refers to government censorship or government prevention of certain stories. According to Vivian (2001), the U.S. Supreme Court has "consistently ruled that prior restraint violates the First Amendment" (p. 431).

Defamation law is intended to provide punishment for speech not protected by the First Amendment. Defamation refers to communication that is so harmful that it significantly tarnishes the reputation of an individual or prevents other persons from associating with the individual (Clement, 2004). Defamation "tends to harm the reputation of another as to lower him in the estimation of the community or to deter third persons from associating or dealing with him" (*Restatement of Torts,* 1977). *Black's Law Dictionary* defines it as "holding up a person to ridicule, scorn or contempt in a respectable and considerable part of the community" (2004). Defamation may expose an individual to public hatred, embarrassment, and ridicule (Wong, 1994).

Defamation may be a result of "news reports, media releases, broadcasts and even speeches" (Middleton, Trager, & Chamberlin, 2000, p. 79). For defamation to occur, the defamatory statement must be communicated to a third party (Clement, 2004).

Essentially, defamation law involves the balancing of two absolute freedoms: the right to privacy guaranteed by the Fourth Amendment and freedom of the press guaranteed by the First Amendment (Craig, 1994). Because plaintiffs must prove actual malice or a reckless disregard for the truth, members of the media are usually afforded greater protection to inform the public (Deem, 2006). Defamation may be a form of oral communication (slander) or written communication (libel).

Elements of and Defenses to Libel

Regardless of the form of the defamatory statement, the communication tarnishes the reputation of a person by lowering his or her

Although defamation by the sport media will not bring about police action against the offender, there may be legal action that results in heavy penalties.

status in the community or by deterring others from associating or dealing with the individual (Clement, 2004). According to Middleton and colleagues (2000), six elements must be established to win a libel suit. These include "1) defamation, defamatory language, 2) identification, the defamatory statement identified the plaintiff, 3) publication, the defamatory statement was published and distributed, 4) fault, the defamation was published as a result of negligence or recklessness, 5) falsity, the defamatory statement was false, a burden only for persons suing for defamation related to matters of public concern, and 6) personal harm, such as a loss to reputation, emotional distress, or the loss of business revenues" (p. 79). Defenses to libel claims include truth, protection for opinion, exaggeration and figurative terms, opinion based on fact, totality of circumstances, absolute privileges for government officials, consent, broadcasts for political candidates, or qualified privileges for journalists (Laucella & Osborne, 2002; Middleton, Trager, & Chamberlin, 2000). (Figure 14.1 summarizes the elements of and the defenses to libel.) If defendants can establish that the defamatory statement was true, they will win

their case. However, defendants may also win if the plaintiff cannot illustrate that the statement was false. As Craig (1994) noted, opinions, even false opinions, are protected by the First Amendment. This was reaffirmed in *Gertz v. Robert Welch, Inc.,* a case discussed in greater detail later in this section.

Public Versus Private Figures: Landmark Cases

An important distinction to make relative to defamation is the status of an individual. Individuals' protection for defamation varies based on their classification as a public or private figure. Public figures do not enjoy the same privacy rights as private individuals. As established in *Gertz v. Robert Welch, Inc.,* two types of public figures exist. Public figures are persons so prominent in society that they are obviously public figures, such as politicians or CEOs of major companies. Public figures are also considered individuals who put themselves at the forefront of a particular issue; such persons are only public figures in respect to matters concerning that particular issue. Examples include presidents or figureheads of charitable organizations or presidents of

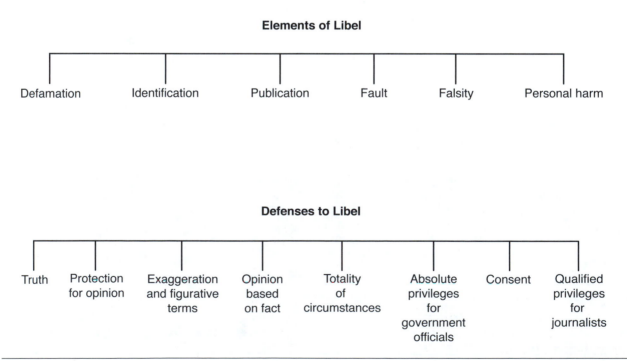

Figure 14.1 Summary of the elements that must be established to win a libel suit and summary of the possible defenses to libel claims.

local community organizations. According to Clement (2004) and Deem (2006), high school athletes, collegiate athletes, professional athletes, coaches, and sport administrators are most often considered public figures.

New York Times v. Sullivan placed defamation law within the scope of the First Amendment. In this landmark case, the Supreme Court ruled that to win a defamation claim, a public official must prove "that the statement was made with actual malice." Actual malice means a reckless disregard for the truth, indicating that the information was published with no attempt to verify its truth. Middleton and colleagues (2000) noted that the ruling meant that false statements that damaged the reputation of an individual were protected by the First Amendment when actual malice could not be established. This means that public figures would be required to show that false statements were published without an attempt to verify their truth. This resulted from the court's philosophy that debate on public issues should be protected (Middleton, Trager, & Chamberlin, 2000). Therefore, sport media entities should ensure that any information published, especially information that may be perceived as negative, is verified and truthful (Nichols et al., 2002).

Curtis Publishing Company v. Butts expanded the ruling in *New York Times v. Sullivan* by extending the defamation standard to public figures. The ruling in *Curtis* as well as rulings in *Chuy v. The Philadelphia Eagles Football Club* and in *Warford v. The Lexington Herald-Leader Company* established that athletes and coaches can be considered public figures. The *Curtis* case involved a story published in *The Saturday Evening Post* that depicted an alleged conversation between University of Alabama football coach Paul "Bear" Bryant and University of Georgia athletic director Wally Butts. The story alleged that the two were overheard on the telephone conspiring to fix the football game between the two universities. Recounts of the alleged conversation indicated that Butts provided Bryant with Georgia's game strategies. Butts sued the newspaper for libel and won the case. However, the ruling shifted the burden of proof for defamation to public

figures and concluded that public officials and public figures should be treated as the same under the law (Laucella & Osborne, 2002; Middleton, Trager, & Chamberlin, 2000). Craig (1994) suggested that the ruling in the case was based on the philosophy that those who, through fame or notoriety, become public figures could exercise significant authority on important societal issues. As a result, open debate and criticism of their actions should be given the same leeway as writings about public officials. As a consequence of the decisions in *Butts,* the First Amendment does not differentiate among suits involving famous people, public figures, and public officials (Craig, 1994).

In *Chuy,* the *Philadelphia Bulletin* had printed an erroneous story stating that Don Chuy, a member of the Philadelphia Eagles football team, had a medical condition known as polycythemia vera, a blood clot condition. The franchise's general manager had informed a sportswriter for the *Philadelphia Bulletin* that Chuy had the condition. The reporter followed up with the team's physician and published the story. The story was distributed by the Associated Press and received widespread publication in newspapers around the United States. Chuy did not actually have the condition, and after reading the article, he had a breakdown and sued the Eagles organization for defamation. In ruling in favor of the *Philadelphia Bulletin,* the Court noted that professional football players were public figures. The philosophy of the court in reaching its decision was based on the fact that professional football garners significant media attention. The Court held that Chuy was a public figure, even though he did not actively seek or desire the media attention and coverage. The Court also stated that professional athletes assume a role of public prominence, especially when they are in the midst of their careers. As Laucella and Osborne (2002) suggested, "Professional sports command a significant amount of public attention...and receive media scrutiny whether they actively seek it or not" (p. 195).

The *Warford* case illustrates that a coach may not always be considered a public figure and that the extent of a coach's status as a public figure may be limited to the time frame of the alleged defamatory statement (Laucella & Osborne, 2002). Reggie Warford was the assistant basketball coach for the University of Pittsburgh. *The Lexington Herald Leader* reprinted an earlier story alleging that Warford had offered a prominent high school recruit money to sign with the team. In hearing the case, the trial court considered Warford a private figure. On appeal, the court reversed this decision and ruled that Warford was a public figure based on his role as a coach and as a recruiter for a Big East Conference university. The Kentucky Supreme Court reversed the decision of the appellate court, stating that at the time of the defamatory statement Warford was a private person. The court noted that his status as a recruiter did not establish that he was a public figure and, therefore, he should be considered a private person. This case, as well as *Butts* and *Chuy*, suggests that athletes and coaches can be considered public figures and as such do not enjoy the same protections as private individuals.

Laucella and Osborne (2002) noted that the *Warford* case illustrates that the status of sports figures is not always clear. The authors noted that the courts use a four-step analysis to determine an individual's status as a limited public or private figure:

1. Isolation of the controversy and determination of the scope of the public's interest

2. An examination of the plaintiff's role in the controversy

3. A determination if the defamatory statement is germane to the plaintiff's role in the controversy

4. An analysis of the extent of the plaintiff's access to channels of communication (Laucella & Osborne, 2002, p. 197)

In today's environment of instantaneous access, sports figures are most often considered public figures and represent matters that are in the general public interest (Craig, 1994; Deem, 2006; Nordhaus, 1999; Robinson, 1998). Matters that are of public interest are also afforded less protection than private matters, as discussed in the next section.

Rosenbloom v. Metromedia, Inc., in 1971 also extended *The New York Times* ruling to include any matter of legitimate public concern or general interest. If a private individual's story related to something of public concern, he or she would have to meet the actual malice standard to win a libel suit (Craig, 1994). As Craig (1994) noted, the court's focus once again centered on an individual's status as a public or private figure. In the 1974 *Gertz v. Robert Welch, Inc.* decision, the Supreme Court ruled that a private figure did not have to meet the actual malice standard. This is because "it was assumed that a public figure would have better access to a forum for a reply to the alleged defamatory statement" (Craig, 1994, p. 533).

Since *Gertz,* the courts have consistently ruled that opinions, even false opinions, are protected (Craig, 1994). According to Craig (1994), after the *Gertz* opinion was given, "there was an absolute privilege requiring every court to distinguish libel claims on whether the printed matter was a fact or an opinion" (p. 534). False opinions are protected by the First Amendment, but false statements are not (Craig, 1994). Many sports talk shows, sports radio shows, and sports columns are grounded on the ability of commentators and columnists to express their opinions and elicit emotional responses in viewers and listeners. Their opinions, even if false, are protected and therefore not subject to defamation claims.

Recently, Lleyton Hewitt, a former top-ranked player on the Association of Tennis Professional's Tour, sued the tour for defamation of character. Hewitt alleged that the ATP defamed him by its comments to the media when he declined to be interviewed at the Cincinnati Masters. Interviews are required by the ATP Tour as part of the official duties of its players. Hewitt believed that the ATP's interview request was "crap," and the ATP noted that other senior players such as Pete Sampras, Andre Agassi, and Roger Federer conducted their interviews (Debelle, 2003). Hewitt, however, has recently changed management groups, and it is speculated he will settle his suit with the ATP (Kaplan, 2005d).

In another case, Time Inc. recently settled its lawsuit with former Alabama football coach Mike Price. Price sued Time Inc. for defamation and slander by a story published in *Sports Illustrated*. The story indicated that Price had spent time in a topless bar in Florida, was intoxicated, and had sexual intercourse at his hotel. As a result of the article, the University of Alabama fired Price. The results of the settlement were not public, but *Sports Illustrated* stands by the validity of its story. Price, however, denies that he had intercourse in his hotel room (Reeves, 2005).

Right to Privacy: Fourth Amendment

As mentioned earlier, defamation cases involve the balancing of freedom of the press with an individual's privacy rights. Supreme Court Justices Louis D. Brandeis and Samuel D. Warren inspired the law of privacy in their 1890 *Harvard Law Review* article entitled "The Right to Privacy." The two expressed concern about gossip and the media's tendency to sensationalize stories. They coined the phrase "the right to be let alone," recognizing right to privacy. Brandeis and Warren (1890) noted that modern advances in technology and communication were placing privacy at greater risk than in the past.

Four Types of Privacy Invasion

As Nordhaus (1999) noted, the right to privacy has evolved to protect against four main types of invasions, which were identified by Prosser (1971). These include:

1. Intrusion into solitude
2. Public disclosure of private facts
3. Depiction in a false light
4. Commercial exploitation of a person's name or likeness, also considered appropriation (Nordhaus, 1999, p. 287)

Proving public disclosure of private facts fares poorly in the United States because it collides with freedom of speech and freedom of the press (Barnett, 1999). "The United States Supreme Court has never upheld, nor have any American courts, a judgment for invasion of privacy based on public disclosure of true facts" (Barnett, 1999, p. 557).

Narrow Degree of Protection for Public Figures

The personal and private lives of athletes at all levels garner significant public interest (Deem, 2006; Nordhaus, 1999; Robinson, 1998). Because of this, information about them is considered a matter of public interest (Nordhaus, 1999). For example, an Associated Press article suggested that a relationship between female tennis players Gigi Fernandez and Conchita Martinez was a well-known secret on the women's tennis tour. Billy Bean made front-page news in *The New York Times* when he publicly acknowledged that he was gay. Sheryl Swoopes' announcement that she was a lesbian also made front-page headlines. At the 2006 Australian Open, rumors and media reports suggested a romantic relationship between tennis standouts Maria Sharapova and Andy Roddick. San Antonio Spurs player Tony Parker's relationship with Eva Longoria has also made national headlines.

Nordhaus (1999) noted that public figures' privacy rights are limited for several reasons, which are described below.

The first rationale is that most public persons seek and consent to publicity. Second, the personalities and affairs of athletes, coaches, and high-profile members of sport entities are viewed as inherently "public." In this sense, the public nature of their occupations is construed as waiving their rights to privacy. Third, the constant exposure that is received, combined with their expectation that such exposure will occur, tends to make athletes, coaches, and high-profile members of sport entities more "psychologically tolerant" of press behavior than they might otherwise be. Finally, the press has a right to inform the public about matters of public interest. As athletes, coaches, and high-profile members of sport entities cultivate their positions in the public spotlight, they generate continued interest in their activities. (pp. 289-290)

Copyright and Trademark

As sport has evolved into big business, sport entities and athletes have realized the importance of protecting their brand image. Copyright and trademarks are used to protect property such as league and team logos, licensed merchandise, and Web site domain names. The sport entity may extend permission to other organizations to use some of the aforementioned property (Clement, 2004). However, copyright and trademark law afford the sport entity protection in the event this property is used without its consent (Clement, 2004; Nichols et al., 2002).

Sport law and sport media scholars point to the Copyright Act, the Lanham Act, and the Trademark Revisions Act as forming the basis for copyright and trademark law. The work of Anderson (1999), Clement (2002, 2004), Nichols et al. (2002), and Nordhaus (1999) provide the framework and context for this section. The Copyright Act stipulates that copyrights should be granted to promote the progress of science and the useful arts (U.S. Constitution, 1787). Section 43 of the Lanham Act prevents the use of words and images that could confuse consumers as to a product's origin (15 USC). The act provides the foundation for the argument that celebrities and athletes should have the right to control their image and that business enterprises cannot use their image without permission. Copyright law allows property owners to reproduce, adapt, distribute, perform, and display their work. However, according to the Fair Use Doctrine, the public may use a copyrighted work without violating the law if it is used for the purposes of criticism, comment, news reporting, teaching, scholarship, or research (Clement, 2004; Nichols et al., 2002).

The Lanham Act was amended in 1988 with the Trademark Revisions Act. This act addressed confusing descriptions and misrepresentations (*Trademark Revisions Act*, 1988). Trademark law protects trademarks, service marks, and collective marks. A trademark is defined as any work, name, symbol, or device or combination thereof adopted and used by a manufacturer or merchant to identify his goods and distinguish them from those manufactured or sold by others (15 USC). As Clement (2004) noted, "Trademarks cover goods; service marks cover services, and collective marks cover goods and services for organizations" (p. 201). The cases of *National Football League v. Primetime 24 Joint Venture, United States Olympic Committee* v. *American Media, Inc.*, and *March Madness Athletic Association v. Sports Marketing International* are a few cases that illustrate the application of trademark law to sport (Clement, 2004). These cases are discussed in the following sections.

The work of Clement (2004) indicates that most often in sport, copyright cases center around performance of athletes, television rights, and unauthorized use of the property. Clement (2004) notes that in *National Football League v. Primetime 24 Joint Venture,* Primetime captured the broadcast signals of the NFL and then transmitted them to a television network in Canada. Additionally, Primetime also broadcast the signals in certain cities in the United States. The NFL argued this broadcast by Primetime violated its copyrights. The court agreed and ruled in favor of the NFL.

Clement (2004) noted that trademark litigation has increased rapidly, and relative to trademark law, most cases in sport will involve name confusion, cancellation, and abandonment. Clement (2002, 2004) outlined several cases involving these issues in sport. In *United States Olympic Committee v. American Media, Inc.*, the U.S. Olympic Committee (USOC) argued that American Media, Inc. violated its trademark by titling its magazine *Olympic USA*. The court ruled in favor of the USOC (Clement, 2004). As Clement (2004) highlighted, in *March Madness Athletic Association v. Sports Marketing International,* the MMAA argued that SMI engaged in cyber squatting, false presentation, trademark infringement, and unfair competition. The court ruled that the phrase "March Madness" was a protectable trademark and that "a strong likelihood of confusion existed between the protected trademark and the web-site, marchmadness.com" (*March Madness Athletic Association v. Sports Marketing International*, 2005, p. 49). In *Playmakers L.L.C. v. ESPN, Inc.* (2004), the court also focused its ruling on likelihood of confusion. Playmakers, a sport agency firm, sued ESPN alleging that the network's series, titled *Playmakers,* was devaluing its brand name. The court ruled that "playmakers" was a common term and, therefore, no confusion existed.

Defamation law, combined with privacy rights, copyright, and trademark law, has led to the need for a right of publicity.

Right of Publicity

Athletes have become celebrities and as such have national and sometimes worldwide appeal. With this growing popularity, athletes have realized the benefits of projecting the "right" image or simply "an image that sells." No longer are athletes limited to endorsing sport products. Tom Brady and his teammates tout the five layers of Visa security, and Jerry Jones pitches Sprint's NFLcast. Andre Agassi and Steffi Graf illustrate the value of Genworth Financial, Maria Sharapova displays the potency of the Canon OneShot camera, and LeBron James drinks Sprite. Former NFL standouts Jason Sehorn and Shannon Sharpe educated the masses in their commercials for Charles Schwab. Tiger Woods promotes Buicks, Yao Ming loves to smile at McDonald's, and Michael Jordan sports Hanes while launching his own line of clothing. Athletes value endorsements and many make more in endorsements than in their player salaries. As noted in chapter 9, endorsements are quite lucrative for athletes, and their image and persona are key in capitalizing on these endorsements. Professional athletes have realized the value of their persona and are using it to generate significant capital. It is of such value that athletes protect their image just as apparel companies protect against unlicensed merchants. The right of publicity is one legal angle used by professional athletes to protect and maintain control of their image.

Definition and Development of Right to Publicity

The right of publicity is defined as the right of "the public figure or the celebrity to control commercial value and exploitation of his name or likeness" *(Estate of Presley v. Russen,* 1981, p. 33). The right of publicity is considered "a right that protects a person against commercial misappropriation of his or her name, likeness, or identity" (Clement, 2004, p. 210). It recognizes athletes' and celebrities' right to control their own image.

Need for Right to Publicity

The courts recognized one's right to publicity in *Haelan Laboratories, Inc., v. Topps Chewing Gum, Inc.* (1953). Haelan had exclusive authorization through contracts with several professional baseball players to use their images on baseball cards that were to be included in their gum packs. Topps, a rival company, persuaded the same players to allow usage of their photographs for the sale of their gum. Haelan then brought action against Topps, alleging breach of contract. Under privacy laws, Haelan had no case against Topps because Haelan could not prove that the players had suffered mental distress, nor had the players authorized the company to sue on their behalf. The court, however, ruled for Haelan because the company's contract with the players authorizing exclusive rights prohibited Topps from using their images. The court ruled that "A man has a right in the publicity value of his photograph, i.e., the right to grant the exclusive privilege of publishing his picture, and that such a grant may validly be made 'in gross.'...Whether it be labeled a 'property' right is immaterial; for here, as often elsewhere, the tag 'property' simply symbolizes the fact that courts enforce a claim which has pecuniary worth. This right might be called a 'right of publicity.'...This right of publicity would usually yield them no money unless it could be made the subject of an exclusive grant which barred any other advertiser from using their pictures" (pp. 5-7).

In 1975, Joe Namath sued *Sports Illustrated,* alleging the magazine violated his right to privacy under New York's Civil Rights law. *Sports Illustrated* ran a series of advertisements around the holiday seasons touting "the man you love, loves Joe" encouraging females to purchase subscriptions for their significant others. The court ruled in favor of *Sports Illustrated,* noting that the photos were incidental advertising and that Namath had been fairly depicted in the photographs. Because of this ruling, no invasion of privacy had occurred. Although Namath lost the case, the dissenting opinion stated that the advertisements were promotional material and that Namath engaged in the business of using his likeness for commercial purposes. The dissenting opinion recognized a person's right to have a personality free from exploitation, even if that personality is newsworthy.

In 1995, Joe Montana sued the *San Jose Mercury News* for commercial misappropriation of name and likeness. The newspaper produced posters commemorating the San Francisco 49ers' four Super Bowl championships in a single decade. The court ruled in favor of the *San Jose Mercury News,* stating Montana had no cause of action because the event was a matter of public interest, that the public had a right to know, and that the press had a right to tell the story. Furthermore, the court noted that the posters were a form of public interest presentation and therefore entitled to protection. The newspaper, the court noted, had a constitutional right to promote itself by reproducing news stories.

ASSESSING TECHNOLOGY'S IMPACT ON LEGAL ISSUES

As discussed in previous chapters, advances in technology have dramatically influenced the manner in which sport entities communicate with key publics, both internal and external. New technology has allowed for levels of interaction that sport consumers often take for granted including real-time sport scores and online fantasy leagues. Although these new media add a dimension to sport communication, they often spur legal debate. This section highlights the legal views regarding real-time sport scores and online fantasy leagues.

Real-Time Scores

Real-time scores include sport information and statistics that may be distributed and accessed instantaneously in a variety of ways. Real-time information allows an instantaneous

The published work of photographers has been the subject of many legal disputes in the sport industry.

© Paul M. Pedersen

link between a sport entity and its key publics. According to Roberts (2004), real-time information also provides a potentially significant revenue source for sport entities. Roberts (2004) suggested that the impact and scope of real-time sport information are largely dependent on the ability of sport entities to hold and retain the legal rights associated with the information related to their events. Roberts (2004) suggested that two cases have shaped the legal philosophy regarding real-time sport information. The cases, *National Basketball Association v. Sports Team Analysis and Tracking Systems, Inc.,* and *Morris Communications Company, LLC v. PGA Tour*, present similar legal issues associated with real-time sport information and have shaped the application of dissemination of this information to the public.

In *National Basketball Association v. Sports Team Analysis and Tracking Systems*, the NBA sued to prevent Motorola and Sports Team Analysis and Tracking Systems (STATS) from disseminating real-time game information via pagers to subscribers. STATS was obtaining the information via the NBA's televised broadcasts. The NBA argued that Motorola and STATS violated their copyrights and trademarks in disseminating the information. The court ruled in favor of STATS and relied on the 1976 Copyright Act when rendering its decision. The 1976 Copyright Act designated that sporting events were not copyrightable events because these events lacked originality. It also noted that a broadcast of a sporting event may be copyrighted, but not the event itself. Therefore, once a game begins, it is in the public domain and, therefore, not copyrightable.

Similar to the NBA case, *Morris Communications Company, LLC v. PGA Tour* centered on the PGA's legal right to distribute and to restrict dissemination of its real-time golf and tournament information by additional entities. Morris Communications sued the PGA Tour, arguing that it monopolized the distribution of its real-time golf scores and tournament information. The PGA Tour argued that it had legal property rights to distribute and to restrict another entity's dissemination of its real-time golf information. It argued that

restricting the dissemination of the real-time golf information was a business strategy, especially because the Tour had developed its own real-time scoring system and implemented steps to post this information on its Web site immediately. The PGA provided this information to media members but restricted them from distributing it for a certain amount of time. The restrictions were used to provide the PGA with a competitive advantage in regard to its real-time scoring and also to serve as a potential revenue source. The court ruled in favor of the PGA, noting that the PGA had a legal right to control the dissemination of its real-time golf information. However, the court also noted that once the real-time information was posted on the PGA's Web site, it was in the public domain and no longer subject to restrictions.

Roberts (2004) and MacDonald (2004) suggested that these two cases highlight the concept of "hot news." The key point is whether sport entities have a legal right to or a solid legal argument for retaining control over information regarding events operated by the entity (Roberts, 2004). Roberts (2004) said this right is relative and may depend on whether the information disseminated is classified as "hot news." Roberts (2004) noted that in the NBA case, the court identified the elements that must be present in order for information to be deemed "hot news":

1. The sport entity generates and acquires the information at an expense.

2. The information is time sensitive.

3. A third party's dissemination of the information would be at the expense of the sport entity.

4. A third party's dissemination of the information directly competes with the dissemination of the information from the sport entity.

5. The quality of the information would be dramatically threatened by the ability of third parties to disseminate the information.

As Roberts (2004) indicated, to truly have legal rights to real-time sport information, a sport entity must illustrate that the information is "hot news" and that no overriding public interest exists. "A promoter should have the legally enforceable right to restrict the dissemination of information about (or even the video image of) its events only if it can show that holding such a right (and its attendant commercial value) is crucial to its willingness to create the event or to collect the information in the first place. Once the promoter can profit sufficiently from expending the effort and resources to produce, market, and sell its sports entertainment product, there appears to be no public benefit from allowing the promoter to use the legal system offensively to reap competitive profits by restricting the flow of information the public wants" (Roberts, 2004, pp. 187-188).

Online Fantasy Sport Leagues

Similar legal battles are brewing relative to fantasy sports leagues and the use of player statistics. Currently, online fantasy sport league sites such as Yahoo Sports and CBS Sportsline pay a licensing fee to the professional sport leagues to use player statistics. This could change in the near future given the outcome of a lawsuit filed by CDM Fantasy Sports alleging that Major League Baseball Advanced Media does not own player statistics that are used for commercial purposes in fantasy games. CDM Fantasy Sports has operated fantasy games for the sport arms of *The Sporting News,* MSNBC, and *USA Today.* CDM chose to sue after MLB Advanced Media denied its request for a license for the 2005 season. Experts note that this case will shape the future of online fantasy games and will determine if sport entities do indeed own the stats of their players (King, 2005c).

PROTECTING REPORTERS' RIGHTS TO LOCKER-ROOM ACCESS

An issue that has often sparked controversy related to the sport media is the issue of the media's access in the locker room. Although

the presence of male sports reporters in a men's locker room had never been challenged, female sports reporters were often harassed and degraded when assigned to cover certain beats and to conduct postgame interviews with male athletes in the locker room. One of the most notable incidents involved Lisa Olson, a reporter for *The Boston Herald.* Olson endured aggressive gestures and vulgar comments when conducting interviews with players for the New England Patriots after a game in 1990. The incident resulted in an attempted cover-up by team management and sparked a national debate. Olson received death threats, and her home and car were vandalized. She later moved to Australia to cover cricket and rugby (Druzin, 2006; Sharp, 1997). Although female sports reporters had fought for and won the legal right to perform the duties of their jobs as journalists in 1978, female sports reporters still face challenges.

In *Ludtke vs. Kuhn* (1978), Time Inc. and Melissa Ludtke, a reporter for *Sports Illustrated,* sued Major League Baseball commissioner Bowie Kuhn after he prohibited her from conducting interviews in the locker room during the 1977 World Series. In 1975, Kuhn had sent a letter to all general managers at league franchises suggesting that baseball should maintain a "unified stand" and not allow female sports reporters into the locker room (p. 7). This letter was in response to the National Hockey League's decision to allow female sports reporters locker-room access following the 1975 All Star Game. Ludtke, covering a 1977 World Series Game between the New York Yankees and the Los Angeles Dodgers, had been told by the Dodgers that she would be allowed postgame access to their locker room. She had also been allowed access to the manager's office in the Yankee's locker room during the American League playoffs. The Commissioner's office informed Ludtke that, because of her gender, she was not allowed to enter either team's locker room after the World Series games. Instead, MLB assigned the public relations director for the Philadelphia Phillies to bring players out of the locker room to speak with Ludtke (p. 8).

In the suit, MLB alleged that the exclusion of female sports reporters was (a) to protect the privacy of those players who are undressed or who are in various stages of undressing and getting ready to shower, (b) to protect the image of baseball as a family sport, and (c) to preserve traditional notions of decency and propriety (p. 16). The court ruled that MLB's policy of excluding female sports reporters "infringed both equal protection and due process rights of Ludtke" (p. 30). The court noted that in denying Ludtke access to the locker room, MLB was denying her the right to perform the duties of her profession and placing her at a competitive disadvantage compared with her male counterparts. MLB's policy "substantially and directly interferes with the right of plaintiff Ludtke to pursue her profession as a sports reporter. Her male counterparts are able to get to the ballplayers fresh-off-the-field when comments about plays may still be in progress" (p. 37). The court further noted, "If defendant's practice of total exclusion is derived, as counsel would appear to suggest, from a mere 'custom', then it surely cannot stand against constitutional attack. The Supreme Court has held that mere administrative convenience cannot justify discrimination on account of sex....Defendant's policy of total exclusion of women sports reporters

from the locker room at Yankee Stadium is not substantially related to the privacy protection objective and thus deprives plaintiff Ludtke of that equal protection of the laws which is guaranteed her by the Fourteenth Amendment" (p. 35).

The court also ruled that the claims by MLB that allowing female sports reporters into the locker room would hinder the family sport image of MLB and not conform to the traditional notions of decency and propriety were "too insubstantial to merit serious consideration" (p. 37). This case provided female sports reporters with the legal rights to conduct the duties of their profession and access locker rooms. Although female sports reporters have the legal rights to perform the duties of their profession, instances still exist where they face harassment from athletes, administrators, and colleagues in the media (Miloch, Pedersen, Smucker, & Whisenant, 2005). The right of members of the media to have locker-room access is essential to perform the duties and responsibilities of their position. Team officials must strike the balance between privacy rights of players in the locker room and the rights of media members to perform their duties. Striking the balance benefits both entities and enhances the symbiotic relationship between sport and the media.

CHAPTER WRAP-UP

Summary

As sport continues to be one of the most prominent aspects of our culture, professional athletes will certainly continue to live life under the watchful eye of the public. Professional athletes today are revered as superheroes and, as such, can generate at least three times their playing salaries in endorsements. The average career span for professional athletes is 3 to 5 years, and they risk injury every time they step onto the field. Thus, they are certainly entitled to maximize profits from their talent and celebrity status and should be able to capitalize on their popularity while in their prime.

Without the ability to protect her persona and reputation, a professional athlete may find her image tarnished, which could ultimately lead to a loss in revenue or dismissal from a team. It is certainly true that professional athletes and celebrities relinquish their privacy rights when choosing to live in the public eye. It is argued that living in the limelight boosts their careers, and thus the public creates their images. However, living life in the public eye should not prevent professional athletes or celebrities from capitalizing on their talents, likeness, and image. They are entitled to earn a living in any manner they choose, and although this choice requires the sacrifice of a private life, it should not prevent them from doing everything possible to generate revenue from that popularity. Athletes' and sport figures' images and reputations are their own, and although the media may distort or create those images and reputation, they do not own them. Similar legal battles are evolving relative to real-time sport scores and player statistics. These legal issues as well as defamation, copyright, trademark, and right of publicity will play a prominent role in shaping the future of sport communication.

This chapter has examined the legal issues surrounding the legal rights of journalists in acquiring, reporting, and publishing information relative to athletes and sport entities. It also examined the legal issues surrounding sport communication stemming from the U.S. Constitution. Furthermore, the chapter analyzed the freedom of the press as it is relates to the sport media and highlighted defamation law. Included in this were an examination of the legal parameters that establish athletes and coaches as public figures and a discussion of the limitations to their privacy rights as public figures. The chapter discussed issues and legal cases pertaining to libel, slander, and right of publicity and analyzed recent legal issues surrounding sport entities' rights to real-time sport information and player statistics.

Review Questions

1. What is defamation? Which legal cases established defamation law?
2. How does defamation law apply to public and private figures?
3. Why are athletes, coaches, and high-profile members of sport entities considered public figures?
4. What rationales exist for affording less strict privacy standards to athletes, coaches, and high-profile members of sport entities?
5. What is the difference between slander and libel?
6. What is the purpose of copyright and trademark law?
7. What are the most common types of cases related to copyright and trademark law in sport?
8. What is right of publicity and how is it applied to professional athletes?
9. What cases have shaped the right of publicity in the United States?
10. What are the legal issues surrounding a sport entity's rights to real-time sport scores and statistics?

Discussion Questions

1. How do privacy rights affect defamation law and right of publicity?
2. How does copyright and trademark law pertain to the media's use of certain images and works?
3. Why is the right of publicity important to an athlete's career?
4. How have player–media relationships evolved? How would you characterize player–media relationships today?
5. Should sport entities have legal rights to real-time sport scores and player statistics? Why or why not?

6. Should athletes, coaches, and high-profile members of sport entities be considered public figures?

7. Should false opinions be protected under the First Amendment?

8. How does the First Amendment empower the sport media to inform the public?

9. How is the balance achieved between freedom of the press and invasion of privacy in sport? How does this balance affect the relationship between sport public figures and the sport media?

10. How would you characterize the sport media's coverage of athletes, coaches, and high-profile members of sport entities? How does this coverage differ? What causes differences in the amount and type of coverage?

Group Activities

1. Have each member of your group collect the sports section of your local newspaper for 1 week. Examine how athletes and franchises are covered. Can you determine trends in coverage? How do the laws governing defamation, copyright, and trademark affect this coverage?

2. Have each member of your group tape commercials during a prime-time broadcast on a major television network. Examine the number of commercials in which athletes endorse products. What type of products do athletes endorse? How do these endorsements impact the athlete's persona and image?

Individual Exercises

1. Select a legal case in the sport industry pertinent to defamation. Summarize the case and provide an overview to the class.

2. Select a sport communication legal case pertinent to copyright. Brief the case and present it to the class.

3. Select a legal case pertinent to a sport trademark or right of publicity. Brief the case and present it to the class.

Internet Sites for Additional Learning

CMG Worldwide: www.cmgworldwide.com/

Federal Communications Commission: www.fcc.gov/

Expert Law: www.expertlaw.com/library/personal_injury/defamation.html

Mark Roesler: www.markroesler.com/

National Sport Law Institute, Marquette University Law School: www.law.marquette.edu

MegaLaw: www.megalaw.com/top/defamation.php

Sport Lawyers Association: www.sportslaw.org/

Sport and Recreation Law Association: http://srlaweb.org/

Bibliography

$2.1. (2005, November 13). *The Indianapolis Star,* p. 1J.

$550,000 fine for Janet exposure. (2004, September 23). *BBC.com.* Retrieved February 23, 2007, from http://news.bbc.co.uk/1/hi/entertainment/tv_and_radio/3681326.stm.

Aaker, D.A. (1991). *Managing brand equity.* New York: Free Press.

Aaron, T.C. (2004). *Factors affecting the performance levels of risk management behaviors of Florida high school athletic directors.* Unpublished doctoral dissertation, Florida State University, Tallahassee.

A-B paces ad spending, Olympic sponsors climb list. (2005, March 21). *SportsBusiness Journal, 7*(45), 9.

About ESPN. (2005). ESPN.com. Retrieved February 23, 2007, from www.joinourteam.espn.com/joinourteam/about_espn.html.

About the 10th anniversary show. (2006). HBO Sports. *REAL Sports with Bryant Gumbel.* Retrieved November 20, 2006, from www.hbo.com/realsports/about/.

About us. (2006). eSports Media Group. Retrieved February 23, 2007, from http://www.e-sports.com/pages/About-Us.

Ackerman, W.C. (1945). The dimensions of American broadcasting. *Public Opinion Quarterly, 9*(1), 1-18.

Acosta, V., & Carpenter, L. (2000, Spring). *Women in intercollegiate sport: A longitudinal study—twenty-three year update.* Unpublished report partially funded by Brooklyn College of the City University of New York and The Project on Women and Social Change of Smith College.

Adams, R. (2004a, April 26). Time Inc. picks *SI* as its top mag. *SportsBusiness Journal, 7,* 35.

Adams, R. (2004b, October 25). *SI* gets the picture for new photo site. *SportsBusiness Journal, 7,* 7.

Adams, R. (2004c, December 20). Perry gave ESPN mag look that set it apart. *SportsBusiness Journal, 7,* 35.

Adams, R. (2005a, March 21). Revenue momentum lands magazines on the 'Hot List.' *SportsBusiness Journal, 7*(45), 8.

Adams, R. (2005b, March 28). ESPN.com celebrates 10-year milestone. *SportsBusiness Journal, 7*(46), 6.

Adams, R. (2005c, April 11). Why does MLB take PR beating? *SportsBusiness Journal, 7*(48), 1.

Adams, R. (2005d, June 13). MLB rocks on, hitting the road with major music tours. *SportsBusiness Journal, 8*(8), 6.

Adler, B. (1927). *Practice and theory of individual psychology.* New York: Harcourt.

Adler, R.B., & Towne, N. (2003). *Looking out/looking in* (10th ed.). Belmont, CA: Wadsworth/Thomson.

Agostini, R. (2005, April 21). Driving forward years after cart-se controversy. Martin has no regrets about challenging PGA. *Modesto Bee,* p. C1.

All-night sports show finds niche. (1989, September 11). *Broadcasting,* p. 118.

Altheide, D. (1996). *Qualitative media analysis* (Vol. 38). *Qualitative research methods.* Thousand Oaks, CA: Sage.

American Press Institute. (2002, September). *The great divide: Female leadership in U.S. newsrooms.* Des Moines, IA: Pew Center for Civic Journalism.

American Psychological Association. (2007). How to work with the media: Tip sheet. Retrieved March 14, 2007, from http://apa.org/journals/media/homepage.html.

Anderson, D. (2005). Sportswriting better than ever, long-time columnist says. *SportsBusiness Journal, 7*(38), 42.

Anderson, D.A. (1994). *Contemporary sports reporting* (2nd ed.). Chicago: Nelson-Hall.

Anderson, P. (1999). *Sports law: A desktop handbook.* Milwaukee, WI: National Sports Law Institute.

Andrews, P. (2005). *Sports journalism: A practical introduction.* Thousand Oaks, CA: Sage.

Apologetic Jackson says 'costume reveal' went awry. (2004, February 2). *CNN.com.* Retrieved February 23, 2007, from http://www.cnn.com/2004/US/02/02/superbowl.jackson/.

Aristotle. (350 bc). *Metaphysics.* Trans. W.D. Ross. Retrieved on November 20, 2006, from http://classics.mit.edu/Aristotle/metaphysics.1.i.html.

Arnett, D.B., & Laverie, D.A. (2000). Fan characteristics and sporting event attendance: Examining variance in attendance. *International Journal of Sports Marketing & Sponsorship, 2*(3), 219-235.

Arnold, M.L., & Shinew, K.J. (1997). Career advancement perceptions held by female middle managers compared to male middle managers. *Journal of Park and Recreation Administration, 15*(3), 40-57.

Atkinson, C. (2005, October 10). Instant replay (almost) for Super Bowl spots. *Advertising Age* (Midwest region edition), *76*(41), 3-4.

Auger, P. (2005). The impact of interactivity and design sophistication on the performance of commercial websites for small business. *Journal of Small Business Management, 43*(2), 119-137.

Babbie, E. (1998). *The practice of social research* (8th ed.). Belmont, CA: Wadsworth.

Badenhausen, K., Gage, J., Ozanian, M.K., Roney, M., & Sundheim, J. (2005, Sept. 1). The business of football. *Forbes.com.* Retrieved November 20, 2006, from www.forbes.com/2005/09/01/sports-football-gambling-cz_05nfland.html.

Badenhausen, K., & Ozanian, M.K. (2005, Nov. 26). The business of hockey. *Forbes.com.* Retrieved November 20, 2006, from http://sports.espn. go.com/nhl/news/story?id=2237348#.

Badenhausen, K., Ozanian, M.K., & Roney, M. (2006, August 31). The business of football. *Forbes.com.* Retrieved November 20, 2006, from www.forbes.com/lists/ 2006/30/06nfl_NFL-Team-Valuations_land.html.

Bagdikian, B. (1997). *The media monopoly* (5th ed.). Boston: Beacon.

Bagdikian, B. (2005, January/February). Grand theft: The conglomeratization of media and the degradation of culture. *Multinational Monitor, 26*(1/2), 35-36.

Baldoni, J. (2003). *Great communication secrets of great leaders.* New York: McGraw-Hill.

Baran, S.J. (2006). Sports and television. Retrieved January 21, 2006, from www.museum.tv/archives/ etv/S/htmlS/sportsandte/sportsandte.htm.

Barnard, C. (1938). *The functions of the executive.* Cambridge, MA: Harvard University.

Barnett, S. (1999). The right to one's own image: Publicity and privacy rights in the United States and Spain. *The American Journal of Comparative Law, 47,* 555-581.

Barr, C.A., & Hums, M.A. (2005). Management principles applied to sport management. In L.P. Masteralexis, C.A. Barr, & M.A. Hums (Eds.), *Principles and practice of sport management* (2nd ed., pp. 19-35). Boston: Jones & Bartlett.

Barrett, D.J. (2006). *Leadership communication.* New York: McGraw-Hill.

Barrett, K. (2005, February 21). NCAA names Williams managing director of public and media relations. Retrieved February 23, 2007, from http://www. ncaa.org/wps/contentviewer?IFRAME_ EMBEDDED=true&CONTENT_URL=http:// www2.ncaa.org/portal/media_and_events/press_ room/2005/february/20050221_bobwilliams.html

Bass, A. (2002). Whose broad stripes and bright stars? Race, nation, and power at the 1968 Mexico City Olympics. In J. Bloom & M. N. Willard (Eds.), *Sports matters: Race, recreation, and culture* (pp. 184-208). New York: New York University.

Bass, A.B. (2001). Flag on the field: The popular construction of the Black athlete. *Journal of Sport History, 22*(8), 299.

Bates, D. (2002). A mini-me history of public relations. Retrieved January 23, 2006, from www. instituteforpr.com/pdf/HistoryofPublic%20Relati on--Institute.pdf.

Battenfield, F.L. (2004). *An ethnographic study of the culture of communication in the sports information office in a Division I-A athletic program.* Unpublished doctoral dissertation, Florida State University, Tallahassee.

Beaver Stadium Press Box. (2006). Penn State Athletics. Retrieved January 20, 2006, from www.gopsusports.com/Football/facilities/ BeaverStadium/StadiumPressBody.cfm.

Beckford, P. (1796). *Thoughts on hare and foxhunting.* London: Jonathan Cape.

Bei, L., Chen, Y., & Widdows, R. (2004). Consumers' online information search behavior and the phenomenon of search vs. experience products. *Journal of Family and Economic Issues, 25*(4), 449-467.

Belts, J.R. (1953). Sporting journalism in nineteenth-century America. *American Quarterly, 5*(1), 56.

Bennett, G., Henson, R., & Zhang, J. (2002). Action sports sponsorship recognition. *Sport Marketing Quarterly, 11*(2), 174-185.

Bennett, G., & Lachowetz, T. (2004). Marketing to lifestyles: Action sports and generation Y. *Sport Marketing Quarterly, 13*(4), 239-243.

Bennett, R. (1999). Sports sponsorship, spectator recall and false consensus. *European Journal of Marketing, 22*(3/4), 291-313.

Benson, M. (2006). *Althea Gibson.* New York: Ferguson.

Benton, J. (2005, October 26). DeBerry: Blacks have edge; after rout, coach says Air Force must recruit speed. *Rocky Mountain News,* p. 1C.

Berardini, C. (2004, July 2). Jill Arrington and Tony Bruno debut in Madden NFL 2005. Retrieved January 21, 2006, from http://news.teamxbox. com/xbox/6205/Jill-Arrington-and-Tony-Bruno-Debut-in-Madden-NFL-2005/.

Bernays, E. (1952). *Public relations.* Norman: University of Oklahoma.

Bernstein, A. (2001, October 29). HBO goes beyond the games. *SportsBusiness Journal, 3,* 8.

Bernstein, A. (2004a, February 23). NFL Network finds plenty to show viewers even when players aren't playing. *SportsBusiness Journal, 7,* 15.

Bernstein, A. (2004b, September 6). GE's bid for future Games looks even brighter in light of Athens profit. *SportsBusiness Journal, 7,* 19.

Bernstein, A. (2005a, January 10). ESPN sees its television viewership reach all-time high. *SportsBusiness Journal, 8,* 9.

Bernstein, A. (2005b, February 14). Super Bowl loses points with men. *SportsBusiness Journal, 8,* 31.

Bernstein, A. (2005c, April 25). NFL restores NBC's clout. *SportsBusiness Journal, 8*(1), 1, 32.

Bernstein, A. (2005d, August 8). Ten technologies that are changing the way people consume sports. *SportsBusiness Journal, 8*(15), 15-19.

Bernstein, A. (2005e, September 12). Comcast's national ad debut is HD sponsorship on "MNF." *SportsBusiness Journal, 8,* 13.

Bernstein, A. (2005f, September 12). Issue to set record for *Sporting News. SportsBusiness Journal, 8*(19), 9.

Bernstein, A. (2005g, September 19). Flexibility a key in new MLB-ESPN deal. *SportsBusiness Journal, 8,* 3.

Bernstein, A. (2005h, October 17). Big decisions, big dollars: Scrambling the TV picture. *SportsBusiness Journal, 8*(24), 1, 6.

Bernstein, A. (2005i, October 31). Media buyers report ho-hum NBA ad market. *SportsBusiness Journal, 8,* 13.

Bernstein, A. (2005j, December 12). NASCAR deals: It's all in there. *SportsBusiness Journal, 8,* 1.

Bernstein, A. (2006, January 9). NBC, ESPN strike deal on Olympic coverage. *SportsBusiness Journal, 9,* 6.

Bernstein, A., & Blain, N. (2002, Autumn). Sport and the media: The emergence of a major research field. *Culture, Sport, Society, 5*(3), 1-30.

Bernstein, A., Fisher, E., & Kramer, S. (2006, January 16). 10 questions and answers for wireless. *SportsBusiness Journal, 8*(36), 15.

Besser, C.N. (2005, June 27). PPM is the next big score for sports TV. *Advertising Age* (Midwest region edition), p. 22.

Betts, J.R. (1953a). Sporting journalism in nineteenth-century America. *American Quarterly, 5,* 39-56.

Betts, J.R. (1953b). The technological revolution and the rise of sport: 1850-1900. *The Mississippi Historical Review, 40,* 231-256.

Big money: Well, they are called the Buckeyes. (2006, January 6). *Indianapolis Star,* p. 1D.

Billings, A.C. (2003). Dueling genders: Announcer bias in the 1999 U.S. Open Tennis Tournament. In R.S. Brown & D.J. O'Rourke III (Eds.), *Case studies in sport communication* (pp. 51-62). Westport, CT: Praeger.

Billings, A.C., & Eastman, S.T. (2002). Selective representation of gender, ethnicity, and nationality in American television coverage of the 2000 Summer Olympics. *International Review for the Sociology of Sport, 37*(3/4), 351-370.

Billings, A.C., & Eastman, S.T. (2003). Framing identities: Gender, ethnic, and national parity in network announcing of the 2002 Winter Olympics. *Journal of Communication, 53*(4), 569-586.

Blake, R.R., & McCanse, A.A. (1991). *Leadership dilemmas—Grid solutions.* Houston: Gulf.

Blanchard, M.A. (Ed.). (1998). *History of the mass media in the United States: An encyclopedia.* Chicago: Fitzroy Dearborn.

Blount, R. (2005, January 28). For Canadians, this is a real struggle. *Minneapolis Star Tribune,* p. 1C.

Blumler J.G., & Katz, E. (1974). *The uses of mass communications: Current perspectives on gratifications research.* Beverly Hills, CA: Sage.

Bonk, T. (2005, November 4). Martin won't be forgotten. *Los Angeles Times,* p. 8.

Bora, M. (2006, January 4). When winning wears well. *Indianapolis Star,* pp. A1, A5.

Boss, S.J. (2002). Television pioneer Roone Arledge '52: Spanning the world. Retrieved February 23, 2007, from www.college.columbia.edu/cct/win99/18.html.

Bostrom, R.N. (1998). *Communication research.* Prospect Heights, IL: Waveland.

Bowden, B., & Bowden, S. (2001). *The Bowden way: 50 years of leadership wisdom.* Atlanta: Longstreet.

Bower, R.T. (1973). *Television and the public.* New York: Holt, Rinehart & Winston.

Bower, R.T. (1985). *The changing television audience in America.* New York: Columbia University.

Boyle, R., & Haynes, R. (2000). *Power play: Sport, the media, and popular culture.* London: Longman.

Bradley, S. (1996, February). Marketers are always looking for good pitchers. *Brandweek,* pp. 36-37.

Brandeis, L., & Warren, S. (1890). The right to privacy. *Harvard Law Review, 4*(5), 193-220.

Brandes, W. (1995, June 2). Advertising: Star power leaves some voice-over artists speechless. *Wall Street Journal,* p. B6.

Branscombe, N.R., & Wann, D.L. (1991). Physiological arousal and reactions to outgroup members during competitions that implicate an important social identity. *Aggressive Behavior, 18,* 85-93.

Brennan, C. (2006). *Best seat in the house.* New York: Scribner.

Brian, D. (2001). *Joseph Pulitzer: A life.* Hoboken, NJ: Wiley.

Brinson, S.L. (2005). From Marconi to Cop Rock: An introduction to broadcasting history. In J.E. Winn & S.L. Brinson (Eds.), *Transmitting the past: Historical and cultural perspectives on broadcasting* (pp. 1-15). Tuscaloosa: University of Alabama.

Britton, P. (2006). *In the groove.* Baytown, TX: Harlequin HQN.

Bronzan, R.T. (1977). *Public relations, promotions and fundraising for athletic and physical education programs.* New York: Wiley.

Brookes, R. (2002). *Representing sport.* London: Arnold.

Brooks, C.M., & Harris, K.K. (1998). Celebrity athlete endorsement: An overview of the key theoretical issues. *Sport Marketing Quarterly, 7*(2), 34-44.

Brown, J. (2005, October 10). Outdoor cable networks find their own space. *Broadcasting & Cable, 135*(41), 16.

Brown, M.T. (1998). An examination of the content of official Major League Baseball team sites on the World Wide Web. *Cyber Journal of Sport Marketing, 2*(1). Retrieved February 23, 2007, from www.ausport.gov.au/fulltext/1998/cjsm/.

Brown, M.T. (2003). An analysis of online marketing in the sport industry: User activity, communication objectives, and perceived benefits. *Sport Marketing Quarterly, 12*(1), 48-55.

Brown, R.S. (2003). Preface. In R.S. Brown & D.J. O'Rourke (Eds.), *Case studies in sport communication* (pp. vii-ix). Westport, CT: Praeger.

Brown, R.S., & O'Rourke, D.J., III. (Eds.). (2003). *Case studies in sport communication.* Westport, CT: Praeger.

Brown, S. (1998, July 20). Sports radio: It pays to play. *Broadcasting & Cable, 128*(30), 50-51.

Bruscas, A. (2005, March 16). Billions at stake in battle over sports on satellite radio. *Seattle Post-Intelligencer.* Retrieved February 23, 2007, from http://seattlepi.nwsource.com/othersports/216168_satellite16.html.

Bryant, J., Comisky, P., & Zillman, D. (1981). The appeal of rough and tumble play in televised professional football. *Communication Quarterly, 29,* 256-262.

Buckner, C. (2006, July 28). Scandal shadows cycling champ. *Knight Ridder Tribune Business News,* p. 1.

Bud Greenspan. (2005). *International Jewish Sports Hall of Fame.* Retrieved February 23, 2007, from www.jewishsports.net/BioPages/BudGreenspan.htm.

Building a career in magazines. (2006). Magazine Publishers of America. Retrieved January 18, 2006, from www.magazine.org/content/files/CareerInMags.pdf.

Bureau of Labor Statistics. (2006). *Occupational outlook handbook* (2006-07). Washington, DC: U.S. Department of Labor.

Burns, K. (2005). *Unforgivable blackness: The rise and fall of Jack Johnson.* Washington, DC: Florentine Films.

Burton, G. (2000). *Talking television: An introduction to the study of television.* New York: Oxford.

Burton, G. (2002). *More than meets the eye: An introduction to media studies.* New York: Oxford.

Burton, G. (2005). *Media and society: Critical perspectives.* New York: Open University.

Butler, J.G. (1999). *Writing sports stories that sell: How to make money from writing about your favorite pastime.* Oxford: How to Book.

Butterworth, M. (2006). Pitchers and catchers—Mike Piazza and the discourse of gay identity in the national pastime. *Journal of Sport & Social Issues, 30*(2), 138-157.

Cahn, S.K. (1993). From the "muscle moll" to the "butch" ballplayer: Mannishness, lesbianism, and homophobia in U.S. women's sport. *Feminist Studies, 19*(2), 343-368.

Callero, P.L. (1985). Role-identity salience. *Social Psychology Quarterly, 48,* 203-215.

Camenson, B. (1985). *Great jobs for communications majors.* Chicago: VGM Career Horizons.

Cann, D.J., & Mohr, P.B. (2001). Journalist and source gender in Australian television news. *Journal of Broadcasting & Electronic Media, 45*(1), 162-174.

Caple, J. (2005). ESPN Page 2: 10 burning questions for Bud Greenspan. Retrieved February 23, 2007, from http://espn.go.com/page2/s/questions/budgreenspan.html.

Careers in the Sports Industry. (2007). Massachusetts Institute of Technology (MIT) Careers Office. Retrieved November 20, 2006, from http://web.mit.edu/career/www/guide/sports.pdf.

Carey, J. (1997). The Chicago School and the history of mass communication research. In E.S. Munson & C.A. Warren (Eds.), *James Carey: A critical reader* (pp. 14-33). Minneapolis: University of Minnesota.

Carey, J.W. (1989). *Communication as culture: Essays on media and society.* New York: Routledge.

Carter, B. (2000). Sportscentury biography: Rozelle made NFL what it is today. Retrieved January 16, 2006, from http://espn.go.com/classic/biography/s/rozelle_pete.html.

Carter, D.M. (1994). *You can't play the game if you don't know the rules: Career opportunities in sports management.* Manassas Park, VA: Impact.

Casazza, M. (2006, October 29). Rod a natural at mastering media: Good relations get message out to recruits. *Knight Ridder Tribune Business News,* p. 1.

Castleman, H., & Podrazik, W.J. (2003). *Watching TV: Six decades of American television* (2nd ed.). Syracuse, NY: Syracuse University.

CBS's McManus takes on the Arledge challenge. (2006, January 9). *SportsBusiness Journal, 8*(35), 42.

Center for Sports Innovation. (2005). Massachusetts Institute of Technology. Retrieved November 20, 2006, from http://web.mit.edu/aeroastro/www/labs/csi/.

Chadwick, H. (2006). *Baseball library.* Retrieved August 22, 2006, from http://www.baseballlibraray.com/baseballlibrary/ballplayers/C/Chadwick_Henry.stm.

Chaffee, S.H. (1996). Thing about theory. In M.B. Salwen & D.W. Stacks (Eds.), *An integrated approach to communication theory and research* (pp. 15-32). Mahwah, NJ: Erlbaum.

Chan-Olmsted, S., & Park, J. (2000). From on-air to online world: Examining the content and structures of broadcast TV stations' web sites. *Journalism & Mass Communication Quarterly, 77*(2), 321-339.

Chappelet, J. (2001). Web-based learning for sport administrators: The example of the SOMIT project. Paper presented at the 11th International Association for Sports Information Congress, Lausanne, Switzerland.

Chelladurai, P. (2006). *Human resource management in sport and recreation* (2nd ed.). Champaign, IL: Human Kinetics.

Chelladurai, P., & Chang, K. (2000). Targets and standards of quality in sport services. *Sport Management Review, 3,* 1-22.

Cheyne, T.L., & Ritter, F.E. (2001, April). Targeting audiences on the Internet. Association for Chicago's Home Plate Virtual Sign Location Out Performs Houston's Placement during World Series Telecasts. Retrieved October 28, 2005, from www.joycejulius.com.

Computing machinery. *Communications of the ACM, 44*(4), 94-98.

Chuy v. The Philadelphia Eagles Football Club. (1979). 595 F. 2d 1265.

Cialdini, R.B., & De Nicholas, M.E. (1989). Self-presentation by association. *Journal of Personality & Social Psychology, 34*, 366-375.

Clarke, M.M. (2005, April 25). More than a game. *Broadcasting & Cable, 135*(17), 38.

Clavio, G., & Pedersen, P.M. (2007). Print and broadcast connections of ESPN: An investigation of the alignment of editorial coverage in *ESPN The Magazine* with ESPN's broadcasting rights. *International Journal of Sport Management, 8*(1), 95-114.

Clement, A. (2002). Contemporary trademark law and sport. *Journal of Legal Aspects of Sport, 12*(1), 1-31.

Clement, A. (2004). *Law in sport and physical activity* (3rd ed.). Dania, FL: Sport & Law.

Coakley, J. (1978). *Sport in society: Issues and controversies.* St. Louis: Mosby.

Coakley, J. (2004). *Sport in society: Issues and controversies* (8th ed.). New York: McGraw-Hill.

Coakley, J., & Dunning, E. (2000). *Handbook of sports studies.* Thousand Oaks, CA: Sage.

Cold Pizza TV. (2005). *ESPN.com.* Retrieved February 23, 2007, from http://www.coldpizza.tv/#.

Collins, J. (2001). *Good to great: Why some companies make the leap . . . and others don't.* New York: HarperCollins.

Collins, P.H. (1994). *Black feminist thought: Knowledge, consciousness and the politics of empowerment.* Boston: Unwin Hyman.

Conrad, M. (2005). *The business of sports: A primer for journalists.* Mahwah, NJ: Erlbaum.

Cooper, A. (2005, March 30). Steroids and the NFL: NFL's possibly insufficient steroid standards. *CBS News Transcripts.* New York: CBS Worldwide.

Corbett, D., & Johnson, W. (2000). The African American female in collegiate sport: Sexism and racism. In D. Brooks & R. Althouse (Eds.), *Racism in college athletics: The African American athlete's experience* (pp. 200-225). Morgantown, WV: FIT.

Covell, D., Walker, S., Siciliano, J., & Hess, P. W. (2003). *Managing sports organizations: Responsibility for performance.* Mason, OH: South-Western.

Covil, E.C. (2005). Radio and its impact on the sports world. *American Sportscasters Online.* Retrieved January 16, 2006, from http://www.americansportscastersonline.com/radiohistory.html.

Cox, J., & Dale, B.G. (2002). Key quality factors in web site design and use: An examination. *International Journal of Quality and Reliability Management, 19*(6/7), 862-889.

Craig, A. (1994). The rise in press criticism of the athlete and the future of libel litigation involving athletes and the press. *Seton Hall Journal of Sports Law, 4*, 527-553.

Craig, J. (2004, April 15). Parents get $1.2 million in puck death. *Columbus Dispatch,* p. 1A.

Craig, S. (2002). *Sports writing: A beginner's guide.* Shoreham, VT: Discover Writing.

Creedon, P.J. (1994a). *Women, media and sport: Challenging gender values.* Thousand Oaks, CA: Sage.

Creedon, P.J. (1994b). Women in boyland: A look at women in American newspaper sports journalism. In P.J. Creedon (Ed.), *Women, media and sport: Challenging gender values* (pp. 67-107). Thousand Oaks, CA: Sage.

Creedon, P.J. (1998). Women, sport, and media institutions: Issues in sports journalism and marketing. In L.A. Wenner (Ed.), *Mediasport* (pp. 88-99). New York: Routledge.

Crepeau, R.C. (2005, December 27). Sport & society. ARETE electronic mailing list. Retrieved November 21, 2006, from http://www.uta.edu/english/sla/s&s051227.html.

Crosset, T.W., & Hums, M.A. (2005). History of sport management. In L.P. Masteralexis, C.A. Barr, & M.A. Hums (Eds.), *Principles and practice of sport management* (2nd ed., pp. 1-18). Boston: Jones & Bartlett.

Crouse, K.C. (2005, February 24). Bonds takes mighty swings but misses badly. *Palm Beach Post,* p. 4C.

Cuneen, J., & Hannan, M.J. (1993). Intermediate measures and recognition testing of sponsorship advertising at an LPGA tournament. *Sport Marketing Quarterly, 2*(1), 47-56.

Cunningham, G.B., & Sagas, M. (2005). Access discrimination in intercollegiate athletics. *Journal of Sport & Social Issues, 29*(2), 148-163.

Curry, T. (2003, December 5). Oakland Raiders' season from hell isn't exactly heaven to beat reporters. *North Gate News Online.* Retrieved November 20, 2006, from http://journalism.berkeley.edu/ngno/stories/001659.html.

Curtis Publishing Company v. Butts. (1967). 388 U.S. 130.

Cutler, N., & Danowski, J. (1980). Process gratification in aging cohorts. *Journalism Quarterly, 57*, 269-277.

Cutlip, S.M., Center, A.H., & Broom, G.M. (2000). *Effective public relations* (8th ed.). Edgewood Cliffs, NJ: Prentice Hall.

Dailey, L. (1999). Designing the world we surf in: A conceptual model of Web atmospherics. *American Marketing Association Conference Proceedings, 10,* 225.

Dailey, L. (2004). Navigational web atmospherics: Explaining the influence of restrictive navigation cues. *Journal of Business Research, 57*, 795-803.

Danzig, A., & Brandwein, P. (Eds.). (1948). *Sport's golden age: A close-up of the fabulous twenties.* New York: Harper.

Davis, A. (2004). *Mastering public relations.* New York: Macmillan.

Debelle, P. (2003). Hewitt's court battle to hot up. *The Age*. Retrieved February 23, 2007, from www.theage.com.au/articles/2003/08/14/1060588526002.html.

Deem, J. (2006). Freedom of the press box: Classifying high school athletes under the Gertz public figure doctrine. *West Virginia Law Review, 108,* 799-829.

DeGaris, L. (2003, December 15). BCS can help itself by helping others. *SportsBusiness Journal, 6*(34), 22.

Dempsey, J.M. (2006). *Sports-talk radio in America.* Binghamton, NY: Haworth.

DeNeui, D.L., & Sachau, D.A. (1996). Spectator enjoyment of aggression in intercollegiate hockey games. *Journal of Sport & Social Issues, 20,* 69-77.

Denham, B.E., Billings, A.C., & Halone, K.K. (2002). Differential accounts of race in broadcast commentary of the 2000 NCAA Men's and Women's Final Four basketball tournaments. *Sociology of Sport Journal, 19*(3), 315-332.

Department of Sport Management Moves into Stylish New Facilities in the Isenberg School. (2004, September 29). *University of Massachusetts Amherst Isenberg School of Management.* Retrieved February 23, 2007, from http://www.isenberg.umass.edu/sportmgt/news/Department_of_Sport__84/.

DeSensi, J.T., Kelley, D.R., Blanton, M.D., & Beitel, P.A. (1990). Sport management curricular evaluation and needs assessment: A multifaceted approach. *Journal of Sport Management, 4*(1), 31-58.

DeVito, J.A. (1990). *Messages: Building interpersonal communication skills.* New York: Harper & Row.

DeVito, J.A. (2005). *Messages: Building interpersonal communication skills* (6th ed.). Boston: Allyn & Bacon.

Dewey, J. (1916) *Democracy and education.* Retrieved January 22, 2006, from www.ilt.columbia.edu/publications/Projects/digitexts/dewey/d_e/chapter01.html.

DirecTV lines up with NFL again. (2004, November 15). *Satellite News, 27*(44), 1.

Disch, L., & Kane, M.J. (1996). When a looker is really a bitch: Lisa Olson, sport, and the heterosexual matrix. *Journal of Women in Culture and Society, 21*(2), 278-308.

Dobrow, L. (2005, February 14). Budding ESPNs target local fans. *Advertising Age, 76*(7), S7.

Dodds, T. (2000, January-February). Opening minds harder than opening doors: Although some still refuse to see, women have made great progress in sports journalism over the years. *American Editor,* 10-11.

Dodds, T. (2005, October 30). The most influential women in Indianapolis sports. *Indianapolis Star,* pp. C1, C4.

Donavan, D., Carlson, B., & Zimmerman, M. (2005). The influence of personality traits on sports fan identification. *Sport Marketing Quarterly, 14*(1), 31-42.

Douglas, S.J. (2002). Letting the boys be boys: Talk radio, male hysteria, and political discourse in the 1980s. In M. Hilmes & J. Loviglio (Eds.), *Essays in the cultural history of radio: Radio reader* (pp. 485-503). New York: Routledge.

Down time for prime time. (2005, October 17). *SportsBusiness Journal, 8,* 10.

Druzin, R. (2006). *Women reporters in the men's locker room: Rugged terrain.* Women's Sports Foundation. Retrieved November 20, 2006, from http://www.womenssportsfoundation.org/cgi-bin/iowa/issues/media/article.html?record=852.

Dunning, E. (1971). *The sociology of sport: A selection of readings.* London: Cass.

Dyreson, M. (1989). The emergence of consumer culture and the transformation of physical culture: American sport in the 1920s. *Journal of Sport History, 16*(3), 261-281.

Eastman, S.T., & Billings, A.C. (1999). Gender parity in the Olympics: Hyping women athletes, favoring men athletes. *Journal of Sport & Social Issues, 23*(2), 140-170.

Eastman, S.T., & Billings, A.C. (2000). Sportscasting and sports reporting: The power of gender bias. *Journal of Sport & Social Issues, 23*(2), 140-170.

Eberhard, W.B., & Myers, M.L. (1988). Beyond the locker room: Women in sports on major daily newspapers. *Journalism Quarterly, 65,* 595-599.

Eder, A. (2007, February 4). Colts and UT star Peyton Manning started his commercial career in Knoxville. *Knight Ridder Tribune Business News,* p. 1.

Edwards, B. (2004). *Edward R. Murrow and the birth of broadcast journalism.* Hoboken, NJ: Wiley.

Edwards, H. (1973). *The sociology of sport.* Homewood, IL: Dorsey.

Egan, P. (1812). *Boxiana.* London: Sherwood.

Eisenstock, A. (2001). *Sports talk: A journey inside the world of sports talk radio.* New York: Pocket.

Eitzen, D.S., & Sage, G.H. (1997). *Sociology of North American sport.* Dubuque, IA: Brown.

Emery, M., Emery, E., & Roberts, N.L. (2000). *The press and America: An interpretive history of the mass media.* Boston: Allyn & Bacon.

Enda, J. (2002, Spring). Women journalists see progress, but not nearly enough: The shortage of women editors reverberates through the ranks. *Neiman Reports,* 67.

Equal opportunities: U.S. Open sees success with men, women. (2005, September 19). *SportsBusiness Journal, 8,* 12.

Eroglu, S.A., Machleit, K.A., & Davis, L.M. (2001). Atmospherics qualities of online retailing: A conceptual model and implications. *Journal of Business Research, 50,* 177-184.

Estate of Presley v. Russen. (1981). 513 F. Supp. 1339.

Evensen, B.J. (1993). Jazz age journalism's battle over professionalism, circulation, and the sports page. *Journal of Sport History, 20,* 229-246.

Evensen, B.J. (1996). *When Dempsey fought Tunney: Heroes, hokum, and storytelling in the jazz age.* Knoxville: University of Tennessee.

Ex-coach confesses illiteracy. (2005, November 4). *Indianapolis Star,* p. D2.

Executives focus on the fan experience. (2005, May 23). *SportsBusiness Journal, 8*(5), 9.

Exit interview: Shapiro on sports. (2005, October 3). *SportsBusiness Journal, 8,* 1.

Facts about newspapers: A statistical summary of the newspaper industry. (2004). Newspaper Association of America. Retrieved January 19, 2006, from www.naa.org/info/facts04/.

Fallows, D. (2004). *The Internet and daily life: Many Americans use the Internet in everyday activities, but traditional offline habits still dominate.* Washington, DC: The Pew Institute and American Life Project.

Feinstein, J. (2004). *Caddy for life: The Bruce Edwards story.* New York: Little Brown.

Fensch, T. (1995). *The sports writing handbook* (2nd ed.). Hillsdale, NJ: Erlbaum.

Field, S. (1999). *Career opportunities in the sports industry* (2nd ed.). New York: Checkmark.

The 50 most influential people in sports business: 2006. (2006, November 18). *SportsBusiness Journal, 9* (29). 17.

Filo, K., & Funk, D. (2005). Congruence between attractive product features and virtual content delivery for Internet market communication. *Sport Marketing Quarterly, 14*(2), 112-122.

Fink, D., & Laupase, R. (2000). Perceptions of website design characteristics: A Malaysian/Australian comparison. *Internet Research, 10*(1), 44.

Fisher, E. (2005a, September 19). 'Glogs' brings color commentary to the web. *SportsBusiness Journal, 8*(20), 7.

Fisher, E. (2005b, October 31). Is sports video next for iPod? *SportsBusiness Journal, 8*(26), 1.

Fisher, E. (2006, January 9). Google gets in the game with NBA. *SportsBusiness Journal, 8*(35), 1.

Fitzgerald, K. (2004, November 8). Viewers game for niche sports. *Advertising Age, 75*(45), S6.

Folkerts, J., & Lacy, S. (2004). *The media in your life: An introduction to mass communication* (3rd ed). Boston: Pearson.

Folkerts, J., Lacy, S., & Davenport, L. (1998). *The media in your life: An introduction to mass communication.* Boston: Allyn & Bacon.

Ford, N. (1998). *Photojournalism as a career.* Retrieved February 23, 2007, from http://NLFord.com/career/intro.shtml.

Forman, I. (2003). Layout. In N. Boyce, I. Forman, D. Gibbons, & A. Roselli (Eds.), *Web graphics for non-designers.* Berkeley, CA: Glasshaus. Chap. 5.

Foss, S.K. (2004). *Rhetorical criticism: Exploration & practice* (3rd ed.). Long Grove, IL: Waveland.

Fountain, C. (1993). *Sportswriter: The life and times of Grantland Rice.* Bridgewater, NJ: Replica.

Fox Sports. (2006). *News Corporation.* Retrieved August 22, 2006, from www.newscorp.com/management/foxsports.html.

Frangi, A., & Fletcher, M. (2002). *So you want media coverage: A simple guide on how to get it and how to handle it.* St. Lucia: University of Queensland.

Freeman, M. (2001). *ESPN: The uncensored history.* Lanham, MD: Taylor.

Frey, J.H., & Eitzen, D.S. (1991). Sport and society. *Annual Review of Sociology, 17,* 503-522.

Fuller, L.K. (2006). *Sport, rhetoric, & gender: Historical perspectives and media representations.* New York: Palgrave Macmillan.

Funk, D.C., & James, J. (2001). The psychological continuum model: A conceptual framework for understanding an individual's psychological connection to sport. *Sport Management Review, 4,* 119-150.

Funk, T. (2005, April 28). Congress to use Panthers' steroid case as test to assess NFL policy. *The Charlotte Observer,* 1A.

Gaines, P. (2004, July 31). Doping: Will the Olympic Games in Athens be clean? *The Record,* p. J1.

Gallico, P. (1946). *Confessions of a story writer.* New York: Knopf.

Gallico, P. (1965). *Golden people.* Garden City, NJ: Doubleday.

Gans, H.J. (1979). *Deciding what's news: A study of CBS Evening News, NBC Nightly News, Newsweek, and Time.* New York: Vintage.

Garner, B.A. (2004). *Black's Law Dictionary* (8th ed.). St. Paul, MN: West Group.

Garrison, B., with Sabljak, M. (1993). *Sports reporting* (2nd ed.). Ames: Iowa State University.

Gelb, A. (2003). *City room.* New York: Putnam.

George, D. (2005, January 14). Limiting access? That's not news. *Palm Beach Post,* pp. 1C, 10C.

Gertz v. Robert Welch, Inc. (1974). 418 U.S. 323.

Gettings, J. (2005). *Civil disobedience: Black medallists raise fists for Civil Rights Movement.* Retrieved January 28, 2006, from www.infoplease.com/spot/mm-mexicocity.html.

Gill, J. (2005, November). Squelching office conflicts. *Inc. Magazine, 40,* 42.

Gillentine, A., & Crow, R.B. (2005). Introduction to the sport industry. In A. Gillentine & R.B. Crow (Eds.), *Foundations of sport management* (pp. 1-9). Morgantown, WV: FIT.

Gillentine, A., Crow, R.B., & Bradish, C. (2005). Communication and media relations in sport . In A. Gillentine & R.B. Crow (Eds.), *Foundations of sport management* (pp. 21-33). Morgantown, WV: FIT.

Gitlin, T. (2000). *Inside prime time.* Berkeley: University of California.

Gladden, J.M., & Funk, D.C. (2001). Understanding brand loyalty in sport: Examining the link between brand associations and brand loyalty. *International Journal of Sports Marketing & Sponsorship, 3,* pp. 67-86.

Gladden, J.M., & Funk, D.C. (2002). Developing an understanding of brand associations in team sport: Empirical evidence from consumers of professional sport. *Journal of Sport Management, 16*(1), 54-81.

Gladden, J.M., Milne, G.R., & Sutton, W.A. (1998). A conceptual framework for assessing brand equity in Division I college athletics. *Journal of Sport Management, 12*(1), 1-19.

Glatzer, J. (2007). *Interview with Bud Collins. Absolute write.* Retrieved March 12, 2007, from www.absolutewrite.com/specialty_writing/bud_collins.htm.

Golden age of radio 1935-50. (2005). Retrieved January 21, 2006, from http://history.acusd.edu/gen/recording/radio2.html.

Goss, B. (1996). Intrapersonal communication. In M.B. Salwen & D.W. Stacks (Eds.), *An integrated approach to communication theory and research* (pp. 335-344). Mahwah, NJ: Erlbaum.

Graduate Programs. (2007). University of San Francisco College of Arts & Sciences. Retrieved March 14, 2007, from http://artsci.usfca.edu/academics/graduate/sport/overview.html.

Grainger, A., & Andrews, D.L. (2005). Resisting Rupert through sporting rituals? The transnational media corporation and global-local sport cultures. *International Journal of Sport Management and Marketing, 1*(1/2), 3-16.

Grant, D., Keenoy, T., & Oswick, C. (1998). Introduction: Organizational discourse: Of diversity, dichotomy and multi-disciplinarity. In D. Grant, T. Keenoy, & C. Oswick (Eds.), *Discourse and organization* (pp. 1-13). London: Sage.

Gratton, C., & Jones, I. (2004). *Research methods for sport studies.* London: Routledge.

Gray, D.P., & McEvoy, C.D. (2005). Sport marketing: Strategies and tactics. In B.L. Parkhouse (Ed.), *The management of sport: Its foundation and application* (4th ed., pp. 228-255). New York: McGraw-Hill.

Greenberg, B.S., & Salwen, M.B. (1996). Mass communication theory and research: Concepts and models. In M.B. Salwen & D.W. Stacks (Eds.), *An integrated approach to communication theory and research* (pp. 63-78). Mahwah, NJ: Erlbaum.

Greenwell, T., Fink, J., & Pastore, D. (2002). Perceptions of the service experience: Using demographic and psychographic variables to identify customer segments. *Sport Marketing Quarterly, 11*(4), 233-241.

Griffin, C.L. (2004). *Invitation to public speaking* (Annotated instructor's edition). Belmont, CA: Thomson Wadsworth.

Gronroos, C. (1991). The marketing strategy continuum: Towards a marketing concept for the 1990s. *Management Decision, 29*(1), 7-13.

Grossman, A. (2005a, November 7). Sports radio stations take their brand extension into publications, even restaurants. *SportsBusiness Journal, 8,* 11.

Grossman, A. (2005b, November 14). Audience grows for sports radio. *SportsBusiness Journal, 8,* 6.

Grossman, A. (2005c, December 19). Sports stations try to scoop up Stern fans. *SportsBusiness Journal, 8,* 9.

Grossman, B. (2005, September 26). Lots of networks want a piece of NASCAR. *Broadcasting & Cable, 135*(39), 18.

Grover, R. (2005, October 17). Mr. touchdown for NFL TV deals. *BusinessWeek,* p. 78.

Growing number of professional sports teams start own TV networks. (2006, January 16). *Bloomington Herald-Times,* p. B2.

Grunig, J., & Grunig, L. (1992). Models of public relations and communications. In J. Grunig (Ed.), *Excellence in public relations and communication management* (pp. 285-326). Hillsdale, NJ: Erlbaum.

Grunig, J., & Hunt, T. (1984). *Managing public relations.* New York: Holt, Rinehart, & Winston.

Guth, D., & Marsh, C. (2003). *Public relations: A values driven approach* (2nd ed.). Boston: Allyn & Bacon.

Guttman, A. (2002). *The Olympics: A history of the modern games.* Urbana: University of Illinois.

Hackman, M.Z., & Johnson, C.E. (2004). *Leadership: A communication perspective* (4th ed.). Long Grove, IL: Waveland.

Hackos, J.T., & Stevens, D.M. (1997). *Standards for online communication: Publishing information for the Internet/World Wide Web/help systems/corporate intranets.* Hoboken, NJ: Wiley.

Haelan Laboratories, Inc. v. Topps Chewing Gum, Inc. (1953), 346 U.S. 816; 74 S. Ct. 26.

Halberstam, D., & Stout, G. (Eds.). (1999). *The best American sports writing of the century.* Boston: Houghton Mifflin.

Halbert, C., & Latimer, M. (1994). Battling gendered language: An analysis of the language used by sports commentators in a televised coed tennis competition. *Sociology of Sport Journal, 11*(3), 298-308.

Hammel, B. (2005, September 18). Chris Schenkel: Goodbye to a hero. *Bloomington Herald-Times,* p. A13.

Halper, D.L. (2001). *Invisible stars: A social history of women in American broadcasting.* Armonk, NY: M.E. Sharpe.

Hammerich, K., & Heinemann, K. (Eds.). (1975). *Texte zur soziologie des sports.* Schorndorf: Hoffman.

Hammersley, M., & Atkinson, P. (2002). *Ethnography: Principles in practice* (2nd ed.). London: Routledge.

Hanan, M. (1980). *Life-styled marketing. How to position products for premium profits.* New York: Amacom.

Hancock, M.M. (2004). How to shoot football—Part I. Photojournalism. Retrieved November 20, 2006, from http://markhancock.blogspot.com/2004/08/how-to-shoot-football-part-i.html.

Harbord, J.G. (1929). The commercial uses of radio. *Annals of the American Academy of Political and Social Science, 142,* 57-63.

Hardin, M. (2005). Stopped at the gate. *Journalism and Mass Communication Quarterly, 82*(1), 62-77.

Hardin, M., Dood, J., Chance, J., & Walsdorf, K. (2004). Sporting images in Black and White: Race in newspaper coverage of the 2000 Olympic Games. *The Howard Journal of Communications, 15,* 211-227.

Hardin, R., & McClung, S. (2002). Collegiate sports information: A profile of the profession. *Public Relations Quarterly, 47*(2), 35-39.

Hardy, S. (1997). Sport in urbanizing America: A historical review. *Journal of Urban History, 23,* 675-708.

Hargie, O., & Dickson, D. (2004). *Skilled interpersonal communication: Research, theory and practice* (4th ed.). London: Routledge.

Harlan, C. (2006, January 4). Paterno's statements trigger reactions. *Pittsburgh Post-Gazette,* p. F4.

Harper, W.A. (1999). *How you played the game: The life of Grantland Rice.* Columbia: University of Missouri.

Harris, J.H. (2002, May 20). Marketing stars and targeting women a winning combination for WNBA. *SportsBusiness Journal, 5,* 11.

Harrison, C., Lee, A.M., & Belcher, D. (1999). Race and gender differences in sport participation as a function of self-schema. *Journal of Sport and Social Issues, 23*(3), 287-307.

Hartley, P. (1999). *Interpersonal communication* (2nd ed.). London: Routledge.

Hassan, S., & Li, F. (2005). Evaluating the usability and content usefulness of websites: A benchmarking approach. *Journal of Electronic Commerce in Organizations, 3*(2), 46-67.

Hattersley, M.E., & McJannet, L.M. (2005). *Management communication: Principles and practice* (2nd ed.). New York: McGraw-Hill/Irwin.

Hawthorne, B. (2001). *The coverage of interscholastic sports.* Austin, TX: Interscholastic League Press Conference.

Heath, R.L., & Bryant, J. (2000). *Human communication theory and research: Concepts, contexts, and challenges* (2nd ed.). Mahwah, NJ: Erlbaum.

Hedrick, T. (2000). *The art of sportscasting: How to build a successful career.* Lanham, MD: Diamond.

Heeter, T. (2005, Sept. 25). Sport letters: Reader is no fan of columnist Kravitz. *Indianapolis Star,* p. 2C.

Heitzmann, W.R. (2004). *Careers for sports nuts and other athletic types* (3rd ed.). Chicago: VGM Career Books.

Helitzer, M. (1999). *The dream job: Sports publicity, promotion, and marketing* (3rd ed.). Athens, OH: University Sports Press.

Henry Chadwick. (n.d.). Retrieved March 3, 2007, from www.baseballlibrary.com/ballplayers/player.php?name=Henry_Chadwick.

Henry Chadwick's Hall of Fame plaque. (2006). National Baseball Hall of Fame. Retrieved August 22, 2006, from www.baseballhalloffame.org/hofers_and_honorees/plaques/Chadwick_Henry.htm.

Hertz, L. (2000, January-February). Measuring progress: Nearly 30 years after Title IX, women no longer have to change minds to prove they can play—or cover—sports, changing habits though has proven more difficult. *The American Editor, 806,* 4-9.

Hessert, K. (1998). *Coach's communication playbook.* Charlotte, NC: Sports Media Challenge.

Hettinger, H.S., & Porter, W.A. (1942). Radio regulation: A case study in basic policy conflicts. *Annals of the American Academy of Political and Social Science, 221,* 122-137.

Hickey, E. (2004, March 16). *Sports Illustrated* digital workflow. Rob Galbraith's digital photography insights. Retrieved November 20, 2006, from www.robgalbraith.com/bins/multi_page.asp?cid=7-6453-6821.

Hiestand, M. (2004, May 19). Baseball's box score making quantum leap. *USA Today.* Retrieved November 20, 2006, from www.usatoday.com/sports/columnist/hiestand/2004-05-19-hiestand_x.htm.

Higgins, J.M., & McClellan, S. (2004, June 7). Welcome to the Olympics. *Broadcasting & Cable, 134*(23), 1.

Higgs, C., & McKinley, B. (2005). Why sport management matters. In A. Gillentine & R.B. Crow (Eds.). *Foundations of sport management* (pp. 11-19). Morgantown, WV: FIT.

Hill, L.A. (2004a, September 6). Building a TV sports empire. *Television Week, 23*(36), 11-12.

Hill, L.A. (2004b, September 6). Clown prince of broadcasting. *Television Week, 23*(36), 12.

Hill, L.A. (2005, July 25). A breakaway success. *Electronic Media, 24*(30), 52-53.

Hillenbrand, L. (2001). *Seabiscuit: An American legend.* New York: Random House.

Hilliard, D.C. (October, 1983). If you've come a long way, why do they still call you baby: Magazine profiles of women professional tennis players. Paper presented at the North American Society for the Sociology of Sport Annual meeting, St. Louis, MO.

Hilliard, R.L., & Keith, M.C. (2005). *The broadcast century and beyond: A biography of American broadcasting* (4th ed.). Boston: Focal.

Hitchcock, J.R. (1991). *Sportscasting.* Boston: Focal.

How we see it: Big challenges, payoffs in selling the 24/7 fan. (2005, March 7). *SportsBusiness Journal, 8,* 38.

Howard, D.R., & DeSchriver, T.D. (2005). Financial principles applied to sport management. In L.P.

Masteralexis, C.A. Barr, & M.A. Hums (Eds.), *Principles and practice of sport management* (2nd ed., pp. 54-77). Boston: Jones & Bartlett.

Hums, M.A., O'Bryant, C.P., & Tremble, L. (1996). Strategies for increasing minorities and women in sport management and physical education teacher preparation programs: Common recruitment and retention themes. *Women in Sport and Physical Activity Journal, 5*(2), 89-97.

Hunnicutt, B.K. (1996). *Kellogg's six-hour day.* Philadelphia: Temple University.

Hunt, T., & Grunig, J. (1994). *Public relations techniques.* Fort Worth, TX: Harcourt Brace.

IEG. (2001a). Niche sponsorships selling cars for Subaru. *IEG Sponsorship Report, 20*(19).

IEG. (2001b). Performance research/IEG study highlights what sponsors want. *IEG Sponsorship Report, 20*(24).

IEG. (2004). IEG/Performance research study finds sponsors earning bigger returns. *IEG Sponsorship Report, 23*(4).

IEG. (2005). Performance research: Sponsors say return on investment is up and they are doing more to prove it. *IEG Sponsorship Report, 24*(4).

If you're a grassquit, they will come. The SportsTravel Files. (2001, April). *SportsTravel, 5*(4), 3.

Inabinett, M. (1994). *Grantland Rice and his heroes: The sportswriter as mythmaker in the 1920s.* Knoxville: University of Tennessee.

Industry Statistics. (2005). Association of American Publishers. Retrieved January 19, 2006, from www. publishers.org/industry/index.cfm.

Infinity boss: Radio still "incredibly vibrant." (2005, March 14). *SportsBusiness Journal, 8,* 34.

Irwin, R.L., Sutton, W.A., & McCarthy, L.M. (2002). *Sport promotion and sales management.* Champaign, IL: Human Kinetics.

Isidore, C. (2005, April 22). NFL's rights might. *CNN Money.* Retrieved January 16, 2006, from http:// money.cnn.com/2005/04/22/commentary/column_ sportsbiz/sportsbiz/.

Jankowski, N.W., & Wester, F. (1991). The qualitative tradition in social science inquiry: Contributions to mass communication research. In K.B. Jensen & N.W. Jankowski (Eds.), *A handbook of qualitative methodologies for mass communication research* (pp. 44-74). London: Routledge.

Jansen, B.J., & Spink, A. (2005). Analysis of document viewing patterns of web search engine users. In A. Scime (Ed.), *Web mining: Applications and techniques.* (pp. 339-354). Hershey, PA: Idea Group.

Jeansonne, J., & Dobie, M. (2005, November 27). The Balco legacy: Significant aftershocks of steroids scandal are still being felt. *Newsday,* p. B8.

Jensen, K.B. (1991). Humanistic scholarship as qualitative science: Contributions to mass communication research. In K.B. Jensen & N.W. Jankowski (Eds.), *A handbook of qualitative methodologies for mass communication research* (pp. 17-43). London: Routledge.

Jensen, K.B., & Jankowski, N.W. (1991). *A handbook of qualitative methodologies for mass communication research.* London: Routledge.

Jewell, R.T. (2006). Sports economics: The state of the discipline. In J. Fizel (Ed.), *Handbook of sports economics research* (pp. 9-20). Armonk, NY: M.E. Sharpe.

Jicha, T. (2004, September 20). When TV came to the ballpark. *Television Week, 23*(38), 33-34.

Johnson, J. (2003). *Web bloopers: 60 common web design mistakes and how to avoid them.* Cambridge, MA: Morgan Kaufmann.

Johnson-Reid, K. (2005a, September 5). Ad-ding it up: Sports magazine advertising count. *SportsBusiness Journal, 8*(18), 16.

Johnson-Reid, K. (2005b, September 19). Sporting summer: Sports films rank among top 15. *SportsBusiness Journal, 8*(20), 12.

Jones, M.J., & Schumann, D.W. (2000). The strategic use of celebrity athlete endorsers in *Sports Illustrated*: An historic perspective. *Sport Marketing Quarterly, 9*(2), 65-76.

Jordan, J.S., & Kent, A. (2005). Management and leadership in the sport industry. In A. Gillentine & R.B. Crow (Eds.), *Foundations of sport management* (pp. 35-54). Morgantown, WV: FIT.

Jordan, L. (1927, July 2). Sports reporting was a scholarly occupation fifty years ago. *Editor & Publisher, 60,* 9.

Jorgensen, S.S. (2005). The world's best advertising agency: The sports press. *Mandag Morgen, 37,* pp. 1-7.

Kahn, R. (1999). *A flame of pure fire: Jack Dempsey and the roaring '20s.* New York: Harcourt Brace.

Kane, M. (1989). The post-Title IX female athlete in the media: Things are changing, but how much? *Journal of Physical Education, Recreation, and Dance, 60*(1), 58-62.

Kane, M.J. (2002). Sociological aspects of sport and physical activity. In J. B. Parks & J. Quarterman (Eds.), *Contemporary sport management* (2nd ed., pp. 107-126). Champaign, IL: Human Kinetics.

Kane, M.J., & Disch, L. (1993). Sexual violence and the reproduction of male power in the locker room: A critical analysis of the Lisa Olson "incident." *Sociology of Sport Journal, 10*(4), 331-352.

Kane, M.J., & Greendorfer, S. (1994). The media's role in accommodating and resisting stereotyped images of women in sport. In P. Creedon (Ed.), *Women, media and sport: Challenging gender values* (pp. 28-44). Thousand Oaks, CA: Sage.

Kane, M.J., & Parks, J.B. (1992). The social construction of gender difference and hierarchy in sport journalism—Few new twists on very old themes. *Women in Sport and Physical Activity Journal, 1*(1), 49-83.

Kaplan, D. (2005a, May 16). Don't adjust TV, open fans. *SportsBusiness Journal, 8,* 1.

Kaplan, D. (2005b, August 22). Nielsen to track the buying habits of NFL fans. *SportsBusiness Journal, 8,* 7.

Kaplan, D. (2005c, August 29). Professional tennis. *SportsBusiness Journal, 8*(17), 17.

Kaplan, D. (2005d, September 5). Hewitt's manager wants end to war with ATP. *SportsBusiness Journal, 8*(18), 12.

Karlin, L. (1997). *The guide to careers in sports* (2nd ed.). New York: E.M. Guild.

Keep dome blue, no aiding the enemy. (2006, January 11). *Indianapolis Star,* p. 1D.

Keller, K.L. (1998). *Strategic brand management: Building, measuring, and managing brand equity.* Upper Saddle River, NJ: Prentice Hall.

Kelley, S.W., & Tian, K. (2004). Fanatical consumption: An investigation of the behavior of sports fans through textual data. In L.R. Kahle & C. Riley (Eds.), *Sports marketing and the psychology of marketing communication* (pp. 27-65). Mahwah, NJ: Erlbaum.

Kelley, S.W., & Turley, L.W. (2001). Consumer perceptions of service quality attributes at sporting events. *Journal of Business Research, 54,* 161-166.

Kellner, D. (1981, January). Network television and American society: Introduction to a critical theory of television. *Theory and Society, 10*(1), 31-62.

Kelly, L., Lederman, L.C., & Phillips, G.M. (1989). *Communicating in the workplace: A guide to business and professional speaking.* New York: Harper & Row.

Kerschbaumer, K. (2004a, September 6). Sports tackle high-def. *Broadcasting & Cable, 134*(36), 28.

Kerschbaumer, K. (2004b, November 8). Slam-dunk graphics. *Broadcasting & Cable, 134*(45), 28.

Kerschbaumer, K. (2005, September 26). Directing NASCAR easy? Not so fast. *Broadcasting & Cable, 135*(39), 20.

Kervin, A. (1997). *Sports writing.* London: A & C Black.

Kieran, J. (1948). Forward. In A. Danzig & P. Brandwein (Eds.), *Sport's golden age: A close-up of the fabulous twenties* (p. ix). New York: Harper.

Kim, S., Shaw, T., & Schneider, H. (2003). Web site design benchmarking within industry groups. *Internet Research, 13*(1), 17-26.

King, B. (2004a, February 2). The best pro team web sites. *SportsBusiness Journal, 6,* 19.

King, B. (2004b, March 1). Fan loyalty: What makes fans tick? *SportsBusiness Journal, 7,* 25.

King, B. (2005a, March 7). World Congress of Sports: The 24/7 fan. *SportsBusiness Journal, 8,* 23.

King, B. (2005b, March 14). Reaching today's fans: Delivery of sports info continues to evolve as fans demand more. *SportsBusiness Journal, 7*(44), 8, 17-21.

King, B. (2005c, September 14). A real fight over fantasy. *SportsBusiness Journal, 8*(19), 16.

King, B. (2005d, Nov. 14). Magazines cater to growing industry. *SportsBusiness Journal, 8*(28), 20.

King, B. (2006, April 17). Reaching the 18-34 demo. *Sports Business Journal, 8*(49), 1.

King, C.R. (2004). This is not an Indian—Situating claims about Indianness in sporting worlds. *Journal of Sport & Social Issues, 28*(1), 3-10.

King, D. (2005). A blog to remember. *Information Today, 22*(1), 27-29.

Kinkema, K.M., & Harris, J.C. (1998). MediaSport studies: Key research and emerging issues. In L.A. Wenner (Ed.), *MediaSport* (pp. 27-54). London: Routledge.

Klapper, J.T. (1948). Mass media and the engineering of consent. *The American Scholar, 17*(4), 419-429.

Kline, R.S. (1996). Effective public relations—A model for business. *Management Research News, 19*(6), 55-60.

Knight Foundation awards $1.5 million to Penn State. (2005, September 29). *CentreDaily.* Retrieved November 3, 2005, from www.centredaily.com/mld/centredaily/news/politics/12775936.htm.

Ko, H., Chang-Hoan, C., & Roberts, M. (2005). Internet uses and gratifications: A structural equation model of interactive advertising. *Journal of Advertising, 34*(2), 57-70.

Komoroski, L., & Biemond, H. (1996). Sponsor accountability: Designing and utilizing an evaluation system. *Sport Marketing Quarterly, 5*(2), 35-39.

Koppett, L. (1994). *Sports illusion, sports reality: A reporter's view of sports, journalism, and society.* Urbana: University of Illinois.

Kotler, P. (1973). Atmospherics as a marketing tool. *Journal of Retailing, 49,* 48-64.

Kovach, B., & Rosenstiel, T. (2001). *The elements of journalism: What newspeople should know and the public should expect.* New York: Random House.

Kravitz, B. (2005, December 4). Good antibiotics will cure bosses of blogging feeling. *Indianapolis Star,* pp. C1, C8.

Kroichick, R. (2005, August 26). Vicious cycle, the saga: Controversy over doping and lawsuits are nothing new for Armstrong. *San Francisco Chronicle,* p. A1.

Krzyzewski, M., & Phillips, D.T. (2000). *Leading with the heart: Coach K's successful strategies for basketball, business, and life.* New York: Warner.

Lacey, K. (2002). Radio in the Great Depression: Promotional culture, public service, and propaganda. In M. Hilmes & J. Loviglio (Ed.), *Essays in the cultural history of radio: Radio reader* (pp. 21-40). New York: Routledge.

Lafayette, J. (2004a, January 19). Sharing Olympics bounty. *Television Week, 23*(3), 14-15.

Lafayette, J. (2004b, August 23). Olympics bring eyeballs to NBC. *Television Week, 23*(34), 3-4.

Lafayette, J. (2004c, August 30). Peacock crowing about Olympics. *Television Week, 23*(35), 4.

Lafayette, J. (2004d, November 1). NBA TV has big plans for season. *Electronic Media, 23*(44), 8-9.

Lafayette, J. (2005a, February 7). NBA TV fans get courtside access. *Television Week, 24*(6), 7-8.

Lafayette, J. (2005b, September 19). ABC's final drive. *Television Week, 24*(38), 65-66.

Lage, L. (2005, November 18). Brawl at the Palace lives in infamy. Retrieved November 20, 2006, from www.chinadaily.com.cn/english/doc/2005-11/18/content_495925.htm.

Lamb, C. (2004). *Blackout: The untold story of Jackie Robinson's first spring training.* Lincoln: University of Nebraska Press.

Lanham Act Article. 15, Section 43(a), (U.S. Constitution).

Lapchick, R. (2004). *2004 Racial and gender report card.* Orlando, FL: Institute for Diversity and Ethics in Sport.

Lapchick, R. (2005). *2005-06 bowl bound teams APR and graduation rates report.* Orlando, FL: Institute for Diversity and Ethics in Sport.

Lardinoit, T., & Derbaix, C (2001). Sponsorship and recall of sponsors. *Psychology & Marketing, 18*(2), 167-190.

Laucella, P., & Osborne, B. (2002). Libel and college coaches. *Journal of Legal Aspects of Sport, 12*, 183-204.

Laucella, P. C. (2004). An analysis of mainstream, black, and Communist press coverage of Jesse Owens in the 1936 Berlin Olympic Games. (Doctoral dissertation, University of North Carolina-Chapel Hill.) *Proquest Dissertations and Theses*, Document ID 845 70 7401.

Laucella, P.C. (2005, Spring). [Review of the book *Blackout: The untold story of Jackie Robinson's first spring training*]. *Journalism & Mass Communication Quarterly, 82*(1), 208-209.

Laverie, D.A., & Arnett, D.B. (2000). Factors affecting fan attendance: The influence of identity salience and satisfaction. *Journal of Leisure Research, 32*(2), 225-246.

Ledbetter, J. (2000, January/February). Wanted: A way of counting that you can count on. *Columbia Journalism Review, 38*(5), 66-67.

Lee, K.C., & Baldwin, J.R. (2004). History of 'speech communication' research: Models and messages. In J.R. Baldwin, S.D. Perry, & M.A. Moffitt (Eds.), *Communication theories for everyday life* (pp. 55-73). Boston: Pearson.

Lefton, T. (2002, April 15). League deals signal change. *SportsBusiness Journal, 5*, 23.

Lefton, T. (2003, September 22). NFL charges MBNA $96M. *SportsBusiness Journal, 6*, 1.

Lefton, T. (2005, May 30). How McDonald's has used sports to package the perfect pitch during most of its 50 year history. *SportsBusiness Journal, 8*(6), 15.

Lefton, T. (2006, January 16). NFL: Sponsors spend $330 M behind XL. *SportsBusiness Journal, 8*(36), 4.

Leonard, W. M. (1998). *A sociological perspective of sport.* New York: Macmillan.

Lewis, M. (1998). High commissioner Pete Rozelle. Retrieved January 16, 2006, from www.time.com/time/time100/profile/rozelle.html.

Li, M., Hofacre, S., & Mahony, D.F. (2001). *Economics of sport.* Morgantown, WV: Fitness Information Technology.

Liberman, N. (2005, August 8). Ranking team websites. Online hits: The best and how they do it. *SportsBusiness Journal, 8*(15), 1.

Lieberman, S., Simons, G.F., & Berado, K. (2004). *Putting diversity to work: How to successfully lead a diverse workforce.* Menlo Park, CA: Crisp.

Likert, R. (1961). *New patterns of management.* New York: McGraw-Hill.

Limon, I. (2005, October 26). Air Force coach investigated for making racial comments. *Albuquerque Tribune*, p. B3.

Lippmann, W. (1922). *Public opinion.* New York: Simon & Schuster.

Lipsyte, R.W., & Levine, P. (1995). *Idols of the game: A sporting history of the American century.* Atlanta: Turner.

Listening to two guys sitting in a bar. (1991, July). *Broadcasting, 29*, 61.

Littlejohn, S.W., & Foss, K.A. (2005). *Theories of human communication* (8th ed.). Belmont, CA: Wadsworth.

Lombardo, B. (1978). The Harlem Globetrotters and the perception of the black stereotype. *The Physical Educator, 35*(2), 60-63.

Lontos, P. (2004). Max your relationship with the media. *Consulting to Management, 15*(4), 29-31.

Lough, N.L. (1996). Factors affecting corporate sponsorship of women's sport. *Sport Marketing Quarterly, 5*(2), 11-19.

Lowery, S.A., & DeFleur, M.L. (1995). *Milestones in mass communication research: Media effects* (3rd ed.). White Plains, NY: Longman.

Lowes, M.D. (2000). *Inside the sports pages: Work routines, professional ideologies, and the manufacture of sports news.* Toronto: University of Toronto.

Lowrie, C.K. (2005, January 15). *Walter Iooss: Shooting from the sidelines. Double Exposure.* Retrieved November 20, 2006, from www.photoworkshop.com/double_exposure/publish/WalterIoossShootingFromTheSidelines.shtml.

Loy, J.W., & Kenyon, G.S. (1969). *Sport, culture and society.* New York: Macmillan.

Ludtke v. Kuhn. (1978). 461 F. Supp. 86.

Ludwig, S., & Karabetsos, J. (1999). Objectives and evaluation processes utilized by sponsors of the 1996 Olympic Games. *Sport Marketing Quarterly, 8*(1), 11-19.

Luschen, G. (2000). Doping in sport as deviant behavior and its social control. In J. Coakley, & E. Dunning (Eds), *Handbook of sports studies* (pp. 461-476). Thousand Oaks, CA: Sage.

Luschen, G., & Weis, K. (1976). *Die soziologie des sports*. Darmstadt: Luchterhand.

Lussier, R.N. (2005). *Human relations in organizations: Applications and skill building* (6th ed.). New York: McGraw-Hill/Irwin.

Luthans, F., Rosenkrantz, S., & Hennessey, H. (1985). What do successful managers really do? An observational study of managerial activities. *Journal of Applied Behavioral Science, 21*(3), 255-270.

MacCambridge, M. (1997). *The franchise: A history of Sports Illustrated magazine*. New York: Hyperion.

MacDonald, C.N. (2004). Gamecasts and NBA v. Motorola: Do they still love this game? *North Carolina Journal of Law and Technology, 5*, 329-349.

Macgregor, J., & Evanitsky, O. (2005). *Sunday money: Speed! lust! madness! death! A hot lap around America with NASCAR*. New York: HarperCollins.

Madden, M. (2003). *America's online pursuits. The changing picture of who's online and what they do*. Washington, DC: Pew Internet and American Life Project.

Making amends. Paterno conciliatory with media, mum on Conner. (2005, September 20). Retrieved on October 4, 2005, http://sportsillustrated. cnn.com/2005/football/ncaa/09/20/paterno.conner. ap/.

Making the switch to magazines. (2006). Magazine Publishers of America. Retrieved November 20, 2006, from www.magazine.org/careers/Career_ Guides___Resources/switch.pdf.

Mamchak, P.S., & Mamchak, S.R. (1989). *Complete communications manual for coaches and athletic directors*. West Nyack, NY: Parker.

Mandese, J. (2005, January 31). Big ticket. *Broadcasting & Cable, 135*(5), 14.

Mann, S. (2003). John Clare's guide to media handling. *Leadership and Organization Development Journal, 24*(7/8), 419.

Manring, K. (2005, Sept. 26). "The Boilermaker" to stand tall at Purdue. *Indianapolis Star*, p. 1B.

March Madness Athletic Association LLC v. Netfire, Inc. (2005) (Sports Marketing International). 162 F. Supp. 2d 560.

Marchand, A. (2005, January 28). "Madness" on the Internet. *New York Post*, p. 72.

Marchionini, G. (1995). *Information seeking in electronic environments*. New York: Cambridge University.

Mason, J.G., & Paul, J. (1988). *Modern sport management*. Englewood Cliffs, NJ: Prentice Hall.

Mateo, M. (1996, July 19). 100 years of gold and glory: Let the celebration begin. *Fort Lauderdale Sun-Sentinel*, p. 1G.

Mateo, S. (1986). The effect of sex and gender-schematic processing on sport participation. *Sex Roles, 15*(7/8), 417-432.

Mathisen, J.A., & Mathisen, G.S. (1991). The rhetoric of racism in sport: Tom Brokaw revisited. *Sociology of Sport Journal, 8*, 168-177.

Mayeda, D.T. (1999). From model minority to economic threat: Media portrayals of Major League Baseball pitchers Hideo Nomo and Hideki Irabo. *Journal of Sport & Social Issues, 23*(2), 203-217.

McCarthy, M. (2005, January 20). No tape delay during halftime show. *USA Today*. Retrieved January 21, 2006, from www.usatoday.com/money/ media/2005-01-20-bowl-cover-side_x.htm.

McChesney, R.W. (1989). Media made sport: A history of sports coverage in the United States. In L.A. Wenner (Ed.), *Media, sports, and society* (pp. 49-69). Newbury Park: Sage.

McCleneghan, J.S. (1994, March 19). Sports columnists sound off. *Editor & Publisher, 127*(12), 72.

McCleneghan, J.S. (1995). The sports information director—No attention, no respect, and a PR practitioner in trouble. *Public Relations Quarterly, 40*(2), 28-33.

McClung, B. (2005, October 31/November 6). Monahan finds his way to Fenway from Deutsche Bank Championship. *SportsBusiness Journal, 8*(26), 26.

McCombs, M.E., & Shaw, D.L. (1972). The agenda-setting function of mass media. *Public Opinion Quarterly, 36*(2), 176-187.

McCracken, G. (1988). *The long interview: Qualitative research methods* (Vol. 13). Newbury Park, CA: Sage.

McDonald, M., Milne, G., & Hong, J. (2002). Motivational factors for evaluating sport spectator and participant markets. *Sport Marketing Quarterly, 11*(2), 100-113.

McFarland, K. (2005, November). The psychology of success. *Inc. Magazine*, pp. 158-159.

McGaughey, R.E., & Mason, K.H. (1998). The Internet as a marketing tool. *Journal of Marketing Theory and Practice, 6*(3), 1-11.

McGillan, R. (2005). Mary Garber: Legendary sportswriter. *Womens Sports Foundation*. Retrieved November 20, 2006, from www. womenssportsfoundation.org/cgi-bin/iowa/issues/ media/article.html?record=798.

McGowan, A. (2004, February 2). The key to building a better Web site? Follow these 5 steps. *SportsBusiness Journal, 7*, 25.

McGowan, A., & Bouris, G. (2005). Sport communications. In L.P. Masteralexis, C.A. Barr, & M.A. Hums (Eds.), *Principles and practice of sport management* (2nd ed., pp. 340-359). Sudbury, MA: Jones & Bartlett.

McGraw, M., & Gullifor, P. (2003). *Courting success: Muffet McGraw's formula for winning in sports and in life*. Lanham, MD: Taylor Trade.

McNeil, R. (2006). Mission. OT Magazine Media Kit. Retrieved January 19, 2006, from www.pbfn.org/OTMediaKit.pdf.

McQuail, D. (1996). *Mass communication theory: An introduction* (3rd ed.). London: Sage.

McQuail, D. (2002). *McQuail's reader in mass communication theory.* Thousand Oaks, CA: Sage.

McQuail, D., & Windahl, S. (1993). *Communication models for the study of mass communications* (2nd ed.). New York: Longman.

Media tracker. (2005, November 21). What teens are reading. *SportsBusiness Journal, 8*(29), 9.

Media tracker. (2007, February 19). Super Bowl. *SportsBusiness Journal,* 11.

Meek, A. (1997). An estimate of the size and supported economic activity of the sports industry in the United States. *Sport Marketing Quarterly, 6*(4), 15-21.

Megargee, S. (2004, October 25). His idea created magazine giant. *Stuart News,* pp. 1C, 3C.

Member bulletin board. (2005, September 15). *The Indiana Publisher, 70*(19), 2.

Messere, F.J. (2005). U.S. policy: Telecommunications Act of 1996. Museum of Broadcast Communication. Retrieved November 20, 2006, from www.museum.tv/archives/etv/U/htmlU/uspolicyt/uspolicyt.htm.

Messner, M.A., Duncan, M.C., & Jensen, K. (1993). Separating the men from the girls: The gendered language of televised sports. In D.S. Eitzen (Ed.), *Sport in contemporary society* (pp. 219-233). New York: St. Martin's.

Messner, M., Dunbar, M., & Hunt, D. (2000). The televised sport manhood formula. *Journal of Sport & Social Issues, 24,* 380-394.

Meyer, P. (2002). *Precision journalism: A reporter's introduction to social science methods* (4th ed.). Lanham, MD: Rowman & Littlefield.

Michman, R., Mazze, E., & Greco, A. (2003). *Lifestyle marketing: Reaching the new American consumer.* Westport, CT: Prager.

Mickey, B. (2006, January 4). Startup stories: Taking on a life of its own. *Folio.* Retrieved January 18, 2006, from http://foliomag.com/index.php?id=396&backPID=392&tt_news=1451.

Middleton, K., Trager, R., & Chamberlin, B. (2000). *The law of public communication* (5th ed.). New York: Longman.

Migala, D. (2004, September 13). If your website doesn't have these features, you're losing business. *SportsBusiness Journal, 7*(19), 15.

Migala, D. (2005a, February). Activation strategies: Discover how teams are assisting sponsors to better activate their sponsorships. *The Migala Report 2*(5), 1-3.

Migala, D. (2005b, October). Sponsor scouting report. *The Migala Report 3*(1), 1-7.

Milbrandt, G., & Stephenson, C. (2001). *Careers in computing.* Toronto: Holt Software.

Miller apologizes for skiing drunk remarks: Olympic gold medal hopeful caused firestorm with "60 minutes" interview. (2006, January 12). The Associated Press. Retrieved January 24, 2006, from http://msnbc.msn.com/id/10820499/.

Miller, P., & Miller, R. (1995). The invisible woman: Female sports journalists in the workplace. *Journalism & Mass Communications Quarterly, 72*(4), 883-889.

Milliman, R.E., & Fugate, D.L. (1993). Atmospherics as an emerging influence in the design of exchange environments. *Journal of Marketing Management, 3,* 66-74.

Miloch, K. (2005). Making it in the minors: Seven simple steps to achieving sustained financial health. *Sport Management and Related Topics Journal, 2*(1), 53-62.

Miloch, K., & Lambrecht, K. (2006). Consumer awareness of sponsorship at grassroots sport events. *Sport Marketing Quarterly, 15*(3), 147-154.

Miloch, K., & Pedersen, P. (2006). Sport information directors and the media: An analysis of a highly symbiotic relationship. *Journal of Contemporary Athletics, 2*(1), 91-103.

Miloch, K.S., Pedersen, P.M., Smucker, M.K., & Whisenant, W.A. (2005). The current state of women print journalists: An analysis of the status and careers of females in newspapers sports departments. *Public Organization Review, 5,* 219-232.

Mindich, D. (1998). *Just the facts: How "objectivity" came to define American journalism.* New York: Columbia University.

Modaff, D.P., & DeWine, S. (2002). *Organizational communication: Foundations, challenges, and misunderstandings.* Los Angeles: Roxbury.

Mogel, L. (2000). *Careers in communications and entertainment.* New York: Simon & Schuster.

Montana v. San Jose Mercury News, Inc. (1995). 34 Cal. App. 4th 790.

Montieth, M. (2005, October 30). Cover boy Artest's night of shame earns him nationwide fame. *Indianapolis Star,* pp. 1, 11.

Morales, M. (2004, October 11). The Latino playing field. *Multichannel News, 25*(41), 58.

Morris Communications Co., LLC v. PGA Tour. (2004). 125 S. Ct. 87.

Mulligan, J.F., & Mulligan, K.T. (1998). *The Mulligan guide to sports journalism careers.* Lincolnwood, IL: VGM Career Horizons.

Mullin, B.J., Hardy, S., & Sutton, W.A. (2007). *Sport marketing* (3rd ed.). Champaign, IL: Human Kinetics.

Muret, D. (2006, September 25). Lexus Experience rolling out with T-wolves. *SportsBusiness Journal, 9*(21), 7.

Murrell, A.J., & Curtis, E.M. (1994). Casual attributions of performance for Black and White quarterbacks in the NFL: A look at the sports pages. *Journal of Sport & Social Issues, 18*(3), 224-233.

Namath v. Sports Illustrated. (1976). 39 N.Y.2d 897.

Nardi, B., Schiano, D., & Gumbrecht, M. (2004). Blogging as social activity, or, would you let 900 million people read your diary? *Computer Supported Cooperative Work, 6*(3), 222-231.

National Basketball Association v. Sports Team Analysis and Tracking Systems, Inc. (1996). 939 F. Supp. 1071.

National Football League v. Primetime 24 Joint Venture. (2000) 211 F.3d 10.

NBCU's Olympics a grand experiment. (2004). *Television Week, 23*(32), 8.

Neff, J. (2005, January 31). Great value at $80,000 per second. *Advertising Age, 76*(5), 4-5.

Nethery, R. (2005, October 31). Big business behind the PBR. *SportsBusiness Journal, 8,* 1.

Neupauer, N.C. (1998). Women in the male dominated world of sports information directing: Only the strong survive. *Public Relations Quarterly, 43*(1), 27-30.

New York Times v. Sullivan. (1964). 376 U.S. 254.

Newspaper Circulation Volume. (2005). Newspaper Association of America. Retrieved January 19, 2006, from www.naa.org/artpage.cfm?aid=1610.

Newspaper readership continues to decline. (2005, November 12). *Business and Industry Reporter,* p. 15.

NFL takes safe route, finds twists and turns. (2005, February 14). *SportsBusiness Journal, 8,* 28.

Nichols, W., Moynahan, P., Hall, A., & Taylor, J. (2002). *Media relations in sport.* Morgantown, WV: Fitness Information Technology.

Nielsen, J. (1993). *Usability engineering.* San Diego: Academic Press.

Nielsen, J. (1997, June 15). Top ten mistakes of web management. *Jakob Nielsen's Alertbox.* Retrieved January 21, 2006, from http://useit.com.

Nielsen, J. (2003, August 25). Usability 101: Introduction to usability. Retrieved January 21, 2006, from http://useit.com.

Nielsen, J. (2004, September 13). The need for web design standards. *Jakob Nielsen's Alertbox.* Retrieved January 21, 2006, from http://useit.com.

Nielsen, J., & Tahir, M. (2001). Homepage usability: 50 websites deconstructed. Indianapolis: New Riders.

Nielsen weekly sports ranking. (2004, September 13). *SportsBusiness Journal, 7,* 14.

Nielsen weekly sports ranking. (2005, February 21). *SportsBusiness Journal, 8,* 12.

Nightingale, D. (1990, May 7). Reds' start a Lou-Lou': Piniella paints a new picture for Rose-colored franchise. *The Sporting News,* 8.

Nixon, H.L. (1982). The athlete as scholar in college: An exploratory test of four models. In A. Dunleavy, A. Miracle, & C. Rees (Eds.), *Studies in the sociology of sport* (pp. 239-256). Fort Worth: TCU.

Nixon, H.L. (2000). Sport and disability. In J. Coakley & E. Downing (Eds.), *Handbook of sports studies* (pp. 422-438). Thousand Oaks, CA: Sage.

Nordhaus, J. (1999). Celebrities' rights to privacy: How far should the paparazzi be allowed to go? *The Review of Litigation, 18,* 285-315.

Noverr, D.A., & Ziewacz, L.E. (1983). *The games they played: Sports in American history, 1865-1980.* Chicago: Nelson-Hall.

NOW upset by Joe Paterno's comments. (2006, January 8). The Associated Press. Retrieved January 24, 2006, from www.statesman.com/sports/content/shared-gen/ap/General_College_Sports_News/FBC_Paterno_NOW.html.

Nylund, D. (2004). When in Rome: Heterosexism, homophobia, and sports talk radio. *Journal of Sport & Social Issues, 28*(2), 136-168.

O'Brien v. Pabst Sales Co. (1942). 315 U.S. 823.

One cyclist's brave candor. (2006, September 15). *Knight Ridder Tribune Business News,* p. 1.

One-on-one, CBS's research guru says DVRs are good for network TV. (2006, August 21-27). *SportsBusiness Journal, 9*(16), 34.

One-on-one with David Halberstam, journalist and author. (2005, October 31). *SportsBusiness Journal, 8*(26), 34.

Oriard, M. (1991). *Sporting with the Gods: The rhetoric of play and game in American culture.* New York: Cambridge University.

Our mission and values. (2005). ESPN.com. Retrieved November 20, 2006, from www.joinourteam.espn.com/joinourteam/about-mission_statement.html.

Ozanian, M.K. (2005a, January 27). The business of football. *Forbes.* Retrieved November 20, 2006, from www.forbes.com/lists/2004/09/01/04nfland.html.

Ozanian, M.K. (2005b, April 1). Soccer team valuations: The richest soccer teams. *Forbes.com.* Retrieved November 20, 2006, from www.forbes.com/2005/04/01/cx_0401soccerintro_print.html.

Ozanian, M.K. (2005c, April 7). The business of baseball. *Forbes.com.* Retrieved on November 20, 2006 from www.forbes.com/2005/04/06/05mlbland.html.

Padgett, B.A. (1998). *Women in sports journalism: Do the barriers still exist?* Unpublished master's thesis, Eastern Illinois University, Charleston, IL.

Paige, T. (2005, August 15). Golden age is now for sports documentaries. *Multichannel News, 26*(33), 16.

Palmeiro tested positive for stanozolol. (2005a, August 2). *Associated Press, Major League Baseball News Wire.*

Palmeiro tested positive for potent steroid stanozolol. (2005b, August 3). *Associated Press, Major League Baseball News Wire.*

Palmer, J. (2002). Web site usability, design, and performance metrics. *Information Systems Research, 13*(2), 151-169.

Papacharissi, Z., & Rubin, M. (2000). Predictors of Internet use. *Journal of Broadcasting and Electronic Media, 44*(2), 175-196.

Parkhouse, B.L., & Pitts, B.G. (2001). Definition, evolution, and curriculum. In B.L. Parkhouse (Ed.), *The management of sport: Its foundation and application* (pp. 2-14). New York: McGraw-Hill.

Paterno turned it around with fresh faces. (2005, November 12). *Bloomington Herald-Times*, p. B2.

Pauly, J. (1997). Introduction on the origins of media studies (and media scholars). In E.S. Munson & C.A. Warren (Eds.), *James Carey: A critical reader* (pp. 3-13). Minneapolis: University of Minnesota.

Pavlik, J.V., & McIntosh, S. (2004). *Converging media: An introduction to mass communication*. Boston: Allyn & Bacon.

Payne, M. (2006). *Olympic turnaround: How the Olympic Games stepped back from the brink of extinction to become the world's best known brand*. Westport, CT: Praeger.

Pedersen, P. (2004b). Keys to running sports and business. *Treasure Coast Business Journal, 20*(26), Z4, Z20, Z50.

Pedersen, P. (2005a). Business of sports: Couple buys into radio by chance. *Treasure Coast Business Journal, 20*(31), Z8, Z24.

Pedersen, P. (2005b). Business of sports: Lawyer tastes life as a sports agent. *Treasure Coast Business Journal, 20*(32), Z1, Z57-58.

Pedersen, P. (2005c). Shaquille O'Neal is a big money-making machine. *Treasure Coast Business Journal, 20*(33), Z1, Z64.

Pedersen, P. (2005d, May 1). Sports advertising: A super sinkhole? *Treasure Coast Business Journal, 20*(37), Z1, Z12.

Pedersen, P.M. (1997). *Build it and they will come: The arrival of the Tampa Bay Devil Rays*. Stuart, FL: Florida Sports.

Pedersen, P.M. (2002a). Examining equity in newspaper photographs: A content analysis of the print media photographic coverage of interscholastic athletics. *International Review for the Sociology of Sport, 37*(3/4), 303-318.

Pedersen, P.M. (2002b). Investigating interscholastic equity on the sports page: A content analysis of high school athletics newspaper articles. *Sociology of Sport Journal, 19*(4), 419-432.

Pedersen, P.M. (2004a). Business of sports: Greg Norman markets image into a corporate empire. *Treasure Coast Business Journal, 20*(23), Z1, Z18.

Pedersen, P.M., Laucella, P.C., Miloch, K.S., & Fielding, L.W. (2007). The juxtaposition of sport and communication: Defining the field of sport communication. *International Journal of Sport Management & Marketing 2*(3), 193-207.

Pedersen, P.M., & Schneider, R.G. (2003). Investigating the academic openings in sport management: An analysis of the field's professorial position announcements and hires. *International Sports Journal, 7*(1), 34-46.

Pedersen, P.M., Whisenant, W.A., & Schneider, R.G. (2003). Using a content analysis to examine the gendering of sports newspaper personnel and their coverage. *Journal of Sport Management, 17*(4), 376-393.

Pedersen, P.M., Whisenant, W.A., & Schneider, R.G. (2005). Analyzing the 2001-02 sport management faculty openings. *International Journal of Sport Management, 6*(2), 154-164.

Pepper, G.L. (1995). *Communicating in organizations: A cultural approach*. New York: McGraw-Hill.

Peterson, R.A., & Merino, M.C. (2003). Consumer information search behavior and the Internet. *Psychology & Marketing, 20*(2), 99-121.

Petty, R.E., Cacioppo, J.T., & Schumann, D. (1983). Central and peripheral routes to advertising effectiveness: The moderating role of involvement. *Journal of Consumer Research, 10*(2), 135-146.

Pierce, D., & Miloch, K. (2006). Gauging public sentiment through letters to the editor. In B. Pitts (Ed.), *Sport marketing in the new millennium. Selected papers from the third annual conference of the Sport Marketing Association* (pp. 133-148). Morgantown, WV: FIT

Pitino, R., & Reynolds, B. (2000). *Lead to succeed: The ten traits of great leadership in business and life*. New York: Broadway.

Pitts, B.G. (1998). An analysis of sponsorship recall during Gay Games IV. *Sport Marketing Quarterly, 7*(4), 11-18.

Pitts, B.G., Fielding, L.F., & Miller, L.K. (1994). Industry segmentation theory and the sport industry: Developing a sport industry segment model. *Sport Marketing Quarterly, 3*(1), 15-24.

Pitts, B.G., & Stotlar, D.K. (2002). *Fundamentals of sport marketing* (2nd ed.). Morgantown, WV: FIT.

Playmakers, L.L.C. v. ESPN, Inc. (2004). 376 F.3d 894.

Poole, M. (2005, May 16). Why try to reach consumers in ways that will only annoy them? *SportsBusiness Journal, 8*, 11.

Pooley, J.C. (1978). *The sport fan: A social psychology of misbehavior* (Sociology of Sport Monograph Series). Calgary: CAPHER.

Pope, N.K., & Voges, K.E. (1997). An exploration of sponsorship awareness by product category and message location in televised sporting events. *Cyber-Journal of Sport Marketing, 1*(1).

Pope, S.W. (1995). An army of athletes: Playing fields, battlefields, and the American military sporting experience. *Journal of Military History, 59*(3), 435-456.

Porter, M.E. (2001, March). Strategy and the Internet. *Harvard Business Review*, pp. 63-78.

Postman, N. (1985). *Amusing ourselves to death: Public discourse in the age of show business*. New York: Penguin.

Povich, S. (1995, May 2). Telling it like it was about Howard Cosell. *The Washington Post,* p. E2.

Powell, M.K. (2003, January 22). Should limits on broadcast ownership change? Yes. *USA Today.* Retrieved January 18, 2006, from Academic Search Premier.

PR Newswire. (2005, May 26). Press release writing tips. Retrieved October 15, 2005, from http://marketingpower.com.

Pratt, J.A., Mills, R.J., & Kim, Y. (2004). The effects of navigational orientation and user experience on user task efficiency and frustration levels. *Journal of Computer Information Systems, 44*(4), 93-100.

Pritchard, M.P., Havitz, M.E., & Howard, D.R. (1999). Analyzing the commitment-loyalty link in service contexts. *Journal of the Academy of Marketing Science, 27*(3), 333-348.

Products and Services Overview. Retrieved February 23, 2007, from www.joycejulius.com/overview.html.

Profile: NBC Sports planning historic television coverage for Summer Olympics. (2004, June 10). NPR *Morning Edition.* Transcript. Retrieved October 31, 2005, from Proquest database.

Prospero, M.A. (2006, January/February). Game on! *Fast Company, 102,* 36.

Publishing. (2006). *Merriam-Webster Online.* Retrieved January 18, 2006, from www.m-w.com/dictionary/publishing.

Prosser, W. (1977). *Restatement of torts.* The American Law Institute, 652.

Rader, B.G. (2004). *American sports: From the age of folk games to the age of televised sports* (5th ed.). Upper Saddle River, NJ: Prentice Hall.

Rainie, L. (2005). *The state of blogging.* Washington, DC: The Pew Internet & American Life Project.

Rainie, L., & Horrigan, J. (2005). *Internet evolution.* Washington, DC: Pew Internet & American Life Project.

Ramo, S. (2005). *Meetings, meetings and more meetings: Getting things done when people are involved.* Los Angeles: Bonus.

Ratermann, D. (1995). *How to get a job in sports.* Indianapolis: Masters.

Real, M.R. (1975). Super Bowl: Mythic spectacle. *Journal of Communication, 25*(1), 31-43.

Real, M.R. (1996). *Exploring media culture: A guide.* Thousand Oaks, CA: Sage.

Real, M.R. (1998). MediaSport: Technology and the commodification of postmodern sport. In L.A. Wenner (Ed.), *MediaSport* (pp. 14-26). London: Routledge.

REAL Sports with Bryant Gumbel. (2006). *Wikipedia.* Retrieved November 20, 2006, from http://en.wikipedia.org/wiki/Real_Sports_with_Bryant_Gumbel.

Reeves, J. (2005, October 10). Former Alabama coach, Time Inc. settle defamation suit. *The Associated Press State and Local Wire.* New York.

Reid, L.N., & Soley, L.C. (1979). *Sports Illustrated's* coverage of women in sports. *Journalism Quarterly, 56,* 861-863.

Reilly, R. (2003a). *Who's your caddy? Looping for the great, near great, and reprobates of golf.* New York: Random House Large Print.

Reilly, R. (2003b, January 27). Under covered. *Sports Illustrated, 98*(3), 94.

Reimer, S. (2006, September 24). Even now, sex and athletics still play on the same team. *Knight Ridder Tribune Business News,* p. 1.

Restatement of Unfair Competition. (1995). *Restatement of Unfair Competition. Appropriation of Trade Values,* (3rd ed.), 38.

Reynolds, M. (2004a, September 6). NBC reached Olympic heights. *Multichannel News, 25*(36), 3.

Reynolds, M. (2004b, November 8). Slicing up a spinoff. *Multichannel News, 25*(45), 18.

Reynolds, M. (2005, August 29). The power of sports is evident everywhere. *Multichannel News, 26*(35), 26.

Rice, G. (1924, October 19). Notre Dame's cyclone beats Army, 13 to 7. *New York Herald Tribune, 1,* 15.

Rice, G. (1948). The golden panorama. In A. Danzig & P. Brandwein (Eds.), *Sports golden age: A close-up of the fabulous twenties* (pp. 1-7). New York: Harper.

Rice, G. (1954). *The tumult and the shouting: My life in sport.* New York: Barnes.

Richard, M. (2003). Modeling the impact of Internet atmospherics on surfer behavior. *Journal of Business Research, 58*(2005), 1632-1642.

Riess, S.A. (1990). The new sport history. *Reviews in American History, 18,* 311-325.

Rintala, J., & Birrell, S. (1984). Fair treatment for the active female: A content analysis of young athlete magazine. *Sociology of Sport Journal, 1*(3), 231-250.

Risse, H. (1921). *Soziologie des sports.* Berlin: Reher.

Ritchie, D.A. (2003). *Doing oral history: A practical guide* (2nd ed.). New York: Oxford University.

Roberts, G. (2004). The scope of the exclusive right to control dissemination of real-time sports event information. *Stanford Law & Policy Review, 15,* 167-188.

Robertson, L. (2006, July 28). To the sports fan, just another fallen hero. *Knight Ridder Tribune Business News,* p. 1.

Robertson, M. (1997). *Stephen Crane, journalism, and the making of modern American literature.* New York: Columbia University.

Robinson, L. (1998). Professional athletes held to a higher standard and above the law: A comment on high-profile criminal defendants and the need for states to establish high-profile courts. *Indiana Law Journal, 73,* 1313-1350.

Robinson, M.J., Hums, M.A., Crow, R.B., & Phillips, D.R. (2001). *Profiles of sport industry professionals: The people who make the games happen.* Gaithersburg, MD: Aspen.

Rodman, G. (2001). *Making sense of media: An introduction to mass communication.* Boston: Allyn & Bacon.

Romanowski admits to using steroids from BALCO. (2005, October 18). *Associated Press, National Football League Newswire.*

Romney, M. (2004). *Turnaround: Crisis, leadership, and the Olympic Games.* Washington, DC: Regnery.

Rosen, D.E., & Purinton, E. (2004). Website design: Viewing the web as a cognitive landscape. *Journal of Business Research, 57,* 787-794.

Rosenbloom v. Metromedia, Inc. (1971). 403 U.S. 29.

Rosenstiel, T., Gottlieb, C., Brady, L.A., & Rosenheim, D. (2000). Time of peril for TV news. *Columbia Journalism Review, 39*(4), 84-92.

Rosner, S.R., & Shropshire, K.L. (2004). *The business of sports.* Sudbury, MA: Jones & Bartlett.

Rothenbuhler, E. (2005). A. C. Nielsen Company: U.S. media market research firm. *The Museum of Broadcast Communications.* Retrieved November 20, 2006, from www.museum.tv/archives/etv/A/htmlA/acnielsen/acnielsen.htm.

Rothenbuhler, E., & McCourt, T. (2002). Radio redefines itself, 1947-1962. In M. Hilmes & J. Loviglio (Eds.), *Essays in the cultural history or radio: Radio reader* (pp. 367-387). New York: Routledge.

Rovell, D. (2006, June 12). Is Danica in danger of being Anna-ized? Retrieved February 23, 2007, from http://sports.espn.go.com/rpm/news/story?series-1&id-2458333.

Rovell, D. (2005, June 9). Students learn about legal issues, negotiations. *ESPN.com.* Retrieved November 29, 2005, from http://sports.espn.go.com/espn/sportsbusiness/news/story?id=2072448&num=2.

Rowe, D. (2004a). *Critical readings: Sport, culture and the media.* New York: Open University.

Rowe, D. (2004b). *Sport, culture and the media: The unruly trinity* (2nd ed.). New York: Open University.

RTNDA-Ball State University Annual Survey. (2005). Washington, DC: Radio-Television News Directors Association.

Rushin, S. (2000, January 10). Rush from judgment. *Sports Illustrated, 92*(1), 24.

Rusinack, K.E. (1998). Baseball on the radical agenda: The *Daily Worker* and *Sunday Worker* journalistic campaign to desegregate Major League Baseball, 1933-1947. In J. Dorinson & J. Warmund (Eds.), *Jackie Robinson: Race, sports, and the American Dream* (pp. 75-85). Armonk, NY: Sharpe.

Ryan, B. (1992, April 4). Knight still applies the off-court press. *Boston Globe,* p. 33.

Ryan, P. (1998, May/June). *ESPN* vs. *Sports Illustrated*: The game is on. *Columbia Journalism Review, 37*(1), 64-66.

Ryerson, D. (2006, January 15). We'll cover topics key to the lives of our readers. *Indianapolis Star,* p. 1E.

Sabo, D., Jansen, S.C., Tate, D., & Duncan, M.C. (1996). Televising international sport: Race, ethnicity, and nationalistic bias. *Journal of Sport & Social Issues, 20*(1), 7-21.

Sailes, G. (1993). An investigation of campus typecasts: The myth of black athletic superiority and the dumb jock stereotype. *Sport Sociology Journal, 10,* 88-97.

Sailes, G. (2000). The African American athlete: Social myths and stereotypes. In D. Brooks & R. Althouse (Eds.), *Racism in college athletics: The African American athlete's experience* (pp. 53-63). Morgantown, WV: FIT.

Salary Guide. (2005). Menlo Park, CA: The Creative Group, Robert Half International.

Salwen, M.B. (1994). Depictions of female athletes on *Sports Illustrated* covers, 1957-1989. *Journal of Sport Behavior, 17*(2), 98-107.

Salwen, M.B., & Stacks, D.W. (1996). *An integrated approach to communication theory and research.* Mahwah, NJ: Erlbaum.

Salwen, M., & Garrison, B. (1998). Finding their place in journalism: Newspaper sports journalists' professional 'problems'. *Journal of Sport and Social Issues, 22*(1), 88-102.

Sandomir, R. (1988, November 14). The $50-billion sports industry. *Sports Inc.,* pp. 11-23.

Sandvig, J., & Bajwa, D. (2004). Information seeking on university web sites: An exploratory study. *Journal of Computer Information Systems, 45*(1), 13-22.

Sarnoff, D. (1941). Possible social effects of television. *Annals of the American Academy of Political and Social Science, 213,* 145-152.

Sasseen, J. (1984, January). Jocks run faster, jump higher and sell better. *Madison Avenue, 25,* 92.

Saussure, F. de (1983). *Course in general linguistics.* C. Bally & A. Sechehaye (Eds.), R. Harris (Trans.). LaSalle, IL: Open Court.

Schaaf, P. (1995). *Sports marketing: It's not just a game anymore.* Amherst, NY: Prometheus.

Scheffelmaier, G.W., & Vinsonhaler, J.F. (2003). A synthesis of research on the properties of effective Internet commerce web sites. *Journal of Computer Information Systems, 34*(2), 23-30.

Schell, L.A., & Rodriguez, S. (2000, Spring). Our sporting sisters: How male hegemony stratifies women in sport. *Women in Sport & Physical Activity Journal, 9*(1), 15-34.

Schneider, T. (2005, April). Economics 201. *SportsTravel, 9*(4), 4.

Schoenfeld, B. (2005, September 5). PR playbook: Forget game notes: Today's communications managers called on to shape teams' images. *SportsBusiness Journal, 8*(18), 35-37.

Schoenherr, S.E. (1999a). History of television. Retrieved January 21, 2006, from http://history.acusd.edu/gen/recording/television1.html.

Schoenherr, S.E. (1999b). Television's split personality. Retrieved January 21, 2006, from http://history.acusd.edu/gen/recording/television4.html.

Schoettle, A. (2005, October). Hip-deep in endorsements. *Indianapolis Business Journal, 26*(30), A1.

School of Journalism and Mass Communication. (2006). University of North Carolina-Chapel Hill. Retrieved January 25, 2006, from http://www.unc.edu/ugradbulletin/depts/sch_journ.html.

Schreiber, A., & Lenson, B. (1994). *Lifestyle and event marketing.* New York: McGraw-Hill.

Schultz, B. (2005). *Sports media: Reporting, producing and planning.* Burlington, MA: Elsevier.

Schwartz, L. (2000). Sportscentury Biography: Billie Jean won for all women. *ESPN.com.* Retrieved November 20, 2006, from http://espn.go.com/classic/ biography/s/King_Billie_Jean.html.

Second best: Top-rated programs of the second quarter. (2005, July 18). *SportsBusiness Journal, 8,* 14.

Seital, F.P. (2001). *The practice of public relations* (8th ed.). Upper Saddle River, NJ: Prentice Hall.

Shank, M.D. (2002). *Sports marketing: A strategic perspective* (2nd ed.). Upper Saddle River, NJ: Prentice Hall.

Shapiro, L. (1995, April 24). Howard Cosell dies at 77: Sportscaster was a magnet for controversy. *Washington Post,* p. A1.

Shapiro, L., & Maske, M. (2005, April 19). "Monday Night Football" changes the channel. *Washington Post,* p. A1.

Sharp, K. (1997). Ex-patriot. *Women's Sports & Fitness, 19*(9), 27-28.

Shearman, M. (1887). *Football: Its history for five centuries.* London: Longman.

Shearman, M. (1889). *Athletics and football.* London: Longman.

Shilbury, D., & Berriman, M. (1996). Sponsorship awareness: A study of St. Kilda football club supporters. *Sport Marketing Quarterly, 5*(1), 27-33.

Shockley-Zalabak, P. (2006). *Fundamentals of organizational communication* (6th ed.). Boston: Allyn & Bacon.

Shoemaker, P.J., & Reese, S.D. (1996). *Mediating the message: Theories of influence on mass media content* (2nd ed.). White Plains, NY: Longman.

Shoham, A., & Kahle, L. (1996). Spectators, viewers, readers: Communication and consumption communities in sport marketing. *Sport Marketing Quarterly, 5*(1), 11-25.

Show, J. (2005, August 29). Sports industry learning how to best use blogs. *SportsBusiness Journal, 8*(17), 08.

Show, J. (2006, September 4). Exclusive survey names Peyton Manning most marketable NFLer. *SportsBusiness Journal, 9*(18), 1.

Shuart, J. (2002). The athlete as hero and celebrity endorser. *Dissertation Abstracts International, 63*(08), 2944. (UMI No. 3062100)

Simons, Y., & Taylor, J. (1992). A psychological model of fan violence in sports. *International Journal of Sport Psychology, 23,* 207-226.

Sloan, L.R. (1979). The function and impact of sports for fans; A review of theory and contemporary research. In J.H. Goldstein (Ed.), *Sports, games, and play: Social and psychological viewpoints* (pp. 219-262). Hillsdale, NJ: Erlbaum.

Slote, B. (1966). First principles. In B. Slote (Ed.), *The kingdom of art: Willa Cather's first principles and critical statements 1893-1896* (pp. 31-112). Lincoln: University of Nebraska.

Smart, B. (2005). *The sport star: Modern sport and the cultural economy of sporting celebrity.* Thousand Oaks, CA: Sage.

Smith, E. (2005, December 12). What's new media. *Indianapolis Star,* p. 1A.

Smith, E.D. (2005, Sept. 26). Media madness: Using all things mass media is Americans' No. 1 activity, Ball State researchers find. *The Indianapolis Star,* pp. C1-C2.

Smith, M. (2006, September 25). AAA sees success with NASCAR. *SportsBusiness Journal, 9*(21), 6.

Smith, R.D. (2005). *Strategic planning for public relations* (2nd ed.). Mahwah, NJ: Erlbaum.

Smith, Y.R. (2000). Sociohistorical influences on African American elite sportswomen. In D. Brooks & R. Althouse (Eds.), *Racism in college athletics: The African American athlete's experience* (pp. 173-197). Morgantown, WV: FIT.

Snyder, C.R., Lassegard, M.A., & Ford, C.E. (1986). Distancing after group success and failure. Basking in reflected glory and cutting off reflected failure. *Journal of Personality and Social Psychology, 51,* 382-388.

Snyder, E.E., & Spreitzer, E. (1978). *Social aspects of sport.* Englewood Cliffs, NJ: Prentice Hall.

Spector, M. (2005, November 9). T.O. little, T.O. late: Terrell Owens wants another chance; unfortunately, he will probably get one. *National Post,* p. B9.

Spencer, N. (2003). "America's sweetheart" and "Czech-mate." *Journal of Sport & Social Issues, 27*(1), 18-37.

Sport Management. (2007). University of Michigan, The Division of Kinesiology. Retrieved March 12, 2007, from www.kines.umich.edu/academics/sm/index.html.

Sport Management Program Review Council. (2000). *Sport management program standards and review protocol.* Reston, VA: NASPE Publications.

Sporting times in Philadelphia-WIP. (1987, December 14). *Broadcasting,* 50-51.

The sports industry. (2007). *SportsBusiness Journal*. Retrieved March 12, 2007, from www.sportsbusinessjournal.com/index.cfm?fuseaction=page.feature&featureId=1492.

Sports law: Sports-related laws and legal cases through the years. (2005). *Sports Business Journal*. Retrieved January 16, 2006, from www.sportsbusinessjournal.com/index.cfm?fuseaction=page.feature&featureId=247.

Sports media: U.S. digital media rights. (2005, November 7-13). *SportsBusiness Journal, 8*(27), 22-23.

Stafford, M., & Stafford, T. (1996). Mechanical commercial avoidance: A uses and gratifications perspective. *Journal of Current Issues and Research in Advertising, 18,* 27-38.

Stafford, T., Stafford, M., & Schkade, L. (2004). Determining uses and gratifications for the Internet. *Decision Sciences, 35*(2), 259-288.

Stanford-Blair, N., & Dickmann, M. H. (2005). *Leading coherently: Reflections from leaders around the world.* Thousand Oaks, CA: Sage.

Stanley, T.L. (2004, May 17). NBC hypes Olympics as hip to youth. *Advertising Age, 75*(20), 1-2.

Stark, P., & Schiffman, M. (2000, May 6). Sports/talk leads in "power ratios." *Billboard, 112*(19), 116-117.

Starr, M. (1999, October 25). Blood, sweat, and cheers. *Newsweek, 134*(17), 42.

Staurowsky, E. (2004). Privilege at play—On the legal and social fictions that sustain American Indian sport imagery. *Journal of Sport & Social Issues, 28*(1), 11-29.

Staurowsky, E.J., & DiManno, J. (2002). Young women talking sports and careers: A glimpse at the next generation of women in sport media. *Women in Sport and Physical Activity Journal, 11*(1), 127-161.

Steiner, B. (2003). *The business playbook: Leadership lessons from the world of sports.* New York: Entrepreneur.

Steiner, G. (1963). *The people look at television: A study of audience attitudes.* New York: Knopf.

Steinfatt, T., & Christophel, D. M. (1996). Intercultural communication. In M.B. Salwen & D.W. Stacks (Eds.), *An integrated approach to communication theory and research* (pp. 317-344). Mahwah, NJ: Erlbaum.

Sterling, C.H., & Kittross, J.M. (2002). *Stay tuned: A history of American broadcasting* (3rd ed.). Mahwah, NJ: Erlbaum.

Stier, W.F. (2001). Sport management: The development of sport management. In D. Kluka & G. Schilling (Eds.), *The business of sport* (pp. 39-56). Oxford, UK: Meyer & Meyer Sport.

Stokes, J. (2003). *How to do media and cultural studies.* London: Sage.

Stoldt, C., Miller, L., & Comfort, G. (2001). Through the eyes of athletics directors: Perceptions of sports information directors, and other public relations issues. *Sport Marketing Quarterly, 10*(2), 164-172.

Stoldt, G., Miller, K., Ayres, T., & Comfort, G. (2000). Crisis management planning: A necessity for sport managers. *International Journal of Sport Management, 1,* 263-266.

Stoldt, G.C., Dittmore, S.W., & Branvold, S.E. (2006). *Sport public relations: Managing organizational communication.* Champaign, IL: Human Kinetics.

Stone, G. (1955, Fall). American sports—Play and display. *Chicago Review, 9,* 83-100.

Stone, G., Joseph, M., & Jones, M. (2003). An exploratory study on the use of sport celebrities in advertising: A content analysis. *Sport Marketing Quarterly, 12*(2), 94-102.

Stotlar, D. (2005). *Developing successful sport sponsorship plans.* Morgantown, WV: FIT.

Stotlar, D., & Johnson, D. (1989). Assessing the impact and effectiveness of stadium advertising on sport spectators at Division I institutions. *Journal of Sport Management, 3,* 90-102.

Strong, P. (2004). The mascot slot—Cultural citizenship, political correctness, and pseudo-Indian sports symbols. *Journal of Sport & Social Issues, 28*(1), 79-87.

Strother, T.E. (1978). The race advocacy function of the black press. *Black American Literature Forum, 12*(3), 92-99.

Strupp, J. (2001, June 11). The changing face of sports. *Editor & Publisher, 134*(24), 10-13.

Stryker, S. (1980). *Symbolic interactionism: A socio-structural version.* Menlo Park, CA: Cummings.

Stump, M. (2005, April 18). How the NBA slices, dices game night. *Multichannel News, 26*(16), 35.

Summit, P., & Jenkins, S. (1998). *Reach for the summit: The definite dozen system for succeeding at whatever you do.* New York: Broadway.

Super Bowl ratings down 4 percent. (2005, February 7). MSNBC.com. Retrieved January 16, 2006, from www.msnbc.msn.com/id/6928502/.

Super Bowl TV ratings and ad rates. (2005, January 31). *SportsBusiness Journal, 8,* 29.

Susman, W.I. (1984). *Culture as history: The transformation of American society in the twentieth century.* New York: Pantheon.

Sutton, B. (2005, October 10). San Antonio's super seller puts it all together. *SportsBusiness Journal, 8*(23), 25.

Sutton, W. (1998). Marketing principles applied to sport management. In L. Masteralexis, C. Barr, & M. Hums (Eds.), *Principles and practice of sport management* (pp. 39-59). Gaithersburg, MD: Aspen.

Sweet, D. (2002a, July 1). Sports gets mixed reviews as place to hype nets. *SportsBusiness Journal, 6,* 19.

Sweet, D. (2002b, November 11). Fabulous Sports Babe still one and only female sports radio host. *SportsBusiness Journal, 5,* 21.

Tagliabue's tenure: The NFL during Paul Tagliabue's reign as commissioner. (2006, July 31). *SportsBusiness Journal, 9,* 32.

Tallack, D. (1991). *Twentieth century America: The intellectual and cultural context.* London: Longman.

Tankel, J.D., & Williams, W., Jr. (1998). The economics of contemporary radio. In A. Alexander, J. Owers, & R. Carveth (Eds.), *Media economics: Theory and practice* (2nd ed., pp. 185-198). Mahwah, NJ: Erlbaum.

Taylor, J. (1992). *How to get a job in sports: The guide to finding the right sports career.* New York: Collier.

Telander, R. (1984). The written word: Player-press relationships in American sports. *Sociology of Sport Journal, 1*(1), 3-14.

Theriault, M.J. (2005). Web site development overview. *American Marketing Association.* Retrieved November 26, 2005, from www.marketingpower.com/content-printer-friendly,php?&Item_ID=996.

Thomaselli, R. (2005). Maria Sharapova. *AdvertisingAge, 76*(45), S18.

Thomaselli, R. (2005, September 19). Outdoor Life could give ESPN run for its money. *Advertising Age, 76*(38), 4.

Till, B.D. (2001). Managing athlete endorser image: The effect of endorsed product. *Sport Marketing Quarterly, 10*(1), 35-42.

Till, B.D., & Shimp, T.A. (1998). Endorsers in advertising: The case of negative celebrity information. *Journal of Advertising, 27*(1), 67-82.

Todd, J. (2005, March 18). Seoul scandal a benchmark in doping history: Ben Johnson is carving out a new career as a clothing designer but he will forever be known as Canada's "disgraced sprinter." *Edmonton Journal,* p. D5.

Top sports movies of 2005. (2005, December 26). *SportsBusiness Journal, 8,* 22.

Torres, R.T., Preskill, H., & Piontek, M.E. (2005). *Evaluation strategies for communicating and reporting: Enhancing learning in organizations* (2nd ed.). Thousand Oaks, CA: Sage.

Towers, W.M. (1981). World Series coverage in New York City in the 1920s. *Journalism Monographs, 73,* 1-29.

Trademark Law Revisions Act (1988). 15 USCS 1051.

Trenholm, S. (1986). *Human communication theory.* Englewood Cliffs, NJ: Prentice Hall.

Trenholm, S., & Jensen, A. (2004). *Interpersonal communication* (5th ed.). New York: Oxford.

Trujillo, N. (1994). *The meaning of Nolan Ryan.* College Station, TX: Texas A&M University.

Trujillo, N. (2003). Introduction. In R.S. Brown & D.J. O'Rourke III (Eds.), *Case studies in sport communication* (pp. xi-xv). Westport, CT: Praeger.

Tuchman, G. (1978). *Making news: A study in the construction of reality.* New York: Free Press.

Tuchman, G. (1991). Media institutions: Qualitative methods in the study of news. In K.B. Jensen & N.W. Jankowski (Eds.), *A handbook of qualitative methodologies for mass communication research* (pp. 79-92). London: Routledge.

Tucker, D. (2006, January 20). Self: Internet is a curse to college sports. *Fort Wayne News-Sentinel.* Retrieved January 24, 2006, from www.fortwayne.com/mld/newssentinel/sports/13673998.htm.

Tuggle, C.A., & Owen, A. (1999). Differences in television sports reporting of men's and women's athletics. ESPN *SportsCenter* and CNN *Sports Tonight. Journal of Broadcasting & Electronic Media, 41*(1), 14-24.

Tuite, J. (1995, July 2). Backtalk, take a long time to admire Gehrig's lengthy feat. *New York Times,* pp. 8, 9.

Turow, J. (1997). *Media systems in society: Understanding industries, strategies, and power* (2nd ed.). New York: Longman.

Ucelli, L. (2002). The CEO's "how to" guide to crisis communications. *Strategy & Leadership, 30*(2), 21-24.

Umstead, R.T. (2005, September 19). *Multichannel News, 26*(39), 4.

United States Olympic Committee v. American Media, Inc. (2000). 156 F. Supp. 2d 1200.

U.S. Open television coverage creates huge exposure return for sponsors. Retrieved September 16, 2005, from www.joycejulius.com.

USTA.com. (2006). USA Schools Program. Retrieved December 8, 2005, from http://usta.com.

Vaillant, D. (2002). 'Your voice came in last night . . . but I thought it sounded a little scared:' Rural radio listening and "talking back" during the progressive era in Wisconsin, 1920-1932. In M. Hilmes & J. Loviglio (Eds.), *Essays in the cultural history of radio: Radio reader* (pp. 63-88). New York: Routledge.

Van Leeuwen, L., Quick, S., & Daniel, K. (2002). The sport spectator satisfaction model: A conceptual framework for understanding the satisfaction of spectators. *Sport Management Review, 5*(2), 99-128.

Van Niekerk, D., Berthon, J., & Davies, T. (1999). Going with the flow: Web sites and customer involvement. *Internet Research, 9*(2), 109-116.

Van Schaik, P., & Ling, J. (2005). Five psychometric scales for online measurement of the quality of human-computer interaction in web sites. *International Journal of Human-Computer Interaction, 18*(3), 309-322.

Vaughn, M. (1995). Organization symbols: an analysis of their types and functions in a reborn organization. *Management Communication Quarterly, 9*(2), 219-250.

Veblen, T. (1899). *The theory of the leisure class.* New York: Macmillan.

Viles, P. (1992, February 10). All-sports radio hits Los Angeles market. *Broadcasting,* 44.

Viseu, J. (2000). *Sport, communication and media: An academic approach.* Paper presented at the 1st International Seminar of Sport Journalism, Lisboa, Portugal.

Vivian, J. (2001). *The media of mass communication.* Boston: Allyn & Bacon.

Von Schilling, J. (2003). *The magic window: American television, 1939-1953.* New York: Haworth.

Wadsworth. (2005). Secrets of the media savvy: Best tips for media interviews. *ASAE and the Center for Association Leadership.* Retrieved February 23, 2007, from http://asaecenter.org.

Wakefield, K.L. (1995). The pervasive effects of social influence on sporting event attendance. *Journal of Sport & Social Issues, 19*(4), 335-351.

Wakefield, K.L., Blodgett, J.G., & Sloan, H.J. (1996). Measurement and management of the sportscape. *Journal of Sport Management, 10*(1), 15-31.

Waller, W. (1932). *The sociology of teaching.* New York: Wiley.

Walsh-Childers, K., Chance, J., & Herzog, K. (1996). Sexual harassment of women journalists. *Journalism and Mass Communication Quarterly, 73*(3), 559-581.

Walsh, C.J. (2006). *No time outs: What it's really like to be a sportswriter today.* Lanham, MD: Taylor Trade.

Wann, D., Allen, B., & Rochelle, A. (2004). Using sport fandom as an escape: Searching for relief from under-stimulation and over-stimulation. *International Sports Journal, 8*(1), 104-113.

Wann, D.L., & Branscombe, N.R. (1990). Die-hard and fair-weather fans: Effects of identification on BIRGing and CORFing tendencies. *Journal of Sport & Social Issues, 14*(2), 103-117.

Wann, D.L., & Branscombe, N.R. (1993). Sports fans: measuring degree of identification with their team. *International Journal of Sport Psychology, 24,* 1-17.

Warfield, S. (2005, October 10). Danica-mania fuels big rise in IRL's ratings. *SportsBusiness Journal, 8,* 33.

Warford v. Lexington Herald-Leader Co. (1990). 789 S.W. 2d 758.

Weber, M. (1958). *The Protestant work ethic and the spirit of capitalism* (T. Parsons, Trans.). New York: Scribner's.

Weis, K. (1986). How the print media affect sports and violence: The problems of sport journalism. *International Review for the Sociology of Sport, 21*(2/3), 239-250.

Weisberg, H.F., Krosnick, J.A., & Bowen, B.D. (1996). *An introduction to survey research, polling, and data analysis* (3rd ed.). Thousand Oaks, CA: Sage.

Welch, M. (2005, November 6). Times' Dodger coverage: It's low, in the dirt. *Los Angeles Times.* Retrieved January 19, 2006, from www.latimes.com/news/opinion/commentary/la-op-tent6nov06,0,6186068.story?coll=la-news-comment-opinions.

Welcome to the SBJ/SBD Reader Survey. (2005, November 21). *SportsBusiness Journal, 8*(29), 13.

Wellner, A.S. (2005). Lost in translation. *Inc. Magazine, 27*(9), 37-38.

Wenner, L.A. (1989). *Media, sports, and society.* Newbury Park, CA: Sage.

Wenner, L.A. (1998a). *Mediasport.* London: Routledge.

Wenner, L.A. (1998b). Preface. In L.A. Wenner (Ed.), *MediaSport* (pp. xiii-xiv). London: Routledge.

Westerbeek, H., & Smith, A. (2005). *Business leadership and the lessons from sport.* New York: Palgrave Macmillan.

Westerbeek, H.M., & Shilbury, D. (2003). A conceptual model for sport services marketing research: Integrating quality, value and satisfaction. *International Journal of Sports Marketing & Sponsorship, 5*(1), 11-27.

Whannel, G. (2002). Sport and the media. In J. Coakley & E. Dunning (Eds.), *Handbook of sports studies.* London: Sage.

What TV ratings really mean. (2006). *Nielsenmedia. com.* Retrieved November 20, 2006, from www.nielsenmedia.com/whatratingsmean/.

Wheat, A. (2003, November 28). Review of REAL Sports with Bryant Gumbel. *Entertainment Weekly.* Retrieved January 23, 2006, from www.ew.com/ew/article/ review/tv/0,6115,547968_3|92386||0_0_,00.html.

Whisenant, W.A., & Pedersen, P.M. (2004a). Analyzing attitudes regarding quantity and quality of sports page coverage: Athletic director perceptions of newspaper coverage given to interscholastic sports. *International Sports Journal, 8*(1), 54-64.

Whisenant, W.A., & Pedersen, P M. (2004b). Traditional managerial activities and interscholastic athletic directors. *Public Organization Review: A Global Journal, 4*(1), 75-84.

White, D.M. (1950). The "gate keeper": A case study in the selection of news. *Journalism Quarterly, 27*(4), 383-390.

Whitney, D. (2004, September 6). Becoming the place for sports. *TelevisionWeek, 23*(36), 26-27.

Whitney, D. (2005, March 21). ESPN and ABC Sports woo clients with ROO. *TelevisionWeek, 24*(12), 17.

Who's watching: Top local markets for Super Bowl XXXIX. (2005, February 14). *SportsBusiness Journal, 8,* 14.

Wielgas, S. (1990). How to create successful media relationships. *Economic Development Review, 8*(4), 50-52.

Wiley, R. (2002, December 9). Arledge's world flowed with ideas. Retrieved November 20, 2006, from http://espn.go.com/page2/s/wiley/021209.html.

Williams, D., & Graham, S. (2006). *The baffled parent's guide to coaching six-and-under soccer.* Camden: McGraw-Hill.

Williams, L.D. (1994). Sportswomen in Black and White: Sports history from an Afro-American perspective. In P. Creedon (Ed.), *Women, media, and sport: Challenging gender values* (pp. 45-66). Thousand Oaks, CA: Sage.

Williams, P. (2005, October 17). How media training pays for athletes. *SportsBusiness Journal, 8*(24), 20.

Williams, P., & Denney, J. (2002). *The paradox of power: A transforming view of leadership.* New York: Warner.

Wilson, P.B. (2007, February 12). QB was Super Bowl XLI exposure king. *The Indianapolis Star,* p. 1D.

Wilstein, S. (2002). *Associated Press sportswriting handbook.* New York: McGraw-Hill.

Witherspoon, P.E. (1997). *Communicating leadership: An organizational perspective.* Boston: Allyn & Bacon.

Wolf, N. (2002). *The beauty myth.* New York: Harper-Collins.

Wong, G.M. (1994). *Essentials of amateur sports law* (2nd ed.). Westport, CT: Greenwood.

Wong, P., Lai, C., Nagasawa, R., & Lin, T. (1998). Asian Americans as a model minority: Self-perceptions and perceptions by other racial groups. *Sociological Perspectives, 41*(1), 95-118.

Wood, J.T. (2004). *Interpersonal communication: Everyday encounters* (4th ed.). Belmont, CA: Wadsworth/ Thomson.

Wooden, J., & Jamison, S. (2005). *Wooden on leadership.* New York: McGraw-Hill.

Woodward, S. (2005, September 12). National governing bodies: The changing face of winter sports. *SportsBusiness Journal, 8,* 19.

Wyner, G. (2002). Segmentation architecture. *Marketing Management, 11*(2), 6-7.

Yang, X., Ahmed, Z., Ghingold, M., & Boon, G. (2003). Consumer preferences for commercial web site design: An Asia-Pacific perspective. *Journal of Consumer Marketing, 20*(1), 10-17.

Ylikoski, T. (2005). A sequence analysis of consumers' online searches. *Internet Research, 15*(2), 181-194.

Yoh, T., Pedersen, P.M., & Park, M. (2006). Sources of information for purchasing golf clubs: Personal and non-personal references. *International Journal of Sports Marketing and Sponsorship, 7*(2), 125-135.

Zacchini v. Scripps-Howard Broadcasting, Co. (1977). 433 U.S. 56.

Zhang, J., Lam, E., & Connaughton, D. (2003). General market demand variables associated with professional sport consumption. *International Journal of Sports Marketing and Sponsorship, 5*(1), 33-55.

Zillman, D., Bryant, J., & Sapolsky, B. S. (1979). Enjoyment from sports spectatorship. In J H. Goldstein (Ed.), *Sports, games, and play: Social and psychological viewpoints* (2nd ed., pp. 241-278). Hillsdale, NJ: Erlbaum.

Zoch, L.M., & Turk, J.V. (1998). Women making news: Gender as a variable in source selection and use. *Journalism and Mass Communications Quarterly, 75*(4), 762-775.

Index

Note: The italicized *f* and *t* following page numbers refer to figures and tables, respectively.

About the Authors

Paul M. Pedersen, PhD, an associate professor of sport communication at Indiana University (Bloomington, Indiana), received his PhD in sport management from Florida State University in 2000. Pedersen began his sport communication career as a sportswriter and sports business columnist and has researched, published, and presented on the activities and practices of many sport organization personnel, specifically those associated with the print media and affiliated with intercollegiate and interscholastic sports. His current research interests focus on hegemony theory and hegemonic practices (how dominant groups secure and maintain power) within the institution of sport.

Pedersen has presented his research at over 35 professional conferences and published more than 40 peer-reviewed articles in national or international academic journals such as the *Journal of Sport Management, International Journal of Sport Management, Sociology of Sport Journal, International Review for the Sociology of Sport,* and *Journal of Sports Economics.* In addition to *Strategic Sport Communication,* he has authored two books: *Build It and They Will Come: The Arrival of the Tampa Bay Devil Rays* (1997) and *Bobby Bowden: Win by Win* (2003).

In addition to authoring more than 400 nonrefereed articles and coauthoring three book chapters, Pedersen is the founding editor of the *International Journal of Sport Communication* (IJSC). He also serves as an editorial review board member for six national and international academic sport journals. He is a member of several professional organizations, including the North American Society for Sport Management (NASSM); American Alliance of Health, Physical Education, Recreation and Dance (AAHPERD); National Association for Sport and Physical Education (NASPE); ICHPER•SD Sport Management and Administration Commission; North American Society for Sport History (NASSH); and Sport Marketing Association (SMA).

Pedersen lives in Bloomington, Indiana, where he enjoys jogging and spending time with his wife, Jennifer, and their four children, Hallie, Zack, Brock, and Carlie.

Kimberly S. Miloch, PhD, is an assistant professor in the nationally recognized sport communication program at Indiana University (Bloomington, Indiana), where her teaching, research, and consulting work focus on sport public relations and sport marketing. In 2002 Miloch earned her PhD in sport management from Florida State University.

Before entering academia, Miloch was the public relations and game operations director for a minor league hockey team. She also worked in communications and marketing for the United States Tennis Association Texas Section.

Miloch is a member of the Sport Marketing Association and an editorial review board member for *Sport Marketing Quarterly, Journal of Legal Aspects of Sport,* and *International Journal of Sport Management.* She also serves as associate editor for *The SMART Journal (The Sport Management and Related Topics Journal).*

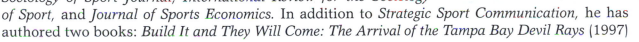

In her free time, Miloch enjoys the outdoors by gardening, attending sporting events with her husband, Matt, and playing competitive tennis. She and her husband are expecting their first child.

Pamela C. Laucella, PhD, is an assistant professor of sport communication, specializing in sport journalism and sport history at Indiana University (Bloomington, Indiana). She earned her PhD in 2004 in journalism and mass communication from the University of North Carolina at Chapel Hill, where she was also a recipient of the Park Fellowship. Before accepting a position at Indiana University, Laucella was an assistant professor in communication studies at Christopher Newport University.

Laucella's work as a freelance sportswriter, sports reporter, and project coordinator for the NFL Players Association's Native Vision Life Skills camp provided firsthand experience for her research in sociocultural, historical, and literary issues in sport journalism and communication. Her research focuses on media portrayals of race. She also studies the media "feeding frenzy" surrounding Division I college coaches and the relationship between coaches and the media.

Laucella has presented at numerous professional conferences in several disciplines and has published in peer-reviewed national and international journals. She is also a member of the Association for Education in Journalism and Mass Communication (AEJMC), American Journalism Historians Association (AJHA), Association for Women in Sports Media (AWSM), National Communication Association (NCA), North American Society for the Sociology of Sport (NASSS), and North American Society for Sport History (NASSH).

Laucella enjoys hiking with her chocolate Labrador, playing tennis, and swimming. When indoors she can be found writing creative nonfiction, playing the violin, or watching ACC sports.